Tottel's Miscellany

Tottel's Miscellany

(1557–1587)

EDITED BY

HYDER EDWARD ROLLINS

VOLUME II

Revised Edition

CAMBRIDGE, MASSACHUSETTS

HARVARD UNIVERSITY PRESS

1965

I had rather than forty shillings I had my book
of Songs and Sonnets here.

Shakespeare

PREFACE

THE first volume of my edition of Tottel's *Miscellany*, containing the text and lists of variant readings, was published in 1928. This second, and final, volume (of Introduction, Notes, and Glossarial Index) was ready for the press at the same time, but has been delayed by my desire to see and collate a new copy of the 1557 edition (*C*) and a copy of a totally unrecorded edition of 1559 (described below as *D**), as well as by the necessarily slow process of reading and correcting the proofs.

In the Introduction and the Notes I have attempted to include only such information as, in my opinion, is essential to a serious and careful study of Tottel's *Miscellany* — not all that would be necessary for a study of the complete works of Wyatt, Surrey, and Grimald. If I seem to have erred by giving too much information, perhaps I may be allowed to plead that comment and annotation are largely a matter of individual taste, that no two scholars would approach the task of editing with exactly the same views and aims, and that it is generally a less serious fault to give too much than too little. Hence the sources of the poems, though nearly all of them have long been known, are usually reprinted in full, in the belief that most students will find it convenient, even in the case of popular authors like Horace and Petrarch, to have this source-material available for comparison with the miscellany poems based upon it. Hence, too, considerable attention has been paid to the variations between the readings of the early editions of the miscellany and the readings, accessible to but few students, in other printed or manuscript texts. But apart from sources and variants, the annotations are reduced to what seems to me almost a minimum of necessary explanation or illustration.

This edition could not have been made without the cordial coöperation of those libraries, public and private, fortunate enough to own copies of the *Songs and Sonnets*. For permission to use their copies, and in several instances to reproduce them in whole or in part, I acknowledge my grateful indebtedness to the authorities of the Bodleian, British Museum, Trinity College (Cambridge), and John Rylands libra-

PREFACE

ries in England, and to the libraries of Mr. Carl H. Pforzheimer, Mr. J. P. Morgan, the late Mr. Henry E. Huntington, and Dr. A. S. W. Rosenbach in America. I wish also to express my thanks to Miss Belle da Costa Greene, of the Morgan library, to Mr. C. K. Edmonds, of the Huntington library, to Mr. F. S. Ferguson, of London, and to Dr. Rosenbach, Professor John L. Lowes, and Professor Albert S. Borgman for help on certain bibliographical details. The specific aid rendered by a few other friendly scholars, as well as by earlier students of the miscellany, is duly indicated in the following pages.

"Learned Homer sometime sleepeth," writes William Averell, schoolmaster, in the preface to *Foure notable Histories* (1590), "and the fastest foote sometime slyppeth, the wysest tongue may catch a tryp, and the wariest penne commit a fault, errour is as naturall, as the correction thereof commendable. Wherefore that which remaineth is, I commit my selfe and my labour to thy good lyking, if thou lyke it, commend it, and vse it, if thou dyslike it, amend it, or refuse it." Thus far the Elizabethan schoolmaster's preface may express my own sentiments, although in subsequent lines he is bumptious in an engaging fashion which only a sixteenth-century author would have dared assume and to which none but sixteenth-century readers would have tamely submitted. My chief thanks are due to Miss Addie F. Rowe, an old friend, whose help in checking the almost innumerable details in this second volume, both in manuscript and in proof, it is difficult to acknowledge warmly enough. To avoid errors in dealing with so many details is, as Averell reminds us, impossible; but at least my blunders are the less numerous because of Miss Rowe's patient carefulness and scholarly alertness.

Hyder Edward Rollins

Harvard University,
    June 19, 1929.

CONTENTS

PHOTOGRAPHIC FACSIMILES

TOTTEL'S *MISCELLANY*

TOTTEL'S *MISCELLANY*

INTRODUCTION

IN the spring and summer of 1557 martyrs' fires were sending a lurid glare throughout England. The melancholy and monotonous chronicle of John Foxe tells of three men and two women who were burned for their religion at Smithfield, London, on April 12. In rapid succession three men were burned in St. George's Fields, Southwark, in May; two men and five women at Maidstone, Kent, on June 18; six men and four women at Lewes, Sussex, on June 22; and three men and four women at Canterbury on June 30.

To the accompaniment of fire and martyrs' shrieks the epoch-making book correctly known as *Songs and Sonnets*, but popularly (since the publication of Arber's edition in 1870) as Tottel's *Miscellany*, made its appearance on June 5. It was concerned chiefly with love; and the rhymes, doleful or airy, in which fictitious lovers wail their supposed woes and recount their supposed joys were eagerly read by the very people who watched the burning of the martyrs — were read so eagerly that in some seven weeks' time two other editions were composed and published. The martyrs' fires died down with the death of the old queen and the coronation of Elizabeth on November 17, 1558, but the poetic fire started by the *Songs and Sonnets* burned more brightly than ever in Elizabeth's reign. At least seven other editions of the book were then published, practically every early Elizabethan poet accepted it as his model, and in time a wonderful outburst of poetry followed.

Mary I has fared badly at the hands of historians, although in the miscellany itself Grimald calls her "The perelesse princesse, Mary quene" (114.10),[1] and Heywood devotes an entire poem (No. 199) to her praise. As early as 1680 *Memoirs of Queen Mary's days* (page 3) remarked: "She lieth Buried in *Westminster*, without any Monument or Remembrance at all; as in her Life She deserved none, so in Her Death

---

[1] References of this sort, consisting of two or more arabic numerals separated by a period, are to pages and lines in the text of volume 1.

Her Memory is rotten; a just Reward for Her who was so cruel and bloody." But the little book of songs and sonnets is a monument or remembrance more lasting than brass or marble.

Tottel's *Miscellany* is one of the most important single volumes in the history of English literature. If its contents as a whole hardly seem to deserve high praise to-day, still its influence demands that it be treated with genuine respect. As the first printed anthology, it is of the greatest historical importance: the beginning of modern English verse may be said to date from its publication in 1557. Hence it is strange that no adequate edition has been made in modern times, and none of any kind in over fifty years.

No fanfares ushered the book into being. Elizabethan printers, to be sure, met with much harsh criticism for their trickery in misleading the public with puffing title-pages. Barnabe Rich, in *Faultes, Faultes, And nothing else but Faultes*, 1606, L4, expressed the popular idea:

Yea, the *Printer* himselfe, to make his booke the more vendible, doth rather desire a glorious Title, than a good Booke: so that our new written Pamphlets of these times, are not much vnlike to a poore Inne in a Countrey towne, that is gorgiously set foorth with a glorious signe; but being once entred into the house, a man shall find but cold intertainment, as well of homely lodging, as of bad fare.

But, although he had perhaps spent some time in assembling the poems, or in having them made fit for the cultivated ear, and although in his preface he asserts that they could vie on equal terms with the poetry of Italy,[1] Tottel did not attempt to give his book typographical distinction or beauty. The title-page is a model of reserve and simplicity, — a model carefully avoided by every later miscellany, — and it is probable that Tottel himself was surprised by the enthusiasm that greeted his little volume. "Il buôn vino," as the proverb has it, "non ha bisogno di frasca." Without any of the typographical allurements that helped later publishers of miscellanies to dispose of their books, Tottel had the satisfaction of selling the entire first edition and of publishing two others in the brief interval between June 5 and July 31, 1557. Here is a book

[1] His preface was widely imitated in later collections of poetry, like *The Paradise of Dainty Devices* (1576) and *A Handful of Pleasant Delights* (1584). Especially numerous were Richard Jones's prefaces. Thus his address "To the Gentlemen Readers" in R. S.'s *Phillis and Flora* (1598) begins: "Courtuous Gentlemen, according to my accustomed manner, which is, to acquaint you with any Booke, or matter I print," etc.

[4]

that resembles a country inn poorly set forth with a cheap sign but equipped inside with splendid entertainment!

I. THE PRINTER, RICHARD TOTTEL

Richard Tottel (or Tothill),[1] born at Exeter about 1530, was a printer of distinction, a charter member of the Stationers' Company (of which he became under-warden in 1561, upper-warden in 1567, 1568, 1574, master in 1578, 1584), and the most notable publisher of law-books of his time. He began to publish about 1550. His sign was the Hand and Star in Fleet Street as early as 1553, and he is said to have secured his patent for law-books in that year. The patent was renewed in 1556 for a period of seven years, and on January 12, 1559, was granted to him for life. In 1554 he printed a folio edition of John Lydgate's *Fall of Princes*, in 1555 he published Stephen Hawes's *Pastime of Pleasure*. From his press came also Thomas Tusser's rhymes on husbandry and "huswifery" (1557 to 1577) and the works of Sir Thomas More (1557). He printed or published, alone or with others, many important non-legal books, including Surrey's translation of the second and fourth books of the *Aeneid* (1557), Arthur Brooke's *Romeus and Juliet* (1562), Richard Grafton's *Chronicles of England* (1562 to 1572), William Painter's *Palace of Pleasure* (1566, 1567), and Sir Thomas North's *Dial of Princes* (1568). This is a distinguished list; but Tottel's best printing is to be found in his law-books, which were extremely numerous.

To most people, however, he is known for the *Songs and Sonnets*, and his immortality is more or less secured by the title of "Tottel's *Miscellany*" now nearly always applied to the work. Of it he issued some seven editions that survive, and perhaps others have disappeared without leaving a trace. The editions later than 1557 injure his reputation for care and accuracy. Each so far surpasses its predecessors in blunders and corruptions that the later editions are practically unintelligible unless compared with the texts of 1557. Such carelessness Jasper Heywood would have us believe typical. In the preface to his translation of

[1] Sketches of his life and publications are in *Bibliographica*, III (1897), 378–384, by H. R. Plomer; in the *Dictionary of National Biography*, by Sir Sidney Lee; and in *The Library* (*Transactions of the Bibliographical Society*, 4th series), VIII (1927), 199–232, by H. J. Byrom.

Seneca's *Thyestes* (1560) Heywood complains bitterly of the errors introduced into his translation of *Troas* (1559) by Tottel. Heywood claims that he himself made the necessary proof-corrections and that, when they were ignored, he said to Tottel,

> within these doores of thyne,
> J make a vowe shall neuer more
> come any worke of myne.

This threat seems to have had no effect on Tottel's happiness or prosperity, and modern scholars[1] have exonerated him from blame in even this instance.

But all the Elizabethan editions of the miscellany could well have been prefaced by such apologetic verses as in "The Printer to the courteous Reader" Robert Walley affixed to the 1581 edition of Barnabe Rich's *The straunge and wonderfull aduentures of Dō Simonides:*

> The faultes are myne, that passed haue the Presse,
> The praise is his, that tooke the paine to penne.

The printers, not the authors, are to blame for most of the corruptions introduced into the texts, although some were no doubt previously made by copyists. More and more errors crowded into each edition after 1557, and for them Richard Turner's *Nosce Te*, (*Hvmors.*), 1607, F4, provides a remedy:

> Reader, some faults (by reason of my absence) escaped by the Printer: I intreat you, if you will, to excuse: if not, correct: the first, if kind; you may: the second, if curious; you must: and easily. If it bee in the ende of the verse, by comparing the meeter: if elsewhere, the sence.

Such remedies, although the authors did not suggest them, must be applied to the text of Tottel's *Miscellany*.

The last two known editions of the *Songs and Sonnets* — those of 1585 and 1587 — were issued by J. Windet and R. Robinson respectively, though Tottel lived until July, 1593. He had for some years been in ill health, as a result of which he retired from business to live in Pem-

---

[1] De Vocht, in his *Jasper Heywood* (Bang's *Materialien zur Kunde des älteren Englischen Dramas*, XLI [1913], pp. xxxix–xl, and cf. pp. 104–105), declares that Tottel in the reprint of *Troas* corrected errors that Heywood failed to detect in the proofs, and that the poet, not the printer, was to blame for the errors that remained. But see R. B. McKerrow's explanation in *Transactions of the Bibliographical Society*, XII (1914), 261.

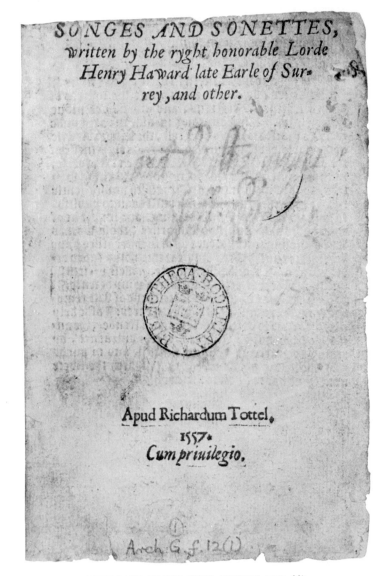

SONGES AND SONETTES,
written by the ryght honorable Lorde
Henry Haward late Earle of Sur=
rey, and other.

Apud Richardum Tottel.
1557.
Cum priuilegio.

Arch. G. f. 12 (1)

TITLE-PAGE OF THE FIRST EDITION 1557 (4)

brokeshire. His last publications were registered at Stationers' Hall in January, 1586; whence it would appear that he had earlier made over his rights in the miscellany to Windet, who in turn assigned them to Robinson. After Tottel's death his patent for law-books was granted (in 1594) to Charles Yetsweirt; his Fleet Street shop passed in 1598 to the printer-publisher John Jaggard.

II. THE 1557 EDITIONS (*ABC*)[1]

A. FIRST EDITION 1557 (JUNE 5)

SONGES AND SONETTES,/ written by the ryght honorable Lorde/ Henry Haward late Earle of Sur=/ rey, and other./ Apud Richardum Tottel./ 1557./ *Cum priuilegio./*

[Colophon] 𝔍mprinted at 𝕷ondon in flete ſtrete/ within 𝕿emple barre, at the ſygne of the/ hand and ſtarre, by 𝕽ichard 𝕿ottel/ the fift day of 𝕵une./ 𝕬n. 1557./ *Cum priuilegio ad impri-/ mendum ſolum./*

Collation: 4°, sigs. A–Dd⁴, unpaged. [A1] title: [A1ᵛ] "*The Printer to the/ Reader.*": A2–D4 Surrey's poems, with "*SVRREY.*" at the foot of D4: [D4ᵛ– M2ᵛ] Wyatt's poems, with "*T. VVYATE the elder.*" at the end of the text on [M2ᵛ], the lower portion of which is blank: M3–[P4ᵛ] Grimald's poems, with "*Songes written by Nicolas Grimald.*" at the top of M3 and "*N. G.*" at the end of the text on [P4ᵛ], the lower portion of which is blank: Q1–[Cc3] poems by anonymous writers, with the heading "*Vncertain auctours.*" at the top of Q1: [Cc3ᵛ–Dd1ᵛ] additional poems by Surrey, with the heading "*Other Songes and Sonettes written by/ the earle of Surrey.*" on [Cc3ᵛ]: DD2–[Dd3] additional poems by Wyatt, with the heading "*Other Songes and ſonettes written/ by ſir Thomas wiat the elder*" on DD2 under the head-line, and "FINIS." at the end of [Dd3]: [Dd3ᵛ] colophon: [Dd4] missing, probably blank.

Running-titles: The full running-title "*Songes and Sonettes.*" appears on A2. Thereafter normally "*Songes*" appears on the verso of each leaf, "*and Sonettes*" on the recto, each sometimes with, sometimes without, a period; they are displaced by section-headings (see the "Collation" above) on M3, Q1, Cc3ᵛ, but not on DD2. "*Songes*" occurs four times (M4, O1, O3, P3) on the recto, "*Songes.*" eleven times (D1, D2, N1–N4, O2, O4, P1, P2, P4); "*and Sonettes.*" appears twice (D1, D2) on the verso.

[1] In the following bibliographical descriptions of *A–I* no attempt has been made at keeping the exact typography of the originals in such matters as "swash" letters, since photographic reproductions of the title-pages themselves are included. The texts of the prefaces, poems, and "tables," as well as the key-words, of *A–I* may be assumed to be in black-letter type unless a specific statement to the contrary is made.

INTRODUCTION

Folio-numbers: None.

Key-words: Incorrect key-words are *If* (F1ᵛ) for *In*, *I am* (L3) for *I can*, *Or* (M4ᵛ) for *Oh*, *Nothing* (T1) for *Thus*. No key-word occurs on Z3ᵛ or at the end of sections devoted to particular authors (D4, M2ᵛ, P4ᵛ, Cc3, Dd1ᵛ, Dd3).¹

Signatures: The first three leaves (except for A1, the title-page) are signed in signatures A, B, E, L, S, V, X, Z, Aa, Bb, with Bb3 misprinted B3; only the first two are signed in H, Y, Cc, Dd (printed Dd.i., as usual, but with the variation of DD.ii.); while all four are signed in C, D, F, G, I, K, M–R, T, with K4 misprinted K3. The numeral ".i." is omitted on the first leaf of B, E, F, M, P.

Copy: Only one copy of *A* is known to be in existence, that in the Bodleian, with the shelf-mark Arch. G.f.12 (1). (Earlier shelf-marks were Tanner 150 and 8°.S.193. Art.) It was bequeathed by Thomas Tanner, Bishop of St. Asaph, who died in December, 1735. The volume — formerly bound with several other books but separately re-bound in March, 1926 — is in fairly good condition. It has, to be sure, been much cut down, so that it measures only about 5¾ by 3⅞ inches; many head-lines are slightly cropped, the first line on Q1ᵛ (122.2) is almost split in two because the paper was wrinkled in the form during printing, and the title-page and the last two leaves are mended; but the text of the poems is legible and almost perfect throughout. The printing is fairly good, perhaps better than that of any subsequent edition: typographical errors are not especially numerous; but in No. 75 one line is omitted, and hence the sonnet-form of the poem is ruined; and in No. 187 a line is omitted after 145.36.

Contents: *A* contains 271 poems, attributed as follows:

To Surrey (Nos. 1–36, 262–265)	40
To Wyatt (Nos. 37–127, 266–271)	97
To Grimald (Nos. 128–167)	40
To Uncertain Authors (Nos. 168–261)	94

Of these poems 30 by Grimald (Nos. 128–132, 135–148, 153, 155–164) appear in *A* only; the remainder are in every subsequent edition (*B–I*).

---

¹ It seems to me unnecessary in the descriptions of *B–I* to list key-words that vary in spelling (or in the omission of a hyphen) from words of the text they point to. For completeness, however, I give those of *A*: *Such* (A3) for *Suche*; *Ye* (G4) for *Yee*; *Since* (G4ᵛ) for *Sins*; *A renouncyng* (I2ᵛ) for *A renouncing*; *He* (P3ᵛ) for *Hee*; *Howe* (T4ᵛ) for *How*; *Well* (V4) for *Wel*; *Saye* (X3) for *Say*; *Manhod* (Z2) for *Manhode*; *Dothe* (Aa2ᵛ) for *Doth*.

SONGES AND SONETTES,

written by the right honorable Lorde
Henry Haward late Earle of Sur-
rey, and other.

Apud Ricardum Tottel.
Cum priuilegio ad impri-
mendum folum.
·1557·

TITLE-PAGE OF THE SECOND EDITION 1557 (*B*)

B. Second Edition 1557 (July 31), First Setting

SONGES AND SONETTES,/ *written by the right honorable Lorde*/ *Henry Haward late Earle of Sur=*/ *rey, and other.*/ *Apud Ricardum Tottel.*/ *Cum priuilegio ad impri=*/ *mendum folum.*/ *.1557.*/

[Colophon] 𝕴𝖒𝖕𝖗𝖎𝖓𝖙𝖊𝖉 𝖆𝖙 𝕷𝖔𝖓𝖉𝖔𝖓 𝖎𝖓 𝖋𝖑𝖊𝖙𝖊/ 𝖋𝖙𝖗𝖊𝖙𝖊 𝖜𝖎𝖙𝖍𝖎𝖓 𝕿𝖊𝖒𝖕𝖑𝖊 𝖇𝖆𝖗𝖗𝖊, 𝖆𝖙 𝖙𝖍𝖊/ 𝖋𝖞𝖌𝖓𝖊 𝖔𝖋 𝖙𝖍𝖊 𝖍𝖆𝖓𝖉 𝖆𝖓𝖉 𝖋𝖙𝖆𝖗𝖗𝖊,/ 𝖇𝖞 𝕽𝖎𝖈𝖍𝖆𝖗𝖉 𝕿𝖔𝖙𝖙𝖊𝖑𝖑/ 𝖙𝖍𝖊 .𝖝𝖝𝖝𝖎. 𝖉𝖆𝖞 𝖔𝖋 𝕴𝖚𝖑𝖞./ 𝕬𝖓. 1557./ *Cum priuilegio ad impri=*/ *mendum folum.*/

Collation: 4°, sigs. A–Gg⁴. [A1] title: [A1ᵛ] "*To the reder.*": A2–[E2ᵛ] Surrey's poems, with "*SVRREY.*" at the foot of [E2ᵛ]: [E3–N1ᵛ] Wyatt's poems, with "*T. VVYATE the elder.*" at the foot of [N1ᵛ]: N2–Ff1 poems by anonymous writers, with "*Songes and Sonettes of*/ *vncertain auctours.*" at the top of N2: Ff1–[Gg1ᵛ] Grimald's poems, with "¶ *Songes written by N. G.*" on Ff1 (after four lines of text) and "*N. G.*" at the end of the text on [Gg1ᵛ]: Gg2–[Gg3ᵛ] "*The table,*" or index of first lines, followed by "FINIS." (in black letter) at the end of [Gg3ᵛ]: [Gg4] colophon; verso blank.

Running-titles: The full running-title "*Songes and Sonettes*" appears on the recto of A2. Thereafter the normal heading for the recto (except on N2: see the "Collation" above) is "*and Sonettes*" (with or without a period), though it appears as "*and Sonnets.*" on A3, as "*and Sonnettes.*" on B1, B2, and as "*and Sone*" [1] on C3. In many of these head-lines the final *s* is defective, particularly on Ff3ᵛ.[2] "*Songes*" (followed by a period on A2ᵛ, C1ᵛ, C2ᵛ [3]) is on the verso throughout. In the final signatures the running-title is "*The table*" (with the misprint "*Tbe*" on Gg2–Gg2ᵛ).

Folio-numbers run from "*Fo.2.*" on A2 to "*Fo.117.*" on Gg1, but leaves 3, 5, 7, 9–12 are unmarked by either prefix or number; furthermore, 5.2 is misprinted for 25, 31 for 33, 33 for 35. The prefix is sometimes "*Fol.*", like "*Fo.*" with or without a period about equally, and the period is sometimes omitted after the numeral.[4]

Key-words: Incorrect key-words are *Yo* (C2ᵛ) for *Your*, *You* (I3) for *Then*, *Doe* (Ff2) for *Do-* or *Doway*. There are no key-words on E2ᵛ, N1ᵛ, Ee1, Gg1ᵛ.[5]

[1] In the Huntington copy "*and Sonettes.*" appears correctly on C3.
[2] These defects are not in the Huntington copy.
[3] In the Huntington copy it appears on C3ᵛ, not C2ᵛ.
[4] The Huntington copy agrees with the foregoing description, except that folios 9–11 are numbered (only the 12 being absent) and that 56 has an inverted 5. The prefix is "*fo.*" on O1–O4 (with the period out of position on O4 because of the misprinted 56).
[5] The Huntington copy differs only in having *Your* on C2ᵛ, *D oe* [sic] on Ff2, and *Why* (an error for *Whych*) on O4ᵛ.

Signatures: Normally only the first two leaves of each signature (except A1, the title-page) are signed; but irregularity is introduced by the signing also of A3, C3, C4, Cc3, Ee3, and Ff3, and by the absence of the usual figure i on the first leaf of C and Dd.[1]

Copies: Two copies of *B* are known,[2] — that in the British Museum (Grenville 11170) and that in the Huntington library.[3] The former, which I have used, is in fair condition, though its margins were once covered with scribbles that have left some traces after being washed.

Contents: *B* contains 280 poems, attributed as follows:

To Surrey (Nos. 1–36, 262–265)	40
To Wyatt (Nos. 37–81, 83–127, 266–271)	96
To Grimald (Nos. 133, 134, 149–152, 154, 165–167)	10
To Uncertain Authors (Nos. 82, 168–261, 272–310)	134

Arrangement: The order of the poems has been completely changed. Thus No. 243 is inserted among Surrey's poems, but with the clear statement that it is an answer by an uncertain author to Surrey's No. 26; while No. 82 has been moved from Wyatt's poems to those of the uncertain authors. Other poems, like Nos. 234 and 261, have been transferred (with new titles) so as to follow the poems they answer. The additional poems of Wyatt and Surrey (Nos. 262–271) that in *A* appeared at the end of the volume are inserted among the other poems by those writers. More striking still, 30 poems by Grimald are dropped, the 10 that remain are transferred to the end of the text, and Grimald's name is displaced by his initials "N. G." To compensate for the omis-

[1] The Huntington copy differs considerably (cf. Greg's comment on p. 14, below). Thus C2 and C3 are misprinted as B2 and B3; no leaf is signed in signature O; P1 is misprinted as H1; T2 and Y1 appear with the unusual punctuation "T.ii," and "Y, i."; Y2 is omitted; "Dd." appears instead of the normal signature "Dd.i." There are a few other variants in punctuation as well.

[2] It may be worth noting that in the sale-catalogue of Joseph Haslewood's library issued by R. H. Evans in December, 1833, lot 1254 is characterized as "Surrey's Songs, *the original edition,* very imperfect." This was presumably a copy of either *B* or *C*. It was bought by Thomas Thorpe for four shillings.

[3] Formerly owned by Sir William Tite, at whose sale (lot 3065) in 1874 it was bought for £46 by the Rowfant library of Frederick Locker (afterwards Locker-Lampson). On April 28, 1905, it passed into the possession of the late Mr. W. A. White, of Brooklyn, who in turn sold it to Mr. Huntington in October, 1923. When Tite owned it (see p. 37 n. 3, below) the book lacked its imprint-leaf and apparently the date on the title-page; but these defects have since been remedied. It contains the book-plate of Locker-Lampson and various manuscript notes by him, Mr. White, and Dr. Rosenbach.

¶ *SONGES AND SONETTES*
written by the right honorable Lorde
Henry Haward late Earle of Sur-
rey, and other.

Apud Richardum Tottell.
Cum priuilegio ad imprimendum
solum. 1 5 57.

sions from Grimald, 39 new poems by uncertain authors (Nos. 272–310) are inserted. The 280 poems are printed in the following order: Nos. 1–26, 243 (by an uncertain author), 262, 264, 265, 27–31, 263, 32–81, 83–113, 266–271, 114–127, 168–177, 179–201, 234, 202–233, 235–241, 244–252, 259, 260, 272–288, 255, 256, 253, 289, 257, 258, 254, 290, 178, 261, 291–296, 82, 242, 297–310, 133, 134, 149–152, 154, 165–167.

The contents and the order of poems in *B* are exactly followed in *C–I*; the page-divisions are identical with those of *C–G*.

C. Second Edition 1557 (July 31), Second Setting

¶ *SONGES AND SONETTES* / *written by the right honorable Lorde* / *Henry Haward late Earle of Sur=* / *rey, and other.* / *Apud Richardum Tottell.* / *Cum priuilegio ad imprimendum* / *folum.* 1557. /

[Colophon] 𝕴𝖒𝖕𝖗𝖎𝖓𝖙𝖊𝖉 𝖆𝖙 𝕷𝖔𝖓𝖉𝖔𝖓 𝖎𝖓 𝖋𝖑𝖊𝖙𝖊𝖋𝖙𝖗𝖊𝖙𝖊 / 𝖜𝖎𝖙𝖍𝖎𝖓 𝕿𝖊𝖒𝖕𝖑𝖊 𝖇𝖆𝖗𝖗𝖊, 𝖆𝖙 𝖙𝖍𝖊 𝖋𝖎𝖌𝖓𝖊 𝖔𝖋 𝖙𝖍𝖊 / 𝖍𝖆𝖓𝖉 𝖆𝖓𝖉 𝖋𝖙𝖆𝖗𝖗𝖊, 𝖇𝖞 𝕽𝖎𝖈𝖍𝖆𝖗𝖉 𝕿𝖔𝖙= / 𝖙𝖎𝖑𝖑, 𝖙𝖍𝖊 .𝖝𝖝𝖝𝖎. 𝖉𝖆𝖞 𝖔𝖋 𝕴𝖚𝖑𝖞. / Anno. 1557. / Cum priuilegio ad impri= / mendum folum. /

Collation: 4°, sigs. A–Gg⁴. [A1] title: [A1ᵛ] "¶ *To the reader.*": A2–[E2ᵛ] Surrey's poems, with "*SVRREY.*" at the foot of [E2ᵛ]: [E3–N1ᵛ] Wyatt's poems, with "*T. VVYATE the elder.*" at the foot of [N1ᵛ]: N2–Ff1 poems by anonymous writers, with "*Songes and Sonettes of* / *vncertain auctours.*" at the head of N2: Ff1–[Gg1ᵛ] Grimald's poems, with "¶ *Songes written by N. G.*" on Ff1 (after four lines of text) and "N. G." at the end of the text on [Gg1ᵛ]: [Gg2–Gg3ᵛ] "*The table.*", followed by "FINIS." (in black letter): [Gg4] colophon; verso blank.

Running-titles: The running-title is regularly "*and Sonettes*" for the recto from A2 to Gg1 (except on N2: see the "Collation" above); it is usually followed by a period,[1] but in five cases (C3, C4, E1, K1, K2) apparently by a comma; it is misprinted "*and Sonettes.*" on A3.[2] "*Songes*" appears on the verso from A2ᵛ to Gg1ᵛ. The head-line of Gg2–Gg3ᵛ is "*The table.*"

Folio-numbers run from "*Fo. 2.*" on A2 to "*Fo 117.*" on Gg1; but leaves 3, 5, 7 are unmarked in any way and the 15 is illegible.[3] Furthermore, 76 is misprinted for 79, 116 for 114, and 114 for 116. Except for a very few cases of

[1] The exceptions are on the first two leaves of R, X, Bb, Ff, and in the Rosenbach copy also N1.
[2] This misprint is not in the Rosenbach copy.
[3] The 15 is correct in the Rosenbach copy.

"*Fo*" the prefix is uniformly "*Fo.*"; and about half of the figures are followed by periods.

Key-words: Incorrect key-words are *You* (I3) for *Then, whic* (O4^v) for *Which,*[1] *On* (Ee4^v) for *One, Doe* (Ff2) for *Do-* or *Doway.* No key-words appear on E2^v, N1^v, Gg1^v, Gg2.

Signatures: Normally only the first two leaves of each signature (except A1, the title-page) are signed, but irregularity is introduced by the signing of A3, B3, C3, C4, by the absence of a signature on Gg2, and in C. ii, Dd. ii, and Ff. i by the unusual punctuation.

Copies: Three copies of *C* are known, that in the Capell collection, Trinity College, Cambridge, that in the library of Mr. Carl H. Pforzheimer, Purchase, New York, and that now owned by the Rosenbach Company of New York and Philadelphia. I have used the first but have also consulted the third, on the title-page of which an old owner has written "Robt. Brome Lichfield."

Contents and Arrangement: In its contents and order of poems *C* is identical with *BD+*; its page-divisions are exactly like those of *BD–G*.

No information about Tottel's *Miscellany* is given in the Stationers' Register (except for one entry on February 18, 1583); for the Stationers' Company had been but recently incorporated in 1557, and no attempt at securing entries of all new publications in the official register seems to have been made so early. There is, indeed, no positive proof that *A* was the first edition, although the evidence tends to make that assumption highly probable.[2]

A bears the date of June 5 in its colophon. Tottel's edition of Surrey's *Aeneid* followed shortly, with the date of June 21. Edward Arber assumed that work on the latter was not begun till *A* had been finished, that the composition of the *Aeneid* took sixteen days, and that, at a similar speed of composition, *A* must have been begun about April 11. There is, however, as Dr. Greg points out,[3] no reason why work on both books may not have been proceeding at the same time; while if *B* and *C* were, as has been suggested, set up almost simultaneously, a quicker rate of composition was possible in Tottel's shop than Arber allowed for.

Fifty-six days after the date given in the colophon of *A* the entire

[1] The key-word is *whi* in the Rosenbach copy.
[2] See p. 20, below.
[3] "Tottel's Miscellany," *The Library*, n. s., v (1904), 123.

first edition had been disposed of, the type distributed, and a second edition, thoroughly revised, set in type and printed. This edition (*BC*) has a colophon with the date of July 31, 1557.

In the introductory notes to his edition (pages xi–xii) Arber remarks:

> The two known copies — one in [*sic*] Grenville Collection, British Musuem [*sic*]; and the other in the Capel Collection, Trinity College, Combridge [*sic*]; vary in some *minutiæ* from each other: but it is incredible that there should be two *distinct* editions finished by the same printer, on the same day. [*Mr. W. A. Wright has collated the first Impression of this Reprint, with the Capell copy. The variations from the Grenville copy, in spelling, are occasional in the bulk of the book, but very numerous in the 39 additional poems.*[1] *Nothing but a comparison of the five or six earliest editions can solve this riddle. Meanwhile we can but believe that one or other of these copies has either a wrong title page or colophon.*]

Now Bohn, editing Lowndes's *Bibliographer's Manual* in 1863,[2] and Hazlitt in 1867 [3] had called attention to variations between *B* and *C*, the latter asserting that they showed *B* and *C* to be distinct editions. Dr. Greg, in the essay already referred to, remarks (page 119): "It is sufficiently evident that Professor Arber had never examined the question for himself, and that when differing from these authorities and pronouncing their statements 'incredible,' he was relying upon purely *à priori* considerations. Now, 'incredible' as it may at first appear that there should be two distinct editions, bearing an identical date, and issuing from the same printing-house, such is nevertheless undoubtedly the case. . . . Either we have to do," he adds (pages 120–121), "with two successive editions, one a close reprint of the other,[4] or else with a work set up in duplicate."

As for duplicate settings, he explains (pages 122–123), "the custom was most likely due to some trades' union regulation for the benefit of compositors. It was not, so far as I am aware, till nearly thirty years later that an ordinance of the Company limited the number of copies

[1] This statement is not true. The spelling of *B* and *C* varies greatly, but it varies as much in the poems common to *ABC* as in those added in *BC*. The italicized passage does not occur in Arber's 1870 reprints (from which the first part of my quotation is taken) but was added to later issues.

[2] v, 2547–2548.

[3] *Hand-Book to Early English Literature*, p. 585.

[4] This, as I show below, was actually the case, though for reasons explained on p. 20 I have kept to the ordinary classification of *B* and *C* as duplicate settings.

to be printed from one setting to 1250 for ordinary works;[1] but the ordinance very possibly did nothing more than give binding force to a generally recognized custom. This would necessitate any work for which a large number of copies were required being set up several times over in rapid succession, and it would be quite likely that if sufficient type were available two settings might be worked off simultaneously. It is even possible that it might be set up in duplicate sheet by sheet and worked. That the second edition of Tottel's Miscellany is a case of duplicate setting I have no doubt."

Dr. Greg observes (pages 126–127) that "there is no single sheet common both to the Grenville and Capell copies." He shows also that the Rowfant (now the Huntington) copy of *B* was printed from the same setting as the Grenville copy. "In a few cases . . . the signatures differ both from the Grenville and Capell copies. It is, however, significant that in all these cases the signature in the Rowfant copy is incorrect,[2] and the variations can therefore be accounted for by supposing the latter to be an early impression from forms which underwent correction before the Grenville copy was printed." Finally, "the misprinted signatures of the Rowfant copy . . . would be far more likely to occur in the original setting than in a mere reprint, and we should therefore be justified in supposing the setting represented by that and the Grenville copies to be earlier than that represented by the Capell." This last remark Dr. Greg characterizes as a conjecture. It can, however, be proved to be a fact.

To make the situation clear: *B* and *C* have identical contents, identical page-divisions, and almost identical verse-arrangement, but differ widely in spelling and punctuation. The problem, then, resolves itself to this: (1) were *B* and *C* set independently from *A*? (2) was *B* set from *A*, *C* from *B*? (3) or was *C* set from *A*, and *B* from *C*? The first query can be ruled out at once: the close agreement of *B* and *C* in page-division and line-arrangement shows the impossibility of their having been set separately and independently from *A*. *B* and *C* drop 30 poems, add 39 others, and upset the order of the 241 poems which they have in common with *A*. With changes of this sort it is inconceivable that two

[1] For this ordinance see Arber's *Transcript* of the Stationers' Registers, II, 43; V, liii. For further information see Greg, "The Decrees and Ordinances of the Stationers' Company, 1576–1602," *The Library*, VIII (1928), 414.

[2] See p. 10 n. 1, above.

compositors working simultaneously from copies of *A* could have pro-
duced two texts so close to each other in appearance and arrangement.
This conclusion will become more certain in the light of the evidence
that follows.

That *B* was set from *C* or *C* from *B* can easily be proved. All the
editions after *A* conclude with a "Table," or index of first lines, which
it would have been useless for me to reprint because it does not index
the text of *A*, the basis of my own edition. Nevertheless, a study of the
Tables in *B* and *C* is indispensable, because it proves conclusively that
one was printed directly from the other. To make the Table the in-
dexer had before him the printed pages of *B* or *C* (at the present stage
of the argument, no matter which), and he merely turned one page
after another, jotting down in the order of their appearance the first
lines that begin with "A," "B," and so on. Then, assigning to each
line a folio-number, he gave his index to the compositor without having
paid any attention to alphabetizing. Hence under each letter from
"A" to "Y" the folio-numbering is progressive, not shifting back and
forth as would have been the case if a correct alphabetical order had
been followed. To make this point clear, the Table of *B* begins as
follows:

*A*Las so al things now.	5
Although I had a chek	10
As oft as I behold	12
Auising the bright	22
Alas madam for steling.	23
Accused though I be.	29
All in thy loke my life	34

And to skip to the end of the "T's":

The vertue of Vlisses	100
To falser eport	100
To walke on doutfull	101
To trust the fained face	102
The blinded boy.	103
The wisest way, thy bote	104
The auncient time com.	113
Therfore when restlesse.	116
The long loue that in my	

Such a crude (but then customary) method of indexing necessarily led to the immediate detection of faulty folio-numbers in the text. In *B*, for example, folios 25, 33, 35, in *C* folios 79, 114, 116, are incorrectly numbered; but in the Table of each edition the poems on these folios are referred to by their correct numbers — a fact that fails to disclose from which edition the Table was compiled. The Tables, however, are exactly alike in the arrangement of pages and lines, as could not have happened, except by a miraculous coincidence, had not one been set from the other.

Still other proofs that one of the Tables is a mere reprint of the other can be given. Thus, in both, No. 81 is indexed as "If euer man" instead of "If euery man"; No. 281 is in both referred to as on folio 95, whereas (since the verso and recto are never indicated) the reference should be 94; No. 217 is in both entered as "O temerous tauntresse" instead of "tauntres"; No. 309 is in both referred to as "Resigne ye dames" instead of "Resigne you dames"; No. 86 begins in both texts with "Once" but in both Tables with "Ones"; in both Tables No. 307 begins with "You" instead of "Ye"; in both "Set me wheras the sun" (No. 12) follows "So cruel prison" (No. 15), although the order should be reversed because No. 15 follows No. 12 in the text; "Stand who so list" should in the Tables, according to the texts of both *B* and *C*, begin with "Stond"; "The stormes are past" (No. 34) is on folio 18 of both texts, and hence in the Tables should precede "The fansie which that I" (No. 36), which is on folio 18ᵛ; "The longer life" (No. 174) should in both Tables read "The lenger life", and "Wiat restes here" (No. 31) should in both read "W. resteth here"; in both Tables the first line of No. 13 is printed in the abbreviated form, "I neuer saw my L. lay." Finally, in both Tables "The long loue that in my" (No. 37) is added at the end of the "T's" with no folio-reference at all; it should have been on the preceding page with the folio-number 19, before the 19 already there.[1] These correspondences could not possibly

---

[1] It is provided with a folio-number for the first time in *H*, though it remains at the end of the "T's." In *I* it remains there still, but with the folio-number changed from 19 to 108 merely because it follows 107. Its position in *BC* indicates that the indexer noticed the omission of the line after his Table had been paged, and that he added it at the end of the "T's" because there was no room for it at the beginning, where it belongs. The folio-numbers in the Tables of *BC*, by the way, are almost identical from beginning to end in arrangement, faulty spacing, and even in slight peculiarities of impression.

have occurred, nor could the exact agreement in abbreviated words and the tolerably close agreement in spelling and punctuation, if one Table had not been set from the other. They prove either that *B* followed *C* or that *C* followed *B;* and, since in *B* there are four misprints ("The flicking fame", "To falser eport", and, on Gg2 and Gg2ᵛ, "Tbe" in the running-title) not found in *C*, it might perhaps not be unreasonable to assume that *C* followed *B*, correcting these errors.

As to spelling, the variations in the two Tables are comparatively slight and unimportant, consisting chiefly in the presence or absence of a final *e*, in the use of a single or a double consonant, or in the interchange of the letters *y* and *i*. It is significant that in many cases the form common to the Tables differs from that common to the *B* and *C* texts. For example, *giltles* (in the texts) appears in both Tables (under the letter "G," index-folio 13) as *giltlesse, breast* as *brest* ("I," 45), *fawlcon* as *falcon* ("L," 35), *birde* as *bird* ("L," 88), *Myne* as *Mine* ("M," 46); *Once* as *Ones* ("O," 33, "Y," 85), *tauntres* as *tauntresse* ("O," 74), *goonne* as *gonne* ("T, 29").[1]

Further evidence that one text was set up from the other is to be seen in the fact that both *B* and *C* have the incorrect key-word *You* for *Then* at I3 (an error that persists through *F*); both have signatures A3, C3, C4 marked in violation of the usual scheme;[2] both (see the Variant Readings) have a curious transposition of the phrases of *A* in lines 30–31, page 143; and both omit the same folio-numbers, 3, 5, 7.

Now which text served as copy for the other? The answer need not be left to assumption or conjecture. A comparison of the pages of *ABC* shows that *B* is much closer to *A* in spelling and arrangement of titles than is *C*. This fact, when reinforced by a line-by-line comparison of the two hundred forty-one poem-titles, proves clearly that *B* was set from *A*. So exact is the agreement of titles in position and line-arrangement (as in Nos. 13, 26, 50, 54, 55, 59, 60, 71, 73–75, 77, 124, 174, 179, 181, 192, 224, 225, 236, 264, 270, all of which in *C* vary slightly in ar-

---

[1] In many cases an old spelling that stands in the Table of *B* has been modernized in that of *C: shold*, for example, is changed to *should* ("A," 35), *shal* to *shall* ("A," 112), *Britle* to *Brittle* ("B," 5), *ded* to *dead* ("L," 89), *wold* to *would* ("T," 75), *fansie* to *fancy* ("W," 100, though in both texts it is *fansy*). Occasionally the opposite change occurs.

[2] *C* also has B3; but it does not, like *B*, print Cc3, Ee3, Ff3, perhaps a sign that *C*, following *B*, corrected these deviations from the rule.

rangement) as to make it certain that the compositor of B worked with his eye on A.[1] That C was set from B is shown by the various instances in which titles of poems — especially of those following a different order from that in A, or of poems not in A — agree in arrangement in B and C. For example, the titles of Nos. 113, 121, 127, 133, 165, 166, 172, 201–203 are arranged alike in BC but differently in A. In the thirty-nine new poems the titles of all but nine (Nos. 275, 277–279, 298–301, 310) are arranged exactly alike in B and C, and even in those nine differ but slightly.[2] Three or four titles (like Nos. 4, 62, 64) have in the three editions small variations of arrangement which are obviously due to mere chance. Such variations would be likely to occur even if one were deliberately trying to make an exact reprint; they could be avoided only by the most painstaking proof-correction.

It is significant, too, that in mechanical details C is more consistent than B, as may be expected when a printed text is used as the copy. Thus in the signatures, — which after the first three letters are normally signed in twos but which in B are managed somewhat irregularly (see page 10, above), — although the compositor of C, with his eye on the sheets of B, not only signs his own A3, C3, C4, as B does, but in his normalizing zeal also signs B3 (as B does not), yet he does not follow B in signing Cc3, Ee3, Ff3. So, too, with the folio-numbers. Although C makes blunders of its own (see page 11, above), it corrects the numbers misprinted by B, normalizes to "Fo." the erratic prefixes in the foliation of B, and restores some of the numbers (9–12, but not 3, 5, 7) omitted by B. But in the use of periods after the folio-numbers C is quite as irregular as B.

The point needs no further laboring. It should be noted, however, that the thirty-nine new poems in B were necessarily set from manuscript; in these C, following the printed text of B, has but a compara-

[1] In the title of No. 13 in A the word *alway* has a slight hiatus between l and w which recurs (though it is perhaps due only to the type) in B but not in C; and the same thing is true of the slight gap between w and i in *with* in the title of No. 71. Furthermore, in the title of No. 174 A has *stat*, with the final t scarcely legible: B emends this to *state*, while C (and hence $D+$) reads correctly *state/ of*. In the title of No. 150 and in many similar cases B changes the y's to i's, and C usually follows suit.

[2] Four of the nine titles (Nos. 278, 299, 300, 310) and several not enumerated above (Nos. 272, 280, 281, 283, 293, 294, 297, 303, 304, 307) show slight variations in spelling, punctuation, or capitalization. In one case, No. 301, C obviously changes the arrangement so as to escape the awkward division in B of *passi/ons*.

tively small number of variations of diction, and (though Arber asserts the contrary [1]) no extraordinary number of variations in orthography. It is significant, further, that in spite of the rearranged and added poems *B* keeps wherever possible the page-arrangement of *A*. According to the custom of the time, *A* itself (and, for that matter, *B–I* as well) was set directly into page, not galley, proof. Hence the repetition in *A*, at the top of signature L4, of two lines of the text from the bottom of signature L3^v.[2]

Now, although *B* unquestionably preceded and served as the copy for *C*, an extremely odd fact remains to be noticed — namely, that *B* has a number of unique readings (compare the list of Variant Readings, as in lines 4, 8, 9, 11, 16, on page 9, and lines 6, 8, 23, on page 12), which *C* discarded in favor of the old readings of *A*. In the new poems (Nos. 272–310) *B* and *C* on the whole agree closely in diction, but even they have (as at 243.19, 247.15, 250.28, 254.16) a few readings that vary. That *B* was set from a carefully revised text of *A* is shown not only by its unique readings but also by the text of No. 200, which in *B* is printed with its final letter capitalized to complete the acrostic. It is possible that, when he came to this poem, the compositor of *C* failed to observe the acrostic, for he eliminated both the final capital and the space (which appears also in *A*) after the initial letter of each line. On the other hand, it may be that the "editor" of *C* intentionally removed these obvious indications of the connection of No. 200 with Edward Somerset, just as he removed the name *Garret* ("Fair Geraldine") which in *B* had been inserted at 12.23. Both *B* and *C* made evident efforts to increase the impersonality of *A*, as in the substitution of *R.* for *Ryce* and *Rise* (192.12, 193.21) and of Grimald's initials for his name. I think it not improbable that the increase in anonymity of *C* over *B* is itself a further indication that *C* came later. Indeed, *C* may be later than July 31, 1557. It was *reprinted* from *B*, and the date of July 31 in its colophon may possibly be only a mechanical reproduction of the colophon of *B*. If some time intervened between the actual printings of *B* and *C*, it would be easier to account for the changes in *C* from the readings of *B* to those of *A*.

---

[1] See p. 13, above.

[2] For a similar error see Barnabe Googe's *Eglogs, Epytaphes, and Sonettes*, 1563, Arber's reprint, p. 127, and other cases noted by R. B. McKerrow, *Introduction to Bibliography*, 1927, p. 65 n.

Whatever the true explanation of this third revision, the fact remains that for all later editions the source was not *B* but *C*. That *C*, or a lost edition based on *C*, was the copy for *D* (and hence indirectly for *D*–I*) is proved not only by the page-divisions, line-arrangement, misprints, and textual readings, but also by the inverted-pyramid form in which Tottel's preface is printed in every edition from *C* to *I*. The choice of *C* as the text to be reprinted hardly seems likely to have been accidental. Tottel must have chosen it deliberately.

To bring these dry, but important, matters to a close, mention should be made of Dr. Greg's conclusion[1] that the "duplicate setting" of *B* and *C* in July "affords strong presumptive evidence that the June edition was the first. It would appear that it was not until this edition was placed on the market that the printer realized what a demand there would be for the book, and had at once to make preparations for a large and rapid supply. This could hardly have happened except in the case of a first edition." Still another indication that *A* was the first edition is seen in its obvious misreading of the original manuscript copy at 191.7, where it has *R. so depe can auoyde*, while *B–I* present the correct reading of *Rodopeian maide*. It may be added also that, since *C* is a reprint of *B*, the two might better be spoken of as distinct editions; but that is so largely a matter of terminology that no urgent reason exists for upsetting the conventional statement that *B* and *C* belong to different settings of the second edition.

III. ELIZABETHAN EDITIONS (*D–I*)

D. THIRD EDITION 1559

¶ *SONGES AND SONETTES*/ *written by the right honorable Lorde*/ *Henry Haward late Earle of Sur=*/ *rey, and other.*/ *Apud Richardum Tottell.*/ 1559./ *Cum priuilegio.*/

[Colophon] ¶ IMPRINTED AT LON-/ *DON IN FLETE-*/ *STRETE*/ within Temple barre at the/ *figne of the hand and ftarre, by*/ *Richard Tottell.*/ *Anno.* 1559./ Cum priuilegio./

Collation: 4°, sigs. A–P⁸ (two sheets being sewed together in each quire). [A1] title:[A1ᵛ] "*To the reader.*": A2–[C2ᵛ] Surrey's poems, with "*SVRREY.*" at the foot of [C2ᵛ]: C3–[G1ᵛ] Wyatt's poems, with "*S. T. wyate the elder.*" at

[1] *The Library*, n. s., v (1904), 128.

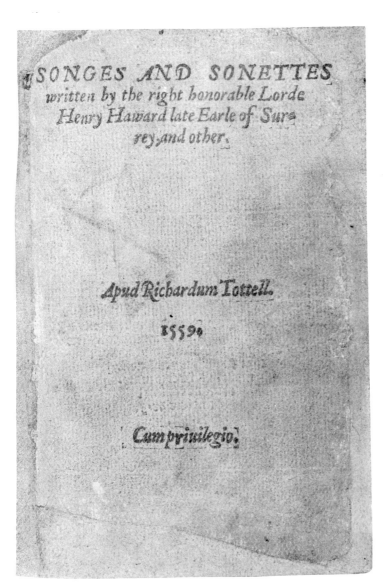

SONGES AND SONETTES
written by the right honorable Lorde
Henry Haward late Earle of Sur=
rey, and other.

Apud Richardum Tottell.

1559.

Cum priuilegio.

TITLE-PAGE OF THE THIRD EDITION 1559 (D)

the foot of [G1ᵛ]: G2–P1 poems by anonymous writers, with "*and Sonettes. of/ vncertaiue* [sic] *auctours.*" (heading combined with running-title) at the top of G2: P1–[P5ᵛ] Grimald's poems, with "*Songes written by N G.*" on P1 (after four lines of text) and "N G" at the end of the text on [P5ᵛ]: [P6–P7ᵛ] "*The table.*", with "Finis" (in black letter) at the foot of [P7ᵛ]: [P8] missing in the two copies I have seen; a modern page with "facsimile" colophon is supplied in the British Museum copy; verso blank.

Running-titles: The running-title for the verso is regularly "*Songes*" from A2ᵛ to P5ᵛ (but it is followed by a period on the verso of every third and fourth leaf);[1] for the recto, from A2 to P5 it is "*and Sonettes.*" (except for G2, on which see the "Collation" above); but on eight pages (A7, B7, B8, F7, F8, G8, H7, I7) it is not followed by a period, while in seven cases (L8, M2, M7, N1, N8, O7, O8) "*and Sonetts.*" appears. "*The table.*" is the head-line of P6–P7ᵛ.

Folio-numbers run from "*fo. 2.*" on A2 to "*fo. 117*" on P5, with the misprints 16 for 19, 37 for 36, 1 for 71, 87 for 76. The prefix also appears as "*Fo.*" or "*Fol.*" (the latter in most cases on the first two leaves of each signature), like "*fo.*" with or without the period, which also is sometimes omitted after the number. Furthermore, in certain figures (as in 11, 12, 21, 63, 66, 81, 103, 114) the type is broken, or out of alignment, or from a wrong font, while in 56 the 5 is printed upside down.

Key-words: Incorrect key-words are *Martia* (B7ᵛ) for *Martiall*, *Am* (B8ᵛ) for *And*, *You* (E3) for *Then*, *Ho* apparently (F2ᵛ) for *He*, *Why* (G8ᵛ) for *Which*, *Oh* (K5ᵛ) for *Of*, *A* (L3ᵛ) for *And*, *When* (O2ᵛ) for *Wher-* (*Wherfore*), *On* (O8ᵛ) for *One*, *Doe* (P2) for *Do-* or *Doway*. On C6 *And* is misprinted *Aud*, on K1 *Within* has an almost unreadable second *i* and the *n* is missing, or else it is meant for *With-*. No key-word appears on C2ᵛ or P5ᵛ. Key-words are likewise missing, because of trimmed or mended pages, on A7ᵛ, A8, K4ᵛ, P6, as well as on the faked page E7ᵛ, of the British Museum copy; but they are printed correctly in the Rosenbach copy.

Signatures: Except for A1, the title-page, the first four leaves of each signature are signed without error; but sometimes, as in K3 and M3, the period after the numeral looks more like a comma, and in one case, K4, it does not appear at all.

Copies: Two copies of *D* are known, (1) that in the British Museum (Grenville 11171), and (2) that now owned by the Rosenbach Company of New York and Philadelphia. In the former Grenville wrote: "This appears to be an unique Copy no other having been yet found with this

---

[1] In the British Museum copy, E7ᵛ (which is a faked page) also has "*Songes.*"; but no period appears in the Rosenbach copy.

date. The earliest date is that of 1557, so that my Copy of 1559 is the second edition." It has various mended pages, while four leaves (E7, G7, I8, P8, as well as part of K4) have been supplied in such clever facsimiles that in the British Museum catalogue and in all other bibliographical works one leaf only, P8, is particularized as modern. P8 has what purports to be a "facsimile" colophon, though the "facsimile" is a reproduction based upon E. The other three leaves — corresponding to pages 72.41–74.32, 131.27–133.31, 164.32–166.31, of my reprint — are likewise "facsimiles" drawn from E,[1] not from another copy of D.

Although I was aware of the faked pages when I made the entries for D in my Variant Readings, I inserted readings from them because I could find no other pages to consult. Since that time (2) has turned up, and through the kindness of Dr. A. S. W. Rosenbach I have been permitted to examine it at my leisure. It contains but two of the leaves (E7 and I8) lacking in (1). An examination of them shows that the readings attributed to D in the Variant Readings [2] should be deleted at 73.20, 29, 74.11, 15, 30, 164.32, 34, 35, 37, 38, 165.6, 23, 27 (first entry only), 35, and that the following additions [3] should be made:

> 73.16 it] it it
> 25 lingred] lingered
> 74.26 listned] listened
> 164.34 pikes] pyckes
> 38 the] *Om.*
> 166.24 bared] barhed

A few entries, too, like those at 17.12 and 42.4, should be omitted, as the text of (2) is quite clear.

The Rosenbach copy is in very bad condition, with every leaf (including the title-page) badly stained and wormed, and with almost every leaf torn and mended. Furthermore, it is incomplete, lacking signatures A2, D7, G7–H1, M6–P8. Still it is valuable because, if for

---

[1] As is proved by the typography and arrangement of the colophon, by entries in my Variant Readings under 74.15, 132.19, 24, 31, and by the spacing and the identical spelling and punctuation of these pages and the corresponding pages in E.

[2] Those listed for D at 73.2, 29, 34, 74.15, 30, 132.13, 16, 19, 22, 24, 31, 133.31, 164.32, 35, 37, 165.6 (second entry), 35, do not appear in D*, which, however, does have the reading listed for E at 132.8.

[3] Only the last of these occurs in D*, which also reads *now* for *the* at 164.38.

no other reason, it supplies four pages which are faked in (1), and be-
cause it clears up a few other readings that are doubtful there. A former
owner, said to have been Edward Capell, made many red-ink cor-
rections in the text, which he had collated with an earlier edition. Both
(1) and (2) belong to the same impression, as is shown by their identity
of collation and misprints.

Contents and Arrangement: The contents and arrangement of *D* are
exactly like those of *BCD*+*, the page-divisions like those of *BCD*-G*.

Characteristics: With *D* the degeneration of the text has been ac-
celerated by careless printing and still more careless proof-reading. It
was set up from a copy of *C* (or some lost edition based on *C*), as a
glance at the Variant Readings and at the page- and line-arrangement
of the two editions clearly proves; [1] but purely through carelessness it
introduces many typographical errors and many unauthorized readings
not found in *ABC*. Its line-arrangement follows that of *C* rather closely,
but in the titles of 21 poems (Nos. 13, 243, 264, 29, 32, 33, 35, 98, 124,
172, 185, 192, 194, 198, 218, 221, 224, 236, 237, 310, 149) it re-arranges
(in most cases very slightly) the lines of *C*. In addition, *D* and all sub-
sequent editions keep the inverted-pyramid form of the printer's
preface that *C*, not *B*, introduced, but they do not keep the para-
graph-signs of *C*. As for typographical errors, *D* omits entire lines, as
34.26, 40.10, 43.6; it combines two lines into one, as at 30.34–35 and
143.30–31; [2] and these errors, as well as others too numerous to mention
here, reappear in every later edition. Many of the blunders made by
D are corrected in *D**, some of them perhaps actually from a compari-
son of the texts of *D* and *C*.[3] It is a bit ironical that at 207.12 *D* has the
correct reading of *to* instead of *by*, and that this one improvement on
the text of *ABC* was not adopted in *D** or *E–I*.

[1] But at 187.25 it (like *D**) has *clarke*, following *B* rather than *C*. I suspect that this
was an inadvertent change from the text of *C*, not an actual borrowing from that of *B*.

[2] In the latter case *BC* (see the Variant Readings) had reversed the order of phrases
in *A*. *D* merely keeps the first line of the new arrangement made in *C* and drops the
second line.

[3] Thus the readings assigned to *D* in the Variant Readings for 7.15, 9.7, 11.4, 13.22,
13.26, 14.7, 14.31, 16.3, 16.33, 18.24, 18.40, 22.39, 25.9, 27.2, 27.7, 31.8, 31.10, etc., are
corrected in *D** to follow those of *C* (and hence many appear later in *E*); as are also, for
example, its misprints at 4.4, 6.6, 9.11, 9.22, 20.13, 20.35, 26.28, 28.39, 30.19.

INTRODUCTION

D*. FOURTH EDITION 1559

¶ *SONGES AND SONETTES*/ *written by the right honorable Lorde*/ *Henry Haward late Earle of Sur=*/ *rey, and other.*/ *Apud Richardum Tottell.*/ 1559./ *Cum priuilegio.*/

[Colophon] ❧ 𝕴𝖒𝖕𝖗𝖎𝖓𝖙𝖊𝖉 𝖆𝖙 𝕷𝖔𝖓𝖉𝖔𝖓/ 𝖎𝖓 𝕱𝖑𝖊𝖙𝖊𝖘𝖙𝖗𝖊𝖙𝖊 𝖜𝖎𝖙𝖍𝖎𝖓 𝕿𝖊𝖒𝖕𝖑𝖊/ barre, at the figne of the/ 𝖍𝖆𝖓𝖉𝖊 𝖆𝖓𝖉 𝖘𝖙𝖆𝖗𝖗𝖊, 𝖇𝖞/ 𝕽𝖎𝖈𝖍𝖆𝖗𝖉 𝕿𝖔𝖙𝖙𝖊𝖑𝖑./ 𝕬𝖓𝖓𝖔. 1559/ Cum priuilegio./

Collation: 8°, sigs. A–P⁸. [A1] title: [A1ᵛ] "*To the reader.*" : A2–[C2ᵛ] Surrey's poems, with "*SVRREY.*" at the foot of [C2ᵛ]: C3–[G1ᵛ] Wyatt's poems, with "*S. T. VVYATE the elder.*" at the foot of [G1ᵛ]: G2–P1 poems by anonymous writers, with "*Songes and Sonettes of*/ *vnc ertain* [sic] *auctours.*" at the top of G2: P1–[P5ᵛ] Grimald's poems, with "*Songes written by N. G.*" on P1 (after four lines of text) and "*N. G.*" at the end of the text on [P5ᵛ]: [P6–P7ᵛ] "*The table.*" with "Finis" (in black letter) at the foot of [P7ᵛ]: [P8] colophon; verso blank.

Running-titles: The running-title for the verso is regularly "*Songes*" from A2ᵛ to P5ᵛ (but it is followed by a period on the third and fourth leaves of C, D, F, H, K, M, O); for the recto, it is "*and fonettes.*" on A3, A7, "*and Sonnettes.*" on A5, "*and Sonets*" on the first and second leaves of C, D, F, H, K, M, O, and "*and Sonettes*" (with or without a period) elsewhere. (Many of the final *s*'s are inverted or else are in an odd font of type.) A section-heading (see the "Collation" above) appears on G2, "*The table.*" on P6–P6ᵛ, "*The table*" on P7–P7ᵛ.

Folio-numbers run from "*Fol.* 2." on A2 to "*fo* 117." on P5, with 26 misprinted as 25, with the first numeral in 13, 14, 18 printed as an italic *i*, with the 4 of 104 torn off, and with an occasional number out of alignment. All the numbers except 49 are followed by periods. The prefix likewise appears as "*fol.*" and "*Fo.*", which like "*Fol.*" and "*fo*" are sometimes followed by a period, sometimes not.

Key-words: None appears on C2ᵛ or P5ᵛ. Incorrect key-words are *Am* (B8ᵛ) for *And, Ladye* (C1ᵛ) for *Layd, O* (C4ᵛ) for *Of, You* (E3) for *Then, why* (G8ᵛ) for *Which, Chere* (L8ᵛ) for *There, Doe* (P2) for *Do-* or *Doway.*

Signatures: The first four leaves of each signature, except for A1 and G3, are signed without error; no period appears before the numeral in I1 and L1.

Copy: Only one copy is known, that formerly in the late Sir George Holford's library, at the sale of which by Sotheby and Company on March 28, 1928, it was bought by the Rosenbach Company for £5000.

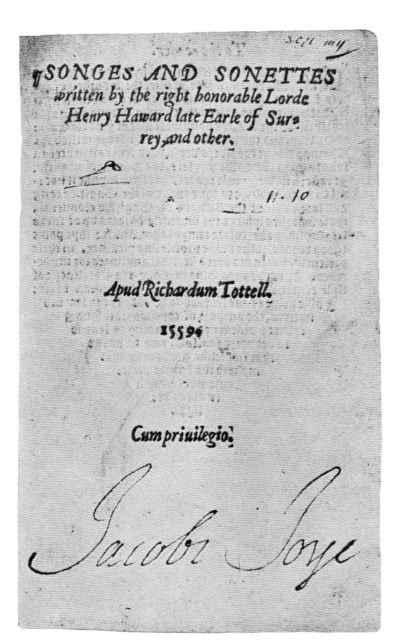

¶SONGES AND SONETTES
written by the right honorable Lorde
Henry Haward late Earle of Sur₌
rey, and other.

Apud Richardum Tottell.

1559.

Cum priuilegio.

Jacobi Joye

TITLE-PAGE OF THE FOURTH EDITION 1559 (*D**)

Sotheby's sale-catalogue of *The Holford Library*, part III, lot 522, repro-
duces the title-page, and gives these details:

A rust-hole in sig. I6, a corner torn from N8 affecting pagination and two
or three words, a tiny wormhole through the last gathering very slightly af-
fecting the text, 18th Century calf, gilt, Horace Walpole's copy with his book-
plate; from the collection of Lord Vernon. . . . On the title is the name of a 17th
Century owner, Jacobi Joye.[1]

It should be added that the first line of the text on A6 is imperfectly
impressed.

This book has always been listed as merely another copy of edi-
tion *D*. After I had made unsuccessful efforts to see it in London dur-
ing 1926, Mr. F. S. Ferguson, as a member of the firm of Bernard
Quaritch, Ltd., secured permission in November, 1927, to examine it
for me at the auction-rooms, and immediately informed me that, al-
though it has a title-page identical in setting with that of *D*, the re-
mainder of the book belongs "to an entirely different edition of the
same year." More recently, Dr. Rosenbach generously turned the book
over to me for study. I have not considered it necessary to print a list
of the variant readings of *D** in the present volume, for although they
are interesting, they have no real authority. Some account of them,
however, is given in notes on pages 22, 23, 26, 29; and whenever in this
second volume an embracive reference like *D*+, *D–G*, or *D–I* appears, it
may be assumed that the reference likewise applies to and includes *D**.

Contents and Arrangement: The contents and arrangement of *D**
are exactly like those of *B*+, the page-divisions like those of *B–G*.

Characteristics: D, as has been said, was set up, directly or indirectly,
from a copy of *C*; and in turn *D**, except for the title-page (which is
identical in setting with that of *D*), was re-set from a somewhat cor-
rected copy of *D*, which it follows very closely in line-arrangement.
Even the short lines, cast in inverted-pyramid form, at the end of the
address "*To the reader*" follow the lines of *D* exactly, though varying
in spelling and punctuation. The same fact distinguishes every page of
the text and the Table. As for poem-titles, only 14 have a different
alignment in *D* and *D**, in spite of their varying spelling and punctua-
tion: three of these (Nos. 22, 185, 310) differ from one another in *C*, *D*,

---

[1] In the *Catalogue of the Classic Contents of Strawberry Hill Collected by Horace
Walpole* (1842) it is lot 143. Thomas Thorpe bought this copy for ten guineas.

and D^*; five (Nos. 14, 29, 32, 33, 237) are alike in C and D^*, six (Nos. 82, 90, 165, 175, 281, 305) are alike in C and D. Hence the variations seem to be accidental in D^*. This edition, furthermore, has also corrected the faulty folio-numbers of its predecessor, — though it makes one new mistake (25 for 26) of its own, — as well as several of its incorrect key-words. It also states in better form the section-heading on G2 (see the "Collation" above), changing the key-word of G1^v to *Songes* in order to point to the new heading; whereas in D the key-word is *Vncer-* (apparently because of *vncertain auctours* in the corresponding section-heading of C), although the heading has the awkward form of "*and Sonettes. of/ vncertaiue* [sic] *auctours.*" D^* follows D in dropping entire lines at 34.26, 40.10, 43.6, and in combining lines 30.34–35 and 143.30–31; but it also drops line 147.19, as do $E+$. A considerable number of the readings introduced by D are corrected in D^* so as to return to the readings of C.[1] On the contrary, D^* (as is natural since it was set in type from that printed text) often adopts the new readings of D.[2] And, of course, it introduces many new and unauthorized variants, a large number of which were taken over by E.[3] Hence without an exact count of the variants it would be difficult to say whether D or D^* has the worse text.

D^*, finally, has a remarkable lot of manuscript notes copied *verbatim et literatim* by Horace Walpole himself [4] from those which, in the Bodleian copy of I, G. F. Nott falsely attributed to John Selden.[5] They are discussed on pages 100–101, below, and several are reproduced (from I) in the Notes.

E. Fifth Edition 1565

1565./ ¶ *SONGES AND SONETTES*/ *written by the right honorable*/ *Lord Henry Hawarde late*/ *Earle of Surrey, and*/ *other.*/ *Apud Richardum Tottell.*/ *Cum priuilegio.*/

---

[1] See p. 23 n. 3, above.

[2] *E. g.*, those listed at 5.15, 6.7, 6.31, 7.3, 8.2, 8.18, 9.6, 11.12, 12.8, 15.34, 17.30, 19.22, 24.41 — all of which reappear in E. It likewise keeps many readings of D — as at 4.10, 4.34, 6.15, 7.16, 10.24, 23.32, 30.5 — that do not reappear in E.

[3] See p. 29 n. below.

[4] Mr. Percivall Merritt, a well-known authority on Walpole, confirms my opinion of this matter. Cf. pp. 100–101, below.

[5] See pp. 36, 38 n. 3.

15 6 5.

¶SONGES AND SONETTES
written by the right honorable
Lord Henry Hawarde late
Earle of Surrey, and
other.

Apud Richardum Tottell.

Cum priuilegio.

TITLE-PAGE OF THE FIFTH EDITION 1565 (E)

[Colophon] ¶ IMPRINTED AT LON-/ *DON IN FLETE-/ STRETE*/ within Temple barre at the/*figne of the hand and ftarre, by*/ *Richard Tottell.*/ *Anno.* 1565./ Cum priuilegio./

Collation: 8°, sigs. A–P⁸. [A1] title: [A1ᵛ] "*To the reader.*": A2–[C2ᵛ] Surrey's poems, with "*SVRREY.*" at the foot of [C2ᵛ]: C3–[G1ᵛ] Wyatt's poems, with "*S. T. VVYATE the elder.*" at the foot of [G1ᵛ]: G2–P1 poems by anonymous writers, with "*vncertain auctours.*" at the top of G2 under the running-title: P1–[P5ᵛ] Grimald's poems, with "*Songes written by N. G.*" on P1 (after four lines of text) and "N. G." at the end of the text on [P5ᵛ]: [P6–P7ᵛ] "*The table,*" with "*Finis.*" (in black letter) at the end of [P7ᵛ]: [P8] colophon; verso blank.

Running-titles: The running-title for the verso from A2ᵛ to P5ᵛ is "*Songes*" (in the Bodleian copy it is trimmed off on L7ᵛ, O3ᵛ, and O8ᵛ, as it is in part on several other pages); for the recto it varies between "*and Sonettes*" and "*and fonettes*", usually with, sometimes without, a period (in the last five signatures it is often partly trimmed off the Bodleian copy). "*The table*" is the head-line of P6–P6ᵛ, "*The table.*" of P7–P7ᵛ.

Folio-numbers run from "*Fo.* 2" on A2 to "*Fol.* 117" on P5 (a few, especially of the later ones, are trimmed off the Bodleian copy in whole or in part); but 23 is misprinted for 13, 26 for 29, 18 for 81, 59 for 95, 115 for 105. The prefix, sometimes with, sometimes without, a period, also appears as "*fo*" or "*fol*", and occasionally a period follows the number. In folio 39 the 9 is either imperfect or from a different font.

Key-words: Incorrect key-words are *Flow* (A5) for *Floring, Am* (B8ᵛ) for *And, Lady* (C1ᵛ) for *Layed, O* (C4ᵛ) for *Of, you* (E3) for *Then, Ye* (E8) for *Yet, Whe* (G2ᵛ) for *Who, To* (G8) for *The, Why* (G8ᵛ) for *Which, Vnt* (H1) for *Vnto, Whose* (H8) for *Who, For* (K6ᵛ) for *Not, That* (L5ᵛ) for *Thus, Chere* (L8ᵛ) for *There, An* (M6ᵛ) for *And, As* (N2ᵛ) for *An, Doe* (P2) for *Do-* or *Doway.*[1] No key-word appears on C2ᵛ, G1ᵛ, P5ᵛ.

Signatures: Except for A1 and G3, the first four leaves of each signature are signed without error (as they are in *D* and *D**).

Copies: Three copies of *E* are known: (1) the Heber copy that recently passed from the Britwell to the Huntington library for £600;[2] (2) the copy formerly belonging to Professor George Herbert Palmer,

---

[1] Something is wrong, also, with the key-word on E3ᵛ; in the rotograph it looks like *End* (or *Eno*) instead of *Euer*; and so it does at the same place in *G*. In the Huntington copy it is clear enough.

[2] It has only the slightest of variations from the foregoing description, as in omitting the period after *elder* at the foot of G1ᵛ.

now in the library of Wellesley College; [1] (3) the copy in the Bodleian. I have used the last-mentioned, in which several head-lines are shaved off, various pages are stained, and the last leaf is mended. This copy has the book-plate of Nathaniel Crynes (†1745), whose name is written on the title-page and stamped at the bottom of folios 97 and 117. The title-page has been badly maltreated: it bears the names of Anne Bowes (twice) and Elizabeth Bowes, besides other names that have been scratched out, the old and new shelf-marks "Crynes 891" and "391," and the disfiguring Bodleian stamp. Hence it is not a beautiful object to look at. On a fly-leaf and on leaves inserted at the end of the book there are various lengthy but unimportant manuscript notes, said [2] to have been written by the antiquarian William Fulman, who died in 1688. The same hand occasionally inserted marginal notes to the poems.

Contents and Arrangement: The contents and arrangement of *E* are identical with those of *B–D*F+*, the page-divisions with those of *B–D*FG*.

Characteristics: E was set up from a copy of *D** (or from some lost edition based upon *D**), as the omission of a line at 147.19 and various

---

[1] I have casually examined this copy, which has various penciled notes by Mr. Palmer, one of them stating that he paid Quaritch £95 for it. An inserted letter from a former Bodleian librarian tells something of the history of the book:

> "Oxford
> "Feb. 15. 1907

"Dear Mʳ Quaritch,
    "The book you sent me *is* a copy of the *1565* edition of the Earl of Surrey's Songs and Sonnets, printed at London by Richard Tottel. Your copy unfortunately wants the titlepage and three leaves at [*sic*] end (two leaves of index, and one leaf bearing the imprint)
    "When Dʳ Richard Rawlinson wrote 'C & P' on the inner front cover the book was in his own possession and was perfect, so it must have been mutilated after his death in 1755.
    "Our copy is complete except that a few of the headlines have been cut into by the ruthless binder, late in the 17th century.
    "This has been no trouble.
> "Very truly yours
> "F. Madan"

Mr. Palmer's copy was perhaps that advertised by Thomas Thorpe in catalogues for 1834, 1835, 1838, 1839, and 1840 at prices ranging from 10*s*. 6*d*. to £1 1*s*.
[2] By John Price, Bodley's librarian (†1813), in a letter to Bishop Percy on December 6, 1797 (J. B. Nichols, *Illustrations of the Literary History of the Eighteenth Century*, VIII [1858], 323).

¶SONGES AND SONETTES
written by the right honorable
Lord Henry Haward late
Earle of Surrey, and
others.

Apud Richardum Tottell.
1567

Cum priuilegio.

TITLE-PAGE OF THE SIXTH EDITION 1567 (F)

other readings prove.[1] But in composing *E* the printer made many additional errors, eliminating or inserting extra syllables, changing words, and dropping a line on no plan, but by sheer carelessness. For example, *E* omits the phrase *alwaies the end* at 234.11, and an entire line at 203.26; it changes *hast* (27.3) to *hall*, *nay* (39.37) to *no*, *Atlas* (90.19) to *Itlas*. These errors, and numerous others, are repeated in every subsequent edition. Some attention, on the other hand, was paid to freeing the text of *E* from obvious typographical errors, in which respect it is superior to the text of *D*.

F. SIXTH EDITION 1567

¶ *SONGES AND SONETTES*/ *written by the right honorable*/ *Lord Henry Haward late*/ *Earle of Surrey, and*/ *others*/ *Apud Richardum Tottell*/ 1567/ *Cum priuilegio*/

[Colophon] ¶ IMPRINTED AT LON-/ *DON IN FLETE-STRETE*/ within Temple barre at the/ *signe of the hand and starre, by*/ *Richard Tottell.*/ *Anno* .1567./ Cum priuilegio./

Collation: 8°, sigs. A–P⁸. [A1] title: [A1ᵛ] "*To the reader*": A2–[C2ᵛ] Surrey's poems, with "*SVRREY.*" at the foot of [C2ᵛ]: C3–[G1ᵛ] Wyatt's poems, with "*S. T. VVYATE the elder.*" at the foot of [G1ᵛ]: G2–P1 poems by anonymous writers, with "*Vncertain auctours.*" at the top of G2, under the running-title: P1–[P5ᵛ] Grimald's poems, with "*Songes written by N. G.*" on P1 (after four lines of text) and "N. G." at the end of the text on [P5ᵛ]: [P6–P7ᵛ] "*The table*", with "Finis." (in black letter) near the end of [P7ᵛ]: [P8] colophon; verso blank.

Running-titles: The running-title of the verso from A2ᵛ to P5ᵛ is "*Songes*"; of the recto, "*and sonettes*" and "*and Sonettes*" in the proportion of about two to one (this is the first time there has been no punctuation in the head-lines); of P6–P7ᵛ "*The table*".

Folio-numbers run from "*fol.* 2" on A2 to "*fo.* 117" on P5. The only error is 23 for 13 (the same misprint is in *E*). Sometimes the prefix is "*Fo.*" or "*Fol.*", and in a few cases there is no period.

Key-words: Incorrect are *T* (A7) for *To*, *Am* (B8ᵛ) for *And*, *O* (C4ᵛ) for *Of*, *In* (C7ᵛ) for *Im-* or *Imprisoned*, *You* (E3) for *Then*, *To* (G8) for *The*, *Why* (G8ᵛ) for *Which*, *Verce* (H6) for *Verses*, *Whose* (H8) for *Who*, *ickle* (K2ᵛ) for

---

[1] *E. g.*, *D** has the readings listed for *E* (some are also in *C*), not those for *D*, in the Variant Readings at 4.11, 5.2, 6.34, 7.15, 7.23, 8.12, 9.7, 9.29, 10.10, 11.4, 12.22, 12.29, 13.22, 14.7, 15.6, 16.3, 16.4, 17.28, 18.24, 19.31, 21.33, 22.8, 24.8, 25.28, 26.36, 27.11, 30.29, 37.2, 89.6, 123.32, 126.16, 170.31, 172.7.

Tickle, Cheere (L8ᵛ) for *There, As* (N2ᵛ) for *An, As* (N6) for *Ah*. No key-words appear on C2ᵛ, G1ᵛ, P5ᵛ.

Signatures: Except for A1 (the title-page) and G3, the first four leaves of each signature are signed without error (as they are in *D–E*).

Copies: Three copies of *F* are known: those in (1) the John Rylands library, Manchester, (2) the Hunterian Museum of the University of Glasgow, (3) the Pierpont Morgan library of New York.[1] The last, the only one I have seen, Miss Belle da Costa Greene suggests may be the Lefferts copy (which is usually said to be untraced). Its first four leaves and last leaf are slightly torn and mended, with various words restored in facsimile. Accordingly, facing page 29 I have reproduced the title-page of (1).

Contents and Arrangement: The contents and arrangement of *F* are identical with those of *B–EG+*, the page-divisions with those of *B–EG*.

Characteristics: *F* was set up from a copy of *E*, as is definitely proved by the errors they have in common. It introduces dozens of verbal changes (like *couered* for *cowarde* at 8.34, *wasteth* for *wisheth* at 127.3, *games* for *flames* at 187. 27, *od* for *on* at 188.9, *walles* for *wastes* at 236.30, *dame* for *dames* at 257.13, and like the omissions of the second *that* and the second *then* at 221.25, 36), which reappear in all subsequent editions. It also abounds in typographical errors. The line-arrangement, too, is obviously adopted from *E*: of the 280 titles of poems, only some 17 differ in arrangement (and those very slightly) from the titles of *E*.

G. Seventh Edition 1574

¶ SONGES AND SONETS/ *written by the right honorable*/ Lorde Henry Haward late/ Earle of Surrey, and/ others./ *Apud Richardum Tottell*/ 1574./ *Cum priuilegio.*/

[Colophon] ¶ Imprinted at London in/ *Fleteſtrete within Tem-*/ ple Barre at the ſigne of/ 𝔱𝔥𝔢 𝔥𝔞𝔫𝔡 𝔞𝔫𝔡 𝔖𝔱𝔞𝔯𝔯𝔢/ 𝔟𝔶 𝔯𝔦𝔠𝔥𝔞𝔯𝔡𝔢/ 𝔗𝔬𝔱𝔱𝔢𝔩𝔩./ Anno. 1574./ *Cum priuilegio.*/

[1] In (1) and (2) the title-page has a period after *others, Tottell,* and *priuilegio* (cf. Greg, *The Library*, v [1904], 132, and the facsimile facing p. 29). In (1) the paragraph-sign at the beginning of the colophon has dropped out. In both copies the key-word on A7 is correct; while in (1) a correct key-word appears on B8ᵛ, an incorrect one (*Ii* for *Im-*) on C7ᵛ. For these variations from my description of (3) I am indebted to the Rylands and Hunterian librarians. The Rylands librarian also kindly permitted me to have rotographs of signatures A–A4, P8, to compare with (3).

¶SONGES AND SONETS
written by the right honorable
Lorde Henry Haward late
Earle of Surrey, and
others.

Apud Richardum Tottell
1574.

Cum priuilegio.

TITLE-PAGE OF THE SEVENTH EDITION 1574 (*G*)

Collation: 8°, sigs. A–P⁸. [A1] title: [A1ᵛ] "*To the Reader.*": A2–[C2ᵛ] Surrey's poems, with "*SVRREY*" at the foot of [C2ᵛ]: C3–[G1ᵛ] Wyatt's poems, with "*S. T. WYAT the elder.*" at the foot of [G1ᵛ]: G2–P1 poems by anonymous writers, with "*Vncertaine auctours.*" at the top of G2 under the head-line: P1–[P5ᵛ] Grimald's poems, with "*Songes written by N. G.*" on P1 (after four lines of text) and "N. G." at the end of the text on [P5ᵛ]: [P6–P7ᵛ] "*The table.*", with "Finis." at the foot of [P7ᵛ]: [P8] colophon; verso blank.

Running-titles: "*Songes and Sonettes.*" is the head-line of A2. Thereafter the verso head-line as far as P5ᵛ is either "*Songes*" or "*ſonges*"; except for "*and Sonettees.*" on A7, the recto head-line to P5 is "*and Sonettes.*" (usually with a period) or "*and ſonettes*" (usually without a period). For P6–P7ᵛ "*The table.*" is the running-title on P6, "The table." on P6ᵛ, "*The Table.*" on P7–P7ᵛ.

Folio-numbers run from "*Fo.* 2." on A2 to "*Fo.* 117." on P5, with 4.1 misprinted for 14, 21 for 22, 68 for 83, 70 for 85, 106 for 114, and in some twenty cases with no period after the figure. The prefix also occurs once as "*Fo*" (B6); on the first and second leaves of signatures B, D, E, H, K, M, O, and on P2, as "*fo.*"; and on the seventh and eighth leaves of the same seven signatures as "*fo.*"

Key-words: Incorrect key-words are *In* (C7ᵛ) for *Im-, than* (E3) for *Then, To* (G8) for *The, Whoso* (H8) for *Who, Nor* (I2) for *Not, To* (L4) for *The, Cheere* (L8ᵛ) for *There, As* (N2ᵛ) for *An, Vnfold* (N3) for *Vntold, As* (N6) for *Ah, Doe* apparently (P2) for *Do-* or *Doway.* No key-word appears on A6, C2ᵛ, G1ᵛ, P5ᵛ. On the key-word of E3ᵛ see above, p. 27 n. 1.

Signatures: The first four leaves of each signature, except of course A1, are signed without error (as in D–F).

Copies: Five copies of G are known: those in (1) the British Museum, press-mark Grenville 11172; (2) the Bodleian, shelf-mark Tanner 149; (3) the Huntington library;[1] (4) formerly in the Britwell library (the Heber copy), which was bought by Messrs. Quaritch on April 12, 1927, for £300; and (5) recently in the John L. Clawson library but now owned by Mr. Owen D. Young, of New York.[2] I have used the fine Grenville copy, but I have also examined the copies in the

---

[1] Formerly in the Locker-Lampson and Beverly Chew libraries. It presents a few variations from (1) in the punctuation of the prefix "*fo.*"

[2] This copy has the book-plates of Clawson and of two earlier owners, Edward Gordon-Duff and Winston Hagen. It measures 6¼ × 3¹⁵⁄₁₆ inches, the top being cropped, and the title-page, N1, and O2 repaired. Mrs. Robinson, Mr. Young's librarian, informs me that there are no important variations between this copy and the description I have given above. A copy of G was also once in the University of Cambridge library, but it disappeared (so the librarian tells me) "long ago." According to a manuscript note in the Rosenbach copy of D it lacked folios 69–73, 104, 112, 113.

Huntington and Bodleian libraries. The Bodleian copy lacks signature A4, but otherwise has only the slightest of variations.[1] Grenville noted: "This edition is of the greatest rarity. Warton & Nott both quote an edition of 1574, but neither of them appears to have seen it.[2] It is the more valuable as it differs in some words of the text from the edition of 1557." In the last sentence "the more" should be instead "very much less."

Contents and Arrangement: The contents and arrangement of *G* are identical with those of *B–FHI*, its page-divisions with those of *B–F*.

Characteristics: *G* was set up from a copy of *F* (or from some lost edition based on *F*), of which it is a close page-for-page reprint. In the "Table" as well as the text it also follows *F* closely in alignment, and only some 15 of its 280 titles vary in arrangement of the lines, and even those but slightly. Retaining most of the errors of its predecessor, it introduces others and adds to the unintelligibility of the text. For example, it substitutes *doleful* for *doubtful* (10.24), *Eche stone* for *eche* (*A* has *Eccho*, 14.3), *do* for *did* (178.33), *that* for *which* (197.4), *is* for *he* (235.19); it omits *the* at 14.10 and *she* at 186.34; it changes *her* to *his* at 246.18, *the* to *in the* at 257.13. In all these cases, and in others too numerous to mention here, *G* is followed by *HI*.

H. Eighth Edition 1585

[Type ornament] SONGES/ AND SON-/*NETS, WRITTEN/* by the Right honourable/ *Lord Henry Haward/* late Earle of Surrey, and/ others,/ [Ornament]/ Imprinted at London by Iohn VVin-/ det. 1585./

[Colophon] Imprinted at London *Anno Domini/* 1585./

Collation: 8°, sigs. A–P⁸. [A1] title: [A1ᵛ] "*To the Reader*": A2–C3 Surrey's poems, with "*SVRREY.*" on C3 (after three lines of text): C3–[G1ᵛ] Wyatt's poems, with "*S. T. WYAT the elder.*" at the foot of [G1ᵛ]: G2–[P1ᵛ] poems by anonymous writers, with "*Vncertaine Auctours.*" at the top of G2

---

[1] Many of its leaves are wormed and stained, many (including the title-page) mended. The colophon on the last leaf is mounted. The margins, too, are closely trimmed; but with a few slight exceptions all the text can be made out. On the title-page an old hand has written the name "Johem Layman."

[2] As a matter of fact, Nott (see pp. 36–37, below) speaks of two separate editions in 1574 as if he had seen both; but his statement cannot be trusted. He had seen *one* edition of 1574, as his collations in *P* show.

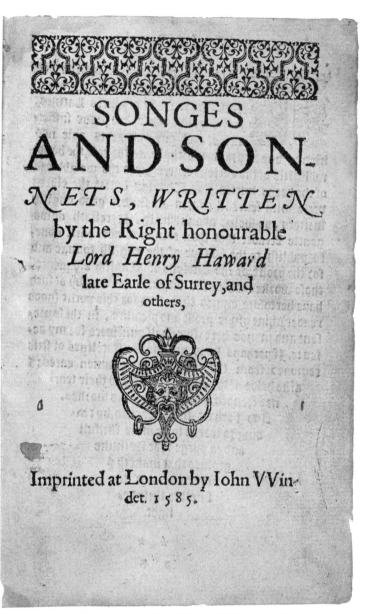

SONGES
AND SON-
NETS, WRITTEN
by the Right honourable
Lord Henry Haward
late Earle of Surrey, and
others,

Imprinted at London by Iohn VVin-
det. 1 5 8 5.

TITLE-PAGE OF THE EIGHTH EDITION 1585 (*H*)

under the head-line: [P1ᵛ–P6] Grimald's poems, with "Songs written by N. G. of the/ ix Muses" (heading combined with poem-title) near the middle of [P1ᵛ], and "*N. G.*" at the end of the text on [P6]: [P6ᵛ–P8] "*The Table*": [P8] colophon; verso blank.

Running-titles: The complete running-title "*Songes and fonnettes.*" appears on A2. Thereafter the rectos have occasionally "*and fonettes*" (never with a period), but in most cases "*and fonnettes.*" (generally followed by a period); "*and ſ nnettes.*" appears on A5, "*and fonenttes.*" on F5. The versos have "*Songes*", usually without a period; but among some fifteen periods that do appear one, on F2ᵛ, stands directly over the *s* of *Songes* instead of after it. "*The Table*" is the running-title of P6ᵛ–P8.

Folio-numbers run from "*fo. 2.*" on A2 to "*fo. 118*" on P6, with 5 misprinted for 8, 38 for 37, 60 for 61, 62 for 63, 64–71 for 65–72, 9 7 for 97. Further, the 7 of 107 is imperfect, and the 2 of 112 is dropped below the line. The prefix "*fo.*" does not vary; but its period is raised out of alignment some ten times, and on C8 the period after the number is likewise raised. Periods are about equally present and absent after the numbers.

Key-words: Incorrect key-words are *of* (A5) for *The* (both rightly in roman, and, were it not for a complicated error by which the last line of A5 is repeated on A5ᵛ, the *of* might be correct), *To* (A7) for *Vn-*, *Why* (E2ᵛ) for *Then*, *Bu* (H1) for *But*, *As* (L1) for *This*, *As* (M4) for *And*. The key-words on A2, L1, O2, P7, and P7ᵛ are blurred; those on A3ᵛ, B2ᵛ, C1ᵛ are torn; none appear on E8ᵛ, G1ᵛ, H4ᵛ, P1, P6.

Signatures: The first four leaves of each signature, excepting A1 and K4, are signed. Contrary to the rule, C5 is also signed. On the first leaf of F and M there is no numeral.

Copies: Six copies of *H* are known. I have not seen those in (1) the Capell collection, Trinity College, Cambridge, (2) the library of Mr H. C. Folger, New York, (3) the Huntington library,[1] (4) the Pierpont Morgan library. I have used the two copies in the British Museum, (5) C.34.a.13 and (6) Grenville 11173. My collations were made from the former (but in the Variant Readings I point out instances where its readings differ from those of the latter), which is a good copy, although its title-page is badly torn and mended. It has the book-plate of Thomas Jolley, F. S. A.

[1] Since writing this sentence I have examined (3), which was formerly in the Locker-Lampson and Chew libraries, and which varies considerably from the foregoing description. For example, its folio-number 97 is correct; its key-words on A2, A3ᵛ, B2ᵛ, C1ᵛ, P7, P7ᵛ are plainly printed; no key-word appears on I7, while that on H1 is misprinted as *B*; on P4ᵛ 117.3 is, by an unusual type-setting error, misplaced *after* the key-word; sig. I3 is not signed.

INTRODUCTION

Contents and Arrangement: The contents and arrangement of *H* are identical with those of *B–GI*, but its page-division and line-arrangement differ from those of every other edition. In most cases it reduces the titles of poems in length, as from four or even five lines to three or two, or from three lines to two; but the wider space between the lines of the text makes *H* run one page longer than *G* or than any other edition. Its titles, furthermore, are awkwardly arranged, several (as those at the end of folios 12, 19ᵛ, 37ᵛ, and 42) being printed partly at the foot of one page and partly at the top of the next, while the title of No. 9, of which only four words appear at the bottom of folio 5, is repeated in full at the top of folio 5ᵛ. Because of the changed foliation a new Table is provided, in which for the first time "The long loue that in my" is furnished with a folio-number, though it is not changed in position.¹

Characteristics: *H* has an abominable text, repeating most of the errors of its predecessors — especially of *G*, from which it was set up — and adding others in almost incredible profusion. An exceptionally careless compositor omitted numerous lines that are in *G*, — as 59.28, 125.8, 139.21, 250.5, — transposed lines 2 and 3 of page 117, made senseless changes like *Macedonians cheife captaines* from the *Macedonians chieftaines* of *G* (117.27), by an involved error at 194.35 repeated a line, and often neglected to indent stanzas. He was slavishly followed by the compositor of *I*.

I. NINTH EDITION 1587

SONGES AND/ Sonnets, written by the/ Right Honorable Lord Henrie/ *Haward late Earle of Sur-/ rey, and others./* [Device]/ ¶ Imprinted at London by/ *Robert Robinſon, dwelling in Fetter/ Lane nere Holborne./* 1587./

[Colophon] None.

Collation: 8°, sigs. A–O⁸. [A1] title; verso blank: [A2] " To the Reader." (the preface is printed for the first time in roman and italic, not black-letter, type): [A2ᵛ]–C2 Surrey's poems, with "*SVRREY.*" at the foot of C2: [C2ᵛ–F7] Wyatt's poems, with "*S. T. WYAT the elder.*" near the end of [F7]: [F7–O2ᵛ] poems by anonymous writers, with the heading "*Vncertayne Authours.*"

¹ In *E–I* this poem begins, "The *one* long love," etc.; but the word *one* never appears in the Tables of *E–I*. Instead, the Table of *I* reads, "The longer love," etc.

SONGES AND

Sonnets, written by the
Right Honorable Lord Henrie
Haward late Earle of Sur-
rey, and others.

¶ Imprinted at London by
*Robert Robinson, dwelling in Fetter
Lane nere Holborne.*
1587.

TITLE-PAGE OF THE NINTH EDITION 1587 (*I*)

on [F7], under the Wyatt signature: [O2ᵛ–O6ᵛ] Grimald's poems, with "Songes written by N. G. of the/ ix. Muses." (heading combined with poem-title) near the middle of [O2ᵛ] and "N. G." at the end of the text on [O6ᵛ]: [O7–O8ᵛ] "*The Table.*" (this index is printed for the first time in roman instead of black-letter type, but with a black-letter capital in place of a roman one to introduce each section), with "FINIS." at the foot of [O8ᵛ].

Running-titles: The running-title throughout A2ᵛ–O6ᵛ is "Songes/ and Sonets."; but "Songes" appears as "Song" on I8ᵛ, while "Sonets" is followed by a comma on ten pages (A5, A6, C7, C8, I6, I7, L5, L6, N5, N6). There is an italic head-line, "*The Table.*",[1] on O7–O8ᵛ.

Key-words: Incorrect key-words are *God* apparently (D3) for *Go, Whree* (E8ᵛ) for *Where, Though* (H3) for *Through, The* (N7) for *Thy, A* (O6ᵛ) for *Alas, O* (O7ᵛ) for *Of.* Those on C1ᵛ, E1ᵛ, and K6ᵛ are blurred. There is no key-word on H1ᵛ.

Folio-numbers run from "fol. 3" on A3 to "fol. 110" on O6 without error or variation, but the 5 of 15[2] is almost blurred out.

Signatures begin with A3 and run by fives to O5; but B5, D4, F5, H5, K5 are not signed at all, and B is the only signature that bears a figure on its first leaf. C5 is signed with a roman, instead of an arabic, numeral; and several figures, as in D2, D3, L3, are so blurred or broken as to be unrecognizable.

Copies: Four copies of *I* are known: those in (1) the Bodleian, (2) the library of Mr. Carl H. Pforzheimer (from the Huth collection), (3) the Drummond collection in the University of Edinburgh, and (4) formerly in the Bridgewater library. The last is said by Seymour de Ricci[3] and Miss Bartlett[4] to be in the Huntington library, but this is a mistake. I have not succeeded in tracing its whereabouts[5] but have worked with (2) and consulted (1). Mr. Pforzheimer's copy (a note in the Huth sale-catalogue says that it "was found in the old wainscot of a baker's house at Chobham in Surrey") has two leaves slightly mended and several lower margins stained, but its text is perfect. The Bodleian copy (8°H.43.Art. Seld.) — in which leaf G is torn

[1] On O7ᵛ the initial letter of *The* is in roman type, but on O8ᵛ it is too badly broken to be read. The Bodleian copy has "*The*" in both places.

[2] Not true of the Drummond copy, which otherwise (according to the librarian of the University of Edinburgh) agrees with my description, and not true of the Bodleian copy.

[3] *The Book Collector's Guide* (1921), p. 308.

[4] *Mr. William Shakespeare* (1922), p. 93.

[5] Presumably this is the copy described in J. P. Collier's *Catalogue, Bibliographical and Critical, of Early English Literature* (1837), pp. 297–298.

in such a manner that a few letters are missing on G1^v — has dozens of manuscript notes and emendations in two or three hands, all of which Curll in 1717 and Nott in 1814 confidently but erroneously assumed to be the notes of the famous antiquary John Selden, and many of which obscure the original readings of the text. Elsewhere in this Introduction [1] and in the Notes are reproduced some of these annotations.

Contents and Arrangement: The contents and arrangement of *I* are identical with those of *B–H*. It has fewer pages than any other edition, thanks to its condensation of titles and to its printing of No. 310 in double columns — the only instance of such printing in any of the editions. Hence the page-divisions of *I* are entirely different from those of *A–G* or *H*.

Characteristics: I was set up from a copy of *H*, retaining nearly all the errors of the latter and making many of its own, as well as a few corrections (for example, returning to the readings of *A* at 233.40, 241.6, 246.2). These corrections were, I think, purely arbitrary, involving no comparison with any earlier edition; but, since among other things the folio-numbers are given without blunders, *I* has a more correct look than has *H*. This correct look is superficial: *I* omits lines at 53.21 and 227.10, makes senseless changes, as from *herauld* (189.3) to *he told*, and otherwise debases the already debased text of *H*. An Elizabethan reader who had *H* or *I* in his hands must frequently have had difficulty in understanding what the poets really meant.

IV. DOUBTFUL ELIZABETHAN EDITIONS

In the "Advertisements" to their 1717 and 1728 reprints (*J, L,* below) the printers Curll mentioned a 1569 edition of the miscellany that they had used. As there seems to be no other evidence of its existence, the references to it made by Brydges,[2] Chalmers,[3] Park,[4] Bliss,[5] and Nott probably came from the Curlls. Nott[6] carelessly asserts that Surrey's

---

[1] See especially pp. 100–101, below.
[2] *Censura Literaria,* I (1805), 244.
[3] *The Works of the English Poets,* II (1810), 322.
[4] Editing Walpole's *Catalogue of the Royal and Noble Authors,* I (1806), 271.
[5] Editing Wood's *Athenae Oxonienses,* I (1813), 158 n.
[6] *The Works of . . . Surrey . . . and Wyatt,* I (1815), cclxxvii–cclxxviii. On p. 286 Nott also speaks of the "first 4to. ed. of . . . 1547."

poems (that is, Tottel's *Miscellany*) "were first printed in June 1557. In the course of that and the following month, they went through no less than four distinct impressions. They were afterwards reprinted in 1665 [*sic*], in 1567 and in 1569, twice afterwards in 1574, again in 1585, and again in 1587." [1] There is, however, no proof whatever of the existence of four editions in 1557, of one in 1569, or of two in 1574. Sir Sidney Lee, in his sketch of Tottel in the *Dictionary of National Biography*, says, "A third edition was issued by Tottel in 1558," [2] but that date is no doubt a misprint for 1559. That other Elizabethan editions than *A–I* were published and have disappeared without leaving a trace seems highly probable. In particular the gaps between 1559 and 1565, 1567 and 1574, look suspicious. [3]

V. EIGHTEENTH-CENTURY EDITIONS (*J–M*) [4]

J. EDMUND CURLL'S EDITION 1717

SONGES *and* SONETTES./ WRITTEN/ By the Right Honorable Lord/ HENRY HAWARD, *late* Earle *of* SURREY./ [Ornament]/ Imprinted at LONDON, in *Fleſtſtrete*, within/ *Temple Barre*, at the Signe of the *Hand* and/ *Starre*, by *Richard Tottell. Anno* 1567./ *Cum Priuilegio./* Re-printed by E. CURLL. *Anno* 1717./

Collation: 8°, pp. viii, 32. P. [i] half-title, "The/ Earl of SURREY's/ POEMS./ Price *One Shilling.*"; verso blank: p. [iii] title; verso blank: p. [v]

[1] Cf. Heinrich Nagel, *Sir Thomas Wyatt und Henry Howard, Earl of Surrey, eine litteratur- und sprachgeschichtliche Studie* (1889), p. 5: "Innerhalb zweier Monate wurden sie viermal aufgelegt und von neuem wurden sie publiziert in den Jahren 1565, 1567, 1569, 1574 (zweimal), 1583 [*sic*] und 1587."

[2] Padelford, *The Poems of Henry Howard* (1920), p. 220, also names a 1558, but not a 1559, edition. He repeats the statement in his 1928 edition, p. 260.

[3] Cf. the entry of "*Songes and Sonnettes*" in the Stationers' Register on February 18, 1583. Sotheby's sale-catalogue (1874, lot 3065) of Sir William Tite's library listed a copy of the *Songs and Sonnets* under the date 1561, remarking: "This is the third edition of the Earl of Surrey's Poems. A former possessor probably wishing it to be considered THE FIRST EDITION (of which only one copy is known) has cropped the small 4to. volume so as to resemble a small 8vo. and to avoid detection of course has cancelled the leaf containing the imprint. According to Lowndes this copy sold for £15." (But Lowndes, in his *Bibliographer's Manual*, v [1863], 2548, had correctly spoken of the copy of 1557 as "now in Mr. Tite's Collection.") In the Tite sale (cf. *The American Bibliopolist*, vi [1874], 91) it brought £46, passing into the Rowfant and, finally, into the Huntington library (see p. 10 n. 3, above). The date 1561 is a bad guess for 1557 (*B*).

[4] These and all subsequent editions, of course, are printed in roman and italic type.

"*Mr.* POPE'*s*/ CHARACTER/ OF THE/ AUTHOR./ IN/ His Poem intituled, *Windſor Foreſt*, inſcrib'd/ to the Lord *Lanſdown*." [eight lines quoted]: p. [vi] "*Advertiſement by the* EDITOR.": pp. [vii–viii] "TO THE/ READER." (Tottel's preface, printed in italics): pp. [1]–32 Surrey's poems, with no heading on p. [1] but with "*SVRREY*." at the end of the text on p. 32.

Running-titles: "To the READER." p. viii; "*SONGES*/ *and SONETTES*." pp. 2–31; "*SONGES*, &c." p. 32.

Signatures: The signatures are [A]–E⁴, with A1–4 unsigned and the first two leaves of B–E signed.

Copies: The British Museum has two copies, with the press-marks 1077.g.13 (2) and 1077.i.26. The former lacks the half-title (pages i–ii); the latter, with the autograph of Thomas Jolley, F. S. A., and the date 1808, has the half-title but lacks pages 9–16 of the text. I own a copy, and there is another in the Harvard College library: in both the half-title is missing. No doubt many other copies exist.

Contents: This reprint contains the forty-one poems (including No. 243, which is not by Surrey) that appeared in the Surrey section of *F*.

In the Advertisement Curll remarks:

In order to give the Publick as correct an Edition as I could of these valuable POEMS, I procured among my Friends Three several *Editions*, printed in the Years 1565, 1567, and 1569,¹ all which I found very full of Typographical Errors, but the most correct, was that of 1567, from which this Edition is printed,² and to which, the *Folio*'s number'd by numeral Figures in the Margin refer. When I had made the Edition of 1567 as correct as I could from the other Two; I heard of a nother Copy in the *Bodleian* Library in *Oxford*, among Mr. SELDEN's Books, wherein were many considerable Amendments, suppos'd to be made by that eminent Person: which I got collated by a learned Gentleman there.³ So that I hope it will appear I have given my Lord SURREY's *Poems* in their Antique Dress, in as careful and accurate a manner as possible: And if these admirable SONGES and SONETTES, meet with a Reception

---

¹ Nothing is known of this edition: see p. 36, above.

² Hence in Lowndes's *Bibliographer's Manual*, ed. Bohn, v (1863), 2548, we are misinformed that the 1567 edition "is considered the most correct of the early editions."

³ A very learned gentleman there assures me that Selden's hand is not one of the two, or perhaps three, represented in the book (*I*). Bodley's librarian, John Price, in describing the volume to Bishop Percy on December 6, 1797 (J. B. Nichols, *Illustrations of the Literary History of the Eighteenth Century*, VIII [1858], 324), declared that "none of these *written* emendations, &c. appear to be in the handwriting of Selden; they rather resemble that of Ascham." Roger Ascham, however, died nineteen years before the 1587 edition of the miscellany was published.

equal to their Merit, they shall be immediately follow'd by the remainder, in the same Volume, written by himself, and his intimate Friend Sir Thomas Wiatt the Elder. To which will be subjoin'd a very full and particular Account of these noble Authors, who have hitherto been undeservedly deny'd the Justice due to their Memories.

London,   *Vale.*
April 13, 1717.

This edition was ultimately due to Alexander Pope. As Warton wrote: "Pope, in *Windsor Forest*, having compared his patron Lord Granville with Surrey, he [that is, Surrey] was immediately reprinted, but without attracting many readers. It was vainly imagined that all the world would eagerly wish to purchase the works of a neglected ancient English poet, whom Pope had called *the* Granville *of a former age*."[1] Curll, accordingly, was discouraged, and he did not "immediately" carry out the promise of his Advertisement. A manuscript note by Haslewood in a copy of *K* (1077. g.13 [1]) suggests that Curll's plans to issue the remainder of the Tottel's *Miscellany* poems were stopped "in consequence of the rival edition by Sewell [*K*], to which in the typographical arrangement it is far superior." Eleven years later his son, Henry Curll, reissued the edition, with a continuation from the poems of Wyatt (see *L*, below).

K. Meares–Brown Edition 1717

POEMS/ OF/ *HENRY HOWARD,*/ Earl of *SURREY,*/ Who Flourifh'd in the Reign of *HENRY*/ the Eighth./ *Printed from a Correct Copy.*/ WITH THE/ POEMS of Sir *THOMAS WIAT*, and/ others his Famous Contemporaries./ To which are added fome Memoirs of his Life/ and Writings./ [Double rule]/ *LONDON:*/ Printed for *W. Meares* at the *Lamb*, and *J. Brown* at/ the *Black-Swan* without *Temple-Bar.* 1717./

Collation: 8°, pp. xvi, 263, +7 unnumbered. P. [i] title; verso blank: p. [iii] dedication to Thomas Duke of Norfolk; verso blank: pp. [v–vi] "The Original/ PREFACE.": pp. [vii]–xvi "MEMOIRS." of Surrey: pp. 1–40 Surrey's poems, with "SONGES/ AND/ SONETTES." at the head of p. 1 and "*Surrey.*" at the foot of p. 40: pp. 41–107 Wyatt's poems, with "Here Beginneth Sir *T. Wyattes* Woorkes." at the top of p. 41 and "*Syr T. Wyatte the Elder.*" at the

---

[1] *History of English Poetry*, ed. Hazlitt, iv (1871), 29.

end of his poems on p. 107: pp. 107–252 poems by anonymous writers, with "Vncertaine Auctors." on p. 107: pp. 253–263 Grimald's poems, with "*Songes written by N. G. of the nine Mufes.*" (heading combined with poem-title) at the top of p. 253, and "*N. G.*" at the end of the text on p. 263: p. [264] blank: pp. [265–269] "THE TABLE.", with "*FINIS.*" at the end: p. [270] "*ERRATA.*" (consisting of fifteen lines).

Running-titles: "PREFACE." p. vi; "*MEMOIRS.*" pp. viii–xvi; "*SONGES and SONETTES.*" pp. 2–16, 18–112, 161–263; "*SONGES and SONNETS.*" p. 17; "*SONGS and SONNETES.*" pp. 113–123, 125–160; "*SONGS and SONNETS.*" p. 124; "THE TABLE." pp. [266–269].

Pagination: Pp. i–vii, 264–270 are not numbered. Furthermore, 131 is misprinted for 121, 158 for 154, 159 for 155, 155 for 158, 154 for 159, 125–140 for 225–240. In the Grenville and Sumner copies 52 is also misprinted for 152, and the figures are set crookedly.

Key-words: Incorrect are *make* (p. xii) for *made* (itself, however, a misprint for *make*), *And* (p. 15) for *Ah*, *The* (p. 40) for *Here*, *No* (p. 143) for *Ne*, *The* (p. 241) for *Tombed*, *Thus* (p. 245) for *This*, *A* (p. 247) for *Her*, *Out* (p. 253) for *But*. (All these key-words are in roman type.) *Wher* (p. 35) for *Where* also appears in the Sumner copy. No key-words occur on pp. xvi, 28, 127, 160, or (in 1077.g.17 only) on p. 3.

Signatures: The signatures are A–S⁸, with A3, A4, and the first four leaves of B–S signed. Instead of Q the mark is Qq.

Copies: This is a rare book. The British Museum has four copies, in one of which is pasted a clipping from a bookseller's catalogue of 1811, offering a copy at the high price of one pound seven shillings. A copy presented to the Harvard College library in 1874 by Charles Sumner has the book-plate of Horace Walpole, and on the fly-leaf, in Walpole's autograph, the "Epitaph written by the Earl of Surrey on one Clere."

The title-page announces, perhaps as a slap at Curll, that a "Correct Copy" of the miscellany has been followed. So incorrect is the text, however, that some labor was involved in discovering what "Correct Copy" the editor attempted to reproduce. A detailed examination of his readings proves that he followed *D**. For example, he omits *vayn most* (126.9), as well as lines 34.26, 40.10, 43.6, and combines lines 34–35 of page 30, — errors that appear in *D–I*. But he also omits line 147.19, as do *D**+, though not, as do *E*+, line 203.26 or the phrase *alwaies the end* (234.11). At 28.3 he has *Wyat*, with *D* and *D**, where *E*+ have *What* (but in his Table he has *What*); while his readings of *tracte* (6.34), *place* (7.23), *no* (37.2) — to name no others — come from *D**. The editor changed words and phrases apparently at random, and did not scruple to insert a new line. For instance, feeling that the sense was incomplete after 143.37, he added "Then throwen benethe the Hyll of Blisse."[1] The editor was George Sewell, hack-writer and M.D. of Edinburgh. His should have been the dubious satisfaction of producing from his "Correct Copy" the most corrupt text issued since 1557.

Two of the British Museum copies have no special points of interest — those with the press-marks Grenville 18047 and 79.a.24. The latter, however, came from the library of George III, and bound with it is an eight-page list of "Books sold by John Darby in Bartholomew-Close." Very interesting indeed are the other two copies.

The first of these (1077.g.17) was owned by the antiquary Thomas Park, whose signature, with the date 1796, is on the title-page. There is also a note asserting that he had "Collated [Sewell's edition] with Mʳ Malone's Copy of the 1ˢᵗ Edit. in 1557." The penciled marginal collations prove that Park consulted *B*, not *A*. He also adds, in the margins, references to the folio-numbers of "the first edition"; but there are no folio-numbers in *A*. This copy, which Park had annotated with the idea of getting out his own edition of the miscellany, passed into the hands of another literary antiquarian, Joseph Haslewood.[2]

Park owned a second copy (now 1077.g.13 [1]), in which he duplicated most of the notes of the foregoing volume. F. G. Waldron, of *Literary Museum* fame, had been an earlier, as Haslewood was a later, owner of this copy. A note by Haslewood on the title-page shows that it came into his possession at "Park's sale at Sotheby May 1829."[3] The notes and collations in this volume are too numerous to particularize. Most of them were made in order to impress some one, presumably a bookseller, with the desirability of a new edition. Thus after enumerating all the editions with which he was familiar from 1557 to 1815, — including Nott's 1815 edition of Surrey and Wyatt "in two quarto volumes, under the bulk of which the modern book-stalls are now groaning," — Haslewood writes: "there is ample room to believe the merit and rarity of the work [that is, Tottel's *Miscellany*], although

[1] For the line supplied here by *I*, see p. 100, below.
[2] See Haslewood's sale-catalogue, 1833, No. 1257.
[3] See Sotheby's *Catalogue of the Miscellaneous Library of a Poetical Antiquary* [Thomas Park], lot 171 (sold on May 9, 1829).

[41]

forming a portion of the national poets,[1] is such, a distinct edition would find a sufficient number of purchasors for 200 copies, but not for one or two thousand, a favourite wholesale number with some well informed, but rather cormorant bibliopolists." The notes were evidently submitted to various booksellers, as well as to Edmund Lodge for use in his historical and genealogical works. In Lodge's hands (as an inserted letter from that guilty man evidences) they suffered "a detention of many days." Haslewood was forced to relinquish his editorial plan. In a final preliminary note he calls attention to Park's penciled comments, and adds: "It seems certain he [Park] projected a new edition, but, on that subject, in talking with publishers, [was] fated like me, 'To talk the more because he talked in vain.'" All of which is but one illustration of the bad luck that has overtaken several prospective editors of Tottel's *Miscellany*.

L. Henry Curll's Edition 1728

THE/ Praise of Geraldine,/ (A Florentine Lady.)/ Being, the celebrated/ LOVE POEMS/ Of the Right Honourable/ Henry Howard,/ Earl of *Surrey*, and Knight of the moſt noble/ Order of the Garter; who was beheaded by/ King Henry VIII, in the Year 1546./ ALSO THE/ Poetical Recreations/ OF/ *Sir* Thomas Wyate,/ CALLED,/ *The* Delight *of the* Muses./ [Rule]/ Faithfully publiſhed from the Original Impreſſion./ Recommended by Mr. *POPE*./ [Rule]/ *LONDON:*/ Printed for Henry Curll in *Clement's-Inn-*/ Paſſage. 1728./

Collation: 8°, pp. vi, 90. P. [i] title; verso blank: p. [iii] "*Mr.* POPE'*s*/ CHARACTER/ OF THE/ AUTHOR./ IN/ His Poem intituled, *Windſor Foreſt*, inſcrib'd/ to the Lord *Lanſdown.*/" [eight lines of the poem quoted]: p. [iv] "*Advertiſement by the* Editor.": pp. [v–vi] "TO THE/ READER." (Tottel's preface): pp. [1]–32 Surrey's poems, with no heading on p. [1] but with "*SVRREY.*" at the end of the text on p. 32: pp. [33]–90 Wyatt's poems, with no heading on p. [33] but with "Sir *T. WYATE the Elder.*" at the foot of p. 90. In the British Museum copy, the only one I have seen, there is a separate Wyatt title-page (verso blank), without a signature-mark or page-number, that belonged after p. 32 though it is bound between pp. 40 and 41. It runs thus: "POEMS/ ON/ Several Occasions./ *By Sir* Thomas Wyate./ In

[1] Perhaps a reference to *M*, below.

EFFIGIEM/ THOMÆ VIATI./ [Three lines of Latin verse.]/ [The "effigy" between the letters T. and V. is reproduced.] / *Aetas* Viati./ *Syderei peteret quum Cœli Regna* Viatus,/ *Tempora luftrorum non dum compleverat Octo./*"

Running-titles: "To the READER." p. vi; "*SONGES/ and SONETTES.*" pp. 2–31, 34–89; "*SONGES,* &c." pp. 32, 90; none on pp. 1, 33.

This edition is a re-issue of *J*, with a fresh title-page and with the Wyatt poems added. The title-page itself is cleverly worded, and should have attracted attention. The book contains all the Surrey–Wyatt poems of *B–I* (including No. 243 and omitting No. 82, in contrast with *A*). It is now extremely rare.

M. ANDERSON'S EDITION 1793

Robert Anderson, *A Complete Edition of the Poets of Great Britain*, 8°, 13 vols., 1792–1794.[1]

Bibliographical information about this work would be superfluous. In volume I (1793), pp. 589–608, are reprinted (along with the original preface of the *Songs and Sonnets*) 41 poems (including No. 243) attributed to Surrey; pp. 611–637, 96 poems (omitting No. 82) attributed to Wyatt; pp. 638–643, 14 poems (Nos. 170, 174, 175, 181, 193, 199, 209–212, 246, 273, 303, 304) attributed to uncertain authors;[2] pp. 643–647, 10 poems attributed to Grimald. Thus the volume contains all the poems printed in the Surrey–Wyatt–Grimald sections of *B–I* and a mere sample of the Uncertain-Authors section.

Anderson attempted to keep the original spelling and punctuation of an unspecified edition. That he followed *D** appears from the following facts: with *D*+ he omits lines 34.26, 40.10, 43.6, and at 11.12 has *A Vow* for *Vow*, at 39.36 *The* for *To a;* but some of his readings, like *estate* (5.2), *Prisoner* (12.29), appear only in *D**+, not in *D*, and some, like *tracte* (6.34), only in *D*–G*, not in *D* or *HI*. Of course he introduces readings, like *The Complainte* (7.10) and *his gloves* (41.5), that do not occur in *A–I*.

[1] Anderson's name does not appear on this title-page, nor does the date (which I have adopted from the British Museum catalogue, although the first volume is dated 1793). Another issue has the title: "*The Works of the British Poets. With Prefaces, Biographical and Critical, by Robert Anderson, M.D.* . . . London: Printed for John & Arthur Arch; and for Bell & Bradfute, and J. Mundell & Co. Edinburgh. 1795."

[2] These same fourteen poems are reprinted in Bell's edition of Surrey (see p. 55, below).

VI. MODERN EDITIONS (*N-V*)[1]

N. PERCY–STEEVENS EDITION 1808

This unpublished two-volume edition is represented by an incomplete copy in the British Museum (Grenville 11568–69). In the first volume Grenville has a note: "Ld Surrey' [*sic*] Poems. by Percy & Steevens 8°. 2 vol. s.a. but 1807. Bishop Percy & Steevens had jointly edited & printed two vol^s of Ld Surrey's & other poems of blank verse prior to Milton, when a fire at the printer's Nichols's in February 1808 consumed the whole impression, of which only *4 copies* (which had been previously delivered) remained[2] — this copy had been sent to Mr Park that he might add some biographical notices — see his MS.S. note —."

In the note referred to, Park comments: "Received from Mr. John Nichols at the desire of Bp Percy, in November 1807; and in February following, the whole impression was swept away in the calamitous fire which consumed the offices and warehouse of the worthy printer. Four other copies are believed to have been preserved." Park's signature also appears on the title-page of volume I, and on a fly-leaf he wrote: "Biog. Notices of *blankverse writers* in this Vol. (To be prefixed,

---

[1] See p. 37 n. 4.

[2] Grenville's is the only copy I know of. It is the same as that listed in Sotheby's *Catalogue of the Miscellaneous Library of a Poetical Antiquary* [Thomas Park], lot 513 (May 9, 1829), and described as "Extremely Rare. Bp. Percy and George Steevens were joint editors of this Work, which was never completed, nearly the whole impression being destroyed by fire, with Mr. Nichols' warehouse, in February 1808." The printer, John Nichols, in a letter addressed to Percy on December 13, 1808 (J. B. Nichols, *Illustrations of the Literary History of the Eighteenth Century*, VIII [1858], 89), writes as if only one copy ("by being on a shelf in my dwelling-house") had been saved from the fire of February 8, and promises to send that one to him. J. P. Collier, however, owned another, two volumes bound as one volume, and described in his sale-catalogue, 1884, lot 824, with the added information that "Mr. Collier, in one of his notes, affirms that this copy contains portions which he has never met with in any other." My student and friend, Mr. B. M. Wagner, kindly informs me that in various catalogues issued by Thomas Thorpe from 1833 to 1845 apparently three different copies (to be distinguished by their binding in boards, russia, or morocco) are often advertised at prices varying from £2 12*s.* 6*d.* to £5 5*s.* The copy in boards, uncut, is described as "a present from the Bishop to J. Rose," and as one of *six* that survived; that in morocco (Thorpe's *Bibliotheca Selectissima*, n. d. [1840?], p. 103), as "the learned prelate's own copy, who has collated it with the editions of 1565 and 1587, and with a manuscript, the variations are noticed in his autograph," and as one of *three* (or, in other catalogues, *six*) that survived.

at the desire of Bp Percy, by T P.)," followed by the list, "Geo. Tur-
bervile/ Geo. Gascoigne/ Barn. Riche/ Geo. Peele/ J. Higgins/ James
Aske/ W^m. Vallans/ Nic. Breton/ Geo. Chapman/ Chr. Marlow/ I.
Nandernoodt [*sic*]/ Gab. Harvey/." No other notes of any kind ap-
pear in the volumes.

Of volume II — which contains poems (not in Tottel's *Miscel-
lany*) by Surrey (pages 1–81) and Wyatt (pages 83–141),[1] as well as
"*POEMS*/ *in Blank Verse*/ (*not Dramatique*)/ *prior to MILTON'S*/
Paradise Lost./ *Subsequent to*/ *Lord SURREY'S in this Volume*,/ *and to*
N. G.'s in the/ *preceding.*" (pages 143–342) — it is not necessary to
speak further. Neither it nor the first volume has a modern title-page.
They are octavos of 272 pages (volume I) and 342 pages (volume II).

Volume I, which alone concerns us, may be described as follows:

Collation: P. [1] title from *C*, "¶ *SONGES AND SONNETTES* [2]/ *written
by the right honorable Lorde*/ *Henry Haward late Earle of Sur-*/ *rey, and other.*/
Apud Richardum Tottel./ *Cum privilegio ad imprimendum*/ *solum.* 1557./":
p. [2] "¶ *To the Reader.*" (Tottel's preface): pp. [3]–40 Surrey's poems, with
"*SURREY.*" at the end of the text on p. 40, the lower portion of which is
blank: pp. 41–111 Wyatt's poems, with "*T. WYATE the elder.*" at the end of
the text on p. 111, the lower portion of which is blank: pp. 112–260 poems
(without heading or subscription) by anonymous writers: pp. 261–272 Grim-
ald's poems, with "¶ *Songes written by* N. G." on p. 261 and "N. G." at the
end of the text on p. 272.

Running-titles: On the verso, from p. 4 to p. 270, the running-title is
"SONGES AND SONNETTES"; on p. 272 "SONGES AND SONNETTES, &c." On the
recto appears "BY THE EARL OF SURREY." pp. 5–39; "BY SIR THOMAS WYAT."
pp. 41–111; "OF UNCERTAIN AUCTOURS." pp. 113–259; "WRITTEN BY N. G."
pp. 261–271.

Key-words: The key-word on p. 3 has been torn out in the Grenville copy;
an incorrect key-word (in roman type), *To* for *I serue*, appears on p. 247.

This edition was an attempted reprint of *C* in the original spelling;
the pagination is changed, but marginal reference is made to the original
folio-numbers of *C*. Percy's interest in the miscellany antedated the
publication of his famous *Reliques* (1765). On March 24, 1763, he en-
tered into an agreement with Tonson to publish an edition of Surrey's
poems (that is, the entire *Songs and Sonnets*) for twenty guineas. Four

---

[1] Pages 82 and 142 are blank.
[2] *C*, however, has the spelling *Sonettes*.

months later (July 12) he wrote to Dr. Thomas Birch, "Mr. Tonson and I are meditating a neat 12mo. edition of the Earl of Surrey's works," mentioning that he had copies of Tottel's 1559 and 1574 editions (D, or D*, and G). On March 1, 1772, Michael Tyson asked R. Gough: "What is Dr. Percy about? I saw, three years ago, proof-sheets of his edition of Lord Surrey. What is become of it?" On August 11, 1792, Percy told Walpole that his nephew, Thomas Percy, was "both able and desirous" to finish the work, the text of which had "been printed off about 25 years," but his letters to George Steevens in 1796–1797 show that he himself had taken up the task again, so that on July 13, 1806, Dr. Robert Anderson, editor of *The Poets of Great Britain*, informed Percy that he had had many inquiries about "your edition of Surrey," to all of which he answered that it was "forthcoming." John Nichols, the printer, brings the story to a conclusion thus: "Dr. Percy had, soon after the year 1760, proceeded very far at the press with an admirable edition of 'Surrey's Poems,' and also with a good edition of the Works of Villiers Duke of Buckingham; both which, from a variety of causes, remained many years unfinished in the warehouse of Mr. Tonson in the Savoy, but were resumed in 1795, and nearly brought to a conclusion; when the whole impression of both works was unfortunately consumed by the fire in Red Lion Passage in 1808." [1] This edition, then, might well have been included in my section on the eighteenth-century reprints; but it was intended for publication in the nineteenth century also. In 1804, according to Thomas Park's "Advertisement" in *Nugae Antiquae*, Tottel's *Miscellany* was "again preparing for public exhibition by the accomplished hand of Bishop Percy." The destruction of his edition was a genuine misfortune, not so much for Percy's own accomplished hand as for that (if it *was* actually engaged in the work) of George Steevens, a scholar of note. [2]

[1] John Nichols, *Anecdotes*, III (1812), 161, 753; VIII (1814), 585; John Bowyer Nichols, *Illustrations of the Literary History of the Eighteenth Century*, VII (1848), 166, 571, VIII (1858), 289.
[2] There seems to be no evidence of Steevens's collaboration: Sir Sidney Lee's comments to the contrary in his sketch of Steevens in the *Dictionary of National Biography* are obviously based merely on Grenville's note in the British Museum copy. The letters Steevens wrote to Percy in 1796–1797 (J. B. Nichols, *Illustrations*, VII, 1 ff.) show that he merely helped the Bishop in finding specimens of pre-Miltonic blank verse, and he died on January 22, 1800. The British Museum catalogue includes the Percy edition under Steevens's name, dating it 1807 — again showing a dependence on Grenville.

ALEXANDER CHALMERS'S EDITION

O. CHALMERS'S EDITION 1810

The Works of the English Poets, from Chaucer to Cowper; Including the Series Edited, with Prefaces, Biographical and Critical, by Dr. Samuel Johnson: and the most Approved Translations. The Additional Lives by Alexander Chalmers, F. S. A., 21 vols., 8°, London, 1810.

Bibliographical information about this work is unnecessary. In volume II, p. 323, Chalmers gives Tottel's preface; pp. 325–337, the 40 poems attributed to Surrey in Tottel's *Miscellany*, as well as No. 243; pp. 369–388, the 96 poems attributed to Wyatt; pp. 396–441, the 133 (not including No. 243) by uncertain authors; pp. 441–444, the 10 poems attributed to Grimald. In his Surrey–Wyatt sections there are also poems by the two not to be found in the miscellany, as well as a memoir of each. In other words, Chalmers reprints C,[1] which he thought to be the first edition, though he interrupts his reprints of Surrey and Wyatt by adding to them poems not in C. The reprint purports to be in the original spelling and punctuation, but is not successfully carried through. It does not, of course, keep the page-division, typography, or line-arrangement of C, and it often divides a poem into separate stanzas.

P. NOTT'S EDITION 1814

Of this edition the British Museum has four partial copies. No modern title-page, no preface,[2] no original covers, are in any of the four. The most nearly complete copy, which has the press-mark 11607.i.7, indicates that the edition was to be in two volumes. The first volume may be described as follows:

Collation: 4°, pp. 1–367. Pp. 1–48 Surrey's poems, with the heading "Songs And Sonnets/ Of The/ Earl of Surrey." on p. 1: p. [49] half-title, "Sir Thomas Wyatt/ The Elder."; verso blank: pp. [51]–136 Wyatt's poems, with the heading "Songs and Sonnets/ Of/ Sir Thomas Wyatt/ The Elder." on p. [51]: p. [137] half-title, "Uncertain Authors."; verso blank: pp. [139]–322 poems by anonymous writers, with the heading "Songs And Sonnets/ Of/

---

[1] This is evident by the absence of any of the unique readings of *B;* by the inclusion of such lines as 34.26, 40.10, 43.6, that are omitted in *D*+; and by the presence of such readings as *turnde* (17.37), *ioynde* (26.13), *chaunced* (36.13), *standes* (37.23), *hath* (42.8). On the other hand, in the title of No. 12 as given by Chalmers ("A Vow to Loue," etc.), the "A" appears first in *D*, and so do *The* (instead of *To a*) in the title of No. 53 and the name of Wyatt in the first line of No. 31; while in the title of No. 15 his reading of *Prisoner* does not come until *D**.

[2] But Nott refers at least twice to a preface: see p. 89, below.

Uncertain Authours." on p. [139]: p. [323] half-title, "Nicholas Grimoald.";
verso blank: pp. [325]–338 Grimald's poems, with the heading "Songs And
Sonnets/ By/ Nicholas Grimoald." on p. [325] and with "N. G.", "FINIS.",
and Tottel's colophon from *B* at the end of the text on p. 338: p. [339] half-
title, "Appendix."; verso blank: pp. [341]–367 "Appendix.": p. [368] blank.
All the headings and half-titles are in large roman capitals.

Running-titles: "Songs And Sonnets./ Earl of Surrey." pp. 2–48; "Songs
And Sonnets./ Sir Thomas Wyatt." pp. 52–136; "Songs And Sonnets./ Un-
certain Authors." pp. 140–322; "Songs And Sonnets./ Nicholas Grimoald."
pp. 324 [326]–338; "Appendix./ Nicholas Grimoald." pp. 342–367. All the
running-titles are in large roman capitals.

Pagination: By an error the half-title "Nicholas Grimoald" and its blank
verso, which should be pp. 323, 324, were not counted (although they have the
signature 2T2 and belong to the original gathering), and are followed by the
numbered pages [323] and 324. Later, when the error was detected, the page-
numbers 327, 328, were omitted, p. 329 following p. 326 and thus restoring the
correct pagination. In other words, the page-numbers run thus: 322, [no num-
bers = 323, 324], [323 = 325], 324 [= 326], 325 [= 327], 326 [= 328], 329, 330.

In 11607.i.7 are preserved also a portion of the Notes that were in-
tended to make Nott's second volume. These pages are numbered
3–24, 41–72. Page 72 ends in the middle of a note on the seventeenth
line of No. 15; from which it appears that Nott's annotations, if carried
out at the same rate with which they began, would have reached enor-
mous proportions. Nevertheless, the gap in pagination between 24 and
41 is misleading; for Nott is discussing No. 8 on page 24 as well as on
page 41, and it seems likely that not more than a page or two is actually
missing and that the numbers 41–72 are press errors. Even Nott, ob-
sessed as he was with the Fair Geraldine, heroine of No. 8, would
hardly have devoted almost fifty pages (25–71) to a discussion of her
charms and of Surrey's slavery.

Nott's reprint was made, in modern spelling and punctuation, from
B. In an appendix (see the Collation above) he also prints the thirty
poems of Grimald that appeared in *A* but were omitted in *B.* His notes
are excellent, and many of them were taken over almost without
change in his edition of Surrey's poems.

A second copy (11604.ff.4) has the complete text (pages 1–367),
plus a duplicate set of pages 49–56 (that is, signature H).

A third copy (11623.ff.1) has only pages 1–48 of the text (all of
Surrey's poems), but these are interleaved with elaborate collations

from other editions of the miscellany. It is noticeable that, although Nott reprinted *B*, in this third copy he has restored the readings of *A* in the text of Surrey's poems, as if sometime he intended to get out an edition based on *A*. A manuscript note explains that he has given in black ink collations from the 1564 (*sic*) edition, in red and blue ink collations from the editions of 1567 and 1574 respectively. But 1564 was a slip of the pen, for the readings Nott gives in black ink are to be found in the edition of 1565 (*E*). Furthermore, the black–red–blue collations for pages 139–338 of Nott's text are preserved in the British Museum's fourth copy (C.60.O.13), on page 338 of which, in collating the date of the colophon (1557), Nott wrote in black ink "1565." That disposes of the mythical 1564 edition.

In both the third and the fourth copy there are also many penciled readings marked "Seld" or "Selden," which are thus, no less than the textual corrections made from *A*, shown to have resulted from a period of study in the Bodleian; for *Seld(en)* is a reference to the manuscript notes in the Bodleian copy of *I*. In C.60.O.13 there is a complete text (pages 1–367) of Nott's reprint, interleaved with very elaborate collations and critical and explanatory notes of great value. Some of the latter were used in his edition of Surrey and Wyatt, others were not (they may possibly be later in date). Separately bound and catalogued as part of C.60.O.13 is a series of manuscript collations made by Nott from editions that I have not attempted to identify.

Some problems of interest arise in connection with *P*. In the British Museum catalogue the editor is said to have been John Nott, M.D. (the uncle of G. F. Nott), the place of publication Bristol, the date 1812. Accordingly, in 1906, Professor Padelford published an article entitled "The Relation of the 1812 and 1815–1816 Editions of Surrey and Wyatt," [1] in which with entire plausibility he argued that G. F. Nott had used without acknowledgment the work of his uncle. This argument could, however, almost be refuted from Nott's statements in the Surrey–Wyatt volumes, where he refers to the edition of Tottel's *Miscellany* in terms that suggest his own editorship; while it is not likely that, if he had been the unblushing plagiarist Mr. Padelford makes him out to be, he would have referred readers to the exact source

---

[1] *Anglia*, XXIX, 256–270. *The Cambridge History of English Literature*, III, 577 (American ed.), also lists the "1812" edition as the work of John Nott.

of his plagiarisms. But Mr. H. J. Byrom has recently proved [1] that the manuscript notes in all four copies of *P* are in the hand of G. F. Nott, and has thus freed his name from the stigma of dishonesty.

The date of *P* is uncertain. The British Museum catalogue evidently gives 1812 on mere guess-work. It also quotes two penciled notes from 11607.i.7 and 11604.ff.4: "This intended Edition was nearly totally destroyed in Bensley's fire," [2] and "Just as it was completed all but the preface, a fire destroyed the whole impression." Bensley, it should be noted, was a London (not a Bristol) printer. He printed Nott's Surrey and Wyatt in 1815–1816. Mr. Byrom observes (page 51) that "the accepted date 1812 for the destruction of the edition should be questioned, for in his bulky notes to the 1815–16 edition of Surrey and Wyatt Nott several times refers to 'Tottel's *Songs and Sonnets*, ed. 1814,' and the page references correspond with [11607.i.7, 11604.ff.4, and C.60.O.13]."

Not before cited in this connection is the evidence of Sir Egerton Brydges, who, editing Davison's *Poetical Rhapsody* in 1814, remarks in his "Advertisement" (page 32) that "'*Tottell's Miscellany*'... is about to re-appear with splendour, aided by the industrious and learned researches of Dr. Nott," — a remark that effectually disposes of the claims advanced for John Nott, M.D. But if any doubt as to the identity of "Dr." Nott remains, it can be removed by a glance at Philip Bliss's edition of the *Athenae Oxonienses* (1813),[3] where we are informed that "the last edition [of Tottel's *Miscellany*], with biographical... and other remarks by Dr. Nott, fellow of All Souls, and prebendary of Winchester, has been lately printed in two volumes, 4to." Perhaps Bliss actually meant *printed*, not published. In any case, A. F. Griffith's *Bibliotheca Anglo-Poetica* [4] of 1815 speaks of "the forthcoming edition, under the skilful editorship of Dr. Nott, which, in the opinion of competent judges, bids fair to become the standard."

There can be no doubt that, so far as the text and part of the notes

[1] "Tottel's Miscellany, 1717–1817," *The Review of English Studies*, III (1927), 47–53.

[2] See Sotheby's sale-catalogue (1874) of Sir William Tite's library, lot 3066, where this copy is (apparently) described. The cataloguer adds that this was "*G. F. Nott's copy, with his autograph signature and notes*," and that it contained also a "Dissertation on English Poetry before the XVIth Century (p. cxxxvii to cclxxxvi)." But that dissertation really belonged to Nott's Surrey volume of 1815, and is not in 11607.i.7.

[3] I, 158 n.

[4] No. 691, p. 329.

are concerned, *P* was in page-proof before Nott published (or at least wrote some of the notes for) his Surrey volume of 1815.[1] But that it had not been published is proved by the numerous references to it in the Wyatt volume of 1816 as "Tottel's Songs and Sonnets, Ed. 1816"[2] and "the late edition of Tottel's Songs and Sonnets."[3] These references indicate that Nott had stopped work on the miscellany to complete the Surrey–Wyatt edition, but that he had expected to issue the former in 1816. For one reason or another he failed to do so. I think it likely that a few of the manuscript notes in *P* are later than 1816, and perhaps that some of the collations are. In 11623.ff.1 Nott, in collating his reprint of *B* with *A*, inserted the readings of *A* in the text itself; and this seems to me to point to a date later than 1816 and, possibly, to an intended reprint based on *A*.

Mr. Byrom believes[4] that *P* "could not have been destroyed in either of the two fires which are recorded to have devastated Bensley's printing offices — on November 5, 1807 (since we know it to have been printed after 1810), or on June 26, 1819 (since it was obviously earlier than the 1815–16 Surrey and Wyatt), and the note prefixed to [11607.i.7] asserting this is a misleading conjecture. The probability is, therefore, that some one else printed the work." "Unless, indeed," he adds in a foot-note, "publication of the edition was for some other reason abandoned, and the story of the fire was a mere invention to explain the absence of perfect copies." As I have shown above, however, *P* was not *published* earlier than 1816. Probably it was never actually published;[5] and it is by no means unlikely that the much-postponed edition was destroyed by the fire of 1819 to which Mr. Byrom refers. I assign the reprint the date of 1814 simply because by that time the text and at least part of the notes were in type.

[1] In the Surrey volume he refers to *P* as the edition of 1810 on pp. 331, 335; of 1813 on p. 369; of 1814 on pp. 251, 286, 296, 307, 310 (twice), 329, 330, 331, 359; as the "late ed." on pp. 310, 360; and as the "new edition" on p. 367.

[2] *E. g.,* pp. 541, 542 (three times), 545 (three times), 559, 562.

[3] *E. g.,* pp. 537, 545, 556.

[4] *The Review of English Studies,* III (1927), 51.

[5] Padelford (*Anglia,* XXIX, 259–260) makes much of the fact that John Nott entered none of his books at Stationers' Hall, while G. F. Nott's Surrey and Wyatt was entered in the Stationers' Rolls immediately after its publication. The non-entry there of *P* suggests that it was not published, though Padelford interprets that fact as evidence of the editorship of John Nott.

INTRODUCTION

Nott was a man of great erudition.[1] How wide his reading was can hardly be appreciated by any one who has not examined the annotated copies of *P*. Mr. Byrom has pointed out the exhaustiveness of Nott's annotations on Grimald, particularly in the matter of sources. Almost equally learned are those, not yet published, on the poems of the uncertain authors.

2. Nott's Edition 1815–1816

The Works/ of/ Henry Howard/ Earl of Surrey/ and of/ Sir Thomas Wyatt/ the Elder./ [Rule]/ Edited by/ Geo. Fred. Nott, D.D. F.S.A./ Late Fellow of All Souls College/ Oxford./ [Rule]/ In Two Volumes./ Vol. I. [Vol. II.]/ [Rule]/ London:/ Printed by T. Bensley,/ Bolt Court, Fleet Street;/ for Longman, Hurst, Rees, Orme, and Brown,/ Paternoster-Row./ MDCCCXV. [MDCCCXVI.]/ (4°)[2]

This edition, though written in a somewhat grandiloquent style, is enormously erudite.[3] It is a mine of information (some of it to modern taste superfluous) about the poems and lives and times of Wyatt and Surrey, a mine to which all present-day students of those poets are heavily indebted. Of course Nott paid no attention to Tottel's *Miscellany* except for its connection with Wyatt and Surrey; that is, he did not edit it completely; but his texts, based on a collation of the manuscripts with the miscellany and printed in modernized spelling and punctuation, were the best that had appeared, and on them later nineteenth-century editors made almost no improvement. They have since been rendered obsolete by the investigations of Miss Foxwell and Mr. Padelford; the biographical sketches, too, have naturally been expanded and, in certain particulars, corrected; and a few additions have

[1] On his life and works see *The Gentleman's Magazine*, n. s., XVII (1842), 106–107, and the *Dictionary of National Biography*.

[2] Volume I contains about nine hundred pages, volume II about eight hundred, and in each there are various illustrations. The pagination is extremely involved and confused, especially in the first volume, where the signatures run as follows: [a⁴], *a*⁴, *b*², b–s⁴, s*², t–20⁴, B–2G⁴, 2G*⁴, 2G**⁴, [2G***⁴], 2H–2Z⁴, 3A–3Q⁴, 3R², *B–X*⁴. In most cases they are signed in twos; 3C3 (on p. 379) is misprinted for 3C2. From this point onward I do not reproduce the typography of the title-pages or give exact bibliographical descriptions.

[3] The irreverent will note with some amusement that in spite of the pious, almost sanctimonious, tone of the preface to volume II, Nott dedicated his work to the Prince Regent.

been made to Nott's notes on sources. But no other one individual has yet done such good work in explaining and illustrating the miscellany poems as did Nott. His edition, made at a time when modern scholarship was in its infancy, merits high admiration and high praise, and in many ways still remains the best that has appeared.

R. SANFORD'S EDITION 1819

Ezekiel Sanford, *The Works of the British Poets*, 50 vols., 12°, Philadelphia, 1819–1823 (vols. 18–21, 23, 25–50, edited by Robert Walsh).

Volume I contains, pp. 283–335, "Select Poems of Sir Thomas Wyat. With a Life of the Author, by Ezekiel Sanford" (Nos. 65–81, 83–123, 266–271); pp. 337–364, "Select Poems of Henry Howard, Earl of Surrey. With a Life of the Author, from Campbell" (Nos. 2, 5, 9, 12, 13, 15, 20, 24, 30, 31). Though Sanford says nothing whatever about the source of his text, he apparently attempted to reproduce that of Chalmers (*O*).

S. ALDINE EDITION 1831

(1) The Poems of Henry Howard/ Earl of Surrey/ [Device]/ London/ William Pickering/ 1831/

Collation: 8°, pp. lxxix, 188, with frontispiece portrait. P. [i] fly-leaf, "The Aldine Edition/ Of the British/ Poets/ [Ornament]/ The Poems of Henry Howard/ Earl of Surrey"/; verso blank: p. [iii] title: p. [iv] imprint: pp. [v]–vii "Contents.": p. [viii] blank: pp. [ix]–x "Index of First Lines.": pp. [xi]–lxxix "Memoir of Henry Howard/ Earl of Surrey."/: p. [lxxx] blank: pp. [1]–188 Surrey's poems (including Nos. 243 and 278).

(2) The Poetical Works of/ Sir Thomas Wyatt/ [Device]/ London/ William Pickering/ 1831/

Collation: 8°, pp. xcvi, 244, with frontispiece portrait. P. [i] fly-leaf, "The Aldine Edition/ Of the British/ Poets/ [Ornament]/ The Poems of Sir Thomas Wyatt"/; verso blank: p. [iii] title: p. [iv] imprint: pp. [v]–xlii "Memoir of Sir Thomas Wyatt.": pp. xliii–lii "Sir Thomas Wyatt's Letter to the Privy Council in 1541.": pp. liii–lxxxvii "Sir Thomas Wyatt's Defence, after the Indictment and Evidence": p. [lxxxviii] blank: pp. [lxxxix]–xcvi "Contents.": pp. [1]–197 Wyatt's poems: p. [198] blank: p. [199] fly-leaf, "Penitential Psalms."; verso blank: pp. [201]–236 Psalms: p. 237 "An Epitaph of Sir Thomas Gravener,/ Knight."/: p. 238 "Sir Antonie Sentleger of Sir T. Wyatt.": pp. 239–244 "Index of First Lines."

Notwithstanding their title-pages, the British Museum catalogue dates these volumes 1830. The editor, who is said to have been Sir Nicholas Harris Nicolas, speaks severely of G. F. Nott's textual methods, and asserts that "the present edition has been printed from the collection of Surrey's pieces by Tottel in 1557, which was the first that appeared." [1] Nicolas quotes Nott's statement that there were "four distinct impressions" in 1557: [2] he gives no further particulars; but he follows the second edition *C*, whereas Nott had favored the readings of *B* as corrected from manuscripts. The Aldine text has no value; for Nicolas arbitrarily switches from one to another of the printed editions, and occasionally borrows from Nott's manuscript readings. In Nos. 7 and 8, for example, he apparently follows *C* (though varying its spelling); but at 9.6 he has *fixed*, which does not appear till *D*; at 9.25 *doth she*, whereas all the editions except *B* (*did she*) have *she doth*; at 12.23 *Garret*, which is found in *B* only. Again, he has *Thomas* [*Wyatt*] at 27.6, 22, where *A–I* read *T. W.*; at 27.34 *the corpse*, of which *the* first occurs in *D*, *corps* in *D**; at 28.3 *Wyatt*, which appears in *D* and *D** only; at 31.8 *wearier*, which is found in no early edition; and he modernizes the spelling, punctuation, and stanza-divisions throughout. Nicolas's work is in all respects inferior to that of Nott: his one contribution lies in his attack on the Fair Geraldine theory that had colored Nott's every comment on Surrey.

Another edition appeared in 1831 with the title: "The Poetical Works of/ Surrey and Wyatt/ [Device]/ Vol I [Vol II]/ London/ William Pickering/ 1831/." Volume I has pages cxiv, 190; volume II, pages xii, 290. The contents and page-arrangement are identical with those of the other Aldine edition; but, since the preliminary matter is shifted so that volume I contains the memoirs of both Surrey and Wyatt, the page-numbering differs.

Other editions based on *S* may be dismissed briefly.

S. (*a*) AMERICAN EDITION 1854

This consists of two volumes (8°, pp. lxxii, 190, and pp. xc, one unpaged leaf, 244, respectively, each with frontispiece portrait), and with the following titles:

(1) The/ Poetical Works/ of/ Henry Howard/ Earl of Surrey./ With a Memoir./ Boston:/ Little, Brown and Company./ New York:

---

[1] Surrey's *Poems*, p. lxxviii.　　　　[2] Page lxxvii.

Evans and Dickerson./ Philadelphia: Lippincott, Grambo and Co./ M.DCCC.LIV./

(2) The/ Poetical Works/ of/ Sir Thomas Wyatt./ With a Memoir./ Boston:/ Little, Brown and Company./ New York: Evans and Dickerson./ Philadelphia: Lippincott, Grambo and Co./ M.DCCC.LIV./

In these volumes the text of *S* is reproduced.

S. (*b*) BELL'S EDITION 1854

The general title-page of Bell's series, as given in his Wyatt volume,[1] is:

The/ Annotated Edition/ of the/ English Poets./ By/ Robert Bell,/ Author of/ 'The History of Russia,' 'Lives of the English Poets,' etc./ In Monthly Volumes, 2*s.* 6*d.* each, in cloth./ London:/ John W. Parker and Son, West Strand./ 1854./

This was issued in twenty-four volumes, 1854–1857. Those that concern us are entitled:

(1) Poetical Works/ of/ Henry Howard, Earl of Surrey/ Minor Contemporaneous Poets/ and/ Thomas Sackville, Lord Buckhurst/ Edited by Robert Bell/ [Device]/ London/ John W. Parker and Son West Strand/ 1854/

(2) Poetical Works/ of/ Sir Thomas Wyatt/ Edited by Robert Bell/ [Device]/ London/ John W. Parker and Son West Strand/ 1854/

In the latter are included all the poems attributed to Wyatt in *B–I*; in the former, all the poems attributed to Surrey in *B–I*, plus Nos. 243 and 278, and, in the "Minor Poets" section of the volume (pages 207–227, 231–256), the ten attributed to Grimald in *B–I*,[2] with the same fourteen poems by uncertain authors (Nos. 170, 174, 175, 181, 193, 199, 209–212, 246, 273, 303, 304) that Anderson prints. Bell remarks (Surrey, page 36): "The text of this edition has been carefully revised and collated with preceding editions [that is, modern editions]; the variances between them and the manuscripts referred to by Dr. Nott have been compared, that which seemed to be the best reading being in all cases adopted; and the original order and headings of the poems, as they were

---

[1] It differs in the Surrey volume by reading "Edited by" in line 5, carrying over "etc." in line 8 as a separate line, and substituting a device for line 9.

[2] They are headed here, as in *HI*, "Songs written by N. G. of the Nine Muses."

first published, have been restored." An examination shows, however, that the order, headings, and readings come direct from the Aldine edition (*S*), so far as it goes. For example, Bell follows *S* in substituting "a wearier lover" for "a wearied lover" in the title of No. 36, although that reading appears in none of the original editions. Occasionally in the Wyatt–Surrey section Bell changed the Aldine text in matters of spelling (especially in putting *ed* for *'d*, thus destroying the movement), capitalization, and punctuation; but his changes apparently represent little or no original work on the text and are all for the worse.[1] Whence came his text for the fourteen poems by uncertain authors I have not tried to discover.

S. (*c*) Gilfillan–Clarke's Edition 1856–1879

(1) The/ Poetical Works/ of/ Sir Thomas Wyatt./ With Memoir and Critical Dissertation./ The Text Edited by Charles Cowden Clarke./ Cassell Petter & Galpin:/ London, Paris & New York./

(2) The/ Poetical Works/ of William Shakspeare/ and the/ Earl of Surrey./ With Memoir and Critical Dissertation./ The Text Edited by Charles Cowden Clarke./ Cassell Petter & Galpin:/ London, Paris & New York./

The British Museum catalogue dates the second volume 1878, but notes that it forms part of "Cassell's Library Edition of British Poets," being "a reprint of the Edinburgh edition of 1856, with a new title-page."[2] Another issue had appeared in 1862 with the imprint, "Edinburgh: James Nichol./ London: James Nisbet and Co. Dublin: W. Robertson./ Liverpool: G. Philip & Son./ M.DCCC.LXII./" According to the same catalogue, Clarke's Wyatt volume was published in 1879, likewise in "Cassell's Library." The earliest copy that I have seen has the title: "The/ Poetical Works/ of/ Sir Thomas Wyatt./ With Memoir and Critical Dissertation,/ by the/ Rev. George Gilfillan./ Edinburgh:/ James Nichol, 104 High Street./ London: James Nisbet & Co. Dublin: W. Robertson./ M.DCCC.LVIII./"

Clarke's two volumes are octavos of pages xlvii, 211, and xl, 316, respectively. In the second, pages [215]–316 are devoted to Surrey. The text used is not specified, but a hasty collation indicates that it was *S*, and that the editing of Gilfillan's 1856 text referred to on the title-pages was extremely superficial.

---

[1] Thus he changed *Lux*, the first word of No. 92, to *Look!*; *The restfull place*, of No. 62, to *Thou! restful place!*; and *What man hath hard*, of No. 68, to *Who hath heard of*.

[2] I have not seen the 1856 edition.

S. (*d*) ALDINE EDITION 1866

(1) The/ Poems of Henry Howard/ Earl of Surrey/ [Device]/ London/ Bell and Daldy Fleet Street/ 1866/

(2) The Poetical Works of/ Sir Thomas Wyatt/ [Device]/ London/ Bell and Daldy Fleet Street/ 1866/

These octavo volumes have pages lxxvi, 180, and civ, 243, respectively. The·"Advertisement" to the former says: "The present work, although substantially a reprint of the Aldine edition . . . published in 1831, has been critically and carefully revised, and some additional notes appended explanatory of words now become obsolete. The Poems have been collated with the edition of the 'Songs and Sonnets,' edited by Bishop Percy and George Steevens [*i. e.*, *N*], as well as by the recent reprint [*T*] of the first edition of 'Tottel's Miscellany,' by John Payne Collier, Esq., whose ready kindness is acknowledged for the loan of the sheets of that rare work." [1] The collation spoken of was superficially carried out: for example, the readings *Garret, the corpse,* [*Wyatt*], *Wyatt* commented on above,[2] are retained from the 1831 text, but *doth she* is changed to *she doth.* Hence the 1866 text has no real authority and is of little value. Its editor is said to have been James Yeowell. A reissue of this edition bears the imprint of Bell and Daldy, York Street, Covent Garden, and (on what authority I do not know) is assigned the date of "1871?" in the Harvard library catalogue.

T. COLLIER'S REPRINT 1867

Seven English/ Poetical/ Miscellanies,/ Printed between 1557 and 1602./ Reproduced/ under the care of/ J. Payne Collier./ [Ornament]/ London./ 1867./ (4°)

Tottel's *Miscellany,* the first of Collier's series, has no separate title-page. It was issued in three parts (which reached the British Museum on April 21, 1868), the first of them (pp. 1–124) accompanied by a "Notice" that announces:

"The cost of the first Part of the Reprint is 10 *s.*; and the other two Parts will, as nearly as possible, be of the same bulk and price. Thus the expense of

[1] Although Collier's reprints (see *T,* below) are dated 1867, the last of them, *A Poetical Rhapsody,* was issued before December 22, 1866 (see *The Athenaeum* for that date, p. 842). [2] At p. 54.

each of the fifty copies (consisting of more than 350 pages) will be, as originally stated, 30 *s.* . . . the price of the whole undertaking has been somewhat enhanced by the unusual cost of an exact transcript, observing all the errors of the press, and the old mistakes of punctuation."

Actually the reprint runs to 299 pages, as follows: p. [1] Tottel's title-page: p. [2] "*The Printer to the Reader.*": pp. [3]–43 Surrey's poems: pp. [44]–124 Wyatt's poems: pp. [125]–164 Grimald's poems: pp. 165–286 poems by uncertain authors: pp. 287–294 additional poems by Surrey: pp. 295–298 additional poems by Wyatt: p. [299] Tottel's colophon; verso blank.

In his "General Introduction" Collier boasts of having "discovered" *A*, whereas Park, Bohn, and Hazlitt certainly knew that it preceded *B* and *C*, while Nott had studied it carefully and in his edition *P* reprinted its thirty unique poems. In *Notes and Queries*, 3d series, x, 224, under the date of September 22, 1866, Collier made further preposterous claims for his reprint:

What purported to be *the first edition* was reprinted by Dr. Sewell in 1717, and by Bishop Percy, Dr. Nott, and Sir Harris Nicolas afterwards; but I discovered a copy which showed that they were all in error, and that the second edition had been all along mistaken for the first, which differs in many essential particulars, and clears away many corruptions. Nobody had ever heard of this *first edition*, and I reprinted it in three parts, at the cost of 72*l.* 10*s.*, or 1*l.* 5*s.* of each of my fifty copies.

Collier's reprint of Tottel's *Miscellany* sold well enough. "I had more claimants for it than I could supply," he explains, "so that here I was not out of pocket"; but with considerable bitterness he complains of the lack of interest in the whole series shown among those who should have been subscribers and buyers.[1]

No doubt Collier deserves some credit, not for discovering, but for making fairly accessible, the text of *A* and in calling attention to its importance; but evidently he knew little or nothing about its variations from *B* and *C*. His assertion that "we have implicitly followed the edition we had the good fortune to discover; and our text represents the true language of the various poets," is, as usual, somewhat exaggerated.[2]

[1] *Notes and Queries*, 3d series, x, 220; *The Athenaeum*, July 28, 1866, p. 113.
[2] So in *The Athenaeum*, July 28, 1866, p. 113, he remarks: "As to type and paper, I boldly assert that the reprints are admirable — quite 'books of luxury,' as the French call them; and as to accuracy of text, I spare no pains to make my reproductions, even as to errors of punctuation, exactly represent the originals." The reprints that I have collated entire are, however, swarming with errors.

I have not collated the entire text with *A*, but a comparison of a dozen or so pages, widely separated in *A* and chosen at random, suggests that his reprint is fairly accurate.

U. ARBER'S EDITION 1870

English Reprints./ Tottel's Miscellany./ Songes and Sonettes/ by/ Henry Howard, Earl of Surrey,/ Sir Thomas Wyatt, the Elder,/ Nicholas Grimald,/ and/ Uncertain Authors./ First Edition of 5th June; Collated with the Second/ Edition of 31st July, 1557./ By/ Edward Arber,/ Associate, King's College, London, F.R.G.S., &c./ London:/ 5 Queen Square, Bloomsbury, W.C./ Ent. Stat. Hall] 15 August,[1] 1870. [All Rights reserved./

Arber's is the best of the modern reprints up to the present time. It gives the text of *A* on pages 1–226 and of the thirty-nine additional poems of *B* on pages 227–271. Notes inserted in the text, in head-lines, and at the foot of the pages call the reader's attention to various changes made by *B* in the text of *A*; on pages ii–v, ix–xvi, 272, some valuable though haphazard biographical, bibliographical, and historical notes are supplied; while pages vi–viii are devoted to a poorly alphabetized, but still fairly serviceable, index of first lines. Issued at an extremely low price and in a convenient small octavo, Arber's reprint has been the only copy of Tottel's book available to the majority of students, — particularly in America, — and it has helped to make Tottel's the best known of the Tudor poetical miscellanies.

So indispensable has it been that to speak severely of its defects would be ungrateful. It must be said, however, that although the reprint purports to be an exact reproduction, it is unsuccessful. It does not, of course, attempt to reproduce the pagination, line-arrangement, or typography of the original, — a fact of no real importance. But even in the matter of typography perhaps some objection might be raised to Arber's methods: for example, the titles of poems in *A* and *B* are everywhere in roman type; this Arber properly represents by italics, though when proper names occur in the titles he arbitrarily prints them in roman letter.[2] Perhaps, too, when he transfers the headings at 93.1

---

[1] Other issues have the date of " 1 October."

[2] In some dozen cases, however, he puts the proper name in italics (as in Nos. 8, 15, 32, 44, 63, 97, etc.); in one case (No. 29) he uses both types for proper names in the same title; in No. 201 he prints *Thestilis* in italics and in No. 234 in roman. But on

and 121.1 into large capitals he gives a somewhat inexact idea of the original.

But there are genuine faults to be pointed out. All through the text misprints are corrected with no notice whatever; and all contractions, like &, $c\bar{a}$, $\dot{w}$, $\dot{y}$, $\dot{y}$, are silently expanded, the last two into the abnormal and indefensible spelling of *ye* and *yat*. Passing over these deviations, I have in volume I, pages 327–335, printed collations of his text with his originals. A glance through that list will show how serious some of his errors are. For instance, he omits words of the original, substitutes words of his own, changes the spelling and punctuation on no ascertainable plan, and introduces various new typographical errors.

All this is bad enough, but the damage is perhaps increased by the foot-notes. In them Arber gives what purport to be variants from the second edition — that is, *B*; for his notes do not recognize the highly significant variations in the readings of *B* and *C*. The impression any careful reader of Arber's reprint gets is that *all* the variants, at least of *B*, are enumerated. This impression is ill-grounded: not a twentieth of them are given, and many that are enumerated have no importance. On page 171, for example, Arber lists seven variants, five of which differ from *A* in capitalization only, one in spelling only, one in both capitalization and spelling. Why these seven are singled out for attention is inexplicable, for in practically every line *A* varies from *B* and from *C* in spelling, capitalization, or punctuation. Furthermore, many of Arber's variants are imaginary: that is, he introduces an incorrect reading into his text, and then in a foot-note calls attention to the correct reading, which he attributes to *B*. As an example, on page 160 he transposes two lines in his reprint of *A*, gives the reading of *B* in a note, and adds, "The rhyme in couplets shows that the Second edition is here the correct reading." In my collations I have marked with an asterisk the numerous other instances of this kind of blundering. Evidently Arber depended on a careless copyist. Then when the first impression of his text was collated with *C*, he failed to consult *A* again, assuming instead that all the readings of his own text were correct.

The plates of this edition were bought by Messrs. Constable and Company, Ltd., who have issued reprints with slightly altered and

p. 226 he reproduces the colophon of *A* exactly as it stands in the original, as he does also the authors' names at the end of sections (31.25, 92.13, 120.22); while in No. 15 he follows *A* even in spelling *windsor* without a capital.

redated title-pages. The first that I have seen has the following title-page:

English Reprints/ Tottel's Miscellany/ Songes and Sonnettes/ by/ Henry Howard, Earl of Surrey/ Sir Thomas Wyatt, the Elder/ Nicholas Grimald/ and/ Uncertain Authors/ First Edition of 5th June, Collated with/ the Second Edition of 31st July 1557/ Edited by/ Edward Arber/ F.S.A. etc. Late Examiner in English/ Language and Literature/ to the University of/ London/ Westminster/ A. Constable and Co./ 1897./

I have a copy with the imprint "Constable and Company Ltd/London Bombay Sydney/ 1921/" and apparently others have been issued in more recent years. These re-issues do Arber less than justice, for the plates are worn so badly that they make his work look more inaccurate than it actually is. Yet the re-issues have served, and no doubt will continue to serve, a useful purpose in providing cheap copies of a valuable miscellany for the general public.

V. MISS FOXWELL'S WYATT 1913

The Poems of/ Sir Thomas Wiat/ Edited/ from the MSS. and Early Editions/ by/ A. K. Foxwell, M.A. (Lond.)/ Lecturer in English,/ Late Lecturer and Tutor at the Ladies' College, Cheltenham/ Vol. 1/ Preface and Text/ [Vol. 11/ Introduction/ Commentary/ Appendixes]/ London: University of London Press/ Published for the University of London Press, Ltd./ By Hodder and Stoughton, Warwick Square, E. C./ 1913/

These octavo volumes have pages xxiv, 400 (with ten illustrations), and xxiv, 272 (with one illustration), respectively.

In 1909 Miss Foxwell issued a small volume called *A Study of Sir Thomas Wyatt's Poems*, giving an account of the manuscripts, the sources, and the metrical characteristics of the poems. Her edition of 1913, a continuation of the *Study*, made all of Wyatt's poems (three of them, in volume 1, pages 319, 325, 327, for the first time) accessible. It provided also some biographical as well as some explanatory material, with reprints of various source-poems, and discussions of Wyatt's prosody based not on Tottel's more or less corrupt texts but upon the manuscripts, some of them holograph. Nineteen of the poems, however, she reprinted from the miscellany.[1] This is the only critical edition of Wyatt yet made, though it was carelessly planned and carelessly printed.

The bibliography attached to the *Study* indicates that Miss Foxwell consulted but four of the early printed editions of Tottel's *Miscellany* (*BDGH*), and it seems likely that for *A* and *B* she relied on Arber's reprint. In any case, her collations of the manuscripts with *AB* are not always to be trusted: they have many faulty readings, a number of which appear to be taken from Arber's inaccurate text. Furthermore, as a glance at the facsimile opposite page 272 of her first volume will show, her transcription of the manuscripts does not uniformly attain literal accuracy.[2] To conclude an ungrateful task of criticism, it may be noted that she is, no doubt pardonably, over-enthusiastic about Wyatt's merits, and that her comments on the influence the printed editions of Chaucer had on Wyatt, as well as some of her biographical interpretations (for example, her reiterated suggestion that the Duchess of Richmond, as in No. 93, represents Wyatt's ideal of womanhood), are sheer assertions that will convince nobody. Faults aside, Miss Foxwell's book is indispensable for any serious student of Wyatt and of the miscellany. To it later editors of the poet will be greatly indebted.

W. Padelford's Surrey 1920

University of Washington Publications/ Language and Literature/ Volume 1 October, 1920/ The Poems of Henry Howard/ Earl of Surrey/ Frederick Morgan Padelford/ [Seal of the University]/ University of Washington Press/ Seattle/ (8°, pp. 238).

---

[1] But in the "Contents," p. xxii, of her first volume of Wyatt's poems, she lists only fourteen as coming from the miscellany. See p. 95, below. It is extremely difficult to follow Miss Foxwell's statements about her texts, but after long study one finds that she reprinted from *A* Nos. 74, 76–78, 80, 81, 84, 101, 105–109, 113, 114, 117, 119, 269, 270, and that of those nineteen only one (No. 101), according to her statements, is also found in MS. No. 101 she declares at 1, 43, appears in MS. Egerton 2711, but in her table of contents (1, xviii) she locates it only in the miscellany and in MS. Additional 28635.

[2] On p. 272, line 3, she prints *save the* as *save thee;* line 7, *hathe* as *hath;* line 9, *ys* as *is;* and in the refrains she prints only one *Say* with a capital instead of both. Again, the facsimiles in volume 1, facing pp. 2 and 45, reveal that she misprints from the former *wherof* (line 3) as *whereof*, *vnarmed* (line 6) as *unarmed*, and from the latter *greuously* (line 3) as *grevously*, *kisse* (line 6) as *kysse*.

In this edition are reprinted, among others, all the poems attributed to Surrey in *A–I* plus Nos. 243 and 282,[1] while in the Appendix Nos. 181 and 201 are given as 'not improbably' by Surrey. No autograph copies of Surrey's poems are known to exist; the manuscripts that do survive are later in date than Tottel's *Miscellany* (except for Nos. 17 and 29 [2]) and no doubt like it contain many revisions or corruptions of the poet's original lines. Accordingly, there can be little certainty as to Surrey's text. Still, as an attempt at the first critical edition of the poems this is a valuable book, and its introductory and explanatory notes are sometimes excellent. Unhappily it is disfigured by many misprints and inexact readings, some of which work disaster with the text of the poems, and several of which were evidently caused by a too close dependence on Arber's reprint of the miscellany. For instance, in both Arber's and Padelford's reprint No. 201 begins "Thestilis is a sely man," whereas *A–I* have "Thestilis a sely man." [3] So, too, in various passages the text of *A*, or of the manuscripts, is not reproduced *literatim;* nor are the collations of *AB* with the manuscripts always exact. Students, however, have cause to be grateful to Mr. Padelford; for, perhaps to a greater degree than any other contemporary scholar, he

[1] The order of poems is altogether different from that of *A–I*, and all the titles are rewritten in shorter form. These titles are in modern spelling; but in the case of Nos. 6, 7, 12, 15, 17, 19, 29 (Padelford's Nos. 4–6, 31, 21, 33, 38) the editor omits the apostrophe in possessive nouns, printing odd forms like "Loves Extremes" and "Lady Surreys Lament." Mr. Padelford has re-issued his work — in what the title-page describes as a "revised edition" — under the date of October, 1928. This book was published too late to be referred to by me. It is hardly a revised edition, but is rather, as p. vii calls it, a "second edition." Except that part of the Introduction has been rewritten, most of the book is unchanged, so that the comments in the foregoing paragraph apply as well to it as to the first edition of 1920. Many new misprints are introduced, various old misprints are retained. Thus Miss A(gnes). K. Foxwell appears as Miss Ada on p. 45, as Miss Ida on p. 222; Harington continues to be misspelled as Harrington (p. 259), Steevens as Stevens (p. 260). John Nott is still said (pp. 260–261) to have edited the "1812" edition of the miscellany, G. F. Nott to have borrowed from that work without acknowledgment; T. Sewell is still credited with having manuscript notes in the British Museum copy of the 1717 edition of the miscellany, which instead G. Sewell edited; and so on. It is too bad that with an opportunity to get out a revised edition (a blissful opportunity that seldom comes to a scholar) the editor failed to take advantage of it.

[2] On which cf. p. 97 n. 1, below.

[3] In his variant readings (p. 170) he gives the reading of *A* at 3.13 as *the shade* instead of *shade* (an error made by Arber); but, curiously enough, he also lists *night* as a variant reading at 3.27, although *night* is the correct reading found in his own text (p. 49), in Arber, and in *A*.

has stimulated interest in Surrey, and by his researches he has made possible a more intelligent study of that poet.

The foregoing books are all that it seems necessary to mention, though a few minor editions of Wyatt and Surrey have been omitted. Works on special topics connected with the miscellany, as well as Dr. Merrill's edition of Grimald, are cited elsewhere in the Introduction or the Notes.

The present edition is based upon a study of the nine sixteenth-century editions,[1] and is the first with a critical apparatus of introduction, notes, glossary, and variant readings. In volume I, I have reprinted the first edition (*A*), as well as the additional poems of the second edition (*B*) from the Grenville copy in the British Museum. In the Variant Readings and Misprints *A* is fully collated with *B–I*, the new poems of *B* with *C–I*. Each edition, then, is in effect collated with every other one.[2]

Although my reprint of *A* does not aim to be an exact facsimile, yet, thanks to the skill and interest of the Harvard University Press (to all the members of which I am deeply obligated), it has much of the appearance and flavor of the original. *A* is reprinted page for page, line for line; but in reprinting the additional poems of *B* it was of course impossible to keep their exact pagination.[3] They are, however, reprinted line for line, and are numbered continuously from the last poem in *A*. The order in which they occur in *B–I* and the signatures on which they appear are indicated elsewhere in this Introduction and in the Notes. The pages in my volumes are so much larger than those of *A* that it was impossible to reproduce the original spacing of words and lines with complete exactness. Nevertheless, they closely imitate the arrangement and spacing of the original head-lines and titles, and vary but occasionally and slightly in the line-arrangement of the verses. For ease of reading and for economy, all the black-letter type in the texts and key-words has been transferred to roman. Apart from that change

---

[1] There were really *ten* sixteenth-century editions if *B* and *C* are counted as separate editions.

[2] *D** is not collated: see p. 25, above.

[3] As a matter of fact, in my reprint pp. 242, 243, 246–258 follow the page-divisions of *B* exactly; so, indeed, do pp. 218–236, except that the rectos of *B* are printed on the versos of my pages, and *vice versa*.

the typography of *A* and *B* is followed exactly, with the title-page and colophon in type-facsimile. Throughout the text the long ∫ has been printed *s*.

The miscellany has, in a word, been reprinted with as few editorial changes as possible. Only the most obvious misprints, like inverted, transposed, or broken letters, or like words faultily run together or separated, are corrected; and even these are noted in the Variant Readings. Other errors are allowed to remain in the text, but are corrected in the Notes or mentioned in the descriptions of the editions on pages 7–12, 16–17, 20–36. Line-numbers and page-numbers are, of course, editorial insertions, as are also the bracketed numbers, from 1 to 310, that precede the titles. The original punctuation is retained throughout.

VII. THE CONTRIBUTORS

For reasons of his own, Tottel made no parade of the authors concerned in his publication: in the first edition he names only three — Surrey, Wyatt, Grimald — and in all subsequent editions replaces Grimald's name with his initials N. G. On the title-pages of all the sixteenth-century editions the only name given is that of "the ryght honorable Lorde Henry Haward late Earle of Surrey," — Wyatt, Grimald, and the uncertain authors being dismissed in the laconic phrase "and other." Probably enough, Surrey's name appears on the title-page, just as his poems come first in the text, because of his rank. But Tottel evidently esteemed Wyatt as highly as Surrey, for he gives them equal attention in his preface, speaking of "the weightinesse of the depewitted sir Thomas Wyat the elders verse." I suggest that he omitted Wyatt's name solely from the fear that it might be confused with that of his son, the unfortunate Sir Thomas Wyatt, usually called "the younger," who in 1554 had been executed for rebellion against Queen Mary. The miscellany throughout reveals an editor who worked nervously with his eye on political conditions and possible censorship. One of the poems (No. 279) seems to be a veiled account of Wyatt's rebellion; another (No. 205) originally mentioned young Wyatt, but the reference was omitted in the miscellany; for, since "Wyatt" was a name with a sound odious to the ears of the government, Tottel would hardly have jeopardized the success of his volume by advertising the connection of the traitor's father with it. Caution, too, is seen in the qualifying phrase of "the elder" that is added after Wyatt's name in the preface, in the titles of Nos. 29, 263, 273, at the top of page 211, and at the end of No. 127.

The miscellany itself bears testimony to the value attached to Wyatt's work by including five poems in his honor, four of them (Nos. 29–31, 263) by Surrey, the fifth (No. 273) by St. Leger. Yet the featuring of Surrey's name on the title-page had a curious effect in exaggerating his importance at the expense of Sir Thomas Wyatt. Thus in *The Defence of Poesy* (about 1580) Sir Philip Sidney, evidently with the entire miscellany in mind, referred to Surrey but neglected Wyatt and Grimald completely; and whenever other Elizabethan critical writers mentioned Wyatt, they usually characterized him as inferior or subordinate to Surrey.[1] That habit continued till at least the middle of the nineteenth century, with Surrey always preceding Wyatt in any discussion of the miscellany, and with editors like Nott and Nicolas christening their editions *The Works of Surrey and Wyatt*. Critical opinion generally went on the calm assumption that the two poets were exact contemporaries, or even that Wyatt was Surrey's disciple; till Nott, whose *penchant* for Surrey kept him from being fair to Wyatt, declared,[2] "Surrey soon became Wyatt's master in poetic composition; but in the first instance he must have been his scholar." *The Edinburgh Review*[3] took Nott to task for editing Wyatt in as great bulk as Surrey:

The credit Dr. Nott might have procured, as an unostentatious enthusiast for great genius, on the strength of his first volume, he is in danger of losing, from the unwarrantable zeal for proportion which he has exhibited in his second. . . . Sir Thomas Wyatt was a man of wit, a shrewd observer, a subtle politician; but, in no true sense of the word, was he a *poet;* and as our object . . . is to consider poets and poetry, we shall here take our leave of him at once.

Actually Wyatt was the older man as well as the pioneer; Surrey was his ardent disciple and a personal friend of the younger Wyatt. Recog-

[1] Thus the compiler of *England's Parnassus* (1600) attributes eleven quotations to Surrey (from Nos. 2, 57, 63, 133, 171, 176, 177, 197, 270); but Charles Crawford, editing the *Parnassus* in 1913, shows that four of them are from Wyatt, one from Grimald, five from mistaken or unknown authors, and (p. 269) only one from Surrey. See the *Parnassus*, pp. 543–544.
[2] In his Wyatt volume, p. lxxxvi.
[3] XXVII (New York, 1817), 392.

nition of these facts is nowaday taken in the conventional order of names, Wyatt and Surrey.

Even yet, however, Surrey's name is the first that comes to mind when the miscellany is mentioned, largely because it is the only name that appears on the title-page. If one suddenly thinks of a poem in that volume, one perhaps almost instinctively associates it with Surrey, less commonly with Wyatt. Such has been the case ever since Elizabethan times. The contributions of Surrey and Wyatt, it should be observed, were printed without any author-headings[1] and were signed only at the end: hence very likely many people failed to grasp the attributions of authorship. The famous poet Michael Drayton, to illustrate, was an admiring student of the *Songs and Sonnets*, part of which he appears to have memorized. Nevertheless, he did not realize that all the poems before the signatures on pages 31 and 92 were Surrey's and Wyatt's respectively, and hence he thought No. 121 was written by Surrey or Sir Francis Bryan, although it is printed as Wyatt's. Drayton's misunderstanding was shared by William Fulman (†1688),[2] whose copy of *E* has on the fly-leaf the note:

From fol. 1. to the end of fol. 18. [Nos. 1–36, 243, 262–265] seemes to be written by the Earle of Surrey, his Name being there added.

From thence to fol. 49. end. seems to be Sir Thomas Wiate the elders, who dyed of the plague at Shirburne 1541. his Name being likewise there added: And the next fol. beginning with the Title of

Uncerteine Authors.

But some perhaps may be intermixed.

HENRY HOWARD, EARL OF SURREY

In *A* forty poems were assigned to Surrey. In *B–I* the number was apparently increased by one when No. 243, with the title of "An answer in the behalfe of a woman of an vncertain aucthor," was inserted among his poems as an answer to No. 26; but the new title clearly states that No. 243 was composed by an unknown author. Various other poems have been attributed to Surrey, as is pointed out in the Notes. For example, by *England's Parnassus* (1600) his name is appended to several selections that do not belong to him,[3] and by *England's Helicon*

---

[1] Except that in *A* (but not in *B–I*) Nos. 262–271 had such headings.
[2] See p. 28, above.
[3] Cf. note 1 on p. 66, above.

INTRODUCTION

(1600) to reprints of Nos. 181 and 201; by George Turbervile, John Weever, and Sir Richard Barckley he is regarded as the author of Nos. 278, 227, and 243 respectively; and in manuscripts he is credited with the composition of Nos. 174 and 282. As none of these ascriptions, however, except perhaps that of No. 282, can be taken seriously, and as No. 9 is very likely the work of Lord Vaux, Surrey's total remains at forty poems. But his importance is not to be measured by quantity, for in this respect he is equalled by Grimald.

Henry Howard, known by courtesy as the Earl of Surrey, was born about 1517 as the eldest son of Thomas Howard, third Duke of Norfolk, by his wife Lady Elizabeth Stafford, daughter of the Duke of Buckingham. His illustrious ancestry, which included royalty, and his equally illustrious family-connections made him the greatest noble of his own age, and contributed to the haughtiness and pride that eventually caused his ruin. Surrey himself, and no doubt others, thought his ancestry fully equal to that of the Prince of Wales (afterwards Edward VI), whose mother was Jane Seymour; for a time it was rumored that he was to marry the Princess (afterwards Queen) Mary; and he was the closest friend of Henry VIII's bastard, Henry Fitzroy, Duke of Richmond, a youth who married Surrey's sister Mary. Other impressive connections may be observed in the sketch of Surrey in the *Dictionary of National Biography*.[1]

The facts of Surrey's life may be passed over rapidly. Educated under his mother's direction by a well-known tutor, John Clerk, Surrey in 1529, at the command of Henry VIII, became companion to the Duke of Richmond, with whom he lived for almost three years at Windsor Castle. His affection for that youth and his grief at Richmond's early death are touchingly recounted in No. 15.[2] Surrey and Richmond accompanied Henry to France in 1532, and were left at Paris for almost a year with the three sons of King Francis I. When they returned to England in October, 1533, Richmond, then about fifteen, was married to Surrey's fourteen-year-old sister, but the early death of the bridegroom made the marriage nominal.

[1] From this work and from Padelford's biographical sketch all my facts have been taken.
[2] See also "A lytyll ballet mayde of ye yong duk' gace," printed from manuscript in *The Yorkshire Archaeological and Topographical Journal*, XI (1891), 201.

HENRY HOWARD, EARL OF SURREY

In the spring of 1532 Surrey had been married to Lady Frances de Vere, daughter of the Earl of Oxford, though because of their youth the two did not live together until some three years later. Their first child, Thomas (afterwards the fourth Duke of Norfolk), was born on March 10, 1536. In that year, too, Surrey perforce acted as earl marshal at the trial of his cousin, Queen Anne Boleyn, served with his father in crushing the rebellion known as the Pilgrimage of Grace, and was confined at Windsor for striking a courtier in the royal grounds of Hampton Court. During this confinement he wrote Nos. 8, 11, 15.

A period of marked royal favor culminating with the king's marriage to Catherine Howard on August 8, 1540, and ending with her execution on February 11, 1542, came to all the Howards. During that time Surrey was made Knight of the Garter, seneschal of the king's domain in Norfolk, and steward of Cambridge University. In July, 1542, he was again imprisoned for striking a courtier, John a Leigh, but was released shortly afterwards, and in the autumn accompanied his father to Scotland on a military expedition, returning to write certain poems (Nos. 29–31, 263) in honor of his master, Wyatt, recently deceased. A bit later he was confined to the Fleet prison for a riot in which he, with the younger Wyatt and other gay gallants, had broken windows about London with "pellets" from their stone-bows, as well as for the offense of eating meat in Lent; and in prison he whiled away the hours in writing a "satire" on London.

Military operations in France filled most of the years 1543 and 1544, with Surrey acting as governor of Boulogne and as lieutenant-general on land and sea of the English Continental possessions, till he was supplanted by his family rival, the Earl of Hertford (later Duke of Somerset and lord protector), as lieutenant-general on land, by Lord Lisle on sea, and by Lord Grey de Wilton as governor. Then, as the health of the king declined, enmity between the Howard and Hertford factions increased. In October, 1546, the latter found a trifling excuse to cause the poet's ruin.

On a charge of high treason he was committed to the Tower, December 12, and his father was also lodged there as an accomplice. The charge was based on the fact that Surrey had put the royal arms and the supposed arms of Edward the Confessor in his escutcheon, modifying the emblems with three silver labels in the first quarter of his arms, a sign used by Prince Edward to distinguish his arms from those of the king. Although later, at the accession of Queen Mary, Parliament passed an act authorizing the use of these arms by the Howards, yet it was alleged at the time that Surrey had expressed a treasonable intention to seize the throne on the death of Henry VIII in defiance of the rights of the prince. He was accordingly indicted for high treason, tried by a hostile jury at the Guildhall on January 13, 1547, condemned to death, and executed on Tower Hill on January 19 before he had reached his thirtieth birthday — his only real crime being that he was the most brilliant and most accomplished aristocrat in England, and that he had too openly boasted of his royal descent. His father escaped execution because of the opportune death of Henry VIII on January 28, shortly after which he was released.

In the midst of a brief and crowded life Surrey found time to write the poems that, thanks almost solely to Tottel's *Miscellany*,[1] made him famous. His special importance comes from the improvements he made on the models set by Wyatt; for his admiration of his master, attested by four poems in the miscellany, did not blind him to the elder writer's defects. It seems likely that Surrey consciously attempted to make his metrical accents fall in general upon words that were accented because of their importance, and upon the accented syllables of those words. He experimented, furthermore, with run-over lines, cesura-variations, and other prosodic matters in such a way as to make Wyatt seem antiquated by comparison and so acceptably as to affect the practice of subsequent poets. His metrical forms, too, were varied; especially noteworthy was his introduction of blank verse into English (in his translation of Virgil's *Aeneid*, books II and IV) and his establishment of the so-called English, or Shakespearean, form of the sonnet. The great advance of Surrey over Wyatt can perhaps best be seen by a comparison of the manuscript copies of Nos. 6 and 37, poems translated from the same sonnet of Petrarch. Modern readers may find Surrey's subjects too conventional or insincere, his images and diction too artificial or naïve, for complete enjoyment; but in the history of English poetry his position is high and secure.

It is not surprising that Surrey rapidly became a figure of romance among the Elizabethans, who regarded him as the first modern verse-

---

[1] At least Nos. 27 and 31 were published before the miscellany was compiled.

writer, as the greatest poet since Chaucer. When the miscellany itself
was published, ten years after his death, his alleged connection with
"Geraldine" was already common rumor, as is shown by the title of
No. 8;[1] further countenance was given to the rumor by Richard Stany-
hurst in the description of Ireland that in 1577 he published in Holins-
hed's *Chronicles;* and from this small beginning sprang the romantic
farrago in Thomas Nashe's novel, *The Unfortunate Traveller, or The
Life of Jack Wilton* (1594),[2] the hero of which meets the Earl of Surrey
in Holland and as a page accompanies him on his travels. Among vari-
ous other impossible episodes, Nashe tells how in Germany Surrey con-
sulted the German alchemist Cornelius Agrippa (who really died in
1535) in regard to Geraldine's welfare and was shown her image in a
magic mirror, "sicke weeping on her bed, and resolued all into deuout
religion for the absence of her Lord"; and how "he published a proud
challenge in the Duke of Florence court against all commers, (whether
Christians, Turkes, Iewes, or Saracens,) in defence of his *Geraldines*
beautie." In the combats that followed, the doughty earl "made all
his encounterers new scoure their armor in the dust: so great was his
glory that day as *Geraldine* was therby eternally glorifid . . . the trum-
pets proclaimed *Geraldine* the exceptionlesse fayrest of women."

Perhaps Nashe told this yarn with tongue in cheek, but the credulity
with which it was accepted for more than two hundred years is amazing.
Thus Michael Drayton, a generous admirer of the miscellany poets,
believed Nashe's story without qualification, and made use of it in his
Englands Heroicall Epistles (1598). One of the poems in that volume,
"*Henry Howard* Earle of Surrey to *Geraldine*" (M6–N2ᵛ), has the fol-
lowing argument:

Henry Howard, that true noble Earle of Surrey, and excellent Poet, falling
in loue with *Geraldine;* descended of the noble family of the *Fitzgeralds* of
Ireland, a faire and modest Lady; & one of the honorable maydes to Queen
Katherine Dowager: eternizeth her prayses in many excellent Poems, of rare
and sundry inuentions: and after some fewe yeares, being determined to see
that famous Italy, the source and Helicon of al excellent Arts; first visiteth
that renowned Florence, from whence the Geralds challenge their descent,

[1] See also the note on 12.23.
[2] R. B. McKerrow's Nashe, II (1904), 187–328 (the quotations are on pp. 254, 271,
278). The novel was registered for publication on September 17, 1593 (Arber's *Tran-
script*, II, 636).

from the ancient family of the Geraldi: there in honour of his mistresse he aduaunceth her picture: and challengeth to maintaine her beauty by deedes of Armes against all that durst appeare in the lists, where after the proofe of his braue and incomparable valour, whose arme crowned her beauty with eternall memory, he writeth this Epistle to his deerest Mistris.

With Nashe and Drayton to vouch for it, belief in the Surrey–Geraldine romance spread until these "lovers" became the English equivalent of Dante and Beatrice or Petrarch and Laura. Thus, during the interregnum Nicholas Hookes, in his *Amanda, a Sacrifice to an Unknown Goddesse*, 1653, F5, referred to the story as follows:

> "Were *Surrey* travel'd now to *Tuskanie*,
> "Off'ring to reach his gauntlet out for thee;
> "If on the guilt tree in the List he set,
> "Thy pretty, lovely, pretty counterfeit,
> "All Planet-struck with those two stars, thy eyne,
> "(Outshining farre, his heav'nly *Geraldine;*)
> "There would no staffe be shiver'd, none would dare,
> "A beautie with *Amanda*'s to compare.

And even into the sober pages of the *Athenae Oxonienses* (1692)[1] Anthony Wood inserted part of Nashe's narrative.

In the eighteenth century it seems to have met with no skeptics. It was evidently in the mind of Elijah Fenton when in 1711 he wrote that "Surrey's numbers glow'd with warm desire";[2] and it was definitely mentioned two years later by Pope in *Windsor Forest*. Hence George Sewell, editing Tottel's *Miscellany* in 1717,[3] wrote smugly of Surrey's romance: "It is uncertain what Success his Passion and his Poetry obtained, but Mr. *Drayton* would made [*sic*] us believe that their Loves were far from being criminal, which I think we at this distance of time ought not in good manners to question." Henry Curll, evidently in the hope of attracting romantic readers, gave to a collection of Surrey's poems that stood immovably on his book-shelves the new title of *The Praise of Geraldine* (1728).[4] Elizabeth Cooper's *Historical and Poetical Medley: or Muses Library* (1738)[5] asserted that Surrey "became first eminent for his Devotion, to the beautiful *Geraldine*,

[1] Ed. Philip Bliss, 1 (1813), 154–155.
[2] "An Epistle to Mr. Southerne," *Poetical Works*, 1779, p. 46.
[3] Pages xii–xiii.   [4] See pp. 39, 42–43, above.   [5] Pages 55–56.

Maid of Honour to Queen *Catherine:* 'Twas she first inspir'd Him with Poetry, and that Poetry has made her Immortal." Horace Walpole, in *A Catalogue of the Royal and Noble Authors of England, Scotland, and Ireland* (1758),[1] accepted the story without question, and his account of Geraldine herself won the approval of Thomas Warton, who retold it in his *History of English Poetry* (1781).[2] George Ellis also fully believed in the love-story when he got out the second edition (1801) of his *Specimens of the Early English Poets,*[3] and Sir Walter Scott included a song based upon it in *The Lay of the Last Minstrel* (1805), canto VI, stanzas 16–20.

Although Alexander Chalmers, editing Surrey in *The Works of the English Poets* (1810),[4] attacked the legend, it nevertheless reached its apogee in the romantic edition of Surrey issued by G. F. Nott in 1815.[5] So thoroughly was Nott obsessed by it that he lost all sense of proportion and evidence, distorting his material, changing the order and titles of poems to make them harmonize with his preconceived ideas, and connecting every love-poem of Surrey's with the always capitalized Fair Geraldine. Perhaps it was not altogether indefensible to give No. 8 the new title of "Surrey declares the Fair Geraldine to be the Mistress of his heart: and describes the place where he first saw, and first began to love her"; but in all other cases Nott drags the maiden in by the hair of the head — drags her into poems where she has no possible business.

Thus No. 262, which obviously is a purely conventional love-lament addressed to no specific person, Nott entitles "Surrey complains of the malice of fortune in separating him from the Fair Geraldine; but assures her that absence shall not diminish his love." A still better example of his contortions is No. 17, which he calls "In the person of a lady anxiously looking for the return of her absent lord, Surrey describes the state of his own mind, when separated from the Fair Geraldine." No. 243, unsigned in the manuscript and specifically attributed to an uncertain author in *A–I*, Nott reprints with the preposterous title, "The Fair Geraldine retorts on Surrey the charge of artifice, and commends the person whom he considered to be his rival, as superior to him in courage and ability."

[1] Ed. Park, 1806, I, 262–267. [2] Ed. Hazlitt, IV, 23–28.
[3] II, 46–47.   [4] II, 311–359. [5] See pp. 52–53, above.

INTRODUCTION

More rhapsodic still are Nott's annotations. A single illustration will suffice. Although it is clear that No. 264 is directed at Lady Stanhope, Nott entitles the poem "Surrey renounces all affection for the Fair Geraldine," juggles evidence in his notes to make it appear that the white wolf refers to the Fitzgerald coat of arms, and concludes the verses to be "an account of a quarrel between Surrey and the Fair Geraldine, which, as we hear nothing of any reconciliation afterwards, was the occasion probably of his renouncing his ill-fated passion."

Nott's romantic extravagance is a blemish on an otherwise admirable edition, and it effectually killed the legend he tried so hard to authenticate.[1] In reviewing his Surrey *The Edinburgh Review* [2] alludes significantly to "the more romantic fables" he relates. Nicolas, editing Surrey and Wyatt in 1831, remarked[3] that Nott's treatment of No. 264 furnished "an amusing instance of first imagining a fact, and then making every circumstance support it. The learned editor, as in most other instances, assumes that Geraldine was the subject of the poem, without a shadow of evidence." At the present time nobody believes in the Surrey–Geraldine tale, which has been formally disproved by Courthope [4] and Bapst.[5]

But Geraldine, or Elizabeth Fitzgerald, herself deserves a word. The youngest daughter of the ninth Earl of Kildare, she was born in Ireland about 1528 and was brought to England in 1533. In 1537 she entered the household of the Princess Mary at Hunsdon, whence she was transferred to that of Queen Catherine Howard in 1540. Surrey is supposed to have met her in March, 1537, and to have written No. 8 (the only poem, except possibly for No. 14, that can definitely be connected with her) in July, when Geraldine was some nine years of age

[1] But see Samuel Rogers, *Human Life*, 1819 (*Complete Poetical Works*, ed. Sargent, 1854, p. 186):

> "Thou, all-accomplished SURREY, thou art known;
> The flower of knighthood, nipt as soon as blown!
> Melting all hearts but Geraldine's alone!"

See also the elaborate account of Geraldine in Mrs. K. B. Thomson's *Celebrated Friendships*, I (1861), 83–90, and the casual belief expressed in the story by Francis Hackett, *Henry the Eighth* (1929), p. 353.

[2] XXVII (1816), 392.
[3] Surrey, p. 47 n.
[4] *A History of English Poetry*, II (1897), 76–79.
[5] *Deux Gentilshommes-Poètes de la Cour de Henry VIII*, 1891, ch. xv.

and Surrey a married man of about nineteen and a father. "The truth probably is," Professor Padelford[1] justly remarks, "that Surrey whiled away an idle hour of confinement by composing a sonnet in compliment to a little girl of nine whose pretty face chanced to have caught his fancy. If he did for the time being accept her as the 'Laura' of his verse, it must have been in a spirit of playfulness. Most of his amatory verse is undertaken largely as a literary exercise, as any student of Renaissance polite verse must appreciate." In 1543, when she was fifteen, Geraldine became the second wife of Sir Anthony Browne, who was sixty, and after his death in 1548 she became the third wife of Sir Edward Clinton, first Earl of Lincoln. She died in March, 1589, and was buried in St. George's Chapel, Windsor Castle.

SIR THOMAS WYATT THE ELDER

Wyatt was by far the most important contributor to the miscellany. In the first edition ninety-seven poems (Nos. 37–127, 266–271) were attributed to him, but in later editions that total was reduced to ninety-six by the attribution of No. 82 to an uncertain author. Other poems, like Nos. 149 and 261, have been loosely assigned to him in one place or another, but the assignments have no weight.

Wyatt[2] was born at Allington Castle, Kent, about 1503, and was sent to St. John's College, Cambridge, in 1516, when he was twelve years old; but the degrees usually assigned to him (B.A., 1518, M.A., 1520) are now said to have been granted instead to a John Wyat.[3] His marriage to Elizabeth Brooke, daughter of Lord Cobham, took place in 1520, but long afterwards he was popularly supposed to be the lover of Anne Boleyn, whom he had met as a boy. His son, later known as the rebel, Sir Thomas Wyatt the younger, was born in 1521.

Barely twenty-one years old, Wyatt was appointed clerk of the king's jewels in 1524, a position which he held until about 1530. During 1525–1526 he was in France, and the next year he accompanied Sir John Russell on a mission to the pope at Rome and the council at Venice. After visiting various other Italian cities, he was taken prisoner by the

[1] *The Poems of Henry Howard, Earl of Surrey*, pp. 189–190.
[2] This sketch is based on the *Dictionary of National Biography* and Miss Foxwell's works.
[3] John and J. A. Venn, *Alumni Cantabrigienses*, IV (1927), 480.

imperial forces and held for ransom; but he escaped to Bologna, and from 1528 to 1532 served as marshal of Calais. Appointed to the Privy Council in 1533, he acted as chief "ewerer" at the coronation of Anne Boleyn, but by her downfall he was brought into trouble. In May, 1536, he was committed to the Tower to be held as a witness against Anne, but was released in June and sent to Allington Castle to remain under his father's charge. Henceforth he grew in favor with Cromwell and the king.

In 1536-1537 Wyatt officiated as sheriff for Kent, but in April, 1537, was appointed ambassador to Spain, and, except for a short visit to England, remained abroad till April or May, 1539. After a brief sojourn at Allington, to which he had succeeded on the death (November 10, 1537) of his father, Sir Henry, he was sent in November, 1539, as envoy to Emperor Charles V. Soon after his return to England (May, 1540) he saw Cromwell disgraced and executed, and he himself was arrested in the following January, imprisoned in the Tower on charges of treason, and deprived of his property. Two months later, however, a full pardon was granted him, and his position with the king seemed secure. But this favor he did not long live to enjoy. Sent in the autumn of 1542 to conduct the imperial ambassador from Falmouth to London, he fell ill on the journey, died at Sherborne, Dorset, and was buried there in the great church on October 11.

None of Wyatt's work was published during his lifetime. His metrical version of the Penitential Psalms, translated from Aretino during 1540-1541, was printed in 1549; but, except to the fortunate possessors of manuscript copies, his lyrics were known only by the selections in the miscellany, a book on which his reputation and influence in Elizabethan times were largely based.

The ninety-six poems in *A–I* consist of sonnets, epigrams, satires, and occasional miscellaneous forms. The inspiration behind most of them is Italian, and of the Italians Wyatt's chief masters were Petrarch and Serafino. In many cases the poems are translated so closely as to suggest mere literary, or language, exercises; for the most partial enthusiast must admit that Wyatt's genius was chiefly derivative. Few of his poems show traces of humanistic influence: of those that do, two epigrams translated from Ausonius and Pandulpho, two moral songs from Seneca and Boethius, two satires suggested (though perhaps indirectly through the Italian) by Horace, and a tiresome "Song of Iopas" indebted to Virgil make up the known total. Because Wyatt had a fondness for elaborate conceits, for grotesque imagery, his reputation has suffered greatly.

Many hard sayings, too, have been directed at his inability to write smoothly flowing lines and at his "carelessness" about accents; but some of this criticism has been based on Tottel's text rather than on Wyatt's, and hence should be ignored.[1] The uncertain accents, the strange pronunciations, the rough movement of his lines, are due to the practice of his time. He is no worse, he is indeed better, than his immediate contemporaries; but in any case he was the pioneer who fumbled in the linguistic difficulties that beset him and prepared the way for Surrey's smoother lines and more pleasing accentuation. Surrey, to be sure, improved on his model, but the importance of the model is only intensified by that fact. As no one at the present day is in danger of underestimating Wyatt's significance in the history of English verse, so no one should be tempted to put too high a value on his intrinsic merit. It is undoubtedly a good thing for his reputation among general readers to-day, as it was in the sixteenth century, that in the miscellany many of his texts were subjected to an editorial process that modernized even though it debased them.

NICHOLAS GRIMALD

So far as the first edition of the miscellany is concerned, Grimald ranks with Surrey in the number of his poems. By Tottel he is credited with the authorship of forty pieces, but it is not unlikely that Nos. 131 and 132 were composed by the N. Vincent and G. Blackwood whose names appear in the titles, instead of by Grimald.[2] In *B–I* his contributions were reduced to ten and his name was replaced by initials. As a result, he became an obscure figure whose very name few Elizabethans knew — a melancholy fact, since he doubtless hoped to be regarded as

---

[1] As, for example, the criticism of No. 37 by Child in *The Cambridge History of English Literature*, III, 191 (American ed.).

[2] Apparently a similar case is that of Barnabe Googe's *Eglogs, Epytaphes, and Sonettes*, 1563 (Arber's reprint, pp. 80–83, 86–87, 92, 102–105), where two poems are by L. Blundeston, three by Alexander Neville, each an "answer" to a poem addressed to the person named as the writer. Other instances will be found in certain volumes by Turbervile and Thomas Howell.

one of the 'fine poets' who, he tells us at 101.10, were so rare in the England of his day.

Grimald was born about 1519 at "Brownshold" (probably Leighton-Bromswold), Huntingdonshire, of an old yeoman family.[1] His elegy on his mother Annes, or Agnes (No. 162), is the chief source of information regarding his early life. He was educated at Christ's College, Cambridge, where he received the degree of B.A. in 1539–1540. In April, 1542, he was incorporated B.A. at Oxford; in May he was chosen probationer-fellow of Merton College; and in 1544 he became a Master of Arts of both Oxford and Cambridge. Cardinal Wolsey's foundation was re-opened in January, 1547, as Christ Church, and to this college Grimald received an appointment as "a senior or theologist" to give lectures on rhetoric in the refectory. He left Oxford in January, 1552, to preach at Eccles (now a suburb of Manchester), and was subsequently appointed chaplain to Nicholas Ridley, Bishop of London.

With the accession of Mary I and the re-establishment of the Roman Catholic church, Ridley with other Protestants was imprisoned, first at London and later at Oxford, whence he sent Grimald copies of everything he wrote. Presently, however, the poet himself was (in 1555) committed to the Bocardo prison in Oxford. That he secured his freedom by recanting his religion seems likely; but much more questionable is the theory that he acted as a spy and brought to their deaths the Protestant martyrs Ridley, Cranmer, Latimer, and others. He died about 1562, as appears from the highly eulogistic elegy published in Barnabe Googe's *Eglogs, Epytaphes, and Sonettes* (1563).

Grimald was a voluminous writer who holds a place of genuine importance in the history of English literature. Unfortunately for him, much of his work is lost and much that is extant is written in Latin; hence the present generation of readers scarcely knows him except for the appearance of his name in the miscellany. Yet important and influential were his Latin plays of *Christus Redivivus* (1543) and *Archipropheta* (1548), as well as his numerous translations from and com-

[1] On Grimald see the *Dictionary of National Biography; Notes and Queries*, 11th series, IV (1911), 275–276, 384; L. R. Merrill, "Nicholas Grimald, the Judas of the Reformation," *Publications of the Modern Language Association of America*, XXXVII (1922), 216–227, and *The Life and Poems of Nicholas Grimald* (Yale dissertation, 1925); C. R. Baskervill's comments on Merrill in *Modern Philology*, XXIII (1926), 377–378, and G. C. Moore Smith's in *The Modern Language Review*, XXI (1926), 81–83.

mentaries on Greek and Latin authors. His English poems are some-what inferior to those of Surrey, but most of them should be judged as metrical translations from Latin rather than as poems. They all, even the touching elegy on his mother, abound in frigid, pedantic references to the classics, and at times in a ponderosity still popularly associated with the academic quill; and they show a limited vocabulary which involves the continual repetition of words.[1] It appears, too, that Grimald had a favorite spelling of his own — especially the use of *oo* for *o* (*Room, soom, coom, twoo, soondry*) — and that he favored northern forms like *tane* and *shinand*. The most interesting of his poems are the two in blank verse (Nos. 165, 166), which after Surrey's translations from the *Aeneid* were the first English poems to be written and published in that meter.[2]

UNCERTAIN AUTHORS

In his reprint of the miscellany (page xvi) Arber declares that the phrase "uncertain authors" was "undoubtedly a designation more of concealment than ignorance"; but I see no basis for that assertion.[3] The editor of *A* must have had a manuscript, or manuscripts, before him in which there were a large number of unsigned poems, the authors of which were totally unknown to him. Some of the poems may well have been signed with the very phrase he uses, for this practice was far from uncommon. For example, poems in MS. Rawlinson Poet. 85, fols. 88, 98, are signed "Incertus author," while most of the contents of that manuscript are ascribed to definite authors; MS. Additional 38823, fol. 58ᵛ, contains a poem headed "Jncerti Authoris," and MS. Ashmole 48 [4] one signed "*Finis, the autor unsertayn.*" Again, a manuscript

---

[1] Courthope (*A History of English Poetry*, II, 151) says: "The pedantry and learned allusion which characterise them are perhaps the earliest notes in English poetry of that manner which culminated in the 'metaphysical' style of Cowley and his contemporaries."

[2] Merrill, pp. 369–374, argues that Grimald's blank verse was published earlier than Surrey's because Tottel issued the two books of Surrey's translation on June 21, sixteen days after the miscellany appeared. Miss Willcock, however, shows (*The Modern Language Review*, XIV [1919], 163–167) that John Day had in all probability published his edition of Surrey's fourth book in 1554.

[3] It is, however, echoed by Child in *The Cambridge History of English Literature*, III, 203 (American ed.), who says that calling the authors uncertain "does not, necessarily, mean that they were unknown."

[4] See Thomas Wright, *Songs and Ballads*, p. 161, Roxburghe Club, 1860.

copy of No. 175 is signed "huomo inconosciuto." It seems reasonable to suppose, then, that the editor of the miscellany found warrant in his "copy" for the phrase "uncertain authors," and that it was a designation of ignorance, not of concealment.

The uncertain authors, it should be observed, show comparatively little knowledge of the Italian poets who had dominated Wyatt and Surrey. Among these contributors, on the contrary, humanistic influence predominates, accounting for their frequent references to classic mythology, as well as for their translations or paraphrases from Ovid, Lucretius, Seneca, and Horace. To uncertain authors ninety-four poems were credited in *A*; and this number was increased in *B–I* by No. 82 plus thirty-nine new pieces, making a total of one hundred thirty-four. Arber identified the authors of three anonymous poems.[1] It is hardly possible that the anonymity of them all will ever be solved, but the following "uncertain" authors are more or less "certain."

J. CANAND, a ballad-writer about whom no biographical information is available, was the author of Nos. 177 and 180.

GEOFFREY CHAUCER wrote No. 238. The poem is given in the miscellany probably from one of William Thynne's editions of his works, and as a result Chaucer here seems no more archaic in style than Wyatt himself. Accordingly, the editor of *A* can hardly be blamed for failing to identify this great "uncertain author."

Sir JOHN CHEKE (1514–1557), tutor to Edward VI, secretary of state, and one of the leading lights of the English Renaissance, was probably the author of No. 284.

WILLIAM GRAY wrote No. 255 and possibly (but not at all probably) No. 256. A ballad-writer of note, a favorite servant of the Protector Somerset, M.P. for Reading, he died on February 1, 1557. His career and works are discussed in Ernest W. Dormer's *Gray of Reading* (1923).

JOHN HARINGTON, father of the epigrammatist and translator Sir John, wrote No. 169 and perhaps others that cannot now be identified. He was an ardent collector of the poems in Tottel's *Miscellany*,[2] who

---

[1] Nos. 199, 211, 212. His identification of Edward Somerset as the author of No. 200 (see the Notes) cannot be accepted.
[2] See "Harington MSS." in the Index.

according to Sir John "could bothe write well and judge well";[1] and various poems attributed to him are reprinted in *Nugae Antiquae*.[2]

JOHN HEYWOOD (1497?–1580?), famous epigrammatist and writer of interludes, was the author of No. 199.

THOMAS NORTON (1532–1584), lawyer and poet, best known for collaborating with Sackville in the composition (about 1561) of the first English blank-verse tragedy, *Gorboduc*, wrote Nos. 257 and 289. Both he and Grimald, by the way, contributed complimentary verses to William Turner's *A perseruatiue or triacle, agaynst the poyson of Pelagius* (1551). Norton's "ditties" are highly praised in the verses (quoted on pages 84–85, below) which Jasper Heywood prefixed as a preface to his own translation (1560) of Seneca's *Thyestes*.

Sir ANTHONY ST. LEGER (1496?–1559), K. G., and lord-deputy of Ireland, wrote No. 273.

D. SAND, if the evidence of *The Paradise of Dainty Devices* (1576) may be accepted, was the author of No. 171. In spite of his voluminous contributions to the *Paradise*, nothing is known of him.

THOMAS VAUX, Baron VAUX (1510–1556) certainly composed Nos. 211 and 212, and perhaps Nos. 9 and 217. All four poems are attributed to him in manuscripts, as is also a twelve-line poem, beginning "Syns by examples daylye we are taught," in MS. Additional 28635, fol. 70ᵛ. The last two poems were apparently unknown to his editor, Grosart, who reprinted Nos. 211, 212, and thirteen poems from *The Paradise of Dainty Devices* as the work of Vaux, in *Miscellanies of the Fuller Worthies' Library*, volume IV (1872–1876).[3]

Thomas Warton loosely remarked [4] that, "from palpable coincidences of style, subject, and other circumstances, a slender share of critical sagacity is sufficient to point out many others" of the uncertain authors. Unfortunately, he contented himself with that vague assertion, and subsequent scholars have lacked the "slender share of critical

---

[1] *A Tract on the Succession to the Crown* (*A.D. 1602*), ed. C. R. Markham, p. 105 (Roxburghe Club, 1880). On p. 101 Sir John gives two specimens of his father's verse.
[2] See pp. 91–92, below.
[3] Grosart (p. 358) declares that No. 9 "has not the ring" of Vaux's poetry, but this is opinion, not evidence.
[4] *History of English Poetry*, ed. Hazlitt, IV (1871), 59.

sagacity" to elucidate it. A few other poets, to be sure, are usually associated with the miscellany, although their specific contributions have not been identified. The most important are GEORGE BOLEYN, Viscount ROCHFORD († 1536), and Sir FRANCIS BRYAN († 1550).

Michael Drayton apparently speaks with authority of Bryan's share in the volume. In *Englands Heroicall Epistles* (1598), signature N1, he has Surrey write to Geraldine, in reference to the "beauteous [Lady Anne] Stanhope":

> And famous *Wyat* who in numbers sings,
> To that inchanting *Thracian Harpers* strings,
> To whom *Phœbus* (the Poets God) did drinke,
> A bowle of Nectar fild vnto the brincke,
> And sweet-tongu'd *Bryan* (whom the Muses kept,
> And in his Cradle rockt him whilst he slept,)
> In sacred verses (so diuinely pend,)
> Vpon thy praises euer shall attend.

In the elegy to Henry Reynolds, appended to *The Battaile of Agincourt*, 1627, page 205, Drayton explicitly mentions Bryan's share in the *Songs and Sonnets:*

> They with the Muses which conuersed, were
> That Princely *Surrey*, early in the time
> Of the Eight *Henry*, who was then the prime
> Of *Englands* noble youth; with him there came
> *Wyat;* with reuerence whom we still doe name
> Amongst our Poets, *Brian* had a share
> With the two former, which accompted are
> That times best makers, and the authors were
> Of those small poems, which the title beare,
> Of songs and sonnets, wherein oft they hit
> On many dainty passages of wit.

Bryan is also named along with Wyatt, Surrey, and others in Francis Meres's *Palladis Tamia*, 1598, fol. 284, as "the most passionate among vs to bewaile and bemoane the perplexities of Loue." It is a pity that his share in the miscellany cannot be identified.[1]

[1] In No. 126 Wyatt mentions Bryan's knowing "how great a grace In writyng is to counsaile man the right." Miss Elsa Chapin, of the University of Chicago, informs me that she has found in a Huntington library manuscript [MS. 183, fols. 7-9^v, formerly owned by Thomas Park and Henry Huth] a poem of one hundred eighty-four lines by

Rochford, ill-fated brother of Henry VIII's queen, Anne Boleyn, is highly praised in verses which Richard Smith prefixed to one of his publications, George Gascoigne's *Posies* (1575):

> Sweete *Surrey* suckt *Pernassus* springs,
> And *Wiat* wrote of wondrous things:
> Olde *Rochfort* clambe the stately Throne
> Which *Muses* holde in *Hellicone*.

The juxtaposition of names suggests that Smith had Tottel's *Miscellany* in mind, though why he should know of any connection between it and Rochford does not appear. It is remarkable that an entire book, Bapst's *Deux Gentilshommes-Poètes de la Cour de Henry VIII* (1891), has been written on Rochford (and Surrey), when not a single one of Rochford's verses is known. To be sure, Bapst argues that Rochford wrote No. 87; but that poem was almost certainly composed by Wyatt.

Of the share that THOMAS CHURCHYARD (1520?-1604) had in the miscellany there can be no doubt. In *A light Bondell of liuly discourses called Churchyardes Charge* (1580), which is dedicated to Surrey's grandson, he speaks of Surrey as "my master (who was a noble warriour, an eloquent Oratour, and a second Petrarke)," telling with pride how he served him as a page for four years, "And usd the penne as he was taught." [1] Churchyard loved Surrey just this side idolatry. [2] To *Churchyard's Challenge* (1593) he prefixes "The bookes that I can call to memorie alreadie Printed" — a list of his own works — including the item, "And many things in the booke of songs and Sonets, printed then [that is, in Mary I's reign], were of my making," and he refers to "An infinite number of other Songes and Sonets, giuen where they cannot be recouered, nor purchase any fauour when they are craued." Churchyard was an honest man, if a poor poet. His word cannot be doubted; and the last quotation is interesting as helping to show how the *Songs and Sonnets* grew into being. Unsigned manuscript copies of poems by various authors no doubt went into the making of the miscellany, and because they were unsigned they were lumped among the compositions of uncertain authors.

Bryan, in which he 'counsels man the right' in a series of proverbial and didactic sayings. Hence she suggests that No. 286, which is of a similar nature, may possibly be Bryan's.

[1] Collier's reprint, pp. 2, 11.
[2] Cf. p. 111, below.

INTRODUCTION

It is not possible to identify Churchyard's "many things." The style of his acknowledged works, however, is extremely mannered, depending for its effects on the over-use of alliteration, proverbs, antithetical or balanced phrases, and — what is more distinctive — piled-up commonplaces or figures that elaborate and suspend the thought. Nos. 82, 178, 188, and perhaps 240, written in such a fashion, suggest his authorship. Another test may be cautiously applied. In 1924 Miss Muriel Byrne discussed "Thomas Churchyard's Spelling,"[1] pointing out the very queer orthography consistently found in his manuscript letters, and showing that his spelling was generally normalized by the compositors but that his characteristic forms do occur sporadically in his printed books.[2] For example, he regularly spelled *are, state, home, hope, like*, as *aer, staet, hoem, hoep, liek*. Professor Moore Smith has suggested to me that on the basis of certain curiously spelled words,[3] as well as of style, Nos. 176, 184, 192, 224, 246 may plausibly be assigned to Churchyard. Not improbably, too, he wrote No. 205, as well as one of the poems on Sir James Wilford (Nos. 182, 189), under whom he had served in Scotland.

I have not identified any other contributors.[4] It is a reasonable guess that among them were EDMUND SHEFFIELD, Baron SHEFFIELD, and Sir CHRISTOPHER YELVERTON. Although no poem by Sheffield (1521–1549) can be recognized, a 'book of sonnets' of his composition is mentioned by Bishop Bale, Thomas Fuller, and others. Yelverton (1535?–1612) is named along with Sackville and Norton in Jasper Heywood's preface to *Thyestes* (1560):[5]

> There Sackuyldes Sonetts sweetely sauste
>   and featly fyned bee,
> There Nortons ditties do delight,
>   there Yeluertons doo flee

---

[1] *The Library*, v, 243–248.

[2] She might well have added that a long poem, "*Thomas Churchyarde Gentleman*, in commendation of this worke," prefixed to Barnabe Rich's *Allarme to England* (1578), has a discreet, printed, marginal note: "*His orthographie and maner of writing* obserued."

[3] E. g., *lief* (129.36), *liekt* (136.34), *liefe, spirites* [pronounced as a monosyllable] (149.6,21), *sprete, lief* (175.11, 20), *wiefly* (193.16).

[4] Sir Sidney Lee, in his sketch of Tottel in the *Dictionary of National Biography*, names William Forrest (on whom see the notes to Nos. 199 and 212) as one of them — perhaps because of a too hasty glance at Arber's reprint, p. xii.

[5] Ed. H. de Vocht, in W. Bang's *Materialen zur Kunde des älteren Englischen Dramas*, XLI (1913), 102.

THE UNCERTAIN AUTHORS

Well pewrde with pen: suche yong men three,
  as weene thou mightst agayne,
To be begotte as Pallas was,
  of myghtie Joue his brayne.

It would be only natural to include THOMAS SACKVILLE, later Lord
BUCKHURST and Earl of DORSET (1536–1608), in the list of "probable
uncertain authors." But there is no advantage in further speculation
of this sort.

The most important contributors were Surrey, Wyatt, Grimald, and
Vaux. Of these all but Grimald were in one way or another connected
with the court: except for his contributions Tottel's *Miscellany* is an
anthology of court-poetry. Furthermore, all four were connected with
Cambridge University, Surrey in the honorary position of steward, the
other three as undergraduates; while, of the uncertain authors men-
tioned above, Cheke, Norton, St. Leger, and possibly Sackville were
Cambridge men. That university, long noted as the mother of poets, is
the foster-mother of the miscellany which ushered modern English
verse into being. Again, the known contributors, except for Grimald
and possibly for Canand, were men of affairs to whom poetry was an
avocation: they wrote not as a profession but because they felt the urge
to write and because it was the thing for men of their class to do. They
penned verses during lives crowded with action, and several of them
experienced the favor as well as the frown of royalty. Wyatt and
Grimald and Surrey became acquainted with prison cells and courts of
law; violent death stared each in the face, and Surrey met his end on
the scaffold. All of which seems prophetic of the literary profession in
Elizabeth's reign, when violence, imprisonment, or legal execution had
its way with Marlowe, Jonson, and Raleigh, among others.

VIII. THE "EDITOR"

It is a striking fact that the two principal contributors to the mis-
cellany had long been dead when it appeared — Wyatt fifteen, Surrey
ten, years. Sir Francis Bryan and Lord Rochford, assumed to be among
the uncertain authors, had died respectively about seven and twenty-one
years earlier, Lord Vaux in the year immediately preceding the publi-
cation. Among other known contributors, John Heywood, Thomas

Churchyard, and Nicholas Grimald were living in 1557 and later. "If to any of these [last] four," observes Arber,[1] "we might assign as a guess, first the existence of the work, in conjunction with the printer; then its chief editing and supervision through the press; it would be to Grimald." The reasons for this guess he sets forth as follows:

We know that he was previously in business relations with the Printer of this work: for Tottel had printed in 1556, Grimald's translation of Cicero's *De Officiis*, dedicated by him, as his humble 'Oratour,' to Thirleby, Bishop of Ely: and on the 23 April 1558, Tottel finished a Second edition of the same work. It is probable, also, that it was to Grimald's position as Chaplain to that genial Bishop, that Tottel was able to put *Cum priuilegio* on so buoyant a book, at a time when the martyrs' fires were luridly lighting up England. Furthermore, the only poems suppressed in the revision, are Grimald's own. It may, therefore, be fairly guessed that Grimald, if not the Originator, was the chief Editor of this Collection of Poetry upon a plan then new to English Literature.

Arber's guess — it is nothing more — is based upon unimpressive reasoning, but it has met with such general acceptance [2] that many people treat it almost as a fact. It assumes that Grimald edited *A*, but no later edition; and speculation has long been rife as to why he was displaced as editor and why thirty of his poems were omitted from *B–I*.

Hermann Fehse, in a dissertation on Surrey,[3] accepts Arber's guess, and explains the changes in the second edition as due to Tottel's desire for greater anonymity in his publication. Wyatt and Surrey, he argues, were dead, and so there was no good reason for concealing their names; the uncertain authors, he believes (though his belief is not well founded), were men of high rank, who wrote poems not for the public but for the pleasure of their friends, and who, accordingly, could not be named. Hence "Nicholas Grimald" was displaced by "N. G." It seems to me likely that a desire for anonymity did play some part in accounting for

---

[1] *Tottel's Miscellany*, p. xv. The "four" include Vaux, who was dead.

[2] See, *e. g.*, W. E. Simonds, *Sir Thomas Wyatt and his Poems*, 1889, pp. 55–56; Greg, in *The Library*, v (1904), 114–115; Child, in *The Cambridge History of English Literature*, III, 202 (American ed.); F. E. Schelling, *The English Lyric*, 1913, p. 40; J. M. Berdan, *Early Tudor Poetry*, 1920, p. 344 n. 1; A. W. Reed, in *The Review of English Studies*, IV (1928), 445. A contributor to *Notes and Queries*, 11th series, IV (1911), 384, speaks of Grimald as "the Elizabethan poet and translator, and editor of Tottel's 'Miscellany,'" and thinks it "probable that most of those [poems] by 'uncertain authors' were by N. G."

[3] *Henry Howard, Earl of Surrey. Ein Beitrag zur Geschichte des Petrarchismus in England*, p. 19 (*Programm der städtischen Realschule I. O. zu Chemnitz*, 1883).

the changes in *BC*. To object, as does Heinrich Kolbe,[1] that, since Rochford and Bryan were dead, they too should have been named is beside the mark; for there are no grounds whatever for believing that Tottel knew of their connection, actual or alleged, with the miscellany. Kolbe's further pronouncements that the editor (by whom he appears to mean Tottel) regarded his book as a 'lyric-erotic anthology,' in which the personality of the poets was unimportant, but that, to secure a favorable reception among buyers, he named the two most famous poets of the time, are far from convincing.

Dr. L. R. Merrill, in an article called "Nicholas Grimald the Judas of the Reformation" (1922),[2] as well as in *The Life and Poems of Nicholas Grimald* (1925), argues that the suppression of Grimald's name and poems was due to his alleged betrayal of Protestant friends to the stake. "It seems more probable," he writes in the latter work,[3] "since Grimald had become *persona non grata* because of his recantation during the Reformation, and because of his having betrayed his friends, the Protestant martyrs, Cranmer, Latimer, and Ridley, to the Roman Catholic prelates, that Tottel, fearing Grimald's name would injure the sale of the book, removed all of his poems with any personal allusions, and for his name substituted his initials."[4] It is hardly just to call Grimald "the Judas of the Reformation," though he probably did recant to save his life. But after his recantation, actual or supposed, he was eulogized by Bishop Bale and Barnabe Googe, both of whom were strongly opposed to Roman Catholicism; and from this fact it follows that Dr. Merrill's suggestion, which has not met with favor,[5] lacks plausibility.

Now Grimald's poems are rather noticeably out of harmony in *A* because of their heavy-footed classicism and their uncourtly tone. Among the other contributors, too, Grimald was out of place: he was a member, not of the court circle, but of the university group. Hence there is considerable point to Miss Gladys D. Willcock's conclusion:

It is a more natural explanation to suppose that it was felt that, in the first edition, too much space and prominence had been given to one who was not a

[1] *Metrische Untersuchungen über die Gedichte der "Uncertain Authors" in "Tottel's Miscellany,"* Marburg dissertation, 1902.

[2] *Publications of the Modern Language Association of America*, XXXVII, 216–227.

[3] Page 366.

[4] A similar suggestion is put forth in J. M. Berdan's *Early Tudor Poetry* (1920), p. 350.

[5] See, for example, C. R. Baskervill in *Modern Philology*, XXIII (1926), 377–378.

member of the order of courtly makers who contributed the bulk of the poems. That Grimald ever acted as supervisor for Tottel is, therefore, more than doubtful.[1]

If Miss Willcock's theory meet with objection, — though it seems more plausible than any hitherto made, — at least one guess is as good as another. In the absence of any facts, I offer an alternative suggestion that the disappearance of Grimald's name and of his highly personal poems was due to his own expressed desire, to his complaints to Tottel, whom evidently he knew well. An ecclesiastic of Grimald's position, whether he was a spy or not, could hardly have relished seeing intimate verses, which he had manifestly kept from the press before 1557, published for the delectation of vulgar readers. For a gentleman to publish original lyrics was at this time regarded as distinctly bad form, and there is no good reason to suppose that Grimald deliberately revolted against that convention. He was *not* unconventional when he published his Latin plays or his translations; and it is a significant fact that nine [2] of the ten poems of his authorship allowed to remain in *B–I* are known to be translations from Latin, four being translated from the famous Calvinist leader, Theodore Beza.

In *BC* (whatever may be true of *A*) Grimald's poems were subjected to the same modernizing touch as was inflicted in *A* upon Wyatt's and Surrey's. Thus *taratantars* (115.13) was changed to *dredfull trompets* — a change that no poet, or at least no poet versed in the classics, as Grimald was, would have thought of countenancing. Again, the northern present participle *shinand* (115.34) was replaced by *shinyng*, and the old proper noun *Alisander* (116.33, 117.38) by *Alexander*. These, and numerous other examples that might be cited, seem to me to point to an editor who, if not identical with the editor of *A*, certainly shared his views and his methods.

Finally, attention should be called to the fairly trustworthy evidence that exactly the same kind of editing or smoothing as (apparently) characterizes Surrey's poems in the miscellany occurs also in the 1557 edition of his translation of the *Aeneid*, books II and IV.[3] Since Tottel

[1] *The Modern Language Review*, XVII (1922), 147.
[2] Nos. 133, 134, 149–152, 165–167. The tenth is No. 154.
[3] Equally striking are the variants that appear in John Day's edition (1554?) of the fourth book. See Miss Willcock, in *The Modern Language Review*, XVII (1922), 144–149; and the collations (based upon her work) in Padelford's *Poems of Henry Howard*, pp. 176–177.

printed both works, surely it is reasonable to believe that, directly or indirectly, he was responsible for the changes which seem to have been made from Surrey's original readings, or else that some other person had already made the changes before the copy came into Tottel's hands. In any case, sheer speculation, and not very probable speculation at that, has connected Grimald with the editorship of the *Songs and Sonnets*.

But other candidates have been proposed for that place. J. P. Collier thought the claim of Thomas Churchyard worth mentioning. In the introduction to his reprint (1867) of *The Firste Parte of Church-yardes Chippes* (1575) Collier says that the miscellany (presumably in its first edition only) "may possibly have been originally edited by Churchyard himself: we only put forward his claim to the discharge of that duty upon conjecture, but there are two or three points in his biography that render it not altogether unlikely. He was at that date about the Court, he had a strong rhyming propensity, he was acquainted with at least several poets, who, like himself, certainly were contributors to that collection, and he was in want of money. Still, if Churchyard had really superintended the publication of so important and popular a volume, we hardly think it probable that he would not somewhere have asserted his right to the distinction." Since Collier evidently did not take his own suggestion seriously, it merits no further consideration here.

G. F. Nott believed that John Harington initiated and edited Tottel's volume. In his edition of Surrey's poems (page cclxxix) Nott says of Harington, "I think he was the person who first gave both Surrey's and Wyatt's poems to the public." Editing Wyatt, he speaks (page 537) of "the conjecture advanced in the preface to the late edition [1] of Tottel's Songs and Sonnets; that the Harington MS. altered by the editor to reduce as much as possible the lines to the Iambic measurement of five equal feet, supplied the text for Tottel's publication." In one copy of *P* (11607.i.7, page 10) Nott, mentioning *Nugae Antiquae* declares: "For the reasons assigned in the preface, the pieces to be found in that publication may be considered as having the authority of a MS." But, unfortunately, no copy of the preface is known to exist.[2]

[1] *I. e.*, *P*, discussed on pp. 47–52, above.
[2] See p. 47 n. 2, above.

INTRODUCTION

Perhaps Nott reasoned somewhat as follows: (1) A manuscript compiled by John Harington formed the basis of Tottel's edition. (2) In the eighteenth century Henry Harington reprinted pieces from Elizabethan manuscripts in his possession, and thus gave to *Nugae Antiquae* the "authority of a MS." (3) Wyatt's own manuscript of the Psalms, written about 1541, passed after his death in 1542 into the possession of John Harington, who caused an edition to be published in 1549, though he had planned it earlier and had secured a commendatory sonnet (No. 29) from Surrey. (4) Since Harington knew Surrey and actually published Wyatt's verses, and since in the manuscripts known to be in his possession (and later owned by Henry Harington) are to be found a large number of the poems that were printed in Tottel's *Miscellany*, it is likely that his manuscripts plus his initiative led to the publication of the book.

Whether or not the last two reasons fairly represent Nott's beliefs is open to some doubt. It is important to recall that the Psalms of Wyatt were printed "at London in Paules Church yarde at the sygne of thee Starre, By Thomas Raynald, and John Harrington,"[1] and that the dedication to the Marquis of Northampton was written by the latter. This Harrington was a London bookseller, who in 1550 published William Hunnis's *Certayne psalmes*.[2] There is no proof that he was identical with the John Harington, poet, whom Nott had in mind; but his sign of the Star, as well as his apparent disappearance from the bookselling trade in 1550, tempts one to believe that he and Tottel, whose sign was the Hand and Star, had some business connections. In that case the original manuscript of the miscellany might have passed through his hands to Tottel.

Nott's faith in John Harington the poet's editorship of the *Songs and Sonnets* seems to have weakened[3] as he learned more about the editorial methods of Henry Harington. To say a word about them is a necessary digression.

The various editions of *Nugae Antiquae: Being a Miscellaneous Collection of Original Papers in Prose and Verse ... By Sir John Harington,*

[1] The title-page is given by Bishop Percy in *N* (the edition described on pp. 44–46, above) and reproduced in Miss Foxwell's Wyatt, I, facing p. 203.
[2] E. G. Duff, *A Century of the English Book Trade*, 1905, p. 66.
[3] Cf. the notes to No. 306.

HARINGTON AND *NUGAE ANTIQUAE*

The Translator of Ariosto, and others who lived in those Times, present some curious problems, which, so far as they concern the poems therein, bear directly on Tottel's *Miscellany.* The first edition, dated 1769, appeared in one volume under the editorship of Henry Harington, a direct descendant of the poet John Harington the elder and of his son Sir John, the epigrammatist and translator of *Orlando Furioso.* Henry Harington possessed at least three manuscripts that had belonged to his poet-ancestors. Two of these are continually referred to in Nott's edition of Surrey and Wyatt as "Harington MS. No. 1" and "Harington MS. No. 2." The first of these, containing the autograph poems of Wyatt as well as No. 29, is now in the British Museum, where it is called MS. Egerton 2711, and where Nott's copy of it is preserved as MS. Additional 28636; the second manuscript has disappeared, but a careful transcript was made of it by Nott and is now MS. Additional 28635. A third Harington manuscript, often used in *Nugae Antiquae,* is now known as MS. Additional 36529.

In his volume of 1769 Henry Harington printed from these manuscripts thirteen poems (Nos. 3, 15, 17, 24, 45, 49, 55, 72, 92, 93, 171, 175, 267) that appear in the miscellany; and three of them (Nos. 17, 171, 175) he explicitly claimed for John Harington the elder, supplying titles and dates to support the ascription: "By John Harington, 1543, for a Ladie moche in Love"; "Elegy wrote in the Tower by John Harington, confined with the Princess Elizabeth, 1554"; and "Sonnet by John Harington, 1554." In 1775 he issued an additional volume (called volume II) in which the following new poems appear: Nos. 65 and 86 rightly ascribed to Wyatt, No. 87 wrongly ascribed to George Boleyn, Lord Rochford, and No. 235 no doubt wrongly assigned to John Harington. *Nugae Antiquae* was newly edited in three volumes in 1779, and this "corrected and enlarged" edition was re-issued in 1792; but in neither were there additional poems from the miscellany. Finally, in 1804 Thomas Park issued a revised edition in two volumes, eliminating all the poems that in the miscellany were definitely assigned to Wyatt and Surrey except No. 87, which he retained and unequivocally ascribed to Rochford. Hence in Park's second volume appear only two of the poems (Nos. 171, 175) that had been claimed for John Harington, though why No. 235 was dropped is not clear to me.

Henry Harington's ascriptions have not the slightest authority.[1] A comparison of his texts with the manuscripts shows that he manufactured titles at will, apparently crediting to John Harington any poem that he had not observed to be attributed to somebody else. No. 171, for example, is unsigned in Nott's transcript, MS. Additional 28635; and in a note in one of the copies of *P* Nott positively states that it was unsigned in the original manuscript owned by Henry Harington. Its ascription to D. Sand in *The Paradise of Dainty Devices* (1576) needs no questioning. In the case of No. 175 the editor's processes seem more dubious than usual. He begins his reprint of it with the second stanza, not the first, thus hiding his tracks from a hasty reader. In the manuscript, however, this poem was carefully signed "huomo inconosciuto," although Nott remarks in one of the copies of *P* that the signature was "in a later hand." Furthermore, Henry Harington emulated Bishop Percy in smoothing and polishing his texts. He changed words at will, often substituted whole lines, and sometimes (as in Nos. 171, 175) discarded entire stanzas. His work, then, has almost no value, and has no authority whatever; but his sins have, of course, no bearing on Nott's belief that John Harington was the editor of the *Songs and Sonnets*.

Nott's suggestion, though it has points in its favor, seems to have been completely ignored. Arber and most later scholars accept Grimald as the editor, and some of them evidently believe that he deliberately chose and compiled for publication the two hundred seventy-one poems found in *A*. For this belief I can see no warrant. Instead, the probability is that *A* was based upon a manuscript, or manuscripts, compiled by some person like Harington for his own use and pleasure. This hypothetical person evidently attempted, but without success, to secure all the short poems of Wyatt, Surrey, and Grimald,[2] and to them he added other poems that happened to be available, perhaps in separate copies, perhaps in one complete manuscript.[3] In one way or another, by accident, gift, loan, purchase, the manuscript so compiled passed into the hands of Richard Tottel. He decided to print it, — just as

[1] Though Charles Crawford, in *Notes and Queries*, 11th series, III (1911), 201, 322, 423, takes the opposite point of view.

[2] Over a hundred poems by Wyatt that are preserved in manuscripts are omitted in the miscellany; five short poems by Surrey are likewise omitted (Padelford's Nos. 10, 32, 35, 36, 47).

[3] Hence the appearance in *A* (and to a less extent in *B–I*) of numerous elegies and other poems out of tone with the "songs and sonnets" that make up most of the book.

some twenty years later another stationer, Henry Disle, published Richard Edwards's manuscript as *The Paradise of Dainty Devices*, — and he exerted himself to make the collection representative and complete. Accordingly, after the body of the book was already in type he secured copies of additional poems by Wyatt and Surrey, which he printed at the end as a sort of appendix or addendum.

It is possible that most of the editing had been done before Tottel saw the manuscript, and that he (or his "corrector of the press") made few alterations beyond giving each poem a title, inadvertently corrupting the text by misprints, and adding Nos. 262–271. In date of composition the poems in the miscellany vary widely: they include not only the early poems of Wyatt but also many (as Nos. 199, 255, 279) that were written in the reign of Mary I. The manuscript followed by Tottel may, then, have been written piecemeal from, say, about 1520 to 1557, in which case editing was necessary after it came into his possession; or it may have been compiled from other copies shortly before 1557, in which case the compiler probably made the editorial changes. Certainly in the sixteenth century few copyists took pains to reproduce texts accurately, and few scrupled to venture upon "improvements" of their own.

But, in the absence of any proof one way or another, I think it not too arbitrary to consider Tottel himself the guiding spirit, or editor, behind the book. Certainly in the whole tradition of English printing from Caxton to Tottel (and later), the combination of editor-printer-publisher in one man was common. In his preface Tottel speaks with evident indignation of those who have 'hoarded up' this beautiful verse as if it were too beautiful for public gaze; in other words, he attacks the anti-publication complex that — for there is no reason to believe otherwise — affected Grimald as a lyric poet as much as it had affected Wyatt, Surrey, Rochford, or Bryan.[1]

[1] Child, in *The Cambridge History of English Literature*, III, 203 (American ed.), asserts that "*Tottel's Miscellany* is the first symptom of the breaking down of this bashful exclusiveness" on the part of the authors. But it seems to me that the miscellany strongly emphasizes that bashfulness, since it was a publication unauthorized by the authors, most of whom were dead. In *The Furies. With Vertues Encomium* (1614) Richard Niccols complains that many people despise all *printed* books of poems: they "esteeme of verses vpon which the vulgar in a Stationers Shop, hath once breathed as of a peece of infection, in whose fine fingers no papers are holesome, but such, as passe

INTRODUCTION

The guess that I have outlined surely agrees better with the time and its traditions, and is surely more plausible, than that which hits upon Grimald as the editor of *A* and some person, or persons, unknown as the editor of *B* and *C*. That Tottel was the editor of *ABC* cannot, of course, be proved: it is merely a reasonable and a safe assumption. Nor would it be unreasonable to suppose that Tottel wrote one or more of the poems in the collection: if he did not write verse, then he was practically unique among the printers of his time, who, like Silas Wegg, dropped into poetry on almost no provocation.

The poems in *A* were thoroughly, but not critically, edited. This editing, or part of it, may, as I have said, have taken place before the verses reached Tottel; it may have been done by Tottel himself, by his "corrector of the press," or by some other agent employed by him. Whoever the editor (and the word *editor* will henceforth be used without reference to any particular theory or person), his chief qualification was the ability to count syllables and accents on his fingers, and thus to make the verses regular. His methods are plainly visible.

Confronted with a series of poems in manuscript, he found them too archaic in rhythm and pronunciation to please his ear, and in order to make them acceptable to himself and to prospective readers he revised lines without mercy. For his text he had no awe, because undoubtedly he felt that his changes improved the work of the original poets. His editorial procedure was similar to that followed by Bishop Percy in his eighteenth-century *Reliques of Ancient English Poetry*. Both editors, judged by the standards of their times, were justified in "improving" their texts, and beyond question the improvements thus introduced helped both the *Songs and Sonnets* and the *Reliques* to attain their remarkable popularity.

The goal at which the editor aimed was regularity, but he did not always attain it. Under his hands Wyatt was therefore the chief sufferer. Wyatt's poems sounded extremely rough because of the irregular

---

by priuate manuscription." And as late as 1627, in his epistle to Henry Reynolds (appended to *The Battaile of Agincourt*, 1627, p. 208), Drayton refused to discuss or praise

> "such whose poems, be they nere so rare,
> In priuate chambers, that incloistered are,
> And by transcription daintyly must goe;
> As though the world vnworthy were to know,
> Their rich composures."

number of syllables in his lines and because of his clumsy accentuation. These defects the editor tried, not always successfully, to eliminate. So far as possible he brought Wyatt up to date, changing the verses, wherever he could, to make them conform to regular iambic movement. Thus No. 39 originally began, "There was never file half so well filed," which in *A* is smoothed to "Was neuer file yet half so well yfiled." This modernizing process, which runs throughout the miscellany, often involved the insertion or the omission of words or entire phrases, the substitution of more recent words for those that were archaic, or the transposition of words and phrases. Sometimes (as in No. 41) a whole line was transposed; and in numerous cases (as Nos. 205, 216, 243, 255) only parts of long poems were given.

The effort to secure a correct iambic movement led the editor into some very strange acts. Thus, he disliked refrains and needlessly omitted those in the originals of Nos. 79 and 225; while in three cases (Nos. 69, 70, 103) poems written by Wyatt as rondeaux he changed into fourteen-line poems that he perhaps thought to be sonnets. Furthermore, he attempted to eliminate rhymes between final syllables; and his insertions, although they usually remove the accent from these final syllables, usually also obscure Wyatt's rhymes in hopeless fashion.[1] That Grimald, a poet and a student of poetry, was the editor responsible for such changes seems to me incredible; but it is easy to believe that Tottel himself, or a "corrector" employed by him, or possibly the original compiler of the manuscript, would have edited exactly in this manner.

Editorial changes of the kind mentioned were most unfair to Wyatt, but at the same time they no doubt enhanced his reputation. In any case, he was known as a poet by the public at large almost solely through Tottel's book, for his only other publication was his version of the Penitential Psalms, translated from Aretino, which appeared in 1549, after his death. Important, also, is the fact that eighteen of his poems (Nos. 74, 76, 77, 78, 80, 81, 84, 105, 106, 107, 108, 109, 113, 114, 117, 119, 269, 270) are preserved in the miscellany only.[2] From it, too, No. 101 is printed by Miss Foxwell, Wyatt's most recent editor, as having a better text than the manuscript version;[3] and in several other

---

[1] *E. g.*, see the notes to No. 94.   [2] Cf. above, p. 62 n. 1.

[3] In spite of the fact that it is in MS. Egerton 2711, which she usually follows to the exclusion of all other texts.

cases the variations between A and the manuscripts are very slight indeed. On the whole, then, the editor's sins against Wyatt are counterbalanced by his benefactions. He did Wyatt a good turn in making him suitable for popular taste; and, whether good or bad, his texts spread Wyatt's name and influence abroad.

A glance through the collations of the poems by Surrey and the uncertain authors, as given in the Notes, suggests that exactly the same tactics were used in editing them as in the case of Wyatt. But, while some of Wyatt's poems are extant in his holograph,[1] no such texts by Surrey and the uncertain authors remain. Indeed, only two of Surrey's poems (Nos. 17, 29) are, if his most recent editor can be trusted, preserved in manuscripts earlier than the reign of Elizabeth — and even for those two that editor followed the texts given in the miscellany and in a late sixteenth-century manuscript. Of the seven manuscripts used by Mr. Padelford, none was written by Surrey, almost none agrees with another or with the printed editions; and so it is impossible to tell exactly what Surrey wrote. But a comparison of the various manuscripts indicates that in many cases they have been subjected to much the same sort of editing as A was. Again, where two or more copies of the anonymous poems are found in manuscript or in print, the variations between them are so great as to prove that an "editor" had busied himself in intended improvements.[2] There is little doubt that Grimald's verses were changed as much as those by the other contributors, although I have found only a single manuscript copy of a poem by him, and that later than A.[3]

The changes made by the editor did no harm, but probably a great deal of good, to the reputation of the poets. Mr. Padelford, in "The Manuscript Poems of Henry Howard" (1906),[4] points out dozens of apparently unauthorized variants introduced by Tottel or his editor. Nevertheless, in his edition of Surrey he reprints twenty-one poems from A, nineteen of which occur only in A–I, and the other two of

[1] Miss Foxwell prints 63 of the Tottel poems (counting No. 64, on which see the Notes) from MS. Egerton 2711, which is partly in Wyatt's own hand, and 6 from MS. Additional 17492, which is contemporary in date with Wyatt. Hence for at least 69 poems her texts have more authority than those in the miscellany. But she prints at least 6 poems from MSS. later than the miscellany.

[2] See, for instance, the notes to Nos. 199, 206, 212, 225, 251.

[3] See the notes to No. 154.

[4] *Anglia*, xxix, 273–338.

which are superior to the texts preserved in manuscript.[1] It is difficult, then, to speak severely of the editor of the miscellany: he found his manuscript texts old-fashioned, and so far as possible he made them conform to contemporary standards. From the point of view of a publisher this was a wise move, the like of which is not unknown even in the present year of grace.

The editor, it is important to observe, also exercised the functions of a censor, removing objectionable references and phrases. Thus at 89.12 *Kitson* was replaced by *the ladde.* The year 1557 was one calculated to make censorship thorough. Hence in *A* all comments on Roman Catholicism were ruthlessly struck out, a fact that no more indicates a Roman Catholic editor than it does a prudent Protestant.[2] Wyatt's lines at 87.37–38 were originally,

> Nor I am not where *Christ* is given in prey
> For money, poison, and treason *at Rome;*

but the italicized words appeared in print as *truth* and *of some.* Likewise William Gray's rabid attack on Roman Catholicism in No. 255 was omitted *en bloc,* while No. 199 was carefully pruned of its references (complimentary though they were) to Queen Mary and No. 205 of its mention of the traitor Wyatt, son of the miscellany poet.

In every previous discussion of the "editor" of the *Songs and Sonnets,* scholars have apparently assumed that editorial supervision was confined to *A,* and that in *B* no changes were made except to drop most of Grimald's poems, to add thirty-nine new poems, to vary the order and titles of certain old ones, and to introduce an occasional new read-

---

[1] The twenty-one are Nos. 2, 5, 9, 10, 14, 16, 17, 18, 20–23, 25, 26, 28, 31, 34–36, 262, 265 (numbered in his edition 2, 23, 7, 1, 8, 13, 21, 24, 18, 12, 25, 16, 17, 26, 42, 46, 37, 39, 9, 19, 28). Nineteen of these (all but Nos. 17 and 28) are found only in *A–I.* Padelford remarks that No. 17 (his 21) is found in MS. Additional 17492 and (incompletely) in MS. Harleian 78, No. 28 (his 42) in MS. Harleian 78; but he reprints both from *A.* Furthermore, he states that No. 29 (his 38) appears in MS. Egerton 2711, No. 282 (his 20, which may *not* be by Surrey) in MS. Harleian 78; but he prints No. 29 from the late sixteenth-century MS. Additional 36529, No. 282 from a 'compilation' of the MS. and *B.* Note also that No. 13 (his 3) in the late MS. he follows lacks its tenth line, which, accordingly, he supplies "conjecturally" from the line in *A.* Since on p. 219 he dates only MS. Additional 17492 and MS. Egerton 2711 earlier than 1558, it appears that *not one* of his texts is pre-Elizabethan, and that the texts in *A–D** are earlier than any he reproduces from manuscript.

[2] H. J. Byrom, in his monograph on Tottel (see p. 5 n.), pp. 204–205, states his opinion that Tottel was a Roman Catholic, or was at least friendly to the old faith.

ing. But the facts are altogether different. The editorial changes in the text of *B* are almost as numerous as those made in the text of Wyatt in *A*. Particularly noteworthy are the striking changes of text that were introduced into *B*, only to be discarded in *C* for the original readings of the first edition.[1]

I shall not attempt to settle all questions. Whether the editor of *A* was identical with the editor of *B* and of *C* is a matter of sheer speculation. In the absence of proof for or against, I feel that probability favors identity of editorship, at least in the case of *A* and *B*. Certainly the editor of *B* had exactly the same standards as the editor of *A*, and his passion for regularity and modernity led to some important changes. It is necessary to keep in mind that the alterations made in *B*, and sometimes in *C*, find almost no warrant in such manuscript copies as have been preserved; they seem to be purely arbitrary — to have been made to please the ear or the eye of the reviser.[2] A slight exception to the foregoing remark occurs at 9.26, where *B* (but not *C*) has *With a* and *ghostly food*, as in the manuscript.

In *BC* many titles (for example, Nos. 178, 234, 243) are rephrased in accordance with the shifted order of poems. Undoubtedly the editor made these changes; they have no manuscript authority, and indeed it is practically certain that all the titles in *A* and *BC* are editorial insertions. Some of them, as in the case of No. 302, are based on a flat misapprehension of which no author could possibly have been guilty. Others, like No. 188, scarcely fit the subject-matter, or, like No. 243, are differently worded in *A* and *BC*, clearly revealing the editor's hand. Furthermore, titles seldom appear in manuscript anthologies of the sixteenth century, and never (so far as I am aware) in such regularity and with such patness as in the printed book.[3] It is worthy of note, too,

[1] See p. 19, above.

[2] Thus the readings of *A* and the MS. are identical at 9.4, 7–9, 16, 22, 12.10, though in all these places *B* differs. It changes, for example, "That in the hart that harborde freedome late" (9.9) to the unintelligible "Feeleth the hart that harborde freedome smart," and "So dothe this cornet gouerne me alacke" (12.10) to the senseless "So doth this corner gouerne my alacke." *A*, *B*, and the MS. have different readings at 9.11, 12.5–7.

[3] So G. T., in Gascoigne's *A Hundreth Sundrie Flowres*, 1573 (ed. B. M. Ward, p. 31), says: "[I] will only recite unto you sundry verses written by sundry gentlemen, adding nothing of myne owne onely a tytle to every Poeme, whereby the cause of writing the same may the more evidently appear."

that Wyatt's own name appears in the titles of Nos. 64 and 116: it would hardly have been inserted by the poet; in any case, his editor, Miss Foxwell,[1] insists that in his holograph manuscript Wyatt "never names [that is, never gives titles to] his poems." Again, if the editor in revising *B* had had any real authority like authors' manuscripts, he could hardly have avoided giving the missing lines, say, at 54.2 and 145.36 (on which see the Notes). In one place, to be sure (after 172.36), he has inserted, evidently from a manuscript, six lines that are not in *A*, and in a few other cases (as at 191.7) he has corrected the text; but elsewhere personal taste is apparently the clue to the revisions. For instance, the editor of *B* obviously did not understand the meaning of *his life to traine* (146.36) when he replaced it with *to end his life;* and there are manifest cases of smoothing at 170.23 ff., where words are lavishly omitted in order to secure a more perfect iambic movement. Again at 62.12, in order to avoid the pronunciation *promésse*, although it is required by the rhyme, *B* changed the line to *now hath kept her prômise* (with the word as before spelled *promesse*). So, too, at 81.23 the insertion of *now* changes the accent of *balance* from the last to the first syllable, and ruins the rhyme.

Why in *C* the original readings of *A* are often restored in preference to those of *B* is a mystery which, in general, I feel incompetent to solve.[2] Occasionally, as in the substitution of *Ladie* (12.23) for *Garret*, the reason may lie in the impersonality or anonymity that both *B* and *C* sought for. An important matter remains to be noticed: a second manuscript, or various manuscripts, served as copy for the thirty-nine additional poems of *BC*. These may have been on separate sheets or in one manuscript. Three of them (Nos. 288–290), being answers to poems earlier printed in *A*, may well have been composed after the publication of that volume.

The editorial methods followed in *ABC* have had admirers in the nineteenth century. Thus Robert Bell, editing the poems of Wyatt in 1854,[3] remarked that "the general superiority of Tottel's edition [superiority, that is, to the manuscripts, one of them holograph, of Wyatt and Surrey] consists in the presentation of a more perfect metre." Since this absurd statement did not seem absurd to an editor in 1854,

---

[1] II, 82.   [2] But see p. 19, above.   [3] Page 80 n.

no wonder that in 1557 the editor (or editors) of *ABC* thought perversion of the manuscripts justifiable.

Finally, an exact parallel to this procedure may be seen in the elaborate manuscript notes made in the text and margins of the Bodleian copy of *I* by two or three hands of different dates.[1] So thoroughgoing are the changes — in many instances involving actual erasure of letters — that in numerous passages it is almost impossible to tell just what printed readings that copy has. The notes often show an utter disregard for what the poets may have written, a sublime confidence in individual powers of emendation. For instance, 26.36 is emended to read "Ne will y̆ ay thus don Phœbus doe lowre," 27.3 to "Take hede of rifte: hale must waters depth finde," 67.32 to "That which with high disdayn you thus refuse." Opposite 4.39 the annotator frankly writes, "J had rather say Jn them their sweete, in me my sorowe springes."

In literally dozens of similar emendations the annotators of this copy proceeded exactly as did the editor (or editors) of *ABC*, changing words or phrases wherever they believed the rhythm or the sense, or both, could be improved. Thus at 3.17 in *My fresh grene yeares, that wither*, the word *yeares* is omitted (as in *F–H*), and to restore the pentameter movement a note suggests *which dothe* for *that*; at 8.34, where *F*+ had changed *cowarde* to *couered*, a note proposes *smothered or scorned*. Occasionally the annotators had consulted some earlier edition,[2] from which (as at 34.26, 53.21, 125.8) they supplied lines dropped in *I*; but more often they depended on their own ingenuity rather than on any printed text. Hence for lines dropped in *I* at 147.19, 227.10, and 250.5 they manufactured "Come then my dearest deare, come spedely to me," "The onely heaven y̆ hear J find," "To hir y̆ it deservd to haue"; while they invented certain lines, as "& most secure in ioye y̆ is" after 143.37. With *I* as an object-lesson, one is inclined to be chary of criticizing unfavorably the procedure of the early editor of *ABC*. He (or they) made no such havoc with the manuscript texts as did the annotators of *I* with a plain, printed text.

The manuscript emendations of *I* were heartily approved of by Horace Walpole,[3] the eighteenth-century owner of *D**, who, wherever

---

[1] See p. 36, above.
[2] Probably *A*, *B*, or *C*. The insertion made at 34.26 does not appear in *D* +.
[3] See p. 26.

his own text gave the slightest excuse, copied them.[1] He was hardly critical in his work: for example, the manuscript suggestions at 227.10 and 250.5 in *I* were due to the omission of lines in the printed text. In *D** the text has no such omissions, but Walpole copied in his margins the notes of *I*, prefixing to that at 250.5 an *or* — "*Or*, To hir y̓ it deserv'd to have." So, too, he reproduced word for word the manuscript readings of *I* at 4.39, 26.36, 27.3, 67.32, 143.37, 147.19; but the line added at 34.26 is absent from *D** because (as the handwriting shows) it was a late addition to *I*, made after he had examined that book.

IX. THE STYLE

Too many pens are represented in the miscellany to make generalizations about its style at all safe. But the most casual reader will, of course, observe the tendency to conceits that runs throughout the work of Wyatt and occasionally in the work of the uncertain authors. Wyatt seldom failed to admire the worst features of his Italian masters, and by translating their stiff figures and images he set a bad example that helped to deform English poetry. When he took his pen in hand, "his conceytes," like those of Anthony Munday's Strabino, "began to come so nimbly together: that he now rolled in his Rhetoricke, lyke a Flea in a blanquet."[2] It may be that he admired the conceited poems of Petrarch and Serafino because they could easily be translated. In one poem (No. 63) he compares his love "to a streame falling from the Alpes"; in another (No. 73), his heart to "the ouercharged gonne"; in a third (No. 97), his life of love to the "vnmesurable mountaines," the Alps. Likewise Lord Vaux adopts this manner in No. 211, with an account of how Cupid laid a regular sixteenth-century siege to the fortress of a lover's heart.

Throughout the book, too, there is much dependence on commonplaces — too much dependence, it would seem to an eye well read in Elizabethan verse. Certain poems, as Nos. 188, 191, 215, are based upon nothing but one trite figure after another, a type of poetry that

---

[1] The emendations and "editorial" comments that are reproduced from *I* in the Notes may, unless a specific remark is made to the contrary, be assumed to appear also in *D**.

[2] *Zelauto*, 1580, P3.

was apparently esteemed beautiful by later writers, like Turbervile and Howell. In fairness, however, one should recall that many of the apparent commonplaces were original and fresh (at least in English) when the miscellany appeared, and lost their freshness only because of continual imitation. Thus hackneyed subjects like Troilus and Cressida, the phoenix, coals that burn in water, and long-besieged and finally yielding towers were not stale in 1557, although they soon became the stock-in-trade of poets and would-be poets. Another stylistic device dear to all English-speaking people, namely, alliteration, decorates almost every line. Sometimes, as in

> O Temerous tauntres that delights in toyes
> Tumbling cockboat tottryng to and fro,[1]

the particular letter is hunted for with the mechanical zeal distinctive of *A Gorgeous Gallery of Gallant Inventions;* but, at least in the work of Wyatt and Surrey, alliteration is seldom used so baldly as this, and as a rule it even lends an aid that may justly be called artful. Puns are also too abundant for modern taste. But No. 186, with its insistent play on the name *White* and the color *white,* surely pleased Elizabethan readers; while even to-day the punning in No. 304, on *Bays,* the poet's mistress, and the *bay,* or laurel, tree, has a moderately pleasing sound.

One of the most interesting features of the miscellany is its widely varied meters and stanzaic forms, a feature in which it was unrivaled for two or three decades. Wyatt in particular was fond of metrical experiments, in the range of which he surpassed even Surrey. Among the most noticeable of his forms are ottava rima in some twenty-four poems,[2] terza rima in three,[3] poulter's measure in two.[4] Though his terza rima has been harshly criticized, its importance as a pioneer effort[5] in English can hardly be destroyed by the criticism. To him also belongs the credit of introducing the jog-trot poulter's measure, which Surrey took over and popularized.

In addition to quatrains, douzaines, and the like,[6] Wyatt has about

[1] No. 217.
[2] Nos. 54–56, 63, 67, 68, 71–73, 85, 88, 90, 92, 93, 109, 110, 112, 114, 115, 116, 120, 121, 123, 267.
[3] Nos. 124–126. [4] Nos. 104, 127.
[5] The twenty-five lines of terza rima in Chaucer's "A Compleint to his Lady" (Skeat's Chaucer, 1, 360–361) hardly deserve mention.
[6] Notice No. 268, every line of which ends with the word *not.*

thirty sonnets of various types, for some of which the editor of the miscellany, rather than Wyatt himself, is accountable. A few of these, like Nos. 69, 70, 103, were originally rondeaux, but were transformed by the editor to queerly rhymed "sonnets." Wyatt seems to have preferred five rhymes, as did Petrarch; but it is noteworthy that, while he gives some variation to the rhyme-schemes of his octave and sestet, he invariably — so far as the miscellany is concerned — ends the sestet with a couplet.[1] The majority of his sonnets are rhymed according to the scheme *abba abba cddc ee;* [2] but one (No. 84) has only three rhymes (*abab abab abab cc*), while six rhymes appear in No. 42 (*abba acca deed ff*). No. 101 is a double sonnet with the repeated rhyme-order of *abba cddc effe gg;* that is, it makes two English, or "Shakespearean," [3] sonnets of the type that Surrey is usually said to have invented, and rightly said to have established in the English tradition.

Of Surrey's sonnets eleven are "Shakespearean"; [4] but Nos. 9, 10, 36 have only three rhymes, No. 2 has only two. Whether these last four were intended to be correct sonnets is a matter of considerable doubt. Surrey shows less metrical ingenuity, less metrical experimentation, than his predecessor. Although he uses various four, six, and seven-line stanzas, he avoids the ottava rima of which Wyatt was so fond; terza rima he employs only once,[5] but poulter's measure, perhaps the most ineffective meter in English, nine times.[6] To Surrey's example is due the flood of dreary sixes and sevens that inundated Elizabethan poetry. Grimald, who may well have known both Wyatt's and Sur-

---

[1] Elizabeth D. Hanscom discusses "The Sonnet Forms of Wyatt and Surrey" in *Modern Language Notes*, XVI (1901), 274–280, basing her remarks on the Aldine edition of those poets. Hence her conclusions apply more to the editors of *A* and the Aldine text than to Wyatt and Surrey. The same is true of Rudolf Alscher's *Sir Thomas Wyatt und Seine Stellung in der Entwickelungsgeschichte der Englischen Literatur und Verskunst,* 1886 (*Wiener Beiträge*, vol. I). But Padelford's article on "The Scansion of Wyatt's Early Sonnets," *Studies in Philology*, XX (1923), 137–152, and, to a less extent, H. B. Lathrop's "The Sonnet Forms of Wyatt and Surrey," *Modern Philology*, II (1905), 463–470, take account of the manuscripts. On Wyatt's models see W. L. Bullock, "The Genesis of the English Sonnet Form," *Publications of the Modern Language Association of America*, XXXVIII (1923), 729–744.

[2] *E. g.*, Nos. 38–40, 45–51, 94–100.

[3] Shakespeare's rhyme-scheme is slightly different (*abab cdcd efef gg*).

[4] No. 13 has exactly the same rhyme-scheme as Wyatt's No. 101. In ten other cases (Nos. 6–8, 11, 12, 14, 29, 30, 32, 263) Surrey uses the regular Shakespearean rhyme-scheme given in the preceding note, though No. 263 has one false rhyme (207.6, 8).

[5] No. 1.

[6] Nos. 4, 5, 18, 19, 22, 26, 33, 264, 265.

rey's compositions through manuscript copies, makes use of poulter's measure in seven poems,[1] the uncertain authors use it in some twenty-five.[2]

Grimald's meters, however, deserve attention. He has heroic couplets in fifteen poems,[3] septenaries in nine,[4] blank verse (with occasional rhymes) in two.[5] Furthermore, he contributes a rhyme-royal stanza,[6] a peculiar douzaine (No. 134) with the rhyme-scheme *aaaaaa bb cc dd,* and three "Shakespearean" sonnets,[7] which, be it noted, have no connection with the theme of love. Among the compositions of the uncertain authors are nine sonnets (five of them "Shakespearean,"[8] four in a scheme of five or six rhymes [9]), two poems in octosyllabic couplets,[10] two in heroic couplets,[11] three in hexameters,[12] and many in septenaries. There are also various other stanza-forms,[13] including ottava rima, dizaines, and douzaines; but the favorite verse, as noticed above, is poulter's measure.

Modern readers are no doubt more interested in the sonnets than in any other literary form in the miscellany; but only slightly less important are its numerous epigrams and satires, those by Wyatt being the first formal examples of each in English. Of considerable interest, too, is the pastoral song of Phyllida (No. 181), which did something toward establishing the type that reached its zenith in *England's Helicon* (1600), an anthology containing nothing but pastoral lyrics.

The subjects used by the three contributors named in the miscellany were in the main prescribed by the authors from whom they translated or adapted. Wyatt and Surrey, familiar by travel and residence with Continental modes, were primarily concerned with love; but, as they

[1] Nos. 128, 138, 151, 152, 154, 155, 158.
[2] Nos. 168, 169, 172, 178, 183, 184, etc.
[3] Nos. 129–132, 135, 136, 143, 149, 150, 157, 160–162, 164, 167.
[4] Nos. 139, 140, 142, 144, 145, 147, 148, 153, 163.
[5] Nos. 165, 166.
[6] No. 159.
[7] Nos. 137, 146, 156.
[8] Nos. 173, 179, 186, 232, 233 (233 is slightly varied).
[9] Nos. 218, 219, 241 (the only sonnet with a regular Italian sestet, *cdecde*), 300.
[10] Nos. 278, 286.
[11] Nos. 245, 281.
[12] Nos. 182, 200, 296.
[13] See also the notes to No. 203.

had the habit of borrowing their concern from writers like Petrarch and Serafino, autobiographical interpretation is in most cases doubtful.[1] Some of Grimald's verses, on the other hand, even when they are translations, are of a more personal nature, and were written with actual people in mind, in spite of the matter-of-factness with which they reproduce their Latin originals. The uncertain authors followed Wyatt and Surrey in ringing changes on amorous themes, but they wrote also on many other subjects. Like Grimald, they devoted poems to the praise of real people, vicariously immortalizing in that fashion ladies named White, Rice, Bays, and Arundel.[2]

Abstract moralizing makes up about a fourth of the entire contents. Oftentimes it takes the form of proverbial philosophy of the kind favored by Dionysius Cato; but formally stated proverbs appear less frequently than in many Elizabethan works. Again, it is paraphrased from Horace or Alamanni. Elegies, too, abound, and seem a bit out of place in a collection where love-songs predominate; but Surrey set the fashion with three elegies on Wyatt, Grimald contributed nine on various individuals,[3] and the uncertain authors eleven.[4] The editor evidently wished to include all of Surrey's poems, whatever their themes; and perhaps he made the same attempt with Grimald's. I suspect that the elegies by uncertain authors were reprinted, not from deliberate choice, but merely because they happened to be available.

The subjects of the miscellany established the vogue for later anthologies, although the proportions in which they were used varied, and although the satires and epigrams had no immediate effect. In *The Paradise of Dainty Devices* and *A Gorgeous Gallery* moralizing poems predominate. Noteworthy, too, are the funeral elegies in all editions of the *Paradise* from 1578 to 1606. *A Gorgeous Gallery* has one elegy, while *The Phoenix Nest* devotes a prose composition to the deceased Earl of Leicester and three long poems to the memory of Sir Philip Sidney. In the miscellanies between Tottel's and *The Phoenix Nest* the love-element is not greatly stressed, probably because the contributors

---

[1] Egon Wintermantel attempted such an interpretation in his *Biographisches in den Gedichten von Sir Thomas Wyatt und Henry Howard, Earl of Surrey*, Freiburg dissertation, 1903.

[2] Nos. 186, 246, 304, 309.

[3] Nos. 156–164. His Nos. 165–167 are likewise "historical elegies."

[4] Nos. 169, 182, 189, 205, 209, 213, 227, 248, 253, 255, 273.

had not enough knowledge of French and Italian to paraphrase or translate their joys and woes, and not enough ingenuity to manufacture them. The *Paradise* and the *Gorgeous Gallery* show a stronger humanistic than Renaissance influence, so that in a sense Grimald, rather than Wyatt and Surrey, is their spiritual father. On the whole, Tottel's *Miscellany* is more akin to *The Phoenix Nest* than to any intervening anthology; its last Elizabethan edition appeared only six years before that beautiful collection.

The diction of the miscellany is extremely archaic. To lexicographers it affords a happy hunting-ground, not exhausted by the editors of *A New English Dictionary*. Although that great work cites, for instance, from the miscellany its earliest examples of *bluntly, bowt, clowt, forepast, intermitted, neck, overthwarts, rakehell, rashly, rife, steaming*, and its only examples of *clergions* ("songsters"), *fantaser, shright* (the infinitive), *stale, unnocht*, yet earlier than any instances noted by it are uses in the miscellany of certain other words, as *begins* (the noun), *eigh*, and *pleasurable*.[1] In spite of the frequent archaisms, however, modern readers will not very often be seriously puzzled by the meaning of passages in Tottel's book, which, compared to the *Paradise* and the *Gorgeous Gallery*, is straightforward and clear. An occasional Italianate or Latin word offers some temporary difficulty, but in the main the miscellany poets knew what they wished to say and said it with comparatively little obscurity and fumbling. In most of the other difficult passages there is a likelihood that the text has been corrupted by the copyist or the Tudor printer. By the latter careless agency the texts of all issues after the second were rendered largely unintelligible; but in the first two editions (*ABC*) there is generally a pleasing swing to the lines that carries them on with rapidity and makes too close analysis or paraphrase seem unnecessary. In its habitual clarity of expression the miscellany has few rivals before the date of *The Phoenix Nest*.

Many separate pieces in the book were composed with music in mind. One of the prettiest is Wyatt's song to the lute (No. 87), with which should be compared No. 65. The editor of the miscellany evidently had no liking for refrains (perhaps because they wasted space in

---

[1] In an unimportant Strassburg dissertation (1894) Franz Hoelper has treated *Die englische Schriftsprache in Tottel's "Miscellany" (1557) und in Tottel's Ausgabe von Brooke's "Romeus and Juliet" (1562)*.

printing), which in themselves point to musical accompaniment, and in several instances he eliminated them.[1] But the further considerations that some of the poems were published as ballads and that musical settings are preserved for others (as for Nos. 17, 87, 173, 201, 212, 251, 265) show that music and the poems usually went together. As songs many of them can be highly praised, and it is unquestionably true that certain faults that worry a reader would hardly be observed if the poem were sung. The miscellany was published in a notably musical age, and part of its popularity no doubt came from the fact that it afforded a matchless collection of new songs, one of which (No. 212) was sung on Shakespeare's stage.

There is some fine poetry in the miscellany. Critics have long waxed enthusiastic over the work of both Wyatt and Surrey, in particular giving to the latter's description of his boyhood at Windsor Castle (No. 15) superlative praise. There is likewise much tiresome, third-rate verse. But historically all of the three hundred ten poems merit commendation. For two decades after its publication Tottel's book was without a serious rival. It was then eclipsed (so far as modern judgment is concerned) by the appearance of *The Shepherds' Calendar* in 1579; but for years after that date Elizabethan readers may well have continued to regard it as a unique "golden treasury." Though not now unique, it is still a treasure-house, the gold in which the passing of almost four centuries has not hopelessly tarnished.

X. THE INFLUENCE

It is hardly possible to overestimate the influence of Tottel's *Miscellany* on sixteenth-century, and hence indirectly on later, English poetry. That the early imitators did not equal their model in excellence is beside the mark, as is also the slight immediate effect which the model had on certain metrical forms. The earliest imitators confined themselves to the simpler meters, like poulter's measure — which had the merit, or the demerit, of making many hacks think themselves poets — and to reproductions of topics or phrases. Yet the appearance of new editions of the miscellany till 1587, when the magnificent outburst of Elizabethan lyricism had begun, kept its influence constant and potent.

[1] As in Nos. 69, 70, 79, 103, 225. But he retained them in Nos. 294, 298.

INTRODUCTION

Tottel's *Miscellany* is largely responsible for this great outburst, and adequately to discuss its influence would be almost to write a history of the first three decades of Elizabethan poetry. Even in the pages of the book itself imitation is manifested. Instances of Surrey's verbal borrowings from Heywood and Wyatt are pointed out in the Notes, but much more numerous are the cases in which the uncertain authors took from Wyatt and Surrey not only subject-matter but also exact phraseology.[1]

Probably the blank-verse and terza-rima poems had almost no effect in ultimately popularizing those measures; nor, considering the infrequency of their occurrence in the miscellany, is this a matter for surprise. It seems remarkable, however, that the most noticeable form in the book, the sonnet, did not spring into immediate favor. Perhaps it was shunned for poulter's measure, septenary couplets, and simple quatrains because of its difficulty — a difficulty that led to some weird "sonnets" in the very pages of the miscellany. Poets like Googe and Turbervile christened their verses "songs and sonnets," but no genuine sonnets can be found among them; and for a time the word *sonnet*[2] meant nothing but a brief lyric.

In the imitative miscellanies that soon sprang up, the same lack of genuine sonnets is noticeable. Earliest in point of time was the lost first edition (1566) of *A Handful of Pleasant Delights*. The 1584 edition borrows from Tottel's *Miscellany* with considerable lavishness, and was undoubtedly inspired by it; yet among the "sundrie new Sonets and delectable Histories, in diuers kindes of Meeter," promised by the title-page of the *Handful*, are no sonnets that Petrarch or Wyatt or Surrey would have recognized. In *The Paradise of Dainty Devices* (1576) only one sonnet is found,[3] and it disappears in all the later editions (1577?–1606) — a striking fact inasmuch as the *Paradise* lifts bodily from the miscellany two poems,[4] as well as various passages and ideas. Possibly Richard Edwards and his collaborators thought sonnets suitable only

---

[1] Various examples are listed also by Heinrich Kolbe, *Metrische Untersuchungen über die Gedichte der "Uncertain Authors" in "Tottel's Miscellany,"* Marburg dissertation, 1902, pp. 3–5.

[2] In the miscellany it appears only on the title-page and in the head-lines, and for its presence in those places Tottel alone must be responsible. Probably he did not realize the importance of this new form which imitated the Italian *sonetto*, but by *sonnet* meant simply a song, or lyric.

[3] Ed. Rollins, No. 38.   [4] Nos. 106, 171.

for frivolous love-topics, and hence eschewed them. But the poets of *A Gorgeous Gallery of Gallant Inventions* (1578) not only borrowed ideas, phrases, and poems[1] from the miscellany, but wrote four sonnets.

While the vogue of new anthologies increased, the original miscellany held its own in popular estimation. Its editions of 1585 and 1587 undoubtedly played some part in keeping the sonnet-form before the minds of poets, and these final sixteenth-century editions came at the very time when the rage for sonnet-sequences was beginning. The popularity of subsequent miscellanies, like *Brittons Bowre of Delights* (1591, 1597), *The Phoenix Nest* (1593), *The Arbor of amorous Deuises* (1594?, 1597), *England's Helicon* (1600), and *A Poetical Rhapsody* (1602), is at least indirect evidence that the influence of Tottel's *Miscellany* operated as strongly at the end of the century as in the middle. The first and the third of these books, compiled by Richard Jones and published under the name of Nicholas Breton, afford direct evidence. Jones had a *penchant* for the miscellany, and he extracted poems from it for these compilations,[2] just as he had done earlier in the case of his *Handful* and his *Gorgeous Gallery*. Furthermore, on Tottel's *Miscellany* were modeled the "garlands" that humble poets collected for the delectation, not of educated or courtly readers, but of the common people. The first of these was the lost 1566 edition of the *Handful*,[3] a frank collection of ballads made by a ballad-poet and issued by a ballad-printer with the common reader chiefly in mind. Others, like Thomas Deloney's *Garland of Good-will* (1593?) and Richard Johnson's *Crown Garland of Golden Roses* (1612), established a fashion that has not yet wholly died in England. Literally hundreds of similar ballad-collections appeared in the three centuries after 1557.

Nor were printers slow to observe another opportunity to exploit the courtly *Songs and Sonnets* as entertainment for the man in the street; for, simultaneously with the editions of 1557–1567, they abstracted some of the poems and issued them as broadside ballads. Thus before 1569 No. 16 was three times registered for publication as a ballad, No. 199 and perhaps No. 212 twice, Nos. 3, 18, 180, 181, 211, 251, 265, and possibly 172 and 286 once; Nos. 16 and 265 were also "moralized"

---

[1] Nos. 206, 207.
[2] See the notes to Nos. 33, 170, 180.
[3] See *Modern Language Notes*, XLI (1926), 327.

or parodied.[1] Obviously, these poems succeeded in pleasing low-class as well as high-class readers.

The earliest Elizabethan poets, like Thomas Sackville,[2] took the miscellany as an infallible guide and text-book. Barnabe Googe, in his *Eglogs, Epytaphes, and Sonettes* (1563) shows the same tendency, but less strongly because he was usually adapting some foreign author. George Turbervile, however, displays in almost every poem the most thorough study of his model. Very often his poems (as well as his titles) are mere paraphrases of those in the miscellany. With more smoothly accented verse than is to be found in either Wyatt or Surrey, he draws out their ideas to tiresome length, taking twenty lines for a theme which they could develop in ten. Nowaday Turbervile would be regarded as a plagiarist: in his own age there was apparently nothing unethical in his action, which he might, if necessary, have defended on the ground that he was modernizing, and thus improving, poems already anti-quated. In any case, he made no effort to hide his tracks; and the "Verse in prayse of Lorde Henrye Howarde, Earle of Surrey," which he included in his *Epitaphes, Epigrams, Songs and Sonets* (1567),[3] ex-presses frankly his whole-hearted admiration:

> WHat should I speake in prayse of Surreys skill,
> Unlesse I had a thousand tongues at will?
> No one is able to depaint at full,
> The flowing fountaine of his sacred skull;
> Whose pen approovde what wit he had in mue,
> Where such a skill in making Sonets grue.
> Eche worde in place with such a sleight is coucht,
> Eche thing whereof he treates so firmely toucht,
> As Pallas seemde within his noble breast
> To have sojournde, and beene a daylie guest.
> Our mother tongue by him hath got such light,
> As ruder speach thereby is banisht quight:
> Reprove him not for fansies that he wrought,
> For fame thereby and nothing else he sought.
> What though his verse with pleasant toyes are fright,
> Yet was his honours life a lampe of light:

[1] See Rollins, *An Analytical Index to the Ballad-Entries, s. v.* "Tottel's *Miscellany.*"
[2] See *The Times Literary Supplement* (London), April 18, 1929, p. 315, for praise of Wyatt and Surrey in a manuscript attributed to Sackville.
[3] Collier's reprint, pp. 16–17.

A mirrour he the simple sort to traine,
That ever beate his brayne for Britans gaine.
By him the nobles had their vertues blazde,
When spitefull death their honors lives had razde:
Eche that in life had well deserved aught,
By Surreys meanes an endles fame hath caught.
To quite his boone and aye well meaning minde,
Whereby he did his sequell seeme to binde,
Though want of skill to silence me procures,
I write of him whose fame for aye endures;
A worthie wight, a noble for his race,
A learned lorde that had an Earles place.

Not quite so literal a borrower was Thomas Howell; but his *Arbor of Amitie* (1568), *Newe Sonets, and pretie Pamphlets* (*ca.* 1568), and *H. His Devises* (1581) bear witness on almost every page to lessons learned from the miscellany poets. Gascoigne likewise reveals his indebtedness, not infrequently paraphrasing and enlarging poems he read there. Other imitators were Timothy Kendall, George Whetstone, and Thomas Churchyard. Kendall, who reproduces whole poems *verbatim* from the miscellany, and yet whose *Flowers of Epigrammes* (1577) pretends to be made up of original translations, must flatly be called dishonest. Churchyard, as has been said, idolized Surrey, declaring in *A light Bondell of liuly discourses called Churchyardes Charge* (1580)[1] that

More heavenly were those gifts he had, then yearthly was his forme;
His corps to worthie for the grave, his fleshe no meate for worme.
An Erle of birthe, a god of sprite, a *Tullie* for his tong,
Me thinke of right the worlde should shake when half his praise were rong.
Oh! cursed are those crooked crafts, that his owne countrey wrought,
To chop of[f] sutche a chosen hed as our tyme nere forthe brought.
His knowledge crept beyond the starrs, and raught to Joves hie trone
The bowels of the yearth he sawe in his deepe breast unknowne:
His witt lookt through eche mans device, his judgemēt grounded was:
Almoste he had foresight to knowe, ere things should come to passe,
When thei should fall what should betied: oh, what a losse of weight,
Was it to lose so ripe a hedde, that reached sutche a height!
In evry art he feelyng had, with penne past *Petrarke* sure,
A fashion framde whiche could his foes to freendship oft alure.

[1] Collier's reprint, pp. 10–11.

INTRODUCTION

Similarly a poet in the *Gorgeous Gallery* (1578)[1] had remarked that
Surrey

scalde, the height of *Ioue* his Throne,
Vnto whose head a pillow softe, became Mount *Helycon*.

And there was also Humfrey Gifford, whose *Posie of Gilloflowers* (1580)
borrows lavishly in titles, subjects, and phrases. His didactic pro-
nouncements on friendship, the life of courtiers, the changeableness of
fortune, as well as his love-poems, not only show little originality but
disclose constant imitation; and an identical comment can be made in
regard to Mathew Grove's *The most famous and Tragicall Historie of
Pelops and Hippodamia* (1587).[2]

Imitation seems too mild a word for Brian Melbancke, in whose
euphuistic novel *Philotimus* (1583) whole passages are lifted *verbatim*
from the miscellany and printed as prose to help carry on the narrative.
Melbancke was a graceless scamp: his borrowings from Tottel's *Mis-
cellany*, which have heretofore escaped notice and which are enumer-
ated in the Notes,[3] are paralleled by his equally shameless pilfering
from the *Paradise*, from Turbervile, Seneca (in the 1581 translation),
Spenser, and others. But fully as barefaced as any of these were the
borrowings of Henry Petowe.[4] As the books in which they occur are
excessively rare, perhaps it may be well to print some of the most
pertinent passages.

In *The Second Part of Hero and Leander. Conteyning their further
Fortunes* (1598), a quarto of twenty-three pages, Petowe attempts to
complete Christopher Marlowe's unfinished poem, remarking that "I
being inriched by a Gentleman a friend of mine, with the true Italian
discourse, of those Louers further Fortunes, haue presumed to finish
the Historie, though not so well as diuers riper wits doubtles would
haue done." But this statement is frank camouflage, and "this my
first labor," as Petowe calls it, draws much of its material from the

[1] Ed. Rollins, p. 63.
[2] Cf. pp. 79 ff. (Grosart's edition) with No. 281; pp. 86 ff. with No. 179; p. 104
with No. 304; pp. 120 f. with No. 154.
[3] See also my article on Melbancke in *Studies in Philology*, extra series, 1 (May,
1929), 40–57.
[4] Some of them are enumerated in *The British Bibliographer*, 1 (1810), 214–217;
Nott's Surrey (1815), p. cclxxxi n.; Dyce's Marlowe (1858), pp. xli–xlii, 398–401.

miscellany. On signatures B4^v–C1, for example, "Then gan *Leander*
to his *Hero* say," plagiarizing from No. 12:

   { (Let me goe where the Sunne doth parch the greene,
   { In temperate heate, where he is felt and seene:
   { Or where his beames doe not dissolue the ice,
   { In presence prest, of people mad or wise.
   Set mee in high, or else in low degree,
   In clearest skie, or where clowdes thickest bee,
   In longest night, or in the shortest day,
   In lustie youth, or when my haires be gray:
   Goe I to heauen, to earth, or else to hell,
   Thrall or at large, aliue where so I dwell,
   On hill or dale, or on the foaming flood,
   { Sicke or in health, in euill fame or good:
   { Thine will I be, and onely with this thought,
   { Content thy selfe: although my chance be naught.)

Hero follows suit, remarking on occasion (C1^v), in the phrases of
No. 102:

   (The piller perisht is, whereto I lent,
   To my vnhap, for lust away hath sent,
   Of all my Ioy, the verie barke and rinde,
   The strongest stay of my vnquiet minde. . . .
   What can I more, but haue a woefull hart,
   My minde in woe, my body full of smart,
   And I my selfe, my selfe alwayes to hate,
   Till dreadfull death doe ease my dolefull state.

Likewise Hero's suitor, Duke Archilaus, angry at her, "breath'd foorth
the venome of his minde" on signature C2, combining Nos. 217 and 215
in the process:

   { (Oh timerous taunters that delights in toyes,
   { Iangling iesters, depriuers of sweete ioyes,
   { Tumbling cock-boats tottering too and fro,
   Grown'd of the graft, whence all my griefe doth grow:
   Sullen Serpents enuiron'd with despight,
   That ill for good at all times doth requite.
   As *Cypresse* tree that rent is by the roote,
   As well sowen seede, for drought that cannot sprout.
   As braunch or slip bitter from whence it growes,
   As gaping ground that raineles cannot close:

As fish on lande to whome no water flowes,
{ As flowers doe fade when *Phœbus* rarest showes,
{ As *Salamandra* repulsed from the fier,
{ Wanting my wish, I die for my desire.)

Poetic justice appears in the line that immediately follows the foregoing speech:

Speaking those words death seiz'd him for his owne.

Two further illustrations of Petowe's method will suffice. On signature D3 Leander remarks to Hero, in the words of No. 178:

To walke on ground where danger is vnseene,
Doth make men doubt, where they haue neuer been.
As blind men feare what footing they shall finde:
So doth the wise mistrust the straungers minde.

No. 261 provides a suitable response (signatures D3–D3^v):

Hero repli'd: (to rue on all false teares,
And forged tales, wherein craft oft appeares,
To trust each fained face, and forcing charme,
Betrayes the simple soule that thinks no harme.)
(Not euery teare doth argue inward paine,
Not euery sigh warrants, men doe not faine,
Not euery smoke doth proue a present fier,
Not all that glisters, goulden soules desire,
Not euery word is drawn out of the deepe,
For oft men smile, when they doe seeme to weepe:
Oft malice makes the minde to powre forth brine,
And enuie leakes the conduits of the eyne.
Craft oft doth cause men make a seeming showe,
Of heauie woes where griefe did neuer growe.
Then blame not those that wiselie can beware,
To shun dissimulations dreadfull snare.
Blame not the stopped eares gainst *Syrens* songe,
Blame not the minde not mou'd with falshood tonge.)

The "second flight" of Petowe's Muse resulted — as he confesses "*To the quick-sighted Readers*" — in *Philochasander and Elanira the faire Lady of Britaine* (1599). He prays:

Oh doe not hurt her [that is, my Muse], though she rudely springs,
For want of skill, but rather pleasure take.

To see an vnflidg'd fowle make shift to flie,
Whose vngrowne plumes all meanes for ayd deny.

This apology is hardly complimentary to the Tottel's *Miscellany* authors, from whom once again Petowe lavishly borrows. Without comment I shall reprint various passages from his rare poem, indicating by bracketed references to the poem-numbers the source in the miscellany.

I. [A4ᵛ]

[1]

Seauen tymes twise tould the bright *Hyperian*
Hath circled the fierie *Zodiacke*,
Seauen times twise seauen, since darting loue began
within those twise seuen dais my poore soules wrack,[1]
    Of an old hurt, yet feele the woūd but green,   [No. 1]
    Wounded by Loue, yet loue hath neuer seen.

[2]

In *Cyprus* springes, where *Beautie* faire once dwelt,   [No. 7]
A well so hot that who so tasts the same,
Were hee of stone, as thawed Ice should melt:
And finde his brest kindled with burning flame.
    Whose feruent heate my cold lymmes so opprest,
    That fell dispaire doth lend me little rest.

[3]

An other well that springes so hot is found,   [No. 7]
Whose chilling venome of repugnant kinde,
Drenches the burning heate of *Cupids* wound,
And with the spot of change infects the minde.
    Whereof my deare hath tasted, to my paine,
    My seruice thus is growen into disdaine.

II. [B1]

[1]

From *Tuskane* came my Ladies worthy race,   [No. 8]
Faire *Florence* was sometimes her auntient seate,
The westerne Ile whose pleasant shore doth face,
Wilde *Cambers* cliffes did giue her liuely heate.
    Fostred she was with Milke of Irish brest,
    And now in famous *Britaine* she doth rest.

---

[1] These opening lines seem to be imitated from "A sonet vpon the Authors first seuen yeeres seruice," printed in Thomas Tusser's *Fiue hundred pointes of good Husbandrie*, 1580, Q3ᵛ–Q4.

INTRODUCTION

[3]

Why did you sleepe, and did not gaze vpon her?
Why did so rare a prise escape your handes?
Why did not waking Centonels cease on her?
Whose sacred lookes all earth on earth commaunds.
   Her faire of kinde, her vertues from aboue,   [No. 8]
   Happy is he that can obtayne her loue.

III. [B1ᵛ]

[1]

The Sun hath twice brought forth his tēder green,   [No. 1]
Twice clad the Earth in liuely lustinesse,
Once haue the windes the trees displayed clean:
And once againe begins their cruelnesse.
   Since I haue hid the harme within my brest,
   My Ladies coy disdaine that hinders rest.

[2]

The winters hurt recouers with the warme,   [No. 1]
The parched greene restored is with shade,
What warmth alas may serue for to disarme,
The frozen heart that mine inflame hath made.
   VVhat colde againe is able to restore,
   My fresh greene yeares that wither more & more.

[3]

Strange kindes of death in life I trie,   [No. 1]
At hand to melt farre of in flame to burne,
And like as time list to my cure applie,
So doth each place whole heapes of woes returne.
   Loue seemes to haue my cure still in scorne,
   VVho liuing die: and dying liue to morne.

IIII. [B2]

[2]

The *Hart* he feedeth by the gentle *Hynde*,   [No. 181]
The *Bucke* doth feede hard by the prettie *Dooe*,
The *Turtle Doue* we neuer see vnkinde,
To him that to her doth affection show.
   I proffer kindnes, yet tis not accepted,
   I loue, yet loue of loue is quite reiected.

[116]

[3]

The harmeles *Ewe* she hath by her the *Ram*,　　　　　　[No. 181]
The younger *Cowe* hath to her make the *Bull*,
The *Calfe* with many a prettie nibling *Lam:*
Vppon the downes doe feede their hunger full.
　But my Loue lou'd prizeth so hie her faire,
　That for her want I cannot but despaire.

V. [B2ᵛ]

[1]

Fvll faire and white she is, and *White* by name,　　　　　[No. 186]
Whose white doth striue the Lillies white to staine,
Who may contemne the blast of blacke defame,
Who in darke night can bring day bright againe.
　Day is not day, vnles her shine giue light,
　And when she frownes, day turnes to gloomy night.

[2]

The ruddie Rose impresseth with clere hewe,　　　　　　[No. 186]
In lippes and cheekes, right orient to behould,
Her sparkling eies dart foorth to worldly view:
Such glimering splendant rayes, more bright thē gold.
　Her lookes the still behoulders eyes amazes,
　Dimming their sights, that on her *Bewtie* gazes.

IX. [B4ᵛ]

[1]

The tyme when this sweet faire her progresse tooke,　　　[No. 2]
Was whē fresh spring that bud & blome forth bring,
With greene had clad the hills, and euery brooke
VVith Christall glyding streames did sweetly spring,
　The Nightingall with feathers new did sing,
　Sommer was come for euery spray did spring.

[2]

The *Bucke* in bracke his Winter coate did cast,　　　　[No. 2]
The *Turtle* to her make hath tould her tale,
The *Adder* all her slough away did wast:
The *Hart* had hunge his olde head on the pale.
　And thus I sawe amonge these pleasant things,
　Each care decaies and yet my sorrowe springs.

[117]

XIII. [C2ᵛ]

[1]

Some men will thinke as due they ought to haue,   [No. 82]
For their true seruice, guerdon and reward,
But I intreate, and loue for loue I craue:
Yet others though vnworthy are prefard.
  I beate the bush, and others catch the bird,
  Reason exclaimes and sweares my hap is hard.

[2]

They eate the honny, I must hold the hiue: [No. 82]
I sowe the seede, and they must reape the corne,
I wast, they win; I drawe, and they must driue,
Theirs is the thanke, and mine the bitter scorne.
  I seeke, they speede: in vaine my winde is spent,
  I gape, they get, I pray and yet am shent.

[3]

I fast, they feede: they drinke, and I still thurst,   [No. 82]
They laugh, I weepe: they ioy, I euer mourne:
They gaine, I loose, I onely haue the worst:
They are whole, I am sicke: they cold, I burne.
  I would, they may: I craue, they haue at will,
  That helpeth them, but hate my hart doth kill.

XIIII. [C3]

[1]

Adew desart, alas how art thou spent?   [No. 303]
Ah droping teares, how wofully you wast,
Poore hart how many scalding sighes are lent
To pricke them forth, that make no speedy hast:
  Ah payned soule, thou gap'st for mickell grace,
  Of her in whome sweete pittie hath no place.

XV. [C3ᵛ]

[1]

VVhen glorious *Phœbus* had the Serpent slaine,   [No. 305]
The wanton God desired *Cupids* bow,
Which sudden strife did turne him to such paine,
That in the end he felt the depth of woe.
  The shaft once shot, he neuer could remoue:
  His woe began in seeking *Daphnes* loue.

[2]

This *Cupid* hath a shaft of perfit kinde,   [No. 305]
Wherewith true-louing makes he gently woundeth.
Whose goulden head hath power ynough to binde,
All loyall harts; such force therein aboundeth.
    An other shafte he hath, that's wrought in spight
    Whose Nature is to quench all sweete delight

[3]

The owne in *Phœbus* tooke a resting place   [No. 305]
In *Daphnes* Brest, the cruell shaft did slumber,
Phœbus sought loue, *Daphne* would not imbrace
His vowed loue could neuer bring her vnder.
    Such is my case? to her I seeke to most
    I loue, she hates, thus is my labour lost.

XVI. [C4]

[1]

As oft as I behold my loue in Maiestie,   [No. 24]
Her sparkling soueraigne bewtie that me bound,
The mores my comfort, though exild I be,
But yet alas the fresher is my wound.
    My soule like *Tantalus* in sorrow wasteth,
    Who sees the goulden fruite, yet neuer tasteth.

Apart from imitations and borrowings, the influence of the miscellany is manifested also by frequent references to its contributors. Enough of these could be collected to make an "allusion-book" of some size, and such a collection would in general reveal sincere respect for Surrey and his achievement, less respect for Wyatt. One exception to this statement is to be found in the superlative praise heaped on Wyatt by the antiquary John Leland in his *Naeniae in mortem Thomae Viati equitis incomparabilis* (1542);[1] and again, about 1691, Anthony Wood called Wyatt "the delight of the muses and of mankind," and eulogized "his admirable skill in poetry."[2] But in Elizabethan times

---

[1] Reprinted in Miss Foxwell's Wyatt, II, 231–240, and in Nott's, II, xcix–cx. In John Pits's "De Illustribus Angliæ Scriptoribus" (the running-title of *Ioannis Pitsei . . . Relationum Historicarum de Rebus Anglicis Tomus Primus*, 1619), p. 922, Leland's praise of Wyatt is echoed, while Surrey (p. 923) is mentioned without praise.

[2] *Athenae Oxonienses*, I (1813), 124–125.

a discordant note was struck only occasionally. Edward Dering's epistle "To the Christian Reader," prefixed to *A Briefe and Necessary Catechisme or instructiō Very needfull to be known of al housholders* (1572), roundly condemned "our Songes & Sonets, our Pallaces of Pleasure, our vnchast Fables, & Tragedies, and such like sorceries," adding, "O that there were among vs some zealous Ephesians, that Bookes of so great vanitie might be burned vp." Likewise, William Webbe evidently had a low opinion of the *Songs and Sonnets*, though he admired *The Paradise of Dainty Devices*. In *A Discourse of English Poetrie* (1586) he refers in laudatory terms to the contributors to the *Paradise*, but those to the *Songs and Sonnets* he ignores completely save for a non-committal reference to "the dyuers workes of the olde Earle of *Surrey*" and a slur at Surrey's translations from the *Aeneid* "without regard of true quantity of sillables." [1] On the contrary, the author of *The Art of English Poesie* (1589) thought the miscellany, at least so far as concerned the poems of Wyatt, Surrey, and Vaux, represented the high-water mark of English verse. No fault at all, in his opinion, could be found with the first two of these ("betweene whom," he declares, "I finde very litle difference, I repute them . . . for the two chief lanternes of light to all others that haue since employed their pennes vpon English Poesie" [2]); and he quotes from them constantly to illustrate the rules and graces of poetry.

Roger Ascham, although like Webbe an opponent of rhyme, generously asserted in *The Schoolmaster* (1570) [3] that Wyatt and Surrey went "as farre to their great praise, as the copie they followed could cary them." Sir Philip Sidney's *Defence of Poesy*, written about 1580 though not published till fifteen years later, reminded readers that they would find "in the Earle of Surries *Liricks*, many things tasting of a noble birth, and worthy of a noble minde." [4] "The Erle of Surrey, that wrat the booke of Songes and Sonettes" is praised also in Geoffrey Whitney's *A Choice of Emblems* (1586). [5] Gabriel Harvey, in *Pierce's Supererogation* (1593), [6] spoke flatteringly of Surrey and Norton. But a Jacobean critic, Edmund Bolton, in his *Hypercritica* (*ca.* 1618) [7] thought the miscellany inferior to Surrey's *Aeneid* translations:

[1] Arber's reprint, pp. 33, 71–72.   [2] Arber's reprint, p. 76.   [3] Arber's reprint, p. 145.
[4] Arber's reprint, p. 62.   [5] Page 196.   [6] *Works*, ed. Grosart, II, 291.
[7] Ed. Anthony Hall, 1722, p. 237.

Before [Sackville] in Age, if not also in Noble, Courtly, and Lustrous *English*, is that of the Songs and Sonnets of *Henry Howard*, Earl of *Surrey* . . . written chiefly by him, and by Sr *Tho. Wiat*, not the dangerous Commotioner but his worthy Father. Nevertheless they who most commend those Poems, and exercises of honourable Wit, if they have seen that incomparable Earl of *Surrey* his *English* Translation of *Virgil's Æneids*, which for a book, or two, he admirably rendreth, almost Line for Line, will bear me witness that those other were Foils and Sportives.

Other writers were much more cordial. For instance, Sir John Harington merely reflected popular opinion when in the preface to *Orlando Furioso* (1591) he wrote that Wyatt and Surrey "are yet called the first refiners of the English tong."[1] Drayton, as has already been shown, highly praises Wyatt, Surrey, and the other miscellany poets in *Englands Heroicall Epistles* (1598) — generous praise from a fine poet. Robert Fletcher speaks in *The Nine English Worthies* (1606)[2] of "the learned pen, Of Princely *Surrey*, once a Poet sweet," as well as of "Sir *Thomas Wyat*, or like gentlemen." Ben Jonson in his *Discoveries*[3] lists among other writers "the elder *Wiat*; *Henry*, Earle of *Surrey*" as "for their times admirable: and the more, because they began Eloquence with us." Finally — though the citations could be almost indefinitely increased — the greatest of all poets had studied the volume, even if he had no exaggerated opinion of its merits. It is Master Slender, not Shakespeare, who "had rather than forty shillings I had my Book of Songs and Sonnets here";[4] but it is Shakespeare himself who by putting No. 212 into the grave-digger's song in *Hamlet* made that poem world-famous. Two centuries later its fame was augmented when Goethe included a version of it in *Faust*.

A temporary decline in the popularity of Tottel's *Miscellany* is evidenced by the fact that, so far as is known, no edition was issued for more than a hundred years after 1587. Early in the eighteenth century, however, thanks largely to Pope's commendation of Surrey, three

[1] In one of his epigrams (ed. N. E. McClure, 1926, pp. 217–218) Harington confesses to having borrowed "some good conceits" from a classic author, and adds,

> "But *Surrey* did the same, and worthy *Wyatt*,
> And they had praise and reputation by it."

[2] Page 51.
[3] Ed. G. B. Harrison, 1923, p. 37.
[4] *The Merry Wives of Windsor*, I. i. 205–206.

editions appeared.[1] They were not especially successful as business ventures, but they did keep the collection before the minds of a few readers. Then Elizabeth Cooper gave considerable space to it in her *Historical and Poetical Medley: or Muses Library* (1738), declaring that "in Purity of Language, and Sweetness of Sound, [Surrey] far surpass'd his Contemporaries, and all that had preceded him. — Nay, I believe no Writer that followed him for many Years, can justly vie with him in either of these Beauties."[2] To illustrate this praise, she reprinted ten of his poems[3] and likewise included four of Wyatt's,[4] although to Mrs. Cooper Wyatt "does not appear to have much Imagination: neither are his Verses so musical or well polish'd as Lord Surrey's."[5] Four poems from the uncertain authors[6] bring to an end her reprints from the miscellany.

Horace Walpole, in *A Catalogue of the Royal and Noble Authors of England, Scotland, and Ireland* (1758),[7] called Surrey "an almost classic author" — a phrase strongly reprehended in *The Gentleman's Magazine* for January, 1759 — and characterized the miscellany as "a small volume of elegant and tender sonnets composed by Surrey; and with them some others of that age, particularly of sir Thomas Wyat the elder, a very accomplished gentleman." Another admirer was Bishop Thomas Percy, who as early as 1763 contemplated getting out an edition of his own,[8] but postponed it no doubt because of his work on the *Reliques of Ancient English Poetry* (1765). In the latter publication[9] Percy included three of Tottel's poems.[10] Among other anthologies Henry Headley's *Select Beauties of Ancient English Poetry* (1787) deserves special mention because the editor not only calls Surrey "the first refiner of our language, and the unrivalled ornament of his age and country,"[11] but also emphatically declares that Wyatt "deserves

[1] See pp. 37–43, above.
[2] Page 56. John Hughes, *The Works of Edmund Spenser*, I (1715), xciv, had likewise spoken favorably of "the Earl of *Surry*'s Lyricks."
[3] Pages 57–69 (Nos. 2, 3, 8, 9, 12, 15, 17, 20, 27, 33).
[4] Pages 70–80 (Nos. 87, 119, 125, 126).
[5] Page 70.
[6] Pages 81–86 (Nos. 170, 174, 193, 199).
[7] Ed. Thomas Park, I (1806), 255, 260–261.
[8] See pp. 45–46, above.
[9] Ed. Wheatley, 1876, I, 179–182, II, 50–53, 75–79.
[10] Nos. 181, 211, 212.
[11] I, lvi. Surrey's Nos. 2, 9, 12 are reprinted at II, 78, 84, 96.

equally of posterity with Surrey for the diligence with which he culti-vated polite letters." [1] This remarkable utterance can hardly be dupli-cated until very recent times. As a final word about eighteenth-century anthologies, George Ellis included in his *Specimens of the Early English Poets* (1790) thirteen poems — two by Surrey, three by Wyatt, eight by uncertain authors.[2] In the second edition (1801) he printed, often in abridged form, twenty-one;[3] and in the third (1803) these same twenty-one increased by four more of Surrey's, six more of Wyatt's, another of Vaux's, five of Grimald's, making a total of thirty-seven.[4]

From 1793, the date of Anderson's English poets,[5] to the present day, the miscellany has met with continual appreciation and study. The numerous editions of it, or of the works of Wyatt and Surrey, have already been sufficiently described. Anthologies — and their name is legion — have helped to familiarize the book.[6] Sixteen of its poems, for example, are included in W. J. Linton's *Rare Poems of the Sixteenth and Seventeenth Centuries* (1883);[7] eight in *The Oxford Book of English Verse* (1900);[8] forty-seven in Edward Arber's *Surrey and Wyatt An-thology* (1900);[9] forty in Mr. Padelford's *Early Sixteenth Century Lyrics* (1907);[10] nineteen in Mr. Norman Ault's *Elizabethan Lyrics from the Original Texts* (1925);[11] three in Mr. Edmonstoune Duncan's *Lyrics*

---

[1] I, lxv-lxvi. Wyatt's No. 125 is reprinted at II, 34-37.

[2] Nos. 2, 20, 57, 87, 107, 175, 181, 199, 210, 214, 257, 298, 303.

[3] Including (in volume II) all but No. 57 from his first edition, plus Nos. 8, 15, 27, 30, 53, 78, 211, 236, 249.

[4] The added poems are Nos. 1, 6, 29, 31, 79, 93, 99, 119, 121, 125, 134, 150, 154, 165, 166, 212.

[5] See p. 43, above.

[6] Four of the poems (Nos. 176, 196, 197, 236) are reprinted in *Censura Literaria*, I (1805), 249-255.

[7] Nos. 53, 79, 82, 128, 170, 174, 175, 185, 199, 229, 244, 249, 250, 294-296.

[8] Nos. 2, 17, 27, 52, 87, 128, 190, 199.

[9] Including 22 by Wyatt (Nos. 50, 52, 54, 59, 64, 66, 68, 69, 77, 86, 87, 91, 93, 97, 103, 105, 115, 116, 121, 124, 125, 270), 19 by Surrey (Nos. 1, 2, 7, 8, 11, 12, 14-17, 19-21, 26, 27, 31, 33, 35, 264), 2 by Vaux (Nos. 211, 212), and 4 by uncertain authors (Nos. 181, 197, 201, 278). Attributions of the authorship of these poems are rather wildly made by Arber. He observes, by the way, that his book should have been called *The Wyatt and Surrey Anthology*, because Wyatt was "the nobler man and the nobler Poet of the two," but isn't so called since it is "customary to say *Surrey and Wyatt*, simply because the former was a Peer." The fashion has changed since 1900.

[10] Nos. 1-4, 7, 8, 10-13, 15, 17, 19, 24, 27, 29, 33, 49, 50, 54, 59, 62, 72, 87, 92-94, 97, 102, 115, 121, 149, 155, 181, 193, 199, 200, 263, 264, 282.

[11] Nos. 2, 10, 17, 20, 27, 33, 50, 52, 53, 87, 128, 171, 190, 199, 212, 235, 236, 244, 257.

from the Old Song Books (1927).[1] Other reprints appear in the innumerable text-books like *Century Readings for a Course in English Literature* (1911). Honorable space is devoted to Tottel's *Miscellany* in histories of English literature, and hence by mere repetition its name looms large in the minds of most students.

None the less, it seems not improbable that much of this interest is historical, and that (to borrow Voltaire's pronouncement on Dante) the reputation of Tottel's *Miscellany* has gone on increasing because it has had few readers.

[1] Nos. 2, 87, 238.

NOTES

NOTES

References consisting of two or more arabic numerals separated by a period (as 9. 3, 98. 7, 117. 35) are to pages and lines of the text in volume I; those of arabic numerals without a period but accompanied by "p." or "page" (as p. 51, page 118) are to pages in the present volume (II). For words and phrases in the text of volume I not commented on in the Notes consult the Glossarial Index.

The sixteenth-century editions of Tottel's *Miscellany* are referred to by the system of letters (explained in more detail on pages 7–12, 20–36, above) that follows:

A 1st edition, June 5, 1557
B 2d edition, July 31, 1557 (British Museum copy)
C 2d edition, July 31, 1557 (Capell copy)
D 3d edition, 1559 (British Museum copy)
*D** 4th edition, 1559 (Holford copy)
E 5th edition, 1565
F 6th edition, 1567
G 7th edition, 1574
H 8th edition, 1585
I 9th edition, 1587

*D** is not considered in the Variant Readings of volume I. It should, then, be carefully observed that in the following Notes *D** is included (see page 25, above) in all embracive references like *C+*, *D+*, *D–G*, *D–I*, and likewise that it has the manuscript readings cited from the Bodleian copy of *I* (see page 26, above), unless a specific remark is made to the contrary.

The following works are cited by catch-titles or abbreviations:

Arber, Edward. *Tottel's Miscellany, English Reprints*, London, 1870. [For complete details see pp. 59–61, above.]

Arte of English Poesie, The, 1589, ed. Edward Arber, *English Reprints*, 1869.

D. N. B. = *Dictionary of National Biography*.

Foxwell, A. K. *The Poems of Sir Thomas Wiat*, 2 vols., University of London Press, 1913. [See pp. 61–62, above.]

Gorgeous Gallery of Gallant Inventions (1578), A [by Thomas Proctor and others], ed. Hyder E. Rollins, Harvard University Press, 1926.

Handful of Pleasant Delights (1584), A, By Clement Robinson and Divers Others, ed. Hyder E. Rollins, Harvard University Press, 1924.

Koeppel, Emil. "Studien zur Geschichte des englischen Petrarchismus im sechzehnten Jahrhundert," *Romanische Forschungen*, v (1889), 65–97.

Lilly, Joseph. *A Collection of Seventy-Nine Black-Letter Ballads and Broadsides, Printed in the Reign of Queen Elizabeth*, 1867. [Lilly wrote the preface and printed the book.]

Melbancke, Brian. *Philotimus. The Warre betwixt Nature and Fortune*, 1583. [See *Studies in Philology*, extra series, 1 (May, 1929), 40–57.]

Merrill, L. R. *The Life and Poems of Nicholas Grimald*, Yale University Press, 1925.

N. E. D. = A New English Dictionary on Historical Principles.

Nott, G. F. *The Works of Henry Howard Earl of Surrey and of Sir Thomas Wyatt*, 2 vols. (vol. I Surrey, vol. II Wyatt), London, 1815–1816. [See pp. 52–53, above; and for an explanation of references to Nott's statements in "11607. i. 7" and "C. 60. O. 13" see pp. 48–49.]

Padelford, F. M. *The Poems of Henry Howard, Earl of Surrey*, University of Washington Press, 1920. [See pp. 62–64, above.]

Paradise of Dainty Devices (1576–1606), The [by Richard Edwards and others], ed. Hyder E. Rollins, Harvard University Press, 1927.

Petrarch. *Le Rime*, ed. Giuseppe Salvo Cozzo, Florence, 1904. [The texts, page-numbers, and poem-numbers of citations from Petrarch come from this book, except in one case specifically noted; but the old-fashioned method of numbering the "sonnets in life" and "in death" has likewise been retained for the possible convenience of students.]

Phoenix Nest, The, 1593, ed. Hugh Macdonald, Etchells and Macdonald, London, 1926.

Rollins, Hyder E. *An Analytical Index to the Ballad-Entries (1557–1709) in the Registers of the Company of Stationers of London*, University of North Carolina Press, 1924. [Printed also in *Studies in Philology*, XXI (1924), 1–324.]

Turbervile, George. *Epitaphes, Epigrams, Songs and Sonets*, 1567 (reprinted by J. P. Collier, 1867).

It is necessary to say a word about the variant readings given in the Notes. When the texts of *AB* are collated with manuscript or early printed copies, punctuation is ignored, and only actual variants in diction (not in orthography, except for a few unusual or doubtful cases) are listed. The texts of *AB* are collated with the modern reprints in accordance with what the editors of those reprints attempted to do. Miss Foxwell, for instance, modernizes punctuation and the use of *u, v, i, j*, usually expands contractions, and omits the original poem-titles; Padelford substitutes punctuation, capitalization, and poem-titles of his own, and expands contractions: these deviations from *AB* are, accordingly, not listed in my collations. Merrill, on the other hand, attempts to reproduce the text of *A* exactly, except in its old use of *u, v, i, j*, and in the expansion of contractions; hence all his variations, even of punctuation, are enumerated.

2.18 *and in moe hereafter*. This phrase may indicate that Tottel knew he had not secured all of Wyatt's and Surrey's poems but hoped to get and publish others later on.

3. 2 (No. 1) *Descripcion of the restlesse state, &c.* In every edition (No. [1] in *B–I*, sigs. A2–A2ᵛ in *B–H*, A2ᵛ–A3 in *I*). The poem is printed by Padelford (pp. 49–50) from a Harington MS. (Additional 36529: see his notes, p. 170, for variants in other manuscript copies), with the following variants:

> 3. 6 furth his] forthe the
>   7 earth] yerthe
>   9 new] now
>   15 mine in flame] my inflame
>   16 able] hable
>   18 hath] to
>   19 in time] somtyme
>   20 In] Yet
>   22 kindes] kynd
>   26 All] Eche:　　seeth] sees:　　heauens] heaven
>   28 It] Him
>   30 tormentes] torment
>   31 And] To
>   32 opprest] represt
>   33 it] yet
>   34 trauailes of mine] travaile of my
>   38 by] in:　　appere] should pere
>   39 in] with:　　pace [1,2]] paas
> 4. 2, 3 the] that
>   3 lace] laase
>   7 found] fynde
>   11 agazed] atgaas
>   14 flee] flye
>   15 venomde] venymd
>   18 tene] will
>   21 my] me:　　els] elles

The poem is written in terza rima.

6–11 *The sonne hath twise . . . healthfulnesse.* Padelford (p. 182) suggests a comparison with Chaucer's *Troilus and Criseyde*, v. 8–11:

> The golden-tressed Phebus heighe on-lofte
> Thryës hadde alle with his bemes shene
> The snowes molte, and Zephirus as ofte
> Y-brought ayein the tendre leves grene, etc.

14–15 *What warmth . . . in flame hath made.* Cf. Petrarch, sonetto in vita 150, lines 1–2 (*Rime*, 202, p. 199):

> D'un bel, chiaro, polito et vivo ghiaccio
> move la fiamma che m' incende et strugge.

23 *At hand to melt.* Koeppel (*Studien*, p. 80) suggests the reading *At hand to freeze* — the antithesis that would be expected. He supports his emendation by a citation from Petrarch's sonetto in vita 169, line 12 (*Rime*, 224, p. 220; also in Petrarch's *Trionfo d'Amore*, cap. III [*Rime*, ed. Carrer, II, 509]),

"s'arder da lunge et agghiacciar da presso," and by one from another poem of Surrey's at 6. 42–43. But no change is really necessary. With lines 22–23 compare also Wyatt at 68. 33, Surrey at 206. 16, and Thomas Watson, *The Hekatompathia*, 1582, K2ᵛ (ed. Arber, 1870, p. 112):

> straunge is my case,
> In mid'st of froast to burne, and freze in flame.

3. 35 *For then, as one that hath the light in hate.* Cf. Petrarch, sestina in vita 1, line 2 (*Rime*, 22, p. 15), "se non se alquanti ch'ànno in odio il sole."

39–4. 2–4 *And in my minde I measure pace, &c.* Cf. Petrarch, sonetto in vita 123, lines 1–4 (*Rime*, 175, p. 179):

> Quando mi vene inanzi il tempo e 'l loco,
> ov' i' perdei me stesso, e 'l caro nodo,
> ond' Amor di sua man m' avinse in modo
> che l'amar mi fe' dolce e 'l pianger gioco.

4. 7–11 *For if I found sometime, &c.* Perhaps suggested by Petrarch, sonetto in vita 137, lines 7–14 (*Rime*, 189, pp. 189–190), the source of No. 50: see p. 169, below.

8 *Those sterres, &c.* With this conceit of the lover's eying the stars for guidance, as does the sailor, compare 175. 16–17 and Petrarch, canzone in vita 8, stanza 4 (*Rime*, 73, p. 82):

> Come a forza di venti
> stanco nocchier di notte alza la testa
> a' duo lumi ch'à sempre il nostro polo;
> così ne la tempesta
> ch' i' sostengo d' amor, gli occhi lucenti
> sono il mio segno e 'l mio conforto solo.

Petrarch no doubt borrowed the idea from Horace's *Carmina*, II. 16.

14–16 *And yf I flee I carie, &c.* Koeppel (*Studien*, p. 80) connects this with Petrarch's sonetto in vita 155, lines 9–14 (*Rime*, 209, p. 209),

> Et qual cervo ferito di saetta
> col ferro avelenato dentr' al fianco
> fugge, et più duolsi quanto più s'affretta, etc.:

and with Virgil's *Aeneid*, IV. 66–69,

> est mollis flamma medullas
> interea, et tacitum vivit sub pectore vulnus.
> Uritur infelix Dido totaque vagatur
> urbe furens, qualis coniecta cerva sagitta.

18 *tene.* The terza rima demands *will*, the reading of the MS.

23 (No. 2) *Description of Spring, &c.* In every edition (No. [2] in

B–I, sigs. A2ᵛ in *B–H*, A3 in *I*). Padelford (p. 45) reprints the poem from *A*, misprinting *flinges* (line 32) as *flings*. Nott (Surrey, p. 280) calls No. 2 "perhaps the most beautiful specimen of descriptive poetry in our language" — surely a great exaggeration.

This "sonnet" — which has only two rhymes (in the peculiar scheme of *abab abab abab aa*), and which is about as much like a rondel as a sonnet, is adapted from Petrarch, sonetto in morte 42 (*Rime*, 310, p. 292):

> Zephiro torna, e 'l bel tempo rimena,
> e i fiori et l'erbe, sua dolce famiglia,
> et garrir Progne et pianger Philomena,
> et primavera candida et vermiglia.
> Ridono i prati e 'l ciel si rasserena;
> Giove s'allegra di mirar sua figlia;
> l'aria et l'acqua et la terra è d'amor piena:
> ogni animal d'amar si riconsiglia.
> Ma per me, lasso, tornano i piú gravi
> sospiri, che del cor profondo tragge
> quella ch' al ciel se ne portò le chiavi;
> et cantar augelletti et fiorir piagge,
> e 'n belle donne honeste atti soavi
> sono un deserto et fere aspre et selvagge.

No. 2 is imitated rather closely in Richard Edwards's "Maister Edwardes his I may not," a poem in the *Paradise*, 1585, pp. 131–132.

4. 31 *The hart hath hong his olde hed, &c.* That is, has shed his antlers.

34 *The adder all her sloughe awaye she slinges.* In his translation of the *Aeneid*, 1557, sig. Cᵛ, Surrey wrote of the adder, "when she her slough had flong."

35 *The swift swalow pursueth the flyes smale.* Cf. Chaucer, *The Parlement of Foules*, line 353, "The swalow, mordrer of the flyës smale."

5. 2 (No. 3) *Descripcion of the restlesse state of a louer.* In every edition (No. [3] in *B–I*, sigs. A3 in *B–H*, A3ᵛ in *I*). Padelford (p. 53) prints the poem from a Harington MS. (Additional 36529), with the following variants:

> 5. 5 me . . . to] did make me
> 9 By ill gydyng, had let my waye
> 10 Mine eyen] Whose eyes
> 11 Had lost me manye a noble praye
> 13 with] by
> 14 The] Their
> 15 The fervent rage of hidden flame
> 16 doe] did
> 17 hath sowen] had sowne
> 18 The brewt therof my frewt opprest
> 19 Ere] Or: buds] bloomes: blowen] blowne
> 20 when] where: eyen] eyes
> 25 glowing] flaming

5. 27 wherin] wherwith
   30 els] elles
   31 specled] sparkled
   33 worshipt] worshipps
   34 norished] nourysheth

No. 3 was perhaps registered at Stationers' Hall in 1564–65 (Rollins, *Analytical Index*, no. 369) as "the complaynte of the Restles lover &c."

5. 36 (No. 4) *Description of the fickle, &c.* In every edition (No. [4] in *B–I*, sigs. A3–A4 in *B–H*, A3ᵛ–A4ᵛ in *I*). Padelford (pp. 59–60) prints the poem from a Harington MS. (Additional 36529), with the following variants:

6. 3 doe] dooth
   5 whom] which
   6 makes the one] cawseth hertes
   7 other] tothers
   8 Whote] Hot
  11 a . . . hel] the darke, diep well
  13 willes . . . beseke] wooll that still my mortall foo I do beseche
  15 lost ere] spilt or
  16 So] Lo: this meanes] these rules: may] can
  18 content] convert: self] will
  20 harmes] harme: dissembling] dissembled
  22 face] faas
  23 chekes] cheke
  25 wote] know
  26 by roate] be roote
  27 furth] forth
  29 doth] can
  31 in] hys
  32 list] lyke: grace] face
  33 pleasures] pleasure: delight the] delightes his: doe] doth
  37 would] colde
  40 with others] withouten
  43 I ¹⁻³] to
7. 2 a yelding] the yeldon
   3 meash] mashe
   4 Or . . . season] Which seldome tasted swete, to seasoned
   5 glimse] glyns
   7 wil] may: may] will
   8 The] That: the] those
   9 The . . . the] That . . . that

Padelford (pp. 186–187) says the poem "is largely indebted" to Petrarch's *Trionfo d'Amore*, III. 151–190, IV. 139–153. He points out borrowings from other Petrarchan sources as well; and Nott (Surrey, p. 297) found still others in the second canto of Ariosto's *Orlando Furioso*.

6. *6–7 golden burning dart, And . . . leaden colde.* On the golden and leaden arrows of Cupid see No. 305 (253. 22 n.), Ovid's *Metamorphoses*, I. 466–471, and the notes in Nott's Surrey, p. 299, and in the *Paradise*, pp. 259–260.

6. 41 *And how the Lion chastised is, &c.* Compare the passage in Chaucer's *Squire's Tale*, F. 490–491,

> And for to maken other be war by me,
> As by the whelp chasted is the leoun.

Skeat (Chaucer, v, 383–384) explained the foregoing lines as a proverb, since they occur in George Herbert's *Jacula Prudentum* (*Works*, ed. Willmott, 1854, p. 328) in the form, "Beat the Dog before the Lion." He also refers to a like expression in Randle Cotgrave's dictionary of 1611 (*s. v. batre*), and cites *Othello*, II. iii. 275–276, "even so as one would beat his offenceless dog to affright an imperious lion." Nevertheless, the chief collections of English proverbs ignore the lion and the dog, and Skeat can hardly be said to have penetrated Chaucer's meaning. It can readily be explained by a glance at Edward Topsell's *The Historie of Foure-Footed Beastes*, 1607, p. 480, in which on the authority of Albertus Magnus (who died in 1280) we are told "that the best way to tame lyons is to bring vp with them a little dogge, and oftentimes to beate the same dogge in their presence, by which discipline, the lion is made more tractable to the will of his keeper." The matter is discussed in *Notes and Queries*, 8th series, VI (1894), 76–77 (see also p. 377, and v [1894], 407), where a French MS. of the thirteenth century is cited as containing the words, "Pour douter (*par crainte*) bat-on le chien devant le lyon"; and in *The Athenaeum*, February 10, 1900, pp. 187–188, where a German reference of 1517 is reproduced—"Das vi das der Lew förcht ist ein hündlin, Wenn man es vor im schlecht, so schmuckt er sich und erschrickt, und gedencket nit an sein stercke."

42–43 *In standyng nere my fire, &c.* See 3. 23 n.

7. 10 (No. 5) *Complaint of a louer, that defied loue, &c.* In every edition (No. [5] in *B–I*, sigs. A4–A4^v in *B–H*, A4^v–A5 in *I*). Padelford (pp. 61–62) reprints the poem from *A*, with the following errors:

7. 21 swete] sweete
  39 litle] little: receaue] receue
8. 8 quod] quoth
  17 relefe] relese

A Harington MS. (Additional 28635, fols. 126–126^v) contains a sequel (apparently incomplete) to this poem, running as follows:

> Dum spero pereo: —   Dum spiro spero: —

> When wynter with his shivering blastes/ the Sommer gan assaile
> with force of myght and rygour greate/ his pleasant tyme to quayle
> and when the lustie greene had left/ eache holt and hill so hye
> and everye pleasaunt place appearde full pale and wan to eye
> the savours sweete and dewye dropps/ that wonted was to be
> in everye field the flowers fayre/ no suche thing can I see

but Boreas with his blustring blast/ eache leafe had layd full loe
that wonted was in Sommer tyme/ full highe on tree to groe
and every birdd hath bound hym self/ no more to strayne his voyce
untyll the pleasant spring shall come/ wheare in he may rejoyce
first gan hym hye the horye frost/ to feoble flowres fearce
whose chilling colde bothe roote and rynde/ of hearb and trie do pearce
eache fowle wext faynt and everye beast/ muste browce wheare he may best
of busshe or bryere to lyck the leaves/ and thinck hym at a feast
the lyttle Emyte slowthfull was/ within the mowle hill hydd
to shrowde it from the wynters blast/ as nature doth her bydde
I meane that weate and wanishe moone/ that then Novembre was
when that eache wight the howse can holde/ and pleasant walkes let passe
eache daye so drowsye was and I/ in dumppes had suche delight
thatt then dispayre his tyme gan spye/ thincking to worke his spight
and thus he sayde thow wretchid man/ whye art thow yet alyve
knowing that fortune is thie foe/ more then I can discryve
for synce thie birth thow knowest best/ what favour thow hast found
att fortunes handes in thyne affaires/ wheare at she ever frownd
and therto hath she made an othe/ even still so to persever
never to be thye ffrend at all/ but as thie foe for ever
no pen can print the peniurie/ ne tongue may yet discryve
the wofull chaunce as yet to come/ of some that bene alyve
yet in the starrs who so can reede/ is wrytten and ygrave
the wretched lyf that thow shalt lead/ till thie retourne to grave
and eke the plannettes seven hath sworne/ eache one to be thie foe
before thow first receavid breath/ yfeared was thie woe
now sence thie wretchid destenie/ thow doste well understand
breviat thie dayes and I dispaire/ shall helpp the heare at hand
whearwith in sowne neare sunck adowne/ had not hope hyed in haste
cryeng what man art thow that wilt/ thie self awaye thus cast
and thus me thought he spake me still/ in wordes as ye shall heare
I hope hath holpen thowsandes ten/ deludid by dispayre
ys this thie greif for love quod he/ or want of worldlye welth
losse of thie ffrend, losse of thye tyme/ or ells for lack of health
what yf thie Ladie thow hast lost/ through her disceaptfull way
another thow mast fynd as true/ as was Penelope
Or if as Cresus thow dost covett/ with ritchesse to rule all
remembre well how horde hath hate/ and clyming ofte doth fall
or if thie frend throughe ficklenesse/ hath broke his faithfull band
knytt then the knott more surer next/ whear as thow takest in hand
ys theise three now the cruell cause/ of this thie mortall payne
or losse of tyme the whiche thow knowest/ will nott begott agayne
what though that fortune froward was/ to the in youthfull race
thye tyme half spent ynoughe remaynes/ if natures lawe take place
where in so wyselye thow mayst worke/ as doth the lyttle Antt
or as the busye bee thow seeste/ whiche never feeleth wantt
so that thow have me hope for aye/ still graffed in thie hart
so shalt thow sone thie dolefull dayes/ to pleasant lyf convart
Throughe hope did Iason take in hand/ an enterpryse moste bolde
three wonders wrought and after wan/ the noble fleese of goolde
Thesius slew the mynitawre/ and David with his slynge
the great Golyas overcame/ through hope they wrought this thing.

7. 33 *the new betrothed birdes ycoupled.* This choice of mates was supposed to take place (as Chaucer's *Parlement of Foules* reminds us) on St. Valentine's day.

8. 9 *Vnwillingly.* The reading *vnwittingly* in *B+* fits the context better.

24 (No. 6) *Complaint of a louer rebuked.* In every edition (No. [6] in *B-I*, sigs. A4ᵛ in *B-G*, A4ᵛ-A5 in *H*, A5 in *I*). Padelford (p. 46) prints the poem from a Harington MS. (Additional 36529), with the following variants:

8. 26 liueth . . . in] doth raine and liue within
27 That] And
30 She, that me taught to loue] But she that tawght me love
32· cloke] looke
35 whereas . . . plaines] where he doth lurke and playne
37 faultlesse] fawtles: paynes] payine
39 his ¹] the: takes his] taketh

No. 6 is translated from Petrarch, sonetto in vita 91 (*Rime*, 140, pp. 154–155):

> Amor, che nel penser mio vive et regna,
> e 'l suo seggio maggior nel mio cor tene,
> talor armato ne la fronte vene:
> ivi si loca et ivi pon sua insegna.
> Quella ch' amare et sofferir n'ensegna,
> e vol che 'l gran desio, l'accesa spene,
> ragion, vergogna et reverenza affrene,
> di nostro ardir fra sé stessa si sdegna.
> Onde Amor paventoso fugge al core,
> lasciando ogni sua impresa, et piange et trema:
> ivi s'asconde et non appar piú fore.
> Che poss' io far, temendo il mio Signore,
> se non star seco infin a l'ora extrema?
> ché bel fin fa chi ben amando more.

No. 37, by Wyatt, is likewise a translation of this sonnet. Padelford (p. 180) remarks that Surrey's translation "is more lively and dramatic than the original. By careful compression Surrey is able to add the thought that Love's arms are those 'wherein with me he fought,' thus securing later the fine contrast between the ease with which Love subdued the lover and his ignominious flight from the presence of the lady."

39 *Swete is his death, &c.* For other phrasings of Petrarch's final line see Ronsard's *Amours* (*Œuvres*, ed. Marty-Laveaux, I, 86), "Belle fin fait qui meurt en bien aimant"; and Desportes's *Diane*, I. 18 (*Œuvres*, ed. Michiels, p. 20), "Douce est la mort qui vient en bien aimant." Cf. the *Paradise*, 121. 19, as well as *The Phoenix Nest*, 1593, p. 71, "No better end, than that which comes by Loue."

9. 2 (No. 7) *Complaint of the louer disdained.* In every edition (No. [7] in *B-I*, sigs. B in *BC*, A5 in *D-H*, A5-A5ᵛ in *I*). Padelford (pp. 46–47) prints

the poem from a Harington MS. (Additional 36529), with the following variants:

> 9. 6 fired] secret
>   11 An other] One, eke: yse] snow
>   16 growen] growne

The unique readings of *B* (listed in the Variant Readings) should be observed.

Nott (in 11607. i. 7, p. 21, as well as in his *Surrey*, pp. 279–280) remarks that the two springs of Cyprus may have been suggested by the two fountains which play so important a part in Boiardo's *Orlando Innamorato*, I. iii, and Ariosto's *Orlando Furioso*, I. 78, XLII. 35–38, 62–65. To quote from *Orlando Furioso*, I. 78 (ed. Pietro Papini, 1916, p. 13):

> E questo hanno causato due fontane
> Che di diverso effetto hanno liquore,
> Ambe in Ardenna, e non sono lontane:
> D'amoroso disio l'una empie il core;
> Chi bee de l'altra, senza amor rimane,
> E volge tutto in ghiaccio il primo ardore.
> Rinaldo gustò d'una, e amor lo strugge:
> Angelica de l'altra, e l'odia e fugge.

For further parallels see the discussion in Pio Rajna's *Le Fonti dell' Orlando Furioso*, 1876, 1900.

9. 17 (No. 8) *Description and praise of his loue Geraldine.* In every edition (No. [8] in *B–I*, sigs. B in *BC*, A5 in *D–H*, A5ᵛ in *I*). Padelford (p. 68) prints the poem from a Harington MS. (Additional 36529), with the following variants:

> 9. 21 shore] showre
>   22 Cambers] Chambares
>   23 Fostered] Ffostred
>   26 With] With a: tasteth costly] tastes gostly
>   31 Her] *Om.*
>   32 can] may

The unique readings of *B* (listed in the Variant Readings) should be observed.

No. 8 is the only poem of Surrey's (but see the notes to No. 14) that can definitely be connected with the "Fair Geraldine," who is discussed on pp. 71–75, above. In *Englands Heroicall Epistles* (1598) Drayton paraphrases much of it; in his notes (N3–N4) he quotes 9. 19–22, 27, 29–30, remarking, "Which sonnet being altogether a description of his [Surrey's] loue, I doe alledge in diuers places of this glosse, as proofes of what I write." In "The Description of Ireland" which he contributed to Holinshed's *Chronicles* (1808 reprint, VI, 46) Richard Stanyhurst reprints No. 8 and identifies its heroine with Lady Geraldine.

20 *Florence was sometyme her auncient seate.* The Fitzgeralds traced

their descent from the Geraldi family of Florence. *Her* is probably the old pronoun-form of *their*.

9. 24 *her dame, of princes blood.* Geraldine's mother, Lady Elizabeth Grey, was the granddaughter of that Elizabeth Woodville who was Edward IV's queen and Henry VIII's cousin.

27 *Honsdon did first present her to mine yien.* The Princess Mary was at Hunsdon in March, 1537, and at Hampton Court (line 29) early in July. Probably Surrey saw the nine-year-old Elizabeth Fitzgerald on these occasions.

30 *Windsor, alas, dothe chase me from her sight.* Because Surrey was confined at Windsor in July, 1537, for striking a courtier within the royal grounds.

31-32 *Her beauty . . . obtaine her loue.* Imitated by the closing lines of a poem in the *Gorgeous Gallery*, p. 56,

> For Beauties sake, sent downe from *Ioue* aboue,
> Thrise happy is hee, that can attayne her loue.

A Harington MS. (Additional 28635, fol. 113) has another copy of the *Gallery* poem, written in honor of "N. N." There the final couplet reads:

> for bewties sake sent downe from heaven above
> thryse happie he, that can attayne her Love.

33 (No. 9) *The frailtie and hurtfulnes of beautie.* In every edition (No. [9] in *B–I*, sigs. B–Bᵛ in *BC*, A5–A5ᵛ in *D–H*, A5ᵛ in *I*). Padelford (p. 47) reprints the poem from *A*, misprinting *dothe* (line 8) as *doth*, and *moste* (line 10) as *most*. There is another copy in a Harington MS. (Additional 28635, fol. 139ᵛ), which is signed "L Vawse." Nott (p. 288) refuses to accept Surrey's authorship; Padelford (p. 181) says that if the poem be "by Surrey, it is not Surrey at his best." Perhaps it is safe to credit the authorship to Lord Vaux.

It seems to me likely that No. 9 was suggested by lines in Seneca's *Hippolytus* beginning (761–763),

> Anceps forma bonum mortalibus,
> exigui donum breve temporis,
> ut velox celeri pede laberis,

and ending (773–774),

> res est forma fugax; quis sapiens bono
> confidat fragili?

The author of *The Arte of English Poesie*, 1589, p. 136, prints an imitation of No. 9, declaring that he wrote it "to daunt the insolence of a beautifull woman."

35-10. 2 *Brittle beautie . . . apt to faile.* Cf. Petrarch, sonetto in morte 63, lines 1–2 (*Rime*, 350, p. 328):

> Questo nostro caduco et fragil bene,
> ch' è vento et ombra et à nome beltate.

10. 3, 8 *Tickell treasure, Iewel of ieopardie.* Cf. Brian Melbancke, *Philoti-mus,* 1583, E3: "treasure is tickle, and a iuell of ieopardy."

14 (No. 10) *A complaint by night, &c.* In every edition (No. [10] in *B–I,* sigs. B^v in *BC,* A5^v in *D–H,* A6 in *I*). Padelford (p. 45) reprints the poem from *A,* misprinting *doutfull* (line 24) as *doubtful.*

No. 10 is adapted from Petrarch, sonetto in vita 113 (*Rime,* 164, p. 172):

> Or che 'l ciel et la terra e 'l vento tace,
> et le fere e gli augelli il sonno affrena,
> notte il carro stellato in giro mena
> et nel suo letto il mar senz' onda giace;
> vegghio, penso, ardo, piango; et chi mi sface
> sempre m' è inanzi per mia dolce pena:
> guerra è 'l mio stato, d' ira et di duol piena;
> et sol di lei pensando ò qualche pace.
> Così sol d' una chiara fonte viva
> move 'l dolce et l' amaro ond'io mi pasco;
> una man sola mi risana et punge.
> Et perché 'l mio martir non giunga a riva,
> mille volte il dí moro et mille nasco;
> tanto da la salute mia son lunge!

Petrarch's sonnet was translated into Latin by Thomas Watson and included in his *Hekatompathia,* 1582, as sonnet 66, beginning, "Dum cœlum, dum terra tacet, ventusque silescit."

30 (No. 11) *How eche thing saue the louer, &c.* In every edition (No. [11] in *B–I,* sigs. B^v–B2 in *BC,* A5^v–A6 in *D–H,* A6 in *I*). Padelford (p. 68) prints the poem from a Harington MS. (Additional 36529), with the following variants:

> 10. 33 Windsor] Windesor
> 35 The] Ech
> 36 blossomd] blossomed
> 11. 3 discouer . . . my] discouered. Than did to
> 4 ioly] ioily
> 6 the] myne
> 7 breakes] brake
> 8 In] And
> 9 vapord] vapored
> 10 whiche] to
> 11 halfebent] have bent

33–34 *When Windsor walles, &c.* Drayton (*Englands Heroicall Epistles,* 1598, N4) quotes these lines as showing that Surrey at Windsor "inioyed the presence of his faire and vertuous mistris . . . by reason of Queene *Katherines* vsuall aboad there, (on whom this Lady *Geraldine* was attending)."

11. 6–7 *the heauy charge of care Heapt in my brest, &c.* Notice Surrey's repetition of this phraseology at 19. 9–10.

11. 9 *My vapord eyes.* Surrey uses *vapored*, meaning misty with tears, again at 27. 35. Cf. also John Studley's *Medea*, act v (in *Seneca His Tenne Tragedies*, 1581, fol. 138), "with vapourde weeping Eye"; and *The Phoenix Nest*, 1593, p. 80, "With vapored sighes, I dim the aire." Nott (Surrey, p. 358) notes several other instances.

12 (No. 12) *Vow to loue faithfully, &c.* In every edition (No. [12] in *B–I*, sigs. B2 in *BC*, A6 in *D–H*, A6–A6ᵛ in *I*). Padelford (p. 47) prints the poem from a Harington MS. (Additional 36529). His text differs so greatly from the text of *A* that I give it below:

> Set we [me] wheras the sonne dothe perche the grene,
> Or whear his beames may not dissolue the ise,
> In temprat heat, wheare he is felt and sene;
> With prowde people, in presence sad and wyse;
> Set me in base, or yet in highe degree;
> In the long night, or in the shortyst day;
> In clere weather, or whear mysts thickest be;
> In lofte yowthe, or when my heares be grey;
> Set me in earthe in heauen, or yet in hell;
> In hill, in dale, or in the fowming floode;
> Thrawle, or at large, aliue whersoo I dwell;
> Sike, or in healthe; in yll fame, or in good;
> Yours will I be, and with that onely thought
> Comfort my self when that my hape is nowght.

The *we* in the first line is a printer's error, and Padelford has *me* in his index, p. 238.

No. 12 is translated from Petrarch, sonetto in vita 95 (*Rime*, 145, p. 159):

> Pommi ove 'l sole occide i fiori et l'erba,
> o dove vince lui il ghiaccio et la neve;
> pommi ov'è il carro suo temprato et leve,
> et ov'è chi cel rende o chi cel serba:
> pommi in humil fortuna od in superba,
> al dolce aere sereno, al fosco et greve;
> pommi a la notte, al dí lungo ed al breve,
> a la matura etate od a l'acerba:
> pommi in cielo od in terra od in abisso,
> in alto poggio, in valle ima et palustre,
> libero spirto od a' suoi membri affisso:
> pommi con fama oscura o con illustre:
> sarò qual fui, vivrò com' io son visso,
> continuando il mio sospir trilustre.

Surrey, appropriately enough, does not translate literally *sospir trilustre*. Petrarch, in his turn, is indebted to Horace's *Carmina*, I. 22:

> pone me pigris ubi nulla campis
> arbor aestiva recreatur aura,
> quod latus mundi nebulae malusque
>   Iuppiter urget;

pone sub curru nimium propinqui
solis in terra domibus negata:
dulce ridentem Lalagen amabo,
dulce loquentem.

There is a similar passage in Propertius, *Elegies*, II. xv. 29–36. Numerous imitations of Petrarch's sonnet occur in French and Spanish as well as in English. Of the last it will suffice to mention the rendition in *The Phoenix Nest*, 1593, p. 82, which begins, "Set me where Phœbus heate, the flowers slaieth." The author of *The Arte of English Poesie*, 1589, p. 231, quotes No. 12, inadvertently assigning it to Wyatt, and concluding, "All which might haue bene said in these two verses.

Set me wheresoeuer ye vvill,
I am and vvilbe yours still."

II. 29 (No. 13) *Complaint that his ladie, &c.* In every edition (No. [13] in *B–I*, sigs. B2–B2ᵛ in *BC*, A6–A6ᵛ in *D–H*, A6ᵛ in *I*). The unique readings of *B* (listed in the Variant Readings) should be observed. Padelford's text (p. 46) comes from a Harington MS. (Additional 36529), and runs thus:

I neuer saw youe, madam, laye aparte
Your cornet black, in colde nor yet in heate,
Sythe first ye knew of my desire so greate,
Which other fances chaced cleane from my harte.
Whiles to my self I did the thought reserve
That so vnware did wounde my wofull brest,
Pytie I saw within your hart dyd rest;
But since ye knew I did youe love and serve,
Your golden treese was clad alway in blacke,
Your smilyng lokes were hid thus euermore,
All that withdrawne that I did crave so sore.
So doth this cornet governe me, a lacke!
In sommere, sonne; in winter, breath of frost;
Of your faire eies whereby the light is lost.

No. 13 is a translation from Petrarch, ballata in vita 1 (*Rime*, 11, p. 8):

Lassare il velo o per sole o per ombra,
Donna, non vi vid' io,
poi che in me conosceste il gran desio
ch'ogni altra voglia dentr' al cor mi sgombra.
Mentr'io portava i be' pensier celati
ch'ànno la mente desiando morta,
vidivi di pietate ornare il volto;
ma poi ch'Amor di me vi fece accorta,
fuor i biondi capelli allor velati,
et l'amoroso sguardo in sé raccolto.
Quel ch' i' piú desiava in voi, m' è tolto;
sí mi governa il velo,
che per mia morte, et al caldo et al gielo,
de' be' vostr' occhi il dolce lume adombra.

[140]

12. 13 (No. 14) *Request to his loue, &c.* In every edition (No. [14] in *B–I*, sigs. B2ᵛ in *BC*, A6ᵛ in *D–H*, A6ᵛ–A7 in *I*). Padelford (p. 48) reprints the poem from *A*, misprinting *gyftes* (line 24) as *gyfts*. The opening lines are a commonplace, telling how heaven had in the lady made a being too perfect to remain long on earth. That idea occurs in Petrarch, sonetti in vita 108, 190 (*Rime*, 159, 248, pp. 169, 238), and elsewhere.

23 *Now certesse Ladie.* In *B* only the reading is *Now certesse Garret*. Strangely enough, however, Nott (and most subsequent editors have followed him) declared that *Garret* appears in the second and third quartos (that is, presumably, *BCD*); while Padelford (p. 181) asserts that "the second and fourth editions" (which, judging from his bibliography on p. 220, are *BCE*) "read *Garret* instead of *Ladie*." To repeat, *Garret* occurs only in *B;* it was a common rendering of the name *Fitzgerald*. Hence Nott, riding his hobby (see pp. 73–74, above), connected the poem with Elizabeth Fitzgerald, the Fair Geraldine of Surrey's supposititious romance and the childish heroine of No. 8. Apparently, however, *B* had no authority whatever for substituting this name for *Ladie*.

29 (No. 15) *Prisoned in windsor, he recounteth, &c.* In every edition (No. [15] in *B–I*, sigs. B2ᵛ–B3ᵛ in *BC*, A6ᵛ–A7ᵛ in *D–H*, A7–A7ᵛ in *I*). Padelford (pp. 69–70) prints the poem from a Harington MS. (Additional 36529), with the following variants:

13.   3 into] unto
        5 seates] sales
       13 grauell] graveld
       15 one] the one: another whelme] overwhelme
       17 meade] meades
       19 trayned with] trayled by
       23 ofte] soft
       25 holtes] holte
       26 auailed] avald
       28 of] a
       29 wide vales] voyd walles
       30 reuiueth in] revive within
       36 night] nightes
       37 the ²] my
       43 doest] didest

In his notes to Surrey's epistle to Geraldine, in *Englands Heroicall Epistles*, 1598, N4, Drayton quotes (from memory, as the verbal changes would indicate) 12. 34–35, 13. 2–6, 17, 21. Of No. 15 Courthope (*A History of English Poetry*, II [1897], 85) enthusiastically remarks: "I know of few verses in the whole range of human poetry in which the voice of nature utters the accents of grief with more simplicity and truth; it seems to me to be the most pathetic *personal* elegy in English poetry."

34 *a kinges sonne.* Henry Fitzroy, Duke of Richmond, the illegitimate

son of Henry VIII by Elizabeth Blount, and the husband of Surrey's sister, Mary Howard.

13. 4 *easie sighes, suche as folke drawe in loue.* Borrowed from Chaucer, *Troilus and Criseyde*, III. 1361–1364:

> Nought swiche sorwful sykes as men make
> For wo, or elles whan that folk ben syke,
> But esy sykes, swiche as been to lyke,
> That shewed his affeccioun with-inne.

The same idea is expressed in James I of Scotland's *Kingis Quhair*, stanza XCVI.

41 *renuer of my woes.* Probably borrowed from Wyatt's expression at 44. 7.

42 *where is my noble fere.* The Duke of Richmond died of consumption on July 22, 1536, aged seventeen. Hence *doest* in line 43 would be better in the past tense, as it is in the MS.

14. 7–8 *And with remembrance of the greater greefe, &c.* A similar sentiment, as Koeppel (*Studien*, pp. 85–86) notes, is found in Dante's *Inferno*, v. 121–123 (*Divina Commedia*, Milan, 1907, p. 49):

> Nessun maggior dolore
> Che ricordarsi del tempo felice
> Nella miseria.

9 (No. 16) *The louer comforteth himself, &c.* In every edition (No. [16] in *B–I*, sigs. B3ᵛ–B4 in *BC*, A7ᵛ–A8 in *D+*). Padelford (p. 51) reprints the poem from *A*, with the following errors:

> 14. 19 Grekes] Greekes
> 22 bloode] blood
> 24 yeres] years: *Padelford tacks this line to the end of the preceding stanza*
> 36 Therfore] Therefore
> 15. 3 Ioyful] Joyful

The author of *The Arte of English Poesie*, 1589, pp. 86, 136, 144, liked the entire poem because "the *Cesure* fals iust in the middle" of the line, because the verses are "made of *monosillables* and *bissillables* enterlaced," and because the iambic movement is "passing sweete and harmonicall." The poem was registered as a ballad called "When raging love" in 1557–58, 1560–61, 1561–62, and what was apparently a "moralization" of it was registered in 1568–69 (Rollins, *Analytical Index*, nos. 2918–2921). To the tune of *Raging love* one of the ballads in the *Handful*, 1584 (pp. 50–51), was written. An imitation of Surrey's poem — composed by Nicholas Balthorp and registered for publication in 1557–58 (Rollins, *Analytical Index*, no. 1619) — begins, "When raging death with extreme paine"; and there is a parody — registered in 1561–62 —

by W. F. (William Fullwood?) called "A new Ballad against Unthrifts" (Lilly's *Ballads*, pp. 153–156), which begins,

> When raging louts, with feble braines,
> Moste wilfully wyl spend awaye.

On the anagram (*W–I–A–T–T*) of Wyatt formed by the initial letters of the five stanzas of No. 16 see the notes to 230. 22, and compare the notes to No. 200.

14. 14–16 *When that my teares, as floudes of rayne, &c.* Cf. Petrarch, sonetto in vita 13, lines 1–2 (*Rime*, 17, p. 12):

> Piovommi amare lagrime dal viso
> con un vento angoscioso di sospiri.

15. 4 (No. 17) *Complaint of the absence of her louer, &c.* In every edition (No. [17] in *B–I*, sigs. B4–B4ᵛ in *BC*, A8–A8ᵛ in *D+*). Padelford (pp. 58–59) reprints the poem from *A*, misprinting *find* (15. 27) as *finde*, *teares* (15. 30) as *tears*, and *doutfull* (16. 5) as *doubtfull*. In *Nugae Antiquae* (1769, pp. 187–188; 1779, 1792, III, 244–245) a copy appears under the unauthorized heading, "By John Harington, 1543, for a Ladie moche in Love" (cf. pp. 90–92, above). A musical setting is given in MS. Additional 30513 (cf. Henry Davey, *History of English Music*, 1895, p. 151).

Padelford (p. 186) remarks: "This poem may have been written . . . for the Countess of Surrey, to voice her impatience at the separation from her husband, during his absence on military duty in France. . . . It is the one poem of Surrey's in the Duke of Devonshire Ms. and is in the hand-writing of Mary Shelton, the sweetheart of Sir Thomas Clere, Surrey's companion, who accompanied him to France. . . . Perhaps the poem was written for Mary Shelton herself, in recognition of her love for Clere, and was inserted in the Ms. after being sent her from France." Koeppel (*Studien*, pp. 82–83) shows that the poem is an adaptation of Serafino's fifth epistle (*Opere*, 1516, fols. 62ᵛ–64, beginning, "Quella ingannata, afflicta, & miseranda Donna, non donna più, ma horrendo monstro"), which in turn was adapted from Phyllis's complaint in Ovid's *Heroides*, II.

14 *In ship, freight with rememberance.* Brian Melbancke, *Philotimus*, 1583, H2ᵛ, borrows lines 14–15, 18–19, as follows: "thus did hee seeme to bee conueyde: in shipe fraught with remembraunce of pleasure past, with scaldinge sighes for want of gale, and stedfast hope that was his sayle."

18–19 *With scalding sighes, for lack of gale, &c.* Cf. Petrarch, sonetto in vita 137, lines 7–8 (*Rime*, 189, p. 189):

> la vela rompe un vento humido, eterno
> di sospir, di speranze et di desio.

15. 31–34 *I stand . . . a mariner loue hath made me.* Cf. Serafino, *Epistles*, v. 37–40 (*Opere*, 1516, fol. 63):

> Ah quante uolte quando el ciel se imbruna
> À meza nocte uscio del freddo lecto
> À sentir le hore, à remirar la luna?
> Facta son marinar per questo effecto.

39 *Alas, now drencheth my swete fo.* Cf. Serafino, *Epistles*, v. 79–80 (*Opere*, 1516, fol. 63ᵛ):

> E se affondato è alcun dal tempo rio
> Chel sappia, dico, ohime, questo è summerso.

Swete fo is a conventional phrase among the sonneteers. Cf. 144. 34, 158. 8, 186. 20, and my notes in the *Paradise*, p. 242.

16. 10 (No. 18) *Complaint of a diyng louer, &c.* In every edition (No. [18] in *B–I*, sigs. B4ᵛ–Cᵛ in *BC*, A8ᵛ–Bᵛ in *D+*). Padelford (pp. 62–64) reprints this poem from *A*, with the following errors:

> 16. 23 iust] just
>   24 without] *misprinted* withoue
> 17. 4 armes] arms
>   7 Wherwith] Wherewith
>   11 poore] pore
>   18 stretcht] stretched
>   23 Wherto] Whereto
>   28 losse] loss
>   37 Wherwith] Wherewith
> 18. 8 restord] restored
>   13 treew] trew
>   15 Angels] angles

He remarks (p. 188) that the poem "is a fusion of one type of the early French *pastourelle*, in which a shepherd complains to another of his hard-hearted mistress, and of one type of the early French *chanson à personnages*, in which the poet chances upon a man who is lamenting an unrequited love. The opening verses, which give the setting, are reminiscent of the *chanson*, although winter has been substituted for the conventional May morning."

No. 18 was registered for publication in 1557–58 (Rollins, *Analytical Index*, no. 1249) as "A ballett, in wynters Juste Retorne." Thomas Howell wrote an imitation, "In vttringe his plaint, he declareth the vncertainty of fained frendship. To the tune of winters iust returne," which was included in his *Newe Sonets, and pretie Pamphlets, ca.* 1568 (*Poems*, ed. Grosart, p. 152). The first two lines are quoted in *The Arte of English Poesie*, 1589, p. 204. Nott thinks that Spenser, in the *Daphnaida*, made "evident and frequent allusion" to the poem.

17. 12 *A shepardes charge, &c.* Repeated in Alexander Neville's *Oedipus*,

iv. iii (*Seneca His Tenne Tragedies*, 1581, fol. 90), "Sometime a charge of sheepe I had, vnworthy though I weer."

17. 17 *sore febled all with faint.* Turbervile borrows this unusual phrase in his *Epitaphes*, etc., 1567, p. 157.

24 *The sonne should runne his course awry, &c.* Cf. Petrarch, sonetto in vita 37, lines 7–9 (*Rime*, 57, p. 62):

> et corcherassi il sol là oltre ond' esce
> d'un medesimo fonte Eufrate et Tigre:
> prima ch' i' trovi in ciò pace né triegua.

28 *a greater losse, than Priam had of Troy.* Nott's suggested emendation, to *Priamus' son of Troy* (that is, Troilus: cf. 18. 12), has points in its favor.

41 *he yelded vp the ghost.* Baptista Guarini, in *Il Pastor Fido*, iii. iii (Fanshawe's translation, 1647, p. 96), makes Amarillis (or Amaryllis) remark that

> "When Lovers talk of dying, it doth show
> "An amorous custome rather of the tongue,
> "Then a resolve of minde (continuing long)
> "To do't indeed.

The present poem is noteworthy for having a lover who actually dies. Hundreds of Tudor lovers, to be sure, threatened to die, but it is to be feared that usually they were like "that old *fainting man* in the [Aesopic] *Fable*, who" (to use the words of *Mercurius Elencticus*, October 4–11, 1648, p. 377) "in the heat of the day threw down his burthen, and called for *death*. But when *death* came to know his *will* of him, said, *it was for nothing, but to help him up with his burthen again.*"

18. 14 *I couered it with bleew.* Blue was the color of true lovers. At the end of each of the three stanzas of his balade "Against Women Unconstant" Chaucer admonishes the ladies, "In stede of blew, thus may ye were al grene." Lydgate (*Troy Book*, i. 2089–2090) says, "They can schewe on [thing], and another mene, Whos blewe is lightly died in-to grene." Just so Mathew Grove (*Poems*, 1587, ed. Grosart, pp. 61, 101) speaks of "the faithful blewe," and adds, "So doth the blewe aye represent, a louing heart alway."

17 (No. 19) *Complaint of the absence, &c.* In every edition (No. [19] in *B–I*, sigs. Cᵛ–C2 in *BC*, Bᵛ–B2 in *D+*). Padelford (pp. 72–73) prints the poem from a Harington MS. (Additional 28635), with the following variants:

18. 20 ye] you: pleasures] pleasure
   24, 26 ye] you
   28 loue and lord] lord and love
   30 That I was wontt for to embrace, contentid myndes
   31 winde] wyndes
   32 Where] Theare: well him] hym well: sone . . . me] safelye me
      hym
   36 do] they

18. 37 when] then: I lye] and stand: where] yf
    38 do] they
    39 That my sweete lorde in daunger greate, alas! doth often lye
19. 2 his faire] T., his
     4 think] thinckes: welcome my lord] Now well come home
     6 atwixt] betwixt
    10 dischargen] dischardgeth: huge] great
    14 Some hydden wheare, to steale the gryfe of my unquyet mynd
    16 I find] there is: good] some
    17 think, by] feele, the
    19 we] that we two
    20 while] tyme: the] that
    21 coniure] convart
    22 ye] you
    23 this] suche

The MS. copy has the signature "Preston". Obviously, however, the poem was written for the Countess of Surrey by her husband during his military service in France, September, 1545–March, 1546.

19. 2 *with his faire little sonne.* Surrey's eldest son, Thomas Howard, born in March, 1536. Observe the MS. reading in the note above.

9–10 *the heauy cares . . . Breake forth.* Notice the similar phraseology at 11. 6–7; and cf. Chaucer, *Troilus and Criseyde*, IV. 236–237,

> And in his brest the heped wo bigan
> Out-breste.

14 *Sum hidden place, &c.* Arber in his edition (p. 19 n.) observes, "Some lines apparently left out here"; but his suggestion is supported by neither the context nor the manuscript copy.

17 *Saue.* The meaning would be clearer, as Nott suggests, if *Saue* were to change places with *but* in line 16.

25 (No. 20) *A praise of his loue, &c.* In every edition (No. [20] in *B–I*, sigs. C2–C2ᵛ in *BC*, B2–B2ᵛ in *D+*). Padelford (p. 56) reprints the poem from *A*, misprinting *coulde* (19. 40) as *could*, *lawe* (20. 8) as *loue*. No. 20 is apparently an imitation of Heywood's No. 199.

28–33 *Geue place ye louers, &c.* In *The Arte of English Poesie*, 1589, p. 203, these lines are quoted as an illustration of the idea that, "if we fall a praysing, specially of our mistresses vertue, bewtie, or other good parts, we be allowed now and then to ouer-reach a little way of comparison as he that said thus in prayse of his Lady."

41–20. 2-5 *The whole effect of natures plaint, &c.* The conceit expressed in these lines is practically duplicated at 28. 34, 126. 23, 155. 38. Melbancke probably had them in mind when he wrote in *Philotimus*, 1583, sig. Hᵛ, "*Dame Nature* howles and weepes bycause the moulde that cast her shape is lost and gone, nor euer can the like be framed againe." Cf. also *A light Bondell of liuly discourses called Churchyardes Charge*, 1580 (Collier's reprint, p. 40), "And maie not Nature breake eche mould that once her hand hath made?"

20. 18 (No. 21) *To the Ladie that scorned her louer.* In every edition (No. [21] in *B–I*, sigs. C2ᵛ–C3 in *BC*, B2ᵛ–B3 in *D+*). Padelford (pp. 50–51) reprints the poem from *A*, but changes *the in* (20. 38) to the *in the* of *B+*. In it Surrey speaks of himself as "a man of warre," a "captain full of might," whence it has been conjectured that he wrote the lines in August, 1542, just before his first military service in Scotland. Perhaps it alludes to the same experience as does No. 264. The chess-figure, on which the poem is based, may owe something to Chaucer's *Book of the Duchess*, lines 617–686. Later Nicholas Breton contributed a poem called "The Chesse Play" to *The Phoenix Nest*, 1593, pp. 28–30. Compare also "A pretty and pleasant Poeme of a whole Game played at Chesse," translated from Vida by G. B. in his *Ludus Scacchiæ: Chesse-play* (1597 [reprinted 1810], sigs. B–E3ᵛ).

38 *the in.* Read *then in* or (with *B+*) *in the.*

21. 15 (No. 22) *A warning to the louer, &c.* In every edition (No. [22] in *B–I*, sigs. C3 in *BC*, B3 in *D–GI*, B3–B3ᵛ in *H*). Padelford (p. 64) reprints the poem from *A*, misprinting *dearely* (line 18) as *dearly, see* (line 28) as *se, fredom* (line 31) as *freedom.*

22. 2 (No. 23) *The forsaken louer, &c.* In every edition (No. [23] in *B–I*, sigs. C3ᵛ–C4 in *BC*, B3ᵛ–B4 in *D–H*, B3–B3ᵛ in *I*). Padelford (p. 54) reprints the poem from *A*.

4–11 *O Lothsome place where I . . . lenger should.* I am indebted to Professor Kittredge for the following paraphrase: "O place [now] loathsome [to me] where formerly I have seen and heard my dear at times when her eye hath made her thought appear in my breast [hath made me feel how she loved me], — her eye [I say] by shining [upon me] with such favor as fortune was unwilling should last any longer between us!"

20–23 *But happy . . . his reliefe.* "But happy is the man who has escaped the suffering which unrequited love can easily inflict upon (well teche) him."

32–35 *And last it may not long, &c.* "The truest thing about love and certainly its greatest injustice is that whoever is prisoner to it may not live long."

23. 5 (No. 24) *The louer describes his restlesse state.* In every edition (No. [24] in *B–I*, sigs. C4 in *BC*, B4 in *D–H*, B3ᵛ–B4 in *I*). Padelford (p. 52) prints the poem from a Harington MS. (Additional 36529), with the following variants:

23. 9 nier] ner
　　12 consume] consumes
　　14 *MS. adds:*

> Like as the flee that seethe the flame
> And thinkes to plaie her in the fier,
> That fownd her woe, and sowght her game,
> Whose grief did growe by her desire.

23. 15 First . . . those] When first I saw theise
    16 my] this
    17 her] these
    18 *MS. adds:*

> Wherein is hid the crewell bytt
> Whose sharpe repulse none can resist,
> And eake the spoore that straynith eche wytt
> To roon the race against his list.

    20 And] *Om.:*   did] dyd me
    27 mine own] my none
    28 on] he
    29 in] for: put] cast
    30 mine] his: *MS. adds:*

> And as the spyder drawes her lyne,
> With labour lost I frame my sewt;
> The fault is hers, the losse ys myne.
> Of yll sown seed such ys the frewte.

In MS. Harleian 78, fol. 27ᵛ, there is a poem of seven stanzas, several of which are practically identical with Surrey's. That poem is reprinted by Miss Foxwell (i, 361–362), Nott (Surrey, pp. 251–252), and Padelford (p. 184). Miss Foxwell (ii, 175–176) thinks it is undoubtedly Wyatt's work, believing that Surrey simply modernized it into No. 24, adding some stanzas derived from an unknown Italian source. Padelford, on the contrary, regards it as "probably a clumsy reworking of Surrey's poem, or an attempt to reconstruct it from memory," but "apparently a mosaic of Petrarchian lines," several of which he points out. Nott believes that in a "spirit of friendly competition" Surrey and Wyatt each translated some piece from the Italian, "or, what seems more likely," each wove various passages from Petrarch into the form of a new ode. Miss Foxwell's text of Wyatt's poem runs thus:

T. WYAT. OF LOVE

> Lyke as the wynde with raging blaste
>   Dothe cawse eche tree to bowe and bende,
>   Even so do I spende my tyme in wast
>   My lyff consumyng into an ende.
>
> For as the flame by force doeth quenche the fyer,
>   And runninge streames consume the rayne,
>   Even so do I myself desyer,
>   To augment my greffe and deadly payne.
>
> Where as I fynde that whot is whot,
>   And colde is colde, by course of kynde,
>   So shall I knet an endles knot.
>   Such fruite in love alas I fynde.

> When I foresaw those christall streames
> 　　Whose bewtie dothe cause my mortall wounde,
> 　　I lyttyll thought within those beames
> 　　So swete a venim for to have founde.
>
> I fele and see my owne decaye,
> 　　As one that bearethe flame in his brest,
> 　　Forgetfull thought to put away,
> 　　The thynge that breadeth my unrest,
>
> Lyke as the flye dothe seke the flame,
> 　　And afterwarde playeth in the fyer,
> 　　Who fyndeth her woo, and sekethe her game,
> 　　Whose greffe dothe growe of her owne desyer.
>
> Lyke as the spider dothe drawe her lyne,
> 　　As labor lost so is my sute
> 　　The gayne is hers the losse is myne,
> 　　Of evell sowne seade suche is the frute.

No. 24 is unblushingly imitated in "A proper Sonet, of an vnkinde Dam-sell," a poem in the *Handful*, 1584, pp. 68–69.

23. 11–14 *As flame doth quenche, &c.* A remark that, no doubt purposely, affirms the exact opposite of its meaning: "As the raging fire quenches the flame and as rain dries up the running streams, just so does the sight of my mistress appease my grief and deadly pain" — that is, it increases my suffer-ings. The idea was perhaps suggested by the opening lines of Petrarch's sonetto in vita 33 (*Rime*, 48, p. 50), "Se mai foco per foco non si spense," etc.

23–26 *As cruell waues full oft be found, &c.* Probably written in imi-tation of Wyatt's lines at 62. 28–29.

31 (No. 25) *The louer excuseth himself, &c.* In every edition (No. [25] in *B–I*, sigs. C4–D in *BC*, B4–B5 in *D–H*, B4–B4ᵛ in *I*). Padelford (pp. 55–56) reprints the poem from *A*, misprinting *by* (23. 34) as *to*, *think* (24. 31) as *thinke*, *felicite* (24. 33) as *felicitie*.

24. 4–5 *to change A falkon for a kite.* "Doe not exchaunge a fawcon for a kite," echoes Turbervile, *Epitaphes*, etc., 1567, p. 53. Cf. the *Gorgeous Gallery*, p. 58, "To seeme a Hauke, and bee a kyte."

27 *the ganders fo.* An old hand in *I* (Bodleian) says, "the sowe or hogge or rather fox."

31 *For think it may not be. Think* is an imperative, as in line 22: "For don't think it possible that I, who am desirous to win and loth to forego your love, should," etc.

42–43 *Yet as sone shall the fire, &c.* Cf. Petrarch, sestina in vita 2, lines 9–10 (*Rime*, 30, p. 32):

> quando avrò queto il core, asciutti gli occhi,
> vedrem ghiacciare il foco, arder la neve.

25. 4 (No. 26) *A carelesse man, &c.* In every edition (No. [26] in *B–I*,

sigs. D in *BC*, B5 in *D–G*, B5–B5ᵛ in *H*, B4ᵛ–B5 in *I*). Padelford (pp. 64–65) reprints the poem from *A*, with the following errors:

> 25. 20 somtime] sometime
> 21 seemd] seemed
> 22 go] grow
> 33 Lorde] Lord

25. 38 *hory heares are powdred, &c.* Probably borrowed from Wyatt (ed. Foxwell, I, 10), "gray heres ben powdered in your sable."

26. 2 (No. 27) *The meanes to attain happy life.* In every edition (No. [31] in *B–I*, sigs. D3ᵛ–D4 in *BC*, B7ᵛ–B8 in *D–G*, B8 in *H*, B7ᵛ in *I*). Padelford (p. 78) prints the poem from a Harington MS. (Additional 36529), with the following variants:

> 26. 4 Martiall] Marshall: that do] for to
> 8 egall] equall: no²] nor
> 13 Trew] *Om.*:   simplenesse] simplicitye
> 15 Where wyne may beare no soveranty
> 16 faithful wife] chast wife, wyse
> 19 Ne . . . ne] Neyther wisshe death, nor

A copy signed "Surre" and beginning "My frende" instead of "Martial" is in MS. Cotton Titus A. xxiv, fol. 80; and, ending with the word "Τέλως," it is written in an Elizabethan hand on the last leaf (Gg4ᵛ) of the Capell copy of *C*. Still another copy, beginning "Warner," is printed ("from a manuscript") in *The Gentleman's Magazine*, xcvii. ii (1827), 392, as is also a poem said to be by Sir John Harington in which, replying to some local charge that the poets in borrowing from the ancients "steall some good conceits from Martiall," he says that the critics must "Match vs at least with honorable theevs," for Surrey, Wyatt, and Heywood did exactly the same thing.

No. 27 was apparently one of the first compositions of Surrey's to be published (but see the notes to No. 31): W. F. Trench ("William Baldwin," *The Modern Language Quarterly*, I [1899], 261) points out that it was printed without Surrey's name at the end of book III in Baldwin's *A treatise of Morrall phylosophye* (1547/8), and with Surrey's name in Wayland's edition of the *Treatise* in 1555 (which I have not seen). Evidently Baldwin, in one way or another, had access to a manuscript copy, not improbably to one given him by the poet.

Surrey's poem was borrowed by Timothy Kendall, *Flowers of Epigrammes*, 1577, C2ᵛ (Spenser Society ed., p. 52), who prints it with a few slight variants:

> 26. 2 The meanes, &c.] To hymselfe
> 13 ioyned] ioynd
> 18 Content thy self with thine estate
> 19 ne] nor

Kendall borrowed it because it is an adequate translation from Martial, x. 47:

> Vitam quae faciant beatiorem,
> iucundissime Martialis, haec sunt:
> res non parta labore sed relicta;
> non ingratus ager, focus perennis;
> lis nunquam, toga rara, mens quieta;
> vires ingenuae, salubre corpus;
> prudens simplicitas, pares amici;
> convictus facilis, sine arte mensa;
> nox non ebria sed soluta curis;
> non tristis torus et tamen pudicus;
> somnus qui faciat breves tenebras:
> quod sis esse velis nihilque malis;
> summum nec metuas diem nec optes.

In the Halliwell-Phillipps collection at the Chetham library, Manchester, there is a broadside (formerly in the Heber ballad-collection), printed by John Awdeley in 1571, with Martial's verses in Latin accompanied by a translation into English and another into Welsh, the latter made by the Welsh poet Simwnt Vychan, or Vachan (1530?–1606). I am grateful to Professor F. N. Robinson for calling my attention to the reprint and the discussion of this broadside, by Evan J. Jones, in *The Bulletin of the Board of Celtic Studies*, III (1927), 286–297. The English version of 1571 runs thus:

> O Martial, thou most mery mate,
> These things do make mans life most blest,
> Goods not gotten by labour great,
> But left by friendes, now gone to rest,
> A fruitfull fielde, a fyre styll drest,
>   For sturdy strife no time to finde,
>   A seldome gowne, a quiet minde.
>
> Strength naturall, a body sound,
> Wyse simplenes, friendes like to thee,
> Prouisions easy to be found,
> A table where no Cookeries bée,
> No dronken night, but from cares frée,
>   No dolefull bed, yet of chast sorte,
>   Sleepe that may make the darknes short.
>
> That thing that thou thy selfe art made,
> And by iust lot pointed to bée,
> Do thou thy selfe firmly perswade,
> Still to remayne in eche degree,
> And let nought be more wisht of thée,
>   The day of death feare not one whit,
>   Nor yet do thou wish after it.

For purposes of comparison I reprint also the rendering made by Sir

Richard Fanshawe in *Il Pastor Fido ... With an Addition of divers other Poems*, 1648, p. 297:

> The things that makes a life to please
> (Sweetest *Martiall*) they are these:
> Estate *inherited*, not *got*:
> A *thankfull* Field, *Hearth* always hot:
> City *seldome*, Law-suits *never*:
> *Equall* Friends agreeing *ever*:
> Health of Body, *Peace* of *Minde*:
> *Sleepes* that till the Morning binde:
> *Wise* Simplicitie, *Plaine* Fare:
> Not *drunken* Nights, yet *loos'd* from *Care*:
> A *Sober*, not a *sullen* Spouse:
> *Cleane strength*, not such as *his* that Plowes:
> Wish onely what thou *art*, to *bee*;
> *Death* neither *wish*, nor *feare* to *see*.

Thomas Randolph's version (*Poems and Amyntas*, 1638, ed. J. J. Parry, 1917, p. 139) should also be cited. Berdan (*Early Tudor Poetry*, pp. 524–526) reprints translations made by Clément Marot before 1544 (*Œuvres*, ed. Pierre Jannet, 2d ed., 1873, III, 89–90), by R. Fletcher in 1656 (*Ex otio Negotium, or Martiall his Epigrams*, p. 93), and by an anonymous writer in 1695 (*Epigrams of Martial, Englished* [by Henry Killigrew, originally issued in 1689], p. 236); he also mentions a translation by Charles Cotton in 1689 (*Poems on Several Occasions*, p. 561). H. H. Hudson ("Surrey and Martial," *Modern Language Notes*, XXXVIII [1923], 481–483) refers to other versions given in John Manningham's *Diary* (ed. Bruce, Camden Society, 1868) under the date of June 9, 1602 (attributed to "Th. Sm."); in *The Dove and the Serpent* (by Daniel Tuville?), 1614, p. 90; and (by Ben Jonson?) in J. P. Collier's *Bibliographical and Critical Account of the Rarest Books*, I, 223. For further details of this sort see the Bohn edition of Martial's epigrams (1897), p. 471, and *Censura Literaria*, IV (1807), 195–196, X (1809), 81–82.

26. 11 *The houshold of continuance.* "An household, or family that is not of recent establishment, and promises to be of duration" (Nott).

20 (No. 28) *Praise of meane and constant estate.* In every edition (No. [32] in *B–I*, sigs. D4 in *BC*, B8 in *D–G*, B8–B8ᵛ in *H*, B7ᵛ–B8 in *I*). Padelford (pp. 78–79) reprints the poem from *A*, misprinting *withdraweth* (line 35) as *withdrawth*.

No. 28 is a translation of Horace's *Carmina*, II. 10. Since the same ode is likewise translated in Nos. 194 and 295, I reprint it below for the convenience of students:

> Rectius vives, Licini, neque altum
> semper urgendo neque, dum procellas
> cautus horrescis, nimium premendo
> litus iniquom.

Auream quisquis mediocritatem
diligit, tutus caret obsoleti
sordibus tecti, caret invidenda
    sobrius aula.

Saepius ventis agitatur ingens
pinus et celsae graviore casu
decidunt turres feriuntque summos
    fulgura montis.

Sperat infestis, metuit secundis
alteram sortem bene praeparatum
pectus. Informis hiemes reducit
    Iuppiter; idem

Summovet. Non, si male nunc, et olim
sic erit: quondam cithara tacentem
suscitat Musam neque semper arcum
    tendit Apollo.

Rebus angustis animosus atque
fortis appare: sapienter idem
contrahes vento nimium secundo
    turgida vela.

26. 22 *Thomas*. The annotator in *I* (Bodleian) explains this as "Sir Tho. Wiatt" (this note is not in *D**), and he has been followed by most of the editors of Surrey. More probably, however, as Padelford suggests, *Thomas* may refer to Surrey's son or his brother.

31 *falne turrets stepe*. "Lofty turrets fall." *Falne*, or *fallen*, is an old form of the third person plural indicative; hence Nott's emendation to *fall* is unwarranted.

27. 4 (No. 29) *Praise of certain psalmes, &c.* In every edition (No. [33] in *B–I*, sigs. D4ᵛ in *BC*, B8ᵛ in *D–H*, B8 in *I*). Padelford (p. 77) prints the poem from a Harington MS. (Additional 36529), with the following variants:

27. 8 Asie rong] Asia range
   9 dan] yf
  10 song] sange
  19 imprinted] yprinted
  20 Ought] Mowght

No. 29 was apparently written as a commendatory poem for Wyatt's *Certayne Psalmes chosen out of the Psalter of David commonlye called thee. vii. penytentiall Psalmes* (printed in 1549), in the manuscript of which it is still to be seen.

9 *In the rich ark dan Homers rimes he placed*. This story is told in Plutarch's life of Alexander and is referred to in his *Morals* ("The First Oration concerning the Fortune or Virtue of Alexander the Great," §4). Nott (Surrey, p. 335) notes that it is mentioned in the opening lines of the dedication to the 1532 edition of John Gower's *Confessio Amantis*. Cf. also Thomas Lodge's *Reply to Gosson*, 1580? (Hunterian Club ed., p. 2), "what made *Alexander*

I pray you esteme of him [Homer] so much? why allotted he for his works so curious a closset?"; George Whetstone, *The Honorable Reputation of a Souldier*, 1585, E4ᵛ, "*Alexander* the great, was so addicted to *Homers Iliades*, as he appointed the most magnificēt Iewell boxe of *Darius* to keepe the same"; Nathaniel Baxter, *Sir Philip Sydneys Ourania*, 1606, A2ᵛ, "Great *Macedon* when he laid by his Launce, Sported himselfe with *Homers* golden verse"; Christopher Brooke, verses on Thomas Coryate in *The Odcombian Banquet*, 1611, sig. H,

> If he liu'd now that in *Darius* casket
> Plac'd the poore Iliads, hee had bought a basket
> Of richer stuffe t'intombe thy volume large.

See also the references in Shakespeare's *1 Henry VI*, i. vi. 24–25, and John Webster's *A Monumental Column*, 1613, line 18.

27. 11 *What holy graue, &c.* This line and its meter are discussed at length in *The Arte of English Poesie*, 1589, pp. 138–139.

13 *the liuely faith, and pure.* Nott cites a similar phrase, "the upright heart and pure," in *Paradise Lost*, I. 18.

21 (No. 30) *Of the death of . . . sir .T. w.* In every edition (No. [34] in B–I, sigs. D4ᵛ in *BC*, B8ᵛ in *D–G*, B8ᵛ–C in *H*, B8–B8ᵛ in *I*). Padelford (p. 80) prints the poem from a Harington MS. (Additional 36529), with the variants of *that livelye hedd* (line 24) for *thy liuelyhed*, and *sowne* (line 25) for *swolne*.

24 *Some, that in presence, &c.* Referring to Wyatt's enemies Edmund Bonner and Simon Heynes, who accused him of various crimes and thus caused his imprisonment in 1540. Lines 24 and 26 are quoted, somewhat inexactly, in *The Arte of English Poesie*, 1589, p. 139, to illustrate the use of dactyls and iambics.

26 *Ceasars teares vpon Pompeius hed.* Suggested by a sonnet of Petrarch's that is the source of No. 45. See 36. 5 n.

34 *And kisse the ground, whereas, &c.* Cf. Chaucer's *Troilus and Criseyde*, v. 1791, "And kis the steppes, wher-as thou seest pace Virgile," etc.

28. 2 (No. 31) *Of the same.* In every edition (No. [35] in B–I, sigs. D4ᵛ–E in *BC*, B8ᵛ–C in *D–GI*, C–Cᵛ in *H*). Padelford (pp. 81–82) reprints the poem from *A*, misprinting *disdayn* (line 4) as *disdain*, *loft* (line 29) as *lost*, *Liued* (line 33) as *Lieud*, *heauens* (line 40) as *heavens*.

Surrey had a passionate admiration and respect for Wyatt, as is attested also by Nos. 29, 30, 263. The present elegy was very likely Surrey's first appearance in print. It originally formed a part of an eight-page booklet (a unique copy of which is in the Huntington library) called "¶An excellent Epi =/ taffe of syr Thomas Wyat, With two/ other compendious dytties, wherin are/ touchyd, and set furth the state/ of mannes lyfe./" (A woodcut portrait follows this title.) The colophon runs, "¶Imprynted at London by Iohn Her =/ forde for Roberte Toye./" Although the pamphlet has no date, it was undoubtedly printed shortly after Wyatt's death in October, 1542. Because of its value as a text printed in Surrey's own lifetime, I give this "Epitaffe" exactly as it stands in the original:

Wyat resteth here, that quicke coulde neuer rest.
　　Whose heuenly gyftes, encreased by dysdayne
And vertue sanke, the deper in his brest
　　Suche profyte he, of enuy could optayne

¶A Head, where wysdom mysteries dyd frame
　　Whose hammers beat styll in that lyuely brayne
As on a styth, where some worke of Fame
　　Was dayly wrought, to turn to Brytayns game

¶A Vysage sterne and mylde, where both dyd groo
　　Vyce to contempne, in vertues to reioyce
Amyd great stormes, whome grace assured soo
　　To lyue vprighte and smyle at fortunes choyse.

¶A Hand that taught, what might be saide in rime
　　That refte Chaucer, the glorye of his wytte
A marke, the whiche (vnperfited for tyme)
　　Some may approche but neuer none shall hyt.

¶A Tonge, that serued in foraine realmes his king
　　Whose curtoise talke, to vertu dyd enflame.
Eche noble harte a worthy guyde to brynge
　　Our Englysshe youth, by trauayle vnto fame.

¶An Eye, whose iudgement, no affect coulde blind
　　Frendes to allure, and foes to reconcyle
Whose pearcynge looke, dyd represent a mynde.
　　with vertue fraught, reposed, voyde of gyle.

¶A Harte, where drede, yet neuer so imprest
　　To hide the thought ẏ might the trouth auaunce
In neyther fortune, lyfte nor so represt
　　To swell in welth, nor yelde vnto mischaunce

¶A valiaunt Corps, where force and beautye met
　　Happy, alas, to happy but for foos.
Lyued, and ran the race that nature set
　　Of manhodes shape, where she the mold did loos

¶But to the heauens, that symple soule is fleed.
　　Which lefte with such, as couet Christe to knowe
Witnes of faith that neuer shalbe deade
　　Sent for our welth, but not receiued so
Thus for our gylt, this iewell haue we lost
　　The earth his bones, the heuen possesse his goost

AMEN.

Peter Betham probably had the foregoing copy of No. 31 in mind when he wrote, in the dedication to *The preceptes of Warre*, 1544 (*Censura Literaria*, VII [1808], 70): "Wyate was a worthye floure of our tounge, as appereth by the mournefulle ballet made of hys death in Englysshe, whyche is mooste wittye, fyne, and eloquent."

28. 3 *W. resteth.* It is curious that only *D* and *D** have the reading (shown to be correct by that of the 1542 text given above) *VVyat resteth*, which *E+* change to *What resteth*.

4 *giftes encreased by disdayn.* That is, increased by his own disdain of them: he did not boast of his gifts.

8 *Whose hammers bet styll in that liuely brayn.* Perhaps a reference to a line in one of Wyatt's poems (ed. Foxwell, I, 306) that is not in *A+*:

> Suche hammers worke within my hed
> That sounde nought els into my eris.

But similar expressions were used by Richard Edwards about 1560 (*Life and Poems*, ed. Leicester Bradner, 1927, p. 103), "When famies [evidently a misprint for *fansies*] hammer bettes there fonde and idle braynes"; by George Gascoigne in 1566 (*Supposes*, v. iv, *Complete Poems*, ed. Hazlitt, I, 247), "he hath so many hammers in his head, that his braynes are ready to burst"; and by Henry Robarts in 1600 (*Haigh for Devonshire*, H3), "*Iames* that had many hammers beating in his braines, was more set a worke by this vnexpected chance." Cf. also Grosart's Breton, I, *n*, 9.

32–33 *Happy, alas, to happy, &c.* Nott shows that Surrey uses these phrases again in his translation of the *Aeneid*, IV. 876.

34 *where she the molde did lose.* The same conceit reappears in No. 20 (19. 41–20. 2-5).

36–37 *Which left . . . Witnesse of faith, &c.* Evidently alluding to Wyatt's translation of the Seven Penitential Psalms (see the notes to No. 29).

40 *The earth his bones, the heauens possesse his gost.* A reminiscence of a familiar passage in Ecclesiastes, xii. 7. A similar idea was expressed in the inscription in memory of Sir Philip Sidney that hung in old St. Paul's Cathedral (see H. H. Milman, *Annals of S. Paul's Cathedral*, 1869, p. 379; *The Dr. Farmer Chetham MS.*, ed. Grosart, II, 180; Thomas Zouch, *Memoirs of . . . Sir Philip Sidney*, 1808, p. 288), the last stanza of which ran:

> His bodie hath England, for she it bred;
> Netherlands his blood, in her defence shed;
> The Heavens have his soule, the Arts have his fame,
> All Souldiers the grief, the World his good name.

Hannah (*The Courtly Poets*, 1870, p. 215) cites "one of the epitaphs on Raleigh" with the lines,

> Heaven hath his soul; the world his fame;
> The grave his corpse; Stukeley his shame.

A similar passage occurs in an "Epitaph" on Sidney by Raleigh: see Hannah, p. 7, and *The Phoenix Nest*, 1593, p. 10.

29. 2 (No. 32) *Of Sardinapalus dishonorable life, &c.* In every edition (No. [37] in *B–I*, sigs. E^v in *BC*, C^v in *D–G*, C^v–C2 in *H*, C in *I*). Padelford (pp. 77–78) prints the poem from a Harington MS. (Additional 36529), with the following variants:

> 29. 5 Thassirian] Th' Assyryans
>   7 on] a
>   8 Did yeld, vanquisht] Vaynquyshed, dyd yelde
>   9 dint] dent
>   14. *Comes after line 18 in Padelford but not in the MS.*
>   15 impacient] vnpacyent
>   17 appalled] appawld
>   18 Murthered] Murdred

"*Sardanapalus*," says Richard Robinson in *The rewarde of Wickednesse*, 1574, K2^v, "the last Assirian King liued too vile a life to bee rehearsed." Melbancke, *Philotimus*, 1583, Aa4, remarks that "*Sardanapalus* king of *Assiria*, one of the richest *Monarchies* in the world, amid his pompous eleuated royalties, was miserably slaine by one *Arbactus*." The story is told at length, among many other places, in Sir Richard Barckley's *A Discourse of the Felicitie of Man*, 1598, pp. 11–13, which represents Sardanapalus as causing himself with his wives and treasures to be burned, whereupon the throne was seized by his lieutenant Arbaces.

19 (No. 33) *How no age is content, &c.* In every edition (No. [38] in *B–I*, sigs. E^v–E2 in *BC*, C^v–C2 in *D–G*, C2 in *H*, C^v in *I*). Padelford (p. 79) prints the poem from a Harington MS. (Additional 28635), with the following variants:

> 29. 27 sighed] sight: doth] did
> 30. 4 wytherd] witheryd
>   5 dented chewes] dynted jawes
>   14 sighed] sight

There is also a copy of the first twelve lines of No. 33 in MS. Cotton Titus A. xxiv, fol. 83. The general idea of the poem was perhaps suggested by Horace's first satire, "Qui fit Maecenas, ut nemo, quam sibi sortem," etc.

A shortened and otherwise considerably changed version of No. 33 appears in *Brittons Bowre of Delights*, 1591, G2–G2^v (1597, F2^v), at the instance, doubtless, not of Breton but of the publisher Richard Jones. It runs thus:

> *A pleasant sweet song.*
>
> L Aid in my restlesse bed,
>   In dreame of my desire:
> I sawe within my troubled head,
> A heape of thoughts appeare.

And each of them so strange,
  In sight before mine eyes:
That now I sigh and then I smile,
  As cause thereby doth rise.

I see how that the little boy,
  In thought how oft that he:
Doth wish of God to scape the rod,
  a tall yong man to be,

I saw the yong man trauelling,
  From sport to paines opprest:
How he would be a rich olde man,
  To liue and lie at rest.

The olde man too, who seeth,
  His age to drawe on sore:
Would be a little boy againe,
  To liue so long the more.

Whereat I sigh and smile,
  How *Nature* craues her fee:
From boy to man, from man to boy,
  Would chop and change degree.

29. 21–23 *if they had skill to vnderstand it.* From Virgil's *Georgics*, II. 458–459, "O fortunatos nimium, sua si bona norint, agricolas!"

24 *Layd in my quiet bed.* Humfrey Gifford's "A Dreame" (in *A Posie of Gilloflowers*, 1580, *Poems*, ed. Grosart, *Miscellanies of the Fuller Worthies' Library*, I, 349–352) begins by imitating this line: "Layd in my quiet bed to rest."

27 *as cause of thought doth ryse.* The past tense *did*, as in *B+* and the MS., is preferable.

28–35 *I saw the lytle boy in thought, &c.* This passage, which was no doubt suggested by Horace, is practically duplicated by a poem in the *Paradise*, p. 62.

30 *his bones with paines opprest.* That is, tired with manual labor, not with infirmity.

30. 12 *Hang vp therfore the bit, &c.* Melbancke, *Philotimus*, 1583, E4ᵛ, borrows this line, combining it with 157. 9: "to see youth hang vp ẙ bitt of wanton tyme, not like ẙ foolish larke, deceiued with swetnes of ẙ call."

18 (No. 34) *Bonum est mihi, &c.* In every edition (No. [39] in *B–I*, sigs. E2–E2ᵛ in *BC*, C2–C2ᵛ in *D–H*, Cᵛ–C2 in *I*). Padelford (p. 76) reprints the poem from *A*, misprinting *growne* (line 24) as *grown*, *pardie* (line 29) as *perdie*, *nyght* (line 32) as *night*. The title in *A* ("It is good for me that thou hast afflicted me") is almost a literal translation of Psalms cxix. 71, "It is good for me that I have been afflicted." In the Vulgate (where the reference is Psalms cxviii. 71) the corresponding verse runs, "Bonum mihi quia humiliasti me."

No. 34 is written on the order of a sonnet: in its seventeen lines there are five rhymes ending with a couplet. Nott (Surrey, pp. 359–361) believes that a line rhyming with 25 is missing after 26, and hence he supplies "Who lives in privacy, is only blest." Even then the syntax and meaning of the whole passage remain obscure. Nott likewise points out that Surrey's son, Henry Howard, Earl of Northampton, asserted this to be the last poem Surrey wrote; but he is inclined to refer its composition to an earlier period of imprisonment than that of December, 1546–January, 1547, which immediately preceded the poet's execution. There is, however, no urgent reason for disputing Northampton's statement.

30. 37 (No. 35) *Exhortacion to learne by others trouble.* In every edition (No. [40] in *B–I*, sigs. E2ᵛ in *BC*, C2ᵛ in *D–H*, C2 in *I*). Padelford (p. 77) reprints the poem from *A*, misprinting *plages* (31. 5) as *plagues*.

31. 2 *My Ratclif.* Nicolas (*Poetical Works of Surrey and Wyatt*, 1 [1831], 68 n.) explains, "Perhaps Sir Humphrey Ratcliffe, one of the gentlemen pensioners." Padelford (p. 193) says, "addressed presumably to Thomas Radcliffe, third Earl of Sussex (b. 1526 [?]), who took part with Surrey in the military operations against France in 1544."

3 *Receue thy scourge by others chastisement.* Nott compares with Tibullus, III. vi. 43–44,

> vos ego nunc moneo: felix, quicumque dolore
> alterius disces posse cavere tuos.

Compare also the proverb, "Fœlix quem faciunt aliena pericula cautum," which is discussed in my notes to the *Gorgeous Gallery*, p. 193.

6 *Salomon sayd, the wronged shall recure.* Nott appears to quote, though with curious deviations, Ecclesiasticus xxvii. 21 (not, as he says, xxvii. 25), "As for a wound, it may be bound up; and after reviling there may be reconcilement: but he that bewrayeth secrets is without hope." The author of Ecclesiasticus was not Solomon but an imitator of Solomon, Jesus, the son of Sirach.

7 *Wiat said.* See 70. 15 and 80. 19.

8 (No. 36) *The fansie of a weried louer.* In every edition (No. [41] in *B–I*, sigs. E2ᵛ in *BC*, C2ᵛ in *D–G*, C2ᵛ–C3 in *H*, C2 in *I*). Padelford (p. 48) reprints the poem from *A*, misprinting *Seemed* (line 12) for *Semed*. The reference in line 21 to "base Bullayn" establishes the date of composition of this sonnet as between September, 1545, and March, 1546 — the period during which Surrey, as lieutenant-general on the Continent, commanded Boulogne. Bapst (*Deux gentilshommes-poètes*, pp. 332–333) considers the sonnet Surrey's lament for his enforced separation from his wife. Nott, as might be expected, tries to connect it with the Fair Geraldine.

19 *my guyde* is probably Reason.

22–23 *as restlesse to remayn, &c.* That is, rather than remain any longer he will willingly bear the pain that (in line 15) he sought to escape.

32. 2 (No. 37) *The louer for shamefastnesse, &c.* In every edition (No. [42] in *B–I*, sigs. E3 in *BC*, C3 in *D–H*, C2ᵛ in *I*). Miss Foxwell (1, 14) prints the poem from MS. Egerton 2711, with the following variants:

32. 5 I] doeth
    6 my] myn: doth] doeth
    8 there] therein: displaying] spreding
    9 learns] lerneth: to ²] *Om.*
    12 takes] taketh
    13 loue to] all unto

The poem is another translation of the Petrarchan sonnet on which No. 6 is based.

    5 *The longe loue, that in my thought I harber.* The movement of this line is rough, though Tottel's editor tried hard to smooth it. In *E+* the attempt was continued by changing the line to read *The one long loue, &c.* That change made *long* unmistakably a monosyllable and accented *harber* on the first syllable, but it left the eighth line unaffected.

    19 (No. 38) *The louer waxeth wiser, &c.* In every edition (No. [43] in *B–I*, sigs. E3 in *BC*, C3 in *D–G*, C3–C3ᵛ in *H*, C2ᵛ in *I*). Miss Foxwell (1, 16) prints the poem from MS. Egerton 2711, with the following variants:

32. 22 Yet was I neuer] Was I never yet: agreued] greved
    23 doth] doeth
    27 haue fixed] yfixed
    28 my sprite] the sperit
    29 boones] bonys
    31 Content . . . withouten] May content you, withoute
    33 you] ye
    34 wrath] disdain: you ¹· ²] ye
    35 haue] hath

The source of No. 38 is Petrarch, sonetto in vita 53 (*Rime*, 82, p. 91):

> Io non fu' d' amar voi lassato unquancho,
> Madonna, né sarò mentre ch' io viva;
> ma d' odiar me medesmo giunto a riva
> et del continuo lagrimar so stancho;
> et voglio anzi un sepolcro bello et biancho,
> che 'l vostro nome a mio danno si scriva
> in alcun marmo, ove di spirto priva
> sia la mia carne, che po star seco ancho.
> Però, s' un cor pien d' amorosa fede
> può contentarve, senza farne stracio,
> piacciavi omai di questo aver mercede.
> Se 'n altro modo cerca d' esser sacio
> vostro sdegno, **erra**; et non fia quel che crede;
> di che Amor et me stesso assai ringracio.

33. 2 (No. 39) *The abused louer, &c.* In every edition (No. [44] in *B–I*, sigs. E3ᵛ in *BC*, C3ᵛ in *D–H*, C2ᵛ–C3 in *I*). Miss Foxwell (1, 21) prints the poem from MS. Egerton 2711, with the following variants:

        33. 5 There was never ffile: half so well filed
              6 any] every
              8 other] othrs: that] *Om.*
              9 loe] *Om.*
             10 pardoned] pardond
             11 of my] *Om.*
             12 led me] did me lede: me misguided] guyded
             13 of] of full
             17 playnd] plained
             18 is] *Om.*

19 (No. 40) *The louer describeth, &c.* In every edition (No. [45] in *B–I*, sigs. E3ᵛ in *BC*, C3ᵛ in *D–H*, C3 in *I*). Miss Foxwell (1, 32) prints the poem from MS. Egerton 2711, with the following variants:

        33. 23 there] ne
             24 perst my] prest myn
             27 Sunne] The sonne
             30 striken] ystricken
             31 Blind] Blynded: and ¹] *Om*
             32 nor] ne
             33 fall] falt
             34 streight] *Om.*
             35 noyse] nay

The poem is very freely adapted from Petrarch, sonetto in vita 200 (*Rime*, 258, pp. 245–246):

                    Vive faville uscian de' duo bei lumi
                    ver me sí dolcemente folgorando,
                    et parte d'un cor saggio sospirando
                    d' alta eloquentia sí soavi fiumi,
                    che pur il rimembrar par mi consumi
                    qualor a quel dí torno, ripensando
                    come venieno i miei spirti mancando
                    al variar de' suoi duri costumi.
                    L' alma nudrita sempre in doglia e 'n pene
                    (quanto è 'l poder d' una prescritta usanza!)
                    contra 'l doppio piacer sí 'nferma fue,
                    ch' al gusto sol del disusato bene
                    tremando or di paura or di speranza,
                    d' abandonarme fu spesso entra due.

No. 40 is imitated in a poem beginning, "The liuelie sparkes of those two eyes," in the *Handful*, 1584, pp. 55–56.

22–24 *The liuely sparkes . . . perst my hart.* Cf. 63. 37–38 n. Miss Foxwell (II, 47) cites another parallel in Dante, *La Vita Nuova*, XIX. 68–71:

Degli occhi suoi, come ch' ella gli mova,
Escono spirti d' amore infiammati,
Che fieron gli occhi a qual che allor gli guati,
E passan si che 'l cor ciascun ritrova.

33. 35 *Of deadly noyse.* For *noyse* read *nay* with the MS.

34. 2 (No. 41) *The waueryng louer wylleth, &c.* In every edition (No. [46] in *B–I*, sigs. E4 in *BC*, C4 in *D–G*, C3ᵛ–C4 in *H*, C3–C3ᵛ in *I*). Miss Foxwell (1, 33) prints the poem from MS. Egerton 2711, with the following variants:

    34. 7 Makes] Maketh
       8 bids] bid
       9 my] myn
      11 lockyng] lacking
      12 So] She: she] as fast: *in the MS. line* 12 *comes after line* 8
      14 ruth] pitie
      15 comfortes] comforteth
      16 And, therewithall bolded, I seke the way how
      17 forth] *Om.*:   I bide] that I suffre

By printing line 12 out of place Tottel gave this sonnet the peculiar rhyme-scheme *abba bbaa cddc ee.* In the MS. the second quatrain rhymes correctly *abba.*

The source of No. 41 is Petrarch, sonetto in vita 117 (*Rime*, 169, pp. 175–176):

Pien d' un vago penser che me desvia
da tutti gli altri et fammi al mondo ir solo,
ad or ad ora a me stesso m'involo,
pur lei cercando che fuggir devria;
et veggiola passar sí dolce et ria,
che l' alma trema per levarsi a volo,
tal d'armati sospir conduce stuolo
questa bella d' Amor nemica et mia!
Ben, s' i' non erro, di pietate un raggio
scorgo fra 'l nubiloso altero ciglio,
che 'n parte rasserena il cor doglioso:
allor raccolgo l' alma; et poi ch' i' aggio
di scovrirle il mio mal preso consiglio,
tanto gli ò a dir che 'ncominciar non oso.

19 (No. 42) *The louer hauing dreamed, &c.* In every edition (No. [47] in *B–I*, sigs. E4 in *BC*, C4 in *D–H*, C3ᵛ in *I*). Miss Foxwell (1, 38) prints the poem from MS. Egerton 2711, with the following variants:

    34. 28 broughtest] broughtes: these] this: seas] mew
      29 to] *Om.*:   tencrease] to renew
      30 delight timbrace] succor to embrace
      32 the other] thothr

34 But thus return] Retorning
35 could] it could
36 do] they

The source of No. 42 is Marcello Filosseno's strambotto (*Sylve*, 1507, I2),

> Pareami in questa nocte esser contento
> che tecco iunxi al disiato effecto
> deh fossio sempre in tal dormir attento
> poi che il ciel non mi porge altro dilecto
> ma il gra*n* piacer mutosse *in* gran torme*n*to
> qua*n*do che solo me trouai nel lecto
> ne duolmi gia chel son*n*o mha ingan*n*ato
> ma duolmi sol che sonno sogno e stato.

35. 2 (No. 43) *The louer vnhappy biddeth, &c.* In every edition (No. [48] in *B–I*, sigs. E4ᵛ in *BC*, C4ᵛ in *D–G*, C4–C4ᵛ in *H*, C3ᵛ in *I*). Miss Foxwell (1, 39) prints the poem from MS. Egerton 2711, with the following variants:

35. 6 Ye] You: swete abundance] habundaunce
7 of] and
8 do way] do away
10 of] in
11 my missehappes vnhappy] the happs most unhappy
14 Stephan] Sephanes
15 of] of the
17 wittes] liff
19 Ioye] Reioyse

No. 43 is paraphrased and greatly expanded by Turbervile (*Epitaphes*, etc., 1567, pp. 195–198) in a poem called "The Lover hoping in May to have had redresse of his woes . . . bewailes his cruell hap."

8–9 *Aryse for shame, &c.*   Cf. Chaucer, *Troilus and Criseyde*, II. 111–112,

> Do wey your book, rys up, and lat us daunce,
> And lat us don to May som observaunce;

also *The Knight's Tale*, A. 1042, 1045,

> For May wol have no slogardye a-night. . . .
> And seith, "Arys, and do thyn observaunce."

11–12 *missehappes vnhappy, That me betide in May.* Wyatt was imprisoned in England in May, 1534, and May, 1536, as well as (probably in May) in Italy in 1527.

13 *As one whom loue list little to aduance.* Cf. Chaucer, *Troilus and Criseyde*, I. 518, "Of hem that Love list febly for to avaunce."

14 *Stephan*, evidently a person who had cast Wyatt's horoscope. The MS. calls him Sephanes.

35. 20 (No. 44) *The louer confesseth him in loue with Phillis.* In every edition (No. [49] in *B–I*, sigs. E4ᵛ in *BC*, C4ᵛ in *D–H*, C4 in *I*). Miss Foxwell (I, 40) prints the poem from MS. Egerton 2711, with the following variants:

> 35. 26 or ¹] to: slack] slake: pace to] passe
>   27 Be] By
>   33 and] my
>   34 doth] doeth

For an imitation of No. 44 by Turbervile see his *Epitaphes*, etc., 1567, pp. 68–69.

The opening lines and the general idea of the sonnet were suggested by Petrarch, sonetto in vita 169, lines 1–4 (*Rime*, 224, p. 220):

> S' una fede amorosa, un cor non finto,
> un languir dolce, un desiar cortese;
> s' oneste voglie in gentil foco accese,
> un lungo error in cieco laberinto.

22–25, 27 *If waker care, &c.* In *The Arte of English Poesie*, 1589, p. 187, these lines are quoted as an example of the device "*Irmus*, or the Long loose," where "all the whole sence of the dittie is suspended till ye come to the last three wordes, *then do I loue againe*, which finisheth the song with a full and perfit sence." Cf. 44. 7–13 n.

29, 31 *Brunet.* Possibly meant for Anne Boleyn.

30 *Phillis.* This lady cannot be identified. Miss Foxwell (II, 52–53) arbitrarily and illogically makes her out to be Mary Howard, Duchess of Richmond, sister of the poet Surrey.

36. 2 (No. 45) *Of others fained sorrow, &c.* In every edition (No. [50] in *B–I*, sigs. F in *BC*, C5 in *D–G*, C4ᵛ–C5 in *H*, C4 in *I*). Miss Foxwell (I, 13) prints the poem from MS. Egerton 2711, with the following variants:

> 36. 7 hartes] *Om.*
>   8 outward] owteward
>   9 Eke Hannibal] And Hannyball, eke: outshyt] shitt
>   13 me] it oft
>   16 that] *Om.*:   laugh] laught: at any] any tyme or
>   17 because] for bicause: none other] nother

No. 45 is translated from Petrarch, sonetto in vita 70 (*Rime*, 102, pp. 105–106):

> Cesare, poi che 'l traditor d' Egitto
> li fece il don de l' onorata testa,
> celando l' allegrezza manifesta,
> pianse per gli occhi fuor, sí come è scritto;
> et Hanibal, quando a l'imperio afflitto
> vide farsi fortuna sí molesta,
> rise fra gente lagrimosa et mesta,
> per isfogare il suo acerbo despitto;

> et cosí aven che l' animo ciascuna
> sua passion sotto 'l contrario manto
> ricopre co la vista or chiara or bruna.
> Però s' alcuna volta io rido o canto,
> facciol perch' i' non ò se non quest' una
> via da celare il mio angoscioso pianto.

An entirely different translation in a Harington MS. (Additional 36529, fol. 45ᵛ) runs thus:

> Cesare what time the wise and valiant hed
> By [From] traitors hand for present hym was broght
> Cloking the Joy the whole world saw [might see,] it wroght
> Outwardlie wept what euer inward bred
> Haniball eke whan he saw fortune fled
> And thempire skorged as no man wold haue thought
> Amides the troupe of wiping eyes he laught
> To slake the rage his kendled furi fed
> So chancith it that eache mind doth assay
> To hyde his harme ẘ cloke of diuerse hew
> As passions pearce ẘ looke now grime now gay
> Therfore [Wherfore] if I chance sing or smile a new
> It is [think it] for that I can none other way
> Couer the plaintes that still my life pursew.

The bracketed words in the foregoing sonnet represent subsequent changes in the text. For a later translation see Davison's *A Poetical Rhapsody*, 1602 (ed. A. H. Bullen, I, 90–91).

　　36. 5 *the traytour of Egypt.* Melbancke, *Philotimus*, 1583, Dᵛ–D2, re-marks: "*Pompey* was cut shorter by y̆ head thē he was, whereof *Petolomie* making merchandise sould it to *Cesar.*" Stephen Batman, *The trauayled Pylgrime*, 1569, D4ᵛ, writes of "*Pompey* . . . which lost his head by *Ptolomeus* feate," and in a marginal note states that Plutarch "sayth, that one Titius slew Pompey, but Polichronicon, that yong Ptolomie did cut of his head, and sent it to Iulius Cesar thinking to haue done him great pleasure, but he was therwith verie sorie." In his life of Pompey, Plutarch asserts that "when one of the Egyptians was sent to present him [Caesar] with Pompey's head, he turned away from him with abhorrence as from a murderer; and on receiving his seal . . . he burst into tears." Plutarch's life of Caesar informs us that when that conqueror "came to Alexandria, where Pompey was already mur-dered, he would not look upon Theodotus, who presented him with his head, but taking only his signet, shed tears." This episode (which, of course, is treated at length in the ninth book of Lucan's *Pharsalia*) became a common-place in English poetry. See the *Paradise*, p. 245, where various illustrations are cited. To them might be added a passage from Lodowick Lloyd's *The Consent of Time*, 1590, p. 389: "It is written that when *Alexander* saw *Darius* dead, hee wept and couered his bodie with his owne cloake: so wept *Iulius Cæsar* when he saw the head of *Pompey.*" Cf. also 27. 26 n.

36. 19 (No. 46) *Of change in minde.* In every edition (No. [51] in *B–I*, sigs. F in *BC*, C5 in *D–H*, C4–C4ᵛ in *I*). Miss Foxwell (1, 17) prints the poem from MS. Egerton 2711, with the following variants:

36. 20 telth] telleth
22 purpose] propose
23 ech] every
27 diuersnesse doth] dyvernes doeth
28 this . . . blamen] that blame this dyvernes
30 you ¹, ²] ye: that] the same
31 doth] doeth

34 (No. 47) *How the louer perisheth, &c.* In every edition (No. [52] in *B–I*, sigs. F–Fᵛ in *BC*, C5–C5ᵛ in *D–H*, C4ᵛ in *I*). Miss Foxwell (1, 22) prints the poem from MS. Egerton 2711, with the following variants:

37. 3 Against] Agayn
4 doth] doeth
5 Neuer appeare] Do never pere
6 to] that: so] *Om.*
7 they] they do
8 But find] And fynde the
9 may I] I may
11 Yet] And yet
12 So . . . remembrance] Remembraunce so foloweth me
13 That] So that: my] *Om.*
14 desteny] destyne: doth] doeth
15 And yet] Yet do

The source of No. 47 is Petrarch, sonetto in vita 15 (*Rime*, 19, pp. 13–14):

Son animali al mondo de sí altera
vista, che 'ncontra 'l sol pur si difende:
altri, però che 'l gran lume gli offende,
non escon fuor se non verso la sera:
et altri, col desio folle che spera
gioir forse nel foco perché splende,
provan l' altra vertú, quella ch' encende.
Lasso, el mio loco è 'n questa ultima schera!
Ch' i' non son forte ad aspectar la luce
di questa Donna, et non so fare schermi
di luoghi tenebrosi o d' ore tarde.
Però con gli occhi lagrimosi e 'nfermi
mio destino a vederla mi conduce:
et so ben ch' i' vo dietro a quel che m' arde.

An entirely different translation of this sonnet in a Harington MS. (Additional 36529, fol. 45ᵛ) runs thus:

Some kind of creaturs haue, so persing sight
They can behold, the glistring [shining] sonne so hie
And some again, cannot abide the bright
Nor come abrode, but when the night drawes nie

One other sort, becawse [by cawse] of shining [flaming] light
Hopes of great sport w̱ᵗ in the [through vaine lust hopes of sport in] fire to flie
And tast's by play, in ernest burning right
Alas and I, ame of this latter Rate
Those lightning [two faire] starrs, to vew I want much myght
And [Yet] for deffence, I know ther is no flight
Nor place so darke, can helpe nor ower so late
Wherfore I yeld, w̱ᵗʰ honor or w̱ᵗ blame
To folow wheare, I shalbe led by fate
All thoughe I know, I go as flie to flame.

The bracketed words represent later changes in the text. Still another transla-
tion was made by the author of *The Arte of English Poesie*, 1589, p. 249, who
observes that the lines have been "very well Englished by Sir *Thomas Wiat*
after his fashion, and by my selfe thus:

"There be some fowles of sight so prowd and starke,
    As can behold the sunne, and neuer shrinke,
    Some so feeble, as they are faine to vvinke,
    Or neuer come abroad till it be darke:
    Others there be so simple, as they thinke,
    Because it shines, to sport them in the fire,
    And feele vnware, the vvrong of their desire,
    Fluttring amidst the flame that doth them burne,
    Of this last ranke (alas) am I aright,
    For in my ladies lookes to stand or turne
    I haue no povver, ne find place to retire,
    Where any darke may shade me from her sight
    But to her beames so bright whilst I aspire,
    I perish by the bane of my delight."

The sonnet is printed throughout in italics.

37. 16 (No. 48) *Against his tong, &c.* In every edition (No. [53] in *B–I*,
sigs. Fᵛ in *BC*, C5ᵛ in *D–H*, C4ᵛ–C5 in *I*). Miss Foxwell (1, 23) prints the poem
from MS. Egerton 2711, with the following variants:

37. 18 still kept thee] have the still kept
    19 thee] have I the
    20 to] right
    23 thou standst] then standest thou: afraied] aferd
    24 one word be sayd] thou speke towerd
    25 It is as in dreme, unperfaict and lame
    26 agaynst] again
    27 I] fayn I
    29 ye] you
    31 doth] *Om.*:   declare] declareth

For an imitation of Wyatt's poem see Turbervile's *Epitaphes*, etc., 1567, pp.
181–182.

No. 48 is translated from Petrarch, sonetto in vita 34 (*Rime*, 49, p. 51):

Perch' io t' abbia guardato di menzogna
a mio podere et honorato assai,
ingrata lingua, già però non m' ài
redduto honor, ma facto ira et vergogna.
Ché quanto piú 'l tuo aiuto mi bisogna
per dimandar mercede, allor ti stai
sempre piú fredda; et se parole fai,
son imperfecte et quasi d' uom che sogna.
Lagrime triste, et voi tutte le notti
m' accompagnate ov' io vorrei star solo;
poi fuggite dinanzi a la mia pace.
Et voi, sí pronti a darmi angoscia et duolo,
sospiri, allor traete lenti et rotti.
Sola la vista mia del cor non tace.

37· 32 (No. 49) *Description of the contrarious passions, &c.* In every
edition (No. [54] in *B–I*, sigs. F^v–F2 in *BC*, C5^v–C6 in *D–G*, C5^v in *H*, C5
in *I*). Miss Foxwell (1, 24) prints the poem from MS. Egerton 2711, with the
following variants:

38. 2 aloft] above the wynde
  3 worlde] worold
  4 lockes nor loseth] loseth nor locketh
  5 holdes] holdeth
  6 lettes] letteth
  8 eye] Iyen: se] se; and
  9 wish] desire: yet] and yet: for] *Om.*
  12 Lo, thus] Likewise: both] boeth

No. 49 is translated from Petrarch, sonetto in vita 90 (*Rime*, 134, p. 147):

Pace non trovo et non ò da far guerra;
et temo et spero, et ardo et son un ghiaccio;
et volo sopra 'l cielo, et giaccio in terra;
et nulla stringo, et tutto 'l mondo abbraccio.
Tal m' à in pregion, che non m' apre né serra;
né per suo mi riten né scioglie il laccio;
et non m'ancide Amore et non mi sferra;
né mi vuol vivo né mi trae d'impaccio.
Veggio senza occhi et non ò lingua et grido;
et bramo di perir et cheggio aita;
et ò in odio me stesso et amo altrui.
Pascomi di dolor, piangendo rido;
egualmente mi spiace morte et vita.
In questo stato son, Donna, per vui.

Petrarch's sonnet is also imitated by No. 301, and is translated by Thomas
Watson in *The Hekatompathia*, 1582, sonnet 40 (ed. Arber, p. 76). See also
Richard Hill's poem in the *Paradise*, p. 80.

  35–36 *I Find no peace, and all my warre is done, &c.* Borrowed by
Melbancke, *Philotimus*, 1583, S3^v: "Ah deare *Aurelia*, my power is too weake

to make any warre, and yet I can find no peace, I am not scorcht with any
fire, and yet no cold adawes my heate." In *The Arte of English Poesie*, 1589,
p. 136, the two lines are quoted as examples of iambic verses constructed
entirely of monosyllables.

38. 4 *That lockes nor loseth, holdeth me in pryson.* "Love, who neither
locks nor unlocks (looseth), holds me in prison" (see Petrarch's fifth line,
above).

14 (No. 50) *The louer compareth, &c.* In every edition (No. [55] in
B–I, sigs. F2 in *BC*, C6 in *D–H*, C5 in *I*). Miss Foxwell (1, 26) prints the
poem from MS. Egerton 2711, with the following variants:

> 38. 18 Through] Thorrough: doth] doeth
>   19 my fo] myn enemy
>   23 doth] doeth
>   24 sighes] sightes
>   25 teares] teris
>   26 Haue] Hath
>   27 and] and eke
>   28 leade] led
>   29 Drownde] Drowned: be my] me

The source of No. 50 is Petrarch, sonetto in vita 137 (*Rime*, 189, pp. 189–
190):

> Passa la nave mia colma d' oblio
> per aspro mare, a mezza notte, il verno,
> enfra Scilla et Caribdi; et al governo
> siede 'l Signore, anzi 'l nimico mio.
> À ciascun remo un penser pronto et rio,
> che la tempesta e 'l fin par ch' abbi a scherno:
> la vela rompe un vento humido, eterno
> di sospir, di speranze et di desio.
> Pioggia di lagrimar, nebbia di sdegni
> bagna et rallenta le già stanche sarte,
> che son d' error con ignorantia attorto.
> Celansi i duo mei dolci usati segni;
> morta fra l' onde è la ragion et l' arte:
> tal ch' i' 'ncomincio a desperar del porto.

21 *And euery houre.* The MS. has *owre*, meaning "oar" (the "remo"
of the source), which the printer has rationalized to *houre*.

31 (No. 51) *Of douteous loue.* In every edition (No. [56] in *B–I*,
sigs. F2–F2ᵛ in *BC*, C6–C6ᵛ in *D–G*, C6 in *H*, C5ᵛ in *I*). Miss Foxwell (1, 27)
prints the poem from MS. Egerton 2711, with the following variants:

> 38. 32 those] these
>   33 abides . . . moistes] is that myn oft moisteth
>   35 To] For to: within] in: worldly] woroldly
> 39. 2 bitter findes the swete] fynde the swete bitter
>   3 there] *Om.*
>   4 then] *Om.*

39. 5 spurs] spurreth: brydleth] bridilleth: eke] *Om.*
     6 Thus is it in suche extremitie brought
     7 In frossen though nowe, and nowe it stondeth in flame
     8 Twixt . . . betwixt] Twyst misery and welth twyst
     9 With seldome] But few
    10 In] With
    11 lo] *Om.*

The source of No. 51 is Petrarch, sonetto in vita 121 (*Rime*, 173, p. 178):

> Mirando 'l sol de' begli occhi sereno,
> ov' è chi spesso i miei depinge et bagna,
> dal cor l'anima stanca si scompagna
> per gir nel paradiso suo terreno.
> Poi trovandol di dolce et d'amar pieno,
> quant' al mondo si tesse opra d' aragna
> vede; onde seco et con Amor si lagna
> ch'à sí caldi gli spron, sí duro 'l freno.
> Per questi extremi duo contrari et misti,
> or con voglie gelate or con accese,
> stassi cosí fra misera et felice.
> M' à pochi lieti et molti penser tristi;
> e 'l piú si pente de l'ardite imprese:
> tal frutto nasce di cotal radice.

38. 33 *Where he . . . moistes and washeth.* Referring to the lady's eyes, where dwells Cupid — he who moistens and bathes (literally, colors, or obscures, and moistens) the lover's own eyes with tears.

39. 11 *Of such a roote lo cometh frute frutelesse.* Petrarch says, "From such a root comes up such a fruit-tree." Wyatt unnecessarily adds that the tree bears no fruit. Cf. 47. 32.

12 (No. 52) *The louer sheweth, &c.* In every edition (No. [57] in *B–I*, sigs. F2ᵛ in *BC*, C6ᵛ in *D–G*, C6–C6ᵛ in *H*, C5ᵛ in *I*). Miss Foxwell (1, 86–87) prints the poem from MS. Egerton 2711, with the following variants:

39. 16 within] in
    17 Once . . . seen] I have sene
    18 once] *Om.*
    19 haue] *Om.*:   them selues] theimself
    21 in] with a
    23 especiall] in speciall
    25 did . . . shoulders] from her shoulders did
    27 And . . . so] Therewith all
    29 for] *Om.*:   awakyng] waking
    30 turnde now through] torned, thorough
    31 bitter] straunge
    34 vnkyndly so] so kyndely
    35 I wold fain knowe what she hath deserved

36 (No. 53) *To a ladie to answere directly, &c.* In every edition (No. [58] in *B–I*, sigs. F2ᵛ–F3 in *BC*, C6ᵛ–C7 in *D–G*, C6ᵛ in *H*, C6 in *I*). Miss

Foxwell (1, 83) prints the poem from MS. Egerton 2711, with the following variants:

> 40. 3, 4 you] ye
>   6 For] And: you] ye
>   7 burns] burneth
>   8 pity or ruth] any pitie
>   12 You] Ye

An answer to Wyatt's poem (beginning, "Of few wourdes *sir* you seme to be") is printed from the same MS. by Nott (Wyatt, p. 77) and Miss Foxwell (1, 83). The latter believes the source of No. 53 to be a douzaine by Mellin de Saint-Gelais (*Œuvres Poétiques*, 1719, p. 231) beginning, "S'amour vous a donné mon cœur en gage." The resemblance between the two poems is slight, even (where it is closest) in the final lines of each:

> S'il ne vous plaist, amis comme devant,
> Un autre aurez, & moy ne pouvant estre,
> Servant de vous, de moy je seray maistre.

    40. 14 (No. 54) *To his loue whom he had kissed, &c.* In every edition (No. [59] in *B–I*, sigs. F3 in *BC*, C7 in *D–G*, C6^v–C7 in *H*, C6 in *I*). Miss Foxwell (1, 46) prints the poem from MS. Egerton 2711, with the following variants:

> 40. 18 therin] then
>   19 Or haue I] Have I then
>   20 not] *Om.*
>   21 Reuenge . . . rediest] Then revenge you: and the next
>   22 my life it shall haue] shall have my lyffe

This epigram is a paraphrase of Serafino's strambotto (*Opere*, 1516, fol. 179^v):

> Incolpa donna amor se troppo io uolsi
>   Aggiungendo alla tua la bocca mia.
> Se pur punir miuoi di quel chio tolsi
>   Fá che concesso replicar mi sia.
> Che tal dolceza in quelli labri accolsi,
>   Chel spirto mio fú per fugirsi uia.
> Só che al secondo tocco uscirá fora
>   Bastar ti dé, che per tal fallo io mora.

    25 (No. 55) *Of the Ielous man that loued, &c.* In every edition (No. [60] in *B–I*, sigs. F3–F3^v in *BC*, C7–C7^v in *D–G*, C7 in *H*, C6 in *I*). Miss Foxwell (1, 47) prints the poem from MS. Egerton 2711, with the following variants:

> 40. 29 wandring] wandering
> 41. 3 the] that: had] *Om.*

Koeppel (*Studien*, pp. 77–78) compares the opening lines of this epigram with Ariosto's *Orlando Furioso*, I. 11 (ed. Pietro Papini, 1916, p. 3):

> Timida pastorella mai sí presta
> Non volse piede inanzi a serpe crudo,
> Come Angelica tosto il freno torse.

The same figure (which seems to be a commonplace) appears also in *Orlando Furioso*, XXXIX. 32 (p. 533), as well as in the *Iliad*, III. 33–36, and in the *Aeneid*, II. 378–381. Surrey, translating the passage in Virgil (1557, B3ᵛ–B4) borrows Wyatt's language:

> Like him that, wandring in the bushes thick,
> Tredes on the adder with his rechlesse foote,
> Rered for wrath swelling her speckled neck
> Dismayd, geues back al sodenly for fere.

41. 4 (No. 56) *To his loue from whom, &c.* In every edition (No. [61] in *B–I*, sigs. F3ᵛ in *BC*, C7ᵛ in *D–G*, C7 in *H*, C6–C6ᵛ in *I*). Miss Foxwell (I, 47) prints the poem from MS. Egerton 2711, with the following variants:

41. 6 nedes] nedeth: threatnyng] threning
10 finde] meit
11 both] boeth
12 reft my] toke from me an
13 then] nowe: one] thon: the other] thothr

The source of this epigram is Serafino's strambotto (*Opere*, 1516, fols. 170–170ᵛ), as Nott (Wyatt, p. 555) indicates:

> À che minacci, à che tanta ira e orgoglio,
> Per questo non farai chel furto renda.
> Non senza causa la tua man dispoglio
> Rapir quel daltri non fú mai mia menda.
> Famme citar dauanti amor chio uoglio,
> Che la ragion de luno & laltro intenda.
> Lei il cor mi tolse, & io gli hó tolto un guanto
> Vorró saper da te se un cor ual tanto.

In his *Epitaphes*, etc., 1567, pp. 179–180, Turbervile paraphrased and expanded No. 56, naming his poem "To a Gentlewoman from whome he tooke a Ring."

14 (No. 57) *Of the fained frend.* In every edition (No. [62] in *B–I*, sigs. F3ᵛ in *BC*, C7ᵛ in *D–G*, C7 in *H*, C6ᵛ in *I*). Miss Foxwell (I, 48) prints the poem from MS. Egerton 2711, with the following variants:

41. 16 the] thy
18 Thought he (*see* 41. 18 n.)] Though they
20 oft times he kindleth] oft knydeleth [?]
21 him self he] Om.

41. 18 *Thought he*. Read *Though thee* (with *B*+), where *thee* can mean either *to thee* or, with the MS., *they*. This phrase is misprinted *Thought he* in *A* only.

22 (No. 58) *The louer taught, &c.* In every edition (No. [63] in *B–I*, sigs. F3ᵛ–F4 in *BC*, C7ᵛ–C8 in *D–G*, C7–C7ᵛ in *H*, C6ᵛ in *I*). Miss Foxwell (I, 78) prints the poem from MS. Egerton 2711, with the following variants:

> 41. 28 The wyndy wordes, the Ies quaynt game
>   29 make] maketh
>   32 seke taccord] seketh to accorde
>   33 thus] *Om.*
> 42. 4 naught doth] yet nothing I
>   7 Should . . . vnto] And should I trust to
>   8 haue] hath
>   9 yet haue] hath
>   11 do I] I do

42. 13 (No. 59) *The louer complayneth, &c.* In every edition (No. [64] in *B–I*, sigs. F4 in *BC*, C8 in *D–G*, C7ᵛ–C8 in *H*, C7 in *I*). Miss Foxwell (I, 79–80) prints the poem from MS. Egerton 2711, with the following variants:

> 42. 16 Both] Boeth
>   18 oft forced ye] ye oft forced
>   19 lo] *Om.:*   my] myn
>   20 Emong whome pitie I fynde doeth remayn
>   24 moisture] moystor
>   26 I endure] to suffre
>   27 hugy] howyy
>   29 alas doth] helas doeth
>   32 thus framed] this joyned
>   33 beauty] beaultie
>   34 No grace to me from the there may procede
>   35 reward] rewarded

No. 59 is based on Serafino's strambotto (*Opere*, 1516, fol. 125):

> Laer che sente el mesto e gran clamore
>   Diuulga in ogni parte la mia doglia
> Tal che per compassione del mio dolore
>   Par che ne treme in arbore ogni foglia,
> Ogni fiero animal posa el furore
>   Che daiutarmi ognun par chabbia uoglia
> Et con mugito stran uoglion le carmi
>   Et uorrian sol parlar per consolarmi.

20 *Amonge whom, such.* In *B*+ *such* is changed to *ruth*, corresponding to *pitie* in the MS.

36 (No. 60) *The louer reioyseth against fortune, &c.* In every edition (No. [65] in *B–I*, sigs. F4–F4ᵛ in *BC*, C8–C8ᵛ in *D–G*, C8 in *H*, C7–C7ᵛ in *I*). Miss Foxwell (I, 81–82) prints the poem from MS. Egerton 2711, with the following variants:

43. 2 not] not well
   5 makst the] causeth: dolourous] dolours
   9 hast set me] me set
   10 by] thy
   11 mindes] mynd: mayst] may: so] *Om.*
   12 For . . . it] And honeste, and it
   14 me trapt] trapped
   15 hapt] happed
   16 hindryng . . . thou] hindering thou diddest
   19 then didst thou] thou diddist
   20 didst] diddist
   21 wouldst] wouldest: wrapt] lapped
   22 hapt] happed

43. 4–6 *Thou fortune with thy diuers play, &c.* It seems likely, as Nott (Wyatt, p. 547) suggests, that Wyatt had in mind Horace's *Carmina*, III. 29,

> Fortuna saevo laeta negotio et
> ludum insolentem ludere pertinax
> transmutat incertos honores,
> nunc mihi nunc alii benigna.

23 (No. 61) *A renouncing of hardly escaped loue.* In every edition (No. [66] in *B–I*, sigs. F4ᵛ–G in *BC*, C8ᵛ–D in *D–G*, C8–C8ᵛ in *H*, C7ᵛ in *I*). Miss Foxwell (I, 77) prints the poem from MS. Egerton 2711, with the following variants:

43. 25 hart] rayn
   27 and wofully] yet shall suretie
   28 Conduyt my thoght of Joyes nede
   29 such] *Om.*
   33 escapt] escaped
   34 he] that: and] *Om.*
   37 my] myn
   38 a part] apart
44. 2 astart] estert
   3 among] emong

44. 4 (No. 62) *The louer to his bed, &c.* In every edition (No. [67] in *B–I*, sigs. G in *BC*, D in *D–G*, C8ᵛ in *H*, C7ᵛ–C8 in *I*). Miss Foxwell (I, 66) prints the poem from MS. Additional 17492, with the following variants:

44. 7 renewer] revyver
   10 myne] and my
   11 remembrer of] remembryng
   14 frosty snowes] frost, the snow
   15 heat of sunne] yet no heate
   16 so great] mete
   17 cure] care
   18 Renewyng] Revyvyng
   19 effectes] affectes: in me they] they do me
   20 Besprent] By sprent: teares] terys

21 But all for nought] Yet helpythe yt not
23 I do] most I
25 Yet that I gave I cannot call agayn
26 from] fro
27 teares] terys

Miss Foxwell overlooked the appearance of this poem in Tottel's *Miscellany*, but she prints (1, 65) from MS. Egerton 2711 a second version of the first eight lines.

No. 62 was suggested by Petrarch, sonetto in vita 178 (*Rime*, 234, p. 227), beginning,

O cameretta, che già fosti un porto
a le gravi tempeste mie diurne,
fonte se' or di lagrime nocturne
che 'l dí celate per vergogna porto.

Turbervile (*Epitaphes*, etc., 1567, pp. 62–64) paraphrased and amplified it in "The Lover to his carefull bed, declaring his restlesse state."

44. 7–13 *The restfull place, &c.* Cf. 13. 41 n. In *The Arte of English Poesie*, 1589, p. 187, these lines are inexactly quoted as an example of the device "*Irmus,* or the Long loose" (cf. 35. 22–25, 27 n.). "Ye see here," the author concludes, "how ye can gather no perfection of sence in all this dittie till ye come to the last verse in these wordes *my bed I thee forsake.*"

28 (No. 63) *Comparison of loue, &c.* In every edition (No. [68] in *B–I*, sigs. G in *BC,* D in *D–G,* C8ᵛ–D in *H,* C8 in *I*). Miss Foxwell (1, 56) prints the poem from MS. Egerton 2711, with the following variants:

44. 32 Of] Off: gathers] gaders
      33 Till] Iyll [?]:   downflowed to] off flowd the
      36 Rage is his raine] His rayne is rage
      37 eschue] estew

Parallels to No. 63 are noted by Miss Foxwell in *Orlando Furioso*, xxxvII. 110 (ed. Pietro Papini, 1916, p. 512), and (much closer) by Koeppel (*Studien,* p. 77) in Ariosto's *Capitoli Amorosi, ca.* 1537, v. 7–15 (*Rime e Satire*, Florence, 1822, pp. 272–273). These passages are respectively:

Come torrente che superbo faccia
Lunga pioggia tal volta o nievi sciolte,
Va ruinoso, e giú da' monti caccia
Gli arbori e i sassi e i campi e le ricolte:
Vien tempo poi, che l'orgogliosa faccia
Gli cade, e sí le forze gli son tolte,
Ch' un fanciullo, una femina per tutto
Passar lo puote, e spesso a piede asciutto.

Ma, come quando alle calde aure estive
Si risolvono i ghiacci e nevi alpine,
Crescon i fiumi al par delle lor rive,
Et alcun dispregiando ogni confine

Rompe superbo gli argini, et inonda
Le biade, i paschi e le città vicine:
    Così quando soverchia, e sovrabbonda
A quanto cape e può capire il petto,
Convien che l' allegrezza si diffonda.

Berdan (*Early Tudor Poetry*, p. 457 n.) refers to still another parallel in one of Ariosto's elegies.

44. 30 *these hie hilles*. The Pyrenees.

36 *Rage is his raine*. "Rage is his restraint; i. e. there is no restraint on his raging" (Nott).

37 *The first eschue is remedy alone*. "The only remedy is to avoid love in the beginning."

45. 2 (No. 64) *wiates complaint vpon Loue, &c*. In every edition (No. [69] in *B–I*, sigs. G^v–G3 in *BC*, D^v–D3 in *D–G*, D–D3 in *H*, C8–D2 in *I*). Miss Foxwell (1, 67–76) prints the first three stanzas of this poem from a Harington MS. (Additional 28635), the remainder from MS. Egerton 2711, with the following variants:

45. 2–4 Love's Arraignment
    6 causde] caused: accited] acited
    7 our] *Om.*
    9 Charged] Changed
    23 prest] pressed
    26 So] O
    27 my . . . ytasted] have my blynde lyfe taisted
    28 semblance] swetenes
    29 fair and] the: made me be] have made me
    30 araced] ataced
    31 From] From all: from] *Om.*
    32 He toke me from rest and set me in error
    33 God . . . regard] He hath made me regarde God muche
    38 Whettyng alwayes] Always whetting: frayle] *Om.*
    39 On] On the
    40 Oh] *Om.*:   had] now had
46. 2 Or] Or els any: to] *Om.*
    3 shalbe changed] shall chaunge
    5 robbeth he my fredom] robbed my libertie
    7 hath] have: in] me in
    8 me hasted] chased me
    9, 10, 11 Through] Thorough
    10 through bitter passions] straite pressions
    11 and ¹] *Om.*
    12 with] *Om.*
    14 All in] In all
    17 my] *Om.*
    18 me] *Om.*:   not] me not
    19 goddes] goodenes
    20 they] *Om.*:   cruell] cruell extreme
    21 fedes] fedeth

22 hower] owre
23 to] for to
24 in] *Om.*
25 guile, and] decepte, and by: thralled] *Om.*
26 since . . . neuer] and syns there never bell
27 Where I ame, that I here not, my playntes to renewe
28 My plaintes] And he: say] say is
29 olde . . . haue] have an old stock
30 is] is alwaye
31 doth] doeth
32 thence] *Om.*
34 noy both] annoye boeth: parauenture other] peradeventure othr
35 the one . . . tother] thone and thothr
36 aduersair] adversary: such] *Om.*
38 troth] trueth
39 may] shall
40 his] *Om.*
41 makes] maketh
43 shames] shameth

47. 2 gain] game
4 therby alone] onely thereby
5 now] *Om.*:   so] greatly
6 quickned I] I quickened
7 as] els, as: els he mought] he might
8 how grete Atride] that Atrides
11 Thaffricane] the Affricane
12 nurture] vertue
15 vnworthy] no dele worthy
16 the] right the
17 sonne yet neuer was] the mone was never
18 of] *Om.*
20 such] suche a
21 so hye might] myght have
25 causde] caused
27 learned, he] he lerned
28 repenteth, now] he repenteth
29 same] *Om.*:   and] and the
31 Sweter then for to in ioye eny othr in all
32 loe thus] *Om.*
33 shall] hath: the . . . further] thunkynd doeth forther
34 A . . . I] I norisshe a serpent
35 now of nature] of his nature now
37 haue I] I have
38 him] *Om.*:   wyse] of wyse
39 once] him
40 gnawen] ynawen
42 Whome now he accuseth he wounted to fere
43 euer] soever

48. 2 holdes] holdeth: whit] wit
3 yet . . . there] there was never: fantome] fantorme
6 rule] ruell: ease] pleasur
7 his gayn] remayn

48. 8 yet] *Om.*
    9 he might vpflie] for to flye
   10 to higher] farther
   13 the] his
   15 sayd, ere] sayed, or
   16 both] boeth
   18 shreke] shright
   19 once] me
   20 ayen] streight
   21 "Not I" quoth he; "but price, that is well worth"
   22 eche other] boeth eche
   23 still] *Om.*
   24 eche . . . haue] have nowe eche othr
   25 now] *Om.*:   thyne onely] onely thy
   26 at the whisted] After thissaid
   28 doth] doeth: a] *Om.*

The source of No. 64 is Petrarch, canzone in morte 7 (*Rime*, 360, p. 337), the first stanza of which (since the whole poem is too long to quote) is given below as a specimen:

> Quel antiquo mio dolce empio Signore
> fatto citar dinanzi a la reina
> che la parte divina
> tien di nostra natura e 'n cima sede;
> ivi, com' oro che nel foco affina,
> mi rappresento carco di dolore,
> di paura et d' orrore,
> quasi huom che teme morte et ragion chiede:
> e 'ncomincio: "Madonna, il manco piede
> giovenetto pos' io nel costui regno:
> ond' altro ch' ira et sdegno
> non ebbi mai; et tanti et sí diversi
> tormenti ivi soffersi,
> ch' alfine vinta fu quell' infinita
> mia patientia, e 'n odio ebbi la vita.

A partial translation of Petrarch's canzone in a Harington MS. (Additional 28635, fol. 17) seems worth quoting for purposes of comparison with No. 64:

> I scited once t' appeare/ before the noble Quene
> that ought to gudge eache mortall life/ that in this world is seene
> That pleasant crewell foe/ that robbeth hartes of ease
> and now doth frowne/ and then doth fawne/ and can both greve and please
> and theare as golde in fyre/ full fynde to eache intent
> Charged w̄ feare and terrour eke/ I did myself present
> As one that doubted death/ and yet did justice crave
> and thus began to unfolde my cawse in hope some helppe to have
>
> Madame in tender youth/ I entrid furst this raigne
> wheare other sweete I never felt/ then greefe and great disdaine
> and eake so sondrie kyndes/ of tormentes did endure
> as lyfe I loth'd, and death desyred/ my cursed case to cure

and thus my wofull daies/ unto this howre have past
In smokie sighes, and scalding teares/ my weried life to waste
O Lord what graces great/ I fledd and eke refused
to serve this crewell craftie Syer/ that doubtles trust abused.

What witt can use suche wordes/ to argue and debate
what tongue express the full effect/ of myne unhappie state
what hand with pen can painte/ t'unsypher this disceate
what hart so hard that wold not yelde/ that once had seene his baite
what great and greevous wronges/ what threates of yll successe
what single sweete mingled with masse/ of doble bitternes
with what unpleasant panges/ with what an horde of paynes
hath he acquaynted my greene yeares/ by his falce pleasant traines

Whoe by resistles powre/ hath forste me sue his dawnce
that if I be not moche abvsde/ had fownd moche better chaunce
and when I moste resolv'd/ to lead moste quyet lyfe
he spoil'd me of discordles state/ and thrust me in truceles strife
he hath bewitch'd me so/ that God the lesse I serv'd
and due respect unto myself/ the further from me swarv'd
He hath the love of one/ so painted in my thought
that other thing I can none mynde/ nor care for as I ought
and all this comes from hym/ both counsaile and the cawse
that whett my yonge desyre so moche/ to th' onour of his lawse.

45. 5 *Myne olde dere enmy, &c.* In *The Arte of English Poesie*, 1589, p. 139, this line is cited as "Myne old deēre ĕnĕ my," etc., in illustration of a dactylic foot.

6 *Afore that Quene.* "Before Queen Reason," as the title of the poem shows. Reason is addressed at 45. 12, 46. 37, 48. 25. Cf. "Loues accusation at the iudgement seat of Reason, wherein the Authors whole successe in his Loue is couertlie described," a poem in J. C.'s *Alcilia*, 1595 (ed. Grosart, pp. 33–41), which begins,

> In *Reasons* Court, my selfe being Plantiffe there,
> *Loue* was by processe summon'd to appeare,

and which is an imitation either of Wyatt or of Petrarch.

33 *God made he me regard lesse, &c.* "He (Cupid) made me love God less than I ought to."

46. 19 *The heauenly goddes.* For *goddes* the MS. has *goodenes*, which corresponds more closely to Petrarch's words, "pietà celeste," "heavenly pity."

47. 2 *in pleasant gain.* The rhyme-scheme is ruined by *gain*: read *game* with the MS.

10 *Whom Homer honored, &c.* "That great Achilles whom Homer honored." The last three words are not in Petrarch. Additions by Wyatt appear also in lines 8–9, and the translation is free throughout.

12 *by much nurture glorious.* Clearly *nurture* is an error for *vertue* (as in Petrarch and the MS.). *B*+ amend to *honour*, and hence change *honor* in line 13 to *actes* (misprinted *artes* in *I*).

47. 16 *the best of many a Milion.* Petrarch says "of a thousand." Wyatt omits Petrarch's comparison of the lady to Lucrece, and inserts an elaborate paraphrase of his own in lines 22–28, ending with the vigorous English phrase, *the ignorant foole.* Lines 34–35 are likewise original.

32 *Of right good sede yll frute, &c.* Cf. Wyatt's remark at 39. 11.

48. 5 *he striueth with the bit.* An English commonplace, added by Wyatt to this paraphrasing passage.

21 *Not I but price.* Wyatt has in mind Petrarch's words, "Io no, ma chi per sé la volse," "Not I, but He who wished her for Himself": *price*, the reward the lady received in heaven, caused her death.

27 *to haue hard your question.* The "question" is similar to the "questions" in Boccaccio's *Filocolo.*

29 (No. 65) *The louers sorowfull state, &c.* In every edition (No. [70] in *B–I*, sigs. G3–G3ᵛ in *BC*, D3–D3ᵛ in *D–H*, D2 in *I*). Miss Foxwell (1, 101–102) prints the poem from MS. Egerton 2711, with the following variants:

49. 6 so] that
    9 Doth] Doeth
    11 saw neuer] never sawe
    15 taste] tasted
    20 Souch] suche: doth] doeth
    22 Souch] *Om.*
    24 Souch] such

31 *Souche.* The oldest hand in *I* (Bodleian) writes in the margin, "& it semeth hir name was Souch, or Chaunce." The editor of the miscellany evidently considered Souch, or Souche, a proper noun, and hence at 49. 20, 22, 24 he put it in parentheses, a sixteenth-century equivalent for quotation-marks (cf. 232. 30 n.). A Mistress Souche (Zouche, Zowche) was one of the "noble ladies" at the court of Queen Jane Seymour (see *Letters and Papers, Foreign and Domestic, of the Reign of Henry VIII,* xii, ii, 340, 374), but the MS. shows that Wyatt was not referring to her. Compare also "Gascoignes prayse of Zouche late the Lady Greye of Wilton" in *A Hundreth Sundrie Flowres,* 1573 (ed. B. M. Ward, p. 86).

49. 26 (No. 66) *The louer complaineth, &c.* In every edition (No. [71] in *B–I*, sigs. G3ᵛ–G4 in *BC*, D3ᵛ–D4 in *D–H*, D2ᵛ–D3 in *I*). Miss Foxwell (1, 103–105) prints the poem from MS. Egerton 2711, with the following variants:

49. 39 stil] all
50. 12 to] unto
    18 her, of] your owne
    23 is] *Om.*
    24 doth] doeth
    26 since so much it doth] forbicause it doeth
    28 troth] trouth: Nought shall] shall not
    29 wretched] very

49. 28 *Where shall I haue, &c.* Nott thinks that the opening lines of this poem may have been suggested by Giusto de' Conti, *La Bella Mano*, 1715 ed., p. 50:

> Chi darà a gli occhi miei sì larga vena
> Di lagrime, ch' io possa il mio dolore
> Sfogar piangendo sì, che poi m' attempre?
> E per quietare il tormentoso core
> Chi darà al petto sì possente lena,
> Che, siccome convien, sospiri sempre?

50. 13 *lyke to like: the prouerb sayeth.* Cf. Alexander Barclay, translating Sebastian Brant's *The Ship of Fools*, 1509 (ed. T. H. Jamieson, II [1874], 35), "For it is a prouerbe, and an olde sayd sawe That in euery place lyke to lyke wyll drawe"; John Lyly, *Euphues. The Anatomy of Wit*, 1578 (*Complete Works*, ed. Bond, I, 197), "Is it not a by woord, like will to like?"; and *The Mirror for Magistrates*, 1587 (ed. Haslewood, I, 304; cf. 379), "Like will to like (for so the Prouerbe sayes)." Barnabe Rich, *The Honestie of This Age*, 1614, p. 33 (Percy Society, 1844, p. 48), refers to "the prouerbe, *Simile Simili gaudet*, like will to like, quoth the Deuill to the *Collier*"; and in this expanded (English) form the proverb usually occurs in sixteenth-century and later works.

34 (No. 67) *Of his loue that pricked her finger, &c.* In every edition (No. [72] in *B–I*, sigs. G4–G4ᵛ in *BC*, D4–D4ᵛ in *D–G*, D4 in *H*, D3 in *I*). Miss Foxwell (I, 45) prints the poem from MS. Egerton 2711, with the following variants:

> 50. 37 sowed] sowde
> 51. 2 She wisht] Wisshed: that] as

Possibly in imitation of No. 67 was written the poem (*ca.* 1653) printed from a manuscript in Arthur Clifford's *Tixall Poetry*, 1813, pp. 19–20:

> Ah, now I find the cause why still you did
> So smile to prick the lawne, or cut the thrid: —
> You were my fate; the needle was your dart,
> The thrid my life, the camberick my hart.

Somewhat similar in theme, as Miss Foxwell notes, is Maurice Sève's (or Scève's) dizaine 332 (*Délie*, 1544, ed. Eugène Parturier, 1916, p. 227):

> Ouvrant ma Dame au labeur trop ardente,
> Son Dé luy cheut, mais Amour le luy dresse:
> Et le voyant sans raison evidente
> Ainsi troué, vers Delie s'addresse.
>   C'est, luy dit elle, affin que ne m'oppresse
> L'aiguille aigue, & que point ne m'offence.
>   Donc, respond il, je croy que sa deffence
> Fait que par moy ton cœur n'est point vaincu.
> Mais bien du mien, dy je, la ferme essence
> Encontre toy luy sert tousjours d'escu.

51. 7 (No. 68) *Of the same.* In every edition (No. [73] in *B–I*, sigs. G4ᵛ in *BC*, D4ᵛ in *D–G*, D4 in *H*, D3 in *I*). Miss Foxwell (1, 45) prints the poem from MS. Egerton 2711, with the following variants:

> 51. 8 What . . . hard] Who hath herd of
> 12 my] myn

She suggests, likewise, that the idea of the epigram (with which compare No. 67) came from lines in John Skelton's *Phyllyp Sparowe* (*Poetical Works*, ed. Dyce, 1 [1843], 57–58); but the suggestion lacks weight. Skelton writes:

> I toke my sampler ones,
> Of purpose, for the nones,
> To sowe with stytchis of sylke . . . .
> But whan I was sowing his beke,
> Methought, my sparow did speke,
> And opened his prety byll,
> Saynge, Mayd, ye are in wyll
> Agayne me for to kyll,
> Ye prycke me in the head!
> With that my nedle waxed red,
> Methought, of Phyllyps blode.

16 (No. 69) *Request to Cupide, &c.* In every edition (No. [74] in *B–I*, sigs. G4ᵛ in *BC*, D4ᵛ in *D–G*, D4–D4ᵛ in *H*, D3–D3ᵛ in *I*). Miss Foxwell (1, 1) prints the poem from MS. Egerton 2711, with the following variants:

> 51. 20 greuous] great
> 21 solemne] holy: takes] taketh
> 23 thee] *Om.*
> 25 all] *Om.*
> 26 iust] *Om.*
> 27 how . . . triumpheth] *Om.*
> 28 but if thee pitie] if pitie the
> 30 great] *Om.*
> 31 doth] doeth
> 32 here] *Om.*:   *MS. adds the refrain* Behold love

As in the case of Nos. 70 and 103, the editor of *A* converted Wyatt's rondeau into a "sonnet" with the weird rhyme-scheme of *aabb aaab aaab ba*.

No. 69 is a free translation of Petrarch, madrigale in vita 4 (*Rime*, 121, p. 125):

> Or vedi, Amor, che giovenetta donna
> tuo regno sprezza et del mio mal non cura,
> et tra duo ta' nemici è sí secura.
> Tu se' armato, et ella in treccie e 'n gonna
> si siede et scalza in mezzo i fiori et l' erba,
> ver me spietata e 'ncontra te superba.
> I' son pregion; ma, se pietà anchor serba
> l' arco tuo saldo et qualchuna saetta,
> fa' di te et di me, Signor, vendetta.

51. 33 (No. 70) *Complaint for true loue vnrequited.* In every edition (No. [75] in *B–I*, sigs. G4ᵛ–H in *BC*, D4ᵛ–D5 in *D–G*, D4ᵛ in *H*, D3ᵛ in *I*). Miss Foxwell (1, 3) prints the poem from MS. Egerton 2711, with the following variants:

    52. 2 troth] trouth
         3 attayn] be tayne
         4 How] *Om.*:   iust] iuste and true
         5 Since] Sythens
         6 both] boeth: crafty] *Om.*
         7 spedes] spedeth: lye and] *Om.*
         8 hye] *Om.*
         9 cloked] *Om.*
        10 troth] trouth: or parfit stedfastnesse] *Om.*
        11 Deceaud] Deceved: false and] *Om.*
        12 meanes] meaneth: faithfull] *Om.*:   doth] doeth
        13 help or] *Om.*
        14 sterne] *Om.*
        15 Where . . . vain] Whose crueltie nothing can refrayn: *MS. adds the refrain* What vaileth trouth?

As in the case of Nos. 69 and 103, the editor of *A* changed Wyatt's rondeau to a "sonnet" with the strange rhyme-scheme *aabb aaab baab ba*, padding out all the lines to five feet and thus making almost a new poem.

    52. 16 (No. 71) *The louer that fled loue, &c.* In every edition (No. [76] in *B–I*, sigs. H in *BC*, D5 in *D–G*, D4ᵛ–D5 in *H*, D3ᵛ in *I*). Miss Foxwell (1, 49) prints the poem from MS. Egerton 2711, with the following variants:

    52. 18 so] *Om.*
        20 the . . . folow] I folow the coles
        21 with willing] against my
        22 both] boeth: furth] *Om.*
        24 laughes he now] now he laugh
        25 Meashed] Mashed: onely torne] all to-torne

The poem is supposed to have been written in reference to Henry VIII's visit to Francis I at Calais in October, 1532 (cf. line 21). Possibly it refers also to Anne Boleyn, with whom Wyatt had once been on terms of intimacy.

    25 *Meashed in the breers, that erst was onely torne.* Miss Foxwell (11, 65) points out that "Tottel completely reverses Wiat's idea" by reading *onely torne.* The MS. reading shows Wyatt to mean that now he is merely caught by the "briars that formerly had torn him severely."

    26 (No. 72) *The louer hopeth of better chance.* In every edition (No. [77] in *B–I*, sigs. H in *BC*, D5 in *D–H*, D3ᵛ–D4 in *I*). Miss Foxwell (1, 50) prints the poem from MS. Egerton 2711, with the following variants:

    52. 28 had] hath
        29 returnes] retornth: hid] *Om.*:   vnder] under the
        31 alowd] allowede
        32 in] into

52. 33 that] the: both] boeth
   34 The willowe eke] And eke the willowe
   35 Doth ¹, ²] Doeth

This poem is a translation of Serafino's strambotto (*Opere*, 1516, fol. 120):

> Sio son caduto interra inon son morto,
>   Ritorna el Sol benche talhor si cele,
> Spero mi dará el ciel qualche conforto,
>   Poi che fortuna hará sfocato el fele,
> Chi hó uisto naue ritornarsi in porto,
>   Dapoi che rotte há in mar tutte soe uele
> El salce anchora el uento abassa & piega
>   Poi se ridriza, & glialtri legni lega.

52. 30–33 *And when Fortune, &c.* These lines are quoted in *The Arte of English Poesie*, 1589, p. 236, as an illustration of "*Etiologia*, or the Reason rend or the Tell cause," with the explanation that they 'first point, then confirm, by similitudes.' Cf. 53. 16–19 n., 121. 15–16 n. Perhaps the poem in general and line 31 in particular refer to Wyatt's imprisonment in the Fleet prison in May, 1534.

53. 2 (No. 73) *The louer compareth his hart, &c.* In every edition (No. [78] in *B–I*, sigs. Hᵛ in *BC*, D5ᵛ in *D–G*, D5 in *H*, D4 in *I*). Miss Foxwell (I, 51) prints the poem from MS. Egerton 2711, with the following variants:

53. 5 most] *Om.*
   8 Crackes] Cracketh: doe] doeth
   9 So doth] right so doeth
  10 ay] *Om.*
  12 inward] now hard: doth] doeth

Turbervile (*Epitaphes*, etc., 1567, p. 74) paraphrases No. 73 in a poem of eighteen lines, beginning:

> Lyke as the gunne that hath to great a charge,
> And pellet to the powder ramde so sore,
> As neyther of both hath powre to go at large.

The source of Wyatt's poem is Serafino's strambotto (*Opere*, 1516, fol. 145ᵛ):

> Se una bombarda è dal gran foco mossa
>   Spirando, ció che troua aterra presto.
> Ma segli aduien chella spirar non possa
>   Se stessa rompe & poco offende el resto.
> Cosi io dentro ardo, el foco è giunto à lossa
>   Sel taccio imor, sel dico altrui molesto.
> Sospeso uiuo, amor mi dá tal sorte,
>   Che altro non è che una confusa morte.

5 *The furious goonne, &c.* Quoted in *The Arte of English Poesie*, 1589, p. 139, as an illustration of the use of one dactylic foot in a line.

53. 13 (No. 74) *The louer suspected of change, &c.* In every edition (No. [79] in *B–I*, sigs. H^v in *BC*, D5^v in *D–G*, D5–D5^v in *H*, D4 in *I*). Miss Foxwell (1, 367) reprints the poem from *A*, misprinting *breake* (line 21) as *break*. Perhaps No. 74 was a sonnet with two lines omitted after line 25.

16–19 *Accused though I be, &c.* In *The Arte of English Poesie*, 1589, pp. 236–237, these lines are quoted as illustrating "Etiologia," on which see 52. 30–33 n.

28 (No. 75) *The louer abused, &c.* In every edition (No. [80] in *B–I*, sigs. H^v–H2 in *BC*, D5^v–D6 in *D–G*, D5^v in *H*, D4–D4^v in *I*). Miss Foxwell (1, 36) prints the poem from MS. Additional 17492, with the following variants:

> 53. 30 to ^1] toke
> 　　31 Therin] Wherin:　　you] she
> 54. 2 *A new line inserted: see note below*
> 　　3 wo yet] care:　　to] for to
> 　　5 To geue] Gyving
> 　　6 your] her
> 　　9 you] the:　　time is] dayes bee

54. 2 *Since with good will, &c.* After this line supply the MS. reading, *To followe her wich causith all my payne*, which was no doubt inadvertently dropped by the printer.

13 (No. 76) *The louer professeth himself constant.* In every edition (No. [81] in *B–I*, sigs. H2 in *BC*, D6 in *D–G*, D5^v in *H*, D4^v in *I*). Miss Foxwell (1, 59) reprints the poem from *A*. The old annotator in *I* (Bodleian) objects to the title, "or rather, A Lady embracinge a gentlemans loue."

23 *That list to blow retrete, &c.* Borrowed in Melbancke's *Philotimus*, 1583, E3^v, "I will not blowe retreate to euery trayne."

24 (No. 77) *The louer sendeth his complaintes, &c.* In every edition (No. [82] in *B–I*, sigs. H2–H2^v in *BC*, D6–D6^v in *D–G*, D5^v–D6 in *H*, D4^v–D5 in *I*). Miss Foxwell (1, 368–369) reprints the poem from *A*, with the following errors:

> 55. 7 Whom] Whan
> 　12 doth] doeth
> 　15 rygour] rigour
> 　17 Wherfore] Wherefore

Nott suggests that when Wyatt wrote No. 77 he "probably had in contemplation" Petrarch's sonnet "Ite, caldi sospiri," which he followed more closely in No. 103. For the commonplace figure at 55. 9–12 Nott likewise gives a plausible parallel from Serafino.

35–55. 2-4 *For though hard rockes among, &c.* On this commonplace (which is repeated at 78. 15–16) see my notes in the *Gorgeous Gallery*, p. 174.

55. 25 (No. 78) *The louers case can not be hidden, &c.* In every edition (No. [83] in *B–I*, sigs. H2^v–H3 in *BC*, D6^v–D7 in *D–G*, D6–D6^v in *H*, D5–

D5^v in *I*). Miss Foxwell (1, 370–371) reprints the poem from *A*, with the following errors:

55. 32 fayn] fain
 39 syde] side
56. 3 no] to
 16 are] ar

56. 14–15 *Your sighes . . . And all to wry your wo.* "You give a far-fetched explanation of your sighs, and you altogether misinterpret (give a false explanation of) your woe" (G. L. K.).

30 (No. 79) *The louer praieth, &c.* In every edition (No. [84] in *B–I*, sigs. H3–H3^v in *BC*, D7–D7^v in *D–G*, D6^v–D7 in *H*, D5^v in *I*). Miss Foxwell (1, 359–360) reprints the poem from *The Court of Venus, ca.* 1542 (or perhaps *ca.* 1557?), with the following variants:

56. 36 ye not] nothing: honestly] honesty: *refrain added* Dysdayne me not
57. 3 This] The: *refrain added* Refuse me not
 6 sins] seyng
 7 *Refrain added* Mystrust me not
 9 *Line missing*
 10 Destroy . . . that] Nor hate me not til [*Evidently parts of lines 9 and 10 of A were run together in the MS.*]
 11 But . . . know] For syth you knew: *refrain added* Forsake me not
 12 that am] being
 13 am] I am
 14 knowne] knowen
 15 not, ne] never: *refrain added* Disdayne me not

33–34 *Disdaine me not, &c.* In *Philotimus*, 1583, C2^v, Melbancke borrows these lines, combining them with an imitation of 62.28–29: "Disdaine me not without desert, nor leaue me not so sodeinly, so do the stony rocks repulse the waues that rush them violently."

38 *Nor think me not to be vniust.* In his *Rare Poems* (1883), p. 229, W. J. Linton suggests that *Nor think* is a misprint for *Forethink*, and that the line means, "Do not be unjust in thinking ill of me before cause shown!" The emendation is ingenious but unnecessary.

57. 16 (No. 80) *The louer lamenteth his estate, &c.* In every edition (No. [85] in *B–I*, sigs. H3^v–H4 in *BC*, D7^v–D8 in *D–G*, D7–D7^v in *H*, D6 in *I*). Miss Foxwell (1, 374–375) reprints the poem from *A*.

23–26 *Regard at length, I you require, &c.* Koeppel (*Studien*, p. 73) finds the source of these lines in Serafino's strambotto (*Opere*, 1516, fol. 159^v, beginning, "Non piú tardar hormai di contentarme"):

Di questa fiamma uogli liberarme,
 Chio uiua in pena piú non è ragione.
Non piú tardar di contentarme in questo
 Due uolte fá el seruitio chil fá presto.

58. 9 (No. 81) *The louer waileth, &c.* In every edition (No. [86] in *B–I*, sigs. H4–H4ᵛ in *BC*, D8–D8ᵛ in *D–G*, D7ᵛ–D8 in *H*, D6–D6ᵛ in *I*). Miss Foxwell (1, 376–377) reprints the poem from *A*, with the following errors:

> 58. 33 to] too
> 59. 2 therfore] therefore
>   3 perill] peril
>   10 my selfe] myself

59. 12 (No. 82) *The louer lamenteth, &c.* In every edition (No. [255] in *B–I*, sigs. Dd–Ddᵛ in *BC*, O–Oᵛ in *D–G*, O2 in *H*, N3ᵛ–N4 in *I*). In all editions except *A* this poem is attributed to an "uncertain author," as a result of which Miss Foxwell (like Nott), finding no manuscript authority, rightly excludes it from her edition. Turbervile imitates the poem in his *Epitaphes*, etc., 1567, pp. 162–165. The annotator in *I* (Bodleian) wrote in the margin of No. 82, "Taken out of Tullye."

22 *My wastefull will is tried by trust.* "My desire — which comes to naught—is proved to be thus unavailing when I trust to enjoy it" (G. L. K.).

29, 31 *They eat the hony, &c.* Cf. Melbancke, *Philotimus*, 1583, D2: "Neither would I haue thee a drone to eate the swete that others sweat for, that y̆ eate y̆ hony, and they hould the hyue, they drawe y̆ driue." The first part of his borrowing may come from the *Paradise*, 1576, p. 86. Cf. also Turbervile, *Tragical Tales* [*ca.* 1574], 1587 (1837 reprint, p. 19):

> I burne the bee, I holde the hyue,
>   the sommer toyle is myne:
> And all bicause when winter commes,
>   the honie may be thine.

60. 5 (No. 83) *To his loue, &c.* In every edition (No. [87] in *B–I*, sigs. H4ᵛ in *BC*, D8ᵛ in *D–G*, D8–D8ᵛ in *H*, D6ᵛ–D7 in *I*). Miss Foxwell (1, 172–173) prints the poem from MS. Egerton 2711, with the following variants:

> 60. 8 The answere] Thanswere
>   14 haue nothing] nothing have
>   17 makes] makethe: *two lines added:*
>
> > Another, why, shall lyberty be bond!
> > Ffre hert may not be bond but by desert
>
>   18 Yet] Nor
>   23 bitter] frendly
>   24 That seithe your frende in saving of his payne
>   26 it] that
>   27 doth] *Om.*

28 (No. 84) *To his ladie cruel, &c.* In every edition (No. [88] in *B–I*, sigs. H4ᵛ–I in *BC*, D8ᵛ–E in *D–G*, D8ᵛ in *H*, D7 in *I*). Miss Foxwell (1, 42) reprints the poem from *A*, with the following errors:

60. 30 kinde] kind
   34 then] *Om.*
61. 2 eke] *Om.*
    5 Therfore] Therefore

No. 84 is written in a somewhat unusual sonnet-form of three quatrains with alternate rhymes of *ab* followed by a couplet with the rhyme *cc*. No other sonnet by Wyatt has this form, which is a kind of link between the Petrarchan and the so-called Shakespearean sonnet; but Surrey used it for Nos. 9 and 10. See also Wyatt's three-rhyme sonnet, No. 43.

   60. 33 *The fierce lyon will hurt no yelden thinges.* A commonplace, which Surrey uses at 208. 25, 33. As a further illustration, Mathew Grove in 1587 (*Poems*, ed. Grosart, p. 87) wrote of the lion,

> who neuer doth delight, with force
> To teare the sely beast y̆ yeldeth to his might,
> But then as victor to returne away.

61. 10 (No. 85) *The louer complaineth, &c.* In every edition (No. [89] in *B–I*, sigs. I in *BC*, E in *D–G*, D8ᵛ in *H*, D7–D7ᵛ in *I*). Miss Foxwell (I, 51) prints the poem from MS. Egerton 2711, with the following variants:

   61. 13 The enmy] Thenmy
       16 offerd] offered
       18 arrowes] arrowe

Koeppel (*Anglia*, XIII [1891], 78) thought the source of No. 85 was Mellin de Saint-Gelais's dizaine (*Œuvres*, 1719, pp. 130–131):

> Pre's [*sic*] du sercueil d'une morte gisante
> Mort & Amour vindrent devant mes yeux,
> Amour me dit, la Mort t'est plus duisante:
> Car en mourant tu auras beaucoup mieux.
> Alors la Mort, qui regnoit en maints lieux,
> Pour me naurer, son fort arc enfonça:
> Mais de malheur sa flesche m'offença
> Au propre lieu où Amour mit la sienne,
> Et sans entrer seulement avança
> Le traict d'Amour en la playe ancienne.

It seems more likely that both Wyatt and Saint-Gelais followed some Italian original not yet discovered. Compare the note on No. 97 (68. 4).

   13 *The enmy of life, decayer of all kinde.* In *The Arte of English Poesie*, 1589, p. 139, this line is quoted as "*Th'ĕnĕmĭe to life destroi er of all kinde*" in illustration of a dactylic foot.

   21 (No. 86) *The louer reioiceth, &c.* In every edition (No. [90] in *B–I*, sigs. I–Iᵛ in *BC*, E–Eᵛ in *D–G*, D8ᵛ–E in *H*, D7ᵛ in *I*). Miss Foxwell (I, 115–116) prints the poem from MS. Egerton 2711, with the following variants:

> 61. 27 but] nought but: ladies] dere
>   30 to] *Om.*
>   32 ouerturnde] overtorned
> 62. 3 wondersly] wonderly
>   14 soueraigne] sufferaunce

62. 16 (No. 87) *The louer complayneth, &c.* In every edition (No. [91] in
B–I, sigs. I^v–I2 in *BC*, E^v–E2 in *D–G*, E–E^v in *H*, D7^v–D8 in *I*). Miss Foxwell
(I, 117–118) prints the poem from MS. Egerton 2711, with the following
variants:

> 62. 21 And] For
>   34 through] thorough
> 63. 5 May chance] Perchaunce: witherd] wethered
>   6 In] The: nightes] nyght
>   13 beauty] beaultie
>   18 both] boeth

No. 87 is a very pretty song, although the identical rhymes of the second
stanza are in careless violation of the usual rhyme-scheme. In Nott's opinion
"it is one of the most elegant amatory Odes in our language. It is as beautifully
arranged in all its parts as any of the odes of Horace." The lute, he points out,
was the instrument to which almost all the early love-songs were sung. In
Nugae Antiquae (1775, II, 252–253; cf. also the editions of 1779, 1792, III, 286–
287; 1804, II, 400–401) it is printed under the heading, "By the Earl of Roche-
ford. In Manuscript, dated 1564." But the evidence of that book is worthless.
From it Horace Walpole turned the poem, "with few alterations, into the style
of the present age," sending his version to Bishop Percy in 1792 (see J. B.
Nichols, *Illustrations of the Literary History of the Eighteenth Century*, VIII
[1858], 291–293).
   In John Hall's *The Courte of Vertue*, 1565, M2^v–M4, No. 87 is moralized as
"A song of the lute in the prayse of God, and disprayse of Idolatrie" (see
Nott's *Wyatt*, pp. 532–534), which begins:

> My lute awake and prayse the lord,
> My heart and handes therto accord:
> Agreing as we haue begon,
> To syng out of gods holy worde.
> And so procede tyll we haue done.

The final stanza runs thus:

> Lorde graunt vs to thy worde to cleaue,
> That no man other doe deceaue:
> And in that zeale that I begunne,
> Lauding our lorde God here I leaue,
> Be styll my lute my song is done.

Hall gives the music for his song on sig. N5^v.

62. 23–24 *As to be heard where eare is none, &c.* Cf. Melbancke's *Philotimus*, 1583, sig. Y^v: "As to bee hearde where eares are none, or Lead to be grauen in Marble stone, so harde it is to heare counsell of you, which may accorde with any good."

24 *As lead to graue, &c.* "It would be more easy for lead, which is the softest of metals, to engrave characters on hard marble, than it is for me to make impression on her obdurate heart" (Nott, p. 545).

28–29 *The rockes do not so cruelly, &c.* Cf. 56. 33–34 n.

63. 5–7 *May chance thee lie witherd and olde, &c.* Probably suggested by Horace's *Carmina*, I. xxv:

> Invicem moechos anus arrogantis
> flebis in solo levis angiportu,
> Thracio bacchante magis sub inter-
> lunia vento.

20 (No. 88) *How by a kisse, &c.* In every edition (No. [92] in *B–I*, sigs. I2 in *BC*, E2 in *D–G*, E–E2 in *H*, D8–D8^v in *I*). Miss Foxwell (1, 52) prints the poem from MS. Egerton 2711, with the following variants:

> 63. 22 feat] seet
> 23 wondrous] wonderous

22–25 *the Bee . . . To finde hony . . . the spider . . . To fetch poyson.* A commonplace dear to the Elizabethans. Cf. Whetstone, in verses prefixed to Kendall's *Flowers of Epigrammes*, 1577, "In flowers fooles (like Spyders) poyson finde: The wise (as Bees) win hony from a weede"; Howell, *H. His Deuises*, 1581 (*Poems*, ed. Grosart, p. 171), "But venomde Spyders poyson take, where Bee doth honey finde"; the title-page of Davison's *A Poetical Rhapsody*, 1602–1621 (see A. H. Bullen's ed., 1, lxi–lxiii); Martin Parker, *Grandsire Graybeard*, 1635, A3, "Be like the *Bee*, sucke out the sweet and good, The ranke refuse, let be the *Spiders* food."

30 (No. 89) *The louer describeth his being, &c.* In every edition (No. [93] in *B–I*, sigs. I2–I2^v in *BC*, E2–E2^v in *D–G*, E2 in *H*, D8^v in *I*). Miss Foxwell (1, 288–289) prints the poem from MS. Additional 17492 (where Nott had failed to find it), with the following variants:

> 63. 33 Vnwarely so] So unwarely
> 34 vpon] apon
> 36 proper] *Om.*
> 38 into] unto
> 64. 3 both] boeth
> 5 fowle] byrde: fleeth] flyeth
> 6 vpon] on: beauty] beaulte
> 7 burnde] burnt
> 9 Inflamde] Enflamed
> 10 through out] therowt
> 11 quakyng] quakynd

    16 doth hold] holdes: sore] so sore
    17 both] *Om.*
    18 do] doeth

Nott (p. 549) points out various borrowings from Petrarch in No. 89, a parallel between 63. 37–38 and Chaucer's *Knight's Tale* (A. 1096–1097), and an imitation in Turbervile's *Epitaphes*, etc., 1567, pp. 11–14.

    63. 36 *My hart was torne out of his proper place.* The MS. and *B*+ agree in omitting *proper*, making the line have four stresses like 64. 3, 7, 11, 15, 19.

    37–38 *Thorow mine eye, &c.* Cf. 33. 22–24; and Chaucer, *The Knight's Tale*, A. 1096–1097:

> But I was hurt right now thurgh-out myn yë
> In-to myn herte.

    64. 20 (No. 90) *To his louer to loke vpon him.* In every edition (No. [94] in *B–I*, sigs. I2^v in *BC*, E2^v in *D–G*, E2–E2^v in *H*, D8^v–E in *I*). Miss Foxwell (1, 58) prints the poem from MS. Additional 17492 (where Nott had failed to find it), with the following variants:

    64. 22 loke] sight
        24 helpe] save
        25 doest] dost
        27 And] For: thy life may last] then maiste thou lyve
        28–29 Sins ton bye tothr doth lyve and fede thy herte,
          I with thye sight, thou also with my smerte.

Koeppel (*Studien*, pp. 72–73) finds the source of No. 90 in Serafino's strambotto (*Opere*, 1516, fol. 125^v):

> Viuo sol di mirarti hai dura impresa,
>   Tu te nascondi, e conuerrá che io mora,
> Ma se saluar mi poi con poca spesa,
>   À che pur fuggi, fuggi un che te adora,
> Che só, se al uiuer mio non dai difesa
>   Io moro, & tu poi me non campi un hora,
> Che lun per laltro uiue, & pasce il core,
>   Io del tuo aspecto, & tu del mio dolore.

    30 (No. 91) *The louer excuseth him of wordes, &c.* In every edition (No. [95] in *B–I*, sigs. I3–I3^v in *BC*, E3–E3^v in *D–G*, E2^v–E3 in *H*, E–E^v in *I*). Miss Foxwell (1, 341–343) prints the poem from MS. Additional 17492 (where Nott had failed to find it), with the following variants:

    65. 6 May] Do
       13 on] of
       15 wordes] worde: you] ye
       16 And if I did] If I saide so
       21 vnto] out of
       22 as farre] afarre

65. 23 his] this
    26 Encrease] Encresst
    32 from] fro
    33 you] ye
    35 my hart to] me to more
    36 this] that: you] ye
    37, 38, 42, 43 You] Ye
66. 3 Lea] Lya

No. 91 is a free translation of Petrarch, canzone in vita 15 (*Rime*, 206, pp. 202–204):

> S' i' 'l dissi mai, ch' i' vegna in odio a quella
> del cui amor vivo et senza 'l qual morrei;
> s' i' 'l dissi, che' miei dí sian pochi et rei,
> et di vil signoria l'anima ancella;
> s' i' 'l dissi, contra me s'arme ogni stella,
> et dal mio lato sia
> paura et gelosia,
> et la nemica mia
> piú feroce ver me sempre et piú bella.
>
> S' i' 'l dissi, Amor l' aurate sue quadrella
> spenda in me tutte et l' impiombate in lei;
> s' i' 'l dissi, cielo et terra, uomini et Dei
> mi sian contrari, et essa ogni or piú fella;
> s' i' 'l dissi, chi con sua cieca facella
> dritto a morte m' invia,
> pur come suol si stia,
> né mai piú dolce o pia
> ver me si mostri in atto od in favella.
>
> S' i' 'l dissi mai, di quel ch' i' men vorrei
> piena trovi quest' aspra et breve via;
> s' i' 'l dissi, il fero ardor che mi desvia
> cresca in me quanto il fier ghiaccio in costei;
> s' i' 'l dissi, unqua non veggian li occhi mei
> sol chiaro o sua sorella,
> né donna né donzella,
> ma terribil procella
> qual Pharaone in perseguir li Hebrei.
>
> S' i' 'l dissi, coi sospir, quant' io mai fei,
> sia pietà per me morta et cortesia;
> s' i' 'l dissi, il dir s' innaspri, che s' udia
> sí dolce allor che vinto mi rendei;
> s' i' 'l dissi, io spiaccia a quella ch' i' torrei,
> sol chiuso in fosca cella,
> dal dí che la mamella
> lasciai fin che si svella
> da me l' alma, adorar: forse el farei.

Ma s'io nol dissi, chi sí dolce apria
meo cor a speme ne l' età novella,
regg' anchor questa stanca navicella
col governo di sua pietà natia,
né diventi altra, ma pur qual solia
quando piú non potei,
che me stesso perdei,
né piú perder devrei.
Mal fa chi tanta fé sí tosto oblia.

I' nol dissi già mai, né dir poria
per oro o per cittadi o per castella;
vinca 'l ver dunque et si rimanga in sella,
et vinta a terra caggia la bugia.
Tu sai in me il tutto, Amor: s' ella ne spia,
dinne quel che dir dei.
I' beato direi
tre volte et quattro et sei
chi, devendo languir, si morí pria.

Per Rachel ò servito et non per Lia;
né con altra saprei
viver; et sosterrei,
quando 'l ciel ne rappella,
girmen con ella in sul carro de Helia.

Nott cites an imitation of Petrarch by Serafino (*Opere*, 1516, fol. 157ᵛ), beginning,

Donna se io dixi mai contra tuo honore
Te mostri à me crudel sempre a piú bella.

64. 33–65. 2-17 *Perdy I sayd it not . . . heauen aboue.* These lines are quoted in *The Arte of English Poesie*, 1589, pp. 221–222, to illustrate "*Ecphonisis.* or the Outcry," with the explanation that "*Petrarche* in a sonet which Sir *Thomas Wiat* Englished excellently well," cast them "in this figure by way of imprecation and obtestation."

65. 20–21 *such warre . . . Troye.* Wyatt's substitution for Petrarch's Pharaoh and the Hebrews.

66. 6 (No. 92) *Of such as had forsaken him.* In every edition (No. [96] in *B–I*, sigs. I3ᵛ in *BC*, E3ᵛ in *D–G*, E3 in *H*, Eᵛ in *I*). Miss Foxwell (1, 62) prints the poem from a Harington MS. (Additional 36529), — where Nott had overlooked it, — with the following variants:

66. 7 Lux] Luckes: thy] your
      9 mought you fall] might ye befall
     10 liked] lykt
     14 and very] so be but

The poem was probably written after the execution in July, 1540, of Thomas Cromwell, Earl of Essex, and before Wyatt was imprisoned in 1541. It expresses truthfully Wyatt's precarious situation.

66. 15 (No. 93) *A description of such a one, &c.* In every edition (No. [97] in *B–I*, sigs. I3ᵛ in *BC*, E3ᵛ in *D–G*, E3 in *H*, Eᵛ in *I*). Miss Foxwell (I, 61) prints the poem from a Harington MS. (Additional 36529), — where Nott had overlooked it, — with the following variants:

66. 17 wonderous] wonders
19 Of liuely loke] With gladsome cheare: repell] expell
20 right good grace] sober lookes
21 word] wordes
23 these perchance] thus might chaunce: tryde] tyde
24 with] the

In this poem Wyatt writes his only description, itself vague, of a woman. An imitation, signed "Jo[hn] Har[ington]," occurs in a Harington MS. (Additional 28635, fol. 72 ᵛ):

A boy that should content me wondrous well
should keep thease rules set down for his behoofe
In fearing God all boys he should excell
and lead a Lyfe unworthy just reproofe
an upright gate a forhed smothe and playn
a countenaunce good wᵗʰ feet even set on ground
a steady ey still hands and setled brayn
an open ear to good enstructions bound
a courteous tounge that talkth trew & playne
An humble harte of guyle voyd evermore
a constant mynde that will refuse no payn
to purchase skyll the fruyt of virtuous lore
and lern to know and know to doe the best
and suche a boy should worthely passe yᵉ rest.

25 (No. 94) *How vnpossible it is to finde, &c.* In every edition (No. [98] in *B–I*, sigs. I3ᵛ–I4 in *BC*, E3ᵛ–E4 in *D–G*, E3–E3ᵛ in *H*, Eᵛ–E2 in *I*). Miss Foxwell (I, 28) prints the poem from MS. Egerton 2711, with the following variants:

66. 27 my] myn
28 ay my] myn
29 That leve it or wayt, it doeth me like pain
30 so] *Om.*
31 black shal it be] shalbe black
32 and] *Om:*   vpon] in
33 backe returne] retorn back
34 his] *Om.*
67. 2 I] that I
4 against] again
5 if] if that
7 That] And

The rhymes sound rough to a modern ear, and the changes introduced by the editor of *A* render them but little more euphonious. Thus by inserting *ay* in line 28 he made the pronunciation *vncertaíne* (necessary for rhyme) almost impossible. In the second edition (*BC*) further unauthorized and unsatisfactory changes appear.

The source of No. 94 is Petrarch, sonetto in vita 37 (*Rime*, 57, p. 62):

> Mie venture al venir son tarde et pigre,
> la speme incerta, e 'l desir monta et cresce,
> onde e 'l lassare et l' aspectar m' incresce;
> et poi al partir son piú levi che tigre.
> Lasso, le nevi fien tepide et nigre,
> e 'l mar senz 'onda, et per l' alpe ogni pesce,
> et corcherassi il sol là oltre ond' esce
> d' un medesimo fonte Eufrate et Tigre:
> prima ch' i' trovi in ciò pace né triegua,
> o Amore o Madonna altr' uso impari;
> che m' ànno congiurato a torto incontra:
> et s' i' ò alcun dolce, è dopo tanti amari,
> che per disdegno il gusto si dilegua.
> Altri mai di lor gratie non m' incontra.

66. 29 *That loue or wait it.* The Italian *'l lassare* and the MS. show that *loue* is a printer's error for *leue* (leave).

31–34 *Alas the snow black shal it be, &c.* Imitated by Turbervile, *Tragical Tales* [*ca.* 1574], 1587 (1837 reprint, p. 397):

> Blacke shall you see the snow on mountains hie,
> The fish shall feed vpon the barren sand,
> The sea shal shrinke, and leaue the Dolphins dry,
> No plant shall prooue vpon the sencelesse land,
> The Tems shal turne, the Sunne shal lose his light,
> Ere I to thee become a faithlesse wight.

Cf. also the oath in Samuel Page's *The Love of Amos and Laura*, 1613 (appended to the 1628 edition of J. C.'s *Alcilia*, N3ᵛ):

> And this I vow, Water shall turne to fire,
> Huge massie mountaines to the clouds aspire;
> The Sun shall leaue his course, the Moon her brightnes,
> Night turne to day, and day shall lose his lightnes;
> Fishes shall fly, birds swim, and Hare shall hunt
> The Hound, which to pursue the Hare was wont:
> Ayre, Earth, Fire, Water, all things which you view,
> Shall change their natures, ere I turne from you.

But the idea, which is voiced by Virgil, Ovid, Seneca, Chaucer, and others, is a commonplace. In line 33 Wyatt substitutes the Thames for the Euphrates and Tigris of Petrarch.

67. 8 (No. 95) *Of Loue, Fortune, and the louers minde.* In every edition (No. [99] in *B–I*, sigs. I4 in *BC*, E4 in *D–G*, E3ᵛ in *H*, E2 in *I*). Miss Foxwell (1, 29) prints the poem from MS. Egerton 2711, with the following variants:

    67. 10 Fortune . . . do] and fortune and my mynde
       11 Eke that] Of that that: and] with: once] *Om.*
       12 Torment . . . that] Do torment me so that I
       13 I hate and] *Om.*
       14 my] myn: while] *Om.*
       19 But daily yet the ill doeth chaunge into the wours
       20 While] And: halfe] the half: now] *Om.*
       21 brittle] brickell
       22 my ¹] myn

Both Miss Foxwell and Nott stigmatize this as one of Wyatt's poorest compositions. They are unable to forgive his putting four *that's* into line 11 (in *A* one *that* is omitted), and Nott is especially disturbed by the licentious rhymes. The source of No. 95 is Petrarch, sonetto in vita 85 (*Rime*, 124, p. 127):

> Amor, fortuna et la mia mente schiva
> di quel che vede, e nel passato volta,
> m' affligon sí ch' io porto alcuna volta
> invidia a quei che son su l' altra riva.
> Amor mi strugge 'l cor, fortuna il priva
> d' ogni conforto: onde la mente stolta
> s' adira et piange; et cosí in pena molta
> sempre conven che combattendo viva.
> Né spero i dolci dí tornino indietro,
> ma pur di male in peggio quel ch' avanza;
> et di mio corso ò già passato 'l mezzo.
> Lasso, non di diamante, ma d' un vetro
> veggio di man cadermi ogni speranza,
> et tutt' i miei pensier romper nel mezzo.

    67. 11 *that . . . that that.* Wyatt was fond of this word. As is pointed out in the foregoing collations, it occurs four times in the MS. version of this line. Cf. also 67. 32, where the MS. has two *that's* together, and note the meaning of *so that* in 67. 34.

    13 *I hate and enuy them.* Unintelligible with the omission of Petrarch's "che son su l' altra riva" — "those who are on the other shore," that is, dead.

    24 (No. 96) *The louer prayeth, &c.* In every edition (No. [100] in *B–I*, sigs. I₄–I₄ᵛ in *BC*, E₄–E₄ᵛ in *D–G*, E₃ᵛ–E₄ in *H*, E₂–E₂ᵛ in *I*). Miss Foxwell (I, 30) prints the poem from MS. Egerton 2711, with the following variants:

    67. 27 With those your Iyes, for to get peace and truyse
       28 Geuen] Profferd: my] myn
       29 In] Emong
       30 you] ye
       31 doth] doeth
       32 that ¹] *Om.*:   that you] that that ye
       34 you] I then: that] nor
       36 calde] called

The source of No. 96 is Petrarch, sonetto in vita 17 (*Rime*, 21, p. 15):

> Mille fiate, o dolce mia guerrera,
> per aver co' begli occhi vostri pace,
> v' aggio proferto il cor; ma voi non piace
> mirar sí basso colla mente altera.
> Et se di lui fors' altra donna spera,
> vive in speranza debile et fallace:
> mio, perché sdegno ciò ch' a voi dispiace,
> esser non può già mai cosí com' era.
> Or s' io lo scaccio, et e' non trova in voi
> ne l' exilio infelice alcun soccorso,
> né sa star sol, né gire ov' altri il chiama,
> poria smarrire il suo natural corso:
> che grave colpa fia d' ambeduo noi,
> et tanto piú de voi, quanto piú v' ama.

As Nott observes, Wyatt substitutes for the last line of this sonnet the last line of Petrarch's 169th sonetto in vita, "vostro, Donna, 'l peccato, et mio fia 'l danno," which he translates again at 68. 35.

67. 37 *wander from his naturall kinde.* That is, die.

68. 4 (No. 97) *The louers life, &c.* In every edition (No. [101] in *B–I*, sigs. I4^v in *BC*, E4^v in *D–G*, E4 in *H*, E2^v in *I*). Miss Foxwell (1, 31) prints the poem from MS. Egerton 2711, with the following variants:

> 68. 6 vnto] to
>   7 So] *Om.*
>   8 hye] of great height
> 10 haue] have full
> 11 doth] doeth
> 13 With] *Om.*: great] with great
> 14 boystous] boyseus
> 15 in] from
> 16 Wilde beastes] Cattell: fierce loue in me] and in me love
> 17 Vnmoueable] Immoveable: they] they are full
> 18 singing] that restles
> 19 passing through] that passe thorough

The source of No. 97 was long thought (cf. also 61. 10 n.) to be Mellin de Saint-Gelais's sonnet beginning,

> Voyant ces monts de veuë ainsi lointaine.

It is now known that both Saint-Gelais and Wyatt independently translated sonetto 3 in Sannazaro's *Rime*, part iii (1531 ed., fol. 49^v), a fact established by Arthur Tilley in *The Modern Language Quarterly*, v (1902), 149, and by L. E. Kastner in *The Modern Language Review*, iii (1908), 273–274. The sonetto runs thus:

> Simile a questi smisurati monti
> E l' aspra uita mia colma di doglie
> Alti son questi, & alte le mie uoglie
> Di lagrime ambedui, questi di fonti

Lor han, di scogli, li superbi fronti
    In me duri pensier, l' amma [anima] coglie
    Lor son di pochi frutti, e molte foglie
    Io pochi effetti a gran speranza aggiunti
Soffian sempre fra lor rabbiosi uenti
    In me graui suspiri, esito fanno
    In me se pasce Amor: in lor armenti
Immobile son io, lor fermi stanno
    Lor, han d' uccelli, liquidi accenti
    Et io la mente, di superchio affanno.

According to Pierre Villey in *La Revue d'Histoire Littéraire de la France*, xxvii (1920), 538–547, the earliest French sonnet dates from 1536, a date that precludes French influence on the sonnets of Wyatt.

    68. 6–9 *Lyke vnto these vnmesurable mountaines, &c.* Quoted in *The Arte of English Poesie*, 1589, p. 142, as an illustration of "*Catalecticke* and *Acatalecticke*" verse, "where in your first second and fourth verse, ye may find a sillable superfluous, and though in the first ye will seeme to helpe it, by drawing these three sillables, (*ĭm mĕ sŭ*) into a *dactil*, in the rest it can not be so excused, wherefore we must thinke he [Wyatt] did it of purpose, by the odde sillable to giue greater grace to his meetre."

    20 (No. 98) *Charging of his loue as vnpiteous, &c.* In every edition (No. [102] in *B–I*, sigs. I4ᵛ–K in *BC*, E4ᵛ–E5 in *D–G*, E4–E4ᵛ in *H*, E2ᵛ in *I*). Miss Foxwell (I, 18) prints the poem from MS. Egerton 2711, with the following variants:

      68. 22 amourous] amours: or if] *Om.*
          24 kindled] kyndelled
          26 distayned] depaynted
          27 if] els in
          28 fear . . . so] nowe fere, nowe shame
          29 If] If a: alas] *Om.*
          31 or sighyng] and sighting
          34 stroy] destroye

Nott points out imitations of this poem in Turbervile's *Epitaphes*, etc., 1567, pp. 68–69, and in Samuel Daniel's fifteenth sonnet to Delia (1592).

    The source of No. 98 is Petrarch, sonetto in vita 169 (*Rime*, 224, p. 220):

S' una fede amorosa, un cor non finto,
un languir dolce, un desiar cortese;
s' oneste voglie in gentil foco accese,
un lungo error in cieco laberinto;
se ne la fronte ogni penser depinto,
od in voci interrotte a pena intese,
or da paura or da vergogna offese;
s' un pallor di viola et d' amor tinto;
s' aver altrui piú caro che sé stesso;
se sospirare et lagrimar mai sempre,

pascendosi di duol, d' ira et d' affanno;
s' arder da lunge et agghiacciar da presso
son le cagion ch' amando i' mi distempre:
vostro, Donna, 'l peccato, et mio fia 'l danno.

An entirely different translation is preserved in a Harington MS. (Additional 36529, fol. 46), which runs thus:

If stable mynd and hart that cannot faine
if sportles plaints that moues unfained desire
if constant will that neuer ment retier
if restles foote in maze that treades in vaine
if face whear in eache thoght is painted plaine
if broken voice that wantes words to require
if now for shame and then for feare in paine
if frawdles searche that fyndeth frutles gaine
if to esteme you than my selfe more deere
if endles sewte that wageles craueth hier
if gref for foode and panges that pearce to neere
if boorn farr of and freese amids the fire
be cawse that I thus helples tourne and tosse
yo^rs is the fawlt and myne the giltles losse.

68. 22 *If amourous fayth, &c.* In *The Arte of English Poesie*, 1589, p. 139, this line is quoted to illustrate the use of a dactylic foot.

27 *my sparkelyng voyce.* One should expect *my speaking voice* (with *E*+). Wyatt does not adequately translate Petrarch's sixth line.

33 *burnyng a farre of, and fresyng nere.* Cf. 3. 23 n.

69. 2 (No. 99) *A renouncing of loue.* In every edition (No. [103] in *B–I*, sigs. K in *BC*, E5 in *D–G*, E4^v in *H*, E3 in *I*). Miss Foxwell (1, 19) prints the poem from MS. Egerton 2711, with the following variants:

69.   9 Hath taught me to sett in tryfels no store
   10 But] And: forth thence] fourth
   15 my] all my
   16 lyst] lusteth

3 *Farewell, Loue, &c.* Quoted in *The Arte of English Poesie*, 1589, p. 144, as an example of "a verse wholly *trochaick*."

11 *go trouble yonger hartes.* Wyatt was about twenty-five in 1528, when (if Miss Foxwell's confusing statements at II, 33 can be accepted) he left England for Calais.

17 (No. 100) *The louer forsaketh his vnkinde loue.* In every edition (No. [104] in *B–I*, sigs. K–K^v in *BC*, E5–E5^v in *D–G*, E4^v–E5 in *H*, E3 in *I*). Miss Foxwell (1, 20) prints the poem from MS. Egerton 2711, with the following variants:

69. 20 lo it to thee was] it was to the
   21 that I should] to
   22 receiue reward] be rewarded

69. 24 And] But: repayd after] payed under
    25 there] *Om.*: nother] othr
    28 by] be: for] *Om.*
    29 pleaseth] please: defaut] a default
    30 departing] parting
    31 doth beleue] belevith
    32 *Partly torn out*

The source of No. 100 is Serafino's strambotti (*Opere*, 1516, fols. 151–151ᵛ) only the first of which is followed at all closely:

> El cor ti diedi non che el tormentassi
>   Ma che fosse da te ben conseruato,
> Seruo ti fui non che me abandonassi
>   Ma che fosse da te remeritato,
> Contento fui che schiauo me acchatassi
>   Ma non di tal moneta esser pagato,
> Hor poi che regna in te poca pietate
>   Non ti spiaccia sio torno in libertate.

> La donna di natura mai si satia
>   Di dar effecto à ogni suo desyderio,
> E sempre ti stá sopra con audatia
>   Del tuo martyr pigliando refrigerio,
> Quanto piú humil li uai tanto piú stratia
>   Perfin che thá sepulto in cymiterio,
> Perche chi pone lo suo amor in femina
>   Zappa nel acqua & nella harena semina.

69. 31–32 *For, he, that doth beleue, &c.* This "gem" is copied in MS. Rawlinson Poet. 108, fol. 7, along with 106. 20 ff. Line 32, "Ploweth in the water," etc. (a close translation of Serafino's "Zappa nel acqua," etc.), is a proverbial expression, numerous examples of which are cited in the *Gorgeous Gallery*, pp. 180–181.

33 (No. 101) *The louer describeth, &c.* In every edition (No. [105] in *B–I*, sigs. Kᵛ in *BC*, E5ᵛ in *D–G*, E5 in *H*, E3–E3ᵛ in *I*). Although this poem occurs in the Egerton MS. from which Miss Foxwell takes many of her other texts, she prints it (1, 43) from *A* instead, introducing the following errors:

70. 8 colour] color
     9 and somthing] And something
    10 lust] luste: to ²] do
    12 assinde] assynd
    17 wherfore] wherefore
    19 there] ther
    20 wheras] wher as
    25 my] the
    28 god] God

This double sonnet — which has only slight variations from the so-called English, or Shakespearean, type (*abba cddc effe gg*) — was, like No. 116, probably written in prison during 1541.

70. 7 *Do fele some force.* Nott (Wyatt, pp. 543–544) suggests that *force* either is used in the extraordinary sense of "secret spring or cause which supplies them with water," or else is an error for *source*. The latter suggestion seems the more plausible.

15 *no toole away the skar can race.* Cf. 31. 7, 78. 11, 80. 19, and *The Firste Parte of Churchyardes Chippes*, 1575 (Collier's reprint, p. 117), "And though some time the surgeon salve did finde To heale the wound (the skarre remaind behinde." See also John Oldham's *Satyrs upon the Jesuits*, 1679 (Satyre III, "Loyala's Will," 1682 ed., p. 70), "A Wound, though cur'd, yet leaves behind a Scar."

30 (No. 102) *The louer lamentes the death, &c.* In every edition (No. [106] in *B–I*, sigs. K^v–K2 in *BC*, E5^v–E6 in *D–G*, E5–E5^v in *H*, E3^v in *I*). Miss Foxwell (1, 41) prints the poem from a Harington MS. (Additional 28635), with the following variants:

> 70. 39 Daily] Dearlye
> 71. 3 carefull] wofull

The source of No. 102 is Petrarch, sonetto in morte 2 (*Rime*, 269, p. 261):

> Rotta è l' alta colonna e 'l verde lauro
> che facean ombra al mio stanco pensero;
> perduto ò quel che ritrovar non spero
> dal borrea a l' austro o dal mar indo al mauro.
> Tolto m' ài, morte, il mio doppio thesauro
> che mi fea viver lieto et gire altero;
> et ristorar nol po terra né impero,
> né gemma oriental, né forza d' auro.
> Ma se consentimento è di destino,
> che posso io piú se no aver l' alma trista,
> humidi gli occhi sempre e 'l viso chino?
> O! nostra vita ch' è sí bella in vista,
> com' perde agevolmente in un matino
> quel che 'n molti anni a gran pena s' acquista!

Wyatt substituted an original final tercet for Petrarch's last three lines. A closer translation of the entire sonnet is to be found in a Harington MS. (Additional 36529, fol. 47):

> The precius piller persiht is and rent
> That contnanste lief and cherd the werid mind
> Like of my losse no age shall euer find
> Thoghe the wolrds [*sic*] eyes a seking all wais went
> Deathe hathe be refte, the worlds cheef glory heere
> Who made the mind w̃ lief the more content
> And now alas no gold no land Empeere

Nor gift so great can that restore is spent
But if the cawse proseed from th' uper place
What can I more then morn that ame constrained
Wͭ wofull tears to waill that wofull case
O britell lief wͭ face so faire I stained
How easly lost th' art in a moment space
That many yeares wͭ muche a doo a tained.

70. 32 *The piller perisht is wherto I lent.* Nearly all commentators see in this line — borrowed though it is from Petrarch — a reference to the execution of Cromwell, Earl of Essex, the lord great chamberlain, on July 28, 1540.

71. 7 (No. 103) *The louer sendeth sighes, &c.* In every edition (No. [107] in *B–I*, sigs. K2 in *BC*, E6 in *D–G*, E5ᵛ in *H*, E4 in *I*). Miss Foxwell (1, 9) prints the poem from MS. Egerton 2711, with the following variants:

71. 11 that] *Om.*
12 be] may be: yet] *Om.*
13 end my wofull] be ende of my
17 fulfil that I desire] *Om.*
21 complaint] plaint
22 from] oute of: disceiuably doth] doeth straynably: *MS. adds:*
Goo, burning sighes

As in the case of Nos. 69 and 70, the editor of *A* changed Wyatt's rondeau to a "sonnet" with (apparently) two rhymes.

The source of No. 103 is Petrarch, sonetto in vita 102 (*Rime*, 153, pp. 164–165):

Ite, caldi sospiri, al freddo core;
rompete il ghiaccio che pietà contende;
et se prego mortale al ciel s' intende,
morte o mercé sia fine al mio dolore.
Ite, dolci penser, parlando fore
di quello ove 'l bel guardo non se stende:
se pur sua asprezza o mia stella n' offende,
sarem fuor di speranza et fuor d' errore.
Dir se po ben per voi, non forse a pieno,
che 'l nostro stato è inquieto et fosco,
sí come 'l suo pacifico et sereno.
Gite securi omai, ch' Amor ven vosco:
et ria fortuna po ben venir meno,
s' ai segni del mio sol l'aere conosco.

Wyatt translates (71. 9–13) lines 1–4 of Petrarch's sonnet but thereafter ignores it.

9–10 *Go burning sighes, &c.* Turbervile, in his *Tragical Tales* [ca. 1574], 1587 (1837 reprint, p. 297), has a poem beginning, "Go burning sighes, and pierce the frozen skie." Melbancke, in *Philotimus*, 1583, Y2, likewise borrows from Wyatt (combining 132. 8 in his passage): "Goe burning sighes vnto their frozen hartes, goe breake the yse with pitties painefull dartes; and when they are within thy reach, giue them the cup of bitter sweete, to pledg their mortall foe."

71. 23 (No. 104) *Complaint of the absence, &c.* In every edition (No. [108] in *B–I*, sigs. K2–K3ᵛ in *BC*, E6–E7ᵛ in *D–G*, E5ᵛ–E7 in *H*, E4–E5 in *I*). Miss Foxwell (1, 180–188) prints the poem from MS. Egerton 2711, with the following variants:

    71. 30 stayed] staide
        31 sored] sory
        32 wight] spryte
        33 depriued] depryffd: desired] desyerd
        34 more] most
    72. 2 mayst once] ons maist
         4 Thus in this] This is the: as yet it] that yet
         5 But] And
         6 se . . . do] perceyve thowrs how thei
         8 the East] thest: shewes] doth show
        11 East ²] thest
        13 weight] whaite: bodies] body
        14 vpon] apon
        15 desired] desird
        17 me . . . I] my whaite that it
        22 enioyed] enioyd
        23 when] wher
        24 And] But
        25 and ¹] in
        27 I never saw the thing that myght my faythfull hert delyght
        29 the ³] and
        30 shene] shining: for] *Om.*
        31 darked] darke
        35 sprong] sprang
        40 transplendant] transparant
        41 colours] colour
        42 the] *Om.*
        43 feares] fiers
        44 sheweth] shewth
    73. 2 eke] that
         3 These] Thes new: most . . . so] wherein most men
         6 for] me
         7 tassay] for to assay
         8 my] myn
        10 wyll] shall
        11 toucheth] towches
        13 shall] do
        15 my] myn
        17 surmount] sormount
        19 doe] doth
        22 gaue . . . erst] did me gyve the courtese gyfft that such
        24 this] that
        25 chere] clere

73. 27 forst] dryven
   35 ragged] craggyd
   37 And] But
   40 And . . . dye] Wherby I fere, and yet I trust
   41 dwelles] lyves
   42 There] Where: somtime, may] may sometyme
74. 2 to] thou
   3 grief] dred: serue] sterve
   6 And if] If that: waighte] whayte: the ²] this

No. 104 is translated from Petrarch, canzone in vita 3 (*Rime*, 37, pp. 38–42), as is pointed out in the notes below.

   71. 25–72. 2–5 *So feble is the threde . . . by trust, am trayned.* From Petrarch's first stanza,

> Sí è debile il filo a cui s' attene
> la gravosa mia vita,
> che s' altri non l' aita,
> ella fia tosto di suo corso a riva:
> però che dopo l' empia dipartita
> che dal dolce mio bene
> feci, sol una spene
> è stato in fin a qui cagion ch' io viva;
> dicendo: Perché priva
> sia de l' amata vista,
> mantienti, anima trista.
> Che sai s' a miglior tempo ancho ritorni?
> et a piú lieti giorni?
> o se 'l perduto ben mai si racquista?
> Questa speranza mi sostenne un tempo:
> or vien mancando, et troppo in lei m' attempo.

   72. 6–19 *The tyme doth flete . . . litle doth remain.* From Petrarch's second stanza,

> Il tempo passa, et l' ore son sí pronte
> a fornire il viaggio,
> ch' assai spacio non aggio
> pur a pensar com' io corro a la morte.
> A pena spunta in oriente un raggio
> di sol, ch' a l' altro monte
> de l' adverso orizonte
> giunto il vedrai per vie lunghe et distorte.
> Le vite son sí corte,
> sí gravi i corpi et frali
> degli uomini mortali,
> che quando io mi ritrovo dal bel viso
> cotanto esser diviso,
> col desio non possendo mover l' ali,
> poco m' avanza del conforto usato;
> né so quant' io mi viva in questo stato.

72. 20–33 *Eche place . . . my wealth doth bate.* From Petrarch's third stanza,

Ogni loco m' atrista, ov' io non veggio
quei begli occhi soavi
che portaron le chiavi
de' miei dolci pensier, mentre a Dio piacque.
Et perché 'l duro exilio piú m' aggravi,
s' io dormo o vado o seggio,
altro già mai non cheggio,
et ciò ch' i' vidi dopo lor mi spiacque.
Quante montagne et acque,
quanto mar, quanti fiumi
m' ascondon que' duo lumi,
che quasi un bel sereno a mezzo 'l die
fer le tenebre mie,
a ciò che 'l rimembrar piú mi consumi,
et quanto era mia vita allor gioiosa,
m' insegni la presente aspra et noiosa!

34–73. 2 *If such record . . . seke redresse.* From Petrarch's fourth stanza,

Lasso, se ragionando si rinfresca
quel ardente desio
che nacque il giorno ch'io
lassai di me la miglior parte a dietro,
et s' Amor se ne va per lungo oblio,
chi mi conduce a l' esca
onde 'l mio dolor cresca?
Et perché pria, tacendo, non m' impetro?
Certo, cristallo o vetro
non mostrò mai di fore
nascosto altro colore,
che l' alma sconsolata assai non mostri
piú chiari i pensier nostri,
et la fera dolcezza ch' è nel core,
per gli occhi, che di sempre pianger vaghi
cercan dí et nocte pur chi gle n' appaghi.

73. 2–16 *and eke . . . fele the smart.* From Petrarch's fifth stanza,

Novo piacer che negli umani ingegni
spesse volte si trova
d'amar qual cosa nova,
piú folta schiera di sospiri accoglia!
Et io son un di quei che 'l pianger giova;
et par ben ch' io m' ingegni
che di lagrime pregni
sien gli occhi miei, sí come 'l cor di doglia.
Et perché a cciò m' invoglia
ragionar de' begli occhi
(né cosa è che mi tocchi
o sentir mi si faccia cosí a dentro),

corro spesso et rientro
colà donde piú largo il duol trabocchi,
et sien col cor punite ambe le luci
ch' a la strada d' Amor mi furon duci.

73. 12 *nought but the case, or skin.* Nott points out that this phrase is not in canzone 3 but occurs elsewhere in Petrarch, and traces it ultimately to Dante, *Paradiso,* I. 19–21:

Entra nel petto mio, e spira tue;
Sì come quando Marsia traesti
Della vagina delle membra sue.

17–28 *The crisped golde . . . trust renewes.* From Petrarch's sixth stanza,

Le treccie d' or, che devrien fare il sole
d' invidia molta ir pieno,
e 'l bel guardo sereno,
ove i raggi d' Amor sí caldi sono
che mi fanno anzi tempo venir meno,
et l' accorte parole,
rade nel mondo o sole,
che mi fer già di sé cortese dono,
mi son tolte; et perdono
piú lieve ogni altra offesa,
che l' essermi contesa
quella benigna angelica salute,
che 'l mio cor a vertute
destar solea con una voglia accesa:
tal ch' io non penso udir cosa già mai
che mi conforte ad altro ch'a trar guai.

18 *streames of pleasant starres.* Glances of her eyes.

21–23 *The wyse and pleasant talk, &c.* Nott explains thus: "That charm of conversation so seldom to be met with, perhaps never in any one but herself, which she was wont courteously to indulge me with, is now taken from me."

29–42 *And yet . . . may take repose.* From Petrarch's seventh stanza,

Et per pianger anchor con piú diletto,
le man bianche sottili
et le braccia gentili,
et gli atti suoi soavemente alteri,
e i dolci sdegni alteramente humili,
e 'l bel giovenil petto,
torre d' alto intellecto,
mi celan questi luoghi alpestri e feri;
et non so s' io mi speri
vederla anzi ch' io mora;
però ch' ad ora ad ora
s' erge la speme et poi non sa star ferma;
ma ricadendo afferma

> di mai non veder lei che 'l ciel honora,
> ov' alberga honestate et cortesia,
> et dov' io prego che 'l mio albergo sia.

73. 30–31 *y̆ firmely do embrace Me from my self.* From Horace's *Carmina*,
IV. 13 (as Nott points out), "Quae me surpuerat mihi."

32 *The swete disdaines, &c.* Nott asserts that this phrase is added from
Petrarch, sonetto in morte 86 (*Rime*, 351, p. 329), "Dolci durezze et placide
repulse."

43–74. 2–6 *My song . . . to her flee.* Somewhat changed from Petrarch's
final stanza,

> Canzon, s' al dolce loco
> la Donna nostra vedi,
> credo ben che tu credi
> ch' ella ti porgerà la bella mano
> ond' io son sí lontano.
> Non la tocchar; ma reverente ai piedi
> le di' ch' io sarò là tosto ch' io possa,
> o spirto ignudo od uom di carne et d' ossa.

74. 7 (No. 105) *The louer blameth his loue, &c.* In every edition (No.
[109] in *B–I*, sigs. K3ᵛ in *BC*, E7ᵛ in *D–G*, E7–E7ᵛ in *H*, E5–E5ᵛ in *I*). Miss
Foxwell (1, 385) reprints the poem from *A*, misprinting *madame* (line 10) as
Madame, *gredy* (line 15) as *greedy*.

22 (No. 106) *The louer curseth the tyme, &c.* In every edition (No. [110]
in *B–I*, sigs. K3ᵛ–K4 in *BC*, E7ᵛ–E8 in *D–G*, E7ᵛ in *H*, E5ᵛ in *I*). Miss Fox-
well (1, 378) reprints the poem from *A*, with the following errors:

> 74. 29 heare] hear
> 75. 4 memorie] memory
>   6 finde] find: geat] get
>   7 foote] fote

Another version appears under the title of "He repenteth his folly," with the
signature W. H. (William Hunnis), in the first (1576), but no later, edition of
the *Paradise*, pp. 65–66. That version omits 74. 30–75. 2, but inserts a new
stanza after 75. 14:

> Thē should not I suche cause haue foūd, to wish this mōstrus sight to se,
> Ne thou alas that madest the wounde, should not deny me remedy,
> Then should one will in bothe remain, to graūt one hart whiche now is twaine.

For verbal variants between the two texts see the *Paradise*, p. 230.

75. 15 (No. 107) *The louer determineth, &c.* In every edition (No. [111]
in *B–I*, sigs. K4–K4ᵛ in *BC*, E8–E8ᵛ in *D–G*, E7ᵛ–E8 in *H*, E6 in *I*). Miss
Foxwell (1, 372–373) reprints the poem from *A*, with the following errors:

> 75. 31 tyll] till
>   33 my selfe] myself
>   37 reward] rewarde

76. 4 a loft] aloft
    7 my self] myself

75. 22 *To serue, and suffer paciently.* This refrain may come (as Miss Foxwell suggests) from Seneca's phrase in *De Moribus*, "Dolor patientia vincitur."

76. 15 (No. 108) *The louer suspected, &c.* In every edition (No. [112] in *B–I*, sigs. K4ᵛ in *BC*, E8ᵛ in *D–G*, E8–E8ᵛ in *H*, E6ᵛ in *I*). Miss Foxwell (1, 379) reprints the poem from *A*, misprinting *deserued* (line 27) as *diserved*, *god* (line 28) as *God*. Possibly the lines refer to the false charges pressed against Wyatt after the execution of Cromwell: the title (manufactured by the printer, not by Wyatt) is obviously misleading.

29 (No. 109) *The louer complaineth, &c.* In every edition (No. [113] in *B–I*, sigs. K4ᵛ–L in *BC*, E8ᵛ–F in *D–H*, E6ᵛ–E7 in *I*). Miss Foxwell (1, 383–384) reprints the poem from *A*, with the following errors:

76. 31 ff. *Speech-tags spelled out in full*
    32 inflamde] inflamed
    34 if] of
77. 2 thy self] thyself
     7 god] God
    13 hart] hert
    15 drieues] drives
    22 should] would
    23 An hart] A hert
    24 doute] doubte

This is a very pretty poem in which a sensual subject is handled with remarkable restraint and purity. Line 28 is Wyatt's comment, not the lover's.

77. 8 *thy grief is mine.* Read *the grief* with *B+*.

29 (No. 110) *why loue is blinde.* In every edition (No. [114] in *B–I*, sigs. L in *BC*, F in *D–H*, E7 in *I*). Miss Foxwell (1, 57) prints the poem from MS. Egerton 2711, with the variant reading (line 30) *chase* for *chose*. Somewhat unreasonably she thinks it "records a deep attachment for some unknown friend, possibly Mary, Duchess of Richmond."

38 (No. 111) *To his vnkinde loue.* In every edition (No. [115] in *B–I*, sigs. L–Lᵛ in *BC*, F–Fᵛ in *D–G*, F in *H*, E7 in *I*). Miss Foxwell (1, 178–179) prints the poem from MS. Egerton 2711, with the following variants:

78. 6 flow] swell
    11 cureles] curid
    13, 14 doest] dost
    18 beloued] belovffd

She overlooks its appearance in *A–I*.

78. 13–14 *thou doest oppresse. Oppresse thou doest.* An interesting example of the rhetorical device chiasmus. See another example at 100. 19.

16 *Fierce Tigre, fell, hard rock.* Cf. 54.35–55. 2–4 n.

78. 22 (No. 112) *The louer blameth, &c.* In every edition (No. [116] in *B–I*, sigs. L^v in *BC*, F^v in *D–H*, E7^v in *I*). Miss Foxwell (1, 53) prints the poem from Wyatt's autograph copy in MS. Egerton 2711 (the only variant is *I sought* for *thou sekest* [line 26] unless, as is not likely, *ledst* [cf. *leadst*, line 27] is the past tense), and also gives a somewhat clearer, if apparently unauthorized, version from MS. Additional 17492:

> Cruell desire my master and my foo,
> Thy self so chaingid. [*sic*] for shame how maist thou see.
> Whom I have sought dothe chase me to and froo:
> Whom thou didst rule nowe rulith the and me:
> What right is to rule thy subjectes soo?
> And to be ruled by mutability?
> Lo wherebye the I doubted to have blame,
> Even now bye dred againe I doubt the same.

She suggests that it was written in imitation of Maurice Sève's dizaine 33 (*Délie*, 1544, ed. Eugène Parturier, pp. 29–30) beginning, "Tant est Nature en volenté puissante"; but the suggestion is hard to credit.

32 (No. 113) *The louer complayneth his estate.* In every edition (No. [117] in *B–I*, sigs. L^v–L2 in *BC*, F^v–F2 in *D–H*, E7^v–E8 in *I*). Miss Foxwell (1, 380–381) reprints the poem from *A*, misprinting *my self* (79. 5) as *myself*, *hath* (line 8) as *have*, *pensif* (line 26) as *pensiv*.

79. 29 (No. 114) *Against hourders of money.* In every edition (No. [124] in *B–I*, sigs. L3^v in *BC*, F3^v in *D–G*, F3 in *H*, F in *I*). Miss Foxwell (1, 60) reprints the poem from *A*.

The original epigram on which the poem is based was long ascribed to Antipater or Statylius Flaccus but now more commonly to Plato: "χρυσὸν ἀνὴρ εὑρὼν ἔλιπεν βρόχον· αὐτὰρ ὁ χρυσὸν ὃν λίπεν οὐχ εὑρὼν ἧψεν ὃν εὗρε βρόχον." It was translated twice by Ausonius (*Epigrammata*, xxii, xxiii), whence Wyatt perhaps took his version. Many other English translations have been made. For example, Timothy Kendall, in *Flowers of Epigrammes*, 1577, G4 (Spenser Society ed., p. 119), included an epigram

> *Translated out of twoo Greeke au-*
> *thors: Plato and Scatilius.*
>
> A Wretched caitiffe, in dispaire,
> 　　went foorth with throtlyng corde
> To make awaie hymself: by hap
> 　　he founde a golden hoarde:
> He ioyfull twas his happie chaunce,
> 　　this hidden hoarde to finde:
> Forsooke his purpose, tooke the gold
> 　　and left the rope behinde.
> The owner when he came, and sawe
> 　　from thence his ruddocks refte:
> For sorrowe hunge hym self with rope,
> 　　that there behinde was lefte.

Coleridge (*Complete Poetical Works*, ed. E. H. Coleridge, II [1912], 971) in 1812 wrote the following translation:

> Jack finding gold left a rope on the ground:
> Bill missing his gold used the rope which he found.

See also the versions by Shelley ("A Man who was about to hang himself") and Courthope (*A History of English Poetry*, II, 58 n.), and those in Latin, Italian, French, German (as well as Greek and English) included in Henry Wellesley's *Anthologia Polyglotta* (1849), pp. 440–442. Melbancke, *Philotimus*, 1583, E3ᵛ, also tells the story, probably borrowing from Wyatt: "One goinge about his busines with an haulter in his hand, chaunced to finde monye which a miser had hid, which money he tooke, aud [*sic*] layde downe the haulter in the place: the olde huddle missing his monye at his next visitation, toke the haulter and hanged himselfe."

79. 38 (No. 115) *Discripcion of a gonne*. In every edition (No. [125] in *B–I*, sigs. L3ᵛ in *BC*, F3ᵛ in *D–H*, F in *I*). Miss Foxwell (I, 58) prints the poem from MS. Egerton 2711.

No. 115 is translated from the Latin of Pandulpho (flourished *ca.* 1500), with its final two lines original. Nott (Wyatt, p. cxxvii) quotes the Latin from Pandulpho's apologue "Bombarda," appended to *Colloquia duo elegantissima*, Basle, 1547, a book inaccessible to me:

> Vulcanus genuit; peperit Natura; Minerva
>   Edocuit; Nutrix Ars fuit, atque dies.
> Vis mea de Nihilo est; tria dant mihi corpora pastum.
>   Sunt nati, Strages, Ira, Ruina, Fragor.
> Dic, Hospes, qui sum! Num terræ, an bellua ponti?
>   An neutrum! aut quo sim facta, vel orta modo.

A slightly different version, which appears along with Wyatt's translation in one of the MSS., is given by Miss Foxwell (II, 73).

80. 10 (No. 116) *wiat being in prison, to Brian*. In every edition (No. [126] in *B–I*, sigs. L4 in *BC*, F4 in *D–G*, F3ᵛ in *H*, Fᵛ in *I*). Miss Foxwell (I, 62) prints the poem from MS. Harleian 78, with the following variants:

> 80. 12 my ²] *Om.*
>   13 would . . . craue] suche musycke wolde crave
>   14 it] *Om.*
>   15 Pore innocence] Innocencie
>   16 iudge I] I judge
>   17 assaultes] assaulted
>   18 am I] I am

It was probably written during Wyatt's imprisonment, January 17–March 21, 1541. Like No. 126, it is addressed to Sir Francis Bryan.

20 (No. 117) *Of dissembling wordes*. In every edition (No. [127] in *B–I*, sigs. L4 in *BC*, F4 in *D–G*, F3ᵛ in *H*, Fᵛ in *I*). Miss Foxwell (I, 382) reprints the poem from *A*, with the following errors:

80. 21 wer] were
    22 ynough] enough
    26 acord] accord

80. 27 (No. 118) *Of the meane and sure estate*. In every edition (No. [128]
in *B–I*, sigs. L4 in *BC*, F4 in *D–G*, F3ᵛ–F4 in *H*, Fᵛ in *I*). Miss Foxwell (1, 366)
prints the poem from a Harington MS. (Additional 28635), with the following
variants:

80. 29 whele] toppe
    30 hye astate] courtes estates
    31 And use me quyet without lett or stoppe
    32 the wanton toyes] such brackishe joyes
81. 2 my . . . slowly] so lett my dayes forthe
     3 And] That: past] done
     4 Let me dye olde] I may dye aged
     5–6 For hym death greep' [?] the right hard by the croppe.
        That is moche knowen of other; and of himself, alas,
     7 He dyeth] Doth dye

Chalmers (*The Works of the English Poets*, 11 [1810], 385) noted that No.
118 is translated from Seneca's *Thyestes* (11. 391–403):

Stet quicunque volet potens
Aulae culmine lubrico:
Me dulcis saturet quies.
Obscuro positus loco,
Leni perfruar otio.
Nullis nota Quiritibus
Aetas per tacitum fluat.
Sic cum transierint mei
Nullo cum strepitu dies
Plebeius moriar senex,
Illi mors gravis incubat,
Qui notus nimis omnibus.
Ignotus moritur sibi.

For other poems on the "low estate" see Nos. 124, 170, 191, 200.

81. 8 (No. 119) *The courtiers life*. In every edition (No. [129] in *B–I*,
sigs. L4–L4ᵛ in *BC*, F4–F4ᵛ in *D–G*, F4 in *H*, Fᵛ–F2 in *I*). Miss Foxwell
(1, 61) reprints the poem from *A*.

16 (No. 120) *Of disapointed purpose by negligence*. In every edition
(No. [130] in *B–I*, sigs. L4ᵛ in *BC*, F4ᵛ in *D–G*, F4 in *H*, F2 in *I*). Miss
Foxwell (1, 55) reprints the poem from MS. Egerton 2711, with the following
variants:

81. 21 aduance] avaunce
    22 Ne could I] Could not it

The opening lines were suggested by sonetto 11 of Petrarch's "sonetti sopra
varj argomenti" (*Rime*, 103, p. 106):

Vinse Hanibal, et non seppe usar poi
ben la vittoriosa sua ventura:
però, signor mio caro, aggiate cura
che similmente non avegna a voi.

They are translated in a Harington MS. (Additional 36529, fol. 47):

Haniball woon and after cold not sew
The victrus lote that happly to him fell
Therfore deer sire take heed and fore see well
That like mischance doo not chance unto you.

The mention of Monzon in line 25 indicates that the epigram was written about 1537, when Wyatt was ambassador to Emperor Charles V.

81. 26 (No. 121) *Of his returne from Spaine.* In every edition (No. [131] in *B–I*, sigs. L4ᵛ in *BC*, F4ᵛ in *D–G*, F4 in *H*, F2 in *I*). Miss Foxwell (1, 57) prints the poem from MS. Egerton 2711, with the following variants:

81. 28 tried] tryd
    29 For . . . saile] With spurr and sayle for I
    30 sheweth] showth
    31 that] which
    32 that leanes] doth lend
    33 I seke] alone
    34 Ioue] love: windes] winges

It was written to celebrate Wyatt's return to England from Spain in 1539. Drayton quotes the poem in the notes to Surrey's epistle to Geraldine in *Englands Heroicall Epistles*, 1598, N4, remarking that it is an "excellent Epigram, which as I iudge either to bee done by the said Earle [of Surrey] or Sir *Frauncis Brian* . . . which as it seemes to me was compiled at the Authors being in Spaine."

27–28 *Tagus . . . Turnes vp the graines of gold.* From Boethius (probably Chaucer's translation), III, meter x.

31 *towne that Brutus sought by dreames.* New Troy, or London, founded by Brutus, the great-grandson of Aeneas (according to the popular legend).

82. 2 (No. 122) *Of sodaine trustyng.* In every edition (No. [132] in *B–I*, sigs. L4ᵛ in *BC*, F4ᵛ in *D–G*, F4–F4ᵛ in *H*, F2 in *I*). Miss Foxwell (1, 340) prints the poem from MS. Additional 17492 (where Nott had overlooked it), with the variant reading of *the untrue* (line 5) for *thuntrue.*

10 (No. 123) *Of the mother that eat her childe, &c.* In every edition (No. [133] in *B–I*, sigs. M in *BC*, F5 in *D–G*, F4ᵛ in *H*, F2–F2ᵛ in *I*). Miss Foxwell (1, 55) prints the poem from MS. Egerton 2711, with the following variants:

82. 13 whiles motherly] whilst moderly
    15 The mother sayth] Sayth thebrew moder
    18 were] wert

Josephus (*The Wars of the Jews*, VI. iii. 4, in his *Works*, ed. Whiston, II [1825], 465–466) tells how Mary, daughter of Eleazer, killed her son, and boiled and ate his body, during the siege of Jerusalem in the year 70 A.D.

82. 21 (No. 124) *Of the meane and sure estate, &c.* In every edition (No. [134] in *B–I*, sigs. M–M2^v in *BC*, F5–F6^v in *D–G*, F4^v–F6 in *H*, F2^v–F3^v in *I*). Miss Foxwell (I, 141–146) prints the poem from MS. Egerton 2711, with the following variants:

82. 23 do] did
   24 sing] sang sometyme: made] *Om.*:   feldishe] feld
   25 forbicause] fobicause [?]
   26 se] seke
   27 greuous] much
83. 2 both] boeth
    3 while] whilest
    4 when her] wher
  11, 20, 25 doth] doeth
  12 labours] laboureth
  13, 17 fedes] fedeth
  15 of] of the
  17 boyle meat] boyled: bake meat] bacon meet: on] *Om.*
  18 therfore no whit of] therof neither
  21 makes she] she maketh
  22 goes] goeth
  24 there] *Om.*
  27 scrapes] scrapeth
  33 towne] townysshe
  40 Amid] Amyddes
  42 lookt] loke
84. 3 the] tho
    7 townemouse] towney mowse: whither] whether
    8 The other] Thothr
    9 wisht] wyshed
  11 The heauen] Thevyn
  16 forgot] forgotten
  21 blindes] blynde
  24, 33, 39 you] ye
  26 with ^{2}] *Om.*
  30, 31 doth] doeth
  32 is it] it is
  34 for] *Om.*:   on ^{1}] upon: on ^{2}] *Om.*
  37 Nor] Ne: set] se
  43 assinde] assigned
85. 5 stickyng] sitting
    9 Poins] Poyngz
  11 his] his high
  13 doth] doeth

The poem is an imitation of the sixth satire of Horace's second book, in which a reference to the fable of the Town Mouse and the Country Mouse is introduced. Possibly Wyatt also knew the rendition of this fable written by Robert Henryson and published before 1500. The tone throughout and many of the actual phrases are Chaucerian. Of John Poyntz, to whom these terza-rima stanzas (as well as No. 125) are addressed, little is known. He belonged, however, to an Essex family of considerable distinction, and was related to Sir Francis Poyntz († 1528) and Sir Anthony Poyntz († 1533), who became important as diplomats. Nott (Wyatt, pp. lxxxiii–lxxxiv) gives some account of him, pointing out that his portrait by Holbein shows him "to have had a remarkably intelligent and expressive countenance," while Miss Foxwell (II, 102) adds that Holbein painted him in "a scholar's garb."

83. 43 *two stemyng eyes*. The adjective was no doubt suggested by the description of the Monk in the Prologue to *The Canterbury Tales* (A. 201–202):

> His eyen stepe, and rollinge in his heed,
> That stemed as a forneys of a leed.

Cf. also John Studley's *Medea*, act III (*Seneca His Tenne Tragedies*, 1581, fol. 128; see also the uses on fols. 153ᵛ, 192ᵛ), "Her firy, scowling, steaming Eyes"; and Melbancke's *Philotimus*, 1583, Iᵛ, "a cat in seing with her steeming eies."

84. 16 *her power, surety and rest*. That is, her poor (in poverty) security and ease. Wyatt is contrasting security in poverty and insecurity in wealth.

25–27 *No, no, although thy head, &c.* Nott (p. 561) thinks these lines are "elegantly imitated" from Horace (*Carmina*, II. 16).

85. 3–4 *seke no more out of thy selfe to finde, &c.* "Cease to look for happiness outside of yourself. You are mad if you do." Cf. Persius, satire I. 7, "nec te quaesiveris extra" (Nott).

8 *depe your selfe in trauell more and more*. Perhaps "enter more deeply into the labor of literary and religious study." Nott thinks the idea may have come from Dante's *Paradiso*, I. 8–9:

> Nostro intelletto si profonda tanto,
> Che retro la memoria non può ire.

11 *to the great God, &c.* Nott calls this whole passage "a beautiful imitation of the following spirited lines of Persius, in his third Satire" (lines 35–38):

> Magne Pater Divum, saevos punire tyrannos
> Haud alia ratione velis, cum dira libido
> Moverit ingenium, ferventi tincta veneno,
> Virtutem videant intabescantque relicta.

19 (No. 125) *Of the Courtiers life, &c.* In every edition (No. [135] in *B–I*, sigs. M2ᵛ–M3ᵛ in *BC*, F6ᵛ–F7ᵛ in *D–G*, F6ᵛ–F7ᵛ in *H*, F4–F5 in *I*). Miss Foxwell (I, 135–140) prints the poem from various MSS. (since Egerton

2711, which she follows so far as it goes, is incomplete), with the following
variants:

85. 22 causes] cause
    27 because] for bicawse: or] and
    28 whom fortune here] to whome fortune
    33 inward doth] doeth inward
    34 of glory that] that of glory
    39 my] me
    40 truth] trothe
    41 nice] vice
86. 2 set] settes
     5 such] do so grete
     8 my] *Om.*
     9 And] Nor
    11 as] *Om.*
    12 and] or
    13 Call] And call: lucre] proffet
    16 that] *Om.*
    20 doth] do
    21 where] when
    22 wealth] wele
    24 in] *Om.*
    25 coward] cowardes
    27 dieth] dythe
    28 Alexander] Alessaundre
    30 Topas] Thopias
    33 laughes] laugheth
    34 frownes] frowneth
    35 both] boeth
    39 to] of
    41 With] With the: ay to cloke] to cloke alwaye
87. 5 faire] *Om.*
     6 curties] courtois
     7 Affirme] And say
    12 rechlesse vnto ech] rekles to every
    20 and] and to
    21 wether] weder
    23, 26 doth] doeth
    26 Saue] Sauf
    27 ordred] ordered
    28 both] boeth
    30 savry] saffry: those] the
    33 that] than [?]
    34 lettes] letteth
    35 takes] taketh: wittes] wit
    36 such . . . beastes] they beestes do so
    37 truth] Christe
    38 of some] at Rome
    40 I am here] here I ame
    41 Among] Emong
    42 myne owne Iohn] my: to] for to

The poem is paraphrased from Luigi Alamanni's tenth satire, "A Thom-maso Sertini" (*Opere Toscane*, 1532, pp. 400–404):

> Io ui dirò poi che d' udir ui cale
> Thommaso mio gentil, perch' amo, & colo
> Piu di tutti altri il lito Prouenzale.
> Et perche qui cosi pouero & solo,
> Piu tosto che 'l seguir Signiori & Regi
> Viuo temprando 'l mio infinito duolo.
> Ne cio mi uien perch' io tra me dispregi
> Quei, ch' han dalla Fortuna in mano il freno
> Di noi, per sangue, & per ricchezze egregi.
> Ma ben' è uer ch' assai gli estimo meno
> Che 'l uulgo, & quei ch' à cio ch' appar di fuore
> Guardan, senza ueder che chiugga il seno.
> Non dico gia che non mi scaldi amore
> Talhor di gloria, ch' io non uo mentire
> Con chi biasmando honor, sol cerca honore.
> Ma con qual pie potrei color seguire
> Che 'l mondo pregia; ch' io non so quell' arte
> Di chi le scale altrui conuien salire.
> Io non saprei Sertin porre in disparte
> La uerità, colui lodando ogni hora
> Che con piu danno altrui dal ben si parte.
> Non saprei reuerir chi soli adora
> Venere & Bacco, ne tacer saprei
> Di quei che 'l uulgo falsamente honora.
> Non saprei piu ch' à gli immortali Dei
> Rendere honor con le ginocchia inchine
> À piu ingiusti che sian, fallaci, & rei.
> Non saprei nel parlar courir le spine
> Con simulati fior, nell' opre hauendo
> Mele al principio, & tristo assentio al fine.
> Non saprei no, doue 'l contrario intendo
> I maluagi consigli usar per buoni,
> Dauanti al uero honor l' util ponendo.
> Non trouare ad ogni hor false cagioni
> Per abbassare i giusti, alzando i praui
> D' auaritia, & di 'nuidia hauendo sproni.
> Non saprei dar de miei pensier le chiaui
> All' ambition, che mi portasse in alto
> Alla fucina delle colpe graui.
> Non saprei 'l core hauer di freddo sinalto
> Contro à pietà, talhor nocendo à tale,
> Ch' io piu di tutti nella mente esalto,
> Non di loda honorar chiara immortale
> Cesare & Sylla, condannando à torto
> Bruto, & la schiera che piu d' altra uale.
> Non saprei camminar nel sentier corto
> Dell' impia iniquità, lasciando quello
> Che reca pace al uiuo, & gloria al morto.

Io non saprei chiamar cortese & bello
   Chi sia Thersite, ne figliuol d' Anchise
   Chi sia di senno & di pietà rubello.
Non saprei chi piu 'l cor nell' oro mise
   Dirgli Alessandro, e 'l pauroso & uile
   Chiamarlo il forte, ch' i Centauri ancise.
Dir non saprei Poeta alto, & gentile
   Meuio, giurando poi che tal non uide
   Smirna, Manto, & Fiorenza ornato stile.
Non saprei dentro all' alte soglie infide
   Per piu mostrar' amor, contr' à mia uoglia
   Imitar sempre altrui se piange, o ride.
Non saprei indiuinar quel ch' altri uoglia,
   Ne conoscer saprei quel che piu piace
   Tacendo il uer che le piu uolte addoglia.
L' amico lusinghier, doppio, & fallace
   Dir non saprei gentil, ne aperto & uero
   Chi sempre parli quel che piu dispiace.
Non saprei l' huom crudel chiamar seuero,
   Ne chi lascia peccar chiamarlo pio,
   Ne che 'l tyranneggiar sia giusto impero.
Io non saprei ingannar gli huomini & Dio,
   Con giuramenti & con promesse false,
   Ne far saprei quel ch' è d' un' altro mio.
Questo è cagion che non mi cal, ne calse
   Anchor gia mai, di seguitar coloro
   Ne quai Fortuna piu che 'l senno ualse.
Questo fa che 'l mio regnio, e 'l mio thesoro
   Son gli 'nchiostri & le carte, & piu ch' altroue
   Hoggi in Prouenza uolentier dimoro.
Qui non ho alcun, che mi domandi doue
   Mi stia, ne uada, & non mi sforza alcuno
   À gir pe 'l mondo quando agghiaccia & pioue.
Quando e' gli è 'l ciel seren, quando e' gli è bruno
   Son quel medesmo, & non mi prendo affanno,
   Colmo di pace, & di timor digiuno.
Non sono in Francia à sentir beffe & danno
   S' io non conosco i uin, s' io non so bene
   Qual uiuanda è miglior di tutto l' anno.
Non nella Hispagnia oue studiar conuiene
   Piu che nell' esser poi nel ben parere,
   Oue frode, & menzognia il seggio tiene,
Non in Germania oue 'l mangiare e 'l bere
   M' habbia à tor l' intelletto, & darlo in preda
   Al senso, in guisa di seluagge fere.
Non sono in Roma, oue chi 'n Christo creda,
   Et non sappia falsar, ne far ueneni
   Conuien ch' a casa sospirando rieda.
Sono in Prouenza, oue quantunque pieni
   Di maluagio uoler ci sian gli 'ngegni,
   L' ignioranza e 'l timor pon loro i freni.

[217]

Che benche sian di 'nuidia & d' odio pregni
  Sempre contro i miglior per ueder poco
  Son nel mezzo troncati i lor disegni.
Hor qui dunque mi sto, prendendo in gioco
  Il lor breue sauer, le lunghe uoglie
  Con le mie Muse in solitario loco.
Non le gran Corti homai, non l' alte soglie
  Mi uedran gir co i lor seguaci à schiera,
  Ne di me hauran troppo honorate spoglie
Auaritia, & liuor, ma pace uera.

Though translated from Alamanni, No. 125 introduces various local and personal touches, as at 86. 20, 23–33, 87. 40–42. It was no doubt written during Wyatt's enforced exile in Kent after he had been released from prison in 1536.

85. 25 *wrapped within my cloke.* Cf. Horace's *Carmina*, III. xxix. 54–55, "mea virtute me involvo" (Nott).

30–33 *I haue alwayes ment, &c.* These obscure lines evidently mean that Wyatt esteems the great less than do the common sort of people, who judge them more by their outward appearance than by their real merits.

41 *all nice.* Read *all vice* with *B–D** and the MS.

86. 10 *Nor turne the worde, &c.* Nott points out that the thought and expression are evidently taken from Horace, *Ars Poetica,* lines 389–390, "delere licebit Quod non edideris; nescit vox missa reverti."

18, 20 *Cato, Liuye.* Wyatt adds Livy and substitutes Cato for Brutus. He handles proper names in the poem very freely, omitting, for example, Alamanni's references to Sulla, Thersites, Aeneas, Maevius, Smyrna, Florence, Provence. Marcus Porcius Cato (Uticensis), Pompey's adherent, committed suicide after the battle of Thapsus in 46 B.C., thus escaping (line 20) "from Caesar's hands." The book (CXIV) of Livy in which this was told is lost, so that (to quote Nott, p. 562) "Wyatt's authority must have been . . . the author of the Epitome to that book, whose words are; Cato, auditâ re, quum se percussisset Uticae et interveniente filio curaretur, inter ipsam curationem, resciso vulnere, expiravit."

30–31 *syr Topas, the story that the knight tolde.* This discriminating comment on two of Chaucer's Canterbury tales is, of course, Wyatt's substitution for Alamanni's "Poeta alto, & gentile, Meuio," etc.

41 *With nearest vertue ay to cloke the vice.* Nott believes this phrase is borrowed from Horace, *Satires,* I. iii. 41–42, "et isti errori nomen virtus posuisset honestum."

42–43 *As to purpose, &c.* On the repetition of these lines at 87. 2–3 see p. 19, above.

87. 16 *I can not, I.* On this common repetition of the pronoun see the examples listed in the *Gorgeous Gallery,* p. 190, and the *Paradise,* p. 239.

87. 26 *a clogge doth hang yet at my heele.* Wyatt was free during his "exile" in Kent, but was formally on parole to his father. The phrase is proverbial, as in John Taylor the Water Poet's *Iuniper Lecture*, 1639, D3ᵛ, "then *you* say *you* cannot be merrie because *you* have such a clog at your Heeles," and *The Rump Despairing, Or The Rumps Proverbs*, 1660, p. 4, "For a Jackanapes cannot be merry when a clog is at his heeles." Cf. also Gabriel Harvey, *The Trimming of Thomas Nashe*, 1597 (*Works*, ed. Grosart, III, 44), "thou hast a clog at thy heele as the prouerbe is."

29 *in Fraunce, to iudge the wine.* Alamanni's words apply to Wyatt's own case; for when the latter poet was at Calais, in 1529, he received permission to export wine.

32 *Rather then to be, outwardly to seme.* "If you will seem honest," Wyatt wrote to his fifteen-year-old son, "be honest, or else seem as you are. Seek not the name without the thing" (see Nott's Wyatt, p. 272).

34–35 *Flaunders chere lettes not, &c.* "I am not in Flanders [Alamanni's "Germania"] where excessive eating and drinking prevent my telling black from white and destroy my wits with beastliness."

37, 38 *truth, of some.* In Wyatt's MS., as in Alamanni's verse, these words are *Christ* and *at Rome.* Of course the editor of *A* made the change in deference to political and religious conditions in 1557. Note Wyatt's comment at 85. 38 that he himself "cannot dye the color black a liar."

88. 2 (No. 126) *How to vse the court, &c.* In every edition (No. [136] in *B–I*, sigs. M3ᵛ–N in *BC*, F7ᵛ–G in *D–G*, F7ᵛ–F8ᵛ in *H*, F5–F6 in *I*). Miss Foxwell (I, 147–151) prints the poem from MS. Egerton 2711, with the following variants:

88.   7 doth] doeth
       12 standst] stondes
       19 mightest] myghtst
       23 dung] the tordes
       24 pearles with] perilles the
       25 So] Then: doth] to
       26 So sackes of dust be filled up in the cloyster
       27 So] That
       28 withouten moysture] withoute moyster
       29 will] woll
       36 knowest] knowst
       37 trouth] trowght
       38 both] boeth
89.   2 dayes] dayes so
        4 saies] say so
        9 calfe] dogge
       12 the ladde] Kittson
       13 withouten] withoute
       14 knowes] knoweth
       16 beginnes] begynneth
       19 coughe] koggh
       20 What] When

89. 24, 32 thou] you
    29 mayest] maist
    34 be] by
90. 2 Laughest] Laughst
     4 Wouldest] Would'st
     8 thou] you
    13 world] worould

This satire, which shows the influence of both Horace (especially *Satires*, II. v) and Chaucer, was perhaps written about 1537. It is supposed to be a dialogue between Sir Francis Bryan (who is described in lines 15–18 on p. 88) and Wyatt. On p. 88, for example, the former speaks from the last half of line 22 through line 31, as well as the first half of line 34, and on p. 90 lines 3–7. In an article on "Particulars respecting Sir Francis Bryan" (*Archaeologia*, XXVI [1836], 446–453) J. P. Collier shows that Bryan had been married to the widow of John Fortescue before he married Joan, Countess of Ormonde; hence he explains 89. 30–31 as a reference to Bryan's "marriage with the widow Fortescue," who may have been older than he. On 90. 9–14 he comments as follows: "This . . . certainly seems meant as a reproof to Sir Francis Bryan, because he did not 'content himself with honest poverty,' and did not 'sometimes' run the risk of 'adversity' by displaying an independent spirit, but kept himself in with all parties, having subsequently been as great a favourite with the Protector Somerset, as he had been with Henry VIII." Miss Foxwell believes that Wyatt's poem led Bryan to write his *Dispraise of the Life of a Courtier* (1548).

88. 13–14 *knowes how great a grace, &c.* Apparently praise of didactic poetry written by Bryan. See my comments on p. 82 n., above.

22 *For swine so groines.* That is, grunts. Cf. Skelton (*Poetical Works*, ed. Dyce, I [1843], 132, 415), "Hoyning like hogges that groynis and wrotes," "the groynninge of the gronnyng swyne."

24 *And driuell on pearles.* Cf. Matthew vii. 6.

25 *of the harpe the asse doth heare the sound.* Cf. Chaucer's Boethius, I, prose iv, "Artow lyke an asse to the harpe?" and *Troilus and Criseyde*, I. 731–735:

> Or artow lyk an asse to the harpe,
> That hereth soun, whan men the strenges plye,
> But in his minde of that no melodye
> May sinken, him to glade, for that he
> So dul is of his bestialitee?

Cf. also John Lydgate's *Here foloweth the Churle and the byrde* (Mychel's ed., 1550?), B2ᵛ, B3ᵛ:

> To here of wysdome thyne eares ben defe
> Lyke to an asse/ that lysteneth to an harpe.

> I holde hym mad/ that bryngeth forth an harpe
> Theron to teche a rude dull asse.

[220]

88. 32–34 *But what and if thou wist, &c.* Cf. the opening lines of Horace's satire (II. v),

> Hoc quoque, Tiresia, praeter narrata petenti
> responde, quibus amissas reparare queam res
> artibus atque modis.

89. 7 *Seke . . . vpon thy bare fete.* Perhaps this means "silently," "with silent tread," in "quiet and stealthy ways."

9 *as to a calfe a chese.* This allusion is not clear to any of the commentators. The MS. reads "as to a dog," etc.

12 *at the ladde.* Nott thinks that the MS. reading, *at Kitson,* may have reference to Sir Thomas Kitson, sheriff of London in 1533, but the wealthy bookseller Anthony Kitson (see E. G. Duff, *A Century of the English Book Trade,* 1905, p. 86) seems a more plausible guess. Omission of the proper noun agrees with the general policy of the editor of *A.*

19–20 *if he coughe to sore, &c.* "A great improvement on the original" (Horace's *Satires,* II. v. 106–109), declares Nott:

> Si quis
> forte coheredum senior male tussiet, huic tu
> dic, ex parte tua seu fundi sive domus sit
> emptor, gaudentem nummo te addicere.

28 *though she curse or banne.* A tautological phrase for curse. Thus Robert Armin, in *The History of the two Maids of More-clacke,* 1609, E3 (*Tudor Facsimile Texts*) writes, "Curse and ban him."

30 *Let the olde mule bite vpon the bridle.* A proverbial expression, examples of which are cited in the *Paradise,* pp. 235–236. Note also that Wyatt wrote a rondeau (Foxwell, I, 10) satirizing a decayed beauty whom he addresses in his first line and in three refrains as "Ye old mule!"

40–42 *As Pandar was.* The reference is to Chaucer's *Troilus and Criseyde,* III. 260–263.

43 *Be next thy selfe.* From Terence's *Andria,* IV. i. 12, "Proximus sum egomet mihi" (Nott).

90. 15 (No. 127) *The song of Iopas vnfinished.* In every edition (No. [137] in *B–I,* sigs. N–Nᵛ in *BC,* G–Gᵛ in *D–G,* F8ᵛ–Gᵛ in *H,* F6–F7 in *I*). Miss Foxwell (I, 189–196) prints the poem from MS. Egerton 2711, with the following variants:

> 90. 17 wanderyng] wandryng
>   19 taught] did teche
>   20 in] in his
>   22, 24, 38 earth] yerth
>   23 powers] powrs
>   24 Repugnant] Repugnant
>   25 mother] moder
>   27 and] *Om.*

90. 28 placed] *Om.*
    32 Carieth] Caryth
    34 Two . . . be] There be two pointes
    36 grounde] round
    37 drawen] draune: the one to thother] ton to tothr
    38 none other] no nothr
    39 be] bene: discriyde] discribd
    40 one] tone: thother] tothr
91. 2 thone to thother] ton to tothr
     3 vpon] apon: the heauens] thevins: do] doth
     4 earth] yerth
     7 be] bene
     8 erryng] wandryng: circle] cyrcles
     9 because] by cawse: repungnant] repugnant
    12 saue] saff
    16 betwene] by twene
    18 seuenth] sevent
    19 gatherth] gaderth
    25 twelue] twelff: thothers] tothrs
    28 bears] berth
    29 eleuen] elefn
    30 fourth] fourt
    31 dayes] day his: her] he
    32 gouerns] governth
    35 vnto] to
    36 starre] stern [?]
    38 fixt] first
    42 these] those
92. 2 them selues] hym sellffes: be layed] ben layd
     4 Saue] Saff
     6 moouynges] moving: the east] thest
     9 twelue] twellff: east ²] thest: carieth] caryth
    10 we] me
    11 the ¹] that
    12 the] *Om.*

This poem, written in awkward poulter's measure, was suggested by Virgil's *Aeneid,* I. 740–747:

> cithara crinitus Iopas
> personat aurata, docuit quem maximus Atlas.
> hic canit errantem lunam solisque labores,
> unde hominum genus et pecudes, unde imber et ignes,
> Arcturum pluviasque Hyadas geminosque Triones;
> quid tantum Oceano properent se tinguere soles
> hiberni, vel quae tardis mora noctibus obstet.
> ingeminant plausu Tyrii, Troesque sequuntur.

The theory of Copernicus was announced in 1530, but his work was first published in 1543. Wyatt may have known nothing of the theory: in any case, his poem is based upon the Ptolemaic system. No doubt, also, he knew Hyginus's treatise on astronomy.

90. 19 *That mighty Atlas taught.* The "antecedent" of *that* is *Iopas*, in line 20.

20 *With crisped lockes.* Wyatt was fond of *crisped* (curled), which he uses also at 66. 22 and 73. 17. Kendall, in *Flowers of Epigrammes*, 1577, sig. K (Spenser Society ed., p. 161), writes of "crisped locks wavde all behinde."

91. 5 *the substance . . . were harde . . . to finde.* Hard, because it differs from each of the "four elements" named in line 4.

31 *the sunne, therin her styckes.* For *her* read *he*, with *B*+ and the MS.

93. 2 (No. 128) *A trueloue.* In *A* only, whence Merrill (p. 375) reprints the poem with the following variations:

> 2, 4 trueloue] true love
> 11 Or I my loue let] Or I let my love let
> 17 Muses] muses

W. P. Mustard, in *Modern Language Notes*, XLI (1926), 202–203, points out that "various fancies" in this poem "may be traced to Virgil, or ultimately to Theocritus," but perhaps "came to Grimald through some such neo-Latin poem as Andrea Navagero's *Iolas*." He compares specifically lines 3–4, 5–8, with *Iolas*, lines 22–23, 68–73.

9–10 *The oke . . . tuning of her lay.* Merrill (p. 416) notes that these lines are borrowed from Virgil's *Eclogues*, VIII. 52–56:

> nunc et oves ultro fugiat lupus, aurea durae
> mala ferant quercus, narcisso floreat alnus,
> pinguia corticibus sudent electra myricae,
> certent et cycnis ululae, sit Tityrus Orpheus,
> Orpheus in silvis, inter delphinas Arion.

21 (No. 129) *The louer to his dear, &c.* In *A* only, whence Merrill (pp. 375–377) reprints the poem with these variations:

> 93. 23 by:] by,
> 94. 2 peeplepesterd] peeplepestered
>   7 somwhere] fromwhere
>   10 hed:] hed,
>   13 thee.] thee,
>   16 dreed?] dreed:
>   17 auaunt.] avaunt,
>   20 minde,] minde.
>   32 ease] eate

The source of this poem is Elegia III (misnumbered IIII) in Theodore de Bèze's (or Beza's) *Poemata* (Paris, 1548), pp. 23–25:

> Cornua bis posuit, bis cæpit cornua Phœbe,
>   Nec tamen es tanto tempore uisa mihi.
> Viuo tamen, si uita potest tibi, Publia, dici,
>   Mœrorem & lachrymas quæ fouet una meas.

Certe dura mihi mors sæpè in uota uocatur:
 Mors finem lachrymis impositura meis.
Non aliter queritur uentrem durare Prometheus,
 Et posito mallet numine posse mori.
Fallor enim, aut quisquis figmenta hæc repperit olim,
 Vulturis est illi nomine dictus amor.
Quæ non uisa mihi est platea? quid in urbe relictum?
 Vrbe tamen tota Publia nulla fuit.
Ergo uel miseram cohibent te coniugis iræ:
 O non tam sæuo fœmina digna uiro!
Vel populosa tibi sordere Lutetia cœpit,
 Et placidi ruris dulcior aura placet.
Forsitan in syluis nostros meditaris amores,
 Et tuto uelles omnia ferre loco.
Ibo igitur, nec me quicquam retinebit euntem,
 Donec sis aliquo sola reperta loco.
Interea manuum serues, collíque colorem,
 Et fieri nigras ne patiare genas.
Tecta incede caput: nam te si cernat Apollo,
 Ardeat in uultus ustus & ipse tuos.
In syluis lauri uestita est cortice Daphne,
 Hei mihi si de te fabula talis erit!
Callisto in syluis summo est compressa Tonanti,
 Ne rogo, ne placeat Iuppiter iste tibi.
Heu quid non timeo? latronum hîc regna teguntur:
 Quisquis es, hinc aufer, prædo cruente, manus:
Actæon doceat uiolati numinis iras:
 Dictynna certe non minor ista Dea est.
Quid loquor? ô nostræ pars maxima, Publia, mentis,
 Non poterunt aures ista ferire tuas.
O utinam præsens uerba obseruare legentis,
 Et frontis possem signa notare tuæ!
Optima tunc nostro spes addi posset amori,
 Et possem mecum dicere, lenis erit.
Perueniam certè quacunque morêris in urbe,
 Siue aliquo potius, Publia, rure lates.
Perueniam, & si non mea per se forma loquatur,
 Fortunæ fiam nuntius ipse meæ.
Quòd si surda preces ausis contemnere nostras,
 Nempe meæ subitò conscia cædis eris.
Attamen hoc media nobis in morte placebit,
 Quòd tu causa meæ, Publia, cædis eris.

It has been conjectured that the Carie addressed in No. 129 had the surname Day which is played upon in No. 130. A contributor to *Notes and Queries*, 11th series, IV, 384, suggests that she may have been Grimald's fiancée, later his wife. It will be observed that Beza's Publia was a married woman, and that Grimald in line 35 changed Beza's *coniunx* to *sire*.

93. 29–30 *So plaines Prometh, &c.* "Just so Prometheus complains that his stomach never fails (but after the vulture has fed on it in the daytime grows

whole again in the night), and, living forever, he had rather die (than exist in such torment)."

93. 31–32 *I erre, or els . . . By that gripes name . . . vnsound.* "Unless I am mistaken, he who first thought of the story (of Prometheus and the 'gripe') called love the vulture." For love is as great a tormentor as Prometheus's vulture.

94. 34 (No. 130) *The louer asketh pardon, &c.* In *A* only. On the Carie Day to whom this poem is possibly addressed see the notes to No. 129. Merrill (pp. 377–378) reprints the poem from *A* with the following variations:

95. 3 blinde] blind: wold] would
   4 fled] fledd
 16 vpon] upon you
 23 hed] head
 24 defautes] defauts
 31 bee.] bee,

The source of the poem is Elegia v (misnumbered vi) in Beza's *Poemata*, 1548, pp. 27–28:

Quisquis amas (aiunt cuncti) fuge corpus amatum,
    Viuere si cæco liber ab igne cupis.
Hei mihi, te quoties fugi, mea Candida, fugi:
    Semper at in nostro pectore regnat amor.
Ecce iterum fateor, fugi te, Candida: uerùm
    Et potui & possum dicere semper, amo.
Siue abeo in syluas, nobis succurrit Adonis,
    Et fit tristitiæ conscia sylua meæ;
Siue placent horti, quot florum hîc millia cerno,
    Tot stimulis captum me premit asper amor:
Narcissum hinc croceum uideo, hinc flentes Hiacynthos,
    Hinc miser ante oculos pulcher Adonis adest:
Magna quidem nostræ fateor medicamina flammæ,
    Sed me qui uincit, uincit & ille Deos.
At si prata iuuant, ô quantas sentio flammas!
    Ardeo tunc flammis totus amoris ego.
Hîc uideor Cereris fugientem cernere natam,
    Hîc uideor furui cernere Ditis equos.
Littora si specto, uitreas tunc cogito Nymphas,
    Feruidáque in medio numina sæpe mari.
Quò magis euado montes sublimis in altos,
    Hoc propior Veneris fit puer ille mihi.
Si placeant urbes, uis ut semel omnia dicam,
    Illic quum uideam plurima, nulla placent.
Illius nunc carpo oculos, nunc illius ora,
    Hæc capite, hæc pedibus displicet, illa genis.
Denique materies si desit, crimina fingo,
    Et quæcunque alijs candida, nigra mihi est.
Quid prodest fugisse igitur, quum Candida praesens,
    Atque adeò lateri sit comes usque meo?

Vmbræ igitur meritò quadret tibi Candida nomen,
    Tale tamen nomen non decet iste color.
Humanum potius debes deponere nomen,
    Vna simul gemino quæ potes esse loco.
Parce, rogo, quæcunque Dea es: subiecit & ipsa
    Anchisi sese, res bene nota, Venus.
Ecce fugam fateor, ueniam ne, Diua, negato,
    Sæpe mihi ueniam Iuppiter ipse dedit.
Ipse quidem prima mox ad te luce reuertar,
    Quásque uoles pœnas, si patiare, feram.

95. 10–11 *In gardens . . . weepyng chere.* Condensed from six lines (9–14) of the Latin.

    14 *dame Ceres ymp.* Proserpine, Dame Ceres' child ("Cereris . . . natam").

    38 (No. 131) *N. Vincent. to G. Black wood, &c.* In *A* only, whence Merrill (p. 378) reprints the poem with the following variations:

95. 38 Vincent.] Vincent: Black wood] Blackwood
96. 3 tell, wherefore] tell wherfore
    7 pan?] pan?)
    8 say,] say
    9 soone] soon
  10 fine:] fine.
  20 Of] Or

The source of No. 131 is Beza's epigram "Ponticus Cornelio de uxore non ducenda" (*Poemata*, 1548, p. 95):

Quum uelis uxorem, Corneli, ducere: quæro
    Coniugium placeat qua ratione tibi.
Scilicet ut deinceps uiuas felicior: atqui
    Fallor ego, aut non hac lege beatus eris.
Vxor enim aut deformis erit, (túne, obsecro, talis
    Si tibi sit coniunx iuncta, beatus eris?)
Aut forma mediocris erit. modus iste, fatemur,
    Optimus, at subitò deperit iste modus.
Aut formosa, ideóque uiris obnoxia mille,
    Et de qua nequeas dicere tota mea est.
Vt sit casta tamen (nemo si fortè rogarit)
    Mille feret natos, tædia mille feret.
Aut sterilis tecum tardos sic exiget annos,
    Nullus ut è multis sit sine lite dies.
His addas caput indomitum, mentémque tenacem,
    Cæteráque à multis quæ didicisse potes.
Desine sic igitur uitam sperare beatam,
    Sit potius cœlebs & sine lite thorus.
Hîc etenim si qua est felicis semita uitæ,
    Fœmineas iuxta non latet illa nātes.

It seems likely that Vincent, whoever he may have been, was the author of No. 131, not Grimald.

96. 5 *I am beguylde, but you take, &c.* "I am deceived if you aren't aiming (at happiness) in the wrong way."

7 *flower of frying pan.* Cf. Henry Medwall, *Fulgens and Lucres, ca.* 1497 (ed. Boas and Reed, 1926, p. 45), "Come forthe ye flowre of the frying pane, Helpe ye to aray vs as well as ye can" (explained by the editors of the play, at p. 95, as "a proverbial phrase for an ugly slut"). The proverb appears also in Breton's *Pasquils Mistresse*, 1600, C3, "If she . . . be the flower of all the frying pan . . . She shal be but the wench, when all is done"; and in Robert Armin's *The History of the two Maids of More-clacke*, 1609, C4 (*Tudor Facsimile Texts*), "Yes flowre it'h frying pan, he stops holes well." Grosart, editing Armin's *Works*, p. 89, changes *pan* to *man*!

22 (No. 132) *G. Blackwood to .N. Vincent, &c.* In *A* only, whence Merrill (p. 379) prints it with the following errors of punctuation:

96. 22 .N.] N.
    34 great:] great,
97. 2 say:] say

The source of the poem is Beza's epigram, "Cornelius Pontico de uxore ducenda" (*Poemata*, 1548, p. 96):

> Vxorem cupiam quum ducere, Pontice, quæris
>   Coniugium placeat qua ratione mihi.
> Deformem nolo, formosam exopto: placebit,
>   Si nequeo pulchram, quæ mediocris erit.
> Formosam, dices, alij mox mille rogabunt,
>   At nulli, quanuis sæpe rogata, dabit.
> Forma perit subito mediocris: id ille queratur
>   Qui præter formam nil muliebre probat.
> Si dederit natos, natos spectare iuuabit,
>   Si sterilis, quid tum? sarcina nostra leuis.
> Cætera quæ narras certè sunt magna, fatemur,
>   Est animúsque tenax, indomitúmque caput.
> Sed sua sunt cunctis connata incommoda rebus,
>   Ipsa etiam damnis commoda plena uides.
> Et me miraris uitam sperare beatam,
>   Si mihi sit deinceps fœmina facta comes?
> Semita uirtutis stricta est, si uera loquuntur.
>   Hæc quoque quam quæro, Pontice, stricta uia est.

It seems likely that Blackwood, whoever he may have been, was the author of No. 132, not Grimald.

Poems on the themes of Nos. 131 and 132 are common. For example, see "Vxor Non Est Ducenda," "Vxor Est Ducenda," in Dr. Walter Haddon's *Poemata*, 1567, I4ᵛ, K–Kᵛ (pp. 70–72), and Turbervile's "To a yong Gentleman, of taking a Wyfe," "The Aunswere, for taking a Wyfe," in *Epitaphes*, etc., 1567, pp. 130–132.

97. 4 (No. 133) *The Muses.* In every edition (No. [271] in *B–I*, sigs. Ff in *BC*, P in *D–G*, P^v–P2 in *H*, O2^v in *I*). Merrill (pp. 379–380) reprints the poem from *A* with the following variations:

> 97.   5 king] King
>   12 dothe] doth
>   14 eare] earr: bindes.] bindes,
>   24 chase.] chase
>   26 dothe enspire] doth inspire

No. 133 is (as Nott notes in C. 60. O. 13) a paraphrase of a poem, "Nomina Musarum," incorrectly attributed to Ausonius and still included in all editions of his works as idyll xx:

> Clio gesta canens, transactis tempora reddit.
> Melpomene tragico proclamat moesta boatu.
> Comica lascivo gaudet sermone Thalia.
> Dulciloquos calamos Euterpe flatibus urget.
> Terpsichore affectus citharis movet, imperat, auget.
> Plectra gerens Erato, saltat pede, carmine, vultu.
> Carmina Calliope libris heroica mandat.
> Uranie coeli motus scrutatur, et astra.
> Signat cuncta manu, loquitur Polyhymnia gestu.
> Mentis Apollineae vis has movet undique Musas.
> In medio residens complectitur omnia Phoebus.

The first two and the last two lines of Grimald's poem appear to be original.

No. 133 is reprinted (from the "second edition" of the miscellany, says Crawford, p. 556) in Allot's *England's Parnassus*, 1600 (ed. Charles Crawford, no. 1194), with numerous unauthorized variants:

> 97.   9 solem] sullen: old] all
>   11 Thaley] Thalia
>   12 like] *Om.:*   last] tast
>   14 eare] eares
>   17 Fine] Fond: liuely] louely
>   18 keeps] beares
>   19 stere] stirre place
>   20 renkes] rankes: in place] *Om.*
>   21 Vranie] Vraine: all] are
>   23 The blessed Eutrope tunes her instrument
>   25 sprite] spirit
>   26 embraceth all] *Om.*
>   27–28 *Om.*

With customary haphazardness, Allot in his text attributes the poem to Surrey: for similar errors see p. 66 n. 1, above, and the notes to Nos. 149, 171, 261, 270, 278.

     5 *Imps of king Ioue, and quene Remembrance.* "Daughters of Jove and Mnemosyne." Hyginus, in his fables, vouches for this parentage, calling Mnemosyne Moneta. See also 100. 26.

97. 28 *that men in maze they fall.* The Graces delight to go abroad in the Muses' garments so that men, seeing them, fall into admiration.

29 (No. 134) *Musonius the Philosophers saiyng.* In every edition (No. [272] in *B–I*, sigs. Ff–Ff^v in *BC*, P–P^v in *D–G*, P2 in *H*, O3 in *I*). Merrill (p. 380) reprints the poem from *A*, misprinting *stil* (98. 4) as *still*, *ylswading* (98. 6) as *ylfwading*. The rhyme-scheme, *aaaaaabbccdd*, is rather unusual.

The "saying" referred to by Grimald — "Verba Musoni philosophi Graeca digna atque utilia audiri observarique; eiusdemque utilitatis sententia a M. Catone multis ante annis Numantiae ad equites dicta" — may be seen in O. Hense's edition, *C. Musonii Rufi Reliquiae*, 1905, pp. 132–133:

Adulescentuli cum etiamtum in scholis essemus, ἐνθυμημάτιον hoc Graecum quod adposui, dictum esse a Musonio philosopho audiebamus et, quoniam vere atque luculente dictum verbisque est brevibus et rotundis vinctum, perquam libenter memineramus: Ἄν τι πράξῃς καλὸν μετὰ πόνου, ὁ μὲν πόνος οἴχεται, τὸ δὲ καλὸν μένει· ἄν τι ποιήσῃς αἰσχρὸν μετὰ ἡδονῆς, τὸ μὲν ἡδὺ οἴχεται, τὸ δὲ αἰσχρὸν μένει.

Postea istam ipsam sententiam in Catonis oratione, quam dixit Numantiae apud equites, positam legimus. quae etsi laxioribus paulo longioribusque verbis comprehensa est praequam illud Graecum, quod diximus, quoniam tamen prior tempore antiquiorque est, venerabilior videri debet. verba ex oratione haec sunt: 'Cogitate cum animis vestris: si quid vos per laborem recte feceritis, labor ille a vobis cito recedet, bene factum a vobis, dum vivitis, non abscedet; sed si qua per voluptatem nequiter feceritis, voluptas cito abibit, nequiter factum illud apud vos semper manebit.'

98. 8 (No. 135) *Marcus Catoes comparison, &c.* In *A* only, whence Merrill (pp. 380–381) reprints the poem with the following variations:

98. 8 comparison] camparison
   11 But] Byt
   17 let] *Om.*
   18 cankerd] cankered
   22 dothe] doth
   29 measure] measures

Antonio Riccoboni, *De Historia Liber. Cum Fragmentis Historicum Veterum Latinorum*, 1579, pp. 122–123, quotes the "comparison" "ex Catonis carmine de moribus" as follows:

Nam vita humana prope uti ferrum est. ferrum si exerceas conteritur; si non exerceas, tamen rubigo interficit. Itidem homines exercendo videmus conteri. si nihil exerceas, inertia, atque torpedo plus detrimenti facit, quàm exercitatio."

30 (No. 136) *Cleobulus the Lydians riddle.* In *A* only, whence Merrill (p. 381) reprints the poem with the following variations:

98. 37 Nor] Now
99. 2 do] doth
   3 sire] fire

Cleobulus (628–558 B.C) was one of the Seven Sages of Greece. His riddle is given in F. W. A. Mullach's *Fragmenta Philosophorum Graecorum*, 1 (1860),

219, thus: "Εἶς ὁ πατήρ, παῖδες δὲ δυώδεκα· τῶν δὲ θ' ἐκάστῳ κοῦραι ἑξήκοντα, διάνδιχα εἶδος ἔχουσαι. Αἱ μὲν λευκαὶ ἔασιν ἰδεῖν, αἱ δ' αὖτε μέλαιναι· ἀθάναται δὲ τ' ἐοῦσαι ἀποφθινύθουσιν ἄπασαι." Mullach translates as follows: "Unus est pater, duodecim autem filii, quorum singulis sexaginta filiae sunt, duplicem formam habentes. Quippe aliae albo colore sunt, aliae nigro: quamvis vero immortales sint, omnes tamen moriuntur." A slightly different version of the Greek riddle is given in Theodorus Bergk's *Poetae Lyrici Graeci*, 4th ed., 1882, III, 201–202; and Greek, Latin, Italian, French, and English versions will be found in Henry Wellesley's *Anthologia Polyglotta* (1849), p. 41. In *A Posie of Gilloflowers*, 1580 (*Poems*, ed. Grosart, *Miscellanies of the Fuller Worthies' Library*, I, 431) Humfrey Gifford gives a version of this riddle which he claims to have "translated out of Italian verse":

> A father once, as bookes expresse,
> Had sonnes twise sixe, nor more nor lesse:
> Ech sonne, of children had scores three,
> Halfe of them sonnes, halfe daughters bee:
> The sonnes are farre more white then snowe,
> The daughters blacker then a crow.
> Wee see these children dayly die,
> And yet they liue continually.

99. 5 *You shall I count an Edipus in wit.* So an "Ænigma, 37" in *Wits A. B. C. Or A Centurie of Epigrams* [1620?], C4, ends,

> Thou shalt be *Oedipus* if thou not misse,
> To tell what kinde of creature this same is.

6 (No. 137) *Concerning Virgils Eneids.* In *A* only, whence Merrill (p. 382) reprints the poem, misprinting *moste* (line 9) as *most*.

21 (No. 138) *Of mirth.* In *A* only, whence Merrill (pp. 382–383) reprints the poem with the following variations:

> 99. 22 Heauy] heavy: smart:] smart;
>   28 beast:] beast.
>   33 leam] beam
>   34 whelmd] whelmed
>   37 eternall] eternal

29 *A mery hert sage Salomon countes, &c.* See Proverbs xv. 15.

100. 2 (No. 139) *To L. I. S.* In *A* only, whence Merrill (pp. 383–384) reprints the poem with the following variations:

> 100. 4 adioynd] adjoyned
>   5 Nymphs] nymphs
>   13 briefe:] briefe;

He suggests (p. 423) that the initials represent "Lady Jane Seymour," daughter of Edward Seymour, Duke of Somerset. Mustard (*Modern Language*

Notes, XLI [1926], 203) calls attention to the resemblance between the two opening lines of No. 139 and Sannazaro's *Epigrams*, III. 2,

> Quarta Charis, decima es mihi Pieris, altera Cypris,
> Cassandra, una choris addita diva tribus.

Grimald credits Lady "I. S." with knowing "full well" Latin, French, Italian, and Spanish, no less than English. Such knowledge was not uncommon in ladies of the aristocracy. As an example, Thomas Heywood in 1640 dedicated *The Exemplary Lives . . . of Nine the Most Worthy Women of the World* to Lady Theophila, wife of Sir Robert Cooke, speaking of

> The severall tongues, in which you so excell,
> *Greeke, Roman, French, Castillian*, and with those,
> *Tuscan, Teutonick*, in all which you pose
> The forreigne Linguist: in the most select
> Both native *Ideom*, and choise dalect [*sic*].

Queen Elizabeth's learning, of course, seems everywhere to have been admired. Charles Gerbier describes it in *Elogium Heroinum: Or, The Praise of Worthy Women*, 1651, pp. 42–43:

> Queen *Elizabeth* of late memory, whose wonderful knowledge, and Learning, was admired by all the Christian Princes that flourished in her time; shee was so well verst in the Hebrew, Greek, Latin, Italian, Spanish, and French languages, that shee needed no Interpreter, but gave her self answer to all such Ambassadors in their own Language, of which those learned Orations in the Latine tongue whiche shee delivered by her own mouth in the two famous Universities do bear a sufficient record in her behalf.

100. 3 *Charis the fourth, Pieris the tenth, the second Cypris, Iane.* A graceful compliment: Lady Jane was the fourth Grace, the tenth Muse, the second Venus. In *Endimion and Phoebe*, 1595 (ed. J. W. Hebel, 1925, pp. 45, 49), Drayton speaks of "The fayrest Graces *Jove*-borne *Charites*," and of Astraea,

> To whom the *Charites* led on the way,
> *Aglaia, Thalia*, and *Euphrozine*.

4 *One to assemblies thre adioynd.* The "three assemblies" were the Graces, the Muses, and Venus, with all of whom (see the foregoing note) Lady Jane was "adioynd" on equal terms.

6 *the quenes most noble grace.* Presumably Mary I, though I cannot find that Lady Jane Seymour was one of her maids of honor (as she afterwards was of Elizabeth).

18 *And if you stay . . . wits will ouergo.* "And if you don't make use of your natural gifts, other ladies (fresh wits) will eclipse your fame." The *doings* of line 17 suggests that her fame as a poet is meant.

23 (No. 140) *To maistres D. A.* In *A* only, whence Merrill (pp. 384–385) reprints the poem with the following variations:

100. 24 fansy] fancy
    25 Britan] Britain
    26 Bothe] Both
    29 ther] their
    32 Allurementes] Allurements
    36 lo] *Om.*
    37 nill] will
101. 2 fansiefourm] fancie fourm
    11 yblest:] yblest,
    13 frendships] friendships
    14 threatning] threatening: tyme] time
    15 mark] marke: depaynt] depaynt,
    16 which,] which

Nos. 140, 141, and 146 are addressed, as the acrostic in No. 141 shows, to Damascene Awdley. Merrill (p. 425) comments: "According to the first she had 'golden gifts of mind,' the second says that she was of 'woorthy race,' while the third pictures her as a lady of 'gorgeous attire.' It seems not unlikely that she was of the noble house of Awdley (Audley), of Staffordshire, in which Eccles lies, the town in which Grimald was licensed to preach in 1551. As this church was one of the most important in that county, it is probable that Grimald came to know various members of the Awdley family. The records of that family do not show any member with the name of Damascene. The name damascene, or damask, which is that of a rose of pink or light red variety, and also that of a fabric of silky surface and elaborate design, popular in mediæval times, may, however, have been only a nickname."

    101. 2 *fansiefourm.* Read as two words, *fancy* (the noun *love*) and *form* (the verb).

    15 *I that daye, with gem snowwhite, will mark.* "The Romans used a white stone or piece of chalk to mark their lucky days on the calendar. Those that were unlucky they marked with charcoal" (Merrill, p. 426). Cf. Horace's *Carmina*, I. xxxvi. 10, "cressa ne careat pulchra dies nota"; Catullus, cvii. 6, "o lucem candidiore nota"; Pliny the Younger's *Epistolae*, VI. xi, "O diem . . . laetum, notandumque mihi candidissimo calculo."

    17 (No. 141) *Of .m. D. A.* In *A* only, whence Merrill (pp. 385–386) reprints the poem with the following variations:

101. 17 .m.] m.
    24 dere.] dere,
    29 outright.] outright,
    30 tyme] time
    32 Yeeld,] Yeeld

On Damascene Awdley see No. 140.

    33 (No. 142) *A neew yeres gift, to the l.M.S.* In *A* only, whence Merrill (p. 386) reprints the poem with the following variations:

101. 38 begoon:] begoon.
102. 6 sound²] found
      7 And,] And: conntrey] countrey

He suggests (p. 427) that Lady Margaret Seymour (cf. Nos. 143, 144) is the person addressed by Grimald.

102. 10 (No. 143) *An other to .l.M.S.* In *A* only, whence Merrill (pp. 386–387) reprints the poem with the following variations:

102. 10 .l.] l.
     12 ryfe] ryte
     28 *Entire line om.*

On the Lady M.S. see the notes to Nos. 142 and 144.

23 *By . . . orders coomly rate.* "By maintaining the comely pace of well-ordered behavior (as opposed to disorder)" (G. L. K.).

31 (No. 144) *To .l.K.S.* In *A* only, whence Merrill (p. 387) reprints the poem with the following variations:

102. 31 .l.] l.
     32 now] nowe: yere,²] yere
     35 wit] with

Nos. 139, 142–145 were apparently written (as Merrill suggests) to four daughters — Jane, Margaret, Katherine, Elizabeth — of Edward Seymour, Duke of Somerset, and his wife, Lady Anne Stanhope (on whom see the notes to No. 264). To them Grimald had addressed his *Carmen Congratulatorium* when the duke was released from the Tower on February 6, 1550. The three eldest of the six sisters (Anne, Margaret, and Jane) were authors of a book of Latin verse on the death of Margaret of Valois (1550). In *Notes and Queries*, 11th series, IV, 384, it is suggested that No. 144 may be addressed to "Lady Katherine Seymour, widow of Henry VIII, who married the Protector's brother, and died in 1548."

103. 2 (No. 145) *To .l.E.S.* In *A* only, whence Merrill (p. 387) reprints the poem with the following variations:

103. 2 .l.] l.
      7 the weeks] *Om.:*   howrs] howrs,
      8 blisfull] blisful

On the person addressed (Lady Elizabeth Seymour?) see the note to No. 144.

9 (No. 146) *To .m. D. A.* In *A* only, whence Merrill (p. 388) reprints the poem with the following variations:

103. 9 .m.] m.
     14 what?] what,:   sins] sincs
     18 suppose,] suppose
     22 by] *Om.*

[233]

Evidently Grimald is here addressing Mistress Damascene Awdley, on whom see the notes to No. 140.

The poem is a paraphrase of Beza's epigram, "Xenium Candidæ" (*Poemata*, 1548, p. 72):

> Vestes diuitijs graues & arte,
> Aptandumué tuo monile collo,
> Aut quos India mittit uniones
> Iani nec queo nec uolo Calendis
> Ad te mittere, Candida, una Bezæ
> Dilectissima Candida. At quid ergo?
> Ipsam nempe animam tibi dicatam,
> Amorísque tui ignibus perustam,
> Quæ pridem tua sit licet, suámque
> Te pridem dominam uocétque, amétque,
> Se rursus tibi, dátque, dedicátque
> Inclusa his numeris Phaleuciorum.
> Quòd si munera raritate censes,
> O Dij quàm tibi grande mitto munus!

103. 24 (No. 147) *To .m. S. H.* In *A* only, whence Merrill (p. 388) reprints the poem with the following variants:

> 103. 24 .m.] m.
> 26 to] *Om.*
> 29 ẏ] ye

I have not identified Mistress Susan H.

104. 2 (No. 148) *To his familiar frend.* In *A* only, whence Merrill (p. 389) reprints the poem, misprinting *coonnyng* (line 3) as *coonyng* and expanding ẏ (line 6) to *yat*. H. H. Hudson (*Modern Language Notes*, xxxix [1924], 393 n.) shows that No. 148 is based upon an epigram by Marc-Antoine Muret, or Muretus (*Poemata*, p. 33, in his *Orationes, Epistolae*, etc., Leipzig, 1660):

> *Calendis Januariis, Jocosum.*
>
> Non tibi pro Xeniis fulvi, pretiosa metalli
> Pondera, non docta signa prolita manu,
> Non lana Assyrio tincta & saturata veneno,
> Non grǝ is argenti lamina munus erit.
> Talia non capiunt generositas munera mentes,
> Talia magnanimi spernere dona solent,
> Cum te igitur, qvam sis excelso pectore nôrim:
> Non mittam ista tibi dona: qvid ergo? nihil.

7 (No. 149) *Description of Vertue.* In every edition (No. [273] in *B–I*, sigs. Ff^v in *BC*, P^v in *D–G*, P2 in *H*, O3 in *I*). Merrill (p. 389) reprints the poem from *A* with these variations:

> 104. 10 price] price,
> 12 mark] marke
> 14 you?] you:

Grimald's epigram is also printed in Kendall's *Flowers of Epigrammes*, 1577, I8ᵛ–K (Spenser Society ed., pp. 160–161), as an original translation from Beza. The only variant is *of* for *whom* (line 10). No. 149 is reprinted (from the "second edition" of the miscellany, says Crawford, p. 556) in Allot's *England's Parnassus*, 1600 (ed. Charles Crawford, no. 1620), with the following variations from *A* in diction:

> 104. 11 rayd] clad
>   12 doublefaced] double fac'd:　　　fare] rare
>   14 Tooles . . . you?] VVhy beare you tooles?

Allot attributed the lines to "S. *Th. Wiat.*" For similar errors of attribution see the notes to No. 133.

The source of the poem is Beza's epigram, "Descriptio Virtutis" (*Poemata*, 1548, p. 68):

> Quǽnam tam lacero uestita incedis amictu?
> 　Virtus antiquis nobilitata sophis.
> Cur uestis tam uilis? Opes contemno caducas.
> 　Cur gemina est facies? Tempus utrunque noto.
> Quid docet hoc frenum? Mentis cohibere furores.
> 　Rastros cur gestas? Res mihi grata labor.
> Cur uolucris? Doceo tandem super astra uolare.
> 　Cur tibi mors premitur? Nescio sola mori.

104. 17 (No. 150) *Prayse of measure-kepyng*. In every edition (No. [274] in *B–I*, sigs. Ffᵛ–Ff2 in *BC*, Pᵛ–P2 in *D–G*, P2–P2ᵛ in *H*, O3–O3ᵛ in *I*). Merrill (pp. 389–390) reprints the poem from *A*, with the following variations:

> 104. 20 mean:] mean,
>   23 sire] fire
>   30 kill.] kill,
>   33 fansies vain,] fancies vain.
> 105. 2 prayzd] prayzed
>   4 chere,] chere.
>   8 medcines] medicines

The source of No. 150 is Beza's Elegia II, "In Mediocritatis laudem" (*Poemata*, 1548, pp. 22–23):

> Non frustrà solita est medium laudare uetustas,
> 　Nam nil laudari dignius orbis habet.
> In medio posita est uirtus hinc indéque fallax:
> 　Tota sinistra uia est, totáque dextra uia est.
> Icare, si patrem esses inter utrumque secutus,
> 　Icarias nullus nomine nosset aquas.
> Si medio Phaëton mansisset calle superbus,
> 　Non esset sæua terra perusta face.
> Nec lenis nimium, nec durat sæua potestas,
> 　Quæ medium seruat, sola perennis erit:

Te nimia, ô Iuli, clementia perdidit olim:
    Occìdit feritas te truculente Nero.
Augustus felix cur multos mansit in annos?
    Nec facilis nimium, nec truculentus erat.
Nec nimis ipse coli, nec sperni Iuppiter optat,
    Sed magis una iuuat mens moderata deos.
Largus opum nullus, nullus laudatur auarus:
    Magnus, in his potuit qui tenuisse modum.
Antonij mensas sic uicit cœna Catonis,
    Et tenuem melior fama secuta larem.
Nec gracilis structura nimis, nec crassa probatur:
    Hæc spectatori displicet, illa ruit.
Vt moderata iuuant, sic ægris pharmaca multis,
    Heu nimium multis, sæpe petita nocent.
Dicere plura nefas credo, nam laude nequaquam
    Efferri immodica sustinet ipse modus.

104. 23 *sire.* Daedalus, the "patrem" of Beza's lines.

29 *Thee, Iulie, once did too much mercy spill.* Julius Caesar after the battle of Pharsalia pardoned his enemies Gaius Cassius and Marcus Brutus, who had been adherents of Pompey, and who later murdered Caesar. Cicero (*Epistolae ad Diversos*, VIII. 15) queries, "Ecquem autem Caesare nostro acriorem in rebus gerendis, eodem in victoria temperatiorem, aut legisti, aut audisti?"

30–31 *Nero, August.* Nero's "rigor" brought about his suicide (to escape public execution) in his fourteenth year as emperor and his thirty-first year of age. Augustus Caesar by holding the golden mean between mercy and severity "well passed" the years from 63 B.C. to 14 A.D.

31–32 *passe, was.* Grimald uses similar rhymes at 109. 37–38, 112. 5–6, 29–30, 114. 26–27.

105. 12 (No. 151) *Mans life after Possidonius, &c.* In every edition (No. [275] in *B–I*, sigs. Ff2 in *BC*, P2 in *D–G*, P2ᵛ in *H*, O3ᵛ in *I*). Merrill (p. 390) reprints the poem from *A*, with the following variations:

105. 12 Possidonius,] Possidonius
    17 feelds] feelde
    18 riche,] riche
    19 poore,] poore

It is reprinted as an original translation from Erasmus's *Chiliades* in Kendall's *Flowers of Epigrammes*, 1577, F7ᵛ (Spenser Society ed., p. 110), with the title of "Best neuer to be borne," with the ten long lines printed as twenty short ones, and with *trauail, and with toyl* (line 17) changed to *toile and trauell* and *lieth* (line 18) to *lyes.* Another translation (beginning, "What course of life should wretched Mortalles take?") is printed in L. E. Kastner's edition of Drummond of Hawthornden's *Poetical Works*, II (1913), 173, but was actually (see James Hutton in *The Modern Language Review*, XXI [1926], 368–372) made by Sir John Beaumont, who likewise translated the original on which No. 152 is based: see his *Bosworth-field*, 1629, pp. 35, 36. Better known than these is Bacon's version in his poem beginning, "The world's a bubble, and the life of man less than a span." Much like No. 151, furthermore, are the two early Elizabethan ballads by I. G. printed in Lilly's *Ballads*, pp. 192–193, 227.

Posidonius (*ca.* 130–50 B.C.) was a Stoic philosopher, accounted the most learned man of his day, and the teacher of Marius, Pompey, and Cicero. Crates, a Cynic philosopher and a pupil of Diogenes, flourished about 320 B.C. J. W. Mackail, *Select Epigrams from the Greek Anthology*, 1906, p. 299, prints the epigram as the composition of Posidippus, saying (p. 420) that it is "a worthless Byzantine tradition" which ascribes the two epigrams (the originals of Nos. 151 and 152) to Heraclitus and Democritus. Mackail's translation of Posidippus's epigram (which begins, "Ποίην τις βιότοιο τάμῃ τρίβον; εἰν 'αγορῇ μὲν") runs thus:

> What path of life may one hold? In the market-place are strifes and hard dealings, in the house cares; in the country labour enough, and at sea terror; and abroad, if thou hast aught, fear, and if thou art in poverty, vexation. Art married? thou wilt not be without anxieties; unmarried? thy life is yet lonelier. Children are troubles; a childless life is a crippled one. Youth is foolish, and grey hairs again feeble. In the end, then, the choice is of one of these two, either never to be born, or, as soon as born, to die.

A Latin version will be found in a book printed at Nuremberg in 1501: *Cratis Thebani Cynici philosophi Epl'e aureis sentencijs referte theologie consenta.iee*, A6ᵛ, where the poem is attributed to Heraclitus. There is a faint possibility that Grimald translated Nos. 151 and 152 directly from the Greek. Both, however, were familiar from the Latin translations made by Erasmus in his *Adagia* (*Opera Omnia*, 10 vols., Leyden, 1703–1706, II, 503–504) and by George Buchanan in the first book of his epigrams (*Poemata*, Leyden, 1621, pp. 129–130). Grimald's titles (and his lines in general) are much like Buchanan's: "E Graeco Possidippi, seu Cratetis," "Contraria sententia verisimilis, ex Metrodoro." Translations into Italian, French, and German have been made by Alamanni, De Baif, and Herder. Nott, by the way (in C. 60. O. 13), points out parallels to the originals of Nos. 151 and 152 in the fifteenth idyll of Ausonius ("Ex Graeco Pythagoricum de ambiguitate eligendae vitae").

105. 24 (No. 152) *Metrodorus minde to the contrarie.* In every edition (No. [276] in *B–I*, sigs. Ff2–Ff2ᵛ in *BC*, P2–P2ᵛ in *D–G*, P2ᵛ–P3 in *H*, O3ᵛ in *I*). Merrill (pp. 390–391) reprints the poem from *A*, with the following variations:

> 105. 28 wee] we: our selues] ourselves
>   32 art thou] thou art
>   34 sires] fires
>   35 dye:] dye,

It is reprinted, like No. 151, in twenty short lines as an original translation from Erasmus in Kendall's *Flowers of Epigrammes*, 1577, F8 (Spenser Society ed., p. 111), with the following variants:

> 105. 27 courts] Court: encreased] encreaseth
>   29 doo] doth
>   30 is gayn to gett] great gaine is got
>   31 knoweth] knowes
>   35 that choys] the choyse

The "saying" will be found, attributed to Democritus, in the Nuremberg volume of 1501, A6ᵛ (cf. the notes to No. 151). The original Greek epigram by Metrodorus, beginning "Παντοίην βιότοιο τάμοις τρίβον· ἐιν ἀγορῇ μὲν," may be seen in Mackail's *Select Epigrams from the Greek Anthology*, 1906, p.300, where it is translated thus:

> Hold every path of life. In the market-place are honours and prudent dealings, in the house rest; in the country the charm of nature, and at sea gain; and abroad, if thou hast aught, glory, and if thou art in poverty, thou alone knowest it. Art married? so will thine household be best; unmarried? thy life is yet lighter. Children are darlings; a childless life is an unanxious one: youth is strong, and grey hairs again reverend. The choice is not, then, of one of the two, either never to be born or to die; for all things are good in life.

106. 2 (No. 153) *Of lawes*. In *A* only, whence Merrill (p. 391) reprints the poem with the following variations:

> 106. 2 lawes] Lawes
>   4 lābes] babes
>   5 heades] heads

He suggests that it refers to Sir Thomas Wyatt's rebellion of 1554.

9 (No. 154) *Of frendship*. In every edition (No. [277] in *B–I*, sigs. Ff2ᵛ–Ff3 in *BC*, P2ᵛ–P3 in *D–G*, P3–P3ᵛ in *H*, O3ᵛ–O4 in *I*). Merrill (pp. 391–393) reprints the poem from *A*, with the following variations:

> 106. 14 brute:] brute.
>   23 dothe] doth: led.] led:
>   26 sickenesse] sicknesse
>   29 fowl] fowle
>   31 blisfull] blissful
>   35 Menetus (*see* Variant Readings)] Menclus
> 107. 2 frend] frend,
>   3 y̌] yat: kinde] kind

There is another copy in MS. Sloane 1896, fols. 39ᵛ–40ᵛ, which varies as follows:

> 106. 9 A Commendacion of friendshippe.
>   11 the] this
>   12 decayd] decayed
>   13 *MS. inserts:*
>   The golden estate of emperors,/ full sone doth weare away:
>   & other precious thinges doe fade,/ freindshippe will never decay.

  20 solace . . . one] may befall, then one for the
  21 mayst] maiest
  24 see] mayest thou
  25 shall] may
  26 sownd] also sound
  27 mayst] mayest: sure] true
  30 sprite] spirite
  32 didst] didest
  33 egall] equall
  35 *Comes after 37 in the MS.*
  36 cause] first cause
107. 5 lo] nowe
  11 sayth] saieth
  12 sins] sithe: kindely] Ioyfull
  13 frendful] freindly

Most of the ideas and proper names in No. 154 are borrowed in Turbervile's poem, "That it is hurtfull to conceale secrets from our Friendes" (*Epitaphes*, etc., 1567, pp. 170–173). The following lines (106. 20–23) are copied in MS. Rawlinson Poet. 108, fol. 7 (cf. 69. 31–32 n.):

   what sweter solace shal befalle then one to fynde
    vppō whose brest thowe mayst expose the secretes of thy mynd.
   He wayleth at thy woo, his tears wth thine be shedde,
    wth ye dothe he all ioys enioye so lefe a lyfe is ledde.

  106. 32 *Scipio with Lelius.* Scipio (Aemilianus) Africanus the younger and Gaius Laelius were life-long friends. They are represented as the interlocutors (though M. Porcius Cato does most of the talking) in Cicero's *De Senectute;* while in the *De Amicitia* Laelius eulogizes and laments Scipio, who had died in 129 B.C., remarking (to follow John Harington's translation of 1550, sig. I), "Truely of all the thynges whiche fortune or nature gaue me, I haue nothyng to matche with Scipioes freendship."

  34 *Gesippus eke with Tite.* The friendship of Gisippus and Titus Quintus Fulvius is celebrated in Boccaccio's *Decameron*, x. 8. For a list of books in which they are featured see *Modern Philology*, VII (1910), 580–581.

  35 *with Menetus sonne Achill, &c.* Referring to the devoted friendship, as told in the *Iliad*, of Patroclus (Menoetius's son) and Achilles.

  36 *Euryalus . . . Nisus . . . Virgil.* See Virgil's *Aeneid*, ix. 176–180.

  107. 4–5 *Cicero . . . to Atticus . . . Of frendship wrote.* Cicero's *De Amicitia* is dedicated to Titus Pomponius Atticus (†32 B.C.), as is also the *De Senectute*. Furthermore, sixteen books of letters addressed to him by Cicero have survived.

  14 (No. 155) *The Garden.* In *A* only, whence Merrill (pp. 393–394) reprints the poem with the following variations:

107. 18 dothe] doth
  23 forow] forowe
  24 downe] down

107. 29 down] *Om.*
    32 bowz] bows
    33 yeeld] yeld
    34 All mirthfull] *One word:*   ayre,] ayre
    36 harts] hartes
    37 drawes] draws
    39 dothe] doth
    40 more,] more

Mustard (*Modern Language Notes*, XLI [1926], 203) observes that No. 155 is a paraphrase of a Latin poem, *De laude horti*, reprinted in Alexander Riese's *Anthologia Latina*, 1906, pp. 101–102 (no. 635):

Adeste Musae, maximi proles Iovis,
Laudes feracis praedicemus hortuli.
Hortus salubres corpori praebet cibos
Variosque fructus saepe cultori refert:
Holus suave, multiplex herbae genus,
Uvas nitentes atque fetus arborum.
Non defit hortis et voluptas maxima
Multisque mixta commodis iocunditas.
Aquae strepentis vitreus lambit liquor
Sulcoque ductus irrigat rivus sata.
Flores nitescunt discolore germine
Pinguntque terram gemmeis honoribus.
Apes susurro murmurant gratae levi,
Cum summa florum vel novos rores legunt.
Fecunda vitis coniuges ulmos gravat
Textasve inumbrat pampinis harundines.
Opaca praebent arbores umbracula
Prohibentque densis fervidum solem comis.
Aves canorae garrulos fundunt sonos
Et semper aures cantibus mulcent suis.
Oblectat hortus, avocat pascit tenet
Animoque maesto demit angores graves.
Membris vigorem reddit et visus capit.
Refert labori pleniorem gratiam,
Tribuit colenti multiforme gaudium.

108. 2 (No. 156) *An epitaph of sir Iames wilford knight.* In *A* only, whence Merrill (p. 394) reprints the poem with the following variations:

108. 2 sir] Sir
     3 wilford] Wilford
     5 and] and the
   11 wight.] wight

On Wilford see also Nos. 157, 182, 189. He was born about 1516, was brought up as a soldier, and fought in the French war of 1544–1545. In September, 1547, he was appointed provost-marshal of the English army invading Scotland under the Protector Somerset, by whom the Scots were disgracefully

A Poeme both pithie and pleasant.

IF right were rackt and ouer-runne,
 And power take parte with open wrong,
 If force by feare doe yeeld too soone,
The lack is like to last too long:

If God for goods shalbe vnplac'd,
If right for riches leaues his shape,
If world for wisdome be imbrac'd,
The guesse is great much hurt may hap.

Among good thinges I prooue and find,
The quiet life doth most abound,
And sure to the contented mind,
There is no riches may be found.

Riches doth hate to be content,
Rule is enmie to quiet ease,
Power for the most part is vnpacient
And seldome likes to liue in peace,

I heard a Shepheard once compare,
That quiet nights he had more sleepe,
And had more merrie dayes to spare,
Then he which ought his Flock of sheepe.

I would not haue it thought heereby,
The Dolphin swim I meane to teach,
Ne yet to learne the Faulcon flie,
I roue not so farre past my reach.

But as my part aboue the rest,
Is wel to wish and good to will:
So till the breath doth fayle my brest,
I shal not stay to wish you still.

  124. 8–11 *I hard a herdman once compare, &c.* Collier (*A Catalogue, Bibli-ographical and Critical, of Early English Literature,* 1837, p. 298) points out an apparent borrowing of this passage in William Warner's *Albion's England,* IV. 20 (1602 ed., p. 96):

  Well wot I, sooth they say that say more quiet nights and daies
  The Shepheard sleeps & wakes than he whose Cattel he doth graize.

These two lines are included in *England's Parnassus,* 1600, in editing which Crawford (1913, p. 472) remarks, "It seems likely that Warner here is alluding directly" to No. 170.

  20 (No. 171) *Comparison of lyfe and death.* In every edition (No. [141] in *B–I,* sigs. N3ᵛ–N4 in *BC,* G3ᵛ–G4 in *D–H,* G–Gᵛ in *I*). Other copies are preserved in (1) MS. Ashmole 48, *ca.* 1555–1565 (*Songs and Ballads,* pp. 36–37, ed. Thomas Wright, Roxburghe Club, 1860); (2) in the *Paradise,* 1576,

pp. 51–52, where it is signed D. S. (D. Sand); and (3) in a Harington MS. (Additional 28635, fols. 10ᵛ–11). Collations follow:

124. 22 that] whiche (2):   doth] doeth (2)
    23 draw] drawythe (1)
    24 plages forepast] plage skarce past (3)
    25 Yelde] Yeldes (1–3)
    26 fele] fynde (3)
    27 The] That (2, 3): endeth] shortnythe (1), shorteneth (2), shortyth (3)
    28 Yet] And (1, 2)
    29 At] All (2)
    30 The Lord be praysed] my God I thanck (3)
    33 doth ¹,²] doeth (2):   doth ²] shall (3)
    34 pleasant] plesand (1):   seme, so swifte that] sown so swyftly (1), semes so swetely (2), seme so swyftlye (3)
    35 that flete] they flytt (1)
    36 nightes] wights (2):   day] daies (2):   daweth] daws (1, 2), drawth (3)
    37 mete] hytt (1)
    38 Doe] Dothe (1)
125. 2 be] lye (3)
    3 drede] shonne (3)
    4 alway] allways (1)
    7 Though . . . doth] But over whome onlye the Lord dothe (1), The hower wherein onely hym self doeth (2):   the . . . alone] hymself doth only (3)
    8 burdens] burthynges (1):   8, 9 doth] doeth (2)
    9 he doth] yt (1)
    10 What . . . spring] what greefes do grow what daungers dayly springe (3):   perilles] perill (2)
    11 sure] safe (3):   dayes] tyme (1)
    12 as] and (2)
    13 were better] ys happyar (1, 2)
    14 a port] the doore (2):   passe] drawe (2)
    16 dere] swet (1), dole (2):   annoy] awaie (2)
    17 that . . . is] yt yeldythe all in (1)
    18 to] in (2):   is] was (1, 3)
    19 likewise] *Om.* (1):   likewise . . . fredome] by death is (was 3) freedome likewise (2, 3)
    20 Wherfore] Therfore (1):   men] flesshe (3)
    21 dissolude] dissolvyd (1, 2):   of] from (3):   fleshy] fleshly (2)
    22 armed] armde (3)
    23 they be] we may be (1)
    25 To] And (2)

There is a reprint in an abbreviated form (consisting of 124. 22–27, 34–39, 125. 14–19) in *Nugae Antiquae* (1769, pp. 95–96; 1779, 1792, III, 269–270; 1804, II, 332–333), with the title, "Elegy wrote in the Tower by John Harington, confined with the Princess Elizabeth, 1554." This title, however, did not occur in the MS. followed by Henry Harington (a transcript of which is now

MS. Additional 28635); it was manufactured by him. Nott, who used the original MS., jotted down in his edition of the miscellany (C. 60. O. 13), "N B. This has no signature of John Harington: nor does it purport to have been written by him from the Tower, as it is said to have been in the Nugae Antiquae." Nevertheless, in the *Nugae* Harington introduced many readings not to be found in the MS. For example, 124. 25 is changed to "But some new grief, still green, doth marr our state."

124. 24 *plages forepast*. This is the earliest use of *forepast*, meaning *past*, given in the *N.E.D.* The word is used again at 137. 18. Cf. also Bartholomew Yonge, marginal note in his translation of Boccaccio's *Amorous Fiammetta*, 1587, P2ᵛ: "Euery thinge refresheth the memory of the Louer of his forepassed and happy life"; and Robert Parry, *Sinetes Passions vppon his fortunes*, 1597, B4, "Long loathed lookes, of my forepassed life."

125. 14–19 *Death is a port, &c.* These lines (with *dere* [line 16] as *neare*, and *is* [line 18] as *was*) are quoted in Allot's *England's Parnassus*, 1600 (ed. Crawford, no. 282), over the signature of "E. of Surrey"; but there is no basis for that attribution (see the notes to No. 133). Lines 14–15 are borrowed, along with various lines from the *Paradise*, p. 52 (cf. p. 217), in Melbancke's *Philotimus*, 1583.

20–24 *with Paul let all men . . . pray, &c.* See 2 Corinthians v. 1 and 2 Timothy ii. 3, iv. 6–8.

26 (No. 172) *The tale of Pigmalion, &c.* In every edition (No. [142] in *B–I*, sigs. N4–N4ᵛ in *BC*, G4–G4ᵛ in *D–H*, Gᵛ–G2 in *I*). There is an unsigned copy in a Harington MS. (Additional 28635, fol. 35ᵛ), with the following variants:

125. 38 wandering] wandringe
126. 3 moued] mov'd
       4 stayde] stayed
       5 might] wolde
       9 coucht] toucht
      12 curious] envious

Perhaps the ballad of "Pygmalyn" that was registered for publication by Richard Jones in 1568–69 (Rollins, *Analytical Index*, no. 2087) was the same as No. 172. Imitated from the latter is William Fullwood's poem, "A secret Louer writes his will, By storie of Pigmalions skill," in *The Enimie of Idlenesse* (1568).

126. 24 (No. 173) *The louer sheweth, &c.* In every edition (No. [143] in *B–I*, sigs. N4ᵛ in *BC*, G4ᵛ in *D–G*, G4ᵛ–G5 in *H*, G2 in *I*). Another copy, with music, will be found in John Forbes's *Cantus, Songs and Fancies*, song 25 (1666, 1682). It differs in so many particulars that I reprint it below (from the 1682 edition, but without reproducing its occasional single letters in italic type):

Like as the Lark within the Marleons foot,
With piteous voice doth chirk her yeelding lay;
Even so do I, since is no other boot,
Rendring my Song unto your will obey.

Your vertue mounts above my force so hie,
That vvith your beauties seas'd I am so sure,
That there remains resistance none in me;
But patiently your pleasure to endure.

And in your vvill my fancie shal depend,
My life and death consists into your vvill:
I rather vvould my life vvere at an end,
Then in dispair this vvay continue still.

Wounded I am, with deadly darts dint,
Fetter'd with fetters, dispairing of relief;
Lying in langor as careful captive tint,
And ye the cause of all my wo and grief,

And since there is no pity more in place,
But that your cruelty doth thrist my blood.
I am content to have no other grace,
But let it out, if it may do you good.

Not so different from No. 173 is the copy (omitting the final two lines) pre-served, with the music, in *The Melvill Book of Roundels*, 1612, ed. Bantock and Anderton, pp. 51–52, 203–204 (Roxburghe Club, 1916).

126. 26 *Lyke as the lark within the marlians foote.* Barnabe Googe, *Eglogs*, etc., 1563 (ed. Arber, p. 103), tells how the merlin

The selye Larke,
doth take by force of flyght,
And hyes to tree,
where as she lodged late,
And on the trem-
blyng Byrde all nyght she stondes,
To keepe her feete,
from force of nyppynge colde.

A song with music in John Hall's *The Courte of Vertue*, 1565, Q2ᵛ, begins:

Like as the larke within the marlions foote
From solace supplanted it were with me,
If thou lord wert not my buckler and boote:
At whose hand I hope saluacion to see.

The conceit is also imitated by Turbervile, *Epitaphes*, etc., 1567, pp. 34–35, in a poem beginning,

Like as the fearefull foule
within the fawcons foote
Doth yeelde himselfe to die,
and sees none other boote,
Even so dread I (my deare);

and by Melbancke, *Philotimus*, 1583, sig. R: "Didst thou neuer read the prop-
erties of the pretie *Merlin*, who holding the Larke all nighte betwene her litle
talantes to kepe her warme, assoone as it is morning vnfastens her holde, &
lettes her flie, and marking which way she takes her flighte, will not all the day
following set winge to that corner?" See also Melbancke's words quoted at
146. 7–10 n.

   127. 2 (No. 174) *Vpon consideracion of the state, &c.* In every edition
(No. [144] in *B–I*, sigs. O in *BC*, G5 in *D–H*, G2 in *I*). A copy in MS. Sloane
159, fol. 23, varies only in having *longer* for *lenger* (line 4) and *merier* for *mery*
(line 13). These two variants, with *the* for *that* (line 20), appear also in the
copy in MS. Rawlinson Poet. 85, fol. 115ᵛ, which is signed "E of Surry." A
copy of the last two stanzas (lines 10–21) is preserved in MS. Additional
26737, fol. 108.

   The author of *The Arte of English Poesie*, 1589, pp. 216–217, highly ap-
proved of the rhetorical echo-device that makes up this poem. It may, he
says, "be called the *marching figure*, for after the first steppe all the rest pro-
ceede by double the space, and so in our speach one word proceedes double to
the first that was spoken, and goeth as it were by strides or paces; it may
aswell be called the *clyming* figure, for *Clymax* is as much to say as a ladder."
Other examples will be found in Googe's *Eglogs*, etc., 1563 (ed. Arber, p. 96),
and in Turbervile's *Epitaphes*, etc., 1567, p. 222.

   13 *The mery minde.* Read *The merrier* with *D+* and the MSS.

   22 (No. 175) *The louer that once disdained, &c.* In every edition
(No. [145] in *B–I*, sigs. O–O2 in *BC*, G5–G6 in *D–H*, G2ᵛ–G3 in *I*). A copy
in a Harington MS. (Additional 28635, fols. 7ᵛ–8ᵛ) has the following variants:

127. 25–30 *MS. reads:*

> Vnto my songe geve eare that wyll
> and deeme my doinges as you please
> for I shall tell yf you be still
> what trade I toke to lyve in ease
> and how those wayes that I way'd best
> in fyne did fayle to myne unrest.

      31 time . . . of] dayes were once and very
128. 4 marked not] reckt no whit: *lines 4 and 6 are transposed*
      6 forced not] toke no care
      7 My . . . thinges] ffrome all suche thinges my hart
      9 to] of
     11 Where fortune laught] their woes I mockt: scorned] skorn'd
     13 smiled] smylde
     14 begiled] begylde
     16 styll] forthe
     21 length] last: spied] spyde
     23 how] saw
     24 still liue] liue still
     26 threw] cast

128. 27 nature neuer] neuer nature
    28 saue] but
    29 as] that
    30 A] an
    32 Her nature] nature her
    33 euen] all
    37 euer] that
    39 greues me] greevythe
    40 sortes] kyndes
    41 salue] heale
    42 But onely she] save she alone
    43 life] healthe
129. 2 saue or slay] heale or hurt euen
    3 But seing] Wherefore synce
    4 bounde] fest
    5 ye] you: ensample] example
    6 That] whiche: fele] fynd
    7 not them] them not
    8 be . . . his] lack powre to flye the

This copy is carefully signed "huomo inconosciuto," but "in a later hand," Nott informs us in C. 60. O. 13. Nevertheless, Henry Harington printed six stanzas from it (corresponding to 127. 31–35, 128. 2, 9–38) in his *Nugae Antiquae*, 1769, pp. 91–92 (1779, 1792, III, 265–266; 1804, II, 334–336), under the unauthorized title of "Sonnet by John Harington, 1554." Since he omitted the first stanza, beginning his reprint with a variant of 127. 31 ("The days were once, and very late"), no detection of his shifty methods has hitherto resulted.

    127. 29–30 *And from the top of all my trust, &c.* George Ballard, *Memoirs of Several Ladies of Great Britain*, 1752, p. 161, says that Mary, Queen of Scots, "wrote these two lines in a window at Fotheringhay [*sic*] castle.

> From the top of all my trust,
> Mishap has laid me in the dust."

Hazlitt, editing Warton's *History of English Poetry*, IV (1871), 65, apparently objects to this statement, and refers vaguely to *Willis's Current Notes*, V (1854), 14. But I see nothing in that book relevant to the passage in question.

    128. 41 *salue the sore.* A commonplace, repeated at 165. 15, 179. 29, 32, 181. 33, 211. 12.

    129. 9 (No. 176) *Of Fortune, and Fame.* In every edition (No. [146] in *B–I*, sigs. O2–O2ᵛ in *BC*, G6–G6ᵛ in *D–H*, G3–G3ᵛ in *I*).

    130. 7 (No. 177) *Against wicked tonges.* In every edition (No. [147] in *B–I*, sigs. O2ᵛ in *BC*, G6ᵛ in *D–H*, G3ᵛ in *I*). A broadside copy, signed "Finis, quod I. Canand" (on the same sheet with No. 180), is reprinted in Lilly's *Ballads*, pp. 149–150. It presents the following variants:

130. 9 slea] flea
    10 faute] fault

11 slaundring] sclaundring
15 warre] hatred
16 Ye] You: rich realmes] good order: and] and eke
17 down right] downeright
19 ye] you
20 liues] liueth

130. 22 (No. 178) *Not to trust to much, &c.* In every edition (No. [247] in *B–I*, sigs. Cc^v in *BC*, N5^v in *D–G*, N6–N6^v in *H*, M8–M8^v in *I*). The poem is made up almost solely of proverbs and commonplaces.

131. 12 *by flaming of the smart.* That is, until my pain, growing unbearable, flames out and expresses itself against my will in words.

13 (No. 179) *Hell tormenteth not, &c.* In every edition (No. [148] in *B–I*, sigs. O2^v–O3 in *BC*, G6^v–G7 in *D–H*, G3^v–G4 in *I*). The poem is imitated in considerably expanded form by Turbervile's "Of the torments of Hell, and the paines of Love" (*Epitaphes*, etc., 1567, pp. 241–244).

20 *The dropsy dryeth. Dryeth* is a noun. Cf. John Hall, *The Courte of Vertue*, 1565, Q2, "Sometyme we call for dryth, Some tyme we aske for rayne."

30 (No. 180) *Of the mutabilitie of the world.* In every edition (No. [149] in *B–I*, sigs. O3–O3^v in *BC*, G7–G7^v in *D–H*, G4–G4^v in *I*). A copy preserved in a Harington MS. (Additional 28635, fols. 118–119) has the following variants:

131. 32 By . . . bed] In dumppes but late wheare as I laye
     36 I] even theare I: wofull] *Om.*
132. 2 wayes] waves: mine] my
       3 this] the
       4 And . . . ygraunted] how sone from wealth ofte graunted
       5 it] yet
       7 my] moche
       8 me] some: my] the
      10 in] an: *lines 9–10 follow lines 11–12 in the MS.*
      11 most straunge of all] a thinge moste straunge
      12 her] the
      13 lenger] longer: her] she
      16 fleyng] *Om.*:   seen] sene trulye
      17 saw] *Om.*:   doe] *Om.*
      18 falleth] lyeth: *lines 17–18 follow 25–26*
      19 my] our
      21–22 *Om.*
      23 dothe] did
      25 eke vertue, how she sat] wheare Atrapose did sytt
      27–30 *MS. adds:*

I saw a lofte vppon the wheele/ honour in highe estate
whose wretched end most eyes behelde/ loe, heare his fynall fate
The happyste man theare I saw then/ who sought no greedy gayne
but with his calling was content/ delighting in the meane
I saw and heard the dolefull crye/ of people in the land
How wickednes the world gan wylde / and had the upper hand

In place of Iudgement theare I saw/ with feare and cruell moode
wheare wrong that blooddye beast was sett/ drincking the giltles blooode
and when all theise with many moe/ I sawe moste perfeitlye
in me my thought eache one had wrought/ a perfect propertie
then sighing said I thus o Lorde/ at thye moste dreadfull dome
when riche and poore bothe good and bad/ before thie seat shall come
thow lyke a just and ryghtuous judge/ there shalt rewarde eache wight
according as he heare hath wrought/ to darknes ells to light.

Alexander Lacy registered a version of No. 180 in 1565–66 for publication
as a ballad called "the fantises of a Trubbled mans hed" (Rollins, *Analytical
Index*, no. 861). That ballad, signed I. C. (that is, John Canand) and printed
on the same broadside as No. 177, will be found in Lilly's *Ballads*, pp. 147–149.
It presents the following variants:

131. 33 had] hath
     34 full] all
     35 then] that
132. 5 how enuy it] eke how Envie
      7 that] fowle
     13 lenger] longer: her] shee
     16 fleyng] flyeng
     19 the] a
     21 gayn] payne
     22 youthfull] youthly
     23 ant] ants: runne] rome
     24 her] their
     28 parfite] perfect

Another copy of No. 180 is included in the rare miscellany known as
Breton's *Arbor of amorous Deuises*, 1597, B3–B3ᵛ. Correcting a few unmis-
takable misprints, I give it below:

Fantasma.

IN fortune as I lay, my fortune was to finde
   Such fancies as my carefull thought, had brought into my minde,
   And when each one was gone to rest, full soft in bed to lie,
      I would haue slept, but then the watch did follow still mine eye:
And sodainly I saw a sea of sorrowes prest,
   Whose wicked waues of sharpe repulse brought me vnquiet rest.
I saw this world, and how it went, each state in his degree,
   And that from wealth graunted is both life and libertie:
I saw how Enuie it did raigne, and bare the greatest price,
   Yet greater poyson is not found within the Cockatrice;
I also saw how that disdaine, oft times to forge my woe,
   Gaue me the cup of bitter sweete, to pledge my mortall foe:
I also saw how that deceit, to rest no place could finde,
   But still constraind an endles paine, to follow natures kinde.
I also saw most strange, how Nature did forsake
   the blood that in her womb was wrought, as doth the loathed snake.

[264]

I saw how fancie would remaine, no longer then her lust,
  And as the winde how she doth change, and is not for to trust:
I saw how stedfastnes did flie, with winges of often change,
  A bird, but truely seldome seene, her nature is so strange:
I saw how pleasant Time did passe, as Flowers in the Mead,
  To day that riseth red as Rose, to morrow lyeth dead.
I saw my time how it did run, as sand out of the Glasse,
  Euen as each hower appoynted is, from tide to tide to passe:
I saw the yeares that I had spent, and losse of all my gaine,
  And how the sport of youthfull playes, my folly did retaine:
I saw how that the little Ant in Summer still doth runne,
  To seeke her foode, whereby to liue in winter for to come:
I saw eke vertue, how she sate the threed of life to spinne,
  Which sheweth the end of euery thing before it doeth begin.
And when al these I saw, with many moe perdie,
  In me my thoughts each one had wrought a perfect propertie:
And then I sayd vnto my selfe, a Lesson this shalbe,
  For other that shal after come, for to beware by me.
Thus al the night I did deuise which way I might constraine.
  To forme a plot that wit might worke the branches in my braine.

132. 8 *Gaue me the cup of bitter swete, &c.* Cf. 71. 9–10 n.

15–16 *I saw, how stedfastnesse did fly, &c.* Borrowed by Melbancke, *Philotimus*, 1583, D2: "Thou seest how *Stedfastnes* doth fly w̄ winges of often chaūg, a flying birde, but seldome seene, her nature is so straung."

23-24 *the litle ant in somer, &c.* On this commonplace see Thomas Howell, 1568 (*Poems*, ed. Grosart, pp. 56–57); Geoffrey Whitney, *A Choice of Emblems*, 1586, p. 175; and the *Gorgeous Gallery*, p. 186.

33 (No. 181) *Harpelus complaynt, &c.* In every edition (No. [150] in *B–I*, sigs. O3ᵛ–O4ᵛ in *BC*, G7ᵛ–G8ᵛ in *D–H*, G4ᵛ–G5ᵛ in *I*). Percy reprinted the poem in his *Reliques*, 1765 (ed. Wheatley, II, 75–79), calling it (though he reprinted next to it Robert Henryson's *Robin and Makyne*) "perhaps the first attempt at pastoral writing in our language," — a remark approved of by Warton in his *History of English Poetry* (ed. Hazlitt, IV [1871], 62), — and asserting that it is "far superior" to Spenser's *Shepherds' Calendar*.

No. 181 was registered as a ballad entitled "Filida was a fayre mayden" at Stationers' Hall in 1564–65 (Rollins, *Analytical Index*, no. 889). It is summarized thus in the last poem in Fullwood's *The Enimie of Idlenesse*, 1568 (1593 ed., R4ᵛ):

I read how *Harpelus*,
  faire *Phillida* did pray:
But she with checking taunts and mockes
  his purpose did gainesay.
The Gods regarding this,
  tooke pittie on his case,
And punished her cruell fact,
  within a little space.

Her heart was shortly set
on fire, with *Corins* loue:
Who passed not a pin for her,
as she did plainely proue.
Whereby she pinde away,
the like may chaunce to you.

In a similar fashion Stephen Batman, *The trauayled Pylgrime*, 1569, C2, writes:

The fatall chaunce and destenie of *Herpelus* his loue,
Auailed not to molifie, although he long did proue,
A thousande moe I coulde recite.

From *B* or some later edition No. 181 was included in *England's Helicon*, 1600 (ed. Macdonald, pp. 42–45), where a number of unauthorized variants were introduced into the text and the signature of "L. T. Howard, Earle of Surrie" added. Furthermore, *England's Helicon* (pp. 45–48) also has a sequel: "An other of the same subiect, but made as it were in aunswere," beginning, "On a goodly Sommers day," and signed by "Shep. Tonie," who is supposed to be Anthony Munday. An imitation of No. 181, "The complaint of the Shepheard Harpalus" (beginning, "Poore *Harpalus* opprest with loue, Sate by a christall brooke"), is to be found in Sir David Murray's *Cœlia*, 1611 (*Poems*, E6–E7, ed. Bannatyne Club, 1823); and as a broadside ballad, signed D. M., it appears also in *The Roxburghe Ballads*, II, 605–607.

134. 25 *your faythfull face.* Read *makes* (= mates) with *B*+.

135. 20 (No. 182) *Vpon sir Iames wilfordes death.* In every edition (No. [151] in *B–I*, sigs. O4ᵛ–P in *BC*, G8ᵛ–H in *D–G*, H in *H*, G5ᵛ–G6 in *I*). On Wilford see No. 156.

136. 4 *er he step vs fro.* For *step* read *stepte* with *B*+.

8 (No. 183) *Of the wretchednes in this world.* In every edition (No. [152] in *B–I*, sigs. P in *BC*, H in *D–G*, H–Hᵛ in *H*, G6 in *I*). There is a copy in MS. Cotton Titus A. xxiv, fols. 81–81ᵛ, with the following variants:

136. 11 was] were
14 gette] clime: hye] eche
15 the] this
17 himself] them selues: hart] harts
20 earth] yearte
23 the] a
24 hordst] hydste
25 Thine] thy: swat] swett

26 (No. 184) *The repentant sinner, &c.* In every edition (No. [153] in *B–I*, sigs. P–Pᵛ in *BC*, H–Hᵛ in *D–G*, Hᵛ–H2 in *H*, G6ᵛ–G7 in *I*). Other copies are in (1) a Harington MS. (Additional 28635, fol. 37ᵛ) and (2) MS. Sloane 1896, fols. 38–39ᵛ. Collations follow:

136. 26–27 durance . . . aduersitie] aduersity prayeth vnto god for mercy (2):
no title in (1)
29 the shell] my youth (2)

    31 grate] call (2)
    32 thee O Lorde alone] thow alone o Lorde (1)
    34 way] race (1):   liekt] lyked (2)
    36 The . . . throwen] The pathe that I pursude/ hath brought (1)
137. 4 and] of (1)
    5 flee] flye (1)
    6 there] *Om.* (2)
    8 no place no houre no] no tyme no place nor (1):   I shal] shall I (2)
    9 shall neuer] noe tyme shall (2)
  10 to craue, to call] to call, to crave (2):   which] that (1):   sayth]
    sayeth (2)
  11 it] you (1)
  13 For] and (1)
  16 receiued] receav'd (1)
  18 the forpassed] me for passed (2)
  19 draw] draweth (2)
  20 lone] loue (2)
  21 threatened] threatned (1, 2)
  25 hope my trust] trust, my hope (2)
  26 saue the soule] sowle to save (1)
  28 all] *Om.* (1)
  29 knowledge eke] eke confesse (1)
  30 I . . . dreade] to love and feare/ I ought (1):   (1) *ends here because
    the page is torn*
  32 walkt] walcked (2)
  33 sprite] spirite (2)

The poem is a mosaic of Biblical expressions, several of which are pointed out below.

    136. 29 *euen frō the shell.* Cf. Melbancke, *Philotimus*, 1583, E*ᵛ*, "to commit wealth to him which yesterday came out of the shell."

    33 *small scourge.* Cf. John ii. 15.

    137. 11 *Knocke and it shalbe heard, but aske, &c.* Cf. Matthew vii. 7–8; Luke xi. 9–10.

    13 *the one wandryng shepe.* Cf. Matthew xviii. 12–13; Luke xv. 3–7.

    17 *for my helpe make haste.* Cf. Psalms xxxviii. 22, xl. 13, lxx. 1, lxxi. 12.

    23 *Not my will lord but thyne, &c.* Cf. Luke xxii. 42.

    25–26 *My fayth my hope, &c.* In *The Arte of English Poesie*, 1589, p. 223, these lines are quoted as an illustration of "*Sinonimia*, or the Figure of store," with the explanation that "Here faith, hope and trust be words of one effect, allowed to vs by this figure of store." Line 26 is indebted to Romans x. 21.

    27 *that thou so dere hast bought.* Cf. Acts xx. 28, 1 Corinthians vii. 23, 1 Peter i. 18–19.

    35 (No. 185) *The louer here telleth, &c.* In every edition (No. [154] in *B–I*, sigs. P2–Q*ᵛ* in *BC*, H2–H5*ᵛ* in *D–G*, H2–H6 in *H*, G7–H2*ᵛ* in *I*). It is imitated by F. G. in the *Paradise*, 1576, pp. 30–31.

Nott (C. 60. O. 13) noted that the source of this poem was Petrarch's canzone in vita 1 (*Rime*, 23, pp. 17–23). Koeppel (*Studien*, p. 88) remarked that No. 185 "das ganze Liebesleben und -leiden Petrarcas erzählt — mit dem einzigen Unterschied, dass der Engländer in die Geschichte seiner Liebe zwischen die Qualen und Zweifel des Werbens und den Tod der Geliebten eine kurze Episode vollen Liebesglückes eingefügt hat."

137. 39–138. 2–15 *Sythe singyng . . . within my hart*. Paraphrased from Petrarch (p. 17):

> Nel dolce tempo de la prima etade,
> che nascer vide et anchor quasi in herba
> la fera voglia che per mio mal crebbe,
> perché cantando il duol si disacerba,
> canterò com' io vissi in libertade
> mentre Amor nel mio albergo a sdegno s' ebbe;
> poi seguirò sí come a lui n' encrebbe
> troppo altamente, e che di ciò m' avenne,
> di ch' io son facto a molta gente exempio.

138. 37, 40 *I spilt no teare, &c. I brake no slepe, &c.* From Petrarch (p. 18):

> lagrima anchor non mi bagnava il petto,
> né rompea il sonno.

139. 22 *The head (alas) dothe still remaine*. A favorite conceit with the Elizabethans, as in J. C.'s *Alcilia*, 1595 (ed. Grosart, p. 9), "hastilie I plucked forth the dart [of Cupid], But left the head fast fixed in my heart."

140. 25 *I gaue my teares*. From Petrarch (p. 21), "a le lagrime triste allargai 'l freno."

30 *Thus dranke I all mine owne disease*. On this punning commonplace see my notes in the *Handful*, p. 97, and the *Gorgeous Gallery*, p. 206.

42–141. 2–3 *Lowde would I cry . . . this grief*. From Petrarch (p. 22), "chiamando morte et lei sola per nome."

141. 9 *Lo, death is painted, &c.* Cf. Petrarch (p. 20), "Morte mi s' era intorno al cor avolta."

19 *that, that shalbe, nedes must fall*. Cf. *Romeo and Juliet*, IV. i. 21, "What must be shall be"; *Twelfth Night*, IV. ii. 17, "That that is is"; Dryden's translation of Horace, iii. 29, st. 8, "what has been, has been."

26–29 *I wrote . . . thyne*. Cf. Petrarch (p. 20):

> ond' io gridai con carta et con incostro:
> Non son mio, no; s' io moro, il danno è vostro.

30–31 *Herewith a . . . did stay*. From Petrarch (p. 21):

> Ben mi credea dinanzi a gli occhi suoi
> d' indegno far cosí di mercé degno;
> et questa spene m' avea fatto ardito.

143. 19 *As to the pleasyng of my thought.* Perhaps this phrase means, "What seemed to me (the highest place of all)."

144. 35 *And earth dothe hide.* From Petrarch, canzone in morte 1, stanza 4 (*Rime*, 268, p. 259): "Oimè, terra è fatto il suo bel viso."

145. 10 (No. 186) *Of his loue named white.* In every edition (No. [155] in *B–I*, sigs. Q^v in *BC*, H5^v in *D–G*, H6 in *H*, H2^v in *I*).

25 (No. 187) *Of the louers vnquiet state.* In every edition (No. [156] in *B–I*, sigs. Q^v–Q2 in *BC*, H5^v–H6 in *D–G*, H6–H6^v in *H*, H2^v–H3 in *I*). In *A+* the poem has only thirteen lines. A copy in a Harington MS. (Additional 28635, fol. 144) supplies the missing line, thus restoring the two rhyme-royal stanzas. Its variants are:

145. 27 which] that
28 yet it] and yet: denyed] denyde
29 receiued] receav'd
30 vnoccupied] unoccupyde
31 which] *Om.:*   applied] applyde
32 Still thus to seke, and] thus may I say I
33 newest] new
34 In wilfull riches I have found povertie
35 In] and in: liue I] I lyved
36 In] in too: lacke my] lacked: *after this line the MS. adds:* nothing but plentie caused my scarsenes
146. 2 am] was
3 that] *Om.:*   shall] should
4 In] in a: suffer] suffred

The first seven lines (145. 27–33) are preserved also in MS. Harleian 78, fol. 29^v, along with an answer solving the "riddle." That copy runs as follows:

A Ridle

What thynge is that that I bothe have and lacke
w^t goodwill graunted and yet yt is denied
always forwarde and yet full fare put backe
Ever more doinge and yet vnoccupied
most slow in that y̆ I have most applied
whearby I lese all that I wyne
ffor y̆ that was readie is now to beginne

Aunswer

Love thou hast wch thou dost lacke
w^t goodwill graunted of her treuly
but yet to graunt her frendes be slacke
So ye be doinge and yet schasely [?]
ffor slothe and fere you cane not wyne
so you ar readie nowe to begyne

146. 5 (No. 188) *where good will is, &c.* In every edition (No. [157] in *B–I*, sigs. Q2 in *BC*, H6 in *D–G*, H6^v in *H*, H3 in *I*).

146. 7–10 *It is no fire that geues no heate, &c.* Borrowed (apparently along with 126. 26–27) in Melbancke's *Philotimus*, 1583, C2ᵛ: "Thus when with fained tunes she hath chirpt her yelden laies, and perceiues that fauning can force no fancie, she will assay another way to flap the in the mouth with flimflam floutes, to dash the out of countenaunce, As that for one: It is no fyre that giues no heate, though it appeare neuer so hotte, and they that runne and cannot sweate, are very drye and leane godwot: but since I lende my loue to losse, fancy (saith she) farewell, adue dastarde."

Miss Elsa Chapin has suggested to me that lines 9–10 ("And they that runne and can not sweate, Are very leane and dry God wot") may perhaps be a reference to Sir Francis Bryan's supposed description of himself at 88. 28, "Though I seme leane and drye, withouten moysture."

15 *New wine will search to finde a vent.* Combined with line 17 and 148. 24–25 in Melbancke's *Philotimus*, 1583, Y2: "Thou maiest aswell be feareles, as he that holds y̆ wolfe by the eares: new wine will seaech [*sic*] to finde a vent, and wit will walke where will is bent: when the winde is not in a good coast, we must ship our oares and further our course: venter & conquer."

25 *There can no want of resident.* That is, no lack of residents (no abundance of soldiers) can defend the castle successfully when Wit and Will and Diligence unite to assault it.

31 (No. 189) *Verses written . . . of sir Iames wilford.* In every edition (No. [158] in *B–I*, sigs. Q2ᵛ in *BC*, H6ᵛ in *D–G*, H6ᵛ–H7 in *H*, H3–H3ᵛ in *I*). On Wilford see No. 156. From line 34 it seems likely that the poem was first issued as a broadside-elegy with a woodcut picture.

147. 12 (No. 190) *The ladye praieth, &c.* In every edition (No. [159] in *B–I*, sigs. Q2ᵛ–Q3 in *BC*, H6ᵛ–H7 in *D–G*, H7 in *H*, H3ᵛ in *I*). The poem was probably suggested by Surrey's Nos. 17 and 19, which it resembles in title and subject.

37 (No. 191) *The meane estate is best.* In every edition (No. [160] in *B–I*, sigs. Q3–Q3ᵛ in *BC*, H7–H7ᵛ in *D–G*, H7ᵛ in *H*, H3ᵛ–H4 in *I*). On this topic see the notes to No. 118.

148. 20–21 *What helps the dyall to the blinde.* Borrowed in Melbancke's *Philotimus*, 1583, Y2ᵛ: "Alas, what helpes the diall the blind, the clock the deafe, or wit him that wantes opportunitie?"

24–25 *Shalbe as free from cares, &c.* See 146.15 n. and, for the proverb, see my notes in the *Paradise*, p. 234. Cf. also *Mercurius Elencticus*, November 5–12, 1647, p. 11, "The Members at Westminster have a Woolfe by the eares." In *The Barons' Wars* (1603), 1, 36, Drayton gives the proverb as "He's mad who takes a lion by the ears."

38 (No. 192) *The louer thinkes no payne, &c.* In every edition (No. [161] in *B–I*, sigs. Q3ᵛ–Q4 in *BC*, H7ᵛ–H8 in *D–G*, H8–H8ᵛ in *H*, H4–H4ᵛ in *I*).

149. 3 *after paynes pleasure prest.* For *paynes* read *paine is* with *B+*.

149. 14 *The pore mā ploweth his groūd for graine.* The rhyme-word *gain* (as in *D**+) might be expected. The idea is a commonplace. Cf. Melbancke, *Philotimus*, 1583, H4ᵛ, "The plowmans toile hath hope that makes him till: Loue hath a sauce that makes his sorrow swete"; A. N., *A true Relation of the Trauels of M. Bush*, 1608, C4ᵛ, "*Spes alit agricolas:* Hope nourisheth the Coun-try-men. The hope of gayne causeth the labouring husbandman, not to feele the scorching heate of the summer, nor the hoary frosts of winter"; and the *Paradise*, 1576, p. 211.

23 *And thus for rest to rage I reche.* "Thus, instead of attaining rest, I attain the opposite of rest, — frenzy."

39 *me ioy thus lesse reioyce.* Read *me ioylesse thus reioyce.*

150. 4 *so fast I folde.* Probably *F*+ are correct in making *I folde* the preterite participle *yfold.*

8 (No. 193) *Of a new maried Student.* In every edition (No. [162] in *B–I*, sigs. Q4 in *BC*, H8 in *D–G*, H8ᵛ in *H*, H5 in *I*). Warton (*History of English Poetry*, ed. Hazlitt, IV, 64) remarks: "Sir Thomas More was one of the best jokers of that age, and there is some probability that this [poem] might have fallen from his pen." Professor H. H. Hudson has called my attention to a shortened version of No. 193 that appears in John Davies of Hereford's *Wit's Bedlam*, 1617, p. 5 (*Complete Works*, ed. Grosart, II [1878], last article). Thence it was reprinted in Samuel Pick's *Festum Voluptatis, Or the Banquet of Pleasure*, 1639, sig. G, and in *Wit's Recreations*, 1640, no. 192 (*Facetiae*, 1817 reprint, II, 106, J. C. Hotten's reprint, n. d. [1874?], II, 111, no. 388). Davies's lines run thus:

Fast and Loose.

Paphus was married all in hast,
And now to wracke doth runne,
So, *knitting* of himselfe *too fast,*
He hath himselfe *undone.*

Davies's title was suggested by some edition later than *A.*

In the margin of the Rosenbach copy of *C* a hand about as old as the copy itself (1557) has written:

gooe feede thie fylthie lustes
wᵗʰ venus fylthie flames
J loue the lawe and muste
J care not for suche dames
gooe tosse thy ladyes trayne
let me aplye my bookes
& see what thowe shalt gayne
when J gayne silluer hookes.

17 (No. 194) ❡*The meane estate is, &c.* In every edition (No. [163] in *B–I*, sigs. Q4–Q4ᵛ in *BC*, H8–H8ᵛ in *D–G*, H8ᵛ–I in *H*, H5–H5ᵛ in *I*). This poem is a translation, more paraphrastic than the translations in Nos. 28 and

295, of Horace's *Carmina*, II. 10 (see pp. 152–153, above). With it might be compared the translation into "attempted" English sapphics as given in John Thelwall's *Champion* (see *The Poetical Recreations of the Champion*, 1822, pp. 107–108), beginning,

> Safely shalt thou, Varro, direct thy vessel,
> Neither seeking rashly the deep, nor steering
> Near the faithless shore, when the storms attack thee,
> Fearfully sailing.

150. 24 *lest harme him happe awayting lest*. I suppose the line (which has no equivalent in Horace) means, "lest harm come to him when he is least expecting it."

28 *he put*. The sense of the passage requires *is put*.

151. 8, 10 *fraught, nought*. This rhyme violates the regular octameter-couplet scheme, making lines 8–11 a quatrain. In lines 13, 15 *blastes, frostes* make a poor rhyme.

20–21 *Not always il . . . rides the racke*. This appears to mean, "It's not ill always, though now, while clouds are driven (by the winds), destruction rides for a time" — an expansion of Horace's sentence (cf. 26. 36), "Non, si male nunc, et olim sic erit."

22–23 *Phebus . . . muse to wake*. Horace writes, "quondam cithara tacentem suscitat Musam neque semper arcum tendit Apollo." Cf. Surrey's translation at 26. 36–38.

28 (No. 195) ¶*The louer refused, &c.* In every edition (No. [164] in *B–I*, sigs. Q4ᵛ–R in *BC*, H8ᵛ–I in *D–G*, I–Iᵛ in *H*, H5ᵛ–H6 in *I*).

30 *I Lent my loue to losse, &c.* This line is commended in *The Arte of English Poesie*, 1589, p. 191: "Whereas this worde *lent* is properly of mony or some such other thing, as men do commonly borrow, for vse to be repayed againe, and being applied to loue is vtterly abused, and yet very commendably spoken by vertue of this figure," that is, "*Catachresis*, or the Figure of abuse."

152. 23 (No. 196) *The felicitie of a mind, &c.* In every edition (No. [165] in *B–I*, sigs. R–Rᵛ in *BC*, I–Iᵛ in *D–G*, Iᵛ–I2 in *H*, H6 in *I*). This poem is of considerable interest, for it is a fairly close translation of the opening lines of the second book of Lucretius's *De Rerum Natura*:

> Suave, mari magno turbantibus aequora ventis,
> e terra magnum alterius spectare laborem;
> non quia vexari quemquamst iucunda voluptas,
> sed quibus ipse malis careas quia cernere suave est.
> suave etiam belli certamina magna tueri
> per campos instructa tua sine parte pericli.
> sed nil dulcius est, bene quam munita tenere
> edita doctrina sapientum templa serena,
> despicere unde queas alios passimque videre
> errare atque viam palantis quaerere vitae,
> certare ingenio, contendere nobilitate,

noctes atque dies niti praestante labore
ad summas emergere opes rerumque potiri.
o miseras hominum mentes, o pectora caeca!
qualibus in tenebris vitae quantisque periclis
degitur hoc aevi quodcumquest! nonne videre
nil aliud sibi naturam latrare, nisi utqui
corpore seiunctus dolor absit, mente fruatur
iucundo sensu cura semota metuque?
ergo corpoream ad naturam pauca videmus
esse opus omnino, quae demant cumque dolorem.

For other (partial) renderings of this passage see Sir Thomas North's translation of Amyot's preface to *Plutarch's Lives*, 1579 (ed. Wyndham, 1 [1895], 17), and Bacon's essay "Of Truth" (1625).

153. 10–11 *Yea . . . delight is spent.* These lines are not in the original.

12 (No. 197) *All worldly pleasures fade.* In every edition (No. [166] in *B–I*, sigs. Rᵛ–R2 in *BC*, Iᵛ–I2 in *D–G*, I2–I2ᵛ in *H*, H6–H6ᵛ in *I*). There is a copy in MS. Cotton Titus A. xxiv, fols. 81ᵛ–82ᵛ, with the following variants:

153. 13 griesly] ougly
14 lusty] tender: earth] yearthe
15 don] do
26 The] then: eates] eth: is Autumn] Autumn is
28 done] doo: whiche] that: had made so] left vs
30 cūtinue] abyde
34 No] what: morne] morow
36 dothe pronounce] gyues of the
38 Nor surged] no sugred
154. 2 thence deliuer] helpe from thense the

No. 197 is a translation (with the omissions specified below) of Horace's *Carmina*, iv. 7, beginning,

Diffugere nives, redeunt iam gramina campis
arboribusque comae;
mutat terra vices et decrescentia ripas
flumina praetereunt.

24–32 *Thē Autumn . . . pleasure gon.* Lines 24–28 represent a considerable expansion of Horace's phraseology, while lines 29–32 are inserted in place of the verses,

Damna tamen celeres reparant caelestia lunae;
nos ubi decidimus,
quo pius Aeneas, quo Tullus dives et Ancus,
pulvis et umbra sumus.

34 *my lyfe shall last.* After this line the translator omits Horace's "Cuncta manus avidas fugient heredis, amico quae dederis animo."

35–40 *For when . . . abyde & dwell.* Horace's verses are:

Cum semel occideris et de te splendida Minos
    fecerit arbitria,
non, Torquate, genus, non te facundia, non te
    restituet pietas.

154. 4 (No. 198) *A complaint of the losse, &c.* In every edition (No. [167] in *B–I*, sigs. R2–R2ᵛ in *BC*, I2–I2ᵛ in *D–G*, I2ᵛ–I3 in *H*, H6ᵛ–H7ᵛ in *I*).

21 *reason rasde through barke and rinde.* "(That day) when my reason was utterly destroyed (by love)." "Bark and rind" seems to have much the same force (cf. 70. 37) as "root and branch."

155. 8–13 *In whose calme streames I sayld, &c.* Borrowed by Melbancke, *Philotimus*, 1583, sig. Y: "I raisde a star whereto direct my course, in whose prospect my tackle faild, my compas brake. I threshed for corne, & all is turnd to chaffe."

24 (No. 199) *A praise of his Ladye.* In every edition (No. [168] in *B–I*, sigs. R2ᵛ–R3ᵛ in *BC*, I2ᵛ–I3ᵛ in *D–G*, I3–I4 in *H*, H7ᵛ–H8 in *I*). There is a copy in MS. Additional 15225, fols. 16–16ᵛ, dating about 1616, which is entitled "here followeth a song in praise of a Ladie," and which has the following variants:

155. 26 you] yea
    37 lampe] lambe
156. 4 well] very well
   15 the] a
   18 redier] ruddier
   20 feast] feastes
   30 in her such] herselfe with
   32 as] soe
   34 Ielifloure a] gilliflower the
   37 this] that

A copy in MS. Harleian 1703, fols. 108–109, made about 1572 by William Forrest, a Roman Catholic priest, is assigned to John Heywood, the well-known epigrammatist and playwright, with the statement that it celebrates Queen Mary I. It differs so greatly from the text in *A* as almost to be a new poem. A reprint follows:

A discription of A most noble Ladye, advowed by John Heywoode: presently who advertisinge her graces, as face, saith of her thus, in much eloquent phrase,

Geue place, ye Ladyes all bee gone,
    shewe not your selues att all,
ffor whye? behoulde, there cometh one
    whose face, yours all, blanke shall.

The vertue of her lookes,
    excelles the precious ston
yee neede none other bookes
    to reade, or looke vpon

In each of her twoe iyes,
  ther smiles a naked boye,
It woulde you all suffice
  too see those lampes of ioye.

Of [sic] all the worlde were sought full farre,
  who coulde finde such a wyght.
Her beutye twinkleth like a starre,
  within the frostye night.

Her couler comes and gose,
  with such a goodly grace
More ruddye then the rose
  within her liuely face.

Among her youthfull yeares,
  shee tryumphes over age,
And yeat shee still appeares,
  boath wyttye, graue, and sage,

J thinke nature, hath lost her moulde,
  wher shee her forme dyd take,
or ells J doubt y̆ nature coulde,
  so faire a creature make,

Shee maye bee well comparde,
  vnto the Phenix kinde,
whose like hath not byn harde,
  that anye nowe can finde,

Jn Lyfe a dyane chaste,
  in truth Penelopeye,
Jn worde and deede steedfaste,
  what neede J more to seye,

At Baccus feast: none may her meete,
  or yeat at anye wanton playe,
Nor gasinge in the open streete,
  or wandringe, as a straye,

The mirth that shee doth vse,
  is mixt with shamfastnesse,
all vyces shee eschues,
  and hateth Jdelnes.

Yt is A worlde to see,
  how vertue can repaire,
And decke such honestee,
  in her that is so faire,

Great sute to vyce, maye some Allure,
  that thinkes to make no fawlte,
Wee see a forte hadde neede bee sure,
  wᶜʰ manye doth assaulte,

They seeke an endlesse waye,
    that thinkes to wynne her love,
As well they maye assaye,
    the stoney rocke to moue.

ffor shee is none of those,
    that settes not bye evill fame,
Shee will not lyghtly lose,
    her truth and honest name,

How might wee doo to haue a graffe,
    of this vnspotted tree,
ffor all the rest they are but chaffe
    in prayse of her to bee.

Shee doth as farre exceade,
    these women now a dayes,
As doth the floure, the weede,
    and more, a thousande wayes.

This prayse J shall her geeue,
    when death doth what hee can,
her honest name shall liue,
    within the mouth of man.

This worthye ladye too beewraye
    a kinges doughter was shee,
Of whom John Heywoode lyste to saye,
    in such worthye degree,

And Marye was her name weete yee,
    with these graces Jndude,
At eightene yeares, so flourisht shee,
    so doth his meane conclude.

This manuscript copy is reprinted, with modernized spelling and punctuation, in Thomas Evans's *Old Ballads*, III (1810), 120–123. From the final stanza ("At eightene yeares") it appears that, since Mary I was born in 1516, Heywood wrote his "Description" in 1534, and hence that Surrey (who was about seventeen in 1534) imitated Heywood in No. 20. Heywood's No. 199 was registered for publication as a ballad about May 11, 1561, under the title of "gyve place you Ladyes" and under the same title in 1566–67 (Rollins, *Analytical Index*, nos. 967, 968).

155. 30–33 *The vertue of her liuely lokes, &c.* Borrowed in Melbancke's *Philotimus*, 1583, C2: "the vertue of her thralling lookes so brauely gloste with glimsing grace, that thou wouldest wishe no other bookes to reade or looke vpon."

35 *Smileth a naked boye.* Love (Cupid) is reflected in her eyes.

156. 18 *More redier to then doth the rose.* That is, more readily; but the MS. has *More ruddye*, D+ have *more ruddier*.

157. 2 (No. 200) *The pore estate to be holden for best.* In every edition (No. [169] in *B–I*, sigs. R3ᵛ in *BC*, I3ᵛ in *D–G*, I4 in *H*, H8 in *I*). A copy,

without a title, in a Harington MS. (Additional 28635, fol. 137) differs in the following particulars:

> 157. 6 fate] state
>   12 haue they] they have
>   13 fele] fynde
>   14 they] the
>   15 the] their
>   16 liues] lyv'ste

Other poems on the topic of the "poor estate" are listed in the notes to No. 118.

The initial letter of each line plus the final letter of the last line spell the name "Edwarde Somerset"; but the acrostic is given completely in *B* only; it is incomplete in *A*, and is not noticed at all in *C–I* or the MS. In his edition of the miscellany (p. vii) Arber listed Edward Somerset among the contributors to that volume; and he has been followed by nearly all subsequent writers, but not by A. F. Pollard, *England under Protector Somerset*, 1900, p. 321. Padelford, for example, in his *Early Sixteenth Century Lyrics*, p. 145, accepts the authorship of "Edward Seymour, Duke of Somerset," saying, "This is the only extant poem of Somerset's, though his papers are voluminous." (Parenthetically, it may be noticed that *Nugae Antiquae* [1769, p. 86; 1779, 1792, III, 259; 1804, II, 328–329] contains "Verses found written by the Lord Admiral Seymour the Week before he was beheaded, 1549"; though Seymour, who became lord high admiral in December, 1542, was not beheaded till 1552. "A Sonet writen upon my Lord admirall Seymour," preserved in MS. Additional 28635, fol. 3, is also printed in *Nugae Antiquae* directly after the "Verses.")

Now the fact that the poem has the acrostic "Edwarde [Duke of] Somerset" is no reason at all for thinking that Somerset was the author: it is far more reasonable to believe that it was written by some one else as a compliment to him. Thus in *The Arbor of Amitie*, 1568 (*Poems*, ed. Grosart, pp. 96–97), Thomas Howell has "A Poesie" with the acrostic *Elisabeth Bradburne* (a fact not noticed by Grosart), and there are other examples in *H. His Deuises*, 1581 (the same work, pp. 237–239). Kendall printed in *Flowers of Epigrammes*, 1577, poems of his own composition which have the acrostics *Henrie Knevet*, *Richarde Woodward*, *Paul Tooley*, *Mary Palmer* (Spenser Society ed., pp. 266–267, 288–290); and Anthony Munday included in his *Mirror of Mutability* (1579) a poem in honor of his patron, Lord Oxford, with the acrostic *Edward de Vere*. Literally dozens of other examples could be cited, but a reference to Grimald's No. 141 and to 14. 9 n. will suffice. The claim of Edward Somerset (whether duke or commoner) for a place among the "uncertain authors" must therefore be dismissed. But a careful reading of No. 200 strongly suggests that the poem was written after the Duke of Somerset's execution in January, 1552: the first stanza seems to discuss his downfall ("Who climbes to raigne with kinges, may rue his fate full sore"), the second stanza to warn men to be content with humble estate.

157. 9 *Deceiued is the birde, &c.* See 30. 12 n.

18 (No. 201) *The complaint of Thestilis, &c.* In every edition (No. [170] in *B–I*, sigs. R3ᵛ–R4 in *BC*, I3ᵛ–I4 in *D–G*, I4–I4ᵛ in *H*, H8ᵛ in *I*). In the second idyll of Theocritus and the second eclogue of Virgil, Thestylis is a shepherdess (John Martyn, editing the eclogues [1829, pp. 15–16 n.] thinks that Thestylis was the cook-maid at Virgil's farm), and hence she appears as "a fair lass" in George Peele's *Arraignment of Paris, ca.* 1584, III. ii. In No. 201, as well as in the reply to it (No. 234), Thestilis is a man's name. A shepherd Thestylis appears also in Lodowick Bryskett's epitaph on Sidney, *The mourning Muse of Thestylis,* 1587 (published in Spenser's *Colin Clout* volume, 1595, G3), and in Francis Sabie's *Pan's Pipe,* 1595, eclogue III. No. 201 was reprinted, with some minor variations, in *England's Helicon,* 1600 (ed. Macdonald, pp. 52–53), as the composition of "L. T. Howard, E. of Surrie." The music for "Thestilis a seely man" (with no further words than these) is given in MS. Additional 4900, fol. 58.

158. 16 (No. 202) ❧*The louer praieth pity, &c.* In every edition (No. [172] in *B–I*, sigs. R4ᵛ–S in *BC*, I4ᵛ–I5 in *D–G*, I5 in *H*, I–Iᵛ in *I*). It is imitated by Turbervile's "To his Love, that Controlde his Dogge for fawning on hir" (*Epitaphes,* etc., 1567, pp. 98–99).

24 *he might her play and moue.* The reading in *B+* is *pray and moue,* which is perhaps correct.

32 (No. 203) *Of his ring sent to his lady.* In every edition (No. [173] in *B–I*, sigs. S in *BC*, I5 in *D–G*, I5–I5ᵛ in *H*, Iᵛ in *I*). The poem was possibly suggested by, and in any case resembles, Ovid's *Amores,* II. 15, "Anule, formosae digitum vincture puellae." It is imitated by Turbervile's "To his Ring given to his Ladie, wherein was graven this verse: My hart is yours" (*Epitaphes,* etc., 1567, pp. 32–33). Dr. Leicester Bradner, in *The Review of English Studies,* IV (1928), 207–208, calls Nos. 203 and 231 "forerunners of the Spenserian stanza."

159. 5 (No. 204) *The changeable state of louers.* In every edition (No. [174] in *B–I*, sigs. S–Sᵛ in *BC*, I5–I5ᵛ in *D–G*, I5ᵛ in *H*, Iᵛ–I2 in *I*).

33 (No. 205) *A praise of Audley.* In every edition (No. [175] in *B–I*, sigs. Sᵛ in *BC*, I5ᵛ in *D–G*, I5ᵛ–I6 in *H*, I2 in *I*). A copy in MS. Additional 23971, fols. 37ᵛ–39, called "An Epitaphe vpon the dethe of Mʳ Thomas Awdeleye," is signed "qd. C.," which may represent (Thomas) Churchyard. The same MS. contains a long treatise on the art of war addressed by Audley to Edward VI. Both works are in one handwriting, probably that of a scribe, "Wyll goodal," whose name is signed on fol. 37. (Another copy of Audley's treatise is in MS. Tanner 103, fols. 30–47, Bodleian library; it has the title, "An introduccion or A. B. C. to the Warre dedicated to kinge Edward the Vjᵗʰ the first yeare of his regne by Thomas Audeley newelie corrected in the

first yeare of Quene Marie by the sayde Thomas Audeley.") Variants between
No. 205 and the MS. follow:

159. 36 lad] ledd
    37 calde] called
160. 4 war long time] warres full Longe
      5 Cald] called: *MS. adds:*

          kynge Henry the viij[th] sent hym to Guynes
              as provest marshall there/
          whose famous deedes in lytle tyme
              dyd floryshe everye where/
          A tutour to thignorant,
              A fathere to them all,
          he tought them howe to lede there men
              as chyefe and principall,
          The worthiest men that yngland brede
              thes manye hundred yeres,
          dyd thinke no skorne to lerne of hym
              as nowe right welle apperes.
          ffrom Guynes the kinge to bullen toke
              This noble mars sonne,
          and placed hym in tholde man
              whan he the Tonne hade wone
          his knowelledge gate suche credytt styll
              The kinge to love hym thane
          One of his privye chamber has
              he made this worthye mane
          and so he was vnto his sonne
              who sent this his lode starr,
          to skotteland as a Counseller,
              in tyme of cruelle warre,

     6 tornay] Jurneye: there] that: refusde] refused
     7 exploit] Expoyete: *after this line the MS. adds:*

          And fyrst of all his trueth was tryede
              his faythe was throwzelye knowen
          whan Wyat dyd foresake the fylde
              & at lenghe [*sic*] his men overthrowen,
          what can be named that vertuous ys
              but he thereof hade parte,
          In everye poyente to Souldyers all
              a mastere of the Arte

     8 fierce] free: the] all
     9 In] A: yet] ye
   10 that] if: defame] dysprayse
   11 life] tyme: *MS. adds:*

          Thoughe fame helde vpe his name a lofte
              yt fortune kepte hym lowe
          and worthye welthe dyd hym forsake
              as his poure ende dyd showe

Some men wolde hys dedes dese*r*ved
　greate recompense to haue
but what lefte he behynd but fame
　when he wente to his grave
Althoughe his meryt*tes* clamed rewarde
　his fortune was so yll,
when othere men there suet*es* obtayned
　he was forgotten stylle,

160. 13 No hard mischaunce] nor no myschange
　　14 loued] beloved:　　mislikt] myslyked
　　15 And . . . not] where ever he went eche man him caled
　　16 doth cause] will haue
　　17 to . . . greuous] for to escape his
　　18 ground] grave
　　19 ygraue in] in stone or:　　shall stand] shalbe
　　20 lies] lyeth:　　hateth] hated:　　vertues] vertuouse
　　21 name in earth] fame one earthe:　　deserues] deserved:

The subject of No. 205 is not John Tuchet (or Touchet), Lord Audley (†*ca.* 1558), or Thomas Audley, Baron Audley (†1544); it is Thomas Audley, a captain at Guisnes. See *Letters and Papers, Foreign and Domestic of the Reign of Henry VIII*, XVII, 275, 325, 331, etc. About February, 1546 (the same work, XXI, pt. I, pp. 118, 200–201), Henry VIII appointed him lieutenant of the Old Man in Boulogne with a salary of thirteen shillings fourpence a day and with ten assistants. He was also gentleman usher to Henry VIII, who willed him two hundred marks (the same work, pt. II, 322; Dasent, *Acts of the Privy Council*, II, 101). On August 21, 1548 (Dasent, II, 217), the Privy Council sent Audley "northward," giving him fifty pounds for the journey; and on September 7, 1549 (Dasent, II, 323), it granted him fifty pounds "in reward for bringing Ket," the rebel. It is somewhat ironical that Audley's name is omitted from the *D. N. B.* "Why, what are thou," asks Barnabe Rich, in *A Right Exelent [sic] and pleasaunt Dialogue, betwene Mercury and an English Souldier*, 1574, sig. B, "that doest not yet know the noble Captaine Audley, whose prouesse and valiaunce, as it hath made him famous to euery inferiour person, so hee is lykewise honoured of each renowned wight"?

160. 6 *What tornay was there.* Though *tornay* (*tourney*) appears in all the editions, sense and the MS. show that the word should be *journey*.

8 *In towne a lambe in felde . . . a lyon.* Cf. Gascoigne, *A Hundreth Sundrie Flowres*, 1573 (ed. Ward, p. 119), "In fielde a lion and in towne a childe, Fierce to his foe," etc.; Gabriel Harvey, *A New Letter of Notable Contents*, 1593 (*Works*, ed. Grosart, I, 277), "The *brauest man* is such a personage, as I haue elsewhere described: A *Lion* in the field, a *Lamme* in the towne," etc.

22 (No. 206) *Time trieth truth.* In every edition (No. [176] in *B–I*, sigs. S*v*–S2 in *BC*, I5*v*–I6 in *D–G*, I6 in *H*, I2–I2*v* in *I*).

Very different versions of this poem appear in the *Gorgeous Gallery*, 1578, pp. 47–48, and a Harington MS. (Additional 28635, fol. 137^v). Below I reprint the one in the *Gallery*, with collations from the MS. in foot-notes:

¶Of a happy wished time.[1]

Eche thing must haue a[2] time, and tyme doth try mens troth,[3]
And troth deserues a special trust, on trust great frenship groth:
And freendship is full fast, where [4] faythfulnesse is found
And faythfull thinges be [5] ful of fruicte, and fruitful things be [6] sound
The sound is good in proofe, and proofe is Prince of prayse,
And woorthy prayse is such a pearle, as lightly not decayes.
All this doth time bring forth, which time I must abide,
How should I boldely credit craue? till time my truth [7] haue tried.[8]
And as a time I found, to fall in Fancies frame,
So doo I wish an [9] happy time, at large to shew the same.
If Fortune aunswer hope, and hope may haue her [10] hire,
Then shall my hart possesse in peace, the time that I desire.

There is a later copy, with the title "Tempus omnia probat. ffestina lente," in MS. Additional 26737, fol. 107. The idea of the poem was perhaps suggested by Ecclesiastes iii. 1–8.

160. 35 (No. 207) *The louer refused, &c.* In every edition (No. [177] in *B–I*, sigs. S2–S2^v in *BC*, I6–I6^v in *D–H*, I2^v in *I*).

Other copies are in (1) MS. Additional 17492, fols. 68–68^v, and (2) the *Gorgeous Gallery*, 1578, p. 45. Each has two stanzas not in *A–I*. The latter copy is entitled "The desperate Louer exclaymeth his Ladyes cruelty and threatneth to kill himselfe." The former, without a title and written in a villainous hand, changes the singular *her* to the plural *the(y)* throughout. Collations follow:

161. 2 youthfull yeres are] ioyful dayes bee (2):   yeres] days (1)
       3 ioyfull dayes] pleasant eres (1), pleasant yeres (2):   are] be (2)
       4 may not last] dothe bot wast (1)
       5 am one] haue won (1)
       6 ioyes are] al ys (1, 2)
       8 Desirous] Desyer (1), Desireth (2)
     11 amids the] in middest of (2)
     12 she dothe] the do (1)
     13 is my most] most I do (1, 2)
     14–17 *follow the new stanza added in* (2) *after line* 25
     15 lyfe] dethe (1, 2)
     16 she] the (1)
     17 That is my] I se my (1, 2):   deadly] ffryndly (1), cruell (2):
     (1) *inserts:*

[1] *Om.* [2] his [3] tryes out mens trouthe [4] never fayles/ when [5] faithfulnesse is
[6] are [7] trothe [8] tryde [9] a [10] his

I se the know my hart
and how I cannot ffain
I se the se my smart
and how I leff yn pane.

161. 18 how] that (2):   she] the (1)
    19 yet she] yt the (1)
    21 She] The (1):   sekes] se (1), seeketh (2)
    22 she doth] the do (1)
    24 nie] by (1)
    25 she] the (1):   *after this line* (2) *inserts:*

I see shee knoweth my harte
   And how I doo complayne,
I see shee knoweth my smarte
   Shee seeth I doo not fayne.

    26 will ye] wold you (1, 2)
    27 She] the (1):   will] wold, (1, 2)
    28 you] shee (2)
    29 she] the (1):   her] ther (1)
    30 with] by (2)
    32 will] would (2)
    33 To . . . good] yff yt myt do them (1), *which adds:*

the shal haue ther reqwest
and I must haue my mend
lo her my blody brest
to ples the ẘ vnkynd

In (2) *the final stanza is:*

Shee shall haue her request
   And I will haue mine ende,
Lo heere my blouddy brest
   To please her most vnkinde.

161. 15 *I see my lyfe also.* The antithesis on which the poem is based shows that *lyfe* should be, as in the other versions, *death.*

    34 (No. 208) *The Picture of a louer.* In every edition (No. [178] in *B–I*, sigs. S2ᵛ in *BC*, I6ᵛ in *D–G*, I6ᵛ–I7 in *H*, I3 in *I*).

    162. 26 (No. 209) *Of the death of Phillips.* In every edition (No. [179] in *B–I*, sigs. S2ᵛ–S3 in *BC*, I6ᵛ–I7 in *D–G*, I7 in *H*, I3–I3ᵛ in *I*). Grove's *Dictionary of Music* (ed. J. A. F. Maitland, III [1907], 708) gives a number of facts about a composer, Philip van Wilder, known as "Mr. Philips," who in 1538 was appointed lutenist to Henry VIII and keeper of His Majesty's musical instruments, and who in 1550 was made a gentleman of the Privy Chamber by Edward VI. Since No. 209 stresses Phillips's skill as a lutenist, it seems not unlikely that this Phillips was Philip van Wilder.

    163. 2 (No. 210) *That all thing sometime finde ease, &c.* In every edition (No. [180] in *B–I*, sigs. S3–S3ᵛ in *BC*, I7–I7ᵛ in *D–H*, I3ᵛ in *I*). The theme

and various lines of this poem remind one of Surrey's No. 265; the style sug-
gests Thomas Churchyard.

163. 21-28 *The owle with feble sight, &c.* Park (in Warton-Hazlitt's *History
of English Poetry*, IV, 63 n.) remarks: "The turn and texture of these stanzas
would appear to be derived from the Gospels of St. Matthew and St. Luke,
viii. 20, and ix. 58."

37 (No. 211) *Thassault of Cupide, &c.* In every edition (No. [181]
in *B–I*, sigs. S3ᵛ–S4 in *BC*, I7ᵛ–I8 in *D–G*, I7ᵛ–I8ᵛ in *H*, I4–I4ᵛ in *I*). A partial
copy in MS. Harleian 6910, fols. 175–175ᵛ (*ca.* 1596), has the following vari-
ants:

> 163. 37-39 *Title om.*
> 164. 4 battry] batterie
>   9 aray] awaye
>   17 the fort] them forth
>   20 Expence of Powder he spar'd not
>   23 discharged] discharging: *MS. ends with line 23*

No. 211 was registered for publication as a ballad, "the Cruell assaulte of
Cupydes forte," in 1565–66 (Rollins, *Analytical Index*, no. 430). A moraliza-
tion called "The Cruel Assault of Gods Fort" (*ca.* 1560), the composition of
the printer-poet John Awdelay, is reprinted in J. P. Collier's *Old Ballads*, pp.
29–37 (Percy Society, 1840), and in H. L. Collmann's *Ballads and Broadsides*,
no. 3 (Roxburghe Club, 1912). In the *Gorgeous Gallery*, 1578, pp. 31–33, there is
"An exellent [*sic*] Sonet, Wherin the Louer exclaymeth agaynst Detraction,
beeing the principall cause of all his care. To the tune, when Cupid scaled
first the Fort," which borrows not only the idea of No. 211 but also several of
its phrases outright.

The author of *The Arte of English Poesie*, 1589, pp. 246–247, in discussing
"*Pragmatographia.* or the Counterfait action", remarked: "In this figure the
Lord *Nicholas Vaux* a noble gentleman, and much delighted in vulgar making,
and a man otherwise of no great learning but hauing herein a maruelous facilli-
tie, made a dittie representing the battayle and assault of *Cupide*, so excel-
lently well, as for the gallant and propre application of his fiction in euery
part, I cannot choose but set downe the greatest part of his ditty, for in truth
it can not be amended." He then quotes 164. 2–23, making some changes in
the text. Percy, reprinting the poem in his *Reliques*, 1765 (ed. Wheatley, II,
50–53), rightly decided that the author was not Lord Nicholas Vaux, but was
Lord Thomas Vaux.

164. 19 *Stode in the rampyre.* "Stood on the rampart." Cf. Churchyard,
A pleasant Discourse of Court and Wars (1596), B3ᵛ, "No walls nor rampire
could hold out A lions hart in manly minde."

165. 13 *youe eye.* Read *your eye.*

16 (No. 212) *The aged louer renounceth loue.* In every edition (No.
[182] in *B–I*, sigs. S4–T in *BC*, I8–K in *D–G*, I8ᵛ–K in *H*, I4ᵛ–I5 in *I*).

This poem is ascribed to Lord (Thomas) Vaux in (1) MS. Ashmole 48, *ca.* 1555–1565 (*Songs and Ballads*, pp. 34–36, ed. Wright, Roxburghe Club, 1860) and (2) MS. Harleian 1703, fols. 100–100ᵛ, the last page of which is dated by the copyist, William Forrest, Roman Catholic priest (cf. the notes to No. 199), October 27, 1572. Other copies are preserved in (3) MS. Additional 38599, fols. 134ᵛ–135 (*ca.* 1611), and (4) MS. Additional 26737, fol. 107ᵛ. The last, which it is not necessary to collate, contains only thirty-two lines arranged in the curious order 165. 18–39, 166. 2–3, 24–27, 4–7. Collations of *A* with the three other MS. copies follow:

165. 16–17 *No title in* (1):   A dyttye or sonet made by the lorde vaws in time of the noble queene Marye rep*r*esentinge the Jmage of deathe (2), A verie pretie songe of an ould man (3)

  18 that] what (1)
  20 requires] requyrth (2)
  21 thinkes] thinke (3)
  23 My] And (1):   be] are (2, 3)
  24 tract] trake (1)
  25 vpon] *wi*thin (2)
  27 clawed] clawd (1, 2), caught (3):   cowche] crutche (1–3)
  28 life] youth (2, 3):   she] he (1, 2), doth (3):   leapes] leape (3)
  30 not] not me (1)
  31 Me as] As she (1), As it (3):   she did] hathe done (1, 3)
  32 are] ys (1)
  33 they haue] yt hathe (1)
  35 This] Thes (1), all (2):   youthly idle rime] youthfull wyldish toyes (3):   rime] ryemes (1)
  36 to me she] on mee hee (2)
  37 these toyes in time] thos trykes be tyemes (1), in tyme these Ioies (3): in time] betyme (2)
  38 brow] browes (3)
166. 2 Say] Saythe (1–3):   will hedge] must lodge (1), hath caught (2)
    4 harbinger] harberger (3)
    5 To] Towardes (1)
    7 Dothe bid] Which bydes (1)
    9 a shrowdyng] wyndinge (2)
  11 For] Of (1):   most] full (1)
  12 the] *Om.* (2)
  13 That] Which (1):   knols] knylles (2), touls (3):   knell] bell (1–3)
  14 wofull] merye (1), wearye (2, 3)
  15 Er] Or (1):   *lines 24–27 follow* 15 *in* (3)
  16 kepers] keper (3):   knit] knytes (1, 3)
  17 That] Which (1), whome (3):   did] doth (2), haith (3):   laugh] laught (3)
  18 me] hyme (1):   clene shalbe] shal be clene (1, 2):   *in* (3) *the line runs*, Which nowe awaie is cleene forgott
  19 I] he (1), *om.* (3):   had not ben] had never be (2), never had (3)
  20 Thus] This (2):   *in* (3) *the line runs*, Which younth [*sic*] I nowe yeelde vpp: 20–23 *follow* 27 *in* (1)

24 Loe here] Behowld (1):   bared] bare head (1, 2), parched (3)
25 signe] skyne (1), signes (2, 3)
26 stoupyng] lympyng (1), crooked (3)
27 Which] That (1–3)
28–31 *Om. in* (1, 3)
32 ye] youe (1–3):   bide] byedes (1), do staie (3):   behinde] begyne (1)
33 ye] youe (1–3):   none] no (3)
34 As ye of claye] but as of claye y' [ye 3] (2, 3):   ye] youe (1):
  were] are (1):   cast] mayd (1, 2):   by] be (1)
35 ye] youe (1):   waste] turne (1–3):   *followed in* (1) *by* Fynys,
  quod lord Vaws.

Lord Vaux's authorship of the poem is also confirmed by George Gascoigne, who in the preface, "To al yong Gentlemen," to his *Posies*, 1575 (*Complete Poems*, ed. Hazlitt, 1, 9), remarks: "What! shoulde I stande much in rehersall how the *L. Vaux* his dittie (beginning thus: *I loth that I did loue*) was thought by some to be made vpō his death bed?"

No. 212 was registered for publication in 1563–64 as a ballad, "the Aged lover Renownceth love," and perhaps on October 19, 1579, as "an olde louers complaynt" (Rollins, *Analytical Index*, nos. 48, 2005). The *Gorgeous Gallery*, 1578, pp. 35–37, contains a poem "to the Tune of I lothe that I did loue." Chappell (*Popular Music of the Olden Time*, 1, 216–217) gives two tunes for this poem, the first from "the margin of a copy of the Earl of Surrey's poems," the second from MS. Additional 4900, fols. 62ᵛ–63. He observes also that "on the stage the grave-digger now sings them to the tune of *The Children in the Wood*," the music for which he prints at 1, 200–201.

Lord Vaux's poem is immortalized, as everybody knows, by the three stanzas which, in an intentionally corrupt form, the first grave-digger sings in *Hamlet*, v. i. 69 ff.:

> In youth, when I did love, did love,
>   Methought it was very sweet,
> To contract, O, the time, for, ah, my behove,
>   O, methought, there was nothing meet.
>
> But age, with his stealing steps,
>   Hath claw'd me in his clutch,
> And hath shipped me intil the land,
>   As if I had never been such.
>
> A pick-axe, and a spade, a spade,
>   For and a shrouding sheet:
> O, a pit of clay for to be made
>   For such a guest is meet.

What might be called a second immortality was conferred on Vaux's poem when Goethe introduced two stanzas of it into *Faust*, part II, v. 6 (*Werke*, ed. E. Schmidt, 1 [1909], 614), where Lemures sings:

Wie jung ich war und lebt' und liebt'
Mich deucht, das war wohl süsse;
Wo's fröhlich klang und lustig ging,
Da rührten sich meine Füsse.

Nun hat das tückische Alter mich
Mit seiner Krücke getroffen;
Ich stolpert' über Grabes Tür,
Warum stand sie just offen!

With the opening line of No. 212 compare the *Gorgeous Gallery*, p. 17 ("Would God I had no cause to leaue that I did loue, Or lothe the thing that likt mee so"), and Alexander Craig's *Amorose Songes*, 1606, I5, ed. Hunterian Club, p. 137 ("Not, that I loath, where I so long did loue").

165. 26 *age with stelyng steppes*. Perhaps Vaux had a good deal to do with popularizing this alliterative phrase. It is used, for example, by T. H. (Thomas Howell?) in *The fable of Ouid treting of Narcissus*, 1560, A2ᵛ ("Wyth stealyng steppes, she [Eccho] foloweth fast"); by Howell in *The Arbor of Amitie*, 1568 (*Poems*, ed. Grosart, pp. 25, 30); by Kendall in *Flowers of Epigrammes*, 1577, E3ᵛ–E4, Spenser Society ed., pp. 86–87 ("Old croked age with stealyng steps, encrocheth on by kynde").

27 *clawed me with his cowche*. Instead of *cowche* all the MSS. and *B+* read *crutch* or *crowch*. Percy, reprinting the poem in his *Reliques*, 1765 (ed. Wheatley, I, 179–182), gave *crowch* in his text, but remarked in a foot-note: "*Crowch* perhaps should be *clouch*, clutch, grasp." Goethe (see just above) borrowed two stanzas for *Faust* from Percy's reprint, and it speaks well for his knowledge of English (as Bayard Taylor, *Faust*, II [1871], 528, remarks) that he emended Percy's text to *crutch*, translating the phrase as "mit seiner Krücke." Shakespeare (see the note to line 16) has *clutch*.

28 *lusty life away she leapes*. The MSS. read *youth* for *life*, which seems more fitting.

166. 4 *The harbinger of death*. On the traditional messengers of death see my notes in the *Gorgeous Gallery*, p. 192, and the *Paradise*, p. 218.

16 *My kepers knit the knot*. Percy suggests, "Alluding perhaps to Eccles. xii. 3"; but the suggestion is far-fetched.

36 (No. 213) *Of the ladie wentworthes death*. In every edition (No. [183] in *B–I*, sigs. T in *BC*, K in *D–G*, K–Kᵛ in *H*, I5–I5ᵛ in *I*). The lady in question was probably Mary, daughter of Sir John Wentworth, of Gosfield, Essex, who on February 9, 1546, became the first wife of Thomas, second Baron Wentworth, of Nettlestead, Suffolk. She died *sine prole* (as the poem tells) about 1555. See W. L. Rutton, *Three Branches of the Family of Wentworth*, 1891, pp. 51, 55, 139. For other Lady Anne Wentworths see the notes to 109. 14.

167. 13 (No. 214) *The louer accusing hys loue, &c.* In every edition (No. [184] in *B–I*, sigs. T–Tᵛ in *BC*, K–Kᵛ in *D–G*, Kᵛ–K2 in *H*, I5ᵛ–I6 in *I*).

167. 16–25 *The smoky sighes . . . swaruyng.* There is a long discussion of this passage in *The Arte of English Poesie*, 1589, p. 85, based upon its meter, "where one verse is of eight an other is of seuen [feet], and in the one the accent vpon the last, in the other vpon the last saue on[e]." The passage is rendered thus:

> *The smoakie sighes, the bitter teares*
> *That I in vaine haue wasted*
> *The broken sleepes, the woe and feares*
> *That long in me haue lasted*
> *Will be my death, all by thy guilt*
> *And not by my deseruing*
> *Since so inconstantly thou wilt*
> *Not loue but still be sweruing.*

Line 16 is also quoted (p. 261) to illustrate alliteration, with *bitter* arbitrarily changed to *trickling*.

26 *To leue me oft.* Probably *oft* should be *off*, the reading of *B+*.

168. 7 *The one, byrdes feedes, the other slayes.* A somewhat similar statement about the holly is made in the *Encyclopaedia Britannica* (11th ed.): "The berries provoke in man violent vomiting and purging, but are eaten with immunity by thrushes and other birds." The Elizabethan herbals are, so far as I can find, silent on this point; but Melbancke (*Philotimus*, 1583, sig. Y) remarks, "The Hollin [*sic*] tree beareth barke, & berries, the one kills birds, the other feedes them."

11 *That Adrianus paynted.* Borrowed by Melbancke, *Philotimus*, 1583, sig. Y: "*Adrianus* painted grapes so artificially, that birds pecked at them, neither could any descerne them, but with diligent marking." The story, however, is usually told of Zeuxis; hence the old annotator of *I* (Bodleian) emended the line to read, *That paynter Zeuxis paynted.*

23 *By Naulus hate so odious.* Professor Magoun has shown me that *Naulus* is a curious error for *Nauplius*, king of Euboea, whose son Palamedes had been falsely accused of treason by Agamemnon, Diomedes, and Odysseus, and stoned to death. The "hate so odious" refers to the revenge Nauplius took on the Greeks, as they sailed from Troy, by placing false lights on the promontory of Caphareus, and thus wrecking many ships. See Propertius, *Elegies*, IV. i. 115, "Nauplius ultores sub noctem porrigit ignes," and the abundant information in Hyginus's fables, cv, cxvi, ccxlix.

26 (No. 215) *The louer for want of his desyre, &c.* In every edition (No. [185] in *B–I*, sigs. Tᵛ–T2 in *BC*, Kᵛ–K2 in *D–G*, K2 in *H*, I6 in *I*). The poem greatly resembles No. 244; perhaps the same man wrote both.

35 *As Chameleon that lackes the ayre so sote.* Turbervile, *Tragical Tales* [*ca.* 1574], 1587 (1837 reprint, p. 298), remarks that the "Chameleon feedes but on the ayre, the lacke whereof is his decay"; and Robert Chester, in *Love's Martyr*, 1601 (ed. Grosart, pp. 112–113, New Shakspere Society, 1878), tells of a species of chameleon:

> The *Stellio* is a beast that takes his breath,
> And liueth by the deaw thats heauenly,
> Taking his Food and Spirit of the earth,
> And so maintaines his life in chastitie,
>> He takes delight to counterfeit all colours,
>> And yet for all this he is venimous.

The blame for this misinformation rests upon Pliny's *Natural History*, XI. 31.

168. 37 *salamandra repulsed from the fyre.* Turbervile (place cited in the foregoing note) says,

> The Salamander cannot liue
>> without the help of flaming fire;
> To bathe his limnes in burning coales,
>> it is his glee and chiefe desire.

See Pliny, X. 86, XXIX. 23.

169. 2 (No. 216) *A happy end excedeth all, &c.* In every edition (No. [186] in *B–I*, sigs. T2 in *BC*, K2 in *D–G*, K2–K2ᵛ in *H*, I6–I6ᵛ in *I*). Tottel printed only the first stanza of a long poem that is preserved in a Harington MS. (Additional 28635, fols. 120ᵛ–121ᵛ). The whole poem runs as follows:

> No wight hym self happie can call
> before the end whiche shewith all.
>
> The sheening season heare to some
> the glorye great even of dew right
> renowned fame throughe fortune wonne
> the glyttring goolde the eyes delight
> the censuall lyfe aye seemyng sweete
> the hart with joyfull dayes replete
> the thinge theare to eache wight is thrall
> the happie end exceadith all.
>
> The merrye meane who so can hytt
> that stable state aye standing sure
> the chaste wyfe by thie syde to sytt
> whose vertue may thy love assure
> suche faithfull frendes as for to trust
> treasure, to serve, but none to rust
> theise guiftes moste rare they vanyshe shall
> the happye end exceedith all
>
> The hardie hartes that Mars doth sarve
> when blooddye battails joyne in fight
> the fyrye strokes for to desarve
> the lawrell greene even of due right
> the Coward knightes turning their backes
> the Victour, of his conquest crackes
> the Valyaunt to the varlett thrall
> the happie end exceadith all.

The symple soule that toylethe still
by sweatt of browes to eate his bread
of Venus lawes hath he no skill
ne Bacchus trobleth nought his head
eache golden hall he doth detest
his thackyd howse hym lyketh best
yf contentacon hym befall
his happie end exceadith all.

In Ceasers seate who lyst to sytt
with Bodkins brought to shamefull end
Catoes cunning and his witt
that with dispaire durst not contend
Hercules honour, and yett be brentt
Ryche as Cresus, in Orientt
whome Syrus made to serve as thrall
the happye end exceadith all

Over thye head now dothe depend
hanging by Subtylle twyned threede
Immortall fame whiche dothe assend
Upp to the Starres who so can reede
Tells contrarye, for aye suche shame
As crewell Nero had by name
So that no wight happie I call
before the end whiche shewith all.

A poem by D. S. (D. Sand) in the *Paradise*, 1576, pp. 25–26, is written in imitation of the MS. copy, which obviously had been in circulation. Its refrain is "The happy ende exceedeth all," and in its fourth stanza it borrows also line 7 of the first MS. stanza, in its fifth, line 7 of the fourth MS. stanza. Another imitation is Thomas Howell's "The Commendation of the meane in all thinges," in *Newe Sonets, and pretie Pamphlets*, ca. 1568 (*Poems*, ed. Grosart, p. 130; cf. also p. 218), which ends:

Which prooues what change or chaunce do fall,
Contented meane exceedeth all.

169. 13 (No. 217) *Against an vnstedfast woman.* In every edition (No. [187] in *B–I*, sigs. T2 in *BC*, K2 in *D–G*, K2ᵛ in *H*, I6ᵛ in *I*). A copy signed "L Vawse" (Lord Thomas Vaux) is in a Harington MS. (Additional 28635, fol. 139ᵛ), with the following variants:

169. 15 that delights] delighting
       16 tottryng] tossinge
       17 iestres depraueres] gesters depravers: swete] all
       18 whence] wheare
       19 enuironned] envenomyd: dispite] spight
       20 doest] will

17 *iestres depraueres.* These are feminine nouns, as is also *tauntres* in line 15.

169. 19 *serpent enuironned ʘ dispite.* The reading of the MS., *envenomyd*, must be adopted.

    21 (No. 218) *A praise of Petrarke, &c.* In every edition (No. [188] in *B–I*, sigs. T2–T2ᵛ in *BC*, K2–K2ᵛ in *D–G*, K2ᵛ in *H*, I6ᵛ in *I*).

    170. 5 (No. 219) *That petrark cannot be passed, &c.* In every edition (No. [189] in *B–I*, sigs. T2ᵛ in *BC*, K2ᵛ in *D–G*, K2ᵛ–K3 in *H*, I6ᵛ–I7 in *I*). This sonnet has the rather odd rhyme-scheme *abba caac deed ff.* There is another copy of it, with no variant readings, in a Harington MS. (Additional 28635, fol. 36ᵛ).

    22 (No. 220) *Against a cruell woman.* In every edition (No. [190] in *B–I*, sigs. T2ᵛ–T3 in *BC*, K2ᵛ–K3 in *D–G*, K3–K3ᵛ in *H*, I7 in *I*).

    30 *causels.* Read *causeles.*

    171. 4 *Slipper and secrete, &c.* This line should have been indented in *A*.

    15–16 *Knowest thou . . . From out my hart that could haue the bereft.* "You know, unkind, that nothing could happen that would tear you from my heart." A line has been omitted after 16, as the faulty ottava rima shows. The printer may have failed to observe the omission because of the defective stanza-indention.

    19 (No. 221) *The louer sheweth what he would haue, &c.* In every edition (No. [191] in *B–I*, sigs. T3–T3ᵛ in *BC*, K3–K3ᵛ in *D–G*, K3ᵛ–K4 in *H*, I7ᵛ in *I*).

    172. 22 (No. 222) *The lady forsaken of her louer, &c.* In every edition (No. [192] in *B–I*, sigs. T3ᵛ–T4ᵛ in *BC*, K3ᵛ–K4ᵛ in *D–G*, K4–K4ᵛ in *H*, I8–I8ᵛ in *I*).

    36 *A wery lyfe here must I passe.* For six new lines added here in *B+* see the Variant Readings.

    173. 23–28 *But since it will not better be, &c.* In *The Arte of English Poesie*, 1589, p. 203, these lines are quoted because they "very pretily" use the figure of "*Hyperbole.* or the Ouer reacher, otherwise called the loud lyer."

    35 (No. 223) *The louer yelden, &c.* In every edition (No. [193] in *B–I*, sigs. T4ᵛ–V in *BC*, K4ᵛ–K5 in *D–H*, I8ᵛ–K in *I*).

    174. 30 (No. 224) *That nature which worketh, &c.* In every edition (No. [194] in *B–I*, sigs. V–Vᵛ in *BC*, K5–K5ᵛ in *D–H*, K–Kᵛ in *I*).

    175. 16–17 *The sters . . . to the mariner, &c.* On this commonplace see 4. 8 n.

    34 (No. 225) *when aduersitie is once fallen, &c.* In every edition (No. [195] in *B–I*, sigs. Vᵛ in *BC*, K5ᵛ in *D–G*, K5ᵛ–K6 in *H*, Kᵛ in *I*). On the anagram (*T–A–W–I–T*) of Wyatt formed by the initial letters of the stanzas see the notes to 230. 22.

    Other copies are in (1) MS. Ashmole 48, *ca.* 1555–1565 (*Songs and Ballads*, pp. 1–2, ed. Wright, Roxburghe Club, 1860), and (2) MS. Additional 17492, fols. 42–42ᵛ. In the former the order of stanzas — each ending with the refrain "So often warnd" — is 2, 4, 6 (not in *A–I*), 3, 5, 1. The new stanza runs thus:

He is in welth that feleth no woe;
　　But I maye synge and thus reporte,
Farewell my joye and plesure to,
　　Thus maye I sing withought comforte;
For sorrowe hath caught me in her sner;
Alas! why colde I not be ware,
　　　　　　　　So often warnd?

Other variants in the two copies are:

175. 34–35 *Title,* Tempore quo fodiebam (1)
　　38 worketh] workes (2)
176.　2 to²] in (1, 2)
　　3 that makes] whyght make (1), wych made (2):　　*after* 3, 9, 15, 21
　　(2) *adds* so offten warnd
　　4 Amid] Amyddes (1), Ameds (2)
　　6 without] to have (1, 2)
　　9 Should] Wolde (1):　　haue] A (2)
　　10 wold] cold (2)
　　11 bring me] have broght (2)
　　12 But] For (1):　　feard] fearedde (1)
　　13 harme] greff (2):　　*the line in* (1) *is* And all is com bye myne owne
　　suyte
　　14 when] wher (2)
　　15 then hapt all] ther I ffownd (2):　　chiefe] cheffest (2):　　*in* (1) *the
　　line is* Then forthwyth came all myne unreste
　　16 neuer] newer [?] (1)
　　18 me] my (1)
　　19 harme] woo and payne (1), payn (2):　　welth] whelt (2)
　　20 There is no] was never (2)
　　21 hath] had (2):　　cause . . . mone] hap to wayll and grown (2):
　　to] *Om.* (1)
　　23 trust no more] not to trust (2)
　　24 My] For (1):　　bred] hathe (1), has (2):　　me] don (1)
　　25 brought] tovrned (2):　　*the line in* (1) *is* And tourned my welthe to
　　great grevance
　　26 whom] that (1, 2):　　spare] here (1)
　　27 when] weane (1):　　his] *Om.* (1), our (2):　　(2) *adds* thus am I warnd

176. 28 (No. 226) *Of a louer that made, &c.* In every edition (No. [196]
in *B–I,* sigs. V2–V2ᵛ in *BC,* K6–K6ᵛ in *D–H,* K2–K2ᵛ in *I*). A copy in a
Harington MS. (Additional 28635, fols. 9ᵛ–10) presents the following variants:

176. 31 you] ye
　　32 And] or:　　present] presentes
　　34 imbrace] enbrace
　　35 the circumstaunce] my case more playne
　　36 them selues that did auaunce] well skyld themselves did payne
　　38 vertues] frindshipps
177.　4 I] than
　　5 none] no
　　9 is] was
　　11 such] all

177. 12 onely that was] that was only
    14 Whom riches] one richesse
    15 to] her
    16 wordes] tearmes
    18 did enioy] had enjoyed
    19 Lord who lyv'd in so pleasant cace
    21 fowle] great
    23 the] a: none] no
    25 as no man by hymsself sett more
    26 so much was] was so moche
    27 when care had creapt in every part
    28 thought of her] frindly thought
    29 neuer care had caused] care had never caws'd
    31 Was] that: so] more
    32 I toke suche care for her alone
    33 That] as
    35 to them selues] unto hym
    36 So my swete graffe] my graffed sweete: growen] growne
    37 Where] that: I] is
    39 transformed] transform'd: to] into
    40 pleased me] pleas'd now me
    41 hart] hope
    43 may] must
178. 4 the more to] for my more
    6 ye] you

178. 8 (No. 227) *Vpon the death of sir Antony Denny*. In every edition (No. [197] in *B–I*, sigs. V2ᵛ in *BC*, K6ᵛ in *D–G*, K6ᵛ–K7 in *H*, K2ᵛ in *I*). A copy in MS. Lansdowne 98, fol. 206ᵛ, called "An Epitaphe of Sʳ Anthony Dennye knyght," varies only in having *farre to* for *gan farre* (line 12), *quitte* for *quite* (line 17). Professor Hudson kindly informed me that this poem is included in John Weever's *Ancient Funeral Monuments*, 1631, p. 852, as a composition of Surrey's. Of Surrey's English verses, says Weever, "take this Essay, being an Epitaph which he made to the memory of Sir *Anthony Denny* Knight, a Gentleman whom King *Henry* the eight greatly affected." The poem is then reprinted, the only variations from the text of *A* being that 178. 15 has *knowne* (with *B–H*) and 178. 17 *quit* for *quite*.

Sir Anthony Denny, favorite of Henry VIII, was born on January 16, 1501, and educated at St. Paul's School, London, and St. John's College, Cambridge. He was a zealous promoter of the Reformation, by which he profited financially. Henry VIII knighted him in France, Septembe. 30, 1544. Denny was appointed one of the executors of Henry VIII's will, and he served as a councilor of Edward VI, dying on October 28, 1549. He was highly praised by Roger Ascham and Sir John Cheke, as well as by the poet Surrey. "The Epitaphe of Sʳ A. Dennie," beginning, "As shipe escaped the powre of tycle wave and wynde," is preserved in MS. Harleian 78, fol. 25ᵛ.

178. 22 (No. 228) *A comparison of the louers paines.* In every edition
(No. [198] in *B–I*, sigs. V2ᵛ–V3 in *BC*, K6ᵛ–K7 in *D–G*, K7 in *H*, K2ᵛ–K3
in *I*).

179. 2 (No. 229) *Of a Rosemary braunche sente.* In every edition (No.
[199] in *B–I*, sigs. V3 in *BC*, K7 in *D–H*, K3 in *I*).

12 (No. 230) *To his loue of his constant hart.* In every edition (No.
[200] in *B–I*, sigs. V3 in *BC*, K7 in *D–G*, K7–K7ᵛ in *H*, K3 in *I*).

22 (No. 231) *Of the token which, &c.* In every edition (No. [201]
in *B–I*, sigs. V3–V3ᵛ in *BC*, K7–K7ᵛ in *D–G*, K7ᵛ in *H*, K3 in *I*). Dr. Leicester
Bradner, in *The Review of English Studies*, iv (1928), 207–208, calls Nos. 203
and 231 "forerunners of the Spenserian stanza."

180. 2 (No. 232) *Manhode auaileth not, &c.* In every edition (No. [202]
in *B–I*, sigs. V3ᵛ in *BC*, K7ᵛ in *D–H*, K3–K3ᵛ in *I*).

4 *Tho.* Read *The* with *B+*.

8–11 *The vnexpert . . . doth leare.* Professor Kittredge paraphrases
as follows: "The inexpert navigator who had never voyaged to unknown
shores, but who nevertheless was not frightened by the dangers of Neptune's
realm, by sailing on the trustless seas in his wandering ship hath taught the
art [of such navigation] to many [persons] whom time too long doth instruct,
that is, who have spent over-much time in learning the art." In other words,
the lucky novice has outclassed the plodding men of experience.

18 (No. 233) *That constancy of all vertues, &c.* In every edition (No.
[203] in *B–I*, sigs. V3ᵛ–V4 in *BC*, K7ᵛ–K8 in *D–H*, K3ᵛ in *I*).

20–25 *Though in the waxe a perfect picture, &c.* Probably this was the
source of Melbancke's remark in *Philotimus*, 1583, G3ᵛ: "A picture portrayed
in wax showes as faire as one ingrauen in marble, but continewes not so
long."

34 (No. 234) *A comfort to . . . Thestilis.* In every edition (No. [171]
in *B–I*, sigs. R4–R4ᵛ in *BC*, I4–I4ᵛ in *D–G*, I4ᵛ–I5 in *H*, H8ᵛ–I in *I*). The
poem is a reply to No. 201, which in *B–I* it follows.

181. 17 *Hie springes may cease from swellyng, &c.* Borrowed in Melbancke's
Philotimus, 1583, sig. Yᵛ: "The Sun which falleth in the West with Eclipse of
his lighte, riseth in the East with his firy garland: high springes may cease
from swelling, but neuer drie away."

18 *stormes of louers yre, do more their loue encrease.* Referring to the
proverbial saying (from Terence), "Amantium irae amoris redintegratio est,"
on which see the *Paradise*, pp. 214–215.

23 *Thinke on Etrascus worthy loue that lasted thirty yeres.* This is evi-
dently the source of the references in the *Gorgeous Gallery*, 1578, p. 82, and
Melbancke's *Philotimus*, 1583, Y3. The former runs:

> *Itrascus* too, full thyrty yeares indurde,
> The panges of loue, within his boyling brest.

Melbancke's words are: "*Etrascus* louing thirtie yeares, could not atchieue his harts desired choise, yet at ẙ end, found reward of his mistris." The old annotator in *I* (Bodleian) glosses—not very plausibly—*Etrascus* as "or Vlisses" and changes *thirty* to *twentie*.

181. 34 (No. 235) *The vncertaine state of a louer*. In every edition (No. [204] in *B–I*, sigs. V4–V4ᵛ in *BC*, K8–K8ᵛ in *D–H*, K3ᵛ–K4 in *I*). This poem is reprinted as the composition of John Harington and entitled "To Isabella Markham, 1549" in *Nugae Antiquae* (1775, II, 256; 1779, 1792, III, 290–291). Isabella Markham became Harington's wife in 1554. The evidence of *Nugae Antiquae* is of little or no value.

182. 28 (No. 236) *The louer in libertie, &c.* In every edition (No. [205] in *B–I*, sigs. V4ᵛ in *BC*, K8ᵛ in *D–H*, K4–K4ᵛ in *I*).

183. 18 (No. 237) *A comparison of his loue, &c.* In every edition (No. [206] in *B–I*, sigs. V4ᵛ–Xᵛ in *BC*, K8ᵛ–Lᵛ in *D–G*, K8ᵛ–L2 in *H*, K4ᵛ–K5ᵛ in *I*).

A ballad similar to this is preserved in a Harington MS. (Additional 28635, fol. 141), a reprint of which may be welcome to some readers; music for it (with the first line only, given as "When Cressed went from Troye") is in MS. Additional 30513, *ca.* 1560:

> Whan Cressyde came from Troye
> in chaunge of Antenour
> as Troylus then did joye
> so joye I at this howre
> and as he pleasure had
> to see her from hym goe
> in lyke cace am I glad
> to parte my lover froe
>
> But yf he weare alas
> an wofull Trojan than
> So I to in this cace
> am now the heaviest man
> and even the man I know
> all thoughe I be another
> yet in this payne and woe
> of right may be his brother
>
> But sence there is no choyce
> but that I must for goe
> whiche moste I did rejoyce
> and moste have loved soe
> what ells remaynes in me
> whiche am so sad a wight
> but even as Troylus he
> to mourne my losse of right
>
> And now for evermore
> to take myself for one
> as Troylus did before
> when Cresyde was once gone

and all the daye to spend
in playntes and lovers cryes
till death shall ryd and send
my spryte above the skyes.

And now and then alas
with teares of both my eyen
to moyste and weete the place
wheare she and I have bene
And then thus for to saye
poore man thow maist well mone
for two they weare to daye
but now theare is but one.

But whan the skriche owle shall
flye from the hollow tree
whiche cry'the to Lovers all
that faithfull lovers be
then shall ye say thus loe
hark man who flyeth about
the beadell of thie woe
Calles now to have the oute.

And out I shall goe then
a wath [sic] man meeke of right
whiche sith the daye began
have watchid for the night
In whiche I might at will
my wofull lif to ridd
bothe sighe and sobb my fill
as wofull Troylus dyd

ffor eache brute beast I see
laid downe to take my rest
may be a meanes to me
to thinck this in my brest
So heare eache thing rest can
as kynd hath taught it soe
Save thow alas poore man
whiche wandrest still in woe

Whiche am as Troylus he
a man in bitter payne
and Troylus still will be
till tyme shall come agayne
and thoughe she did not mynd
to come her truthe to save
yet shall she me thus fynd
Trew Troylus to my grave./

On the same order is the ballad called "A new Dialogue betweene Troylus and Cressida" that appears in Thomas Deloney's *Strange Histories*, 1612, K2ᵛ–Lᵛ.

    184. 13 *Making two fountayns of his eyes*. This figure is a commonplace in Italian and French sonnets. Cf., for example, Petrarch, sonetto in vita 110

(*Rime*, 161, p. 170), "oi occhi miei, occhi nọn già, ma fonti"; Du Bellay, *L'Olive*, lv, "O tristes yeulx, que n'estes-vous fonteines?"; De Baif, *Œuvres* (ed. Marty-Laveaux, 1, 160), "O mes yeux, non plus yeux, mais de pleurs deux fontaines." See also 209. 38.

185. 26 (No. 238) *To leade a vertuous . . . life.* In every edition (No. [207] in *B–I*, sigs. X2 in *BC*, L2 in *D–H*, K5ᵛ in *I*). The old annotator in *I* (Bodleian) writes, "Mʳ Jo: Wyse. taken out of Chawcer." I do not understand the significance of "Mʳ Jo: Wyse," although most later students have observed Chaucer's authorship. Since, however, Arber failed to mention Chaucer in his edition of the miscellany, that great name seldom appears as one of the "uncertain authors." Tottel's text differs considerably from the versions given in the editions of Chaucer issued by Richard Pynson in 1526 and William Thynne in 1532, 1542, and about 1545. It agrees more closely with Thynne's than Pynson's text, however, so that I give collations below with the 1532 edition:

> 185. 26–27 ❡Good counsayle of Chaucer
> 28 Flee] Flye ye
> 29 to thee . . . though] vnto the good if
> 31 Praise] Preace: blinde in] blent ouer
> 32 Fauour] Sauour
> 33 others well canst] other folke shal
> 34 shall the] the shal
> 36 hope] truste
> 37 standeth] stondeth
> 38 against] agayne
> 39 against] with
> 186. 2 first] *Om.*
> 3, 10 shall the] the shal
> 8 giue thankes to] and thanke
> 9 Weane well] Weyue: honest life ay] lette thy gost the
> 10 So] And: shall the] the shal

In modern editions this "balade" is entitled "Truth," and is accompanied by Chaucer's "Envoy." Its indebtedness to Boethius is discussed in Skeat's Chaucer, 1. 550–553.

32 *Fauour, &c.* The reading should be *Sauour*, making the line mean, "Have a relish for no more than it may behove you (to taste)" (Skeat, 1, 551).

34 *trouth shall the deliuer.* The refrain comes from John, viii. 32.

36 *her that turneth as a ball.* The goddess Fortuna.

37 *Great rest standeth in litle busynesse.* Proverbial. See the numerous examples cited in my notes in the *Paradise*, 1576, p. 251.

39 *Striue not as doth a crocke against a wall.* Skeat (1, 552) calls this "an allusion to the fable in Æsop about the earthern and brazen pots being dashed together. An earthen pot would have still less chance of escape if dashed against a wall."

186. 11 (No. 239) *The wounded louer, &c.* In every edition (No. [208] in *B–I*, sigs. X2–X2ᵛ in *BC*, L2–L2ᵛ in *D–H*, K5ᵛ–K6 in *I*).

187. 2 (No. 240) *The louer shewing of the, &c.* In every edition (No. [209] in *B–I*, sigs. X2ᵛ–X3 in *BC*, L2ᵛ–L3 in *D–H*, K6–K6ᵛ in *I*). The old annotator in *I* (Bodleian) objects to the title that "Jt semeth rather to be of one nere desperation for some evill dede or at the least sorowfull &c."

23 *both play and singe.* Intelligible, but *both* is probably a misprint for *doth*.

26–27 *As smallest sparckes, &c.* On the proverb see the *Paradise*, pp. 201–202.

34–37 *But since the mill, &c.* Borrowed by Melbancke, *Philotimus*, 1583, R4ᵛ, "But since the Myll will needes about, the pinne whereon the Mill doth goe, I will assay to strike it out, and so the Myllne to ouerthrowe."

188. 2 (No. 241) *The power of loue ouer gods them selues.* In every edition (No. [210] in *B–I*, sigs. X3 in *BC*, L3 in *D–H*, K6ᵛ in *I*). This is a strict Petrarchan sonnet, rhyming *abba abba cde cde*. It is of considerable interest, furthermore, because I have observed that it is a translation of Seneca's *Hippolytus*, lines 296–308 (first chorus):

> Thessali Phoebus pecoris magister
> egit armentum positoque plectro
> impari tauros calamo vocavit.
> induit formas quotiens minores
> ipse qui caelum nebulasque fecit:
> candidas ales modo movit alas,
> dulcior vocem moriente cygno;
> fronte nunc torva petulans iuvencus
> virginum stravit sua terga ludo,
> perque fraternos nova regna fluctus
> ungula lentos imitante remos
> pectore adverso domuit profundum,
> pro sua vector timidus rapina.

The merit of the translation in No. 241 can perhaps best be seen by comparing it with that of John Studley (*Seneca His Tenne Tragedies*, 1581, fol. 60ᵛ):

> Sir *PHOEBVS* vvhilome forst in *Thessail* Land
> To Sheepeherds state *ADMETVS* Heirdes did driue,
> His mourning Harp depriude of heauenly Hand
> With ordred Pipe his Bullockes did reuiue.
> Euen hee that trayles the dusky riding rack,
> And wieldes the swaying Poles with swinging swift
> How oft did hee faynde fourmes put on his back
> And heauenly Face with baser countenaunce shift.
> Sometime a Byrde with siluer shining wings,
> He fluttering flusht, and languishing the death
> With sweete melodious tuned voyce hee sings,
> When silly *Cygnus* gaue vp gasping breath.

> Sometime also wyth curled forhead grim
> A dallying Bull, he bent his stouping backe
> To maydens sport, through deepest Seas to swim
> Whyle horny houe made shift like Ore slacke
> Through waters wyld his brothers perlous cost
> Wyth forward glauncing breast the stream he brake,
> And least he should his tender pray haue lost,
> Her troublus thought did cause his heart to quake.

The general idea and the specific figures in the poem are almost identical with those of No. 281; indeed, they were poetic commonplaces. Thus Petrarch's canzone in vita 1 (the source of No. 185) concludes (*Rime*, p. 23):

> Canzon, i' non fu' mai quel nuvol d'oro
> che poi discese in pretiosa pioggia,
> sí che 'l foco di Giove in parte spense. . . .

Compare, further, Turbervile's *Epitaphes*, etc., 1567, p. 7:

> There may you plainely see
>   how Joue was once a swanne
> To lure faire Leda to his lust
>   when raging loue beganne:
> Some other when a bull
>   Some other time a showre
> Of golden drops, as when he coyde
>   the closed Nunne in towre.

Barnabe Barnes, *Parthenophil and Parthenope*, 1593, sonnet 63 (*Poems*, ed. Grosart, p. 43), writes:

> Ioue for Europaes loue tooke shape of Bull,
> And for Calisto playde Dianaes parte
> And in a golden shower, he filled full
> The lappe of Danae with cœlestiall arte.

Exactly the same illustrations appeared in two poems in *The Phoenix Nest*, 1593, pp. 73–74, and Lodge's *Phillis*, 1593, sonnet 34 (*Complete Works*, ed. Hunterian Club, II, v, 51), both of which, however, are translations from Ronsard's *Amours* (*Œuvres*, ed. Marty-Laveaux, I, 12).

188. 18 (No. 242) *Of the sutteltye of craftye louers.* In every edition (No. [256] in *B–I*, sigs. Dd^v–Dd2 in *BC*, O^v–O2 in *D–G*, O2–O2^v in *H*, N4–N4^v in *I*).

24 *dogge vnto the bow.* Professor Magoun points out to me similar expressions in *The Canterbury Tales*, D. 1369, E. 2013–2014: "For in this world nis dogge for the bowe," "he gooth as lowe As ever dide a dogge for the bowe." Skeat (Chaucer, V, 325) explains, "a dog used to accompany an archer, to follow up a stricken deer."

189. 25 (No. 243) *Of the dissembling louer.* In every edition (No. [27] in *B–I*, sigs. D^v in *BC*, B5^v in *D–H*, B5–B5^v in *I*). If the evidence of *A–I* is to be

accepted, Surrey was not the author of this poem: it is a reply to his No. 26, which it follows in *B–I*, but the title in those editions (see the Variant Readings) carefully assigns the poem to an "uncertain author." I see no reason to dispute that assignment, even though I observe that eight lines (189. 30–37) are quoted in Sir Richard Barckley's *A Discourse of the Felicitie of Man*, 1598, p. 499, with the plain statement that they were written by Surrey. Barckley remarks:

those ambitious and vaine-glorious men that hunt after offices of rule and charge, without due consideration of their owne insufficiencie, and vnworthinesse to beare rule, euen in meane callings also, are aptlie reprehended by the Earle of *Surrey*, thus:

> *For with indifferent eyes,*
> *My selfe can well discerne,*
> *How some in stormes to guide a ship,*
> *Do seeke to take the sterne.*
> *VVhose practise if t'were proued,*
> *In calme to guide a barge,*
> *Assuredly beleeue it well,*
> *It were too great a charge.*
> *And some I see againe,*
> *Sit still, and say but small,*
> *VVho could do ten times more then they,*
> *That say they can do all.*
> *VVhose goodly gifts are such,*
> *The more they vnderstand,*
> *The more they seeke to learne and know,*
> *And take lesse charge in hand.*

It seems to me almost certain that Barckley mentioned Surrey, not from any knowledge of the authorship of No. 243, but purely because Surrey's name came to his mind (as it does to that of a modern reader) when he referred to the *Songs and Sonnets*.

Padelford included No. 243 in his edition of Surrey (pp. 65–66), printing it from a Harington MS. (Additional 28635, fol. 23). That MS. supplies the following variants:

189. 26 giltlesse] *Padelford misprints* glitlesse
    31 seke for] styckes [*Padelford* stycke] not
    32 practise . . . proued] skill and conninge tryed
    33 Assuredly . . . well] they wolde son shan [*MS. doubtful, Padelford* shaw], you shold sone see
    35 could] can
    38 fletes] slyttes [*Padelford* flyttes]
    39 full] right
190. 2 With] in
    3 ioynde] mett

190. 6 *Eighteen lines added:*

> muche lyke untruth to this/ the storye doth declare
> wheare th' elders layd to Susans chardge/ meete matter to compare
> They did her both accuse/ and eke condempne her to
> and yet no reason right nor truthe/ did lead them so to do
> and she thus judged to dye/ toward her death went forthe
> ffraughted wth faith a pacient pace/ taking her wrong in worthe
> but he that dothe defend/ all those that in hym trust
> Did raise a Childe for her defence/ to shyeld her from th' unjust
> and Danyell chosen was/ then of this wrong to weete
> How, in what place and eke with whome/ she did this cryme com*m*ytt
> he caws'd the Elders part/ the one from th' others sight
> and did examyne one by one/ and chardged them bothe say right
> Vndr a Mvlberye trye/ it was fyrst sayd the one
> The next namde a Pomegranate trye/ whereby the truth was knowne
> Than Susan was dischardg'd/ and they condempn'd to dye
> as right requeares and they deserve/ that fram'de so fowll a lye
> and he that her preserv'd/ and lett them of their lust
> hath me defendyd hetherto/ and will do still I trust./

As the story of Susanna and the Elders, from the apocryphal book of Daniel, was one of the most popular stories in Tudor England, it is difficult to see why the editor of *A* omitted the foregoing eighteen lines.

190. 7 (No. 244) *The promise of a constant louer.* In every edition (No. [211] in *B–I*, sigs. X3–X3^v in *BC*, L3–L3^v in *D–H*, K6^v–K7 in *I*). Perhaps the same author wrote this poem and No. 215; they are much alike in all particulars.

19 (No. 245) *Against him that had slaundered, &c.* In every edition (No. [212] in *B–I*, sigs. X3^v–X4 in *BC*, L3^v–L4 in *D–G*, L3^v–L4^v in *H*, K7–K7^v in *I*). There is a copy in a Harington MS. (Additional 28635, fols. 108^v–109^v) with the following variants:

> 190. 24 or] and
>   25 .R.] lyer
>   29 lied] lyde
>   31 no nor neuer] nor euer did or
>   33 charge so large] over chardge
>   36 the] thee
>   37 dedes] deede
> 191. 4 Collatiue] Collatyne: wife] wyse
>   5 trayterous] Traytours
>   6 Cartage] Carthage: fordid] undid
>   7 R. so depe can auoyde] Rodapeiane mayde
>   9 crokest] crokst: agaynst] agayne
>   10 brag] cadge
>   11 voyce] foyse
>   16 shouldest] shuldst
>   21 delight] delightes
>   25 treade] leade

    26 here auowe] advowe
    27 settest] sett
    32 in] the: eke] to
    42 trouth] trothe: floorist] florisht
    43 stande] stode: the] thie
192. 2 one] worme
    4 on thee may light] may light on thee

190. 25 *Of her for whom thou .R., &c.* The pentameter movement of the line shows that *R.* stands for some two-syllabled word like *Robert* — if, indeed, it should not be *liar*, as in the MS.

30–32 *neuer honge the bow vpon the wall, &c.* That is, the lady you have slandered has not broken her vow of chastity: a discarded bow would indicate that she had deserted Diana.

38 *Lurker of kinde like serpent, &c.* On this commonplace (already used at 6. 24) see my notes in the *Gorgeous Gallery*, p. 186.

191. 4 *Of Collatiue.* The proper spelling, *Collatine*, is in *D+*. "*Colatine* was the husband of *Lucrece*," Richard Robinson obligingly informs us, and in *The rewarde of Wickednesse*, 1574, sig. F, he tells the story.

7 *the R. so depe can auoyde.* A senseless remark due to a compositor who could not read his manuscript "copy." *B+* and the MS. have *the R(h)odopeian maid.* The reference is to Phyllis, daughter of King Sithon, who, when Demophoön failed to come to marry her, hung herself and was metamorphosed into an almond tree. Her epistle in Ovid's *Heroides* (II. 1) begins, "Hospita, Demophoön, tua te Rhodopeïa Phyllis."

15 *yrkesome wormes.* "Loathsome reptiles." John Studley, *Medea*, act IV (*Seneca His Tenne Tragedies*, 1581, fol. 134), speaks of "filthy byrdes of irkesome miry mud."

43 *the wretched part.* For *the* read *thy* with *B+* and the MS.

192. 2 *Hath spotted vs, &c.* "All men (all of us) are disgraced because you (vile slanderer) are a man."

11 (No. 246) *A praise of maistresse Ryce.* In every edition (No. [213] in *B–I*, sigs. X4–Y in *BC*, L4–L5 in *D–G*, L4ᵛ–L5 in *H*, K7ᵛ–K8ᵛ in *I*). The style of this poem (see also the comments on p. 84, above) suggests Thomas Churchyard. He was fond, too, of eulogizing court-ladies, as in *A Pleasant conceite penned in verse* (1593).

193. 25 (No. 247) *Of one vniustly defamed.* In every edition (No. [214] in *B–I*, sigs. Y in *BC*, L5 in *D–G*, L5–L5ᵛ in *H*, K8ᵛ in *I*). A copy in a Harington MS. (Additional 28635, fol. 37) has only one variant — *by* for *thy* in line 35.

34 *to trie.* Read *so trie.*

35 *Thus kind thy craft.* For *thy* perhaps one should read *by* with *C+* (cf. line 31).

194. 7 *G. by name.* This cloudy poem seems to be addressed to a man, not a woman. One would like to believe that he was the Gray who contributed (see p. 80, above) to the miscellany, and who is referred to as *G.* at 200. 33.

194. 15 (No. 248) *Of the death of the late county of Penbroke.* In every edition (No. [215] in *B–I*, sigs. Y–Y^v in *BC*, L5–L5^v in *D–G*, L5^v in *H*, K8^v–L in *I*). In *B+* the word *county* is properly changed to *countess.* The lady in question was Anne Parr, whose sister Catherine was one of the numerous wives of Henry VIII. Anne married Sir William Herbert, first Earl of Pembroke, about 1534, died at Baynard's Castle, London, on February 20, 1551/2, and was buried with great state in St. Paul's Cathedral on February 28 (G. E. C., *Complete Peerage*, VI [1895], 216–217). The opening lines of this elegy remind one of the words with which Milton begins his lament for Lycidas.

195. 2 (No. 249) *That eche thing is hurt of it selfe.* In every edition (No. [216] in *B–I*, sigs. Y^v–Y2 in *BC*, L5^v–L6 in *D–H*, L in *I*).

20 (No. 250) *Of the choise of a wife.* In every edition (No. [217] in *B–I*, sigs. Y2 in *BC*, L6 in *D–G*, L6–L6^v in *H*, L^v in *I*).

23 *men to heare delight.* The rhyme-scheme demands *men delight to heare.*

196. 6–7 *go, wo.* This rhyme violates the scheme of the stanzas. *Fate, state* would fit both the rhyme-scheme and the sense.

8 (No. 251) *Descripcion of an vngodlye worlde.* In every edition (No. [218] in *B–I*, sigs. Y2–Y3 in *BC*, L6–L7 in *D–G*, L6^v–L7 in *H*, L^v–L2^v in *I*).

Other copies are in (1) MS. Ashmole 48, *ca.* 1555–1565 (*Songs and Ballads*, pp. 57–59, ed. Wright, Roxburghe Club, 1860); (2) MS. Sloane 1896, fols. 35^v–38, *ca.* 1576; (3) MS. Additional 15225, fols. 56–58, *ca.* 1616. Tottel's text (*A–I*) has 74 lines. (1) omits six of these but adds 14 new lines. It ends with a prayer for King Philip and Queen Mary, is older than the text of *A*, and no doubt represents the original poem, which in *A* was thoroughly revised by the author or, more probably, by the editor. (2) has 72 lines; (3) has 88 lines, including all those of *A* in addition to the 14 new lines (slightly varied) of (1). There are an enormous number of variants which, — although they show how freely texts were "edited" in the sixteenth century, — without enthusiasm, I give to the bitter end:

> 196. 8–9 *Title: none in* (1), A Discripcion of the wickednesse of this world (2), A dittie most excelent for euerie man to reade/ that dothe intend for to amende & to repent with speede to the tune of a rich marchant man or John come kiss me now (3)
> 10 loues] lovithe (1, 3)
> 11 hear] se (1, 3):   semeth] sem (1, 2):   wōderous] right wondrous (2), wondrous (3)
> 12 in] and (1)
> 13 harts] brestes (2)
> 14 amongs] amongst (2), amonge (3):   hye] he(1)
> 15 deceite] deceites (3):   pore] weake (1, 3)
> 16 sugred] forged (3):   16–18 *reduced in* (1) *to* Suche spyte in sugeryde tongis, which bryng men ofte to care

17 which] that (3):   vnspied] vnspyde (3)
18 restlesse sute for] sute for wretles (3):   sute] state (2):   bringeth
    men] bringe men oft (3)
19 slippry] slyppery (1–3):   can we not] we cannot (1, 3)
20 bolstrynge] bolsteringe (3):   of the] up of (1, 3)
21 threatnyng] threatenynge (1)
22 Such . . . estate] Suche clymyng to estate, suche discorde daly wraghte
    (1)
23 all mixt] mixed (3):   23–36 om. in (1)
24 prollyng] prowling (2, 3)
25 cruell] overthwart (3):   truth] plaine (3):   hearde] saw (3)
26–27 Om. in (2)
29 foles do] follys (1)
30 plenty] plentithe (1):   so] of (3)
31 Such . . . expresse] Howe welthe declynithe [declines 3] towarde decay,
    what [noe 3] tong can well expres (1, 3)
32 markt] merkyd (1), marked (3):   troubles] trobble (1, 3)
33 were] was (1, 3):   *after this line* (1) and (3) *insert:*

Such poverty abrowde, and fewe men takyth [takes 3] them in;
Suche juels warne and [when 3] poore men want, which [that 3] ys both shame and syne;
Suche pryntynge off [of 3] good bookys, such praychyng synn to sle [flee 3];
Suche ronnynge hedlong into hell [Such runinge yet headlong to hell 3], it pittiethe me to se.

34 which] such (1):   euer gapes] gapynge (1), gapeth still (3):   for]
    after (1)
35 *After this line* (1) *and* (3) *add:*

Suche prolynge [prowling 3] for fate farmes, such dublyng of small rente;
Suche heppis of golde in sum mens handes [hand 3], yete no man ys contente.
Suche byldyng [knitting 3] of fear bowars [faire browes 3], suche honger kepte in hallys;
Wher nydy men have fownde relyffe, nowe may the [you 3] se bar wallys.

36 will] wyte (1, 3):   will in tender] wilfulnesse in (2)
37 sortes] sectes (1, 3):   among] amongst (2)
38 Such . . . craft] Suche crafte in cloake of symplenes (2):   falshed]
    reconsylyng (1, 3)
39 sene within mens] immagynede within mans (1, in mans 3):
    hartes] harte (1, 3)
197. 3 thinkes] thinkythe (1):   take those goods] haue this good (3):
    which] that (3):   must] shall (1, 3)
    4 which] that (3)
    5 breke] los (1):   slepes] slepe (2)
    6 one] won (1):   amonges] among (1, 3), amongst (2):   hath]
    haue (1–3):   welth and ease] ease and wealth (3)
    7 which toyleth] that toyle full (1, 3)
    8 falles] fallyth (1)
    9 Thus] and (3):   pore] poware (1):   fortune geues] God givith
    (1), god doth giue (3):   the] them (1, 3)
    10 thinkes] thinketh (1)
    12 those] they (2):   liue] lyves (1):   are] be (1, 3)
    13 time] space (3):   falles] failes (3):   do] that (1), the (3):   fade]
    vade (2)

197. 14 is] ar (1, 3):   this] the (3):   will] doth (1, 3)
  15 may] doth (1, 3):   strike] place (3):   *after this line* (1) *and* (3) *add:*

Yf that the boughe do breake be whiche the yous [by which they vse 3] to clym;
For God doth exsalte and overthrowe [exalts & overthrowes 3] as he syeth caus [sees place 3] and tym.
The tymes apoyntyde be, and alteryde in ther kynde,
Be [by 3] Godes forsyght and provydence, whos knowlege [iudgmentes 3] fewe can fynde.

  16 feares] fearythe (1):   full] right (3)
  17 There] here (3):   so] *Om.* (1):   earth] yerth (1):   changeth] chaungys (1):   as] lyke (1, 3)
  18 pore] poware (1)
  19 haue] hathe (1)
  20 They] Ofte tymes they (2):   fayre] fear (1):   seke] seekes (3):   suck] shed (2)
  21 And . . . hell] his children wishe him ofte in earth (2)
  22 The] Muche (2):   the ¹] *Om.* (1, 3), worldly (2):   spirite] sprite (1)
  23 And] soe (3):   men] doe (3):   that gropeth for] which grope [groped 3] after (1, 3):   the] *Om.* (3)
  24 is still] ofte tymes is dedly (2):   enuied] hated (2), envide (3):   by] with (1):   which] that (1–3)
  25 fawning] fanyde (1, 3):   spech] speece [*sic*] (3):   are] be (1, 3)
  26 fine] time (3):   proue] knowe by profe (2):   haue] hath (1, 3)
  27 The slepe full sownde and fearithe leaste [haue lesse feare 3] that hath [haue 3] not moche to loys (1, 3)
  28 As] The (3):   time] the worlde (1), world (3):   would] wyll (1, 3)
  29 liue in pore estate] be a pleane poor man (1, 3):   pore] meane (2)
  30 those troblesome] thes troblous (1), these troubleous (3)
  32 our] won (1):   in] to (3)
  33 may we] we may (3):   such] lyk (1, 3):   to] and (1, 3):   with him in] into the (1, 3):   snare] sknare (1)
  34 thinkes] thinkithe (1)
  35 wethered] withered (2, 3):   that] which (1–3):   cannot bide a] which can abyde no (1)
  37 playd] played (2):   our] his (1, 3)
  38 Who trustes] To trust (1, 3):   him] them (1, 3):   then mad] men made (1)
  40 seme as] semith (1), seemed (3):   are] ar very (1)
  41 Though] although (3):   ÿ] *Om.* (1, 3):   earth] yerthe (1):   bringes] bryng (1, 3):   it beareth many] its wondrous full of (2)
  42 from mischief to] that will at all (3)
  43 But . . . or] they set their mindes on worldlie cares and (3):   flee the seas of] loys the seale off (1):   or] and (1)
198. 2 that] so (2, 3)
  3 styrres] stirrith (1):   shal] doth (1, 3):   *after line 3* (1) *adds:*

Thus hear I mak an ende, wisshing for grace and helthe;
God save Philepe our kyng and Mary our quyne, and eke the commenwelthe.

    (3) *adds:*

Thus heere I make an end wishinge for grace and health
  to keepe our king [James I] from all his foes and eake the common wealth

Perhaps this tiresome poem was suggested by a long passage in Skelton's *Speke, Parrot* (*Poetical Works*, ed. Dyce, II [1843] 22–25), nearly every line of which begins with "So many" or "So myche." The two passages are identical in idea. No. 251 was registered as a ballad, under the title of its first line, on September 4, 1564 (Rollins, *Analytical Index*, no. 2949). The tunes to which it was to be sung are named in the collations to 196. 8–9, above: the music for *John, come kiss me now* will be found in Chappell's *Popular Music of the Olden Time*, I, 147–148 (also in MS. Additional 38539, fol. 12); that for *The rich merchant man* in Chappell, I, 381–382.

197. 36 *Though that the flood be great, the ebbe as lowe doth ronne.* On this proverb see the *Paradise*, p. 254.

198. 4 (No. 252) *The dispairyng louer lamenteth.* In every edition (No. [219] in *B–I*, sigs. Y3–Y3ᵛ in *BC*, L7–L7ᵛ in *D–G*, L7ᵛ–L8 in *H*, L2ᵛ–L3 in *I*). Similar to this poem, and possibly suggested by it, is Raleigh's famous lyric in *The Phoenix Nest*, 1593, p. 72, beginning:

> Calling to minde mine eie long went about,
> T'entice my hart to seeke to leaue my brest,
> All in a rage I thought to pull it out,
> By whose deuice I liu'd in such vnrest.

199. 4 (No. 253) *An epitaph of maister Henry williams.* In every edition (No. [241] in *B–I*, sigs. Bb3–Bb3ᵛ in *BC*, N3–N3ᵛ in *D–G*, N3ᵛ–N4 in *H*, M6 in *I*). Henry's father, John Williams, sheriff of Oxfordshire, was apparently knighted soon after November 15, 1538 (W. A. Shaw, *The Knights of England*, II [1906], 50). He was keeper of the king's jewels, M.P. for Oxfordshire during 1547–1554, an ardent supporter of Queen Mary in the Northumberland–Lady Jane Grey rebellion, and lord chamberlain of Philip II's household. He was created Baron Williams of Thame early in 1554, and appointed lord president of Wales in February, 1559. Dying at Ludlow Castle on October 14, 1559, he was buried at Thame on November 15. His first wife, Elizabeth Edmunds, widow of Andrew Edmunds of Essex, had died on October 25, 1556. Her second son, Henry, the subject of the present poem, married Anne Stafford, daughter of the first Baron Stafford, and died without issue on August 20, 1551. Sir Thomas Hoby, of *The Courtier* fame, had intended to travel on the Continent with him; but, this plan going awry, he met Henry and his brother Francis ("which died bothe in England the yere 51") at Padua on August 15, 1548 (*Travels and Life*, ed. Edgar Powell, pp. 7, 8, Camden Society, 1902). For another elegy on Williams see 237. 21 n. (No. 289).

9 *feare from frendes. B+* read *feare for frendes*, which is probably correct. In either case the incomplete sentence means, I suppose, something like "Free us from the fear that our friends may fail or disappoint us."

34 (No. 254) *Against a gentlewoman, &c.* In every edition (No.

[245] in *B–I*, sigs. Bb4–Bb4ᵛ in *BC*, N4–N4ᵛ in *D–G*, N4ᵛ–N5 in *H*, M7–M7ᵛ in *I*). For an answer to this poem see No. 290.

200. 2–3 *her bolstred name . . . Had stuffe to shew that praise did hight.* "Although I once gave slight credit to what rumor said of her, believing that her puffed-up reputation stood for real praiseworthy stuff, I find I was mistaken." Cf. Melbancke, *Philotimus*, 1583, sig. Y, "I thought their boulstered names had stuffe to show, y̎ *praise* did hight."

18 *she is such as geason none.* The context plainly shows that the line means, "She is such as has no rarity." In *G+* the phrase is changed to *a geason:* "she is not at all such a rarity."

29 *By cocke and pye.* A common oath, used also at 239. 23. *Cock* is a corruption of *God; pie* originally meant a collection of rules in the pre-Reformation church. Cf. Henry Robarts, *Haigh for Devonshire*, 1600, K3, "sweare not so vainely: yea, and nay, Cock and Pye, are sufficient for honest dealers."

30 (No. 255) *An epitaphe written by w. G., &c.* In every edition (No. [239] in *B–I*, sigs. Bb2ᵛ in *BC*, N2ᵛ in *D–G*, N3–N3ᵛ in *H*, M5ᵛ in *I*).

A copy in MS. Lansdowne 98, fol. 206, entitled "An Epitaphe made by William Grey, lyeng on his deathe bed, and by him appointed to be set on his tombe," was printed by F. J. Furnivall in *Notes and Queries*, 4th series, IV (1869), 194, with the following variants:

200. 33 G.] Grey
    34 Emong] Among
201. 2 shortnyng] shortener
    10 may] might
    11 this] the

Another copy, from MS. Sloane 1207, fols. 9–10, is printed in Furnivall's *Ballads from Manuscripts*, I, 435–437, and thence in Ernest W. Dormer's *Gray of Reading*, 1923, pp. 125–128. In both reprints it is mistakenly said to be from MS. Sloane 1206. This copy has no title or signature, but is preceded by a long poem (in the same hand) which has "Wm. Gray" in its title and is signed "Gray." In the Sloane MS. the present poem varies in the following particulars:

200. 33 lieth G.] Lyes gray
    34 Emong] Amonge
    35 Which] that
201. 5 they were but] were very
    7 tong] tonges
    9 here] stell
    10 whom] ho

The following new stanzas (I follow Furnivall's text) are then added:

> Yet now at the Last hathe gotten Rest
>   Amonge the ffathers olde,
> with clottes of yerthe apon his brest,
>   nott ffelynge hott nor colde,

Nor fferynge ones the porgynge plase
　　Devysed by the pope,
Bwtt in the marsy & the grase
　　of chryst that is my hoppe.

As ffor the pardons and his mass
　　Wyche wher his cheffe chase,
Lett chryston men nott on them pass,
　　thé be butt the popes draff

The holly oyle, hose consett*es*,
　　his mede shall be butt smale:
beleve nott his sacrement*es*,
　　nor his sacrymentaule.

As ffor the Rest of popesnes —
　　to longe now to Ressytt —
Lett chryston men *with* qwytnes
　　this pass them over qwytt,

And trwst, — in that yow shall ffynd good,
　　yf sole helthe ye well wen, —
yeven chrystes merett*es*, & his blud
　　that was shed ow*er* solles to kepe ffrom sen.

ffor that is that *that* allwayes moste,
　　yf we well chryst attene,
pwtt all yow*er* conffydence & trwst
　　All theng*es* ell*es* ar bwtt vene.

This is the ende of grat & smaule,
　　to torne as I am now:
ffrom yerthe we cam, to yerthe we shall,
　　no man knothe whan nor howe.

Yett was I once as now ar ye,
　　yeven losty ffrom my berthe;
shyche as I ame, syche shall ye be;
　　all ye shall torne to yerthe.

Therffore leve hee accordingely,
　　As holly wrytt dothe tell,
And then shall god aswredly
　　kepe yow ffrom dethe & hell.

To leve as on sholde allway dye,
　　Yt wer a blesed trade;
to change ower dethe ffor Lyfe so hey;
　　no batter change is mayd.

ffor All the worldly theng*es* ar vene,
　　in them ther is no trwst;
ye se all stattes awhyle Remenethe,
　　and then thé torne to dwst.

Yf Lwst & Lykynge myght be bowght
   ffor syllu*er* or ffor golde,
still to Indever yt wolde be sowght:
   what kyng*es* wolde then be olde?

Bwtt all shall pass & ffoulou me, —
   this is most s*er*tin trwthe, —
bothe hyghe & Lowe, & Ieche degre,
   the age and Ieke the youthe.

Yf yow be ffound mett or vn-mett
   Agynst the dredffull ower,
As ye be ffound, so shall the swettar
   be s*er*ved w*ith* the sower.

All this is sayd to mend ow*er* harthis,
   that shall [it] her or sey,
And then Acordinge to yow*er* part*is*
   to ffoulow dethe w*ith* me.

As in the case of No. 125, the editor of *A* prudently omitted the author's attacks on Roman Catholicism.

It will be observed that both in the Lansdowne MS. and in *B*+ Gray is said to have written the poem on his death-bed; but not much faith is to be put in that statement. Thus Lord Vaux was said to have written No. 212 as he was dying, but George Gascoigne ridiculed the simple people who believed that report (see above, 165. 16 n.). Thus, too, in various editions of the *Paradise*, pp. 95–96, 251–253, the Earl of Essex was named as the "death-bed author" of a poem that actually came from the pen of Francis Kinwelmarsh. It is interesting, however, that the last four stanzas of the Sloane MS. version of No. 255 are (with slight changes) chiseled on a stone slab beneath an old mural monument in the parish church of Sonning. That fact is chronicled by Dormer (pp. 55–56), who with great seriousness vindicates Mrs. Gray from the aspersions cast upon her by the poem. He shows, also (pp. 59–62), that she had been married twice before she became Mrs. Gray, and was married once after Gray's death. She died as Mrs. Agnes Ockham, perhaps on February 28, 1579 (1579/80?). See No. 256.

201. 12 (No. 256) *An aunswere.* In every edition (No. [240] in *B–I*, sigs. Bb3 in *BC*, N3 in *D–G*, N3ᵛ in *H*, M5ᵛ–M6 in *I*). The poem is a reply to No. 255. Dormer, p. 129, reprints it (somewhat inexactly) from Arber's edition as the composition of Gray. Of Gray's authorship there is no proof at all: the probabilities are against it, even if No. 255 was not a death-bed production. A copy in MS. Lansdowne 98, fol. 206, as printed by Furnivall in *Notes and Queries*, 4th series, IV (1869), 194, has the following variants:

201. 17 causelesse cause thee] cause the causeles
    20 blist] bleste: to] now to
    32 can not] in no case can

201. 33 (No. 257) *Against women either good or badde.* In every edition (No. [243] in *B–I*, sigs. Bb3^v–Bb4 in *BC*, N3^v–N4 in *D–G*, N4–N4^v in *H*, M6^v in *I*). Arbitrarily attributed to Gray by Dormer, who reprinted it (following Arber's text) in his *Gray of Reading*, p. 130. In MS. Cotton Titus A. xxiv, fol. 80^v, there is a copy with the signature of (Thomas) Norton. These variants occur:

> 202. 4 age] tim
>   6 good] greate
>   11 Sith] bothe
>   12 Bring] Worke

35–36 *A Man may liue thrise Nestors life, &c.* Imitated by Kendall, *Flowers of Epigrammes*, 1577, C4^v (Spenser Society ed., p. 56), "Then, then, full often wouldst thou wishe thrice *Nestors* yeares to liue"; and by Melbancke, *Philotimus*, 1583, D3^v, "A man may liue thrice *Nestors* yeares, thrice wander out *Vlisses* race, ere he gaine that by seruice, that sometime hath bene a common pencion."

202. 14 (No. 258) *An answere.* In every edition (No. [244] in *B–I*, sigs. Bb4 in *BC*, N4 in *D–G*, N4^v in *H*, M6^v–M7 in *I*). This reply to No. 257 is arbitrarily assigned to Gray by Dormer, who reprints it from Arber in *Gray of Reading*, p. 131.

32 (No. 259) *The louer praieth his seruice, &c.* In every edition (No. [220] in *B–I*, sigs. Y3^v–Y4 in *BC*, L7^v–L8 in *D–H*, L3–L3^v in *I*).

203. 2 *Procryn that some tyme serued Cephalus.* Evidently written with Ovid's *Metamorphoses* (vii. 794–862) in mind. Later (about 1568) Thomas Howell wrote "The lamentable historie of Sephalus with the Vnfortunat end of Procris. To the tune of Appelles," a poem included in his *Newe Sonets, and pretie Pamphlets* (*Poems*, ed. Grosart, pp. 146–149); and in 1595 Thomas Edwards published his *Cephalus and Procris* (ed. Roxburghe Club, 1882).

13 *after pray.* In lines 11–17 of the second stanza the rhyme-scheme is confused. The poem is in three nine-line stanzas, so that the paragraph-divisions should come at lines 11 and 20 but not at line 17.

29 (No. 260) *Description and praise of his loue.* In every edition (No. [221] in *B–I*, sigs. Y4–Y4^v in *BC*, L8–L8^v in *D–H*, L3^v in *I*). This poem of twenty-seven lines is written in three rhymes (some of them faulty according to modern pronunciation), the third appearing only in the final couplet.

31–32 *Lyke the Phenix . . . With golde and purple.* Cf. Petrarch, sonetto in morte 53 (*Rime*, 321, p. 299),

> È questo 'l nido in che la mia fenice
> mise l'aurate et le purpuree penne?

and canzone in morte 3, stanza 5 (*Rime*, 323, p. 303),

> Una strania fenice, ambedue l' ale
> di porpora vestita e 'l capo d' oro.

204. 23 (No. 261) *An answere to a song, &c.* In every edition (No. [248] in *B–I*, sigs. Cc2 in *BC*, N6 in *D–G*, N6ᵛ–N7 in *H*, M8ᵛ–N in *I*). The poem is a reply to No. 178, which (with a shortened title) it follows in *B–I*.

205. 3–4 *Oft malice makes the minde, &c.* Quoted in Allot's *England's Parnassus*, 1600 (ed. Crawford, no. 392), over the initials T. W., which may mean either Thomas Watson or Sir Thomas Wyatt, but which, as the following note shows, are not to be trusted.

5–6 *Oft craft can cause the man, &c.* These lines (with *distreined* as *distaind*, *did* as *doth*) are quoted in *England's Parnassus*, no. 191 (cf. the foregoing note), over the initials S. T. B. Perhaps these letters are a misprint for S. F. B., — that is, Sir Francis Bryan, who is known to have been a contributor to the miscellany; but, since Allot assigned lines 3–4 to T. W., he cannot be trusted here, especially in view of his errors in regard to the authorship of Nos. 133, 149, 171, 270, 278.

206. 3 (No. 262) *The constant louer lamenteth.* In every edition (No. [28] in *B–I*, sigs. Dᵛ–D2 in *BC*, B5ᵛ–B6 in *D–H*, B5ᵛ in *I*). Padelford (p. 57) reprints the poem from *A*, with the following variations:

206.   6 Wherin] Wherein
        26 hote] hot

11 *Spite draue me into Borias raigne.* "This probably alludes to the military expedition to Scotland on which Surrey accompanied his father in the early autumn of 1542, shortly after his imprisonment in the Fleet for quarreling with John a Leigh" (Padelford, p. 185).

19–20 *His beames in brightnesse, &c.* Cf. Petrarch, sonetto in morte 87, lines 1–2 (*Rime*, 352, p. 330):

Spirto felice che sí dolcemente
volgei quelli occhi piú chiari che 'l sole.

26 *the hote desire.* Cf. Petrarch, sonetto in vita 180, line 5 (*Rime*, 236, p. 228), "il mio caldo desire."

29 (No. 263) *A praise of sir Thomas wyate, &c.* In every edition (No. [36] in *B–I*, sigs. E–Eᵛ in *BC*, C–Cᵛ in *D–G*, Cᵛ in *H*, C in *I*). Padelford (p. 80) prints the poem from a Harington MS. (Additional 36529), with the following variants:

206. 31 knowledge] scyence: not] not so
        32 were that] where they
        33 conuert] reverte
        34 Wende] Wan
        35 no voyde] in no
207.   8 we . . . traine] deserve they monnis blame
        9 their brestes] thy brest
        10 they do] doo the

As may be seen from the foregoing collations, the text of *A* is corrupt.
Possibly it has some such meaning as this: "If, in the rude and ignorant age,
Jove in Crete and others — who taught the arts of humanity for our advan-
tage — thought (without reason) that their temples would be (gratefully)
honored after their death; if virtue, even in barren ungrateful times, never
lacked some to praise her endless fame — a goodly means both to deter us from
sin and to inspire us to follow her steps; then shall not, at the present day,
Wyatt's friends lament — the only debt the dead may claim of the living —
the extinction of the rare wisdom he employed for our advantage, teaching us
of Christ and leading us to the company of virtue? When he lived, his face
angered envious people; even now (that he is dead) with envy they attack his
dead body (cinders)."

207. 11 (No. 264) ❡*A song written by the earle of Surrey, &c.* In every
edition (No. [29] in *B–I*, sigs. D2–D3 in *BC*, B6–B7 in *D–H*, B5ᵛ–B6ᵛ in *I*).
Padelford (pp. 73–75) prints the poem from a Harington MS. (Additional
28635), with the following variants:

> 207. 15 can] to
>   16 late] theare
>   18 the] this: pleased] lyked
>   19 he] it: well] me
>   22 whales] whale his
>   23 of] a
>   24 coy] fearce
>   25 Vnto] Toward
>   30 With that] Wheare with
>   32 hadst] hadest: before] beforne
>   33 nor] and: forlore] forlorne
>   35 Go] But: where] *Om.*:   finde] seeke oute
>   36 With that] Forthwith: began] begounne
>   38 wrath] rage
> 208.   4 ye] you
>   10 haue heard] dothe know
>   12 strong] both strong
>   14 whom] who
>   15 lese his life] seeke his death
>   16 liues doe] lyfe, to
>   17 willes] will: ar] is: died] dyed right
>   18 now I doe] well I may: moueth] movid
>   21 other] others: ye] you
>   22 our kyndes] my kynd
>   24 fled] fedd: slay] flee
>   27 on] of
>   28 coyed] coy
>   29 trapt] traynd: with] bye
>   30 lust] list: loue] bow
>   31 of currant sort] a currant fawne
>   35 nor ¹] or: nor ²] that
>   38 ruse] rew

208. 39 This] Thus: ne] no
   40 And for reuenge therof] In the revendge wherof
   41 I] A
   42 luck] happ
209. 2 and bow] to low
   3 ye] you: sailes] saile
   4 Sith] Syns
   5 go . . . shepe] of symple sheepe go slake your wrath
   8 aucthor] awthour: the] this
   9 for] by

In *Englands Heroicall Epistles*, 1598 (Surrey to Geraldine), Drayton has Surrey mention "beauteous *Stanhope*, whom all tongues report, To be the glory of the English Court." In his notes (N3ᵛ) Drayton writes: "Of the beauty of that Lady, hee [Surrey] himselfe testifies in an Elegie which he writ of her, refusing to daunce with him, which hee seemeth to alegorize vnder a lyon & a wolfe. As of himselfe he saieth

A Lyon saw I late, as white as any snow.

And of her [207. 22–24 quoted]." Earlier Drayton explained that the white lion was on one of the Howard badges. There is little doubt that Surrey wrote the poem against Lady Anne Stanhope, who later became the wife of Edward Seymour, Earl of Hertford and Duke of Somerset; and Bapst (*Deux gentils-hommes-poètes*, pp. 370–371) presents evidence to date it in August, 1542. Nott, as always, drags the Fair Geraldine into the poem by the hair of the head, explaining that her refusal to dance with Surrey brought about the final rupture in their relations. See p. 74, above.

207. 12 *by a lady*. Only D has the correct reading, *to a lady*.

16 *A Lion*. The heraldic emblem of the Howard family; hence Surrey himself.

23 *A fairer beast of fresher hue, &c*. In *The Arte of English Poesie*, 1589, p. 136, this line is quoted as a good example of "*monosillables* and *bissillables* enterlaced." See another example in the notes to No. 16.

208. 5 *with his pawes a crowned king deuoured*. A reference to the poet's grandfather, Thomas Howard, who defeated James IV of Scotland in the battle of Flodden Field (1513).

11–15 *for loue one of the race did end his life, &c*. Referring to Thomas Howard, son of the Duke of Norfolk and the poet's half-uncle, who was committed to the Tower in June, 1536, for having become engaged to Lady Margaret Douglas, Henry VIII's niece, without that monarch's knowledge or consent. He died in prison about two years later.

14 *This gentle beast likewise*. In B+ *likewise* is needlessly changed to *so dyed* to agree with the context.

20–21 *lure me to the trade, &c*. "Lure me to follow the course which for many years you craftily made others trace (follow)."

208. 25 *I can deuour no yelding pray, &c.* Cf. 60. 33 n. and 208. 32–33. Turbervile, *Tragical Tales* [*ca.* 1574] 1587 (1837 reprint, p. 300), remarks, "The noble minded Lion kils no yeelding beast by crueltie"; *Willobie His Avisa*, 1594 (ed. G. B. Harrison, 1926, p. 125), "The raging Lyon neuer rendes The yeelding pray, that prostrate lyes." This characteristic of the lion is vouched for also in Pliny's *Natural History*, VIII. 19, and in Topsell's *The Historie of Foure-Footed Beastes*, 1607, p. 467.

31 *to such beasts of currant sort, &c.* The MS. reading (see above) is not explained by Padelford. Nott holds it to be "preferable to that of the printed copies, though the passage is not intelligible even as it now stands." He suggests that the line should read, "And to such beasts accouchant fawn, as should seek travail bright." The old annotator in *I* (Bodleian) emended the line to read, "And to such beasts of cravan sort theie will their travell hight."

38 *shal ruse.* Evidently *ruse* is a misprint for *rue*, the reading in *B+* and the MS.

41 *I thousand.* Read *A thousand* with *B+* and the MS.

209. 10 (No. 265) *The faithfull louer declareth, &c.* In every edition (No. [30] in *B–I*, sigs. D3–D3ᵛ in *BC*, B7–B7ᵛ in *D–G*, B7–B8 in *H*, B6ᵛ–B7ᵛ in *I*). Padelford (pp. 66–67) reprints the poem from *A*, with the following errors:

> 209. 36 doe] do
>   38 y̆ᵗ] yat
> 210. 15 forgetfulnes] forgetfulness
>   24 delay] delaye

There are other copies in MS. Ashmole 176, fols. 97–97ᵛ; with music in *The Melvill Book of Roundels*, 1612, ed. Bantock and Anderton, pp. 47–48, 199–200, Roxburghe Club, 1916 (forty short lines corresponding, with considerable changes, to 209. 15–28, 33–34, 31–32, 35–36); and with music in John Forbes's *Cantus, Songs and Fancies*, song 1 (1666, 1682, differing in many details from *A*, especially in the last half of the poem). A manuscript of "Scottish Musick" once owned by Dr. Burney and dated 1627–1629 (see *The Gentleman's Magazine*, XCIII [1823], 122) contained the music for "Give caire does cause men cry." No. 265 was registered for publication as a ballad, "yf Care may Cause men crye," in 1557–58; and an imitation or moralization called "Care Causethe men to Crye newly altered" was registered in 1562–63 (Rollins, *Analytical Index*, nos. 262, 1213). It is apparently imitated in No. 210. But Surrey himself seems to refer in his opening line to a poem by Wyatt (Foxwell, I, 129–130) beginning,

> Hevyn and erth and all that here me plain,
> Do well perceve what care doeth cause me cry.

19–21 *For all thynges hauing life, &c.* A similar idea is expressed in the six opening lines of Petrarch's sestina in vita 1 (*Rime*, 22, p. 15):

A qualunque animale alberga in terra,
se non se alquanti ch' ànno in odio il sole,
tempo da travagliare è quanto è 'l giorno;
ma poi che 'l ciel accende le sue stelle,
qual torna a casa et qual s'anida in selva,
per aver posa almeno infin a l'alba.

Petrarch and Surrey made these expressions a commonplace in Elizabethan poetry. They are repeated at 163. 5–8.

209. 35–36 *Then as the striken dere, &c.* Perhaps the source of Melbancke's remark in *Philotimus*, 1583, Y2ᵛ: "The stricken Deare withdrawes himself to die, and so will I." See also 163. 9, and cf. Sackville, in *The Mirror for Magistrates*, 1563 (ed. Haslewood, II, 342), "Like to the dere that stricken with the dart, Withdrawes himselfe into some secret place," and *Hamlet*, III. ii. 282, "let the stricken deer go weep." Lines 35–36 and 210. 24–25 are quoted in *The Arte of English Poesie*, 1589, p. 248, as examples of "generall *resemblance*, or bare *similitude*."

38 *the stremes of those two welles.* Cf. 184. 13 n.

210. 32 *to serue vntill my brethe.* This apparently means, "to serve until my final breath"; but (as Nott suggests) *brethe* may be an error for *death*, the subject discussed in lines 33–37.

37 *I do bequeth my weried ghost to serue her afterwarde.* Cf. Chaucer, *Troilus and Criseyde*, IV. 319–322,

but when myn herte dyeth,
My spirit, which that so un-to yow hyeth,
Receyve in gree, for that shal ay yow serve;
For-thy no fors is, though the body sterve;

and *The Knight's Tale* (A. 2768–2770),

But I biquethe the service of my gost
To yow aboven every creature,
Sin that my lyf may no lenger dure.

211. 4 (No. 266) *Of his loue called .Anna.* In every edition (No. [118] in *B–I*, sigs. L2 in *BC*, F2 in *D–H*, E8 in *I*). Miss Foxwell (I, 48) prints the poem from MS. Egerton 2711, with the following variants:

211. 8 Anna] aunswer
9 The only] And eke the
10 My loue that medeth] A love rewardeth
11 will you] would ye
12 salue, and eke] helth eke and

For other riddles see Nos. 115 and 268. Nott (Wyatt, p. 560) suggests that No. 266 may have been an early poem written on Anne Boleyn.

6 *What word is that, that changeth not.* The word *Anna* is a palindrome. John Taylor, in *The Nipping or Snipping of Abuses (Works*, 1630,

Spenser Society ed., p. 404) says: "*This line is the same backward, as it is for-*
ward, and I will giue any man fiue shillings apiece for as many as they can make
in English:

> Lewd did I liue, & euil did I dwel."

211. 13 (No. 267) *That pleasure is mixed with euery paine.* In every edition
(No. [119] in *B–I*, sigs. L2ᵛ in *BC*, F2ᵛ in *D–G*, F2 in *H*, E8 in *I*). Miss
Foxwell (1, 54) prints the poem from MS. Egerton 2711, with the following
variants:

> 211. 16 Sometyme ber flowers fayre and fresh of hue
> 　　17 is also] offtyme is
> 　　18 And causith helth in man for to renue
> 　　19 Ffire that purgith allthing that is unclene
> 　　20 hurt . . . be] hele and hurt: and if thes bene
> 　　22 euery] evry

The source of No. 267 is Serafino's strambotto (*Opere*, 1516, fol. 117; also
in Poliziano's *Le Stanze*, etc., ed. Carducci, 1912, p. 606):

> Ogni pungente & uenenosa spina
> 　　Se uede à qualche tempo esser fiorita,
> Crudel ueneno posto in medicina,
> 　　Piú uolte torna lhom da morte uita,
> El foco che ogni cosa arde & ruina,
> 　　Spesso risana una mortal ferita,
> Cosi spero el mio mal me fia salute,
> 　　Chogni cosa che noce há pur uirtute.

17 *Poison is also put in medicine.* Compare with this line and with
the thought of the entire poem Thomas Norton's verses prefixed to William
Turner's *A perseruatiue or triacle, agaynst the poyson of Pelagius*, 1551, which
begin:

> And euen as lerned leches do oftentymes
> (Triall techeth dayly tofore our eyes)
> Put in poyson, to make for medicines:
> So make their bale thy boote.

23 (No. 268) *A riddle of a gift geuen by a Ladie.* In every edition
(No. [120] in *B–I*, sigs. L2ᵛ in *BC*, F2ᵛ in *D–G*, F2 in *H*, E8 in *I*). Miss
Foxwell (1, 49) prints the poem from a Harington MS. (Additional 28635),
with a single variant — the omission of *which* (line 26). A copy (not known
to her) in MS. Rawlinson Poet. 172, fol. 3ᵛ, has the same title as in *A* but pre-
sents the following variant readings:

> 211. 29 giue] gaue
> 　　30 And] *Om.*:　　it] *Om.*
> 　　31 this is] is this

In the margin of *I* (Bodleian) the second and later annotator wrote, "J
think it is a Kysse." For other riddles see the notes to No. 266. George

Gascoigne imitated No. 268 in his *Posies*, 1575 (*Complete Poems*, ed. Hazlitt, 1, 365):

A Riddle.

A Lady once did aske of me
This preatie thing in priuitie:
Good sir (quod she) faine would I craue
One thing which you your selfe not haue;
Nor neuer had yet in times past,
Nor neuer shall while life doth last.
And if you seeke to find it out,
You loose your labour out of doubt:
Yet if you loue me as you say,
Then giue it me, for sure you may.
Meritum petere, graue.

In *The Gentleman's Journal*, July, 1692, p. 20, Peter Motteux tells his readers: "I shall be obliged to you, if you give me a Solution of that ['Ænigma'] which follows. It was written by the Earl of *Surrey*, about 130 Years ago. I have been desired to explain it, but shall be glad to find your Thoughts concur with mine, before I disclose them." He then reprints Wyatt's "Riddle" (with slight variations of diction). In his next issue (August, p. 24) Motteux remarks: "I have received several Explications of the Earl of *Surrey's* Riddle in my last; some think it one thing, some another; for my part, I must own my self partly of the sentiment of an honourable Person, who believes that it refers much to Mr. *Cowley's Verses*.

"*Thou thing of subtile slippery kind,*
Which Women lose, and yet no Man can find.

"And as the Lady had it not to give, I suppose that she pretended at least to give it him to make the blessing the greater."

212. 2 (No. 269) *That speaking or profering, &c.* In every edition (No. [121] in *B–I*, sigs. L2ᵛ in *BC*, F2ᵛ in *D–G*, F2–F2ᵛ in *H*, E8–E8ᵛ in *I*). Miss Foxwell (1, 386) reprints the poem from *A*, misprinting *dothe* (line 6) as *doth*.

11 (No. 270) *He ruleth not though he raigne, &c.* In every edition (No. [122] in *B–I*, sigs. L3 in *BC*, F3 in *D–G*, F2ᵛ in *H*, E8ᵛ in *I*). Miss Foxwell (1, 387) reprints the poem from *A*, with the following errors:

212. 17 empyre] Empyre: Indian] Inlian
21 minde] mind
25 the] thee: workyng] working
26 bee] be
27 foule] foul: conquere] conquer
28 golde] gold
31 selfe] self

The poem is based on Boethius (as Nott points out in his Wyatt volume, p. 551), probably on Chaucer's translation: stanza 1 corresponds to Boethius,

III, meter 5; stanza 2 to III, meter 6; stanza 3 to III, meter 3. The first stanza of No. 270 is quoted in Allot's *England's Parnassus*, 1600 (ed. Crawford, no. 877) over Surrey's name, which in the notes (p. 443) Crawford corrects to Wyatt's. Crawford adds that "the style of this poem is remarkably like that of a poem in Sir Thomas Elyot's *Governour*," beginning, "Though that thy power stretcheth both far and large." For the numerous blunders Allot makes in the ascriptions of the passages he quotes, see *England's Parnassus*, pp. 543–544, and above, 205. 5–6 n.

212. 32–34 *thy couitise And busye bytyng . . . do thy death profet.* "Your covetousness and sharp corroding desire yet would never cease, nor your death be any profit to your wretched life." Chaucer's words are: "never ne shal his bytinge bisinesse for-leten him whyl he liveth, ne the lighte richesses ne sholle nat beren him companye whan he is ded."

213. 2 (No. 271) *whether libertie by losse of life, &c.* In every edition (No. [123] in *B–I*, sigs. L3–L3ᵛ in *BC*, F3–F3ᵛ in *D–G*, F2ᵛ–F3 in *H*, E8ᵛ–F in *I*). Miss Foxwell (1, 364–365) prints the poem from a Corpus Christi College (Cambridge) MS., with the following variants.

213. 6 within] in
       7 her foe] and
      10 Lo] Certes: seke] do seke
      14 is] is the: but] *Om.*
      15 better to] oute of daunger yet to
      16 Than bide in] Rather than with
      17 For small pleasure moche payne to suffer
      18 Rather] Soner: thinketh] thinccketh it
      20 By lengthe of lyff yet shulde I suffer
      21 I do but wait a] Adwayting
      22 Oft] *Om.*:   do] *Om.*:   in one] within an
      23 oppressed me now] me oppressed
      25 wholy] utterlye
      27 where] in: lengthes] lengthe of
      28 these] *Om.*:   euyls] ylles
      29 that here dothe] you that here her
      30 What saye ye] Your advise you: the] *Om.*
      31 cage] cage in: the] *Om.*:   opprest] to be opprest
      32 to] for to

With this poem — which belongs to the "lover's-dilemma type" favored by the troubadours — compare the moral of John Lydgate's *Here foloweth the Churle and the byrde* (Mychel's ed., 1550?), B4ᵛ, where the bird says,

> For better is fredome/ with lytel in gladnesse
> Than to be thrall/ with all worldly rychesse.

No. 271, as Professor J. N. D. Bush points out in *The Philological Quarterly*, v (1926), 327, is imitated in the following passage from George Pettie's *A Petite Pallace of Pettie his Pleasure*, 1576 (ed. Gollancz, 1, 123–124): "And as the bird enclosed in cage, the cage door being set open, and the hawk her enemy

sitting without watching for her, between death and prison piteously op-
pressed standeth in doubt whether it be better still to remain in prison, or to
go forth to be a prey for the hawk, so stand I in doubt whether it be better by
losing life to get liberty, or by living to become thrall and bond, and live in
continual torment and vexation of mind."

213. 28 *chuse the best.* The proverb demands the reading *lest,* that is, *least*
(cf. also line 30).

217. 2 (No. 272) *The louer declareth his paines, &c.* Not in *A* (No. [222]
in *B–I,* sigs. Y4ᵛ–Z in *BC,* L8ᵛ–M in *D–H,* L3ᵛ–L4 in *I*). A copy in a Har-
ington MS. (Additional 28635, fols. 117–117ᵛ) presents the following variants:

> 217. 2 The louer, &c.] Of purgation
> 10 boile] boylde: leade againe] sckalding lead
> 12 with deadly paine] from foote to head
> 15 their] theise
> 23 be] are: kept] put
> 24 are aungels] Angells be
> 25 know I] I know
> 218. 3 thousand] thousandt
> 12 So that I know] syth I know not
> 18 And as I am] Beholding heare this

218. 22 (No. 273) *Of the death of sir Thomas wiate, &c.* Not in *A* (No.
[223] in *B–I,* sigs. Z in *BC,* M in *D–G,* M–Mᵛ in *H,* L4ᵛ in *I*). A copy in MS.
Harleian 78, fol. 15, runs as follows:

> Sʳ Antonie Sentlenger of Sʳ T.W.
>
> Thus lyvethe the deade that whilome lived here
> Emonge the deade that quick go on the grownde
> Thoughe he be deade yet dothe he quicke appere
> by immortall fame ẏ deathe cane not confounde
> his lyf for aye his fame in trompe shall sounde
> thoughe he be deade yet is he thus alive
> no deathe cane ẏ lyf from Wiattes lyf deprive

With various unauthorized changes, the foregoing verses (the final word in
which was first written as *depart* and then corrected to *deprive*) were printed
in the unpublished Percy-Steevens edition of *C* (II, 112), in the 1831 edition
of Wyatt and Surrey (II, 238), and elsewhere. "Sir Anthony Sentlyger, deputie
of Irelande," says *The Firste Parte of Churchyardes Chippes,* 1575 (Collier's
reprint, p. 128), was "a wyes and noble knight," as well as a personal bene-
factor to Churchyard.

31 (No. 274) *That length of time, &c.* Not in *A* (No. [224] in *B–I,*
sigs. Z–Zᵛ in *BC,* M–Mᵛ in *D–G,* Mᵛ in *H,* L4ᵛ in *I*).

34 *softe.* Read *oft* with *D+.*

219. 6 (No. 275) *The beginning of the epistle of Penelope, &c.* Not in *A*
(No. [225] in *B–I,* sigs. Zᵛ in *BC,* Mᵛ in *D–H,* L4ᵛ in *I*). These Alexandrines
are a translation of Ovid's *Heroides,* I. 1–12, beginning,

> Haec tua Penelope lento tibi mittit, Ulixe;
> Nil mihi rescribas ut tamen; ipse veni!

In Turbervile's translation of the *Heroides*, 1567, sig. A, the corresponding lines run thus:

> To thee that lingrest all too long,
>   thy Wyfe (*Vlysses*) sendes:
> Gayne write not, but by quick returne
>   for absence make amendes.
> To Greekish Nymphes that hatefull Troie
>   is now to ruine brought:
> Scarce mought the King and all his wealth
>   requite the wrong they wrought.
> O that the surging Seas had drencht
>   that lustfull Lecher tho:
> When he to *Lacedemon* came
>   imbarckt, and wrought our wo.
> Then should I not haue layde my limmes
>   in desert coutch alone:
> Ne made complaint that *Phœbus* steades
>   to slowe to glade had gone.
> Then should no Beldames distaffe made,
>   my Wydowish hande so faynt:
> Whilst I to waste the wearie night,
>   with spinning was attaynt.
> When stoode I not in worser awe
>   in deede than was befell?
> Aye loue is passing full of feare,
>   though euery thing be well.

219. 21 (No. 276) *The louer asketh pardon, &c.* Not in *A* (No. [226] in *B–I*, sigs. Z^v in *BC*, M^v in *D–G*, M^v–M2 in *H*, L5 in *I*). Koeppel (*Studien*, p. 88) shows this poem to be a translation of Petrarch, sonetto in vita 1 (*Rime*, 1, p. 1):

> Voi ch'ascoltate in rime sparse il suono
> di quei sospiri ond' io nudriva 'l core
> in sul mio primo giovenile errore,
> quand' era in parte altr' uom da quel ch' i' sono;
> del vario stile in ch' io piango et ragiono,
> fra le vane speranze e 'l van dolore,
> ove sia chi per prova intenda amore,
> spero trovar pietà non che perdono.
> Ma ben veggio or sí come al popol tutto
> favola fui gran tempo; onde sovente
> di me medesmo meco mi vergogno:
> et del mio vaneggiar vergogna è 'l frutto,
> e 'l pentersi, e 'l conoscer chiaramente
> che quanto piace al mondo è breve sogno.

Like No. 277, No. 276 is apparently an attempt to write a sonnet, though it is in septenary couplets.

An entirely different translation in a Harington MS. (Additional 36529, fol. 45) runs thus:

> You that in rime dispersed here the sownd
> of wonted sighes that whylome eas'd my hart
> in my greene yeares whilest youthe tooke errours part
> whan I strayd farr from that course synce I fownd
> of the sere sort wheare in I plead and plaine
> somtyme ẘ hope somtyme ẘ heuy mynd
> at you I say whear youth did euer raine
> pitie I troust as well as pardon fynde
> howb' it I know what brewts ther haue ben bred
> abrode of me long tyme, wherby not seeld
> euin at my self shame staynes my cheeks ẘ red
> such ar the frewts which those uain coourses yeeld
> repentance eke, and knowledge printed deepe
> that eache worlds Joy is but a slombring sleepe.

220. 2 (No. 277) *The louer sheweth, &c.* Not in *A* (No. [227] in *B–I*, sigs. Z2 in *BC*, M2 in *D–H*, L5 in *I*). A copy in a Harington MS. (Additional 28635, fol. 37) has the following variants:

220. 6 mine] my
    9 none] no
  10 plight] flight
  12 vewed] vew'd: approcht] approche
  16 which fleest] that flyeste
  17 vnweaponed] vnweap'nyd

Koeppel (*Studien*, p. 88) shows this poem to be a translation of Petrarch, sonetto in vita 3 (*Rime*, 3, p. 2):

> Era il giorno ch'al sol si scoloraro
> per la pietà del suo factore i rai;
> quando i' fui preso, et non me ne guardai,
> che i be' vostr' occhi, Donna, mi legaro.
> Tempo non mi parea da far riparo
> contra colpi d'Amor; però m'andai
> secur, senza sospetto: onde i miei guai
> nel commune dolor s'incominciaro.
> Trovommi Amor del tutto disarmato,
> et aperta la via per gli occhi al core,
> che di lagrime son fatti uscio et varco.
> Però, al mio parer, non li fu honore
> ferir me de saetta in quello stato,
> a voi armata non mostrar pur l'arco.

Like the foregoing poem (No. 276), No. 277 is a "sonnet" in septenary couplets.

18 (No. 278) *The louer describeth, &c.* Not in *A* (No. [228] in *B–I*, sigs. Z2–Aaᵛ in *BC*, M2–M5ᵛ in *D–G*, M2–M6 in *H*, L5–L8ᵛ in *I*). In his *Epitaphes*, etc., 1567 (p. 192), Turbervile has a poem beginning,

> Though noble Surrey sayde
> that absence woonders frame,
> And makes things out of sight forgot,
> and thereof takes his name.

This is a reference to 224. 26, and Nott accordingly printed the poem in his edition of Surrey. Turbervile's loose statement is not worth taking seriously. He merely had one of the poems of the *Songs and Sonnets* in mind and attributed it to Surrey because Surrey's name instinctively came to him.

In *The Arte of English Poesie*, 1589, p. 186, 225. 22–25, 28–29, are quoted as examples of "*Polisindeton*, or the Coople clause," so-called "for that euery clause is knit and coupled together with a coniunctiue."

220. 28 *And laughes vpon the earth anone.* Nott suggests that the author had in mind Lucretius, *De Rerum Natura*, III. 21–22, "semperque innubilus aether integit, et large diffuso lumine rident."

30 *the teares of her own kinde.* That is, dew.

221. 40 *Saue I alas.* The phrase recurs at 3. 29 and 209. 23.

222. 11 *That lacke the thing should comfort me.* The same idea is expressed at 10. 29.

29 *As nay.* Read *as may* with C+.

224. 4 *old pamphlets.* Not dry prose tracts, but poetical verses. See Thomas Proctor's use of the word in the *Gorgeous Gallery*, p. 79.

225. 30–34 *On thee she speakes, &c.* Nott suggests a borrowing from Terence's *Eunuch*, I. 191, 193–196:

> egone quid velim?
>
> . . . .
>
> dies noctisque me ames, me desideres,
> me somnies, me exspectes, de me cogites,
> me speres, me te oblectes, mecum tota sis:
> meus fac sis postremo animus quando ego sum tuos.

227. 20 (No. 279) *Of the troubled comon welth, &c.* Not in *A* (No. [229] in *B–I*, sigs. Aaᵛ–Aa2ᵛ in *BC*, M5ᵛ–M6ᵛ in *D–G*, M6–M7 in *H*, L8ᵛ–Mᵛ in *I*). A copy in a Harington MS. (Additional 28635, fols. 138ᵛ–139ᵛ) has the following variants:

227. 28 set] did sett
228. 13 sad] *Om.*
   17 demed] deemde
   19 stroied Troians] Troyans stroyed
   24 of²] eke of
   34 cloke] clooke
   37 oreturneth] over turneth
   42 midst] myddes: this] his
229. 6 welth] health
   18 ease] case

The poem was probably written about the rebellion of Sir Thomas Wyatt the younger (son of the poet), which began on the official announcement, January 15, 1554, of Queen Mary's marriage to Philip II, and ended with his surrender on February 8. Wyatt was executed on April 11, and the poem must have been written shortly afterwards. But 228. 31 may perhaps indicate that Lady Jane Grey's rebellion is aimed at. Many of the details about Troy sound as if they were borrowed from Surrey's translation of the second book of the *Aeneid*.

227. 40 *Treason in Anthenor and Eneas*. According to some accounts, Aeneas was led by his hatred of Paris into betraying Troy to the Greeks: Antenor, when sent on a mission to negotiate peace with Agamemnon, arranged with that king and Odysseus to deliver the city into their hands.

228. 12–13 *compted . . . As sad deuines in matter but of sport.* "They were accounted serious diviners in matters that were merely trivial." People thought that Cassandra and Laocoön were taking matters of no import too seriously.

229. 20 (No. 280) *The louer to his loue, &c.* Not in *A* (No. [230] in *B–I*, sigs. Aa2ᵛ in *BC*, M6ᵛ in *D–G*, M7 in *H*, Mᵛ–M2 in *I*).

31 (No. 281) *The louer sheweth, &c.* Not in *A* (No. [231] in *B–I*, sigs. Aa2ᵛ–Aa3 in *BC*, M6ᵛ–M7 in *D–G*, M7–M7ᵛ in *H*, M2 in *I*). With the subject-matter see the notes to No. 241, and compare John Dickenson, *The Shepheardes Complajnt*, ca. 1595 (*Prose and Verse*, ed. Grosart, p. 18): "IUPITER himselfe . . . felt the force of his aspiring Nephewes fatall weapons, else would he not haue courted LEDA in the shape of a Swanne, wafted EUROPA in forme of a Bull, descended into DANAES lap like a goulden showre." Dickenson's comment is somewhat like a passage in the *Octavia* (lines 200–207), a play long attributed to Seneca.

230. 22 (No. 282) *The louer disceiued by his loue, &c.* Not in *A* (No. [232] in *B–I*, sigs. Aa3–Aa3ᵛ in *BC*, M7–M7ᵛ in *D–G*, M7ᵛ–M8 in *H*, M2–M2ᵛ in *I*). Nott (C. 60. O. 13) observes that in MS. Harleian 78, fol. 30ᵛ, a copy of this poem has the signature H. H. and "therefore may be ascribed to the Earl of Surrey." It really has H. S. (Henry Surrey), — not an uncommon way of referring to the poet, — in the margin opposite the first line. In the same MS. No. 28 is signed H. S. Padelford accepted this poem as Surrey's, reprinting it in *Anglia*, XXIX, 336–337, in *Early Sixteenth Century Lyrics*, 1907, pp. 41–42, and in his edition of Surrey, pp. 57–58. In the last work he constructed a text of his own from *A* and the Harleian MS. Collations with the MS. follow:

230. 26 finde] seeke
27 that] the
28 seke] say
29 case] cause
31 bewaile] repent
33 wanton, raging] *Transposed*
34 me] I

35 Scilla] Cillas seas
37 hauen] heauen
39 Much like] lyke vnto
231. 2 her] his
3 So] for
6 there now] *Transposed*
8 as] is
9 As] that
10–15 *Om.*

The initial letters of the stanzas of No. 282 (cf. Eleanor P. Hammond, "Poems 'Signed' by Sir Thomas Wyatt," *Modern Language Notes*, XXXVII [1922], 505–506) form the anagram *I–A–W–T–T*, possibly indicating that Wyatt was the author. For similar cases see Surrey's No. 16, as well as Nos. 225 and 296 by uncertain authors. What credence, if any (cf. the notes to No. 200), should be given to this type of signaling is doubtful.

230. 29–30 *Since Troylus case.* The author says he thought his sweetheart was a Penelope, himself a Ulysses; but he finds her false like Cressid, himself faithful and deserted like Troilus.

231. 16 (No. 283) *The louer hauing enioyed his loue, &c.* Not in *A* (No. [233] in *B–I*, sigs. Aa3ᵛ–Aa4 in *BC*, M7ᵛ–M8 in *D–G*, M8–M8ᵛ in *H*, M2ᵛ–M3 in *I*).

232. 18 (No. 284) *Totus mundus in maligno positus.* Not in *A* (No. [234] in *B–I*, sigs. Aa4–Bb in *BC*, M8–N in *D–G*, M8ᵛ–Nᵛ in *H*, M3–M4 in *I*). The title (which, by the way, is the legend accompanying the first emblem in Francis Quarles's *Emblems*, 1635) comes from the first Epistle of John, v. 19 (Vulgate), "Et mundus totus in maligno positus est." Thomas Lodge, in *Wits Miserie*, 1596, sig. B (*Complete Works*, ed. Hunterian Club, IV, 7), remarks: "that true sentence is frustrate, *Totus mundus in maligno positus est,* The whole world is set on mischiefe."

A copy, with the same title as in *A*, is in MS. Rawlinson Poet. 82, fols. 1ᵛ–2ᵛ; it presents only a few unimportant variants:

233. 9 gainst] against
12 are] is
32 Flattry] flatterie
38 be we] we be

At the end of the poem is the phrase, "τῷ Θεῷ μόνῳ δόξα." Nothing else is included in the MS. except (fol. 3) the following lines:

Sir John Cheek.
Who can persuade, where treson is aboue reson;
and Might ruleth right; and it is had for
lawful, whatsoever is lustful; and commotioners
is better, then Commissioners; and common
Wo is nam'd Common Welth.
Gabriel Haruey.

The foregoing passage may indicate that Sir John Cheke wrote No. 284, and that the Rawlinson MS. is in the handwriting of Harvey. Such, at any rate, was the opinion of the compiler of the Bodleian *Summary Catalogue of Western Manuscripts*, III (1895), 299.

232. 30 *Duty by* (*will not*), *&c.* The parentheses are used where we should now use quotation-marks; the MS. has (*WIL NOT*). Cf. 48. 31 n.; Melbancke's *Philotimus*, 1583, sig. T, "O let not (*was*) worke all delight, let (*is*) and (*shall*) haue part in pay"; and *The Phoenix Nest*, 1593, p. 6, "This word (*was slaine*) straightway did moue."

39 *A wise man saith not, had I wist.* Numerous examples of this proverb are cited in my notes to the *Paradise*, pp. 182–183.

234. 5 *as chickens vnder the hen.* Cf. Matthew xxiii. 37.

8 (No. 285) *The wise trade of lyfe.* Not in *A* (No. [235] in *B–I*, sigs. Bb in *BC*, N in *D–G*, N^v in *H*, M4 in *I*).

12 *Wit bought is of to dere a price.* Referring to the proverb, "Wit's never good till it be bought," on which see my notes in the *Paradise*, p. 189. Cf. also Gascoigne's *A Hundreth Sundrie Flowres*, 1573 (ed. Ward, 1926, p. 98), "Bought wytte is deare."

24 (No. 286) *That few wordes shew wisdome, &c.* Not in *A* (No. [236] in *B–I*, sigs. Bb–Bb^v in *BC*, N–N^v in *D–G*, N^v–N2 in *H*, M4–M4^v in *I*). The opening line suggests a possible connection between this poem and the ballad of "who lest to leave at Ease and lede a quyett lyf &c." that was registered for publication in 1566–67 (Rollins, *Analytical Index*, no. 2947). In MS. Additional 38813, fols. 1–2 (in J. P. Collier's handwriting, however), there is a ballad on the same theme as No. 286. It is said to be copied from "a contemp: MS. in the possession of Mr. Bright," is signed "master Knight," and begins,

> It hath beene ofte both sayde & soonge
> Take heede what woords do pas the toonge.

No. 286 has borrowings from Proverbs (compare especially 235. 20–21 with Proverbs xvii. 28) and possibly from Cato's *Disticha de Moribus*, I. 3,

> Virtutem primam esse puta compescere linguam:
> Proximus ille deo est, qui scit ratione tacere.

31 *bestrow them well.* This may mean *bestrew*, but *C+* read *bestow*.

235. 4–5 *Two eares, one tong onely, &c.* Edmund Tilney, in *The Flower of Friendship*, 1568, C3–C3^v, remarks: "*Xenophon* sayeth, that nature gaue vs two eares, and but one mouth, to the intent we should heare more, than we ought to speake." He is echoed by Howell, in *The Arbor of Amitie*, 1568 (*Poems*, ed. Grosart, p. 5): "that siluer sentence of the Philosopher *Zeno* . . . that nature had giuen vs two eares and one mouth, to the entent, that we should heare more than we vtter in wordes." In Plutarch's *Morals* ("On Listening to Lectures," §3) we read: "It is a common saying that Nature has

given each of us two ears and one tongue, because we should do less talking than listening." Cf. also Thomas Lodge, *Wits Miserie*, 1596, M4 (*Complete Works*, ed. Hunterian Club, IV, 87), "It was noted by AESCHILUS the Trage-dian, that God in our bodies hath planted two eies, two eares, two nosthrils, and the braine aboue the tongue, to giues [*sic*] vs to vnderstād, that we ought rather see, hear, and conceiue, then speake"; and Gabriel Harvey, *The Trim-ming of Thomas Nashe*, 1597 (*Works*, ed. Grosart, III, 60), "Nature gaue thee two eares and but one tongue, because thou shouldest heare more then thou shouldest speake."

235. 10 *Words wisely set are worth much gold.* Cf. Proverbs xxv. 11.

26 (No. 287) *The complaint of a hot woer, &c.* Not in *A* (No. [237] in *B–I*, sigs. Bbᵛ–Bb2 in *BC*, Nᵛ–N2 in *D–G*, N2–N2ᵛ in *H*, M4–M5 in *I*).

29 *A Kinde of coale, &c.* Similar natural phenomena are mentioned in Melbancke's *Philotimus*, 1583, B4ᵛ, L3ᵛ, T2: "In *Fraunce*, there is a Well of such chilling coldnes, that it wil conuert wood into stone, and yet oftentimes, flakes of flaming fier haue bene sene to issue from it"; "the wels which be in *Norwaye*, whose licour is so grose, and extreme could, that if wood be cast in them they turne it to yron"; "There are found certeine stones in a riuer in *Pontus*, which thē take on fire, when ẙ wind is greatest, and by how muche ẙ more they are couered in water, by so muche the fearcer and brighter they burne." In *Willobie His Avisa*, 1594 (ed. G. B. Harrison, 1926, p. 89), we read of "canal cole,"

> There is a cole that burnes the more,
> The more ye cast colde water neare.

See also Pliny's *Natural History*, II, 107–110.

236. 31 (No. 288) *The answer.* Not in *A* (No. [238] in *B–I*, sigs. Bb2–Bb2ᵛ in *BC*, N2–N2ᵛ in *D–G*, N2ᵛ–N3 in *H*, M5–M5ᵛ in *I*).

237. 10 *the bauen blase. Bauen*, meaning brushwood (hence, quickly dying out), is used also by Turbervile (Ovid's *Heroides*, 1567, 18ᵛ), "kindeled Torches shone With Bauen blase"; by Francis Meres (*Palladis Tamia*, 1598, fol. 150ᵛ), "As the Bauin is but a blaze: so beautie"; and in *The Play of Dicke of Devonshire*, ca. 1626 (A. H. Bullen, *A Collection of Old English Plays*, II, 35), "our *Spanish* ovens are not heated with one Bavyn." Many other examples are cited in M. P. Tilley's *Elizabethan Proverb Lore* (1926), p. 69.

21 (No. 289) *An other of the same.* Not in *A* (No. [242] in *B–I*, sigs. Bb3ᵛ in *BC*, N3ᵛ in *D–G*, N4 in *H*, M6ᵛ in *I*). The title is explained by the fact that in *B–I* the poem follows No. 253. There are other copies of this elegy in (1) a Harington MS. (Additional 28635, fols. 139ᵛ–140) and (2) MS. Cotton Titus A. XXIV, fol. 79ᵛ. The latter is signed "finis. norton." Collations follow:

237. 23 lore] love (1)
24 we] they (1), the (2):   hye] gye (2)
25 and] to (1, 2)
26 that] the (1)

237. 27 and] withe (2):   worldly] wordly (2)
       28 withstand] resist (1, 2)
       30 me] my (1)
       35 on] in (2)
       40 will] shall (1, 2):   for] of (1, 2)
       41 Now] thus (2)

238. 2 (No. 290) *The answere.* Not in *A* (No. [246] in *B–I*, sigs. Bb4ᵛ–Ccᵛ in *BC*, N4ᵛ–N5ᵛ in *D–G*, N5–N6 in *H*, M7ᵛ–M8 in *I*). The poem is an answer to No. 254, which it follows in *B–I*.

7 *No minde of meane.* "No moderate, well-balanced mind," that is, no mind that kept the golden mean. The phrase is opposed to *heat of braine* (G. L. K.).

10–11 *Fansy forced . . . light to get.* "Love (desire) impelled by the false report that she was easy to win."

19 *This laud had lied if you had sped.* "This praise (of the lady's chastity) would have been falsified if you had succeeded (in winning her)."

26 *you blame brute of brutish traine.* "It is brutish (stupid) of you to blame report (which declared that she was virtuous), when it turns out that the report was true."

239. 3–4 *Good should by geason, &c.* "Good should win no place because of its rarity, nor should that which is good be not esteemed (made nought) if it is common instead of rare."

12–13 *Ye will repent, and right for done. Ye . . . shame.* "You will repent, and rightly; for you have done a deed that deserves shame." There should be no punctuation after *done* (G. L. K.).

19 *your thrall.* Read *you thrall* with *D+*.

24 (No. 291) *The louer complaineth, &c.* Not in *A* (No. [249] in *B–I*, sigs. Cc2–Cc3 in *BC*, N6–N7 in *D–G*, N7–N7ᵛ in *H*, N–Nᵛ in *I*).

241. 4 (No. 292) *The louer wounded of Cupide, &c.* Not in *A* (No. [250] in *B–I*, sigs. Cc3–Cc4 in *BC*, N7–N8 in *D–G*, N7ᵛ–N8ᵛ in *H*, Nᵛ–N2ᵛ in *I*).

243. 8 (No. 293) *Of womens changeable will.* Not in *A* (No. [251] in *B–I*, sigs. Cc4 in *BC*, N8 in *D–G*, N8ᵛ in *H*, N2ᵛ in *I*).

19 *To make death surgeant for my sore.* Borrowed in Melbancke's *Philotimus*, 1583, Y2ᵛ: "no remedie remaines, but death must be surgeon of thy sore." Cf. also 1 *Henry VI*, II. iv. 53, "Opinion shall be surgeon to my hurt."

22 (No. 294) *The louer complayneth, &c.* Not in *A* (No. [252] in *B–I*, sigs. Cc4–Cc4ᵛ in *BC*, N8–N8ᵛ in *D–G*, N8ᵛ–O in *H*, N2ᵛ–N3 in *I*). The rhyme-scheme (*aaaa baba caca baba dada*) is peculiar.

29 *My mouthes of mirth.* For *mouthes* read *months* with *D–G*.

30 *My times.* For *times* we should expect *tunes.* The two words are so much alike in manuscript that the printer may have misread his copy.

244. 6 *Hath rest my dame.* For *rest* read *reft* (taken away by death).

244. 8 (No. 295) *Of the golden meane.* Not in *A* (No. [253] in *B–I*, sigs. Cc4ᵛ in *BC*, N8ᵛ in *D–G*, O–Oᵛ in *H*, N3 in *I*). It is, like Nos. 28 and 194, a translation of Horace's *Carmina*, ii. 10 (given on pp. 152–153, above).

18 *Of lofty ruing towers the fals the feller be.* Obviously *ruing* is a printer's error for *rising*, since the poet was translating Horace's "celsae . . . turres." He means, "the falling of lofty-rising towers is more terrible (than the falling of low towers)."

28 *Ceast siluer sound, &c.* For the meaning of this line see the translations at 26. 37–38 and 151. 22–23, as well as the Latin quoted in a note to the latter passage.

33 (No. 296) *The praise of a true frende.* Not in *A* (No. [254] in *B–I*, sigs. Cc4ᵛ–Dd in *BC*, N8ᵛ–O in *D–G*, Oᵛ–O2 in *H*, N3–N3ᵛ in *I*). There is a copy in MS. Sloane 1896, fols. 40ᵛ–42, with the following variants:

> 244. 33 *Title:*　　A true freind is a rare Juell
> 　　35 that] doth:　　weyes] wey
> 　　36 by . . . rise] is worthy to aryse
> 245. 5 to forgo] for to goe
> 　　11 alayde] alayed
> 　　13 thy] thine
> 　　20 loues] loueth
> 　　24 haue] fynde
> 　　25 that thou can craue] thou doe it mynde
> 　　29 sayth] sayeth

The old annotator in *I* (Bodleian) notes, "Taken out of Tullye," referring, I suppose, to Cicero's *De Amicitia.* Many of the phrases, too, could well have been taken from "Of a Happy Life," chapter xviii, in Seneca's *Morals.* On the anagram (*W–W–I–T–A*) of Wyatt formed by the initial letters of the first five stanzas see the notes to 230. 22 n.

245. 29 *Such man to man a God, &c.* I have found no examples of this proverb, though Professor Kittredge reminds me of a similar statement in Virgil's *Eclogues*, i. 7, "erit ille mihi semper deus." As *an other self to thee* in line 28 proves, the author had in mind the *De Amicitia*, xxi, 80: "quod nisi idem in amicitiam transferetur, verus amicus numquam reperietur: est enim is qui est tamquam alter idem."

34 (No. 297) *Of the vanitie of mans lyfe.* Not in *A* (No. [257] in *B–I*, sigs. Dd2–Dd2ᵛ in *BC*, O2–O2ᵛ in *D–G*, O2ᵛ–O3 in *H*, N4ᵛ in *I*). A copy in MS. Sloane 1896, fol. 42, has the following variants:

> 245. 37 Whereon] wherupon
> 　　40 elde] age
> 246. 2 vnto] into
> 　　5 whylome] sometymes
> 　　11 rasde] rased:　　adowne] doune
> 　　13 caryon] body

246. 16 (No. 298) *The louer not regarded, &c.* Not in *A* (No. [258] in *B–I*, sigs. Dd2^v–Dd3 in *BC*, O2^v–O3 in *D–G*, O3–O3^v in *H*, N5 in *I*).

247. 11 *With cost.* Read *Which cost* with *D–G*.

15 *derst you brake.* For *durst* read *erst* with *C+*.

17 (No. 299) *The complaint of a woman, &c.* Not in *A* (No. [259] in *B–I*, sigs. Dd3 in *BC*, O3 in *D–G*, O3^v in *H*, N5–N5^v in *I*).

35 (No. 300) *The louer being made thrall, &c.* Not in *A* (No. [260] in *B–I*, sigs. Dd3–Dd3^v in *BC*, O3–O3^v in *D–G*, O4 in *H*, N5^v in *I*).

248. 16 (No. 301) *The diuers and contrarie passions, &c.* Not in *A* (No. [261] in *B–I*, sigs. Dd3^v in *BC*, O3^v in *D–G*, O4 in *H*, N5^v–N6 in *I*). The poem is an imitation of the Petrarchan sonnet that Wyatt translated in No. 49, or perhaps of No. 49 itself.

34 (No. 302) *The testament of the hawthorne.* Not in *A* (No. [262] in *B–I*, sigs. Dd3^v–Dd4^v in *BC*, O3^v–O4^v in *D–G*, O4–O5 in *H*, N6–N7 in *I*). Tottel or his editor gave this poem its title from the first line, interpreting *haw* as *hawthorn*. With that interpretation the *N. E. D.* agrees, though it has no further example before 1821. But (as Berdan, *Early Tudor Poetry*, p. 434 n., observes) the poem has no connection whatever with a hawthorn, and "I Sely Haw" evidently means something like "I, unfortunate worthless man." The testament-form suggests, ultimately, French influence. For a genuine tree-testament, this time of a "pore crabbe-tre," see Thomas Wright's *Songs and Ballads*, pp. 169–171 (Roxburghe Club, 1860).

249. 24 *she will withsaue.* That is, vouchsafe, as in Hall's *The Courte of Vertue*, 1565, F5^v, K6 ("O lorde witsafe my voyce to here," "If thou witsafe nowe me to save"), and Whetstone's *The Honorable Reputation of a Souldier*, 1585, A4^v ("And if this Booke, you do witsafe to reade").

250. 36 (No. 303) *The louer in dispeire, &c.* Not in *A* (No. [263] in *B–I*, sigs. Dd4^v–Ee in *BC*, O4^v–O5 in *D–G*, O5^v in *H*, N7 in *I*).

39 *how do ye washe?* Rhyme demands *waste*.

251. 29 (No. 304) *Of his maistresse .m. B.* Not in *A* (No. [264] in *B–I*, sigs. Ee–Ee2 in *BC*, O5–O6 in *D–G*, O5^v–O6^v in *H*, N7–N8 in *I*). The lady's name was apparently Bays. An imitation of this poem, also on a Mistress Bays, will be found in the *Paradise*, pp. 60–61.

253. 14 (No. 305) *The louer complaineth, &c.* Not in *A* (No. [265] in *B–I*, sigs. Ee2–Ee2^v in *BC*, O6–O6^v in *D–G*, O6^v–O7 in *H*, N8–N8^v in *I*).

16 *the serpent* is, of course, Python, in memory of his conquest over which Phoebus Apollo founded the Pythian games.

19 *The story* of Apollo and Daphne is that told in Ovid's *Metamorphoses*, 1. 452–567.

22 *This Cupide hath a shaft of kinde.* Cf. 6.6–7 n., and Thomas Watson, *The Hekatompathia*, 1582, sonnet 63 (ed. Arber, p. 99):

> Loue hath two shaftes, the one of beaten gold,
> By stroake wherof a sweete effect is wrought:
> The other is of lumpishe leaden mould,
> And worketh none effect, but what is nought.

253. 36 *He burnt with heat, she felt no fire.* Cf. Turbervile, *Tragical Tales* [*ca.* 1574], 1587 (1837 reprint, p. 20), "She felt no flame, when he, good man, did burne."

37, 39 *fro, so.* These words violate the rhyme-scheme, which is *abacbc*.

254. 14 (No. 306) *A praise of .m. M.* Not in *A* (No. [266] in *B–I*, sigs. Ee2ᵛ–Ee3 in *BC*, O6ᵛ–O7 in *D–G*, O7–O7ᵛ in *H*, N8ᵛ–O in *I*). Perhaps this poem suggested that called "In the prayse of a beautifull and vertuous Virgin, whose name begins with M.", in the *Gorgeous Gallery*, 1578, pp. 56–57. Nott (C. 60. O. 13) wrote: "Why not M:ʳˢ Markham. The name would suit the metre: In w:ᶜʰ case this piece would belong to John Harington. The harmony of the versification, and the delicate taste of some of the thoughts and expressions might justify the conjecture." The conjecture seems to me good, though Nott himself later crossed out the note.

16 *Of right my thought.* The reading should be *Of right methought*, as in *C+*.

27 *to seme.* Rhyme and sense require *to seen* (that is, to be seen).

40 *As rage of flame not Nilus stremes, &c.* Professor Kittredge comments: "For *not* read *nor:* 'Her looks would impress in hearts of flint such feelings as neither the rage of fire nor the streams of the Nile could increase in as many years as Nestor's.' This is merely hyperbole for the maximum of such feelings, which are so intense that the most powerful agencies could never intensify them further."

255. 6 (No. 307) *An old louer, &c.* Not in *A* (No. [267] in *B–I*, sigs. Ee3 in *BC*, O7 in *D–G*, O7ᵛ–O8 in *H*, O in *I*).

12–15 *But trill the ball before my face, &c.* Evidently imitated by Melbancke in *Philotimus*, 1583, C2ᵛ: "What trylle the ball againe my Iacke, and be contente to make some play, and I will lulle the on my lappe, with hey be bird now say not nay."

38 *Is like to bring a foole to bed.* Proverbial, as in Breton's *Pasquils Mistresse*, 1600, B3ᵛ, "if her beautie . . . like a glasse, be euery woodcockes gaze, By fond affectes to bring a foole to bed."

256. 2 (No. 308) *The louer forsaketh, &c.* Not in *A* (No. [268] in *B–I*, sigs. Ee3ᵛ in *BC*, O7ᵛ in *D–G*, O8–O8ᵛ in *H*, O–Oᵛ in *I*). The poem is based largely on proverbs and hawking-terms.

38 (No. 309) *The louer preferreth his lady, &c.* Not in *A* (No. [269] in *B–I*, sigs. Ee3ᵛ–Ee4 in *BC*, O7ᵛ–O8 in *D–G*, O8ᵛ–P in *H*, Oᵛ–O2 in *I*). A court lady named Arundell is mentioned in a poem attributed to Richard Edwards. She appears as a maid of honor in the expense-account of Mary I's

funeral (see Leicester Bradner, *The Life and Poems of Richard Edwards*, 1927, p. 95), and was perhaps Mary, daughter of the Earl of Arundel, later the wife of Thomas Howard, Duke of Norfolk. She may have been the Arundel referred to in No. 309; but compare Turbervile's praise of Elizabeth Arundel in his *Epitaphes*, 1567, pp. 14–15.

257. 10 *Priams sonnes* should probably read *Priams sonne*, as the reference seems to be to Paris (and Helen).

258. 2 (No. 310) *The louer lamenteth, &c.* Not in *A* (No. [270] in *B–I*, sigs. Ee4ᵛ–Ff in *BC*, O8ᵛ–P in *D–G*, P–Pᵛ in *H*, O2–O2ᵛ in *I*).

38 *Let dead care for the dead.* Cf. Matthew viii. 22, Luke ix. 60.

APPENDIX

ADDITIONAL NOTES

Originally printed as the first part of "Marginalia on Two Elizabethan Poetical Miscellanies" in *Joseph Quincy Adams Memorial Studies* (1948), pp. 457 ff.; reprinted here by kind permission of the Folger Shakespeare Library. A few notes calling attention to mistakes in the first printing have been omitted, since appropriate corrections have now been made in the type. A number of notes have been inserted in brackets to show the present (1964) location of copies of sixteenth-century editions which have changed hands or come to light since 1948; this information has been supplied by Professor William A. Jackson, Librarian of the Houghton Library of Harvard University.

References are to pages of volume II, but page and line references (like 18.20) to the text of volume I have sometimes also been given. The Additional Notes are not covered by the Glossarial Index.

ADDITIONS TO THE INTRODUCTION

4 The conventional statement that Tottel's was "the first printed anthology" needs qualification. See the discussions by R. H. Griffith, E. M. Tillyard, and R. A. Law in *The Times Literary Supplement*, July 5, July 12, 1928, pp. 504, 520, December 26, 1929, p. 1097; Griffith and Law's "'A Boke of Balettes' and 'The Courte of Venus,'" University of Texas *Studies in English*, No. 10 (1930), pp. 5–12; and Sir E. K. Chambers, *Sir Thomas Wyatt and Some Collected Studies* (1933), pp. 111–9, 207–28.

12 [The second copy of *C* now belongs to the Carl H. Pforzheimer Foundation, New York City, and the third to Mr. A. A. Houghton, Jr., New York City.]

19 For the identical error of repetition of lines mentioned in note 2 see Nicholas Breton, *The workes of a young wyt* (1577), G1–G1ᵛ.

21 [The second copy of *D* is now in the library of Mr. H. Bradley Martin, New York City.]

24 Two other copies of the fourth edition, 1559 (*D**), are now known: (2) Lord Harlech, Brogyntyn; (3) Mr. Carl H. Pforzheimer, Purchase, New York. John Hayward, *English Poetry, A Catalogue of First & Early Editions* (1947), p. 8, says that Lord Harlech's copy is a "variant issue with undated title-page," and that the Pforzheimer copy, also undated, agrees with it in everything except for "L1 being signed with a single period as in the dated issue." [Copy (1) now belongs to Indiana University; (2) to the Estate of Howard Samuels, London; (3) to the Carl H. Pforzheimer Foundation.]

27–28 [A fourth copy of *E* is in the library of Shrewsbury School, Shrewsbury, England.]

30 A copy of the sixth edition, 1567, was sold in Topham Beauclerk's sale (*Bibliotheca Beauclerkiana* [1781], lot 3453) for £3. The cataloguer notes: "This Copy was presented by Mr. Tho. Rawlinson to Mr. Matt. Prior, and by him given to the late Mr. West, P. R. S." It is untraced, as are the Christ Church, Oxford (stolen), and the Burgh-Heber-Utterson copies.

31 [Copy (4) of *G* is now at the Carl H. Pforzheimer Foundation; copy (5) is in the New York Public Library. Two other copies (6, 7), one of them imperfect, are in the Folger Shakespeare Library, Washington, D. C.]

33 Four other copies of the 1585 edition are now known: (7) Matthew Prior–J. M. Rice–Britwell–C. H. Pforzheimer; (8) Lord Fitzwilliam, Wentworth Woodhouse; (9) Heber-Utterson-Corser-Harmsworth-Folger Library; (10) Lord Feilding–A. A. Houghton, Jr. (see *The Times Literary Supplement*, July 16, 1938, p. 484, and Edgar H. Wells and Company, Catalogue 47 [March, 1940], item 102). John Hayward, *English Poetry*, p. 9, states that another copy, "said to be at Arundel Castle, cannot be traced." [Copy (2) is now in the Folger Shakespeare Library; (7) is at the Carl H. Pforzheimer Foundation; (8) is in the library of Mr. Robert H. Taylor, Princeton, New Jersey. An imperfect copy is at Yale University.]

35 Another copy (Tooke-Heber-Utterson) of the 1587 edition is at Arundel Castle; it is described by Hayward, *English Poetry*, p. 9. [Copy (2) is now at the Carl H. Pforzheimer Foundation. Five other copies of *I* are known: (6) Inner Temple Library, London; (7) Aberdeen University, Scotland; (8) Bristol Reference Library, England; (9) Hull University, England; (10) Preston Public Library, England.]

37 The supposititious edition of 1569 is listed in Sir Egerton Brydges' edition of *England's Helicon* (1812), p. ix, whence Nott may have got his misinformation.

37–42 My account of the editions of 1717 has been corrected in certain small, but interesting, points by Professor George Sherburn's note, "Songes and Sonnettes," *The Times Literary Supplement*, July 24, 1930, p. 611.

The title-page of the 1728 edition ends: "Printed for HENRY CURLL in *Clement's-Inn*–/ Paſſage. 1728. Price Two Shillings./" The last three words have been almost completely erased from the British Museum copy, and hence did not show in the photostat which I followed, but are clear enough in the copy which I bought in December, 1929. In it, too, the Wyatt title-page correctly comes after p. 32.

44 The Lehigh University Library has a copy of the first volume of Percy's 1808 edition, as well as a small part of the second volume: see *Notes and Queries*, cxlviii (1925), 349. Those interested in Percy's edition should consult Heinz Marwell's *Thomas Percy* (Göttingen, 1934); Hans Hecht, *Englische Studien*, lxx (1935), 330 f.; Arthur Tillotson's *The Correspondence*

of Thomas Percy & Edmond Malone (1944), pp. 141, 214, 224 f.; and especially Cleanth Brooks's "The History of Percy's Edition of Surrey (*Tottel's Miscellany*)," *The Correspondence of Thomas Percy & Richard Farmer* (1946), pp. 175–200.

50 In the preface to *Heliconia* (1815), volume i, Thomas Park says, "A complete edition of the poems of Lord Surrey is now preparing by Dr. Nott, who possesses every requisite for the undertaking."

59–61 A rechecking of Arber's reprint with the original shows that to my list of his variations (as given in volume i, pages 329–35) the following additions or corrections should be made:

64.24 thy] they	112.16 gan] can
72.32 me,] me	117.6 death,] death
76.31 Arber has "Lo(uer)."	135.20 sir] Sir
83.28 scarse] scarce	156.12 farre,] farre.
33 loude?] loude:	202.15 Vlisses] Vlysses
101.30 tyme] time	213.2 of] or
108.2 sir] Sir	237.31 My] May

65 f. Compare Thomas Fuller, *The History of the Worthies of England* (1662), p. 81 ("Kent"): "Sir THOMAS WIAT, Knight, commonly called the *Elder*, to disting[u]ish him from Sir *Thomas Wiat* (raiser of the Rebellion (so all call it) for it did not succeed). . . ."

72 See also the accounts of Surrey and Geraldine in William Winstanley's *The Lives Of the most Famous English Poets* (1687), pp. 49–56; Charles Gildon's *The Complete Art of Poetry* (1718), i, 83; Theophilus Cibber's *The Lives of the Poets of Great Britain and Ireland* (1753), i, 46–53; Anna Jameson's *Memoirs of the Loves of the Poets* (1829; 1879), chap. xii, pp. 144–53; Edward Moxon's *Sonnets* (1835), p. 16; R. F. Housman's *A Collection of English Sonnets* (1835), p. 305; *Atkinson's Casket* (Philadelphia), April, 1836, p. 175, reprinting from the Dublin *Satirist* (which I have not seen) a poem called "The Earl of Surrey to the Lord of Kildare's Daughter"; Stanhope Busby's *Lectures on English Poetry* (1837), p. 25; and so on. Mrs. Cooper wrote on Surrey in the first edition of *The Muses Library* (1737), i, 55 f.

75 For Geraldine's portrait (by Hans Eworth) see the publications of the Walpole Society, ii (1912–3), 31, and plate XXIIIa. Mrs. C. C. Stopes, *The Life of Henry, Third Earl of Southampton* (1922), pp. 495 f., says that Geraldine married Browne when he was about forty-three or forty-four, not sixty.

76 Richard Sherry, *A treatise of Schemes & Tropes*, A3–A3ᵛ (the preface is dated December 13, 1550), praises the English of Chaucer, Gower, Lydgate, Elyot, and adds: "What shuld I speake of that ornamente Syr Thomas Wyat? which beside most excellente gyftes bothe of fortune and bodye, so flouryshed in the eloquence of hys natiue tongue, that as he passed therin those wyth whome he lyued, so was he lykelye to haue bene equal

wyth anye other before hym, had not enuious death to hastely beriued vs of thys iewel."

79 For a further discussion of whether or not Grimald's blank verse was published before Surrey's see Herbert Hartman, *Surrey's Fourth Boke of Virgill* (1933). He dates the book (p. xiv) "*circa* September 1554."

Poems ascribed to unknown authors ("Incerti Authoris") will also be found in MS. Additional 38823, fols. 8, 48, MS. Harleian 7392, fols. 24ᵛ–25, and *Naps upon Parnassus* (1658), A4; while a quotation in Robert Allot's *England's Parnassus* (1600, ed. Charles Crawford [1913], p. 246) is signed "I[ncerti]. Authoris," and MS. Additional 28635, fol. 55, contains "Certayne verses made by uncertayne autours wrytten out of Charleton his booke." In this connection I observe that in MS. Additional 27407, fol. 129, Sir Walter Raleigh's "Wrong not, dear empress of my heart," is signed "Finis quod sumbodie."

80 Another of the "uncertain authors" has been identified as John Hall, from whose book, *The Proverbs of Solomon* (1549), A5–A7, Nos. 285 and 286 were taken. See my note, "Tottel's 'Miscellany' and John Hall," in *The Times Literary Supplement*, January 14, 1932, p. 28.

Four other poems ascribed to Sir John Cheke occur in MS. Additional 28635, fols. 133ᵛ–134.

81 There is a poem signed "Qᵈ Norton" in Huntington Library MS. H.M.8 (folios not marked). For further poems (note 1) of John Harington see Sir John Harington's *Orlando Furioso* (1591), F3, N5.

82 On Bryan see Elsa Chapin in University of Chicago *Abstracts of Theses, Humanistic Series*, viii (1932), 428–33.

92 These arguments about Henry Harington as an editor have been upset by my friend Professor Ruth Hughey. Her brilliant article, "The Harington Manuscript at Arundel Castle and Related Documents," *The Library*, 4th Ser., xv (1935), 388–444, contains many other new facts of great value for students of Tottel's book.

98 The statement that "it is practically certain that all the titles in ...[Tottel's *Miscellany*] are editorial insertions" needs qualifying so far as concerns Grimald. A. W. Reed, in *The Year's Work in English Studies*, x (1931), 156, correctly points out that "no one but Grimald could have supplied the titles of many of those [poems] that are his. There is no evidence, for example, except in the title of the poem on his mother that her name was Annes." The point is well taken, but the appearance of titles composed by Grimald does not in the least indicate that Grimald edited the book ("there is, of course, no proof that Grimald was Tottel's editor," Reed agrees). The editor — whether "Tottel himself, . . . his 'corrector of the press,' or ... some other agent employed by him," as I say on page 94 — perhaps followed Grimald's holograph copies, or else copies made from them. The fact that, in so doing, he printed the names and initials of Grimald's

relatives and friends and patrons — that is, made public property of strictly personal verse — very likely caused Grimald to protest to Tottel and to demand the exclusion of this verse from the second edition. Grimald's authorship of the titles is, in my opinion, further convincing evidence tending to prove that he could not have edited the book; but according to Hallett Smith, *The Huntington Library Quarterly*, ix (1946), 234 n., none is needed, since Miss Hughey's article (see above) "disposes of the theory that Grimald was the editor."

106 On the diction of the Tottel poets see the excellent discussion in Veré L. Rubel's *Poetic Diction in the English Renaissance* (1941), pp. 47–95.

108 The assertion that Barnabe Googe wrote no formal sonnets is incorrect: see P. N. U. Harting, *English Studies*, xi (1929), 100–02, and H. H. Hudson, *Modern Language Notes*, xlv (1930), 542 f., and *Publications of the Modern Language Association of America*, xlviii (1933), 293 f. The word *sonnets* (compare note 2) also appears in the section headings at 206.1 and 211.1.

112 In the *Jahrbuch der deutschen Shakespeare-Gesellschaft*, xliv (1908), 154 f., Joseph de Perott has written "Über die Quelle von Henry Pettowe's 'Hero and Leander.'"

120 Another objector to the miscellany was Archbishop Matthew Parker, who in preliminary verses to his own work, *The whole Psalter translated into English Metre* (1567?), writes,

> Ye songes so nice: ye sonnets all,
>   of lothly louers layes:
> Ye worke mens myndes: but bitter gall,
>   by phansies peuishe playes.

On sig. G2ᵛ, however, he refers to "Henrie Haward Earle of Surrie in his Ecclesiastices," quoting four lines.

121 Compare Edward Phillips, *Theatrum Poetarum* (1685), 2C10ᵛ, "*Henry Howard* . . . deserves . . . , had he his due, the particular Fame of Learning, Wit, and Poetic Fancy, which he was thought once to have made sufficiently appear in his publish'd Poems, which nevertheless are now so utterly forgoten, as though they had never been Extant, so Antiquated at present, and as it were out of fashion is the style and way of Poetry of that Age."

122 Compare Lewis Theobald, *The Censor*, iii (1717), 184,

[The first book is] a Reviv'd Collection [1717 (K)] of *Poems* of the Earl of *Surrey*, Sir *Thomas Wiat*, and some other of their Contemporaries, who have stood the Test of about a *Century* and an *half*; and who, tho' under the Disadvantage of a Language not entirely polish'd, will, from their Strokes of Nature, deserve to please in every Age,

and Charles Gildon, *The Laws of Poetry* (1721), p. 32, "After him [Chaucer] we had no man that made any figure in *English* verse, till the *Earl* of *Surrey*, in the time of *Henry* the eighth, who very much improv'd our *English* numbers." George Ellis, *Specimens of the Early English Poets* (1790), p. 1, like Walpole, remarks that Surrey "is considered as the first English classic."

ADDITIONS TO THE NOTES

131 Partial translations of the Petrarchan sonnet, "Zephiro torna," and so on, are made in Nicholas Yonge's *Musica Transalpina* (1588) and Thomas Watson's *Italian Madrigals Englished* (1590).

133 Other examples of the proverb are in Robert Cawdrey's *A Treasurie Or Storehouse of Similies* (1600), B3ᵛ, "Like as they that go about to make Lyons tame, do vse to beate little whelpes before them, and to make them to couch, that so the Lyons seeing, they may do so also"; *Gods Handyworke in Wonders* (1615), C3, "But it pleased God, to beate the Dogge before the Lyon, to punish the least sinners before the greatest"; and Stephen Jerome's *The Arraignement of the Whole Creature* (1631), H3ᵛ, "as the *Lyon* is *instructed*, when the *Dog* is beat before him." See also *Modern Language Notes*, lv (1940), 209 f., 481.

136 "Peirce Plainman, an obscure Gentleman," in *A Latter Discovery of Ireland* (1646), N4, quotes No. 8 as follows:

Ireland hath long fostered two as Noble Families as is perhaps of *Europe*, to wit, the *Geraldines*, and the *Boteliers:* The house of the *Geraldines* is somewhat touched in the Sonnet of Surry, upon the Earl of *Kildares* Sister, *viz.*

> From Tuscane *came my Ladyes worthy race;*
> Fair Florence *was sometime her ancient seat:*
> The Western Isle, whose pleasant Shore doth face
> Wilde Cambres Cliffes, *did give her lively heat.*

144 Compare with 16.14 f. and 3.8 John Dennys, *The Secrets of Angling* (1613; Thomas Westwood's reprint [1883], p. 24):

> And blustering *Boreas* with his chilling cold,
> Vnclothed hath the Trees of Sommers greene;
> And Woods, and groues, are naked to behold,
> Of Leaues and Branches now dispoyled cleane:
> So that their fruitfull stocks they doe vnfold,
> And lay abroad their of-spring to be seene.

146 With 18.20 f. compare Thomas Howell, *Newe Sonets, and pretie Pamphlets (ca.* 1568), F3 (*Poems*, ed. A. B. Grosart [privately printed, 1879], p. 149), "Deare Ladies steppe your foote to myne,/ To mourne with me your hartes inclyne." With the conceit beginning at 19.41 compare the novel *Eromena* (1683), B6ᵛ: "*Eromena* . . . , a Lady that Nature only created for Man to wonder at; and when created, she broke her Mould, so that since she has not been able to produce her equal."

150 With 25.9 compare George Chapman, *The Widow's Tears* (*ca.* 1608), III, i (*Plays and Poems*, ed. T. M. Parrott [1914], ii, 397), "What, wrapp'd in careless cloak." In John Wayland's edition, *The tretise of Morall Phylosophy, contayning the sayinges of the wyse. Newlye perused and augmented by William Baldwyn fyrst auctoure therof*, n.d. (1555?), M5ᵛ, No. 27 is headed, "The thinges that cause a quiet life, written by Marciall, and Englished by lord Henry Erle of Surrey."

152 Compare the translation of the original of No. 28 ("You better sure shall liue, not euermore") given in Sidney's *Arcadia* (1598), 2R4ᵛ–2R5 (A. Feuillerat's Sidney [1922], ii, 307).

154 H. H. Hudson (*Modern Language Notes*, xlv [1930], 543) observes that Surrey's first line (28.3) translates the epitaph placed on the Milan tomb of Jacopo Trivulzio (died 1518), which Camden gives in his *Remains* (1614), p. 359.

156 The exact words of Peter Betham, *The preceptes of warre* (1544), A7, are: "Wyate was a worthye floure of our tounge, as appereth by the mornefulle ballet made of hys death in Englysshe, whyche is mooste wyttye fyne and eloquent." They occur in his dedicatory epistle, which is dated December, 1543. For an explanation of 28.3 f. as hendiadys see S. G. Putt, *Modern Language Review*, xxxiv (1939), 66 f.

159 Compare 30.28 with the *Aeneid* I.203, "forsan et haec olim meminisse juvabit."

173 A greatly changed copy of No. 59 was included in John Attey's *The First Booke of Ayres* (1622; E. H. Fellowes, *English Madrigal Verse* [1920], p. 310).

175 John Grange, *The Golden Aphroditis* (1577), G4ᵛ, combines lines 44.13, 20 and 209.24. He also borrows at G3 seven lines (209.24–6, 31 f., 35 f.) from No. 265. See my article in *Harvard Studies and Notes in Philology and Literature*, xvi (1934), 194 f.

209 Compare with No. 114, James Sandford, *Houres of recreation* (1576), B2:

One *Marke Antonio Batistei*, an Italian, hauyng lost fyue hundreth crounes in a drowned shippe, went as desperate to hang himselfe: But beeing aboute to fasten the roape to a beame, he founde there hidden by chaunce a thousande crownes: wherfore he beeyng exceeding ioyfull and merrie, tooke them, and exchaungyng the haulter for the crownes, went awaye. Nowe beholde, not long after, the owner came thyther to see them and handle them, who not fynding them, but in theyr place seeyng a halter, was ouercome with so greate sorowe, that withoute any more adoe hee hoong hymselfe with it.

Variants of the story occur in William Painter's *The Palace of Pleasure* (1567), tome ii, novel 11, and in the popular ballad of "The Heir of Linne."

220 With 88.25 compare Sir Thomas Chaloner, *The praise of Folie* (1549), D4ᵛ, I1, R1, "wisemen be as vnapte for all publike offices and af-

faires, *as an asse is to finger an harpe,*" "An other *lyke an asse to the harpe,*"
"these iayes would chatter this greke tau*n*t agaynst him, *An asse to the harpe.*"

227 With 96.7 compare Thomas Nashe, *Pierce Penilesse* (1592; *Works*,
ed. R. B. McKerrow [1910], i, 181), "you had been as faire as the floure of
the frying pan."

228 The Latin epigram translated in No. 133 was usually included in
fifteenth- and sixteenth-century editions of Virgil (e.g., the 1507 ed., Paris,
fol. 197ᵛ), and it appeared also in John Penkethman's translation, *The
Epigrams Of P. Virgilius Maro* (1624), B7ᵛ–B8. John Grange, *The Golden
Aphroditis* (1577), quotes a line of it, referring to "*Virgill* in his Epigrams"
(B1), and translates it entire on L4. One line is quoted in E. K.'s "April"
gloss to Spenser's *The Shepherds' Calendar* (1579), and another in "Novem-
ber." Thomas Heywood, *Gunaikeion* (1624), F6–F6ᵛ, gives both the Latin
(by "Virgill") and a poetical translation. See G. P. Shannon, *Modern Lan-
guage Quarterly*, viii (1947), 43–5, for speculations on the exact Latin source
of "Nicholas Grimald's List of the Muses."

229 H. B. Lathrop, *Translations from the Classics into English* (Uni-
versity of Wisconsin *Studies in Language and Literature*, No. 35, 1933), pp.
102 f., gives another source for the "saying" at 97.29 — Aulus Gellius, *Noctes*
XVI.2. For 98.8 he cites (p. 103) the same work, XI.2. With 98.30 compare
also the *Greek Anthology* XIV.101 (I cite the numbering of the Loeb Classical
Library edition), and Diogenes Laertius (trans. C. D. Yonge [1901], book i,
pp. 41 f.).

230 (99.5) The date of *Wits A. B. C.* is 1608, the author Richard West.

231 With the opening lines of No. 139 compare the *Greek Anthology*
V.95, and Ausonius (*Opera Omnia* [1823], p. 140), Epigram 121 ("Tres fuerant
Charites: sed dum mea Lesbia vixit, Quatuor: ut periit, tres numerantur
item").

237 Translations of the originals of Nos. 151 and 152 ("What life is
the liefest — The needy is full of woe," "What life list ye to lead — in good
Cytie & towne") are in MS. Harleian 6910, fol. 166ᵛ (*ca.* 1596). Others are
given in Peter Motteux's *The Gentleman's Journal*, December, 1693, pp. 411 f.

238 In the following passage from *Euphues. The Anatomy of Wit*
(1578), Lyly (*Complete Works*, ed. R. W. Bond [1902], i, 197) is perhaps
summarizing Grimald's poem (No. 154):

I cannot tell, whether the immortall Gods haue bestowed any gift vpon mortall
men, either more noble, or more necessary, then friendship. Is ther any thing in the
world to be reputed (I will not say compared) to friendship? Can any treasure in
this transitorie pilgrimage, be of more valewe then a friend? in whose bosome thou
maist sleepe secure without feare, whom thou maist make partner of all thy secrets
without suspition of fraude, and pertaker of all thy misfortune without mistrust of
fleeting, who will accompt thy bale his bane, thy mishap his misery, the pricking of
thy finger, the percing of his heart.

240 The Latin original of No. 155 occurs in nearly all the early editions of Virgil, and is translated in John Penkethman's 1624 version of Virgil's epigrams.

244 On Amphinomus and Anapus (III.27) see the *Greek Anthology* III.17; on Cleobis and Biton (III.30), III.18.

255 With 120.8 compare George Whetstone, *Aurelia* (1593), A4, "*Sweete* Pithos *tongue, and* Dians *chaste consent.*"

257 Lines 124.8–11 occur also in MS. Harleian 7392, fol. 42. 124.13 is based on the Latin proverb, "Delphinum natare doces."

260 With the poem beginning at 126.26 compare the verse and the emblem in Henry Peacham's *Minerva Britanna* (1612), 2B2.

265 The plot of No. 181 is retold at considerable length in Humphrey King's *An Halfe-penny-worth of Wit*, "The third Impression" (1613), C3ᵛ–D1. King begins,

> Hast thou not heard a song of *Phillida*,
> Of *Herpilus*, and eke *Coren?*
>   why these, my sonne, be they.
> The one is *Coren*, that once tooke
>   delight his Hawkes to lure. . . .

267 No. 185 is apparently imitated, or summarized, by a poem (No. 28) in *The Paradise of Dainty Devices* (1576), C3ᵛ–C4 (ed. Rollins [1927], pp. 30 f.).

268 With 141.19 compare a poem in MS. Harleian 6910, fol. 100 (*ca.* 1596), beginning, "Now what shalbee, shall bee: there is no choyse"; Humphrey King, *An Halfe-penny-worth of Wit* (1613), A3ᵛ, "that which will bee shall bee"; Beaumont and Fletcher, *The Scornful Lady* (*ca.* 1610), III, i, 279, "What must be, must be."

271 W. L. Renwick, in *The Modern Language Review*, xxv (1930), 487, suggests a connection between No. 193 and Alciati's *Emblemata* (Paris, 1618), No. 108, p. 489, "In Studiosum captum Amore."

274 Brian Melbancke, *Philotimus* (1583), R2, borrows 154.2 f. thus: "*Cynthia* could not call her son *Hyppolitus* out of Hell, nor *Theseus* his frende *Perithous.*"

277 Thomas Seymour, Lord High Admiral, was beheaded on March 20, 1549. In the notes he is confused with his brother Edward, Duke of Somerset, the Protector, who was beheaded on January 22, 1552.

278 Melbancke, *Philotimus* (1583), D2–D2ᵛ, borrows 157.36 f. thus: "*Cresus* . . . was imprisoned as a captiue, shackled with boultes, and faine to yeelde his goods into his enemies handes."

280 Expressions similar to 160.8 will be found in George Whetstone's *Sir Phillip Sidney* (1586), C3 (*Frondes Caducae*, Auchinleck Press, 1816); Nicholas Breton's *Strange Fortunes* (1600; *Works*, ed. Grosart [1879], ii, *d*, 5); and *The Arbor of Amorous Devices* (1597), B4ᵛ. See also the last page of

William Webster's *The Most Pleasant And Delightful Historie of Curan . . .
and . . . Argentile* (1617).

283 L. J. Jones, in *The Times Literary Supplement*, June 11, 1925,
p. 400, writes: "I possess a painting by Francesco Albani (1578–1660) which
is generally acknowledged to be an illustration of 'Cupid's Assault.'" He
thinks that Lord Vaux's poem (No. 211) had an Italian original. "A learned
friend has an impression of having seen an Italian poem entitled 'La Fortezza
del Cupido,' but is unable to find it."

287 With 168.7 compare George Whetstone, *Aurelia* (1593), B2:

in sundry places in proper colours was ingraued his deuise, which was *A Holly tree,
full of red beries: and in the same, a fluttering Mauis fast limed to the bowes.* with this
posie in french, *Qui me nourit, me destruit:* And in verie deede, the beries of the tree
feedeth this bird, and the barke maketh Lime to fetter her.

For Nauplius (168.23) see also the *Greek Anthology* IX.289, 429.

290 Dr. F. B. Williams, Jr., points out to me the similarity of lines
172.1–7 to Chaucer's *Troilus and Criseyde*, iii, 1373–9.

293 With 181.23 compare Robert Allot, *Wits Theater of the little
World* (1599), K7v–K8:

Estrasco a Romaine, borne dumbe, loued Verona a Latine, borne also dumbe, who
lyking each other, came & visited each other, by the space of thirty yeeres, vvithout
the witting of any person, then died the husband of the Lady Verona, & the wife of
Estrasco, they married, & of them descended the noble linage of the Scipios. *Aurelius.*

294 With 181.36 f. compare John Hall, *The Proverbs of Solomon* (1549),
C4v, E8, "And as the riuers greate & depe encrease by rage of rayne," "The
fluddes . . . swel by rage of raine."

315 (211.23) Melbancke, *Philotimus* (1583), X2, makes Laida write
to her faithless lover, "I gaue thee that, which then I had not, and thou
receiuedst y^t, which thou tookst not" — that is, her maidenhead.

317 No. 271 is copied from the Corpus Christi MS. in the eighteenth-
century MS. Additional 5843, fol. 72, with the note: "The following *Copy of
Verses*, supposed by Mr Nesmith, *Fellow of Benet College*, to have been wrote
by *Cromwell Earl of Essex*, are in the *MS Library of that College, Miscellany Y*."

320 Marguerite Hearsey, *The Complaint of Henry Duke of Bucking-
ham* (Yale Studies in English, vol. lxxxvi [1936], p. 119), suggests that No. 278
was composed by Thomas Sackville.

322 Melbancke, *Philotimus* (1583), D1v, borrows 229.30 thus: "Then
take time while thou hast it, the haucke may checke y^t now coms faire to
fyst."

324 Another version of No. 286 is printed from Corpus Christi College
MS. No. clxviii in James Goodwin's *Six Ballads, with Burdens* (1844), pp. 1–3,
6–8 (Percy Society, vol. xiii), and attributed to Richard Cox, Bishop of Ely;
but see the note, above, on 80. Goodwin also observes (pp. xi f.) that the same

manuscript contains Nos. 125 and 271, signed "C. W." and "C." Other statements of the two ears, one tongue commonplace at 235.4 f. are in Richard Taverner's *Flores aliquot sententiarum ex variis collecti scriptoribus* (1540), A7ᵛ, William Baldwin's *A treatise of Morall Phylosophye* (1550), K7ᵛ, Isabella Whitney's *A sweete Nosegay* (1573), C4ᵛ, Lodowick Lloyd's *The pilgrimage of Princes* (1573), P1, James Sandford's *Houres of recreation* (1576), B1ᵛ, and Robert Hayman's *Certaine Epigrams* (1628), E1 (translated from John Owen).

329 A. W. Reed, in *The Year's Work in English Studies*, x (1931), 156, suggests that the Mistress M. of No. 306 was the Mistress Mancell praised in a poem by Richard Edwards (Thomas Park, *Nugae Antiquae* [1804], ii, 392–4; Leicester Bradner, *The Life and Poems of Richard Edwards* (Yale Studies in English, vol. lxxiv [1927], p. 102), and that Edwards also wrote No. 306.

GLOSSARIAL INDEX

References like 9 (8) or 112 (32) are to pages and lines of the text in volume I; if followed by an "n.," as 9 (8) n., 112 (32) n., a note on the word, or words, in question will be found in the present volume. References not followed by a figure, or figures, in parentheses are to pages of volume II. Initial *i* and *j*, *u* and *v*, are treated respectively as the same letter.

The glossary has been prepared with the idea of making readily accessible a large amount of lexicographical material (most of which, to be sure, offers no difficulties to any educated person) and of serving somewhat the same function as a concordance to the text of the miscellany.

A, interj., *ah*, 112 (38)

a, prep., *on (in)*, 118 (26), 138 (43), 139 (12), 161 (10)

A., D., Mistress, poems addressed to, 100 (23) n., 101 (17) n., 103 (9) n.

aback, hold, v. phr., *restrain*, 163 (32); put aback, *rejected*, 145 (29)

abate, v., *subtract*, 114 (32)

abbreviations, explanation of those, used, 127 ff.

abode, v., *suffered*, 19 (18)

abuse, the figure of: *see* catachresis

Acca Laurentia, 111 (35) n.

accited, v., *summoned*, 45 (6)

accompt, s., v., *account*, 13 (42), 22 (37), 150 (17), 229 (18), etc.

accumbred, pp. adj., *encumbered*, 72 (42)

Achilles, 47 (10) n., 106 (35) n., 113 (23), 181 (12)

acold, adj., 113 (10), 161 (10)

across, adv., *embracing (arms)*, 15 (28), 85 (16)

acrostic or anagram poems, examples of, 157 (2) n., 175 (34) n., 323

Actaeon, 94 (18)

adawth, v., *subdueth*, 151 (16) (the first example in the *N.E.D.*)

adieu, interj., 250 (38)

Admetus, king of Thessaly, and his (supposed) daughter, referred to, 188 (5)

Adonis ('Adone'), 95 (8)

adown, adv., *down*, 14 (21), 246 (11)

adrad, pp., *afraid*, 108 (5)

Adrianus, 168 (11) n.

adversair, s., *adversary*, 46 (36)

advertisement, s., *warning*, 31 (5)

Aeneas ('Ene,' 'Eneas'), 90 (17), 113 (24), 173 (13), 227 (40) n., 244

Aeneid, the: *see* Virgil

Aesop, fable of the pots by, 185 (39) n.

affect, affects, s., *love, passion*, 28 (23), 84 (42), 194 (2), 254 (39)

afore, adv., *before*, 92 (3), 142 (22), 205 (19)

afore, prep., 45 (6)

after, prep., *according to*, 105 (12)

afterdays, s., 114 (15)

afterfall, s., *later happening*, 111 (5)

afterweal, s., *future good fortune*, 210 (27)

against, prep., *before*, 191 (9). *See* ainst

Agamemnon's daughter, *Iphigenia*, 14 (22)

agazed, pp., *amazed*, 4 (11)

agilted: *see* aguilted

agrieved ('agreued'), pp., *distressed*, 8 (19), 32 (22)

Agrippa, Cornelius, 71

aguilted ('agilted'), pp., *made accessory to* (Latin *conscius*), 94 (31)

aie: *see* ay

aim, s., *(by) design*, 6 (9)

ainst, prep., *against*, 60 (32)

aknow, v., *recognize*, 118 (38)

Alamanni, Luigi, 105, 219, 237; poem by, translated, 216 ff.

Albertus Magnus, 133

Alcilia: *see* C. (J.)

Aldine editions, the, of Wyatt and Surrey, 53 f., 57, 103 n. 1

Alexander (Alisander) the Great, 27 (7), 86 (28), 116 (33), 117 (38), 153 f., 165; Zoroas and, a poem, 115 (8) n.

GLOSSARIAL INDEX

Arbor of Amorous Devices, The (by Breton [*q.v.*] and others), 109; borrowings of, from the miscellany, 256 f., 264 f.

Archaeologia, 220

Archilaus, Duke, and Hero, 113

arctic ('Artike'), adj., 90 (40)

areard, pp., *erected*, 113 (18)

Aretino, Pietro, 76, 95

Arge, i. e., *Argos, or Greece*, 111 (30)

Ariosto, 132, 136, 172, 175 f.

ark, s., *chest*, 27 (9)

Armin, Robert, 221, 227

armonie, s., *harmony*, 221 (22)

arow, adv., *in order*, 192 (19)

array ('aray'), s., *military order*, 152 (32), 164 (9)

art, s., *business, craft*, 46 (40)

Art of English Poesie, The (attributed to Puttenham), 120, 127; pronouncements of, on the miscellany, 137, 140, 142, 144, 146, 154, 164, 167, 169, 175, 179, 184 f., 188, 193, 198 f., 255, 261, 267, 272, 283, 287, 290, 312, 314, 321

Artike: *see* arctic

Arundel, Earl of: *see* Fitzalan

Arundel, Elizabeth, 330

Arundel (Arundell), Mistress, poem on, 257 (24), 329

as, conj. adv., *when*, 16 (16)

as, conj., *as if*, 16 (19), 125 (4), 166 (19)

a scance: *see* askance

Ascham, Roger, 38 n.3, 120, 245, 292

Asia ('Asie'), 27 (8)

askance ('a scance'), adv., 83 (42)

Aske, James, 45

aslake, v., *suppress, drive away*, 244 (24)

aspects, s., *beneficent influence (of planets)*, 226 (34)

assemble, s., *assembly*, 192 (19)

assembly, s., 100 (4) n.

assinde (assigned), pp., 70 (12), 77 (34), 78 (4), 79 (3)

assuage ('asswage'), v., *pass away*, 30 (9)

Assyrian, 29 (5), 157

astart, v., *escape*, 44 (2)

astate, s., *estate*, 80 (30), 171 (25), 244 (15)

astonied, pp., *astonished*, 254 (33)

astronomy, Wyatt and, 222

at, prep., *from, by the example of*, 89 (12)

atcheue (achieve), v., 181 (24)

Athenaeum, The, 57 n., 58 notes, 133

Atlas, 90 (19) n.

Atride, i. e., *Agamemnon*, 47 (8)

attaint, v., *harm, impair*, 16 (21), 98 (21)

Atticus, Titus Pomponius, 107 (4) n.

atween, prep., *between*, 104 (34)

atwixt, prep., *between*, 19 (6)

auctoritie, s., *authority*, 69 (12)

Audley, Thomas, Baron Audley, 280. *See* Touchet

Audley ('Awdeleye'), Thomas, Captain, elegy on, 159 (33) n. *See* Awdley

aught, v., *owed*, 162 (18)

augur, s., *seer*, 119 (25)

August: *see* Caesar

Ault, Norman, 123

Ausonius, Decimus Magnus, 76, 209, 237; poem by, translated, 97 (4) n.

avail, s., *safety, benefit*, 15 (20), 103 (6) (The *N.E.D.* explains 15 (20) as *avale, disembarkation*, but is clearly wrong. Surrey's "swete port of his auail" is a translation of Petrarch's *Rime*, 14, line 7, "al dolce porto de la lor salute.")

availed, pp., *slackened*, 13 (26)

avale ('auayl'), v., *flow down*, 27 (35)

avance, avaunce, v., *advance*, 22 (12), 28 (28), 50 (14), 89 (36), 129 (19), 150 (34), 176 (36)

avaunt, interj., 94 (17)

avaunt, s., v., *boast*, 58 (11), 60 (20)

Avern (Hades), 117 (15)

avising ('auisyng'), pres. p., *gazing at* (Italian *mirando*), 38 (32)

avow ('auowe') v., *declare, swear*, 191 (26), 226 (22), 231 (17)

Awdeley, John, printer, 151, 283

Awdley (Audley), Damascene, poems to, 100 (23) n., 101 (17) n., 103 (9) n. *See* Audley

awe, under, prep. phr., 8 (6), 85 (24)

awry, adv., *obliquely*, 72 (10)

axith, v., *asketh*, 186 (5)

ay ('aie'), adv., 26 (23, 36), 44 (32), 65 (13), 66 (28), 244 (14), etc.

ayelife, s., *life forever*, 93 (30) (not in the *N.E.D.*)

ayen (again), adv., 48 (20); *(spoke) in reply*, 117 (4)

B., G., *Ludus Scacchiae*, 147

B., M., Mistress, poem on, 251 (29) n.

B., S. F., 310

Bellona, goddess, 115 (29)

ben: *see* been

bend, v., *pass away*, 72 (6)

bended, bent, pp. adj., *crescent (moon)*, 81 (32), 91 (41)

bene: *see* been

Bensley, T., 50 f.

bent, s., *curve*, 204 (3). *See* bended

berain ('berayne'), v., *wet (with tears)*, 13 (38)

Berdan, J. M., 86 n.2, 87 n.4, 152, 176, 328

bereft, v., *deprived of (by death)*, 243 (25); *killed*, 109 (28), 125 (31); *pulled*, 168 (30), 171 (16); *snatched away (by death)*, 194 (34)

berent, v., *rend, tear*, 157 (34)

Bergk, Theodorus, 230

bering: *see* bearing

berive (bereave), v., 199 (14)

berne ('beurn'), s., *warrior*, 116 (30)

beset, v., *set with (pearls)*, 100 (34); *surrounded with*, 249 (40)

beside ('byside'), adv., *in addition to*, 239 (7)

besprent, pp., *sprinkled, suffused*, 44 (13, 20), 133 (33), 164 (11)

bestrow, v., *bestrew*, 234 (31) n.

bet (beat), v., 28 (8), 207 (36)

betell bee: *see* beetle-bee

Betham, Peter, 156

betide ('betyd'), v., *happened to* 203 (4)

betimes, adv., 57 (25)

beurn: *see* berne

bewedded, pp., 107 (29)

bewrapt, pp., 110 (23)

bewray, v., *reveal*, 5 (14), 72 (41), 151 (37), 159 (2), 230 (19), 247 (27)

Beza (Bèze), Theodore de, 88; poems by, translated by Grimald, 93 (21) n., 94 (34) n., 95 (38) n., 96 (22) n., 103 (9) n., 104 (7) n., 104 (17) n., 108 (18) n., 115 (2) n., 118 (9) n., 120 (17) n.

Bible, uses of the, in the miscellany, 88 (24) n., 156, 159, 230, 259, 267, 281, 283, 286, 296, 300, 323 ff., 330. *See* Psalms

Bibliographica, 5n.

Bibliographical Society, England, *Transactions*, 5n., 6 n. See *Library*

biden, v., *remain (constant)*, 225 (6); 'bydeth,' *lives*, 51 (22)

bind, wood doth, v. phr., Italian *legni lega*, 52 (35)

Birch, Thomas, 46

Biton: *see* Cleobis

Blackwood, G., poem addressed to, 95 (38) n.; supposed author of a miscellany poem, 96 (22) n., 77

blank verse, the effect of, 108; Grimald's, 79, 104, rhymes in, 115 (12) n.; Surrey's, date of its publication, 70, 79 n.2

blase, blaser: *see* blaze(r)

blast, s., *a blasted (withered) condition*, 173 (4); *musical sound*, 97 (23); *slander*, 145 (13); *storm*, 190 (17)

blast, v., *sound (as on a trumpet)*, 207 (2)

blaze ('blase') ill, v. phr., *spread scandal abroad*, 238 (37)

blazer ('blaser'), s., *one who proclaims lies*, 191 (36)

blear one's eye, v. phr., *hoodwink*, 126 (19), 255 (11)

blee, s., *looks* (Latin *forma*), 96 (31)

bleew: *see* blue

blend, pp., *blinded*, 193 (39)

blent, pp., *blended*, 100 (31), 102 (26); *blinded*, 242 (43)

blin ('blyn'), v., *cease*, 173 (24)

blind maze, s. phr., *a labyrinth*, 68 (25)

Bliss, Philip, 36, 50, 72 n.1

blist, pp., *blessed*, 179 (31), 201 (20)

blome (bloom), v., 254 (24)

blontly: *see* bluntly

Blount, Elizabeth, 142

blue ('bleew'), adj., s., *livid ("black and blue")*, 94 (9); *a sign of true love*, 18 (14)n.

Blundeston, L., 77 n. 2

bluntly ('blontly'), adv., *stupidly*, 130 (28) (the first example in the *N.E.D.*), 255 (36). (Cf. *Churchyard's Charge*, 1580 [Collier's reprint, p. 47]: "Who bluntly bites a baite, and swallows up a hooke.")

blyn: *see* blin

board ('boord'), s., *table*, 120 (16)

Boas, F. S., 227

Boccaccio, 180, 239, 259

bode, v., *suffered*, 183 (24)

Bodleian library, Oxford, its copies of the miscellany, 8, 27 f., 31 f., 35 f., 38

boe (bow), s., 253 (17)

Boethius, 76, 220, 296; Wyatt's borrowings from, 81 (27 f.) n., 212 (11) n.

Bohn, H. G., 13, 38 n.2, 58, 152

Boiardo, M. M., 136

boile, pp. adj., *boiled*, 217 (10)

boisteous ('boysteous,' 'boystous'), adj. *boisterous*, 14 (20), 68 (14), 194 (9)

bolded, pp., *emboldened*, 34 (16)

Boleyn, Anne, Queen, 83; and Surrey, 69; and Wyatt, 75 f., 183, 314. *See* Brunet

Boleyn, George, Viscount Rochford, supposed contributor to the miscellany, 82 f., 85, 87, 91, 93, 189

bolstering ('bolstrynge'), verb. n., *upholding*, 196 (20)

bolstred (bolstered), pp. adj., *puffed up (by flattery)*, 200 (2) n.

Bolton, Edmund, 120 f.

Bond, R. W., 181

bondes (bounds), s., 175 (3)

Bonner, Edmund, Bishop, 154

boon, s., *entreaty*, 111 (24)

boones (bones), s., 32 (29)

boord: *see* board, bourd

boot ('bote'), s., *advantage, remedy*, 40 (32), 126 (28), 168 (33)

boots it, impers. v., 95 (26); booteth, 233 (8)

bord: *see* bourd

Boreas ('Borias'), 16 (14), 206 (11) n.

bote: *see* boot

boule: *see* bowl

Boulogne, France, Captain Audley and, 280; Surrey as governor of, 69, 247. *See* Bullayn

bourd ('bord,' 'boord'), s., *jest*, 40 (4), 49 (39), 60 (25)

bout ('bowt'), s., *circuit, orbit*, 91 (22) (the first example in the *N.E.D.*)

bowes, s., *boughs*, 252 (2)

Bowes, Anne and Elizabeth, 28

bowl ('boule'), s., *ball, bullet*, 53 (6) (the first example in the *N.E.D.* is dated 1623)

bowt: *see* bout

boxomnesse: *see* buxomness

boysteous, boystous: *see* boisteous

Bradburne, Elisabeth, 277

Bradner, Leicester, 156, 278, 293, 330

brags, s., 19 (29)

braid, at a, prep. phr., *on a sudden*, 141 (39)

brake, s., *curb (of a bridle)*, 178 (24); *thicket*, 4 (32)

brake, v., *was broken*, 27 (29)

brand, s., *torch (of love)*, 193 (39). *See* bronde

Brandon, Henry, second Duke of Suffolk, 245

Brant, Sebastian, 181

brasten, v., *burst*, 240 (5)

brats, s., 96 (13), 105 (21)

braught (brought), v., 114 (7)

brave, adj., *splendid, costly*, 115 (36)

breadeth (breedeth), v., 258 (8)

break ('breke') thy mind, v. phr., *express your thoughts*, 191 (24)

breers: *see* briers

bren, v., *burn*, 55 (37), 56 (5)

brend, pp., *burned*, 140 (10)

brent, v., *burned*, 52 (18), 247 (3)

Breton, Nicholas, 45, 147, 156, 227, 329. See *Arbor, Brittons*

Brian: *see* Bryan

bride, s., *burd, woman*, 188 (8)

Bridgewater, Earl of: *see* Egerton

briers ('breers'), s., 52 (25), 130 (28)

bright, adj., *beautiful*, 9 (28), 13 (5), 101 (27)

brine, boiled, s. phr., *tears (of envy)*, 205 (3) n.

bring me in, to, inf. phr., *deceive*, 255 (8)

bringer-in, s., *provider*, 88 (6)

Briseis ('Brises') and Achilles, 181 (12)

Britain ('Britan'), 9 (25), 28 (10), 30 (36), 100 (25); adj., *Briton*, 114 (11)

Britaynes, Brittons, i. e., *Englishmen's*, 136 (6), 254 (24)

British Bibliographer, The, 112 n.4

British Museum, its copies of the miscellany, 10, 21, 31, 33, of reprints of, 38, 40 ff., 44 ff., 47 ff.

brittle, adj., *dangerous*, 24 (15); *evanescent*, 9 (35)

Brittons Bowre of Delights (by Breton [*q. v.*] and others), 109; borrowings in, from the miscellany, 157 f.

Britwell library: *see* Christie-Miller

brokes (brooks), s., 153 (16)

Brome, Robert, 12

bronde, s., *brand (q. v.), torch*, 186 (21)

brood, s., *offspring*, 105 (33), 109 (16)

Brooke, Arthur, 5

Brooke, Christopher, 154

Brooke, Elizabeth, Lady Wyatt, 75

Brooke, Thomas, Baron Cobham, 75

cheer ('cheare,' 'chere'), s., *countenance, expression of the face*, 3 (38), 6 (20), 13 (15), 95 (11), 120 (4), 243 (11), etc.; *food and drink*, 87 (34), 105 (4); *jollity*, 107 (38)

cheered ('chered'), pp., 110 (37)

cheezil: *see* chisel

Cheke, John, Sir, contributor to the miscellany, 80, 85, 323 f.; on Denny, 292

chepe: *see* cheap

chere: *see* cheer

chess, poem on, 147

Chester, Robert, 287 f.

Chew, Beverly, his copy of *G*, 31 n.1, of *H*, 33 n.

chews, s., *jaws*, 30 (5) (not in the *N. E. D.*, but cf. *chavel*)

chiasmus, examples, of, 78 (13–14) n.

Child, H. H., 77 n. 1, 79 n.3, 86 n.2, 93 n.

chisel ('cheezil'), s., 99 (13)

choose ('chuse'), s., *choosing, selection*, 233 (20)

chop and change, v., *change*, 29 (35); *chopt a change, made an exchange with*, 241 (11)

chorlish: *see* churlish

chose (choose), v., 7 (36), 188 (30), 207 (14), 213 (9), 224 (22)

Chreseid: *see* Cressida

Christ, 28 (36), 147 (29), 207 (8), 220 (5)

Christendom, 87 (40)

Christie-Miller, S. R. (Britwell library), his copy of *E*, 27, of *G*, 31

Churchyard, Thomas, alleged share of, in the miscellany, 83 f., 86, 278, 283, 301; curious spelling of, the, 84; editorship of the miscellany by, theory of the, 89; praise by, of Surrey, 111; quoted, 146, 201, 283, 318; Wilford and, 241

churlish ('chorlish'), adj., 24 (23)

chuse: *see* choose

Cicero, Marcus Tullius, Grimald's translation from, 86; mentioned or quoted, 107 (4) n., 187, 236 f., 239; poem indebted to, 327; poems on, 118 (9) n., 120 (17) n.

Ciminelli (or Cimino), Serafino dei, Aquilano, 76, 101, 105, 185; poems indebted to, 143 f., 171 ff., 184 f., 191, 193, 200, 315

Ciprus: *see* Cypria

Circe's cup, *drunkenness*, 193 (39)

civil swoord, reskued from, v. phr., *rescued from civil war*, 118 (14)

clack, s., *a mill-hopper alarm-bell*, 187 (25, 32)

Clarke, C. C., edition by, of Wyatt and Surrey, 56

clattering, adj., *chattering*, 46 (41)

claw by the back, v. phr., *flatter, fawn upon*, 41 (16)

Clawson, J. L., his copy of *G*, 31

clean ('clene'), adv., *completely*, 17 (29)

clearly ('clerely'), adv., *completely*, 159 (31)

Cleobis and Biton, 111 (30) n.

Cleobulus's riddle, poem on, 98 (30) n.

cleped, v., *called*, 93 (32) n.

Clere, Thomas, Sir, 143; Surrey's epitaph on, 40

clergions, s., *young song-birds*, 221 (5) (the only example in the *N. E. D.*)

clerk, s., *scholar*, 116 (2)

Clerk, John, and Surrey, 68

Clifford, Arthur, *Tixall Poetry*, 181

climbing figure, the, example of, 127 (2) n.

Clinton, Edward, first Earl of Lincoln, 75

Clio, 97 (9)

clives, s., *cliffs*, 26 (32), 230 (35)

close, v., *enclose, express*, 193 (27)

Clotho, the Fate, 112 (35)

cloudy, adj., *frowning*, 34 (14)

clout (*cloth*), pale as a, adj. phr., 222 (36) (the first example in the *N. E. D.*)

coal, canal, strange properties of, 235 (29) n.

coardes: *see* cords

coarse: *see* corse

coast ('cost'), s., 157 (14)

Cobham, Baron: *see* Brooke (Thomas)

cock and pie, by, exclam., 200 (29) n., 239 (23)

cockatrice, s., 132 (6)

cockboat, s., 169 (16)

Cokayne, G. E. (G. E. C.), 302

Coleridge, E. H., 210

Coleridge, S. T., 210

Collatine ('Collatiue') and Lucrece, 191 (4) n.

Collection of Seventy-nine Black-letter Ballads, A (printed by Joseph Lilly), 127, 143, 237, 262, 264

Collier, J. P., 35 n.5, 44 n.2, 83 n.1, 110 n.3, 111 n., 146, 152, 201, 241, 257,

283, 318, 324; alleged discovery by, of *A*, 58; on Bryan, 220; on Churchyard as editor of the miscellany, 89; reprint by, of *Seven English Poetical Miscellanies*, discussed, 57 ff.

Collmann, H. L., 283

colours, s., *falsehood*, 86 (39)

columbine, s., 133 (14)

comen ('commen'), pp., *come*, 184 (21), 185 (16). *See* cumne

commodious, adj., *advantageous*, 168 (21)

common weal, s., *the state or nation*, 115 (5)

common wealth, s., *general good*, 86 (22); *nation*, 227 (20)

compass, s., *moderation, correct course of life*, 26 (22)

compass, v., *encompass*, 146 (34), 189 (17)

compted, pp., *accounted*, 228 (12) n.

conceit, s., *opinion*, 128 (15); *pretty or witty expression*, 100 (32), 109 (38)

conceits in the miscellany poets, 101

concupiscence, 27 (17)

conduit of the eyes, s. phr., *the tear-ducts*, 205 (4)

connyng: *see* cunning

Constable and Company, re-issue by, of Arber's reprint of the miscellany, 60 f.

constance, s., *constancy*, 24 (41)

conster, v., *construe, explain*, 211 (31)

Consul Marcus, i. e., *Cicero (q. v.)*, 118 (17)

consume, v., *dry up*, 23 (12); v. i., *burn away*, 131 (17), 235 (34); *expire, end*, 124 (38)

consumingly, adv., *rapidly destroyed by fire*, 58 (3) (the first example in the *N. E. D.*)

Conti, Giusto de', 181

continuance, s., 26 (11) n.

contrairs, s., *contraries*, 248 (32)

contrarious, adj., 37 (32-33)

contributors, the, to the miscellany, discussed, 65 ff.; their avoidance of publication, 88, 93

convert, v. i., 76 (34)

cony, s., 84 (36), 163 (17)

Cooke, Robert, Sir, and Lady Theophila, 231

coom (come), v., 94 (26, 28), 95 (8, 36), 116 (33, 40), 119 (22, 27)

cooning: *see* cunning

Cooper, Elizabeth, on Geraldine, 72 f.; reprints from the miscellany by, 122

Copernicus and Wyatt, 222

Copinger, W. A., 242

cords ('coardes'), s., *rigging of a ship*, 38 (26)

Corin and Phyllida, poem on, 132 (33)

Coriolanus, Gaius Marcius, 111 (23) n.

cornet, s., *head-dress*, 11 (34) (the first example in the *N. E. D.*), 12 (10)

corps, corpse, s., *dead body*, 108 (31), 113 (10), 115 (19), 136 (3), 160 (18), 178 (18), 249 (14), etc.; *living body*, 28 (31), 95 (2), 99 (35), 108 (7), 146 (34), 162 (24), 210 (34), 237 (35), 249 (8), etc.

corse ('coarse'), s., *body*, 219 (15); *corpse*, 18 (10), 27 (34), 191 (6)

Coryate, Thomas, 154

cost: *see* coast

cosyn: *see* cousin

Cotgrave, Randle, 133

Cotton, Charles, 152

coucht, pp., *couched, concealed*, 126 (9)

cough, v., 89 (19) n.

could, v., *knew*, 121 (35)

countenance ('countinaunce'), s., 94 (23)

counterfeit action, the: *see* pragmatographia

countervail, v., *equal*, 106 (11)

countinaunce: *see* countenance

county, s., 194 (15) n.

couple-clause, the: *see* polysyndeton

coursing, pres. p. adj., *swiftly moving*, 114 (12)

Court of Venus, The, 186

Court of Vertue, The: *see* Hall (John)

courteous ('curteis,' 'curties'), adj., 73 (22), 87 (6)

Courthope, W. J., 74, 79 n.1, 141, 210

courtier, the life of a, poems on, 81 (8), 85 (19), 88 (2)

cousin ('cosyn'), s., 89 (33)

couth ('kouth'), pp., *known*, 101 (19)

covered, adj., *cloudy*, 99 (32)

coverts, s., 107 (31)

covet, v., *wish*, 28 (36)

covitise, s., *covetousness*, 212 (32) n.

cowche, s., 165 (27) n.

Cowley, Abraham, 316; Grimald compared to, 79 n.1

cowslips, s., 133 (14)

coyed, pp. adj., *coy*, 208 (28)

Day, 'Carie' (*q. v.*), 224 f.

Day, John, printer, 79 n.2, 88 n.3

dayne: *see* deign

days, lucky and unlucky, and the Roman calendar, 101 (15) n.

deal ('dele'), s., *part, portion*, 75 (2), 80 (31)

Deane, William, 245

dear ('dere'), adj., *of great worth*, 59 (6)

dearworth, adj., *beloved*, 112 (38) (the last example in the *N. E. D.*)

death, the dance of, 125 (6); the harbinger of, 166 (4) n.; life and, compared, a poem, 124 (20); sleep's sister or brother, 109 (7) n.

deathday, s., 98 (36)

debate, s., *friendly contest*, 11 (4); *quarreling*, 26 (16), 106 (29), etc.

Deborah ('Debore'), a prophetess who judged Israel, 102 (33)

deburs, v., *disburse, pay*, 89 (25)

decay, s., *death*, 109 (18)

decay, v., *make weak, impair*, 98 (27); *vanish*, 244 (32)

decayer of all kind, s. phr., *destroyer of everything in nature*, 61 (13)

deceavable: *see* deceivable

deceitless, adj., 204 (31)

deceivable ('deceauable'), adj., *deceitful*, 45 (22)

deem ('deme,' 'demen'), v., *judge*, 87 (34) n., 159 (32), 186 (2), 242 (6), etc.

deep ('depe'), v., *busy oneself in*, 85 (8) n.

deepwitted ('depewitted'), adj., 2 (9)

deface, s., *shame*, 177 (21)

deface, v., *put to shame, surpass*, 170 (18)

defame, s., *ill fame*, 98 (3); *slander*, 145 (13)

defame, v., 160 (10)

defaut, s., *default, defect*, 30 (22), 69 (29), 95 (24)

defend, v., *fend off, keep at bay*, 99 (23), 107 (32)

defenst, pp., *defended*, 220 (16)

defied ('defide'), v., *renounced, set aside*, 188 (7)

define, v., *state precisely*, 18 (27)

deign ('dayne'), v., 203 (14)

dele: *see* deal

delf ('delph'), s., *pit*, 170 (28)

Deloney, Thomas, 109, 295

deme: *see* deem

demean, v., 8 (4)

demen: *see* deem

Democritus, epigram ascribed to, 237 f.

Demophoön and Phyllis, 301

Denny, Anthony, Sir, elegy on, 178 (8) n.

dented, pp. adj., *hollow, sunken*, 30 (5) (the only example in the *N. E. D.*)

depaint ('depaynt'), v., *adorn*, 101 (15); pp., *colored*, 204 (12)

depart, v., *divide*, 110 (11); *send away*, 225 (7); *separate from the body*, 113 (9), 249 (12)

depe: *see* deep

Dephne: *see* Daphne

depraveress ('depraueres'), s., *a female depraver*, 169 (17) n. (the only example in the *N. E. D.*)

dere: *see* dear

De Ricci, Seymour, 35

Dering, Edward, 120

derlinges: *see* darlings

descried ('discriyde'), v., 90 (39)

descrived, pp., *described*, 99 (18)

desert, adj., *forsaken*, 34 (6)

despairing ('dispearyng'), pres. p., 38 (30)

despite ('despight'), s., 17 (10)

despoiled ('dispoyled'), pp., *disrobed*, 13 (9); *stripped of leaves*, 3 (8)

Desportes, Philippe, 135

destroy ('distry'), v., 99 (3)

determed, pp. adj., *determined*, 30 (23)

Devereux, Penelope, daughter of the first Earl of Essex ("Stella"), 256

Devereux ('Deuerox'), Richard, elegy on, 122 (37) n.

Devereux, Robert, second Earl of Essex, 256

Devereux, Walter, first Earl of Essex, 256, 308

Devereux, Walter, third Baron Ferrers, Viscount Hereford, 256

devines: *see* divines

devise, s., *figure, story*, 93 (31) n.; *intention, wish*, 38 (6), 254 (18); *purpose*, 36 (20)

devise, v., *contrive*, 7 (36), 18 (9); *imagine*, 91 (2); *ponder over, plan*, 125 (33, 37)

De Vocht, H., 6 n., 84 n.5

dial ('dyall'), s., *face of a clock or a sundial*, 148 (20) n.

Diana ('Dyane'), 100 (4), 154 (2), 156 (8), 190 (26, 31), 257 (23). *See* Dictynnaes, Phoebe

dice, what chance comes on the, i. e., *whatever event may happen*, 18 (23)

Dick of Devonshire, 325

Dickenson, John, 322

Dictionary of National Biography (D. N. B.), 5 n., 37, 46 n.2, 52 n.1, 68, 75 n.2, 78 n., 84 n. 4, 242, 245 f., 280

Dictynnaes, *Diana's*, 94 (18). *See* Diana

did ('dyd'), v., *compelled*, 71 (29)

Dido, 90 (17), 173 (11). *See* Carthage

dight, pp., *repaired*, 82 (32)

dike, s., *ditch*, 87 (28)

diligent, s., *Diligence*, 146 (23)

dint, s., *noise of thunder*, 151 (5); *stroke*, 29 (9), 219 (5), 241 (8); *stroke of lightning*, 33 (30)

Diodorus Siculus, 252

Diogenes, 237

disarmed, pp. adj., *weaponless* (Latin *inermis*), 119 (7)

disarne: *see* discern

disceivably, adv., *deceivably*, 71 (22)

disceive, v., *deceive*, 130 (33), 230 (22)

discern ('disarne'), v., 70 (10)

discriyde: *see* descried

disease ('disseyse'), s., *lack of ease*, 10 (26), 21 (27)

diseased, pp. adj., *uneasy*, 148 (3)

disges, v., *disgest, endure*, 152 (10)

Disle, Henry, printer, 93

disparst: *see* dispersed

dispearyng: *see* despairing

dispersed ('disparst'), pp., 145 (18)

display, v., *undress (by removing a glove:* Italian *dispogliare)*, 41 (9)

displeasaunt, adj., 30 (30)

disport, s., 11 (5)

dispoyled: *see* despoiled

disprove ('disprooue'), v., *disapprove of*, 111 (19)

disseyse: *see* disease

distain ('distayn'), v., *defile*, 167 (9); *paint, reveal*, 68 (26); *stain*, 35 (24)

distrain ('distrein'), v., *oppress, subdue*, 14 (13), 205 (6) n.

distry: *see* destroy

divers, adj., *changing (waxing and waning)*, 91 (40)

diverseness, s., *changeableness*, 36 (27 f.)

divines ('deuines'), s., *prophets*, 228 (13)n.

do, v., *cause*, 51 (5), 71 (29)

doe ('doo'), s., 134 (27)

doings, s., *poetical compositions*, 100 (17), 231

dole, s., *dealing, course of life*, 102 (20)

doling ('dolling'), pres. p., *grieving for*, 151 (36)

dome: *see* doom, dumb

dompes: *see* dumps

don, done, v., *do*, 147 (9) 153 (15, 28)

doo: *see* doe

doolfull, adj., *doleful*, 107 (36), 109 (7, 24), 110 (37), 113 (21), 155 (12)

doom ('dome'), s., *decision, judgment*, 18 (16), 85 (11), 100 (20), 102 (19), 153 (35), 201 (22), 254 (18); lively domes, *quick-witted people*, 12 (20)

doon, inf., *to be done*, 147 (9)

Dormer, E. W., 80, 306, 308 f.

doubleness, s., *duplicity*, 52 (4, 9)

doubt, s., *anxiety*, 244 (32)

doubt ('dout'), v., *fear*, 41 (25), 47 (41), 78 (30 f.), 119 (20)

doubtful, adj., *fearful*, 7 (9), 8 (31), 16 (5), 82 (13), 148 (2)

Douglas, Margaret, Countess of Lenox, 312

douteous, adj., *doubtful, fearful*, 38 (31)

Dove and the Serpent, The, 152

Dover, England, 52 (21)

do way, v., *do away with*, 35 (8), 77 (25), 105 (35), 246 (20 ff.), 247 (2, 14); *go away, stop*, 207 (34), 246 (26, 33)

down, bed of, 83 (11), 88 (19)

downflowed, pp., 44 (33)

downsent, inf., 117 (15)

Doyle, J. E., 245

drave, v., *drove*, 61 (20), 206 (11) n., 219 (25)

Drayton, Michael, on Geraldine and Surrey, 71 f., 136, 138, 141; on Surrey and Lady Stanhope, 312; on the authorship of certain miscellany poems, 67, 82, 212; quoted, 94 n., 231, 270

dread ('drede'), s., *(no) doubt*, 185 (34), 186 (3, 10)

dreadful ('dredfull'), adj., *full of fear*, 203 (9)

drench, v., *drown*, 15 (39); *overwhelm (in sloth)*, 29 (14), *(in sleep)*, 221 (26)

drenching, adj., *that which overwhelms or drowns*, 122 (13)

drent, pp., *drowned*, 153 (4)

drieve: *see* drive

GLOSSARIAL INDEX

drifts, s., *crafty actions*, 188 (26)

drive ('drieue'), v., 77 (15), 78 (26); *cause*, 219 (36); *hold one's course toward*, 206 (17)

drivel, s., *foolish talk*, 226 (18) (the first example in the *N. E. D.* is dated 1852)

drivel, v., *slaver*, 88 (24) n.

drops, silver, s. phr., figurative for *dew*, 13 (17)

dropsy, adj., *dropsical*, 131 (20) n.

Drummond, William, of Hawthornden, 236 f.; his copy of *I*, 35

Dryden, John, 268

dryeth (dryth), s., *thirst*, 131 (20) n. (the first example in the *N. E. D.*)

Du Bellay, Joachim, 296

Dudley, John, Viscount Lisle (later Duke of Northumberland), 69

Duff, E. G., 90 n.2, 221

dull, v., *deaden*, 99 (28)

dumb ('dome'), adj., 147 (17), 252 (12)

dumps ('dompes'), s., *melancholy fits*, 97 (24), 99 (28), 107 (36), 222 (34)

Duncan, Edmonstoune, 123 f.

duplicate settings and the miscellany, 13 ff.

durance, s., *endurance (of toil)*, 136 (26)

dure, v., *endure*, 114 (15), 125 (2)

dyall: *see* dial

Dyane: *see* Diana

Dyce, A., 112 n.4, 182, 220, 305

dyd: *see* did

dyde (dyed), v., 153 (14)

each one ('echone'), pron., 116 (21)

eachwhere ('echwhere'), adv., *on each side* (Latin *utrumque*), 115 (28)

earnest and game (jest), betwixt, 39 (8)

earthed, pp., *buried*, 136 (3)

easy sparks of flame, s. phr., *sparks easily kindled*, 6 (8)

echo-device, the, example of, 127 (2) n.

ecphonesis, or the outcry, example of, 64 (33)–65 (2–17) n.

Edinburgh Review, The, on Geraldine, 74, on Wyatt, 66

Edinburgh University, its copy of *I*, 35

Edipus: *see* Oedipus

editor, the, of the early editions of the miscellany, methods and aims of, 88 f., 94 ff., theories about, 85 ff.

editorial methods of the present edition, 64 f.

Edmunds, Andrew and Elizabeth, 305

Edward IV, king of England, 137

Edward VI, prince and king of England, 114 (35 n., 43), 68, 70, 80, 282; Captain Audley and, 278; Denny and, 292

Edwards, Richard, 93, 108, 131, 156, 329. See *Paradise*

Edwards, Thomas, 309

eek: *see* eke

eft, adv., *again*, 151 (6), 188 (14)

egal, adj., *equal*, 90 (26), 105 (3), 106 (33), 121 (13); *well-matched* (Latin *par*), 26 (8)

Egerton, F. H., eighth Earl of Bridgewater, his copy of *I*, 35

Egypt, the traitor of, 36 (5) n.

Egyptian astronomer, an, Zoroas, poem on, 115 (8)

eigh, interj., 94 (16) (the earliest example in the *N. E. D.* is dated 1750)

eight, numeral, *eighth*, 92 (5)

eke ('eek'), adv., *also*, 4 (27), 6 (25), 98 (15), 114 (40), 119 (4), etc.

eld, s., *old age*, 245 (39)

Eleazer: *see* Mary

elect, pp., *chosen*, 12 (24)

elegies and epitaphs, 12 (29), 27 (21), 28 (2), 108 (2)–115 (7), 120 (17), 122 (37), 135 (20), 146 (31), 159 (33), 162 (26), 166 (36), 178 (8), 194 (15), 199 (4), 200 (30), 206 (29), 218 (22); discussed, 105

Elizabeth, princess and queen of England, 3, 91, 258; the learning of, praised, 231; treatment by, of Essex, attacked, 256

Elizabeth (Woodville), queen of England, 137

Ellis, George, on Geraldine, 73; reprints by, from the miscellany, 123

else ('els,' 'elles'), adv., 11 (23), 34 (24), 41 (10), 47 (7), 49 (36), 57 (38), etc.

Elyot, Thomas, Sir, 317

embassadors, s., 189 (11)

emong, prep., *among*, 102 (37), 116 (38), 200 (34)

empressed, pp. adj., *oppressed*, 8 (16) (the last example in the *N. E. D.* is dated 1475)

Encyclopædia Britannica on holly, 287

endite, v., *write*, 16 (30)

Ene: *see* Aeneas

Eneids: see Virgil

engins, s., *tricks*, 188 (37)

[356]

GLOSSARIAL INDEX

fawcon: *see* falcon
faynted: *see* fainted
feared ('ferde'), pp., *frightened*, 84 (3, 9), 255 (26)
feares: *see* fierce
feast, s., *delight*, 12 (35)
feastfull, adj., *festive*, 109 (23), 110 (36)
feat, adj., *dexterous*, 63 (22)
feat, s., *act (of writing)*, 99 (10)
feater, adj., *more skilful*, 150 (13)
feator, s., *feature*, 254 (33)
featured, pp. adj., *fashioned*, 126 (14)
fee, s., *reward (in love)*, 78 (36), 135 (9); fees ('feese'), *goods, wealth*, 89 (13)
feel ('fele') s., *sense*, 193 (33)
feel ('fele'), v., *taste*, 87 (30)
Fehse, Hermann, 86
feint, v., *feign*, 179 (6)
feldishe: *see* fieldish
fele, felen: *see* feel
feller, adv., 244 (18) n.
Fenton, Elijah, 72
ferde: *see* feared
Ferdinand I, king of Bohemia, 245, 247
fere, s., *companion, mate*, 7 (36), 13 (42) n., 96 (6), 97 (6), 100 (4), 107 (9), 110 (6), 207 (14, 35); *fear*, 210 (5)
Ferguson, F. S., 25
Ferrers ('Ferres'), Lord: *see* Devereux
fers: *see* fierce
ferse, s., *queen (in chess)*, 20 (32 f.) (Cf. Chaucer's *Book of the Duchess*, lines 654 f., 723)
fervent, adj., *intense (cold)*, 44 (15), *(heat)*, 107 (32); fervent powers, Latin *fervida numina*, 95 (17)
fet, pp., *fetched, brought*, 236 (33); v., *bring up*, 49 (29), 56 (14), 165 (6)
fethe (faith), s., 180 (32)
fetrers, s., *fetters*, 80 (13)
fieldish ('feldishe'), adj., *rural*, 82 (24)
fierce ('feares,' 'fers'), adj., 72 (43); adv., 244 (19)
fierly: *see* firely
fift, numeral, *fifth*, 91 (28)
file, s., *woman*, 170 (10)
filed, pp. adj., *false*, 227 (36); *polished, finished*, 125 (32)
Filosseno, Marcello, 163
fine, s., *end*, 152 (20); in fine ('fyne'), *in short*, 95 (24), 197 (26)
fineness, s., Finesse, Subtlety, 192 (35)

fingerfeat, s., *handicraft*, 101 (25) (not in the *N. E. D.*)
fired flame, s. phr., 9 (6)
firely ('fierly'), adv., *ardently*, 45 (14) (the last example in the *N. E. D.* is dated 1435)
Fitzalan, Henry, twelfth Earl of Arundel, 241, 245, 330
Fitzalan, Henry, Lord Maltravers ('Mautrauers'), elegies on, 113 (34) n., 115 (2) n.
Fitzalan, Mary, Duchess of Norfolk, 330
Fitzgerald, Elizabeth: *see* Geraldine
Fitzgerald, Gerald, ninth Earl of Kildare, 74
Fitzgerald, Geraldine (Elizabeth): *see* Geraldine
Fitzgerald, Joan, Countess of Ormonde, 220
Fitzroy, Henry, Duke of Richmond, 68, 141 f.
Flanders' cheer ('Flaunders chere'), s. phr., 87 (34) n.
fleering ('flering'), adj., *mocking*, 200 (22)
fleet ('flete'), v., *die out*, 237 (10); *flit, hasten*, 67 (18), 72 (6), 124 (35), 150 (11), 189 (38); *float*, 114 (12), 150 (23), 231 (14)
fleeting ('fletyng'), pres. p., adj., *floating*, 148 (15); *inconstant*, 148 (5)
flering: *see* fleering
fleshy, adj., *fleshly*, 125 (21) (the first example in the *N. E. D.* is dated 1604)
Fletcher, Robert (fl. 1603), 121
Fletcher, Robert (fl. 1656), 152
flete: *see* fleet
fleyng (flying), adj., 129 (29)
flight, s., *movement (turning of fortune's wheel)*, 243 (12)
floorist: *see* flourished
Florence, Italy, 9 (20); Surrey's alleged jousting at, 71
flourished ('floorist'), pp., 191 (42)
foe, my sweet, etc., 15 (39) n., 67 (26), 140 (21), 144 (34), 158 (8), 186 (20)
fole: *see* fool
Folger, H. C., his copy of *H*, 33
foltring: *see* faltering
fond, adj., *foolish*, 59 (23), 99 (31), 105 (22), 194 (2)
fone, s., *foes*, 117 (37), 118 (38)
fool ('fole'), s., 154 (32), 196 (29)

[358]

foolish ('folish'), adj., 198 (3)

foord: *see* ford

foot, step in your, or set your, v. phr., *join in the song or chorus*, 18 (21, 26) (the first example of *foot* in this sense given in the *N.E.D.* is dated 1552)

for, prep., *instead of*, 98 (25); *of*, 140 (4); *since*, 17 (31), 77 (35)

for because, conj., *because*, 21 (7), 72 (24), 73 (9), 82 (25), 209 (8)

for that, conj., *because*, 159 (7); what for that, *what of that*, 140 (4)

for to, prep. (before infinitive), 3 (14), 6 (30 f.), 16 (17), 17 (20), 37 (3), 42 (35), 52 (14), 57 (29), 62 (6), 69 (28), 72 (28, 30, 39), 73 (6), 76 (5), 83 (23), 85 (41), 159 (13), 162 (13), etc.

for why, conj., *because*, 150 (22)

Forbes, John, borrowings by, from the miscellany, 259 f., 313

force, s., *ability*, 126 (30); *matter, importance*, 70 (13), 87 (27), 122 (30), 129 (20); *necessity*, 23 (21); *?source*, 70 (7) n.; *waterfall, cascade*, 44 (33) (the first example in the *N.E.D.* is dated 1600); of force, *necessarily*, 43 (29), 75 (18), 162 (32), 178 (29), 209 (23); of force, *to hunt in the open with the hounds in full cry*, 13 (28) (the first example in the *N.E.D.* is dated 1575)

force ('forse'), v., *care for*, 128 (6), 211 (29), 220 (9), 221 (31), 233 (2); *love*, 133 (11, 17), 251 (10); *pursue*, 221 (29)

forced face, with, adv. phr., *with faces hiding their grief (tears) in forced calm* (Latin *invitus*), 118 (22)

ford ('foord'), s., 112 (29) n.

fordid, v., *maltreated*, 16 (36), 191 (6)

fordon, pp., *annihilated*, 219 (11)

forecast, s., *foresight*, 108 (12)

foreman, s., 204 (15)

forepast ('forpassed'), pp. adj., *past*, 124 (24) n. (the first example in the *N.E.D.*), 137 (18)

forepointed, pp. adj., *predestined*, 102 (36) (the first example in the *N.E.D.* is dated "c. 1550")

forereading, s., *foreseeing*, 112 (13) (the first example in the *N.E.D.*)

foretime, s., *past ages*, 111 (31) n. (the first example in the *N.E.D.* is dated 1853)

forewatched: *see* forwatched

forewind, s., *favorable wind*, 244 (31) (the first example in the *N.E.D.* is dated 1561)

forged, pp. adj., *deceptive, lying*, 196 (27), 204 (28), 242 (15)

forger, s., *fabricator of lies*, 54 (19), 191 (35), 192 (7)

forgone, pp., *lost (by death)*, 110 (4)

forlet, v., *put an end to*, 146 (33)

forlore, pp., *lost*, 141 (16), 144 (29), 207 (33)

forow: *see* furrow

forpassed: *see* forepast

Forrest, William, priest, 84 n. 4; miscellany poems copied by, 274 ff., 284

forst: *see* force (v.)

Fortescue, John, 220

Fortuna, goddess, poems on, 58 (9), 61 (21), 67 (8), 129 (9); the wheel of, 243 (12)

fortunable, adj., *fortunate*, 103 (25)

fortune, referred to, 76 (3), 102 (27), 138 (17 ff.), 155 (17), 157 (28), 185 (36) n.

forwatched ('forewatched'), pp. adj., *wearied with watching*, 133 (32)

Foster, Joseph, 243

foul ('foule,' 'fowl'), adj., *disagreeable*, 87 (21), 93 (5); *ugly, odious*, 96 (26), 98 (3, 19), 119 (42), 125 (21), 191 (12, 25)

fouleth ('fowlth'), v., *defaces*, 151 (14)

fountain, s., *source of a river*, 66 (33); *springs*, 68 (9); to make fountains of one's eyes, 184 (13) n.

fourt, numeral, *fourth*, 114 (30)

fowl, s., *bird*, 37 (2), 119 (14), 125 (37), etc. See foul

fowlth: *see* fouleth

Foxe, John, 3

Foxwell, Agnes Kate, 52, 75 n.2, 90 n.1, 95, 99, 119 n.1, 148, 150, 156, and *passim* 160–221, 313–317; edition of Wyatt by, described, 61 f., collations with, 128; reprints of poems from *A* by, list of, 62 n.1

fraighted: *see* freighted

frame, s., *profit, good condition*, 47 (4); out of frame, *in disorderly fashion*, 192 (39)

frame, v., *deceive*, 134 (13); *discipline, train*, 102 (17), 136 (5); *prosper, succeed*, 86 (36), 184 (10); frame a form, *make a model*, 99 (17)

GLOSSARIAL INDEX

France, 84 (2), 87 (29) n., 108 (16). *See* Boulogne, Calais, Landrecies, Montreuil

Francis I, king of France, 68, 183

fraught, pp., *freighted, laden,* 28 (26), 73 (8), 151 (8), 159 (26), 242 (27)

fray, v., *frighten,* 93 (9)

freat, freate, v., *rage, fume,* 47 (8), 79 (25), 85 (18), 96 (35); *vex,* 207 (9), 218 (9). *See* fret

freight ('freyght'), pp., *laden,* 15 (14), 121 (14)

freighted ('fraighted'), pp., *laden,* 25 (32)

frekes, s., *men,* 108 (16)

French, Frenchmen, 100 (9), 108 (5)

frequent, v., *busy oneself with,* 100 (9)

fret ('frette'), freat (*q. v*) v , *consumed,* 195 (11); *rub, wear,* 26 (25), 190 (11)

freyght: *see* freight

friend ('frende'), s., *lover, sweetheart,* 21 (24), 64 (24), 176 (32 ff.), 190 (18); a true, described, 244 (33)

friendful ('frendful'), adj., 107 (13)

friendship ('frendship'), s., *love,* 176 (31); poem in praise of, 106 (9) n., 244 (33) n.

fro, prep., 16 (4), 37 (18), 60 (14), 73 (35), 136 (4), 155 (19), etc.

front, in first, prep. phr., Latin *in primo fronte,* 116 (32)

frot ('frote'), v., *chafe,* 151 (15)

fruit ('frute'), s., *offspring,* 96 (32)

fruitless ('frutelesse'), adj., *childless,* 96 (14)

fry, v., *heat, burn,* 101 (36)

frying-pan, flower of the, 96 (7) n. (apparently not in the *N. E. D.*)

fulfil, v., *fill full,* 73 (36), 107 (37)

Fuller, Thomas, 84

fullfatted, adj., 115 (15) (apparently not in the *N. E. D.*)

Fullwood, William, 143, 259; imitation by, of a miscellany poem, 265 f.

Fulman, William, manuscript notes in *E* by, 28, 67

fume, s., *smoke, anger,* 6 (31), 235 (36), 236 (32, 40), 239 (34), 246 (14)

furder, adv., *further,* 112 (30)

furder, v., 15 (19), 58 (22)

Furnivall, F. J., 306, 308

furor, furour, s., *fury,* 73 (34), 78 (2)

furrow ('forow'), s., 107 (23); v., *plow the waves with a ship,* 219 (14)

furth, adv., *forth,* 3 (6), 4 (26), 6 (27), 7 (28), 52 (22), 152 (15), 153 (25), 221 (3), etc.

furtherance, s., 194 (32)

furththrow, v., *throw forth,* 186 (32) (not in the *N. E. D.*)

G., poem attacking, 194 (7) n.

G., F., 267

G., I., 237

G., W.: *see* Gray

gadding as a stray, *wandering like a loose woman,* 156 (23)

gadling, s., *wayfarer,* 40 (29) (the first example in the *N. E. D.*)

Gaeta, 244, 254

gain ('gayn'), prep., *against,* 116 (16)

gain, s., *?advantage, benefit,* 60 (26); misprint for *game,* 47 (2) n.

gainstrive ('gaynstriue'), v., *oppose, harm* (Latin *nocere*), 119 (17)

gainward, prep., *towards, facing,* 81 (30) (the only example in the *N. E. D.*)

game, s., *entertainment,* 209 (8); *jesting, jest,* 5 (13), 39 (8), 62 (39), 134 (9), 180 (14), 187 (29); win the game, *achieve success,* 135 (26)

gan, v., *began, did,* 7 (18, 38), 8 (4), 16 (14, 26), 17 (14), 74 (30), 95 (6), 101 (16), 112 (16, 24), 114 (27), 115 (13), etc.

gander's foe, 24 (27) n.

gape, v., *await eagerly but unsuccessfully,* 246 (28); *long for,* 59 (19, 34), 85 (7)

garden, poem on a , 107 (14) n.

garlands and the miscellany, 109

Garret, 141

Gascoigne, George, 45, 83, 98 n.3, 308; imitation by, of the miscellany, 111, 315 f.; on Lord Vaux, 285; quoted, 156, 180, 280, 324

gate, v., *got,* 253 (38)

gear, s., *things, articles,* 104 (5)

geason, adj., *rare,* 10 (7), 200 (18) n.

geason, s., *rarity,* 239 (3) n. (the last of two examples in the *N. E. D.*)

geat (get), v., 75 (6)

gend(e)reth, v., *engenders,* 116 (9)

generate, pp., *conceived and born,* 82 (18)

Gentleman's Magazine, The, 52 n.1, 122, 150, 313

Gentlemen's Journal, The, 316

George III, king of England, his copy of *K*, 41

George IV, king of England (as Prince Regent), Nott's edition dedicated to, 52 n.3

Geraldi family, the, of Italy, 72, 137

Geraldine, Fair (Fitzgerald, Geraldine or Elizabeth), 48, 54, 136 ff., 141, 159, 212, 312; romance of, 71 ff.; Surrey's poem to, 9 (17)

Geraldine, The Praise of, 42 f.

Gerbier, Charles, 231

Gesippus: *see* Gisippus

gesse: *see* guess

gest: *see* guest

gests, s., *exploits (histories)*, 27 (10)

ghost ('gost,' 'goste'), s., *soul (of a dead person)*, 17 (41), 28 (40), 108 (30), 120 (3), 210 (37), etc.; *(of a living person)*, 22 (31), 36 (31), 137 (15), 147 (21)

Gibbs, Vicary, 245

Gifford, Humphrey, imitation by, of the miscellany, 112, 158, 230

Giles, J. A., 245

Gilfillan, George, edition by, of Wyatt and Surrey, 56

gillot ('gyllot'), s., *wanton woman*, 200 (28) (the first example in the *N. E. D.*)

gillyflower ('ielifloure'), s., 156 (34)

gins, v., *begins*, 47 (35), 164 (39), 181 (19), 220 (31)

gins ('ginnes'), s., *traps*, 205 (22)

girded, pp., *pierced*, 115 (32)

Gisippus ('Gesippus') and Titus Quintus Fulvius, 106 (34) n.

gitterns, s., *guitar-like instruments*, 162 (29)

glad, s., *joy*, 39 (9)

gladdest, adv., 251 (25)

gladsome, adj., 136 (4)

Glasgow University, Hunterian Museum, library, its copy of *F*, 30

glead (gleed), s., *fire*, 37 (15)

gleaves ('gleaus'), s., *glaives, swords* (Latin *enses*), 115 (23), 118 (33)

glims, s., *gleams (of the eyes)*, 257 (7)

glimsing, pres. p., *glancing*, 22 (8)

glode, pp., *glided*, 112 (28)

glome, v., *gloom, frown*, 26 (29)

glose: *see* gloze

gloss, s., *deceptive appearance*, 54 (21)

gloze ('glose'), v., *falsify*, 54 (20)

gnash, v., *grind the teeth in anger*, 117 (22)

gnawing, s., *torment*, 19 (14)

go, v., *walk*, 87 (23), 89 (18), 136 (2), 177 (6), 218 (25)

go to, interj., 78 (12)

godhead, s., *divine personality*, 188 (4); *God*, 217 (22)

Goethe, borrowings by, from the miscellany, 121, 285 f.

gogen gift, s., *gudgeon-gift, a gift for gudgeons or credulous persons*, 149 (11)

Gollancz, Israel, Sir, 317

gonne: *see* gun

good, s., *dear one*, 60 (23), 77 (21); *property*, 41 (8), 197 (21)

Goodal, Will, 278

Googe, Barnabe, 19 n.2, 77 n. 2, 247, 260 f.; on Grimald, 78, 87; borrowings by, from the miscellany, 108, 110

goom, s., *gome, man*, 105 (2)

goonne: *see* gun

Gorboduc, 81

Gordon-Duff, Edward, his copy of *G*, 31 n.2

Gorgeous Gallery of Gallant Inventions, A (ed. Rollins, *q. v.*), 102, 105 f., 112, 127, 159, 185, 200, 218, 265, 268, 301, 321; borrowings in, from the miscellany, 109, 137, 281 ff., 285 f., 293, 329

gost, goste: *see* ghost

Gough, R., 46

govern, v., *influence, direct*, 12 (10)

governance, s., *control*, 15 (16), 26 (9)

Gower, John, 153

Graces, the, 93 (18), 97 (27), 100 (21)

graff, s., *plant, shoot*, 123 (20), 156 (36), 169 (18), 171 (9), 177 (36)

graffed, graft, pp., adj., *grafted*, 30 (23), 181 (16)

Grafton, Richard, 5

grange ('graunge'), s., *storehouse* (fig.), 171 (10)

grant ('graunt'), v., *confess* (Latin *fateor*), 95 (6)

Granta, *the River Cam, here used for Cambridge University*, 112 (25)

Granville, George, Baron Lansdowne, reprints of the miscellany poems dedicated to, 38 f., 42

grate, v., *greet, cry out (pray) for*, 136 (31), 240 (36), 242 (35). *See* greeted

graunge: *see* grange

graunt: *see* grant

grave, v., *carve*, 125 (30, 35, 37), 193 (10), 210 (9); *engrave*, 62 (24) n.; *impress*, 55 (14)

gravel(ed) ground, s. phr., 13 (13)

Gravener, Thomas, Sir, 53

graveness, s., *gravity*, 114 (6) (the first example in the *N. E. D.* is dated 1577)

graving ('grauyng'), s., *sculpturing*, 99 (10)

Gray, Agnes (Mrs. William), 308

Gray, William (W. G.), contributor to the miscellany, 80, 194 (7) n., 200 (30) n.; censorship in the poem of, 97; poems wrongly attributed to, 308 f.

Grayes, *Greeks*, 120 (6) n.

greave, s., *leg-armor*, 117 (19); ('greves') *thickets*, 203 (15, 28)

Greece ('Grece'), 125 (29), 126 (5), 202 (10)

Greek Anthology, 237 f.

Greekish ('grekish'), adj., *Grecian*, 168 (24), 228 (23)

Greeks ('Grekes'), 14 (19, 29), 227 (26), 228 (17, 19, 23), 246 (10)

green ('grene'), adj., *newly made*, 4 (20); *youthful and vigorous*, 3 (17), 21 (18)

green, s., *green trees, shrubs, etc.*, 4 (27), 7 (16), 11 (15), 61 (14)

Greene, Belle da Costa, 30

greenness ('grenes'), s., *immaturity*, 159 (21)

grees, s., *degrees* (astronomical) 116 (17)

greeted, v., *wept*, 108 (26). *See* grate

Greg, W. W., 10 n.1, 12 ff., 20, 30 n., 86 n.2

grene, grenes: *see* green(ness)

Grenville, Thomas, his copies of *B*, 10, 13 f., of *D*, 21, of *G*, 31 f., of *H*, 33, of *K*, 40 f., of *N*, 44 ff.

greves: *see* greave

Grey, Arthur, fourteenth Baron Grey de Wilton, the wife of (Elizabeth Zouche), praised by Gascoigne, 180

Grey, Elizabeth, Countess of Kildare, 137

Grey, Jane, Lady, 305, 322

Grey, William, thirteenth Baron Grey de Wilton, 69, 241

griesly: *see* grisly

grieues (griefs), s., 149 (30)

Griffiths, A. F., 50

Grimald, Annes (Agnes), elegy on, 111 (12) n., 78

Grimald, Nicholas, 3, 65 f., 92 ff., 277; "editor" of the miscellany, theories of his being the, 86 ff., 95; life and works of, 77 ff., 85; manuscript of a poem by, 96; meters of, 103 f.; orthographical peculiarities of, 79; poems by, in the first edition, 93 (2)–120 (21), order of, and omissions, in later editions, 8, 10 f.; reputation of, subordinated to Surrey's, 66; rhymes, poor, in the work of, 236; style of, the, 79; subject-matter of, the, 105; text of, the, how treated in the old editions, 88, 96

gripe, s., *grip*, 160 (17); *torment*, 81 (5); *vulture*, 93 (32) n.

grisly ('griesly,' 'gryzely'), adj., *frightful*, 120 (15), 153 (13)

groins, v., *grunts*, 88 (22) n.

grones (groans), s., 115 (28)

Grosart, A.B., 81, 112 n.2, 120 n.6, 144 f., 156, 158, 179, 188, 190, 219, 227, 230, 265, 268, 271, 277, 280, 286 f., 289, 298, 309, 322, 324 f.

gross, adj., *solidly built* (Latin *crassus*), 105 (6)

Grove, George, Sir, 282

Grove, Mathew, 145, 188; imitations by, of the miscellany, 112

grunts, s., *cries of pain* (Latin *dolor*), 115 (28)

gryzely: *see* grisly

Gualterus de Castellione, Philippus (Philippe Gualtier de Lille or de Châtillon), the *Alexandreis* of, translation from, by Grimald, 115 (8), reprinted, 248 ff.

Guarini, Baptista, 145

Guatier de Châtillon: *see* Gualterus

guerdon, s., 248 (14)

guess ('gesse'), v., *suppose, think*, 34 (13), 100 (33)

guest ('gest'), s., *fellow*, 252 (42); *visitor (love)*, 121 (10)

guie: *see* guy

guise ('guyse,' 'gyse'), s., *apparel*, 95 (23); *manner*, 33 (29)

gun ('gonne,' 'goonne'), s., 53 (5); description of a, 79 (38) n.

gushen, v., *gush*, 240 (9)

guy ('guie'), inf., *guide, steer*, 244 (9)

guyse, gyse: *see* guise

gyllot: *see* gillot

H., Susan, Mistress, poem on, 103 (24) n.

H., T., 286. *See* Howell

H., W.: *see* Hunnis

ha, interj., 110 (10), 200 (22), 239 (10)

Hackett, Francis, 74 n.1

Haddington, Scotland, battle of, 108 (15) n.

Haddon, Walter, 227; poem translated from, 113 (34), 245 f.

Hagen, Winston, his copy of *G*, 31 n. 2

hair ('heare,' 'heeres,' 'heyres'), s., 11 (22), 25 (38), 30 (8), 119 (35), 133 (29), 152 (2), 157 (34), 165 (25), 192 (24), 257 (16)

hale, v., *haul, pull*, 155 (6), 240 (11)

Hall, Anthony, 120 n.7

Hall, John, *The Court of Vertue*, moralizations of the miscellany poems in, 189, 260; quoted, 263, 328

Halliwell-Phillipps, J. O., 151

halseth, v., *esteems, is content with* (Latin *diligit*), 26 (26)

halt, v., *limp*, 188 (23)

Hammond, Eleanor P., 323

Hampton Court palace, 9 (29) n., 137

Handful of Pleasant Delights, A (ed. Rollins, *q. v.*), 4 n., 127, 252, 268; borrowings in, from the miscellany, 108 f., 142, 149, 161

handiwork ('handy warke'), s., 165 (14)

Hannah, John, 156 f.

Hannibal, 36 (9), 47 (9); referred to, 81 (18 f.), 164 f.

Hanscom, Elizabeth D., 103 n.1

hap, s., *chance, fortune*, 7 (35), 43 (8 ff.), 70 (36), 75 (38), 79 (24), 118 (29), 149 (17), 175 (37), etc.; *lucky chance*, 66 (27), 142 (4, 19), 230 (37), 232 (17)

hap ('happe'), v., *happen*, 43 (8 ff.), 79 (24)

harbinger of death, the, 166 (4) n.

hard: *see* heard

hard by, adv., 248 (26)

hardiness, s., *audacity*, 32 (12)

hargabush, s., *harquebus*, 164 (36)

Harington, Henry, editor of *Nugae Antiquae, q. v.*

Harington, John, contributor to the miscellany, 80 f., 256, 329; editor of the miscellany poets, Nott's theory, 89 ff.; poem by, in manuscript, reprinted, 194; poems attributed to, in *Nugae Anti-*

quae, 90 ff., 143, 258 f., 262, 294; translation (*The Book of Friendship*) of Cicero by, quoted, 239

Harington, John, Sir, 80 f., 90 f.; on his father's poem in the miscellany, 256; on Wyatt and Surrey, 121; poem by, quoted, 150

Harington MSS.: *see* MSS. Additional 28635, 28636, 36529, MS. Egerton 2711

harm, s., *grief*, 8 (20)

Harpalus ('Harpelus') and Phyllida, a pastoral poem, 132 (33) n.

harps, v., *plays on the harp*, 151 (23)

Harrington, John, printer, 90

Harrison, G. B., 121 n.3, 313, 325

harty: *see* hearty

Harvard College library, its copies of *J* and *K*, 38, 40

Harvey, Gabriel, 45, 120, 219, 280, 323 ff.

hase (has), v., 72 (41); used for *have*, 41 (33)

Haslewood, Joseph, 39, 181, 314; his copy of the miscellany, 10 n.2; manuscript notes by, in *K*, 41 f.

hatch, s., *gate, door*, 59 (20)

hatched, v., *cut in parallel lines*, (fig.) *tormented*, 133 (34)

hateless, adj., 11 (4) (the first example in the *N. E. D.* is dated 1580)

haunted, pp., *frequented*, 3 (37)

haw, s., 248 (36), 328

hawbart, s., *halberd*, 84 (26)

Hawes, Stephen, 5

hawthorn, the testament of a, a poem, 248 (34) n.

hay, s., *net for trapping rabbits*, 84 (36)

haynous: *see* heinous

Hazlitt, W. C., 13, 39 n., 58, 73 n.2, 81 n.4, 156, 262, 265, 271, 283, 285, 316

head ('hed'), s., *antlers*, 4 (31) n.; on head, *ahead, headlong*, 255 (36)

Headley, Henry, 122 f.

heale, s., *welfare*, 225 (24)

health, s., *good luck, welfare*, 40 (34), 211 (21); *safety*, 7 (9), 18 (29)

heaped, pp., *added to*, 111 (36)

heapy, adj., *full of heaps*, 231 (29)

heard ('hard'), v., 48 (27), 51 (8), 124 (8)

heare: *see* hair

hearse ('hersse'), s., *bier*, 250 (6)

heart-griping ('hertgripyng'), adj., 114 (17)

GLOSSARIAL INDEX

holly tree, the, and its properties, 168
(5 ff.), 287

holt, s., *wooded hill*, 13 (25), 188 (9)

home-hasting, adj., 199 (26)

homely guest, adj., *unpretentious fellow*,
252 (42)

Homer, 27 (9) n., 47 (10) n., 99 (8): *Iliad*,
the, cited, 172, 239

honest, adj., *virtuous*, 193 (22)

honestly, adv., *honorably*, 56 (36)

honesty ('honeste,' 'honestie'), s., *chas-
tity*, 238 (17); *honor*, 23 (36), 43 (12)

hongersterven: *see* hungerstarven

Honsdon: *see* Hunsdon

hood, s., *head-covering*, 239 (5)

Hookes, Nicholas, 72

hoont (hunt), v., 93 (19)

hoopt, pp., *encircled (with a crown)*, 84
(25)

hoord: *see* hoard

Horace, 77, 80, 105, 130, 139 f., 232, 268;
poems translated or imitated from,
152 f., 157 f., 174, 190, 207, 213 f., 218,
220 f., 272 ff., 327

horde: *see* hoard

hore: *see* hoar

hote (hot), adj., 8 (31), 9 (4), 56 (5), 68
(15), 121 (30), etc.

Hotten, J. C., printer, 271

hourd: *see* hoard

house, s., *one of the twelve parts (or
"houses") of the sky*, 116 (21)

hove, v., *linger*, 13 (2)

Howard, Catherine: *see* Catherine

Howard, Edward, ninth Duke of Norfolk,
39

Howard, Henry, Earl of Surrey, *Aeneid*
of, the: *see* Virgil; allusions to, enumer-
ated, 110 ff., 119 ff.; blank verse of, the,
date of its publication, 70, 79 n.2;
Churchyard's relations with, 83; edi-
tions of: *see* Tottel's; Geraldine and,
71 ff.; Harington and, 90 f.; imitations
by, of Heywood, 146, 276, of Wyatt, 3
(23) n., 13 (41) n., 23 (23-26) n., 25
(38) n., 28 (8) n., 172, 313; imitations
of, in the miscellany, 147 (12) n., 163
(2) n., 313; life and works of, 67 ff., 85;
mentioned, 212, 241, 255, 272, 285;
meters and stanzaic forms of, 70, 103;
named alone on the title-page, reasons
why he is, 65, and the effect on his

reputation, 66 f., 299; named elsewhere
in the miscellany, 2 (8), 31 (24), 206
(2), 207 (11 f.); poems by, the, in the
miscellany, 3 (2)-31 (23), 206 (2)-210
(37), last of, written, 159, order of,
in the second and later editions, 8,
10 f.; manuscript copies of, omitted by
Tottel, 92 n.2, manuscript sources of,
96 f., and how "edited," 88 f., 96 f.,
published in his lifetime, 150, unique
copies of, 96 n. 1, wrongly attributed to,
67 f., 259, 261, 266, 278, 292, 299, 316 f.,
321, Wyatt the subject of certain of,
66; Shelley, a "servant" of, 247; son-
nets of, 103, 188; style of, 102 ff.; value
of the work of, 70. *See* S. (H.)

Howard, Henry, first Earl of Northamp-
ton, 159

Howard, Mary, Duchess of Richmond, 62,
68, 142, 164, 208

Howard, Thomas, second Duke of Nor-
folk, 312

Howard, Thomas, third Duke of Norfolk,
68 f., 241, 310

Howard, Thomas, fourth Duke of Nor-
folk, 69, 146, 330

Howard, Thomas, Lord, son of the second
Duke of Norfolk, half-uncle of the poet
Surrey, 312

Howell, Thomas (T. H.), 77 n.2, 102, 144,
190, 265, 277, 309, 324; imitation by, of
the miscellany, 111, 289

Hudson, H. H., 152, 234, 271, 292

hue ('hewe'), s., *face*, 9 (28), 13 (5), 257
(13)

Hughes, John, 122 n.2

hugy, adj., 42 (27), 147 (21)

hungerstarven ('hongersteruen'), pp. adj.,
starved, 131 (22)

Hunnis, William (W. H.), 90, 207

Hunsdon ('Honsdon'), Hertfordshire, 9
(27) n.

Hunterian Club, 153, 286, 298, 323, 325

Hunterian Museum: *see* Glasgow

Huntington, Henry E., library of, its
copy of *B*, 9 n.1-5, 10, 37 n.3, of *E*, 27,
of *G*, 31, of *H*, 33, of an epitaph on
Wyatt, 154 f.

hurtful, adj., *baleful*, 116 (18) n.

Huth, Henry, 82 n.; his copy of *I*, 35

Hutton, James, 237

Hyacinth, 95 (11)

[365]

Hyads ('Hyades'), 111 (37), 244
hye: *see* hie
hyght: *see* hight
Hyginus, 222, 228, 287
Hypolitus: *see* Hippolytus
hyre: *see* hire

I, repetition of, 87 (16) n.
Jaggard, John, printer, 7
James I, king of Scotland, 142
James IV, king of Scotland, 208 (5) n.
Jamieson, T. H., 181
Jane (Seymour), queen of England, 68, 180
jangling, pres. p., *quarreling*, 169 (17)
Jannet, Pierre, 152
Janus, the god, 101 (38), 103 (3)
jape, make a, of, v. phr., *make a joke of, make light of*, 83 (21)
Icarian beck, *Icarian Sea*, 104 (24)
Icarus ('Icar'), 104 (23) n.
idol, s., *image (of death)*, 109 (26); *sculptured image*, 126 (15)
ieewell (jewel), s., 111 (18)
ieifloure: *see* gillyflower
jeopardy ('ieopardie'), s., 10 (8)
Jerusalem, Mary of, eats her child, a poem, 82 (10) n.
jestress ('iestres'), s., *a female jester*, 169 (17) n. (the only example in the N. E. D.)
Jesus, son of Sirach, 159
Jewry, 27 (18)
Ilium, 228 (6). *See* Troy
ill-suading ('ylswading'), adj., *tempting to evil*, 98 (6)
imp ('ymp'), s., *child*, 93 (16), 95 (14) n., 97 (5) n., 100 (21), 111 (29); *evil spirit in hell*, 131 (19); *young man*, 109 (27), 114 (28)
inborne, adj., 96 (36)
inconstance, s., 238 (6)
incontinent, adv., *immediately*, 58 (2)
indexing, the manner of, in the early editions of the miscellany, 15 f.
Indian, 103 (11), 212 (17, 30)
indifferent, adj., *impartial*, 189 (30); *ordinary* (Latin *mediocris*) *in looks*, 96 (8, 9, 27)
infeft, pp., *given up entirely (to you)*, 171 (12) (earlier figurative use than any cited in the N. E. D.)

injust, adj., *unjust*, 16 (11)
inow: *see* enow
inpresseth ('inpreaseth'), v., *mingles with*, 145 (15)
intend ('entend'), v., *express in words*, 88 (35); *understand*, 193 (37)
intent ('entent'), s., 85 (32) n.; *use*, 33 (6)
intermitted, adj., *interrupted*, 194 (18) (the first example in the N. E. D.)
interyield ('enteryeld'), v., 237 (16)
Johnson, Richard, 109
Johnson, Samuel, 248
Jolley, Thomas, his copy of *H*, 33, of Curll's reprint, 38
Jones, Evan J., 151
Jones, Richard, printer, 4 n., 109, 157, 259
Jonson, Ben, 85, 121, 152
Iopas, the song of, a poem, 90 (15) n.
Josephus, 213
Jove, 81 (34), 91 (26), 93 (17), 94 (14), 95 (35), 97 (5) n., 102 (37), 104 (33), 107 (15), 110 (20), 111 (37), 114 (25), 119 (15), 188 (11 ff.), 206 (32), 230 (5, 9), 244 (23); Jove's imp, or daughter, *Venus*, 100 (21, 30). *See* Jupiter.
Joye, Jacob, 25
Iphigenia, allusion to, 14 (22)
Irish, 9 (23)
irksome ('yrkesome'), adj., *loathsome*, 191 (15) n.
irmus, or the long-loose, examples of, 164, 175
Israel, 229 (19)
issue, s., *outlet*, 56 (3)
Italians, 2 (5)
Itrascus, 181 (23) n.
Judith, the apocryphal heroine, slayer of Holofernes, 102 (33)
juggling ('iuglyng'), s., *deception*, 150 (14)
Iulie: *see* Caesar, July
July ('Iulie'), 114 (31)
Juno, 90 (18)
Jupiter, 151 (4), 229 (35). *See* Jove
ivory ('yuery,' 'yuorie'), adj., 126 (6), 204 (8)
iwis ('ywys,' 'ywis'), adv., *certainly, indeed*, 25 (21), 41 (8), 225 (23)
iye: *see* eyen

K., G. L.: *see* Kittredge
kaies, s., *keys*, 165 (11)

Leland, John, 119

Lelius: *see* Laelius

lenger, adj., *longer*, 17 (33), 22 (11), 48 (28), 59 (21, 35), 69 (16), 127 (4), 132 (13), 135 (36), 139 (9), etc.

lengest, adj., *longest*, 180 (29)

length, v., *prolong*, 171 (36), 213 (27)

lent, v., *leaned*, 70 (32)

lere ('leare'), v., *teach*, 180 (11) n.

lese: *see* leese

lesse, s., *loss*, 243 (33)

lesse, v., *lessen*, 35 (26)

lest (least), adv., 71 (12), 79 (18), 92 (4), 136 (35), 150 (24) n., 176 (12), 188 (21), 193 (18)

let, v., *cease*, 149 (6), 212 (33); *deprived*, 193 (35); *hinder*, 72 (36), 87 (34) n.; *prevent*, 6 (14), 116 (18) n.; let thee weet, *give you to understand*, 207 (34)

letcher: *see* lecher

Letters and Papers . . . Henry VIII, 180, 241, 247, 280

lever: *see* liefer

leves, v., lives, 244 (15)

lewd ('leude'), adj., *base*, 239 (10); *evil, vicious*, 125 (17), 238 (31); *ignorant*, 232 (32)

leze: *see* leese

Library, The, 5 n., 12 n.3, 14 n.1, 20 n.1, 30 n., 84 n.1, 86 n.2. *See* Bibliographical Society

Libyk, adj., *Lybian*, 90 (18)

licour: *see* liquor

Lide: *see* Lydia

lief ('leef,' 'leefe'), adj., *agreeable*, 106 (23); *dear*, 14 (2); *glad*, 128 (10), 179 (20)

lief, liefe, s., *life*, 129 (36), 149 (6), 175 (20)

liefer ('leefer,' 'leuer'), adj., *more pleasing, dearer*, 69 (10), 105 (23), 139 (42); adv., *more gladly*, 93 (30)

liefsome ('leefsom'), adj., *delightful*, 19 (3)

lieve ('leeue'), v., *believe*, 195 (31)

lift, v., *lifted*, 178 (18)

light, adv., *easy*, 238 (11)

light, v., *disembark*, 90 (18); *fall*, 256 (13); *fall to the lot of*, 192 (4); *happen*, 208 (42), 239 (31); *lighten*, 7 (29); *sit down*, 205 (19); *strike*, 244 (19)

lightly, adv., *quickly*, 148 (33); *readily, easily*, 195 (31)

lightning, adj., *murderous* (Latin *fulmineus*), 115 (23)

like, s., 151 (38)

like ('lyke'), v., *love*, 158 (21); *please* (impersonal), 94 (2), 114 (22), 119 (30), 145 (7)

liked ('liekt'), v., 136 (34)

Lilly, Joseph: *see* Collection

limbs ('lims,' 'limes'), s., 107 (37), 158 (4)

Lincoln, Earl of: *see* Clinton

Linton, W. J., 123, 186

liquor ('licour'), s., *juice*, 83 (19); *water*, 107 (24)

Lisle, Lord: *see* Dudley

list, s., *pleasure*, 139 (17)

list ('lyst'), impers. v., *it pleases*, 61 (25), 69 (16), 85 (35), etc.

live, on, prep. phr., *in life*, 250 (34)

livelihead ('liuelyhed'), s., *living presence, life*, 27 (24) (the first example in the N. E. D.)

livelihood ('liuelod'), s., 82 (25)

lively, adj., *animated*, 66 (19), 72 (21), 73 (18), 97 (17), 155 (30) n., 156 (19); *lifelike*, 19 (7), 99 (18); *living*, 27 (13), 207 (9), 218 (27); *vigorous*, 28 (8), 99 (25), 171 (37); *warm and vigorous*, 3 (7), 9 (22), 147 (31); *vivid*, 257 (33, 39)

lively, adv., *in lifelike fashion*, 29 (26), 120 (2), 126 (9)

livelyhed: *see* livelihead

liver, s., *one who is living*, 145 (7)

lives, adj., *living*, 147 (20), 151 (33)

Livy, Titus, 86 (20) n.

Lloyd, Lodowick, 165

loathful ('lothfull'), adj., *hideous* (Latin *informis*), 244 (23)

loathly ('lothly'), adj., *unwilling* (Latin *invitus*), 120 (4)

Locker-Lampson, Frederick (Rowfant library), his copy of *B*, 10 n.3, 14, 37 n.3, of *G*, 31 n.1, of *H*, 33 n.

lodesman, s., *pilot*, 175 (17)

Lodge, Edmund, 42

Lodge, Thomas, 153 f., 298, 323, 325

loft, adj., *raised aloft, elevated*, 28 (29), 224 (27) (the first of two examples in the N. E. D.)

londe (land), s., 186 (22)

lone (loan), s., 137 (20)

long, of, adv. phr., *a long time*, 130 (15)

long, v., *belong*, 11 (5), 218 (13), 226 (39); *desire to be*, 123 (6)
long-gathered, pp., 117 (10)
long-loose, the: *see* irmus
lookers-on, s., 252 (20)
loose, pp., *lost*, 105 (33)
loose ('lose'), adv., 128 (24), 155 (21)
loose ('lose,' 'lowse'), v., 38 (4), 153 (38)
lore, s., *doctrine*, 69 (5); *learning*, 101 (5); *lesson*, 235 (18), 237 (23), 244 (16)
lothfull: *see* loathful
lothly: *see* loathly
loud-liar, the, example of, 173 (23–28) n.
louring, adj., *frowning*, 240 (32), 245 (30)
lovde ('loude'), v., *loved*, 173 (7)
love, v., error for *leue (leave)*, 66 (29) n.
lovers'-dilemma poem, a, 317
lower ('lowre'), v., *frown*, 26 (36)
lowly cheer, s. phr., *modest appearance*, 238 (18)
Lowndes, W. T., 13, 37 n.3, 38 n.2
lowse: *see* loose
Lucan, 165
Lucrece, 191 (4–5), 193 (17), 180
Lucretius, borrowings from, 80, 272 f., 321
lukewarm, adj., 113 (10)
Lupa, 111 (35) n.
lure, a falcon's, 159 (8), 256 (25)
lure, v., *recall (a hawk) by the lure*, 133 (16), 256 (30)
lurk, v., *be concealed* (Latin *teguntur*), 94 (16), (Latin *latet*), 96 (21)
lurker, s., *one who lies in ambush*, 190 (38) n.
lurking, pres. p., *hiding*, 159 (12), 163 (22)
lust, s., *base desire*, 29 (6), 106 (14); *pleasure, caprice*, 12 (33), 32 (10), 35 (7), 59 (28), 84 (30), 86 (35), etc.; *wish, desire*, 6 (18), 7 (26), 84 (29), 106 (6), 132 (13), 174 (25), 246 (15), etc.
lust, v., *wish*, 70 (10), 208 (30)
lustiness, s., *beauty*, 3 (7)
lusty, adj., *beautiful*, 81 (32); *delightful*, 87 (24), 93 (5), 171 (35); *vigorous*, 11 (22), 93 (5), 153 (14)
lute, Wyatt's song to the, 62 (16)
Lux, a falcon, 66 (7)
luyster, s., *luster*, 101 (30)
Lyaeus ('Lyai'), 111 (39) n. *See* Bacchus
Lydgate, John, 5, 145, 220, 317
Lydia ('Lide'), Lydian, 98 (30), 157 (36)

lyke: *see* like
Lyly, John, 181
Lysippus, Greek artist, 99 (8)
lyst: *see* list

M., Mistress, poem on, 254 (14) n.
M., D.: *see* Murray
McClure, N. E., 121 n.1
Macdonald, Hugh, 128, 266, 278
mace, s., *club* (really, according to Horace, a stroke of lightning), 151 (5)
Macedoins: *see* Macedonians
Macedon, the, *Alexander the Great (q. v.)*, 27 (7), 115 (23), 117 (22)
Macedonians ('Macedoins'), 115 (18), 116 (28)
Mackail, J. W., 237 f.
McKerrow, R. B., 6 n., 19 n.2., 71 n.2
mad, worse than, 175 (29), 197 (38)
Madan, F., 28 n.1
Magdalene ('Maudlē'), St. Mary, 102 (33)
Magoun, Jr., F. P., 287, 298
maierome: *see* marjoram
maim ('maym'), s., *calamity*, 105 (21)
maistres, maistresse: *see* mistress
Maitland, J. A. F., 282
make, s., *mate*, 4 (29), 194 (38), 207 (20), 219 (9)
make, v., *do*, 252 (30)
makeless, adj., *matchless*, 254 (31)
malice, v., *seek to injure*, 8 (9) (the first example in the *N. E. D.*)
Malone, Edmond, 41
Maltravers ('Mautrauers'): *see* Fitzalan
man, s., *servant, lover*, 40 (12), 54 (6), 121 (26), 185 (18)
manifold, adv., *in many degrees, very much*, 86 (29), 142 (35)
manner ('maner'), adj., *kind of*, 36 (25), 47 (38), 100 (31), 120 (20)
Manningham, John, 152
manuscript notes in *C*, 150, 271, in *E*, 28, 67, in *D** and *I*, 26, 36, 100 f., 149, 153, 185, 187, 287, 294, 296 f., 313, 315, 327
manuscripts, the, of the miscellany poets, how treated, 94 ff.
manuscripts, list of the, cited: Additional *4900*, 278, 285; Additional *15225*, 274, 302 ff.; Additional *17492* ("Duke of Devonshire MS."), 96 n.1, 97 n.1, 143, 174, 185, 190 f., 209, 212, 281, 290; Ad-

ditional *23971*, 278; Additional *26737*, 261, 281, 284; Additional *28635* (a copy of "Harington MS. No. 2"), 62 n.1, 81, 91 f., 137, 145, 157, 176, 201, 211, 258 f., 261, 263, 266, 269, 277, 281, 289 ff., 299 ff., 311, 315, 318, 320 f., 325, reprints from, 133 f., 137, 178 f., 194, 263 f., 288 f., 294 f.; Additional *28636* (a copy of "Harington MS. No. 1"), 91; Additional *30513*, 143, 294; Additional *36529* ("Harington MS."), 91, 97 n.1, 129, 131 f., 135 f., 138 ff., 141, 147, 150, 153 f., 157, 193 f., 310, reprints from, 165 ff., 199, 201 f., 212, 320; Additional *38539*, 305; Additional *38599*, 284; Additional *38813*, 324; Additional *38823*, 79; Ashmole *48*, 79, 257, 284, 290, 302 ff.; Ashmole *176*, 313; Burney, 313; Corpus Christi College (Cambridge), 317; Cotton Titus A. xxiv, 150, 157, 255, 266, 273, 309, 325; Duke of Devonshire, i. e., Additional *17492 (q. v.)*; Egerton 2711 ("Harington MS. No. 1"), 62 n.1, 91, 95 n.3, 96 n.1, 160–164, 166–176, 180–184, 187–190, 194–200, 202 f., 208–215, 219, 221, 314 f.; Farmer (Chetham library), 156; French, a, of the thirteenth century, 133; Harleian *78*, 97 n.1, 148, 210, 269, 292, 318, 322; Harleian *1703*, 274, 284; Harleian *6910*, 283; Huntington *183*, 82 n.; Lansdowne *98*, 292, 306, 308; Rawlinson Poet. *82*, 323; Rawlinson Poet. *85*, 79, 261; Rawlinson Poet. *108*, 200, 239; Rawlinson Poet. *172*, 315; Sloane *159*, 261; Sloane *1206*, 306; Sloane *1207*, 306 ff.; Sloane *1896*, 238 f., 266, 302 ff., 327; Tanner *103*, 278

marching figure, the, example of, 127 (2) n.

Marcus, i. e., *Cicero (q. v.)*, 118 (17) n. *See* Cato

Margaret of Valois, 233

Marius, Caius, 237

marjoram ('maierome'), s., 2 (25)

Markham, C. R., 81 n.1, 256

Markham, Isabella (Mrs. John Harington), poems alleged to be addressed to, 254 (14) n., 294

marlian: *see* merlin

Marlowe, Christopher, 45, 85, 112

Marot, Clément, 152

marriage, poems for and against, 96 (2, 22), 150 (8), 195 (20)

Mars, 91 (28), 93 (14), 186 (15)

Martial, epigram translated from, 26 (2) n.

Martius, 111 (23) n.

Marty-Laveaux, C. J., 135, 296, 298

Martyn, John, 278

martyr ('martir'), s., 222 (8, 16); *a constant sufferer (in love)*, 184 (7), 223 (12)

martyrs, the Marian, and the miscellany, 3; Grimald's alleged betrayal of, 78, 87

Mary, the Blessed Virgin, 102 (34)

Mary, daughter of Eleazer, of Jerusalem, 213

Mary I, princess and queen of England, Arundel (Mrs.) and, 329 f.; Audley's treatise dedicated to, 278 f.; Geraldine and, 74, 137; Grimald and, 78; Howard family, the, and, 70; Heywood's poem on, 155 (24) n.; name of, in the miscellany, 100 (6) n., 114 (10, 30), removed, 97, 302; poems contemporary with, 93; reputation of, and the miscellany, 3 f; Surrey and, 68; Williams and, 305; Wyatt's rebellion and, 65, 322

Mary, queen of Scots, the acquaintance of, with the miscellany, 262

masheth, v., *mesheth, catches in a net*, 148 (35) (the first example in the *N. E. D.*)

masked, v., *was enmeshed*, 128 (16) (the first example of "absolute" use in the *N. E. D.*)

massy, adj., 93 (19)

mate, s., *checkmate*, 20 (22), 21 (14)

matter ('mater'), s., (Latin *materies*) 95 (24)

Maudlē: *see* Magdalene

maugre, prep., *in spite of*, 237 (39)

Mausolean, adj., *like the tomb of Mausolus, king of Caria*, 113 (19) (the first example in the *N.E.D.*)

Mautravers: *see* Maltravers

Mavorses, *Mars's*, 116 (20)

Mavortian, adj., *martial*, 111 (6)

May, the unluckiness of, to Wyatt, a poem, 35 (2), 163

maym: *see* maim

maze, s., *amazement, admiration*, 97 (28) n.

mean, adj., *medium*, 26 (20); *moderate*, 26 (12); *ordinary*, 96 (30); the golden mean, poems in praise of, 26 (2, 20), 104 (17), 150 (17), 244 (8) n.; the mean (*poor*) estate, poems praising, 80 (27) n., 82 (21), 123 (28), 147 (37), 157 (2) n., 197 (18 ff.)

mean, s., *center*, 86 (40); *golden mean*, 104 (20 f., 28); *means*, 114 (38); *lament, complaint*, 79 (11), 236 (32); *tenor*, 233 (33); of mean, 238 (7) n.

meaning, vbl. n., *intention*, 59 (16)

meant ('ment'), v., *aimed, directed*, 92 (6); *intended*, 85 (30), 203 (16)

Meares, W., printer, 39

meash (mesh), v., *entangle*, 7 (3), 52 (25)

measure-keeping, s. phr., *observing the golden mean*, 104 (17 f.)

mede (meed), s., 22 (27)

medeth (meedeth), v., *rewards*, 211 (10)

Medwall, Henry, 227

Melbancke, Brian, borrowings of, from the miscellany, 112, 128, 138, 143, 146, 157 f., 165, 168 f., 185 ff., 190, 202, 210, 214, 259, 261, 265, 267, 270 f., 274, 276, 287, 293 f., 297, 306, 309, 314, 326, 329; quoted also at 324 f.

Meleager, the son of Neoptolemus, an officer of Alexander the Great, 117 (28)

mell, v., *mingle*, 102 (8)

Melpomene, 97 (13)

Melvill Book of Roundels, The, copies of miscellany poems in, 260, 313

Memoirs of Queen Mary's Days, 3

Memphite, adj., *of Memphis (Egypt)*, 116 (2)

Menoetius's ('Menetus') son, *Patroclus*, 106 (35) n.

ment: *see* meant

Mercurius Elencticus, 145, 270

Mercury, the planet, 91 (36). *See* Cyllene

mercy, v., *be merciful to*, 12 (27)

merely (merrily), adv., 221 (8)

Meres, Francis, 82, 325

merlin ('marlian'), s., 126 (26) n.

Merrill, L. R., 64, 78 n., 128, 223–255 *passim*; on Grimald as the "editor" of the miscellany, 87

Merritt, Percivall, 26 n.4

meseems ('me semes'), impers. v., 73 (6), 105 (10)

mesh: *see* masheth, meash

messengers of age, 30 (8)

mete, v., *measure*, 5 (6), 72 (28)

metrical and verse-forms in the miscellany, 102 ff.

Metrodorus, 105 (24) n.

meve, v., *move*, 51 (28), 152 (17), 212 (21)

Michiels, Alfred, 135

middle stream, s. phr., *the main ocean* (Latin *altum*), 244 (10)

mids, middes, s., *midst*, 97 (25), 133 (35)

million, many a, s. phr., *a very large number*, 47 (16) n. (Cf. Chaucer, *The Sumner's Prologue*, line 21, "many a millioun.")

Milman, H. H., 156

Milton, John, 154, 302; blank-verse earlier than, 45

mind ('mynde'), v., *remember*, 125 (8); *think of* (Latin *cogitare*), 95 (16), 100 (25)

mindful, adj., 109 (36)

Minerva ('Minerue'), goddess, 80 (2), 101 (25), 103 (19), 112 (21), 116 (43) n.; *wisdom*, 193 (38). *See* Pallas

ming, v., *call to mind, mention* (Latin *narrare*), 96 (34); *meng, produce (honey) by mixing*, 4 (36)

Minos, 153 (36)

Mirror for Magistrates, The, 181, 314; Sackville's "Induction" to, 242

mirth, a poem in praise of, 99 (21)

mischanced, pp., *made unfortunate*, 35 (15) (the first example in the *N. E. D.*)

misease, s., *lack of ease*, 31 (13), 88 (40)

misfall me, it, impers. v., *(if) misfortune happen to me*, 203 (24)

misseek ('misseke'), v., *seek wrongly*, 84 (39)

mistress ('maistres,' 'maistresse'), s., 47 (22), 52 (14), 192 (11), 193 (23), 253 (12)

Mnemosyne's daughters, *the Muses*, 100 (26). *See* Remembrance

mo, moe, adv., *more*, 2 (18), 19 (38), 25 (36), 48 (39), 89 (22), 102 (5), 105 (10), 108 (28), 124 (9, 10, 37), etc.

moan ('mone'), v., 176 (18, 21), 177 (37)

Modern Language Association of America, *Publications*, 78 n., 87 n.2, 103 n.1

Modern Language Notes, 103 n.1, 109 n.3, 152, 223, 230 f., 234, 240, 323

Modern Language Quarterly, The, 150, 197

Modern Language Review, The, 79 n.2, 88 n.3, 197, 237

ones, adv., *once*, 3 (8), 17 (15, 19), 18 (26), 34 (24), 198 (31), 226 (27), 248 (19, 31)

onlesse (unless), conj., 119 (24)

or, adv., conj., *ere*, 93 (11), 128 (37), 144 (25), 162 (7), 167 (32), 186 (31), 246 (34), 249 (12); or . . . or, 94 (9), 165 (15)

orators, s., *petitioners*, 189 (4)

orderly, adv., *in regular succession*, 220 (35)

order's comely rate, by, 102 (23) n.

Oreads, the, mountain nymphs, 100 (5)

Orestes, 106 (37)

orient, adj., *glowing, ruddy*, 145 (16)

Ormonde, Countess of: *see* Fitzgerald (Joan)

oste, s., *host*, 229 (27)

other, pron., *others*, 79 (4, 10, 16, 20, 22, 28), 159 (16), 206 (32); other some, *some others*, 208 (21)

otherwhere, adv., *elsewhere*, 192 (20)

ought, s., *aught, any part*, 75 (3), 123 (2), 248 (15), etc.

ought, v., *owed*, 256 (34); *owned*, 124 (11)

out, interj., 107 (11)

outcry, the: *see* ecphonesis

outgate, s., *egress*, 93 (35)

outshit ('outshyt'), v., *shut out*, 36 (9). *See* shit

overblown, v., *blown away*, 30 (20) (the first example in the *N. E. D.* is dated 1596)

overfervent, adj., 114 (9)

overfierce ('ouerferse'), adj., 104 (32)

overgo, v., *overtake*, 187 (32); *surpass*, 100 (18) n.

overmeek, adj., 104 (32)

overpass, v., *pass*, 112 (6)

overreacher, the, example of, 173 (23–28) n.

overrun, pp., *killed*, 14 (28)

overthwart, adj., *contrarious, adverse*, 44 (19), 49 (8), 244 (30)

overthwarts, s., *rebuffs, adversity*, 26 (33) (the first example in the *N. E. D.*)

overweighed ('ouerwayd'), pp., *weighed down with*, 242 (33)

Ovid, 80, 132, 143, 195, 301, 325, 328; his *Art of Love*, 188 (32); poems imitated or translated from, 158 (32) n., 203 (2) n., 219 (6) n.

Oxathres ('Oxate'), 115 (26) n.

Oxford, 112 (29) n.; Earl of: *see* Vere

Oxford Book of English Verse, The, 123

pacient: *see* patient

pack, truss up thy, v. phr., *pack up your wares (like a pedler)*, 30 (15)

Padelford, F. M., 37 n.2, 52, 68 n.1, 88 n.3, 92 n.2, 129–159 *passim*, 277, 299, 310–313, 322; edition by, of Surrey, 62 ff., collations with, 128; Geraldine, on, 75; manuscripts of Surrey, on the, 96 f.; John and G. F. Nott, on, 49 f., 51 n.5; reprints by, of the miscellany poems, 123; Wyatt's sonnets, on, 103 n.1

Page, Samuel, 195

pageant, s., *part played by one in the drama of life*, 197 (37)

page-proofs, the miscellany set directly into, 19

paint ('paynt'), v., *create*, 20 (3); *describe*, 27 (13), 97 (8), 101 (29), 120 (2), etc.; *flatter*, 86 (13); paint colors, *deceive*, 5 (29); paint the mold, *adorn the earth*, 107 (26)

painted, pp., *revealed*, 141 (9); painted thoughts, *?thoughts revealed by blushes*, 6 (21)

Painter, William, 5

Palamades and Nauplius, 287

pale, s., *rail-fence*, 4 (31)

palindrome, a, examples of, 314 f.

Pallas, 93 (14), 101 (5), 257 (35). *See* Minerva

palm, reaped the, v. phr., *gained the victory*, 180 (7)

Palmer, G. H., his copy of *E*, 27 f.

Palmer, Mary, 277

palm-play, s., *a game resembling tennis, played with palms of the hands instead of racquets*, 13 (9) (the first example in the *N. E. D.*)

pamphlets, s., 224 (4) n.

Pan, 86 (28)

Pandar, 89 (40) n.

Pandulpho (Pandolfo Collinutio or Collenuccio), epigram translated from, 79 (38) n.

Papini, Pietro, 136, 172, 175

paradise, 38 (35)

Paradise of Dainty Devices, The, by Richard Edwards (*q. v.*) and others (ed. Rollins, *q. v.*), 4 n., 81, 92 f., 105 f., 120, 128, 132, 135, 144, 165, 168, 187, 207, 218, 221, 270 f., 286, 293, 296 f.,

GLOSSARIAL INDEX

305, 308, 324, 328; borrowings by, from the miscellany, 108 f., 257 ff., 267, 289

paragon ('parragon,' 'peragon'), s., 160 (15), 170 (4), 172 (21), 200 (7)

paramour, s., *sweetheart*, 133 (3)

paraventure, adv., *peradventure*, 46 (34)

parceive, v., *perceive*, 207 (22)

parcel, s., *a small piece, a bit*, 2 (4), 4 (18)

pardie, pardy, interj., 30 (29), 132 (27), 172 (39). *See* perdie

parentheses used for quotation-marks, 324

parfit, parfite: *see* perfit

Paris of Troy, 179 (24), 202 (4, 22, 27), 219 (13), 231 (26), 254 (26), 257 (10) n.

Park, Thomas, 36, 46, 58, 73 n.1, 82 n., 122 n.7, 283; manuscript notes by, in copies of *K*, 41 f., in Percy's edition, 44 f.; *Nugae Antiquae*, changes in his edition of, 91

Parker, Henry, eighth Baron Morley, 245

Parker, Martin, 190

Parnassus ('pernasse'), s., fig. for *Cambridge*, 112 (27)

Parr, Anne, Countess of Pembroke, elegy on, 194 (15)n.

Parr, Catherine: *see* Catherine

Parr, William, first Marquis of Northampton, 90

parragon: *see* paragon

Parry, J. J., 152

Parry, Robert, 259

parsever: *see* persevere

Parsons (*alias* Dolman), Robert, Jesuit, 256

part, s., *melody*, 233 (33)

Parturier, Eugène, 181, 209

pass, v., *put to shame, surpass*, 86 (29), 93 (6), 115 (13), 170 (5), 218 (6); bring to pass, 230 (15)

past not, neg. v., *didn't care or mind*, 23 (35), 128 (23)

pastoral, a, in the miscellany, 104, 265

pastourelle, a, 144

patient ('pacient'), adj., *persistent*, 149 (18) (the first example in the *N. E. D.* is dated 1590)

Patroclus, 106 (35) n.

Paul, St., 125 (20)

pay, s., *reward*, 194 (19); *satisfaction, liking*, 95 (21)

payzed: *see* peised

pear, v., *appear*, 94 (28)

peares: *see* peers

peas, pease, s., *peace*, 110 (31), 124 (7), 130 (2)

peason, s., *peas*, 10 (5). *See* pese

Peele, George, 45, 278

peep ('pepe'), v., *make a sound*, 233 (33)

peers ('peares,' 'peres'), s., 100 (11), 114 (35)

peevish ('peuishe'), adj., *foolish*, 192 (38)

peised ('payzd,' 'payzed'), pp., *weighed, deliberated*, 102 (19), 105 (3)

Peitho ('Pitho'), goddess of persuasion, 120 (8) n.

pellets, s., *bullets*, 164 (16)

pelow: *see* pillow

Pembroke, Earl of: *see* Herbert (William), Parr (Anne)

Penbroke (Pembroke): *see* Parr (Anne)

Penelope, 19 (35), 156 (9), 230 (26); epistle of, to Ulysses (*q. v.*), a poem, 219 (6) n.

people-pestered, adj., 94 (2)

pepe: *see* peep

peragon: *see* paragon

Percy, Thomas, Bishop, 28 n.2, 38 n.3, 92, 94, 189; reprints by, from the miscellany, 122, 265, 283, 286; unpublished edition by, of the miscellany, 44 ff., 57 f., 90 n.1, 318

Percy, Thomas, the younger, 46

Percy Society, 181, 283

perdie ('perdy,' 'perdee'), interj., 49 (10), 58 (27), 64 (33), 118 (14), etc. *See* pardie

peres: *see* peers

perfit ('pfit,' 'parfit,' 'parfite'), adj., *perfect*, 20 (2), 27 (15), 37 (2), 52 (10), 69 (6), 102 (26), 126 (4), 132 (28), 169 (31), 170 (17), 172 (5), 174 (34)

perfitly, adv., 49 (12)

perfitness ('parfitness'), s., *perfection*, 121 (17), 126 (7)

Periothous: *see* Pirithous

pernasse: *see* Parnassus

persaunt, adj., *perceant, piercing*, 5 (15)

Perses, *Persians*, 115 (20, 30)

persevere ('parseuer'), v., 69 (7), 198 (28)

Persia, 27 (7)

Persians, Alexander's fight with the, 115 (11, 18), 117 (36)

Persius, 214

[375]

pervart, v., *pervert*, 160 (12)

pese, s., *pease, one pea*, 24 (8). *See* peason

Petowe, Henry, borrowings of, from the miscellany, 112 ff.

Petrarch, poems in praise of, 169 (21), 170 (5); edition of, used, 128; mentioned, 70, 72, 76, 83, 101, 103, 105, 108, 245; imitations or translations from, 129 ff., 132, 135, 137 ff., 140 f., 143, 145, 149, 154, 160 ff., 164–170, 175, 178 ff., 182, 185, 188, 191 ff., 195 ff., 198 f., 201 f., 204–207, 211 f., 268 f., 295 f., 297 f., 309 f., 313 f., 319 f., 328

Pettie, George, borrowing by, from the miscellany, 317

pevishe: *see* peevish

Pforzheimer, C. H., his copy of *C*, 12, of *I*, 35

Phaeton, son of Apollo, 104 (25)

phantom ('fantome'), s., *dream*, 48 (3)

Pharaoh, 229 (19)

Phebe, Phebus: *see* Phoebe, Phoebus

phenix: *see* phoenix

Philip II, king of Macedonia, 252

Philip II, king of Spain and England, 302, 305, 322

Phillida: *see* Phyllida

Phillips, a musician, elegy on, 162 (26) n.

Phillis, Wyatt's poem to, 35 (20), 164. *See* Phyllis

Phillis and Flora, 4 n.

Philological Quarterly, The, 317

phisike: *see* physic

Phoebe ('Phebe'), 93 (23), 191 (10). *See* Diana

Phoebus ('Phebus'), 26 (36), 72 (31), 97 (25), 101 (35), 112 (22), 119 (14), 120 (4), 151 (22) n., 168 (36), 191 (10), 204 (17), 244 (27), 253 (16 n., 26 ff.), 257 (17); Phoebus' fowl, *the raven*, 119 (14); Phoebus' spear, *sunbeams*, 72 (31). *See* Apollo

phoenix ('phenix'), the, 148 (32), 156 (5), 203 (31) n., 250 (31)

Phoenix Nest, The, 105 f., 109, 128, 135, 139 f., 147, 157, 298, 305, 324

phrenzy (frenzy), s., 117 (14)

Phrygian, 111 (33)

Phyllida ('Phillida') and Harpalus, a pastoral poem, 132 (33) n.

Phyllis: *see* Demophoön, Phillis

physic ('phisike'), s., *medicine*, 246 (20, 32)

pick ('pike,' 'pyke'), v., 89 (21), 196 (24)

Pick, Samuel, 271

pickax ('pikeax'), s., 166 (8)

pie ('pye'), s., 200 (29) n., 239 (23)

Pieris, *one of the nine Pierides, who being defeated in a contest with the Muses were transformed into birds*, 100 (3) n.

pight, pp., *pitched, placed*, 111 (37), 204 (3), 242 (37)

Pigmalion: *see* Pygmalion

pike: *see* pick

pikeax: *see* pickax

Pilgrimage of Grace, the, 69

pillow ('pelow'), tells her tale to her, i. e., *talks (of her lover) to herself when in bed*, 225 (40)

pine, s., *torment*, 162 (2)

pine, v. t., *inflict torment on*, 75 (26)

pineapple tree, translating Horace's *pinus*, a *pine-tree*, 244 (17)

Pinkie, battle of, Wilford and, 241

Pirithous ('Periothous'), and Theseus, 107 (2), 154 (3)

pitfall ('pitfoll'), s., 149 (33)

Pitho: *see* Peitho

Pits, John, 119 n.1

plage, s., *net, snare*, 22 (26) (the only example in the *N. E. D.* is dated 1608)

plain ('playn'), v., *lament, complain*, 3 (36), 4 (16), 8 (35), 16 (5), 33 (17), 42 (15), 48 (5), 50 (38), 63 (7), 67 (16), 93 (29), etc.

plainness ('playnesse'), s., *honesty*, 189 (29)

Plato, 69 (5), 209

Plautus, 109 (37)

play, make you, v. phr., *make sport for you, be jested at*, 255 (13)

playnesse: *see* plainness

pleasans, s., *pleasance, pleasure*, 107 (21)

pleasurable, adj., 100 (32) (the first example in the *N. E. D.* is dated 1579)

plight, s., *healthy condition*, 102 (26), 165 (32); *situation*, 185 (9)

Pliny the elder, 288, 313, 325

Pliny the younger, 232

Plomer, H. R., 5 n.

plump, on a, prep. phr., *in a band or troop* (Latin *agmen*), 115 (26)

plunge, be put unto his, v. phr., *fall into danger or distress*, 130 (29)

Plutarch, 153, 165, 244, 273, 324 f.

Pluto, 95 (15), 131 (18)

Poetical Rhapsody, A, edited by Francis Davison, 50, 57 n., 109, 165, 190

Poins: *see* Poyntz

pointel ('poyntel'), s., *pencil,* 99 (13)

polisindeton: *see* polysyndeton

Poliziano, Angelo, 315

Pollard, A. F., 277

Pollux: *see* Castor

Polychronicon, by Ranulf Higden (the reference is to book III, chapter xli), 165

Polyhymnia ('Polymnie'), 97 (19)

polysyndeton ('polisindeton'), or the couple-clause, examples of, 321

Pompey, 36 (6), 165, 218, 236 f.; Pompeius, *Pompey's,* 27 (26) n.

ponder, v., *weigh (on scales),* 6 (9)

poore (pour), v., 226 (19)

Pope, the (Clement VII), 75

Pope, Alexander, his praise of Surrey, 38 f., 121 f.; on Geraldine, 72

Popillius ('Popilius') Laenas, Gaius, 118 (39) n., 120 (14)

Posidippus, epigram by, 237

Posidonius, poem said to be translated from, 105 (12) n.

post, s., *post-rider,* 209 (21)

poudred: *see* powdered

pound, s., *enclosure for strayed cattle,* 255 (21)

powdered ('poudred'), pp., *sprinkled,* 25 (38), 162 (21)

Powell, Edgar, 305

power, adj., *poor,* 84 (16) n.

powr, s., *power,* 101 (3), 102 (4), 104 (27), 106 (13)

powr, v., *pour,* 88 (5)

poyntel: *see* pointel

Poyntz, Anthony, Sir, and Sir Francis, 214

Poyntz ('Poins'), John, poems addressed to, 82 (21) n., 85 (19)

pragmatographia, or the counterfeit action, example of, 163 (37) n.

Praise of Geraldine, The, 42 f.

pray (prey), s., 5 (11), 41 (7), 159 (11), 188 (35), 203 (13) n., 208 (25 n., 37), 209 (4), 220 (12); in pray, *as a prey,* 87 (37)

pray (prey), v., 208 (6)

prease, prese: *see* press

preface, Tottel's, to the miscellany, imitated, 4 n.

present, adv., *instantly,* 119 (5)

press ('prease,' 'prese'), s., *crowd,* 81 (12), 85 (23), 185 (28), 192 (27), 193 (13)

press ('prease'), v., *hasten,* 31 (14), 32 (7), 116 (27), 188 (35)

prest, adj., adv., *at hand,* 11 (18), 131 (36), 148 (8), 149 (3); *quickly,* 100 (36); *ready,* 45 (23), 125 (23), 134 (43), 135 (38), 164 (16)

prest, pp., *oppressed,* 248 (19, 23)

Preston, a miscellany poem signed, 146

presumptuous, adj., 119 (40)

pretence, s., *claim to authority,* 8 (9)

pretend, v., *indicate,* 254 (37); *intend,* 37 (7)

prey-seeker, s., *robber,* 94 (17)

Priam ('Pryam'), 12 (35), 17 (28) n., 18 (12), 184 (20), 219 (12), 254 (20), 257 (10) n.; allusion to, 228 (4 f.)

price, s., 48 (21) n.; in price, *in esteem,* 104 (10), 219 (35), 246 (5); at price for, *ready to bargain,* 255 (33)

Price, John, 28 n.2, 38 n.3

pricely, adj., *choice,* 101 (16)

prick, s., *dart,* 255 (3)

prick and prune, v. phr., *dress the feathers with the beak,* 154 (31)

prime, adj., *early, youthful,* 114 (34)

primetide, s., the spring, 112 (2), 116 (10)

process, by, prep. phr., *in the course of time, slowly,* 58 (3)

Procris ('Procryn'), 203 (2) n.

Proctor, Thomas, 321

procure, v., *cause, bring about,* 118 (4), 195 (35), 210 (3)

profet, s., *profit,* 212 (34) n.

proffering, vbl. n., *making a (lover's) proposal,* 212 (2)

prolling, s., *prowling,* 196 (24)

Prometheus, 93 (29) n., 131 (24)

pronouncing proves (proofs), i. e., *giving evidence of,* 242 (28)

proper, adj., *own,* 63 (36) n.

Propertius, Sextus, 140, 287

property ('propartie'), s., 69 (13)

Proserpine, 95 (14) n.

prospect, s., *sight,* 155 (12)

prosper, v., *cause to be prosperous,* 102 (4)

proufe, s., *proof,* 66 (12)

prove, v., *find to be true through trial*, 55
(21), 79 (12), 123 (38), 197 (26); *make
trial of*, 138 (3), 217 (27); *prosper*, 170
(25)

proverbs, proverbial phrases, common-
places: absence works wonders, 224
(26); amantium irae amoris, etc., 181
(18) n.; ant, the, works in summer to
prepare for winter, 132 (23 f.) n.; bag
and baggage, with, 165 (2); bark and
rind, 70 (37), 154 (21) n.; bavin blaze,
a, soon dies, 237 (10) n.; bit, to strive
against the, 48 (5) n.; bite upon the
bridle, let the old mule, 89 (30) n.;
blind, the, the dial doesn't help, 148
(20); blind, the, fears what footing he'll
find, 130 (26); blind, the, where leads,
comes a fall, 233 (28); bonum est mihi
quod humiliasti me, 30 (18) n.; boughs,
to climb rotten, 69 (16), 131 (8), 205
(18); burn away from the fire, to freeze
near it, to, 68 (33) n.; Caesar's tears
over Pompey's head, 165; candle, to
compare a, with the sun, 20 (17);
change a falcon for a kite, to, 24 (4 f.)
n.; chastisement, let others', be thy
scourge, 31 (3) n.; chip of chance (for-
tune), to weigh, more than a pound of
wit, 87 (19); clog, a, hangs at my heel,
87 (26) n., 139 (4); cock and pie, by, 200
(29) n.; cold as a stone, 222 (40); con-
stant dripping wears away a stone, 55
(9 ff.), 218 (33 ff.); crocodile tears, 205
(7 f.); crop and root, 40 (34); deaf, who
speaks to the, wastes his words, 146
(29); death's door, to bring one to, 99
(30); deer, the stricken, withdraws him-
self alone, 209 (35–36) n.; defense, none
needed, against chained prisoners, 60
(32); dog, beat the, before the lion, 6
(41) n.; dog unto the bow, as a, 188
(24) n.; dolphin, to teach the, to swim,
124 (13); drink, to, one's own disease,
140 (30) n.; eel's tail, slippery as an, 10
(6); eyes, to make one's, fountains, 184
(13) n.; falcon, to teach the, to fly, 124
(14); flood, the highest, has the lowest
ebb, 197 (36) n.; flower of the frying-
pan, 96 (7) n.; foelix quem faciunt
aliena pericula cautum, 159; fool, a, has
two tongues and one ear, 235 (7), 324 f.;
fool to bed, bring a, 255 (38) n.; gape

while others eat the fruit, 162 (13);
gods, the, love drives, to take many
shapes, 229 (31) n., 298; gold, every
glistering doesn't give (show), 204 (36);
grapes on brambles or briers, seek for,
84 (34); great rest stands in little busi-
ness, 185 (37) n.; had I wist, 232 (39) n.;
hammers beat in one's brains, 28 (8) n.;
happy end, a, exceedeth all, 169 (12);
harp, like an ass to the sound of a, 88
(25) n.; haste is waste, 27 (3); hawk,
the, that now comes to the fist may
check, 229 (30); he who winks isn't
blind, 56 (6 f.); head, the, of Cupid's
dart remains behind when the dart is
plucked from one's breast, 139 (22) n.;
highest tree (hall, house, etc.) have the
quickest falls, are soonest struck by
lightning, etc., 150 (35 ff.); honey, they
eat the, I hold the hive, 59 (21, 31) n.;
lamb, a, in town, a lion in the field, 160
(8) n.; like will to like, quoth the devil
to the collier, 50 (13) n.; lion, a, at-
tacks no yielding prey, 60 (33) n., 208
(25 n., 32 f.); lion, a, is chastised by
beating the whelp, 6 (41) n.; longer, the,
I watch, the worse I speed, 59 (21); look
before you light or leap, 205 (19), 255
(28, 32); madman, a, isn't fit to guide a
naked sword, 256 (22); match a candle
with the sun, to, 20 (17); mould, Na-
ture loses her, despairing of equaling
one of her men or women, 19 (41 ff.), 28
(34) n., 126 (23), 155 (38); of two evils
choose the least, 213 (28) n.; pale as a
clout, 222 (36); pleasure, every, has
some pain, 211 (13); plow in the water,
sow in the sand, 69 (32) n.; plow, to, a
barren field is madness, 131 (3); plows
for gain, the poor man, 149 (14) n.;
poison is put into medicine, 211 (17) n.;
reap, to, and others take the sheaves,
134 (17); remember the end, 234 (11);
rolling stone, a, gathers no moss, 88
(7 f.); row, to, beyond one's reach, 124
(15); salve the sore, to, 128 (41) n.; say-
well and do-well are two things, 235
(24); scar remains, the, 70 (15) n.; seed,
from good, comes ill fruit, 47 (32) n.;
serpent, a, lurks under the green, 6
(24), 190 (38) n.; short horns to hurtful
heads, 256 (19); sow seed and others

reap, 59 (30), or reap no corn, 251 (22); sparks, the smallest, make the greatest flames, 187 (26 f.) n.; speak and speed, 212 (5); spending hand, a, needs a bringer-in, 88 (5 f.); spiders get poison, bees honey, from the same flower, 63 (22–25) n.; spurn (kick) against an awl, 185 (38); stars, a sign to the mariners of calm, 175 (16 f.) n.; still man, the, oft hath wrong, 186 (38); stir, to, an oar in every man's boat, 198 (3); stream, to try to turn the, 8 (5); strive against the stream, 129 (32), 233 (9); that that shall be must be, 141 (19) n.; tiger, nursed by a, bred among rocks, 78 (16) n.; time, there's a, for each thing, 160 (23); time tries truth, 159 (32), 160 (22) n.; totus mundus in maligno positus, 232 (18) n.; truss up thy pack, 30 (15); water in a sieve, like, 90 (14); wealth brings friends, 245 (30); weeds grow where good herbs can't, 233 (5); well to wish and well to have, 124 (17); whale's bone, white as, 207 (22); wit bought (by experience) is dear, 234 (12) n.; wolf, to hold a, by the ears, 148 (25) n.; words, few, show wisdom, 234 (24) n. *See also* 130 (22) n., 256 (2) n.

proyne, v., *prune, preen,* 154 (31)

Pryam: *see* Priam

Psalms, the, 158; Wyatt's metrical version of, 76, 90, 95

psaltery ('sawtrey'), s., 188 (7)

Ptolemaic system of astronomy, Wyatt and the, 222

Ptolemy XII and Pompey, 165

purchase, v., *try to bring about or secure,* 27 (12)

purpose, as to, i. e., *in conversation,* 83 (38)

purpurde, pp., *empurpled (with blood),* 115 (19)

pursuit ('pursute'), s., *course of life,* 106 (15)

Puttenham (?), Richard, alleged author of *The Art (q. v.) of English Poesie*

pye: *see* pie

Pygmalion ('Pigmalion') and Galatea, a poem on, 125 (26) n.

pyke: *see* pick

Pylades and Orestes, 106 (37)

Pynson, Richard, printer, 296

Pyramus and Thisbe, 27 (36)

Pyrenees mountains, Spain, 44 (30) n.

Pythias, 106 (34)

Python, the serpent, 253 (16) n.

quadrate, adj., 116 (12) n.

quail, v., *die,* 93 (30); *quell,* 7 (15)

Quaritch, Ltd., Bernard, 25, 28 n.1, 31

Quarles, Francis, 323

queint, inf., *be quenched,* 250 (7)

quent, pp., *quenched,* 52 (20)

quest, s., *inquest, trial,* 204 (15)

question, s., 48 (27) n.

quick, adj., *animated,* 99 (27); *alive,* 28 (3), 218 (25)

quick, s., *the living,* 130 (9), 207 (6)

quickness ('quicnesse'), s., *life,* 99 (24)

quishes, s., *cuisses, thigh-armor,* 117 (20)

quit, v., *get rid of,* 36 (12), 56 (11)

quite, adv., *completely,* 177 (28)

quite, v., *quit, rid of,* 60 (15); *took away,* 178 (17)

quod, v., *quoth,* 7 (20), 8 (8), 16 (22), 17 (9), 48 (19, 21, 27), 83 (8, 32 f., 35), etc.

R., a slanderer, 190 (25) n.

R. so depe can auoyde, 191 (7) n., 20

raarnesse: *see* rareness

race, s., *course of life,* 28 (33), 31 (18), 105 (26), 106 (6), 147 (8), etc.; *family,* 9 (19), 207 (17), 208 (4, 11); outrun the race, *finished one's life,* 102 (36)

race, v., *erase,* 70 (15), 257 (38); *raze,* 202 (28)

Rachel, wife of Jacob, 66 (2)

rack, s., *storm,* 151 (21) n. (the last example in the *N. E. D.* is dated 1513)

Radcliffe, Thomas, third Earl of Sussex, 159

ragged, adj., *jagged (hills),* 73 (35)

raign: *see* reign

railed ('reyled'), v., *gushed,* 117 (21)

rain ('rayne'), croak against the, 191 (9)

raine: *see* reign, reins

raised ('raysde'), v., *sighted,* 155 (10)

Rajna, Pio, 136

rakehell, adj., *rakehelly, dissolute,* 11 (5) (the first example in the *N. E. D.*)

Raleigh, Walter, Sir, 85, 156 f., 305

ramp, s., *vulgar woman,* 201 (28)

rampire, s., 164 (19) n.

Randolph, Thomas, 152

ranged in array, v. phr., *drawn up in military formation*, 152 (32)

rare ('rere'), adj., *fine, excellent* (ironical), 247 (14)

rareness ('raarnesse'), s., *rarity*, 103 (22)

rased ('rasde'), v., *razed, cut*, 154 (21) n.

rash, adv., 135 (24)

rashly, adv., *rapidly*, 17 (3) (The first example in the *N. E. D.*, where the second is dated 1691. Cf. Richard Robinson, *A Golden Mirrour*, 1589 [ed. Thomas Corser, p. 37, Chetham Society, 1851]: "Thus rashly rushing vp for feare, from thence my way did take," "Thus runninng [*sic*] rashly in this race.")

Ratclif, Surrey's poem to, 31 (2) n.

Ratcliffe, Humphrey, Sir, 159

rate, s., *manner of action*, 102 (23)

rate, v., *conceive of*, 111 (3)

rathe, all to, adv. phr., *too quickly*, 58 (31) (the last example in the *N. E. D.*)

raught, v., *clutched*, 17 (38); *snatched away*, 154 (18)

Rawlinson, Richard, his copy of *E*, 28 n. 1

ray, s., *glance of the eye*, 206 (20)

rayd, pp., *arrayed, dressed*, 104 (11)

rayghne: *see* reign

Raynald, Thomas, printer, 90

rayne: *see* rain

rayns: *see* reins

readier ('redier'), adv., *more readily*, 156 (18) n.

rear ('rere'), v., *raise, cause*, 240 (10)

reason, s., *speech, statement*, 226 (24)

Reason and Love, a poem, 45 (2), 179

reason-rend, the: *see* etiologia

rebated, v., *abated*, 119 (34)

rebel, s., *rebellion*, 8 (19)

rechless: *see* retchless

recount, v., *draw, get* (Latin *traho*), 114 (2)

recourse, s., *recurrence*, 103 (8); *return*, 240 (2)

rect, adj., *straight, erect*, 149 (24) (the only example in the *N. E. D.*)

recure, s., *healing*, 163 (11), 186 (14); *help*, 147 (4); *remedy*, 78 (16)

recure, v., *be cured*, 31 (6); *cure*, 43 (32), 131 (10), 159 (14), 174 (29)

rede, v., *advise*, 20 (29), 185 (33)

redier: *see* readier

redress, s., *aid, remedy*, 17 (3), 42 (26), 52 (13), 134 (16), 246 (38), etc.

redress, v., *relieve*, 44 (14); *set right*, 65 (37), 185 (35)

reduceth, v., *leads back*, 3 (19)

Reed, A. W., 86 n.2, 227

referred ('refarde'), pp., *conveyed back*, 210 (36) (the first example in the *N. E. D.*)

reflexion, s., *echo of the voice*, 42 (16)

refrain ('refrayne'), v., *hold back*, 44 (25), 248 (7)

refrains omitted by the "editor," 95

reft, v., *deprived of*, 28 (16), 239 (18, 21); *snatched away*, 41 (12)

refuse, s., *refusal, objection to*, 208 (39)

rehearse ('reherse'), v., *utter*, 118 (19), 193 (29)

reign ('raine,' 'raign,' 'rayghne'), s., v., 84 (17), 87 (15), 97 (16), 251 (12), 258 (12); *kingdom, empire* (Italian *imperio*), 36 (10)

reined, v., *guided, governed*, 32 (11)

reins ('raines,' 'rayns'), s., 119 (12), 186 (24)

reject, pp., *rejected*, 8 (3)

release ('relesse'), s., 243 (27, 31, 35), 244 (3, 7)

relent, v., *grow less*, 58 (4); *grow soft (yield)*, 75 (11); *lessen*, 70 (39)

Remembrance, Queen, *Mnemosyne (q. v.)*, 97 (5) n.

remorce, v., *show pity*, 185 (11)

remove, v., *flee*, 95 (6); *make inconstant in love*, 208 (14); *move aside*, 8 (38), 170 (27)

Remus: *see* Romulus

rendering, pres. p. adj., *submissive*, 126 (29)

renk, s., *rink, man*, 97 (20), 117 (29)

renowmed, adj., *renowned*, 99 (9), 114 (4), 169 (7)

rent, v., *rend*, 74 (8, 11), 164 (24); *torn*, 70 (36)

repair ('repayre'), s., *concourse of men to (Troy)*, 14 (30)

repeat, v., *rehearse* (Latin *meditari*), 94 (5)

repent, s., 235 (3)

repose, v., *place*, 103 (18)

reposed, pp., *firmly fixed*, 28 (26)

represt, adj., *downcast*, 28 (29)

repugnant, repugnant, adj., *opposite*, 9 (12), 90 (24), 91 (9)

require, v., *ask (vengeance) for* (Latin *reposcere*), 119 (29); *demand*, 18 (25), 58 (20); *entreat*, 57 (23); *make love-suit to*, 96 (29)

rere: *see* rare, rear

resident, s., 146 (25) n.

resolve, v., *consider*, 7 (38)

resound, v., *make sound out*, 109 (24)

rest, v., 244 (6) n.

retchless ('rechlesse'), adj., *heedless*, 16 (26), 31 (2), 40 (30), 87 (12), 254 (18)

retreat, v., *carry away* (Latin *ferre*), 94 (5)

return, v., *go away (disappear)*, 78 (11)

returnable, adj., *capable of being returned*, 33 (14) (the first example in the *N. E. D.*)

revart, v., *revert, change*, 174 (5)

reve, v., *reave, deprive*, 239 (28), 245 (3)

reven, pp., *riven, torn asunder*, 194 (23)

revenger, adj., 117 (26)

reverse, v., *send back*, 54 (30)

revert, v., *turn away (be revoked)*, 50 (4)

revested, pp., *reclothed*, 10 (35)

Review of English Studies, The, 50 n.1, 51 n.4, 86 n.2, 278, 293

Revue d' Histoire Littéraire, La, 198

reyled: *see* railed

Reynolds, Henry, 82, 94 n.

Riccoboni, Antonio, 229

Rice ('Rise,' 'Ryce'), Mistress, poem in praise of, 192 (11) n.

Rich, Barnabe, 4, 6, 45, 84 n.2, 181, 280

Rich, Hugh, Sir, 245

richesse, s., *wealth*, 26 (6), 171 (31)

Richmond, Duchess of: *see* Howard (Mary); Duke of: *see* Fitzroy

rid, v., *free oneself*, 74 (19), 147 (35); *get rid of*, 93 (28), 258 (11); *kill*, 16 (37); *ride*, 114 (12); *take away*, 10 (29), 16 (22), 136 (2)

riddles, poems in the form of, 79 (38), 98 (30), 211 (23) n., 269

Ridley, Nicholas, Bishop, 78, 87

Riese, Alexander, 240

rife ('ryfe'), adv., *common*, 108 (8), 191 (18), 206 (31); *easily, or speedily*, 102 (12); *easy*, 194 (28) (the first example in the *N. E. D.*)

rifest, adv., *most frequently* (the Latin has *saepius*), 150 (36), 244 (17)

rift ('ryft'), take in a, v. phr., *furl a rift (reef) or sail*, 27 (3)

right, adv., *directly*, 17 (43); *exactly*, 184 (7)

right over, adv. phr., Latin *oppositus*, 115 (36)

right so, adv., 103 (6)

rightway, the gates of my, s. phr., *the jaws* (which are the "gates" of the passage that leads straight up from within the body), 30 (6) (not in the *N. E. D.*)

rightwisely, adv., *righteously*, 67 (3)

rigor, s., *harsh dealing, cruelty*, 104 (30)

rind ('rynde'), s., 70 (37), 154 (21) n.

riot ('ryot'), range at, v. phr., *act without restraint*, 171 (17)

rise, v., *raise*, 241 (25)

Rise: *see* Rice

rive, v., *split asunder*, 26 (30)

riveled ('riueld'), pp. adj., *wrinkled*, 89 (26)

riveth, v., *destroys*, 210 (14)

road ('rode'), s., *harbor*, 118 (25)

roar ('rore'), s., *confusion*, 35 (29)

roate, by, prep. phr., *by rote or heart*, 6 (26)

Robarts, Henry, 156, 306

Robinson, F. N., 151

Robinson, Mrs. N. L., 31 n.2

Robinson, Richard, 157, 301

Robinson, Robert, printer, 6 f.

Rochford, Viscount: *see* Boleyn

rode: *see* road, rood

Rogers, Samuel, 74 n.1

roll, v., *ponder over, think of*, 210 (10)

Rollins, H. E., 108 n.3, 110 n.1, 112 n.1, n. 3, 132, 142, 144, 259, 264 f., 276, 283, 285, 305, 313, 324; reprint of the miscellany by, editorial methods of the, 64 f. See also *Gorgeous, Handful, Paradise*

Roman calendars, 111 (36)

Roman Catholicism, the effect of, on the miscellany, 97, 308

Rome ('Room'), 47 (9), 111 (23), 118 (19), 119 (2 n., 11, 19, 25, 29)

Romulus and Remus, 244

rondeaux, Wyatt's, edited into sonnets, 95, 103, 182 f., 202

rones (runs), v., 248 (27). *See* roon

Ronsard, Pierre de, 135, 298

rood ('rode'), s., 83 (35)

Room: *see* Rome

rooms ('roumes'), s., *offices, appointments*, 196 (18)

roon (run), v., 119 (13), 152 (17), 228 (9). *See* rones

Rose, J., 44 n.2

roseal ('rosiall'), adj., 156 (16)

rosemary, s., 179 (2)

Rosenbach, A. S. W., 10 n.3, 11 n.1–3, 25; his copy of *C*, 12, 271, of *D*, 21 ff., 31 n.2, of *D**, 24 ff.

rosiall: *see* roseal

rote (root), s., 202 (7), 254 (36)

roumes: *see* rooms

rounds ('rowndes'), s., *orbits*, 92 (3)

rout, s., *band, crowd*, 97 (20), 98 (36), 117 (31), 118 (21, 34), 131 (18), etc.

row, s., *company*, 25 (35); on row, *in order*, 125 (6)

Rowfant library: *see* Locker-Lampson

rowndes: *see* rounds

Roxburghe Ballads, The, 266

Roxburghe Club, 79 n.4, 81 n.1, 256 f., 260, 283 f., 290, 302, 309, 313, 328

rue on or upon, v., *pity*, 3 (4), 4 (21), 31 (12)

rueful ('rufull'), adj., 16 (27), 114 (18)

ruff (rough), adj., 152 (2)

ruing, pres. p., 244 (18) n.

rule, s., *disorder*, 192 (31) (the first example in the *N. E. D.* is dated 1567)

Rump Despairing, The, 219

ruse, 208 (38) n.

Russell, John, Sir, 75

ruth, s., 13 (17), 34 (14), 208 (13), 240 (12), 241 (34), 251 (12), etc.

Rutton, W. L., 242, 245, 286

Ryce: *see* Rice

ryfe, ryft: *see* rife, rift

Rylands, John, library, its copy of *F*, 30

ryot: *see* riot

S., D.: *see* Sand

S., E., Lady, poem to, 103 (2) n.

S., H. ("Henry Surrey"), poems signed, 322

S., H., Mistress, poem to, 103 (24) n.

S., I., Lady, poem to, 100 (2) n.

S., K., Lady, poem to, 102 (31) n.

S., M., Lady, poems to, 101 (33) n., 102 (10) n.

S., R., *Phillis and Flora*, 4 n.

Sabie, Francis, 278

Sackville, Thomas, Earl of Dorset, Baron Buckhurst, 81, 84 f., 110, 242, 314

sad, adj., *sober, serious*, 210 (19), 228 (13) n.

sadly, adj., *soberly*, 193 (15)

safeguard, s., *safety*, 119 (9)

Saint-Gelais, Mellin de, 171, 188, 197

St. Leger (Sentleger), Anthony, Sir, 53, 66; contributor to the miscellany, 81, 85, 318

St. Valentine's day and birds, 7 (33) n.

salamander ('salamandra'), s., 168 (37) n.

sallet (salad) herbs, 107 (19)

Salomon (Solomon), King, 31 (6) n., 99 (29) n., 160 (9)

salveth, v., *salutes*, 19 (7)

sample, s., *example in action*, 205 (21)

sampler ('samplar'), s., 51 (2)

sance, prep., *sans, without*, 99 (9)

Sand, D. (D.S.), contributor to the miscellany, 81, 92, 258; imitation by, of the miscellany, 289

Sanford, Ezekiel, edition by, of the miscellany poems, 53

Sannazaro, Jacopo, translations from, 197 f., 231

sapience, s., 117 (36)

Sardanapalus, poem on, 29 (2) n.

Sargent, Epes, 74 n.1

sat me on, it, impers. v., *it was fitting for me*, 16 (17). *See* sits

satires, examples of, 82 (21)–90 (14), 104

Saturn, the planet, 91 (22, 27)

Saturnian, adj., *baleful (like Saturn)*, 111 (6) (the first example in the *N. E. D.*)

savor, s., 252 (3)

savry, adj., *savory*, 87 (30)

saws, s., *lines, sayings*, 100 (13); *stories*, 111 (22); *wise comments*, 152 (36); *words*, 117 (17)

sawtrey: *see* psaltery

'sayed ('sayd'), pp., *assayed*, 143 (40)

sayen, inf., *say*, 19 (31)

scace, adv., *scarcely*, 29 (13)

scape, v., *escape*, 22 (21), 29 (29), 38 (5), 69 (10), 131 (2), 140 (3), 149 (20), etc.

Scève: *see* Sève

Schelling, F. E., 86 n.2

Schmidt, Erich, 285

science, s., *knowledge*, 117 (10)

scilla: *see* Scylla

(B) of, 19, variant, and misprints of D*, 25 (of all other editions: *see* 1, 263–326); registered at Stationers' Hall, 12, 37 n.3; revisions, the, made in the second edition (B) of, 10 f., and C, 19 f.; second edition of (BC), relationship of the different impressions of the, 12 ff.; sonnets in, 103 f.; sources of the poems in: *see* Alamanni, Beza, Ciminelli, Filosseno, Gualterus, Haddon, Horace, *Laude*, Lucretius, Ovid, Petrarch, Virgil, etc.; style of, the, 101 ff.; subjects treated in, the, 104 ff.; tables of, the, discussed, 15 ff.; titles of poems in, whence derived, 98 f.; types of literature in, 103 ff.; typography of the early editions of, the, 4 ff., 290. *See also* ballads, censorship, music

Touchet (Tuchet), John, Baron Audley, 280

tourney ('tornay,' 'turney'), s., 160 (6) n., 189 (18)

Tower, the, of London, 208 (12)

townish, adj., *living in a town*, 82 (26)

toy, s., *idle fancy*, 129 (33), 165 (37), 258 (7); *mocking speech*, 128 (9), 169 (15); *trifling action*, 80 (32)

Toy, Robert, printer, 154

trace, s., *manner of life*, 202 (20); *path of the sea*, 244 (10); *practice, action*, 159 (19), 189 (12); the common trace, *the usual course of life*, 81 (4)

trace, v., *follow*, 208 (21)

traced, pp., *lured* (Italian *m'atrasse*), 45 (29)

tract, s., *passage (of time)*, 165 (24)

trade, s., *course of life*, 202 (6), 208 (20) n., 234 (8); *habit*, 159 (19)

train ('trayn'), s., *army* (fig.), 54 (23) n.; *follower*, 170 (26); *trap, deception*, 5 (17), 7 (6), 52 (11), 196 (24), etc.

train ('trayn'), v., *attended by*, 13 (19) (the first example in the *N. E. D.* is dated 1593); *deceive*, 72 (5), 152 (18), 168 (24), 186 (30), 192 (35); *deceive by death*, 146 (36); *draw*, 73 (26)

transplendent, adj., *resplendent*, 72 (40) (the first example in the *N. E. D.*)

travail ('trauell'), s., 3 (28, 34), 4 (5), 22 (27), 28 (22), 67 (7), etc.

travail, v., *travel*, 197 (7)

tread, v., *copulate*, 191 (25); *crush under foot*, 104 (16)

Trench, W. F., 150

tress, s., *locks of hair*, 66 (22)

tried, pp. adj., *refined (gold)*, 81 (28)

triedly, adv., *in an experienced manner*, 135 (38) (the last example in the *N. E. D.*)

trill, v., *spin, revolve*, 255 (12) n.

trim ('trym'), v., *keep in order*, 105 (32)

Trinity College, Cambridge, its copy of C, 12 f., of H, 33

Troilus ('Troylus'), 17 (28) n., 18 (12), 230 (29) n.; poems on, 183 (18) n.

Trojan knight, *Aeneas*, 90 (17). *See* Troyan

troned, pp., *enthroned*, 152 (35)

troth, s., 52 (2, 10), 76 (19), 79 (8), 225 (15)

trots, v., *journeys*, 88 (15)

Troy, 12 (35), 14 (19), 17 (28), 47 (8), 65 (21), 168 (25), 179 (26), 183 (22), 202 (11), 219 (11), 227 (23 ff.), 231 (26), 246 (9), 254 (20), 257 (11). *See* Ilium

Troy, New, *London*, 212

Troyan, adj., s., 183 (27), 202 (22, 28), 227 (25, 38), 228 (19); Troyan boy, *Paris*, 179 (24). *See* Trojan

Troylus: *see* Troilus

trudge, v., 30 (15)

truss, s., *quiver of arrows*, 77 (33)

truss, v.: *see* pack

trust, pp., *trussed*, 192 (24)

try, v., *find or prove by experience*, 3 (22), 70 (8), 91 (37), 127 (8)

trym: *see* trim

Tudor Facsimile Texts, 221, 227

Tullius ('Tullie'), 118 (35), 120 (18, 21). *See* Cicero

tunes of, v., *draws music from*, 97 (23) (the first example in the *N. E. D.* is dated 1701)

Turbervile, George, 45, 68, 77 n.2, 102, 108, 128, 227, 261, 287 f., 298, 313, 319 ff., 325, 330; borrowings by, from the miscellany, 110 f., 145, 149, 163 f., 167, 172, 175, 184, 187, 191, 195, 198, 202, 239, 260, 263, 278, 329. *See* T. (G.)

turn the word, v. phr., 86 (10) n.

Turner, Richard, 6

Turner, William, 81, 315

turney: *see* tourney

turtle, s., *dove*, 4 (29)

GLOSSARIAL INDEX

wiefly: *see* wifely

wife, choosing a, a poem on, 195 (20)

wifelihead ('wiuelyhed'), s., *wifely quality*, 194(27) (the first example in the *N.E.D.*)

wifely ('wiefly'), adj., *womanly*, 193 (16)

wight, s., 7 (28), 97 (34), 114 (28, 43), 116 (31), 117 (4), etc.

Wilford, James, Sir, epitaphs on, 108 (2, 18, 22) n., 135 (20) n., 146 (31) n.; Churchyard and, 84

will, v., *desire, wish*, 96 (26), 152 (21)

Willcock, Gladys D., 79 n.2, 87 f.

Williams, Francis, 305

Williams, Henry, epitaph on, 199 (4) n.

Williams, John, first Baron Williams of Thame, 199 (28), 305

Willis's Current Notes, 262

Willmott, R. A., 133

Willobie's Avisa, 313, 325

willow, to wear a wreath of, i. e., *in sign of disappointed love*, 133 (39)

Wilton, Jack, Nashe's hero, Surrey, and, Geraldine, 71

wind, take my, v. phr., *walk in the open air*, 122 (19)

Windet, John, printer, 6 f.

Windsor Castle, 9 (30) n., 10 (33) n., 12 (29, 33)

wines, v., *winds, steers*, 150 (25)

wink, v., *sleep*, 203 (19)

Wintermantel, Egon, 105 n.1

wist, v., *knew, known*, 88 (32), 208 (28), 209 (3), 232 (39)

wit, s., *judgment*, 84 (35); *wisdom*, 24 (7), 28 (16), etc.

wite, v., *blame*, 24 (3)

with, prep., *on behalf of*, 96 (23)

withered ('wethered'), pp. adj., 197 (35)

withsaue, v., *vouchsafe*, 249 (24) n. (This is the only example in the *Century Dictionary;* the *N. E. D.* has only two examples — both from Wyatt — but see the note on 249 [24].)

Wit's A. B. C., 230

Wit's Recreations, 271

wivelyhead: *see* wifelihead

wo worth, interj.,16 (28,30),48(20),154(8)

woe, v., *woo*, 189 (21)

wold, wolden, v., *would*, 117 (38), 167 (3)

Wolsey, Cardinal, 78

womanhood, womanhead, s., 47 (18), 194 (25)

womanish, adj., *effeminate*, 29 (14)

womb, s., *stomach*, 93 (29) n.

wombed, pp., *hidden as in a womb*, 228 (22) (the first example in the *N. E. D.*)

won ('wonne'), v., *dwell*, 96 (21), 244 (13). *See* woon

wonders, wondersly, adv., *wondrously*, 18 (3), 62 (3), 84 (8), 101 (8), 114 (5)

Wood, Anthony, 36 n.5, 50, 72, 119

wood, adj., *crazy*, 178 (25); *ferocious*, 256 (19)

woodness, s., *violence, fury*, 122 (13)

Woodville, Elizabeth: *see* Elizabeth

Woodward, Richard, 277

woon, v., *dwell (see* won*)*, 94 (27), 223 (5); *won*, 117 (40), 152 (18), 218 (16)

woorrier: *see* worrier

wordly, adj., *worldly*, 136 (13)

work, v., *cause, bring about*, 224 (26); *toss, roll*, 10 (20), 240 (3)

working, pp., *living, conducting oneself*, 97 (31, 35)

worms, s., *serpents*, 191 (15) n.

worn, adj., *experienced in* (Latin *exercitus*), 118 (21) (this meaning is not given in the *N. E. D.*)

worn, pp., *past, spent*, 4 (37) (the first example in the *N. E. D.* is dated 1611)

worrier ('woorrier'), s., *an animal that "worries" or bites his victims*, 189 (8)

worth, s., *?property, possession*, 221 (5) (the first example in the *N. E. D.* is dated 1592; Nott explains the meaning as *family, brood);* take in worth, *bear patiently*, 23 (21)

worth, v., *befall*, 16 (28, 30), 48 (20)

wot ('wote,' 'wat'), v., *know*, 6 (25), 43 (2), 49 (36), 64 (16), 65 (2), 77 (8), 105 (8), 129 (38), 146 (10), etc.

would you (*or* ye) wist, I, i. e., *I wish you knew*, 208 (28), 209 (3)

wrack ('wrake'), s., 155 (15), 179 (26), 245 (4)

wrapped within my cloak, 85 (25) n.

wrasteth, v., *wresteth, gives a new turn to*, 25 (29)

wraths, s., 73 (32)

wreak ('wreke'), s., *injury*, 37 (21)

wreathed ('wrethed'), pp. adj., *intertwined*, 38 (27)

wreck, v., *wreak, revenge*, 50 (21)